THE ROUTLEDGE HANDBOOK OF ASIAN AMERICAN STUDIES

The Routledge Handbook of Asian American Studies brings together leading scholars and scholarship to capture the state of the field of Asian American Studies, as a generation of researchers have expanded the field with new paradigms and methodological tools.

Inviting readers to consider new understandings of the historical work done in the past decades and the place of Asian Americans in a larger global context, this ground-breaking volume illuminates how research in the field of Asian American Studies has progressed. Previous work in the field has focused on establishing a place for Asian Americans within American history. This volume engages more contemporary research, which draws on new archives, art, literature, film, and music, to examine how Asian Americans are redefining their national identities, and to show how race interacts with gender, sexuality, class, and the built environment, to reveal the diversity of the United States. Organized into five parts, and addressing a multitude of inter-disciplinary areas of interest to Asian American scholars, it covers:

- a reframing of key themes such as transnationality, postcolonialism, and critical race theory
- U.S. imperialism and its impact on Asian Americans
- war and displacement
- the garment industry
- Asian Americans and sports
- race and the built environment
- social change and political participation
- and many more themes.

Exploring people, practice, politics, and places, this cutting-edge volume brings together the best themes current in Asian American Studies today, and is a vital reference for all researchers in the field.

Cindy I-Fen Cheng is Associate Professor of History and Asian American Studies at the University of Wisconsin-Madison. She is the award-winning author of *Citizens of Asian America: Democracy and Race during the Cold War* (New York University Press, 2013).

THE ROUTLEDGE HANDBOOK OF ASIAN AMERICAN STUDIES

Edited by Cindy I-Fen Cheng

Routledge
Taylor & Francis Group
NEW YORK AND LONDON

First published 2017
by Routledge
711 Third Avenue, New York, NY 10017

and by Routledge
2 Park Square, Milton Park, Abingdon, Oxon, OX14 4RN

Routledge is an imprint of the Taylor & Francis Group, an informa business

© 2017 Taylor & Francis

The right of the editor to be identified as the author of the editorial material, and of the authors for their individual chapters, has been asserted in accordance with sections 77 and 78 of the Copyright, Designs and Patents Act 1988.

All rights reserved. No part of this book may be reprinted or reproduced or utilised in any form or by any electronic, mechanical, or other means, now known or hereafter invented, including photocopying and recording, or in any information storage or retrieval system, without permission in writing from the publishers.

Trademark notice: Product or corporate names may be trademarks or registered trademarks, and are used only for identification and explanation without intent to infringe.

Library of Congress Cataloging in Publication Data
Names: Cheng, Cindy I-Fen, editor.
Title: The Routledge handbook of Asian American studies / edited by Cindy I-Fen Cheng.
Description: New York : Routledge, 2017. | Includes bibliographical references and index.
Identifiers: LCCN 2016031678 (print) | LCCN 2016050569 (ebook) | ISBN 9780415738255 (alk. paper) | ISBN 9781315817514
Subjects: LCSH: Asian Americans—History. | Asian Americans—Ethnic identity. | Asian Americans—Social conditions. | Asian Americans—Politics and government.
Classification: LCC E184.A75 R68 2017 (print) | LCC E184.A75 (ebook) | DDC 973/.0495—dc23
LC record available at https://lccn.loc.gov/2016031678

ISBN: 978-0-415-73825-5 (hbk)
ISBN: 978-1-315-81751-4 (ebk)

Typeset in Bembo
by Florence Production Ltd, Stoodleigh, Devon, UK

To all educators and students working to advance meaningful
and transformative education

CONTENTS

List of Tables   *x*
Notes on Contributors   *xi*
Acknowledgments   *xiv*

Introduction: On Reclaiming the Political Project of Asian American Studies   1
Cindy I-Fen Cheng

PART ONE
Shifting Paradigms   19

1. On Racial Stereotyping   21
   Leslie Bow

2. On the Asian American Question   39
   Joshua Chambers-Letson

3. Postcolonialism and Asian American Studies   52
   Erin Suzuki

4. Diaspora as Frame and Object of Analysis in Asian American Studies   65
   Martin Joseph Ponce

5. American Antipodes: Anna Kazumi Stahl's *Flores de un solo día*   83
   Michelle Har Kim

PART TWO
War, Colonization, and U.S. Imperialism   101

6. The Vietnam War and The "Good Refugee"   103
   Yen Le Espiritu

7	Refugee Memoryscape: The Rhetoric of Hmong Refugee Writing *Chong A. Moua*	117
8	Prosecuting the Khmer Rouge: Cambodian American Memory Work *Cathy J. Schlund-Vials*	129
9	Asian Settler Colonialism's Histories *Bianca Kai Isaki*	142
10	The Strange Career of the Filipino "National": Empire, Citizenship, and Racial Statecraft *Rick Baldoz*	154
11	The Arab American Experience: From Invisibility to Heightened Visibility *Louise Cainkar*	166

PART THREE
Globalization, Global Restructuring, and the Question of National Belongings — 185

12	Popular Music, Globalization, and Asian/America *Christine Bacareza Balance*	187
13	The Sports Loyalty Test: Asian Athletes and Asian American Cultural Politics *Rachael Miyung Joo*	198
14	Jeremy Lin, Global Asian American *Timothy Yu*	211
15	Beneath Each Layer of Cloth: Chinese Women in the New York City Garment Industry *Margaret M. Chin*	221

PART FOUR
Representations Within and Across Nations — 231

16	The Globality of Af-Pak: U.S. Empire and the Muslim Problem *Junaid Rana*	233
17	The Japanese American Transnational Generation: Rethinking the Spatial and Conceptual Boundaries of Asian America *Michael Jin*	246

18	Migration, Citizenship, and Sexuality in Asian/America *Yu-Fang Cho*	260
19	From Noxious Quarters to Affluent Ethno-burbs: Race and Space in Asian American History *Shelley Sang-Hee Lee*	273
20	The Invention of the Model Minority *Ellen D. Wu*	285

PART FIVE
Social Change and Political Participation   303

21	Asian American Studies and/as Digital Humanities *Lori Kido Lopez and Konrad Ng*	305
22	Asian American Queer and Trans Activisms *Jian Neo Chen*	318
23	"Other": Reconsidering Asian Exclusion and Immigrant Rights *Sujani K. Reddy*	328
24	Afro-Asian Solidarity through Time and Space: Roads Taken and Not Taken *Yuichiro Onishi*	342
25	The Political Participation of Asian Americans *Pei-te Lien*	355

Index   *367*

TABLES

15.1 NYC Chinese Population, 1940–2010   224

CONTRIBUTORS

Christine Bacareza Balance is Associate Professor of Asian American Studies at the University of California, Irvine. Her writings on Imelda Marcos, Asian American YouTube artists, and spree killer Andrew Cunanan have appeared in *Women and Performance*, *Women Studies Quarterly*, and *Journal of Asian American Studies*. She is the author of *Tropical Renditions: Making Musical Scenes in Filipino America* (Duke University Press, 2016).

Rick Baldoz is Associate Professor of Sociology at Oberlin College. He is the author of *The Third Asiatic Invasion: Empire and Migration in Filipino America, 1898–1946* (New York University Press, 2011), which won book awards from the American Sociological Association and the American Library Association. He is currently working on a monograph about the 1965 Hart-Celler Immigration Act, examining this historical legislation against the backdrop of Cold War politics, anti-colonial insurgency, and domestic civil rights mobilization.

Leslie Bow is Vilas Distinguished Achievement Professor and Mark and Elisabeth Eccles Professor of English and Asian American Studies at the University of Wisconsin-Madison. She is the author of the award-winning *'Partly Colored': Asian Americans and Racial Anomaly in the Segregated South* (New York University Press, 2010); *Betrayal and Other Acts of Subversion: Feminism, Sexual Politics, Asian American Women's Literature* (Princeton University Press, 2001); and editor of *Asian American Feminisms* (Routledge, 2012).

Louise Cainkar is Associate Professor of Sociology and Social Welfare and Justice at Marquette University and President of the Arab American Studies Association. She has published widely on Arab Americans, Muslim Americans, and the global Arab diaspora. Her book, *Homeland Insecurity: The Arab American and Muslim American Experience after 9/11* (Russell Sage Foundation, 2009), was honored by the Arab American National Museum.

Joshua Chambers-Letson is Assistant Professor of Performance Studies at Northwestern University. He is the author of *A Race So Different: Law and Performance in Asian America* (New York University Press, 2013), winner of the 2014 Outstanding Book Award from the Association of Theater in Higher Education, and is working on a book about the Marxism of minoritarian performance.

Jian Neo Chen is Assistant Professor of English at The Ohio State University, Columbus. His work explores strategies for trans and queer cultural activism at the turn of the 21st century, with the expansion of neoracist U.S. state capitalism across sectors of the transnational economy and embodied social life.

Cindy I-Fen Cheng is Associate Professor of History and Asian American Studies at the University of Wisconsin-Madison. She is the award-winning author of *Citizens of Asian America: Democracy and Race during the Cold War* (New York University Press, 2013).

Margaret M. Chin is Associate Professor of Sociology at Hunter College and the Graduate Center at the City University of New York. With degrees from Harvard and Columbia, she studies family, Asian Americans, and children of immigrants. She is the author of *Sewing Women: Immigrants and the NYC Garment Industry* (Columbia University Press, 2005) and is currently working on an ethnography on the second generation Asian American professional.

Yu-Fang Cho is Associate Professor of English and Global and Intercultural Studies at Miami University of Ohio, Oxford. She is the author of *Uncoupling American Empire: Cultural Politics of Deviance and Unequal Difference, 1890–1910* (SUNY Press, 2013) and articles in *American Quarterly*, *Journal of Transnational American Studies*, *Meridians*, and *Journal of Asian American Studies*, among many others. She is also the co-editor of the 2017 special issue of *American Quarterly*, "Reorienting Global Imaginaries in American Studies."

Yen Le Espiritu is Professor of Ethnic Studies at the University of California, San Diego. An award-winning author, she has published widely on Asian American panethnicity, gender and migration, and U.S. colonialism and wars in Asia. Her most recent book is *Body Counts: The Vietnam War and Militarized Refuge(es)* (University of California Press, 2014).

Bianca Kai Isaki writes and researches at the intersection of Hawaiian rights, environmental law, and queer studies. She received her doctorate from the University of Hawai'i at Manoa in 2008 in Political Science with a dissertation entitled "A Decolonial Archive: Asian Settler Politics in a Time of Hawaiian Nationhood." She graduated summa cum laude from the William S. Richardson School of Law in 2013.

Michael Jin is Assistant Professor of Global Asian Studies and History and a member of the Diaspora Studies Cluster at the University of Illinois at Chicago.

Rachael Miyung Joo is Assistant Professor of American Studies at Middlebury College. Her research focuses on sports, media, and race in transnational contexts. Her book, *Transnational Sport: Gender, Media, and Global Korea* (Duke University Press, 2012), details how sports shape ideas of global Koreanness in the United States and South Korea.

Michelle Har Kim is an independent scholar who lives in the Los Angeles area. The recipient of a 2016 Translation Grant from the National Endowment of the Arts, she is currently working on a Spanish-to-English rendition of *Banderas detrás de la niebla*, the final book of poetry by the celebrated Peruvian poet José Watanabe.

Shelley Sang-Hee Lee is Associate Professor of History and Comparative American Studies at Oberlin College. She is the author of the books *Claiming the Oriental Gateway: Prewar Seattle and Japanese America* (Temple University Press, 2010) and *A New History of Asian America* (Routledge, 2013).

Pei-te Lien is Professor of Political Science, Asian American Studies, and Feminist Studies at the University of California, Santa Barbara. Born and raised in Taiwan, she is the author of numerous publications on the political participation and representation of Asian and other nonwhite Americans.

Contributors

Lori Kido Lopez is Assistant Professor of Media and Cultural Studies in the Communication Arts Department at the University of Wisconsin-Madison. She is also an affiliate of the Asian American Studies Program and the Gender and Women's Studies Department. She is the author of *Asian American Media Activism: Fighting for Cultural Citizenship* (New York University Press, 2016).

Chong A. Moua is a Ph.D. candidate in the History Department at the University of Wisconsin-Madison. Her dissertation explores how Hmong refugees from the Southeast Asian War reveal the violence of U.S. democracy and freedom and upend the nationalist discourse of the United States as a nation of refuge for displaced and exiled immigrants.

Konrad Ng is Executive Director of the Doris Duke Charitable Foundation's Shangri La, a Center for Islamic Arts and Cultures. He was the former director of the Smithsonian Institution's Asian Pacific American Center and was a professor of creative media at the University of Hawai'i's Academy for Creative Media.

Yuichiro Onishi is Associate Professor of African American & African Studies and Asian American Studies at the University of Minnesota, Twin Cities. He is the author of *Transpacific Antiracism* (New York University Press, 2013).

Martin Joseph Ponce is Associate Professor of English at The Ohio State University, Columbus where he has served as Coordinator of the Asian American Studies Program and Sexuality Studies Program. He is the author of *Beyond the Nation: Diasporic Filipino Literature and Queer Reading* (New York University Press, 2012).

Junaid Rana is Associate Professor of Asian American Studies at the University of Illinois at Urbana-Champaign. He is the author of the book *Terrifying Muslims: Race and Labor in the South Asian Diaspora* (Duke University Press, 2011), and winner of the 2013 Association of Asian American Studies Book Award in the Social Sciences.

Sujani K. Reddy is Associate Professor of American Studies at State University of New York at Old Westbury. She is author of *Nursing and Empire: Gendered Labor and Migration from India to the United States* (University of North Carolina Press, 2015) and co-editor of *The Sun Never Sets: South Asian Migrants in an Age of U.S. Power* (New York University Press, 2013).

Cathy J. Schlund-Vials is Professor of English and Asian/Asian American Studies and Director of the Asian and Asian American Studies Institute at the University of Connecticut. In addition to numerous articles and book chapters, she is the author of two monographs: *Modeling Citizenship: Jewish and Asian American Writing* (Temple University Press, 2011) and *War, Genocide, and Justice: Cambodian American Memory Work* (University of Minnesota Press, 2012). She is currently the President of the Association for Asian American Studies.

Erin Suzuki is Assistant Professor of Literature at University of California, San Diego. Her research focuses on the intersections of American, Asian American, and indigenous Pacific Islander literatures and cultures. Her current book project is *Sacred Travelers: Indigenous Diaspora and the Transpacific Imagination*.

Ellen D. Wu is Associate Professor of History and Director of the Asian American Studies Program at Indiana University Bloomington. She is the author of *The Color of Success: Asian Americans and the Origins of the Model Minority* (Princeton University Press, 2014).

Timothy Yu is Professor of English and Asian American Studies and Director of the Asian American Studies Program at the University of Wisconsin-Madison. He is the author of the poetry collection *100 Chinese Silences* (Les Figues, 2016) and of *Race and the Avant-Garde: Experimental and Asian American Poetry since 1965* (Stanford University Press, 2009).

ACKNOWLEDGMENTS

My deepest gratitude to all the contributors to the volume. I would also like to thank my colleagues at the University of Wisconsin-Madison for fighting to keep Asian American studies a vibrant curriculum. Finally, I want to thank my students who made teaching Asian American studies meaningful and transformative.

INTRODUCTION: ON RECLAIMING THE POLITICAL PROJECT OF ASIAN AMERICAN STUDIES[1]

Cindy I-Fen Cheng

The Routledge Handbook of Asian American Studies situates itself within the expansive collection of Asian American anthologies that aims to increase classroom instruction of Asian American studies. Notably, Asian American anthologies have also had a vital hand in bringing coherence and defining values that would shape the academic field of Asian American studies. In fact, a critical genealogy of the field lies not just with the institutionalization of Ethnic Studies following the Third World Liberation Front-led strike in 1968 on the campus of San Francisco State University. It also lies with the publication of *Roots: An Asian American Reader* in 1971 by the UCLA Asian American Studies Center. Together with the 1974 publication of *Aiiieeeee!* and the 1976 release of *Counterpoint*, these assemblages began the foray into defining the mission, productive potential, and goals of Asian American studies. *The Routledge Handbook of Asian American Studies*, with its compilation of essays, builds on this aspect of Asian American anthologies. In addition to being a teaching tool, it offers a moment of reflection on the field, highlighting its realignments, growth, and possibilities. The goal of this rumination is to advance the political project of Asian American studies to transform the terrain of higher education.

Roots is in many ways a befitting title for the first published Asian American anthology. It not only named the goal of getting at the "'roots' of issues facing Asians in America," but the seeds planted also laid the groundwork for shaping the wide-ranging and often contested directions of Asian American studies.[2] Importantly, this premier volume of published essays conceived Asian American studies as a body of knowledge that was not exclusively tied to an institutionalized field of study on college campuses. Published after the 1968 San Francisco State Strike and the establishment of the Asian American Studies Center at UCLA, the editors of *Roots* saw the growing student demand for more Asian American studies courses on college campuses as one component, albeit an important one, of a broader call voiced by "social workers, organizers, lawyers, businessmen, workers, and housewives" for appropriate materials on Asian American issues.[3] In the final portion of this three-section anthology that surveyed an array of contemporary communal concerns, the expressed desire of the Asian American Political Alliance to steer the newly created Asian Studies Division within the interim Ethnic Studies Department at UC Berkeley to focus on Asians in the U.S. was juxtaposed with essays that addressed the need for more Asian American women leaders, the oppressed working conditions of Filipino farmworkers, and how the push for urban renewal was threatening ethnic spaces such as the Kalama Valley in Hawaii and Chinatown and the I-Hotel in San Francisco. By framing this aggregate body of knowledge as meeting the larger communal demand for works that upended society's neglect of Asian American concerns, this anthology conceived Asian American studies to be foremost the domain of Asian Americans who were working to serve their communities by combatting racism and economic injustice.

Besides featuring topics that identified Asian American concerns, *Roots* sought to bring attention to the varied perspectives, approaches, and sources of its essays. As editor Franklin Odo noted in his preface to the volume, only some of the essays drew on scholarly methods to ground their findings while others relied on personal reflections to recount the state of Asian Americans. This observation keenly saw the task of reclaiming the assorted perspectives of a neglected subject as tied to reforming the approaches and sources used to generate that body of knowledge. To study Asian Americans and their concerns was thus to call into question the tools used to produce legitimate knowledges and, in particular, viable scholarly knowledges. In light of how *Roots* equated Asian American concerns with combatting racism and economic injustice, this ethos further revealed the cultural politics that molded the whos, hows, and whats of Asian American studies, creating in its wake a makeshift heritage for the emergent field. Accordingly, the dictum "to return to one's roots" became a charge that Asian American studies remain tied to serving the community and to forging paradigms that shape how we made sense of the world and who and what we saw in it.

Five years later, the UCLA Asian American Studies Center followed its release of *Roots* with the 1976 publication of *Counterpoint: Perspectives on Asian America*. In this new anthology, Asian American studies came wholly to denote an institutionalized field of study in higher education. The importance of this shift from a more open-ended understanding of Asian American studies lay in how the university was nominally given the reigns to be the producers and teachers on matters related to Asian Americans. In some ways, no real shift appeared to have occurred in the conception of Asian American studies from the publication of *Roots* to *Counterpoint*, given the pervading assumption during that time that scholars of Asian American studies who worked and taught at universities shared the same goals as activists who labored in the community or outside the halls of higher education. The expectation was that Ethnic Studies scholars would transform higher education and unseat the effects of economic racism while advocating for the interests of racially and economically disenfranchised populations.

As editor Emma Gee remarked in the preface to this anthology, the emergence of Asian American studies in colleges and universities grew out of and was inseparable from social movements of the sixties and seventies and its attendant call to reclaim the histories and experiences of people of color. However, she recognized that Asian American studies was a "pioneering venture" and lacked a clear direction. Still, discernible trends abounded. The purpose of *Counterpoint* was to assemble works that captured some of these trends and bring coherence to the institutionalized field of Asian American studies.[4] Notably, this endeavor to create continuity within a field that was admittedly still without an apparent direction revealed how the accepted kinship between academics and activists needed to be regularly affirmed so that it appeared as a commonplace understanding. It also underscored the important role that early Asian American anthologies played in shaping and laying bare the values that fashioned this emergent field. As *Counterpoint* took on this monumental task, it featured works from an impressive array of professionalized academics, independent scholars, community activists, and artists. It further devoted the bulk of the reader to showing how scholar-activists were reframing the terms of knowledge production through scholarly and creative interventions so that the histories and social conditions of Asian Americans would be made visible. In its segment on contemporary issues, it included a section on education that connected the struggle for the institutionalization of Ethnic Studies to the activism of community organizations that have long labored to offer

Introduction

English language classes to recent Asian immigrants and tutorials to help economically disadvantaged Asian immigrant youths adjust to mainstream American schools. While nascent in development, the trends that were underscored in this 1976 anthology showed the field of Asian American studies to be firmly entrenched in a heritage of community activism and of developing critical approaches to bring to the fore Asian American issues.

About a decade would pass before the release of a new series of Asian American anthologies that featured selected papers first presented at the annual meeting of the Association for Asian American Studies. In the 1988 inaugural issue entitled, *Reflections on Shattered Windows: Promises and Prospects for Asian American Studies*, which published papers presented at the 1987 Association for Asian American Studies conference, editor Gary Okihiro called for "a new dispensation for Asian American studies." Twenty years had passed since the institutionalization of Ethnic Studies. Asian American studies, as this anthology revealed, was in need of a new direction. Okihiro detailed the values and goals of this conferment by stating,

> The authors remind us that Asian American studies arose out of struggle, out of a critique of American society and the education system that buttresses it, and out of a profound commitment to community. They also point to the changes undergone since the founding, both within the world-system and within our expanding and diversifying communities. They urge a conceptualization of Asian American studies that embraces the tradition together with an informed understanding of our present condition. That new synthesis, embodied in Asian American studies programs, the curriculum, and research, will serve us well in shaping our destiny.[5]

As Okihiro drew on the assembled works to peer into the windows shattered by strikers of the 1968 San Francisco State Strike, what he saw were reflections of Asian American studies at a crossroads. The declaration that Asian American studies arose from struggle, from a critique of U.S. society and its education system, and from a commitment to community no longer functioned as a recitation of a common understanding. Rather, it became a point of departure to ponder whether scholars of Asian American studies have "strayed from that tradition or whether that tradition required reformation."[6] What prompted this dilemma was the awareness that even though academic institutions persisted to oppose incorporating the demands of student and community activists of decades passed, the social and political milieu of the eighties was not conducive to the kinds of social activism of the sixties and seventies. The declaration that Asian American studies arose from struggle, in this view, was an expressed hope that the institutionalized field of Asian American studies does not abandon this legacy given how the fight was far from over, even as it acknowledged that the field was moving away from the roadmap laid out by scholar-activists of the sixties and seventies.

While Okihiro framed this crossroads as a "synthesis" between tradition and its departures, other authors of this 1988 volume proclaimed it the "crisis" of Asian American studies. Citing Italian political theorist Antonio Gramsci, Michael Omi defined "crisis" as the condition where "the old is dying and the new cannot be born."[7] For Omi, the crisis of Asian American studies captured in part the breakdown of the prevailing belief in the shared experience of Asian Americans and the sobering awareness of the different life experiences between a third-generation Japanese American and a recent Hmong refugee. Added to the dissipating belief in a uniform community bounded together by shared experiences was the growing split between campus and community endeavors. The once coordinated efforts of academically oriented Asian Americanists who worked to raise consciousness and build a new Asian American political and cultural identity in the classroom, so that politicized students would return to the community and support activist-orientated Asian Americanists to build alternative institutions, had fractured. Omi attributed this rift to the changing climate of both the academy- and community-based organizations. For academics, many succumbed to the mounting pressures to professionalize along traditional lines in order to secure tenure while community-based organizations watered down their radical visions as they navigated through local, state, and federal politics. These changes, Omi argued, led to the erosion of a shared goal for the development of alternative institutions. The institutionalization of Asian American studies thus not only strayed from radically transforming higher education, but it also moved away from cultivating the growth of non-traditional community-based organizations. Compounding this fissure was the embrace of mainstream politics by grassroots activists who once rejected the "bourgeois sham" of electoral politics. With these effects in mind, Asian American studies lost its coherent vision.[8]

Omi identified a final concern to characterize the crisis of Asian American studies, where the predicament of the field lay not with the old dying but with the difficulties of producing the next generation of scholar-activists. For author Don Mar, this crisis is evidenced by the rise of what he called "The Lost Second Generation of Asian American Scholars." Mar attributed the formation of this lost generation to two factors. The first cause extended beyond the problem of job scarcity and addressed the shortage of viable employment opportunities given the tenuous structure of Asian American studies programs nationwide. To underscore the shakiness of Asian American studies programs, Mar explained how most existed as "nomadic programs" that consisted of the ever-revolving door of visiting lecturers who were largely hired on an annual basis with the promise that a permanent position was "just around the corner.[9] While some programs appeared to be stable with the hiring of permanent personnel, Mar observed how these "fortress programs" belied the way college administrators, after funding the initial creation of permanent positions to quell student protests, had refused to provide any further support, forcing these programs to exist as a "fortress of solitude" on college campuses.[10] Finally, Mar described the growth of "mix-match programs" where the development of Asian American studies built on the hiring of Asian American studies scholars within traditional disciplines with the understanding that the primary commitment of these scholars was to their hiring department. Not only did this hiring structure limit the time and energy of scholars to foster Asian American studies but it also pushed them to develop scholarship in conformity with the dictates of traditional disciplines. Mar pointedly observed how this prevented many from publishing in Asian American studies journals for fear of risking their intellectual credibility.

Notably, Mar advanced a second reason to explain not just the rise of a lost second generation of Asian American studies scholars but also why this group was bound to be "lost." As Mar noted, this second generation of scholars were trained to embrace radical paradigms that pushed against the boundaries of traditional disciplines and challenged the terms and credibility of their knowledge productions. As many second generation scholars rejected the approaches of traditional disciplines and advanced new methods to recover the suppressed histories of Asian Americans and examine their current conditions, the commitment to forging critical perspectives meant that they could not return "home" again. The sense of disciplinary and departmental unbelonging thus accounted for the formation of a lost group of Asian American studies scholars. Importantly, traditional disciplines often worked to reinforce this structure of alienation by branding Asian American studies scholars as less scholarly, ill-trained academics who were limited by their particular interests while those in traditional disciplines held the clear-eyed view of the larger picture. This branding led Mar to quip that

> a stay in Asian American studies is akin to spending time teaching at a Siberian university. The reasoning is that if you were really a good sociologist, historian, psychologist, or

whatever, you would have spent time teaching and doing research in the discipline, and not some "soft" area like Asian American studies. Thus, the Asian American scholar lacks legitimacy in that scholar's original discipline. He or she can never "go home" to the traditional discipline. The net effect is that the Asian American scholar drops out of academics entirely.[11]

Despite this bleak appraisal of the future of Asian American studies scholars, Mar prescribed some possible solutions such as the development of more sophisticated political strategies outside of student protests to create employment opportunities for scholars. Another plan of action entailed the adoption of what Mar called a "holding arrangement."[12] Drawing on the example of his colleague, Mar detailed how some scholars made a deliberate choice to pick a non-Asian American topic for their dissertation in order to be attractive to traditional disciplines. This approach led to the hiring of his colleague in a mix-match program where he could still teach Asian American studies courses while meeting the demands of the traditional department. Interestingly, this latter strategy circled back to deepen Omi's assessment on why the old was dying. As certain negotiations functioned as intentional schemes, they revealed how necessity often drove the move away from old goals. But instead of death and the inability to form anew, this calculated shift sought to sustain and advance the institutionalization of Asian American studies. What was reproduced may be for some a grave disappointment from the desired ideal. Nevertheless, the deviation did not chart as a matter of course the abandonment of the old, even as it opened doors to redefine and reclaim the political project of Asian American studies.

Taken together, the insights of Omi and Mar are instructive for the current state of Asian American studies. In this early examination of the crisis of Asian American studies, the institutionalization of Ethnic Studies and of Asian American studies, in particular, could not be fully reduced to or narrated as a single event. Rather, as Omi, Mar, and other authors of the 1988 volume revealed, not only was the institutionalization of Asian American studies an ongoing struggle twenty years after its founding on the campus of San Francisco State University, but the values that shaped the development of the field and what constituted meaningful and transformative education were also in flux. The stated reasons for the breakdown in the belief in a community unified through shared experiences and between campus and community endeavors to create alternative institutions were the changing social and political milieu of the eighties and the increasingly diverse demographics of Asian Americans. Omi's discussion of the different life experiences between a third-generation Japanese American and a Hmong refugee, for instance, pointed to how, aside from immigration reforms, U.S. Cold War interventions in the affairs of Southeast Asia had prompted the influx of displaced people to the U.S., altering the makeup of Asian America.

However, the fractures that took place could not be wholly attributed to the external factors of demographic changes and the rise of New Conservatism or neoconservatism of the eighties. This was because the conception of Asian American panethnicity of the sixties and seventies already betrayed an East Asian bias.[13] This bias was famously imprinted with the release of both the 1974 *Aiiieeeee!* and the 1991 *The Big Aiiieeeee!*. In these two anthologies of Asian American literature edited by Jeffery Paul Chan, Frank Chin, Lawson Fusao Inada, and Shawn Wong, the category of Filipino American literature was first introduced as a discrete section, apart from the discussion of Asian American literature, and then dropped altogether from the 1991 publication such that Chinese and Japanese American literature came to stand in for Asian American literature.[14] Within this context, the rupture that took place within Asian American studies did not result in the abandonment of the political but in furthering the field's transformative potential. This was because the insistence against a single narrative of the Asian American experience went above calling attention to the varied life experiences of communities and individuals and interrogated the very values and socio-political contexts that rendered certain communal and life experiences invisible while others emerged as definitive. The analytic of difference thus fostered a critique of normative structures so that the logics, histories, and life experiences of the marginal could come to light.[15] It sought to resist reproducing the frameworks that buried the histories and concerns of Asian Americans and in so doing, carried forward a founding mission of the field even as it unsettled the core belief in a discernible, coherent Asian American community.

In some ways the rupture that took place during the eighties was a buildup for an even bigger fallout that occurred ten years later following the decision of the Association of Asian American Studies to award its literature prize to *Blu's Hanging* by Lois-Ann Yamanaka. After much protest, the Association of Asian American Studies retracted the award over the book's racist depictions of Filipinos and left in its wake a splintered field as supporters of the novel considered the revocation an infringement on artistic expression, stifling multidimensional representations of Asian Americans. While the issues surrounding the *Blu's Hanging* controversy were complex and in no way coherent, the dominant framework that emerged to account for the dissension took on the shape of a campus/community divide where scholarly concerns were pitted against community concerns.[16] In light of this framework, the issues that arose over *Blu's Hanging* advanced the crisis of the eighties, laying bare not just an incoherent community of scholars and activists but also the unintelligibility of "Asian American." Beyond interrogating the authority to define communal histories and concerns, these issues prompted a reassessment of the political efficacy of lumping together diverse and competing life experiences and communal interests into one representative category. Notable scholars such as Kandice Chuh and Viet Thanh Nguyen have addressed the representational crisis that emerged following the *Blu's Hanging* controversy.[17] More recently, Mark Chiang and Christopher Lee have revisited this controversy to assay the political function of academic work, with Chiang examining how intellectual autonomy is often at odds with community accountability and Lee analyzing why identity still matters within Asian American studies despite the crisis over representation.[18]

Notwithstanding the significance of this 1998 rupture and the generative conversations that it invoked, I would like to return to the eighties and to the crisis that was documented with the 1988 release of *Reflections on Shattered Windows*. This return is important because I consider the eighties a pivotal moment to chart not just the fractures and departures that took place within Asian American studies but also the continuities. In short, I look to this period to tie the critical perspectives developed by a founding generation of Asian American scholars to current ones. *The Routledge Handbook of Asian American Studies*, with its assemblage of essays, highlights how, aside from the analytic of difference, the frameworks of denationalization and the transnational have been critical to sustaining the way Asian American studies arose from a critique of U.S. society to form new paradigms to reclaim Asian American concerns and combat economic racism. Markedly, the eighties, as seen in Mar's discussion of the lost second generation of Asian American studies scholars, also highlighted the ongoing struggle for the institutionalization of Asian American studies, foregrounding the political economy that fostered a structure of unbelonging for Asian American studies programs, scholars, and scholarship. This volume also considers how the sense of "unbelonging" that Mar described has led to a conception of interdisciplinarity that aims to keep the institutionalized field of Asian American studies open to scholars who could never go "home" again. To that end, *The Routledge Handbook of Asian American Studies* reclaims the heritage of Asian American studies.

Introduction

Critical Perspectives

One of the most striking features of *Roots* was how it began with the formation of an Asian Americanist critique.[19] In the opening section of this three-section anthology on identity, editor Amy Tachiki discussed how U.S. national memory had largely ignored the participation of Asian Americans. Because of this erasure, Tachiki found it curious, ironic even, that there was a surge of articles hailing Asian Americans as the nation's most successful minority. Writing in 1971, Tachiki recounted how the release of "Success Story of One Minority Group in the U.S." by *U.S. News and World Report* five years earlier paved the way for similar stories to appear in major news outlets such as the *New York Times* and *Newsweek*. Like all stereotypes, the creation of the "success image of Asian Americans," she argued, prioritized certain parameters and ignored others.[20] What these stories covered up with their focus on how Asian Americans, unlike other minorities, had managed to achieve high educational and economic standing was the persistence of racism and how Asian Americans professionals were still subjected to various forms of institutional subordination and segregation.

Tachiki further probed the context that gave rise to the "success myth." She noted how the 1966 *U.S. News and World Report* feature was published shortly after the release of the McCone Commission report on the Watts uprising such that the Asian American success myth worked to uphold the belief that blacks were the problems of society and responsible for the Watts unrest. Rather than challenge the underlying value structure that propagated economic racism and prompted blacks to protest institutionalized racism, the success myth of Asian Americans reinforced the belief that "American democratic capitalism guarantees self-determination for all its people." Tachiki concluded,

> By accepting the distorted picture of Asian American success, America rationalizes its racist behavior—and fools itself that it is responsive to the people. Furthermore, the Asian model of assimilation frees the white majority from assuming responsibility for its own oppressiveness, since it implies that nonwhite minorities have to *earn* their rights to American society and it shifts the cause for minority problems away from society and onto minority communities.[21]

As Tachiki rejected the misleading caricature of Asian Americans, she replaced it with a critique. By interrogating the context and underlying values that gave rise to the Asian American model minority myth, Tachiki compellingly forged an Asian Americanist critique of U.S. democratic capitalism. In so doing, she conceived Asian American studies to dismiss racist love and thwart attempts to suppress examinations of the effects of economic racism and blame racialized communities for society's ills.

In a similar fashion, editor Buck Wong drew on his introductory remarks to the history section to issue a critique of U.S. society, stating that "as long as people believed in the popularized concept of democracy, they will not question any of the mechanisms of the governing process.[22] This "apotheosis of American democracy," Wong argued, had damaging consequences for Asian Americans. Like Tachiki, Wong considered how the model minority stereotype compromised the ability of Asian American experiences to generate different views of U.S. society. He found it problematic the way the success myth manipulated Asian American histories and achievements to buttress claims about the superiority of U.S. democracy and to cultivate an unquestioned adherence to its governing systems. Wong noted how "history" was not a neutral retelling of past events but operated as a "concept" with values guiding the retelling of past events. As mainstream news outlets as well as scholars used the success myth to frame the narration of the past, they produced what Wong described to be a generic recollection of how Asian Americans "faced and overcame much prejudice in society" and how this progress "served as an example of the responsiveness of the democratic system."[23]

The casualty of this retelling of Asian American history lay not in the use of history to highlight positive changes that occurred in society. Wong contended that it was founded on the use of the past to disguise the persistence of racism. History functioned as an effective cloak because it allowed for the acknowledgment of racism only to relegate it as a thing of the past, a social ill that society had fixed and moved away from. Rather than portend the kinds of changes that society needed to make in order to increase the overall livelihood of its peoples, the success myth sustained the status quo and warded off calls for institutional changes. As Wong shrewdly remarked, "Through such a manipulation of the Asian identity, the desired result is to have the Asian riding in the back of the bus and digging it."[24]

Wong's appeal to reclaim Asian American history began in this way with a critique of the uses of historical memory. The project of reclaiming the participation of Asian Americans in the country's development required a different framework to guide the crafting of historical memory, a framework that refused to lavish praise on the mechanisms of democratic capitalism. Notably, Wong would prescribe the development of a singular Asian immigrant experience to call attention to how all Asian Americans came from a shared past of economic exploitation and racism. Together with the reflections of Eddie Wong, editor of the final section on community, the development of this common history promised to produce beneficial results, powering the need for resistance and social movements to upend the effects of economic racism.[25]

Interestingly, this conception of the Asian American identity laid the groundwork for the growth of Asian Americanist critiques. Driving the reformulations of existing paradigms was the desire not to reproduce the very exclusionary mechanisms that rendered marginal Asian American experiences. But the quest to call into question the operating assumptions of the field proved to be a double bind. This was because the advancement of a paradigm of difference for the purpose of recovering the varied and conflicting life experiences of Asian Americans buried by the master narrative of the Asian American experience had ruptured a foundational premise of a field. Continuity, in this view, was only possible through ruptures. Along with the analytic of difference, questions over the assimilationist paradigm would further fracture Asian American studies, only to create in its wake frameworks that deepened the analysis of power structures and how they reproduced social unevenness through the visible and the invisible.

While both Amy Tachiki and Buck Wong strongly criticized how the assimilation paradigm and its promotion of the Asian American success myth had covered up institutional racism while reaffirming the responsiveness of U.S. democratic capitalism, they nevertheless espoused the way this framework distinguished Asians as Americans and contested the caricature of Asian Americans as the foreigners-within. To reclaim the history of Asian Americans thus entailed not just constructing a shared experience of economic exploitation and racism; it also included demonstrating how Asian Americans struggled against racism, successfully shed away attachments to countries of origin, and claimed America. This cultural nationalist approach is exemplified by two anthologies on Asian American literature, the 1974 *Aiiieeeee!* and the 1991 *The Big Aiiieeeee!*, edited by Chan, Chin, Inada, and Wong. It also framed Ronald Takaki's 1989 *Strangers from a Different Shore* and his retelling of the Asian American experience.[26]

Around the time of the release of Takaki's book, the Association for Asian American Studies published its third anthology in 1991 that featured papers first presented at the 1989 Annual Conference of the Association for Asian American Studies.[27] To commemorate three decades of Asian American studies, the volume brought together papers that addressed the conference theme, "Comparative and Global Perspectives of the Asian Diaspora." Notably, with its focus on the "international dimension" of the Asian American experience, this 1991 volume documented another major shift that was taking place within the field. As literary scholar Sau-Ling C. Wong described in her 1995 piece "Denationalization Reconsidered," the shift away from a cultural nationalist approach and towards a diasporic one marked a key theoretical crossroads of Asian American studies.[28] Careful not to ascribe too much weight to how theoretical developments shaped field formation, Wong cited Sucheta Mazumdar to underscore how "the very genesis of Asian American studies was international," given the way scholar-activists of the sixties and seventies linked the battle for Ethnic Studies to the global struggle for decolonization and self-determination.[29] Wong also noted how immigration historians have long adopted frameworks that connected national developments to global happenings.

With these points in mind, what this theoretical crossroads revealed was a shift in the cultural politics of the field where the political efficacy of claiming America at the expense of Asia no longer brought about the transformative results that earlier scholars envisioned. Rather, demographic shifts and global restructuring created different realities of economic racism and racial formations that altered the terrain of and advocacy for social change. Wong compellingly detailed the shifts that took place where the cultural nationalist approach eased and the diasporic framework gained prominence. But what her piece is best known for is the concluding section outlining some reservations about the over-emphasis on the fluidity of borders and identities. While denationalization may be effective for lifting restrictions of the cultural nationalist approach, allowing for more nuanced understandings of identity formations and political activism that takes into consideration the experiences of first-generation immigrants and the economies that maintain attachments to more than one country, Wong showed how the exchanges between and among nations were far from even. Rather, the ease of moving back and forth between countries often exemplified the privilege of upper-class travelers whereas the restrictions of national borders were more keenly felt by those without disposable income. As Wong called attention to the factors that contributed to the uneven exchange between nations, she adopted a transnational understanding that mined the various power structures at work to shape the uneven movement of ideas and people. Denationalization, in this view, did more than widen the landscape for identity formations. It sustained the political project of Asian American studies to forge a critique of U.S. society, unseating the belief in American exceptionalism while keeping critiques of economic racism relevant in the global age.

Shifting Disciplinary Terrains

Importantly, the growth of Asian American studies was brought about not only by the changing perspectives and theoretical frameworks of the field but also by unsettling the way disciplinary boundaries defined viable academic knowledge and the approaches used to generate that knowledge. The need to shift disciplinary boundaries in order for Asian American concerns to come to light was a matter that the 1976 publication of *Counterpoint* took up. Like *Roots*, *Counterpoint* dedicated the first part of this anthology to highlighting the critical perspectives of the field, beginning with three essays and a handful of book reviews delineated as "critiques." Interestingly, the featured essays did not center their critiques on examining how U.S. democratic capitalism was compromising the retelling of Asian American histories. Instead, they focused on revealing the limits of disciplinary knowledges. A productive aspect of this inquiry is the focused attention on sources and methods, situating Asian American studies as a field that interrogated the mechanisms that have rendered Asian Americans marginal. Like the ethos that drove scholar-activists to fight for the institutionalization of Ethnic Studies, the demand was not simply for inclusion but for a fundamental shift in the values that governed higher education, values that also shaped how we know what we know. While this inquiry led to the unbelonging of Asian American studies programs, scholars, and scholarship, it also fostered the development of Asian American studies as an interdisciplinary field committed to critiquing normative disciplinary structures of the academy.

For instance, historian Yuji Ichioka, while wedded to using historical approaches to generate truth claims, was deeply aware of their limits for recovering the past experiences of minority groups. In his *Counterpoint* essay entitled, "A Buried Past," Ichioka declared his expressed hope for Asian American history stating,

> Ideally it should entail a search for a meaningful historical past—the debunking of old distortions and myths, the uncovering of hitherto neglected or unknown facts, and the construction of a new interpretation of that past.[30]

To that end, he did a thorough survey of English-language works on Japanese American history for common themes, approaches, and sources used in the writing of that history. From this investigation, Ichioka concluded that there was an overabundance of works on Japanese American internment during WWII. Missing were in-depth studies of first generation Japanese immigrants that went beyond the context of the exclusion movement, where history was something that they shaped and not something that happened to them. The recovery of this buried past required different tools. Specifically, the task of centering Japanese Americans' activities and pursuits necessitated the use of different primary sources and in particular, Japanese language sources. While scholars of immigration history had already adopted these changes when researching and writing about European immigrants, Ichioki noted how historians have yet to make these changes when studying Asian immigrants.

Similarly, sociologist Lucie Cheng Hirata in her *Counterpoint* essay entitled, "The Chinese American in Sociology," called out the discipline of sociology for developing models of normal behavior through the lens of white America. Minority issues were thus seen as deviations from the norm, requiring socialization and social control to fix the differences. The belief that minority groups such as the Chinese were an inferior race further complicated analysis of whether they could change their deviant ways to be like other white Americans. Hirata issued a pointed critique at how some liberal sociologists addressed this racist thinking by reinforcing stereotypes of the Chinese as model minorities or narrowly casting them as part of the educated elite, perturbed by associations with nineteenth-century laborers. Because these seemingly positive caricatures did not fundamentally unsettle the values that defined normal behavior, they upheld the assimilation model and left intact racist sociological analysis. For Hirata, the discipline needed to embrace a different approach such as cultural pluralism where sociological inquiry does not begin with an exemplary model of normative behavior. Moreover, community studies needed to go beyond a black/white paradigm and consider how Chinatowns shaped community formation. Beyond the appeal to consider race more broadly, Hirata advanced the importance of examining Chinatowns through the frameworks of institutional racism and internal colonialism, rejecting the racist culture of poverty paradigm for perpetuating the perceived pathology of black ghettos.[31]

As the analysis of Ichioka and Hirata showed, the project of recovering buried histories and concerns included shifting the terrain of disciplinary knowledges. Importantly, this task took a steeper turn as the field contended with not only problematizing the operating assumptions of traditional disciplines but also how the unearthing of biased approaches unsettled the truth claims of all disciplines. This turn has its beginnings with the way early anthologies like *Counterpoint* often included a section on Asian American literature, recognizing that creative inventions, like historical and sociological accounts, were essential to making sense of Asian American experiences. "Third World writings," argued editor Bruce Iwasaki, "provided a critique of America from people who are uniquely prepared to provide one, discouraged from doing so, and able to illuminate how these two conditions are related."[32] In many ways, Iwasaki advanced the analysis of editors Chin, Chan, Inada, and Wong and their 1974 *Aiiieeeee!*, which was published two years prior to the release of *Counterpoint*. As the editors of *Aiiieeeee!* and later, *The Big Aiiieeeee!*, set forth to define the term Asian American literature, they ignited a debate over the facticity of truth-claims. The insights generated from this debate crucially bolstered the development of an interdisciplinary approach for Asian American studies.

In the 1974 anthology, editors Chin, Chan, Inada, and Wong sought to unfold the tradition of Asian American literature and make known the proficiency of Asian American writers. They defined Asian American literature as creative writings by American-born Chinese and Japanese authors and to a lesser extent, by Filipino American authors. The editors also delineated Asian American literature as creative works that did not pander to the interests of white readers and reproduce Orientalist caricatures of Asian Americans. Rather than develop the tradition of Asian American literature in conformity with the movements of mainstream American literature, Chin, Chan, Inada, and Wong established their own frameworks to distinguish the trends of Asian American literature.[33] Still, social context was important and they drew on events in U.S. history to explain, for instance, how WWII was a favorable time for Chinese American literature and an adverse one for Japanese American literature and how the U.S. colonial takeover of the Philippines gave rise to Filipino American literature. The editors, moreover, utilized historical time to demarcate the gradual shift of works written primarily for white readers and works that highlighted the interests of Asian Americans. Interestingly, the detailing of this shift also functioned as a reproach of readers and the publishing industry to stop confusing works written by Chinese-born authors as Chinese American literature and of Chinese American authors to cease describing their social proclivities as quintessentially Chinese. It was with these points in mind that prompted the editors to decry the "tyranny of language" not only for denigrating writings that featured the idioms of Asian Americans as works that showed the failure of Asian American writers to grasp fully the English language, but also for the way Third World anthologies continued to feature in their Chinese American sections the writings of a Chinese from China.[34] It was also with these points in mind that prompted scholars of Asian American studies to dub *Aiiieeeee!* as exemplary of the cultural nationalist approach.

Notably, editors Chin, Chan, Inada, and Wong continued the quest to define the authoritative Asian American writer and literature and fight against their marginalization with the publication of the 1991 follow-up anthology, *The Big Aiiieeeee!* But what the 1991 anthology brought to the fore far exceeded its stated aim of outing Maxine Hong Kingston and other female authors as among the "fake" Asian American writers given how *The Women Warrior* painted an inaccurate portrait of Chinese culture and was not, as Frank Chin argued, an exact autobiographical sketch of Kingston's life but a marketing tool to sell books.[35] This was because the search to distinguish the authentic from the inauthentic in Asian American literature revealed an epistemic dilemma of the field. It placed the need for Asian Americans to define their history and culture on their own terms against the project of interrogating the values behind all truth-claims. As Chin appealed to an empirical outside to creative inventions in order to justify his version of the real, he betrayed in part the mission of scholar-activists who sought to show through the institutionalization of Ethnic Studies how knowledge was a manifestation of social power. Thus, even though Chin and the rest of the editors of *The Big Aiiieeeee!* endeavored to advance the credibility of Asian American literature, their attempts to situate themselves and their works as part of the authentic tradition of Asian American literature were predicated on suppressing how *The Women Warrior* revealed gaping holes in that tradition in its failure to recover Asian American women's voices and points of views. Thus, what Chin promoted was an approach to racial equality where the interests of Asian American feminists were subsumed and forestalled for the greater good of a male-led Asian America.[36]

Not coincidentally, a similar epistemic dilemma erupted following the 1989 publication of Ronald Takaki's *Strangers from a Different Shore*. A year after its release, *Amerasia* dedicated an entire issue to exploring questions over who possessed the authority to define a communal history and what kinds of sources and approaches one could and should use to generate that history.[37] Questions were thus raised about how Takaki had based his truth claims about a community on a handful of interviews rather than on a random representative sample of Asian Americans, and about his failure to acknowledge the contributions of colleagues in the writing of this communal history. But, as literary scholar Elaine Kim noted, the problem with *Strangers from a Different Shore* exceeded concerns over source selection and citational practices. It was the assumption that there was a transparent non-politicized approach to knowledge production. Kim thus found troubling the way Takaki had positioned himself as a neutral mediator giving voice to the voiceless, where the use of oral histories and autobiographies cloaked his role as the master interpreter of life events. For Kim, the danger of assuming the position of a neutral storyteller went beyond Takaki's elevation of history above literature and rested on his reliance on the disciplinary mechanisms of history to make truth claims appear as unmediated facts. But as Kim compellingly showed, much of Takaki's retelling of Asian American history belied his patriarchal framework given how Asian American women were on the whole presented as extensions of men with little or no agency of their own.[38]

With these points in mind, what was shown by the assortment of critiques that followed the publication of *The Woman Warrior* and *Strangers from a Different Shore*, two definitive works of Asian American literature and history, was how the task of unsetting disciplinary terrains had advanced Asian American studies as a field that sought not just to reclaim the histories and concerns of Asian Americans but also the values that rendered them invisible. This sensitivity towards the conditions and consequences of knowledge production formed one basis of the development of Asian American studies as an interdisciplinary field, while the other basis sees interdisciplinarity as the neutral merging of different disciplines that some would call "multidisciplinary." As the dilemma between "history" and "literature" revealed, the split between the way scholars understood these two modes of disciplinary formations had also charted competing meanings of interdisciplinarity. For some, history worked to ground and ascertain the assertions of literature while literature breathed life into historical writings. For others, historical writings, like literature, are interpretations of life events that require examinations into the values that guide the storytelling in order to guard against reproducing exclusionary paradigms. At the heart of this dilemma is the quandary about just what the institutionalization of Asian American studies within higher education is supposed to signify and accomplish. It asks whether Asian American studies is to exist as just another disciplinary formation, attesting to the ability of higher education to "change" and expand its fields of study, or whether Asian American studies is to exist as a site that continued to interrogate the way the academy is reinforcing social inequalities.[39]

The Routledge Handbook of Asian American Studies builds on the shifts that have taken place during the eighties and nineties, advancing foremost an examination into how the denationalized and transnational frameworks have impacted Asian American scholarly work. It further promotes the advancement of Asian American studies as an interdisciplinary field that is committed to recognizing the political nature of all knowledge production in order to keep open the possibility of transforming higher education with its attention to the production of social inequalities and to exploring different meanings and paths towards social justice. This anthology organizes its collection of essays around five thematic sections to showcase some of the analytical trends and directions of the field. It connects Asian Americanist critiques with critical perspectives to analyze the growth of U.S. capitalism brought about by war, imperialism, and global restructuring and explores the consequences of these changes through Asian American representations within national and transnational terrains. Finally, this anthology explores how shifts within Asian American communities have engendered different conceptions of and avenues to achieving social justice. By providing a snapshot of the field of Asian American studies and its productive potentials, this anthology looks to foster critical conversations in classrooms about social power, inequalities, and justice.

Overview of Sections

The essays featured in Part One highlight a set of critical terms and concepts that are shifting the paradigms of Asian American studies. Besides advancing analytical frameworks to assay the values shaping U.S. national development, the essays draw on Asian American racial formations to forge transnational frameworks that cultivate not only a hemispheric understanding of Asian America but also a deeper awareness of the ways in which U.S. economic development is tied to that of Asia and the Pacific. This section opens with Leslie Bow's examination of what has become a foundational outset of Asian Americanist critiques: "stereotype." Bow effectively argues that the harmful consequences of "negative" and "positive" racial representations rest not in their misrepresentations but in their overdetermining of culture above economic stressors such as the uneven allocation of resources and the lack of infrastructural development. A critical interrogation of racial stereotypes is thus needed to unsettle the values that uphold normative structures of governance. For Joshua Chambers-Letson, "law" is another mechanism that works to promote American democratic capitalism. He entreats critical race theorists to appraise the effectiveness of achieving economic and racial justice through civil rights reforms, asking the difficult question of whether political emancipation through law only reforms racial capitalism to allow for the class ascension of racialized minorities and their greater participation as capitalist consumers. Erin Suzuki interrogates in her article the racial representations of Asian Americans as inscrutable foreigners and privileged post-racial subjects to reveal how they trace the growth of American capitalism and colonization. Suzuki develops this lens to examine Asian America as a postcolonial formation for the purpose of critiquing the way U.S. foreign policy initiatives in Asia and the Pacific endeavored to regulate the global flows of capital, commodities, and communities. Martin Joseph Ponce advances this inquiry through the study of Asian diaspora. Ponce develops how a diasporic framework bolsters the transnational and denationalized approaches of Asian America studies, noting their importance not just for building greater understanding between U.S. and Asian studies but also for undermining U.S. national belonging as the most desired endpoint for displaced populations. Finally, Michelle Har Kim broadens understandings of a transnational Asian America to include Latin America. Through her elegant reading of Anna Kazumi Stahl's *Flores de un solo dia*, Kim argues that the reorientation of Asian American studies around *castellano* or the Spanish language disrupts the reign of anglophonicity and the homolingual to shape what constitutes Asian American literature, revealing instead the social power that fashions how we know and what we know.

Part Two builds on the critiques of the previous section with critical perspectives on U.S. expansionist efforts through war, imperialism, and colonization. As Yen Le Espiritu pointedly argues in her piece, during this moment of renewed U.S. imperialism, it is imperative to undercut the way mainstream media have cast Vietnamese refugees as the "good refuge" to reinforce

Introduction

U.S. rescue fantasies and justify military intervention. Chong Moua supports this call for critical refugee studies and constructs a Hmong refugee memoryscape to highlight stories about displacement rather than rescue. Besides revealing the devastating impact that U.S. covert operations in the Secret War in Laos had inflicted, these tales forge a sense of community for the warn-torn and geographically dispersed Hmong. Cathy J. Schlund-Vials builds on the importance of memory work in her examination of how U.S. covert operations in Cambodia and support of the Khmer Rouge propelled the Cambodian genocide. Schlund-Vials details how the cultural productions of 1.5 and second generation Cambodian Americans are working to prosecute the Khmer Rouge and the U.S. in ways that the Khmer Rouge tribunals have failed to do. Importantly, Bianca Kai Isaki broadens critiques against U.S. imperialism to cultivate the importance of decolonization efforts. For Isaki, this endeavor goes beyond supporting the Hawaiian sovereignty movement and entails decolonizing Asian Americans studies so that the experiences of early Asian immigrants in Hawai'i are directed to highlight the inner workings of settler colonialism instead of promoting the multicultural agenda of the U.S. liberal state. Rick Baldoz uncovers in his essay the contradictory values of U.S. racial statecraft that saw the colonial takeover of the Philippines as an important step towards advancing racial capitalism even as nativist sentiments worked to block the importation and use of racialized cheap labor. As this contradiction manifested in the ambiguous citizenship of Filipinos as nationals to denote both their marginalized status in U.S. society and their elevated position in relation to other Asian groups, Baldoz considers how racial statecraft works to prevent the social closure of citizenship and undermine national sovereignty. Finally, Louise Cainkar shows how the 9/11 attacks initiated the heightened scrutiny of Arab and Muslim Americans and not discriminatory treatment against them, which was prevalent long before the attacks. Given how this acute visibility tracks the expansion of U.S. empire through economic restructuring and political domination, Cainkar details how the study of Arab and Muslim Americans aligns with the political project of Asian American studies to critique U.S. imperialism.

In Part Three, the development and effects of globalization and global restructuring are examined through changes that took place in the material conditions of working-class Asian Americans. Additionally, they are shown to manifest in Asian American identity formations to detail the variegated connections between the national and the transnational. As Christine Bacareza Balance duly notes, globalization is not a new phenomenon but an ongoing process where, for instance, the globalizing power of popular music taps into the ways "Asia America" signifies both national and transnational belongings. Balance charts three periods, spanning the 1850s to the present, where technological advancements and sociopolitical forces shape the circulation of popular music to historicize how Asian Americans made use of popular music to signify "Asianness," "Americanness," and the exchanges between the two. For Rachael Joo, the rise of Asian athletes such as Yao Ming and Yuna Kim who have competed in North American commercialized sports and achieved top-level celebrity status exemplifies current manifestations of global Asianness. Joo develops its significance for exposing how Asian difference is at once marketable because of its foreignness and because it could be used to affirm the American Dream. Contrary to the way "global" signifies a denationalized understanding, Joo details how global Asianness generates new Asian nationalisms among Asian Americans who have little or no ties to Asia. Timothy Yu, while recognizing how NBA star Jeremy Lin participates in promoting his global Asianness appeal, highlights how Lin has also used popular media to proclaim his identity as an Asian American. Yu explores the significance of this racial identification and details how the circulation of Lin's global Asian Americanness exposes not just U.S. racial disparities but also the way racial hierarchies structure the uneven exchange between "Asia" and "America." Lastly, Margaret Chin offers an insightful look at the way global restructuring during the 1990s not only undercut the growth of unionized shops in New York City's garment industry but also propelled the development of "quick time" orders where domestic workers stayed competitive in the global market by replenishing popular items quickly so that manufactures did not have to wait for overseas production and shipment. But, as Chin notes, Chinese women garment workers lost this competitive edge after the 9/11 attacks and the 2008 recession, which saw the demise of the garment industry, leaving many unemployed while others found work in New York's service industry.

Part Four continues the examination of how war, imperialism, and global restructuring shape the representations of Asian Americans within and across national borders. It begins with Junaid Rana's analysis of anti-Muslim racism and how it exposes the way white supremacy is tied to the global project of U.S. imperialism. Rana employs the U.S. foreign policy construct of Af-Pak, which grouped Afghanistan and Pakistan as a single theater of operations in the War on Terror, to show how it shaped the demographics of Little Pakistan in Brooklyn, New York to be a composite of South Asians, Afghans, and ethnic Pashtuns. As this spatialization lumped the plurality of ethnicities under the rubric of "Muslim," Rana details how Little Pakistan became an extension of U.S. imperialism, working to assimilate Muslims into a white norm. Michael Jin in his essay unsettles the U.S. national focus of Japanese American history by examining how WWII and questions over Nisei loyalty forged transnational connections. Jin draws on an understudied group of Niseis who left for Japan before the attack on Pearl Harbor to highlight how these Nisei strandees, like those in the U.S., were stripped of their American citizenship and forced to serve in the Japanese army. Questions over Japanese American loyalty, thus, gave rise to a transnational formation of denationalized Niseis. Yu-Fang Cho further enriches the study of transnational racial formations by analyzing how the ethos of heterosexual domesticity regulated the kinds of Asian men and women that were allowed to immigrate to the U.S. Cho pointedly details how during the post-1965 era, this ethos continued to govern Asian immigration for the purpose of developing a transpacific reproductive economy. Shelley Sang-Hee Lee reorients the focus back to examining how race and space shaped the U.S. national belonging of Asian Americans. Lee explores Chinatowns and Ethno-burbs as sites that have worked not only to marginalize Asian Americans from mainstream society but also to build a sense of community for Asian Americans, prompting redefinitions in the terms of national belonging. Lastly, Ellen Wu offers a fresh analysis of the historical origins of the model minority myth to examine it as a product of the changes taking place in the nation's domestic and foreign policies from WWII to the Vietnam War and the desire of Chinese and Japanese Americans to be accepted as legitimate members of U.S. society.

In the final section of this anthology, the featured essays provide a look at the various approaches to social change and political participation. Lori Kido Lopez and Konrad Ng in their piece develop the need for Asian Americans studies to advance as a digital project given the rising influence of technology in shaping the knowledge production of race and nation. They argue that the development of Asian American studies as Digital Humanities necessitates treating technology not as a tool but as a discursive formation that is defined through social power and disseminates normative ideologies. Jian Neo Chen builds on the importance of advocating for social change by examining Asian American queer and trans activisms. Chen provides a cogent analysis of how a queered Asian American consciousness emerged during the mid-to-late 1990s as a reworking of LGBT Asian Pacific American politics to push for non-normative understandings of sexual practices and gender expressions and the overall messiness of sexual and gender desires. But the rise in the visibility of trans Asian Americans in the 2000s came at a time of disconnect among mainstream LGBT movements that saw white dominance over emergent transgender movements and the privileging of binary transitions as the primary mode of transgender expressions. These shifts muted the struggles and experiences of trans Asian Americans but, as Chen contends, they also energized the need to build new coalitions to challenge transphobia and cis-heterosexism. Sujani Reddy, in her examination of the Asian immigrant rights movement, makes a compelling case to use Asian/Pacific/American prisoners as a starting point for organizing. Reddy considers this a politically efficacious move given how the nation has become a carceral state and how the dismantling of the "good" and "bad" immigrant construct is imperative to advancing the rights of all immigrants and not just those who conform to and advance the interests of the U.S. liberal state. For Yuichiro Onishi, the path towards social justice entails looking back at the roots of Afro-Asian solidarity that saw the convergence of Black radicalism and Third World internationalism. It also requires interrogating the values that broke down this solidarity and in particular, the way the model minority construct has worked to mute Black critiques against institutionalized racism. The project of moving forward then, as Onishi contends, calls for a renewed understanding of the importance of Afro-Asian solidarity and the development of activism along multiple color lines. This section concludes with Pei-te Lien's review of Asian American political participation. While early Asian American activists focused on grassroots organizing over electoral politics as the main avenue of social change, Lien details how current trends emphasize political participation through voting. This shift not only heightens the importance of understanding the voting patterns of Asian Americans but it also ties the political participation of Asian Americans to other processes such as naturalization and voter registration.

With this assemblage of essays, *The Routledge Handbook of Asian American Studies* provides a sample of some decisive critiques and critical perspectives of Asian American studies. It draws on these works to show how the field of Asian American studies is committed to interrogating the growth of American democratic capitalism in this age of global restructuring and its attendant affects in reorienting national and transnational articulations and belongings. Given the changes in community and identity formations as well as in the modes and technologies of knowledge production, this anthology provides a variegated look at the different paths to social change and justice. Taken together, the aim of this volume is to reclaim the transformative potential of the institutionalized field of Asian American studies. It builds on the legacies of scholar-activists of the sixties and seventies that sought to affect change through education and pedagogy. The expressed hope is that this reader will work as an effective teaching tool, enlivening classroom discussions over social inequalities and the possibilities for change and an equitable future.

Notes

1 I would like to thank Leslie Bow for her insightful comments and feedback on an early draft of this introduction.
2 Franklin Odo, "Preface," in *Roots: An Asian American Reader*. Amy Tachiki, Eddie Wong, Franklin Odo, and Buck Wong (Eds.) (Los Angeles, CA: UCLA Asian American Studies Center, 1971), vii.
3 Ibid.
4 Emma Gee, "Preface," in *Counterpoint: Perspectives on Asian America*. Emma Gee (Ed.) (Los Angeles, CA: UCLA Asian American Studies Center, 1976), xiii.
5 Gary Okihiro, "Introduction," in *Reflections on Shattered Windows: Promises and Prospects for Asian American Studies*. Gary Y. Okihiro, Shirley Hune, Arthur A. Hansen, and John M. Liu (Eds.) (Pullman, WA: Washington State University, 1988), xviii.
6 Ibid.
7 Michael Omi, "It Just Ain't the Sixties No More: The Contemporary Dilemmas of Asian American Studies," in *Reflections on Shattered Windows: Promises and Prospects for Asian American Studies*. Gary Y. Okihiro, Shirley Hune, Arthur A. Hansen, and John M. Liu (Eds.) (Pullman, WA: Washington State University, 1988), 33.

Introduction

8 Ibid., 33–35.
9 Don Mar, "The Lost Second Generation of Asian American Scholars," in *Reflections on Shattered Windows: Promises and Prospects for Asian American Studies*. Gary Y. Okihiro, Shirley Hune, Arthur A. Hansen, and John M. Liu (Eds.) (Pullman, WA: Washington State University, 1988), 38.
10 Ibid., 39.
11 Ibid., 41.
12 Ibid., 42.
13 For a comprehensive account of the building of Asian American panethnicity, see Yen Le Espiritu, *Asian American Panethnicity: Bridging Institutions and Identities* (Philadelphia, PA: Temple University Press, 1992).
14 See Frank Chin, Jeffrey Paul Chan, Lawson Fusao Inada, and Shawn Wong (Eds.) *Aiiieeeee!: An Anthology of Asian American Writers* (Washington, DC: Howard University Press, 1974. Reprint, New York: Mentor, 1991) and *The Big Aiiieeeee!: An Anthology of Chinese American and Japanese American Literature* (New York: Meridian, 1991).
15 See Lisa Lowe, "Heterogeneity, Hybridity, Multiplicity: Marking Asian American Differences," *Diaspora* 1:1 (1991): 24–44 and *Immigrant Acts: On Asian American Cultural Politics* (Durham, NC: Duke University Press, 1996).
16 For a comprehensive account of the *Blu's Hanging* controversy, see Mark Chiang, *The Cultural Capital of Asian American Studies: Autonomy and Representation in the University* (New York: New York University Press, 2009), 173–211.
17 See Kandice Chuh, *Imagine Otherwise: On Asian Americanist Critique* (Durham, NC: Duke University Press, 2003) and Viet Thanh Nguyen, *Race and Resistance: Literature and Politics in Asian America* (New York: Oxford University Press, 2002).
18 See Mark Chiang, *The Cultural Capital of Asian American Studies: Autonomy and Representation in the University* (New York: New York University Press, 2009) and Christopher Lee, *The Semblance of Identity: Aesthetic Meditation in Asian American Literature* (Stanford, CA: Stanford University Press, 2012).
19 For an excellent account of the importance and development of Asian Americanist critiques, see Kandice Chuh, *Imagine Otherwise: On Asian Americanist Critique*.
20 Amy Takichi, "Introduction," in *Roots: An Asian American Reader*. Amy Tachiki, Eddie Wong, Franklin Odo, and Buck Wong (Eds.) (Los Angeles, CA: UCLA Asian American Studies Center, 1971), 1.
21 Ibid.
22 Buck Wong, "Introduction: Asian Americans and the Apotheosis of American Democracy," in *Roots: An Asian American Reader*. Amy Tachiki, Eddie Wong, Franklin Odo, and Buck Wong (Eds.) (Los Angeles, CA: UCLA Asian American Studies Center, 1971), 131.
23 Ibid.
24 Ibid.
25 See Eddie Wong, "Introduction," in *Roots: An Asian American Reader*. Amy Tachiki, Eddie Wong, Franklin Odo, and Buck Wong (Eds.) (Los Angeles, CA: UCLA Asian American Studies Center, 1971), 247–250.
26 See Ronald Takaki, *Strangers from a Different Shore: A History of Asian Americans* (New York: Penguin, 1989).
27 See Shirley Hun, Hyung-chan Kim, Stephen S. Fugita, and Amy Ling (Eds.), *Asian Americans: Comparative and Global Perspectives* (Pullman, WA: Washington State University Press, 1991).
28 Sau-Ling C. Wong, "Denationalization Reconsidered: Asian American Cultural Criticism at a Theoretical Crossroads," *Amerasia Journal* 21:1 & 2 (1995): 1–27.
29 Sau-Ling C. Wong, "Denationalization Reconsidered: Asian American Cultural Criticism at a Theoretical Crossroads," *Amerasia Journal* 21:1 & 2 (1995): 3. See also, Sucheta Mazumdar, "Asian American Studies and Asian Studies: Rethinking Roots" in *Asian Americans: Comparative and Global Perspectives*. Shirley Hun, Hyung-chan Kim, Stephen S. Fugita, and Amy Ling (Eds.) (Pullman, WA: Washington State University Press, 1991), 29–44.
30 Yuji Ichioka, "A Buried Past: A Survey of English-Language Works on Japanese American History," in *Counterpoint: Perspectives on Asian America*. Emma Gee (Ed.) (Los Angeles, CA: UCLA Asian American Studies Center, 1976), 14.
31 See Lucie Cheng Hirata, "The Chinese American in Sociology," in *Counterpoint: Perspectives on Asian America*. Emma Gee (Ed.) (Los Angeles, CA: UCLA Asian American Studies Center, 1976), 20–26.

Introduction

32 Bruce Iwasaki, "Introduction," in *Counterpoint: Perspectives on Asian America*. Emma Gee (Ed.) (Los Angeles, CA: UCLA Asian American Studies Center, 1976), 452.
33 See Frank Chin, Jeffrey Paul Chan, Lawson Fusao Inada, and Shawn Wong, "Introduction: Fifty Years of Our Whole Voice," in *Aiiieeeee!: An Anthology of Asian American Writers*. Frank Chin, Jeffrey Paul Chan, Lawson Fusao Inada, and Shawn Wong (Eds.) (Washington, DC: Howard University Press, 1974. Reprint, New York: Mentor, 1991), 1–38.
34 Ibid., 23–24.
35 See Frank Chin, "Come All Ye Asian American Writes of the Real and the Fake," in *The Big Aiiieeeee!: An Anthology of Chinese American and Japanese American Literatures*. Jeffrey Paul Chan, Frank Chin, Lawson Fusao Inada, and Shawn Wong (Eds.) (New York: Meridian, 1991), 1–61.
36 For an excellent analysis of the autobiographical controversy of Maxine Hong Kingston's *The Woman Warrior*, see Laura Hyun Yi Kang, *Compositional Subjects: Enfiguring Asian/American Women* (Durham, NC: Duke University Press, 2002), 29–70. For a wonderful examination of the tensions between feminism and ethnic nationalism, see Leslie Bow, *Betrayal and Other Acts of Subversion: Feminism, Sexual Politics, and Asian American Women's Literature* (Princeton, NJ: Princeton University Press, 2001).
37 For a complete look at the essays featured in the forum reviewing Ronald Takaki's *Strangers from a Different Shore*, see *Amerasia* 16:2 (1990): 63–156.
38 See Elaine Kim, "A Critique of *Strangers from a Different Shore*," *Amerasia* 16:2 (1990): 101–111.
39 For an excellent discussion on the importance of interdisciplinarity, see Joe Parker and Ranu Samantrai, "Interdisciplinarity and Social Justice: An Introduction," in *Interdisciplinarity and Social Justice: Revisioning Academic Accountability*. Joseph D. Parker, Ranu Samantrai, and Mary Romero (Eds.) (Albany, NY: SUNY Press, 2010), 1–23. See also Julie Thompson Klein, *Interdisciplinarity: History, Theory, and Practice* (Detroit, MI: Wayne State University, 1990); Julie Thompson Klein, *Humanities, Culture, and Interdisciplinarity: The Changing American Academy* (New York: SUNY Press, 2005); and Joe Moran, *Interdisciplinarity* (New York: Routledge, 2002).

PART ONE
Shifting Paradigms

1
ON RACIAL STEREOTYPING

Leslie Bow

As an adult, graphic novelist Gene Yang was startled to discover his childhood rendering of an ethnic joke in an old sketchbook. In his cartoon, a buck-toothed Mandarin giggles, "Me Chinese. Me play joke. Me go pee pee in your Coke."[1] A Chinese American, Yang puzzled over his ability to access American racial stereotypes while refusing to see them as self-implicating. Was the stereotype such a gross exaggeration that it bore no relationship to his self-conception? Or is this wishful thinking? Caricature would find pointed use in his first graphic novel, *American Born Chinese*: Chin-Kee, the excruciating embodiment of all Chinese stereotypes, is sent to test the novel's self-hating protagonist. Their encounter culminates in a kung-fu movie parody, a battle symbolizing Asian Americans' struggle with the reviled form of misrepresentation popularly known as the stereotype.

Not surprisingly, in its very definition, stereotyping invokes race: it represents "oversimplified opinion, affective attitudes, or uncritical judgment (as of a person, a race, an issue, or an event)" (*Websters*). Unlike the archetype, the stereotype is neither a primary nor an ideal projection but a reduction without variation; repetition without change is inherent to its form. While we rely upon categorizing in order to make sense of the world, racial stereotypes are now largely understood to represent inaccurate biases that both deindividualize and dehumanize. Reifying notions of group difference, stereotyping enables hierarchy by constructing and reinforcing distinction. It establishes a foundation for prejudice by explicitly or implicitly ranking peoples as superior or inferior.

A cultural arm of white supremacy, racial stereotypes nevertheless impersonate as immutable, transhistorical, as it ever was. While they are historically specific, they are often represented as reflecting timeless traits or ascribed to genetic inheritance. As stereotypes converge with belief in biological differences, they reflect antiquated, eugenicist views of evolutionary distinctions between peoples, race as "species" difference. For example, the representation of Filipino and Hawaiian primitivism justified nineteenth-century U.S. imperialism.[2] Propaganda surrounding Japanese patriotic fanaticism contributed to the internment of Japanese Americans as "enemy aliens" during World War II.[3] The perception that Asian Americans are good at math derives from 1965 immigration reforms that privileged labor pools in technology and medicine, reforms that resulted in increased immigration from Asia (Ong and Liu 1994). In spite of this historicity, Asians are represented as "naturally" sly, clever, or frugal, just as they are "naturally" mathematically inclined and technologically advanced or primitive and childlike; emotionally repressed or happy-go-lucky; effeminate and timid or inherently cruel and immune to pain; uncoordinated, poor drivers or good with their hands. Note that contradiction never worried the work of the stereotype.

It is not simply that fixity alleviates anxieties surrounding difference by attempting to make the unknown knowable, but that stereotypical beliefs justify actions towards racial groups. They do not merely reflect, but *produce* culture; stereotyping serves an ideological role linked to social control. Psychologist Richard Lee expresses a generally held view stating, "Stereotypes of any group are inherently inaccurate because they try to shoehorn all members of the group being stereotyped into a single conception while ignoring the wide diversity within the group. Moreover, some stereotypes are simply wrong and are perpetuated by the majority group in order to bias perception of the targeted group" (Richard Lee 2013: n.p.). Lee's view speaks to two truisms underlying dominant conceptions of stereotypes: they are both factually and morally "wrong." Identifying stereotypical content surrounding Asian Americans and mobilizing around the offensive racial image is still an activist necessity. Yet at one level, both the question of accuracy—stereotype as *false* generalization—and of ethics—*good* images vs. *bad* ones—cloud the more abstract stakes underlying racial stereotyping. How might we deepen the analytic frame of race studies by looking beyond the content of racial stereotypes either to establish their inaccuracy or evaluate their degrees of offense?

Asian American encounters with the racial stereotype suggest the complexities underlying categorization, complexities that enrich our understanding of the "damaged knowledge" that is the racial stereotype (Mithlo 2008). Is the move to stereotype "just human nature"? How do cognitive and linguistic structures underlying stereotyping reflect racial profiling? Are "positive" stereotypes also harmful? Where does the productive cultural generalization end and stereotyping begin? Any analysis of the content of Asian stereotypes circulating in the U.S. should not obfuscate their purpose: representation enables the exercise of power. In what follows, I briefly explore the content of stereotypical imagery, a project that is ongoing and always incomplete, but, more importantly, the desiring structures that underlie it.

Structures of Typing: Othering, Alterity, Syllogism

The racial stereotype serves a productive function; it is a *useful* if pernicious fiction. Edward Said's allegory of Self and Other in *Orientalism* (1978) neatly articulates the political stakes underlying the attempt to establish distinctions between peoples. Here, constructing a notion of the "barbarian" enables an unspoken norm, the "civilized":

> A group of people living on a few acres of land will set up boundaries between their land and its immediate surroundings and the territory beyond, which they call "the land of the barbarians." In other words, this universal practice of designating in one's mind a familiar space which is "ours" and an unfamiliar space beyond "ours" which is "theirs" is a way of making geographical distinctions that can be entirely arbitrary ... [The] imaginative geography of the "our land–barbarian land" variety does not require that the barbarians acknowledge the distinction. It is enough for "us" to set up these boundaries in our own minds; "they" become "they" accordingly, and both their territory and their mentality are designated as different from "ours."
>
> Said 1978: 54

The actual content that defines "us" from "them" is arbitrary to the abstract processes of differentiation. What is significant is that the Other serves the purpose of self-definition. In *Orientalism*, Said makes this point more historically, arguing that European identity during and after the Enlightenment was formed through projections about the "Orient." Said defined "Orientalism" as a discourse primarily about the Middle East produced by English, French, and German literature, science, politics, and sociology. This discourse did not only serve to justify European colonial endeavors but produced another effect: "European culture gained in strength and identity by setting itself off against the Orient as a sort of surrogate and even underground self" (Said 1978: 3). The stereotype fixes difference not for its own sake, but in order to secure what passes as the norm.

The structure of racialization implied by Hegel's master-slave dialectic and invoked by psychoanalyst Franz Fanon likewise highlights relationally defined identity or what is often deemed alterity or "Othering." If the colonized "is a Malagasy," Fanon wrote, "it is because the white man has come" (Fanon 1991:98). To make an analogous point, he echoes Jean-Paul Sartre in asserting, "It is the anti-Semite who makes the Jew" (Fanon 1991: 93). Whether articulated through nationality, region, skin color, ethnicity, or religion, difference emerges out of a dialectical relationship with an invisible center or norm. Similarly, Slavoj Zizek highlights the purpose underlying anti-Semitic stereotypes in noting that "all the phantasmic richness of the traits supposed to characterize Jews (avidity, the spirit of intrigue, and so on) is here to conceal not the fact that 'Jews are really not like that', not the empirical reality of Jews, but the fact that in the anti-Semitic construction of a 'Jew', we are concerned with a purely structural function" (Zizek 1989: 99). This "structural function" is the making of alterity; a key insight of structuralist feminism, for example, is the notion of gender alterity: "Man" (X) as the norm against which "Woman" (Not X) becomes defined. The fallout of accepting this X/Not-X binary is accessibly portrayed in Dr. Seuss's story of the hapless Sneetches whose fluctuating senses of self-worth hinge upon an arbitrary mark: "You could only play if your bellies had stars/And the Plain-Belly children had none upon thars" (Seuss 1961: 5). That is, the mark of (often visual) difference can be arbitrary; what is important is the social meaning ascribed to it and the degree to which one internalizes that meaning.

Unveiling this structure makes clear that racial stereotypes are not merely negative or derogatory towards a specific group, but productive on behalf of another; in the U.S., they help establish white identity through negation. Toni Morrison makes this clear in recognizing the role that African Americans play in the national imaginary. In *Playing in the Dark: Whiteness and the Literary Imagination*, she writes, "The fabrication of an Africanist persona is reflexive; an extraordinary meditation on the self" (Morrison 1992: 17). Positing racial difference in a medium such as literature does not simply reflect or reinforce preexisting views, it also serves a more abstract purpose in establishing white identity via contrast: what it is *not*. I focus here on the structures of alterity, but I want to note that they are triggered by larger material and economic forces at specific points in history. Defining and scapegoating populations serves the economic interests of the elite; specific case studies of this dynamic appear in this volume (Cheng 2016).

Examples of human classification based on the projection of racial, religious, or geographic difference are historically specific and contextual. Does this specificity prove or disprove the generally held idea that the move to classify or "type" represents a "universal" human trait? Attempting to understand the logic of anti-Semitism after the Holocaust, Sartre relates the following anecdote: "A young woman said to me: 'I have had the most horrible experiences with furriers; they robbed me, they burned the fur I entrusted to them. Well, they were all Jews.'" Unpacking the logic underlying her bias, he asks, "But why did she choose to hate Jews rather than furriers? Why Jews or furriers rather than such and such a Jew or such and such a furrier?" His answer: "Because she had in her a predisposition toward anti-Semitism" (Sartre 1970: 11–12). Sartre's work goes on to explore the "predisposition" towards prejudice as it derives from environment; here, the anti-Semitic beliefs circulating in Europe prior to

World War II. Exploring how children learn social biases, anthropologist Lawrence Hirschfeld offers another explanation to Sartre's question, "why did she choose to hate Jews rather than furriers?": "The answer evidently involves the realization that the intuitive object of a prejudice is more likely to be a kind of thing rather than a property of that thing" (Hirschfeld 1988: 628). Surprisingly, Hirschfeld's answer points to noncontextual, linguistic logic: we are more likely to assign (here, negative) value to things (e.g. people) rather than their properties (in this case, occupation). Race and ethnicity, he notes, are "psychologically privileged" insofar as they are seen to be "inalienable aspects of a person's being" (Hirschfeld 1988: 628). This is not to affirm the often-repeated truism, "Stereotyping is just human nature." Rather, it is to say that forming stereotypical belief reflects not only historical context, but structures of language and cognition.

This is also distinct from positing that human beings are innately racist, a truism that often allows people to throw up their hands on racial issues as if there is nothing that can be done. Nevertheless, classifying people into distinct groups and assigning these groups value can be seen as a function of cognition. The volume of academic studies exploring how young children apprehend social categories like race and ethnicity speaks to the "universal" processes of categorization as a means of understanding the world. But I would suggest that those processes also reveal the faulty reasoning underlying racial stereotyping among adults. Studies in the racial perceptions of children confirm psychologists Kenneth Clark and Mamie Clark's broadest 1939 hypothesis that between the ages of three and four years, children are able to distinguish people "in terms consonant with race," a phenomenon evidenced across cultures (Hirschfeld 1988: 616). When children use racial definitions inconsistently or unconventionally, we find it to be cute, innocent, and humorous. Yet children's perception of race and ethnicity relies upon the same over-application of generalization that likewise informs the less funny adult use of racial stereotypes. Categories become catchalls for the unfamiliar; for example, Spanish might stand in for all "foreign" languages (Ramsey 1987). In one 1987 study, developmental psychologist Patricia Ramsey found that one boy began an interview by stating that Chinese children were Japanese; he then deemed black children to be Japanese. By the end of the interview, "he was referring to all children that he did not know as Japanese" (Ramsey 1987: 63). In this case, ethnic difference, no matter its content, was invoked as a way to define the child's "out-group," those different from himself.

More significant to the underlying logic of stereotyping, Ramsey also found that children ages three to seven often use "transdeductive reasoning" in associating groups of people with traits or behaviors. For example, one white child insisted that Chinese people always ate in restaurants because her only contact with them had been at a Chinese restaurant; she was "unable to think simultaneously of Chinese people as eating both at restaurants and at home, even though she was able to see that she herself ate at restaurants sometimes, but not all the time" (Ramsey 1987: 62). The child's single experience with Chinese people was generalized to all who shared their visual difference. Children's use of transdeductive logic reflects phases of cognitive development that increases in sophistication over time (Aboud 1988): they sort people according to "naïve biology" most often based on surface cues such as skin color or eye shape. Researchers found that children under the age of seven are more likely to group people according to race than other forms of visible difference such as gender, clothing, or morphology (Ramsey 1987; Hirschfeld 1995). When this over-application of type takes on negative resonance, developmental psychologists are reluctant to label young children's biases as reflecting the "prejudices" held by adults[4] because the over-exaggerated group characteristics that children assign to racial-ethnic groups are inconsistent. This inconsistency is attributed to age-related cognitive levels, to brain development and the inability to focus on more than one attribute at a time (Ramsey 1987; Aboud 1988). Looking at stereotyping from this angle of "innocent" over-generalization produces a perhaps startling conclusion: *stereotyping reflects an inability to process complex pieces of information.*

That is, racial stereotyping relies on faulty deduction. Ramsey recounts that after an altercation with one of his two black classmates, a white five-year-old informed his mother that "brown people always fight." He connected two pieces of information, the fight and his opponent's skin color, in order to form the logical deduction that "people who are alike in one respect must be similar in all respects" (Ramsey 1987: 62). This required the child to ignore information that contradicted this connection: "He was unable to consider at that time that he also had fights with white classmates and there was a Black child with whom he did not fight" (Ramsey 1987: 62). Linking African Americans and violence, the child in Ramsey's study absorbed prevailing social attitudes of his environment and, more to my point here, he applied transdeductive logic to his experience in ways that, not surprisingly, converged with those attitudes. From the point of view of a five-year-old, the belief that "brown people always fight" is innocent enough but it takes on serious implications when held by adults, particularly those in positions of institutional power such as law enforcement: a form of stereotyping, racial profiling reflects faulty deductive logic.

To demonstrate, an acquaintance once shared with me a traumatic memory from junior high school: "Black kids always tried to beat me up." Because I had taught in the community where he grew up, I was surprised by his account. Students of color were voluntarily bussed into the community from the inner city; I knew that they did not endure the long ride to the suburbs in order to pick fights, much less in groups. As we talked, it became apparent that the man's generalized statement was based on the following logic:

Sammy always tried to beat me up.
Sammy was black.
Therefore, black kids always tried to beat me up.

As in the previous example, "blackness" became the salient feature linked to one individual's behavior; other qualities of Sammy's that might have informed his bullying, e.g. his being male, an upper-classman, or a jock, for example, did not figure in the man's deductive conclusion formed in adolescence and held into adulthood. A black child had bullied him: race became the single marker of that child's behavior. One individual became all black kids. In this sense, racial stereotyping is connected to faulty logic or syllogistic thinking.

Syllogisms reflect logical arguments that rely upon deductive reasoning: if two propositions, one major and one minor, are assumed to be true, then a conclusion based on those propositions is likewise assumed to be true. The most common example is:

- All men are mortal. (Major premise)
- Socrates is a man. (Minor premise)
- Therefore, Socrates is mortal. (Conclusion deduced).

Put more abstractly, the deductive logic of the syllogism is:

- A is predicated of all B.
- B is predicated of all C.
- *Then* A is predicated of all C.

Expressed thus, neither the potential inaccuracy nor the political nature of the above sequence is apparent. In fact, Socrates *was* mortal so there is nothing controversial about this deductive logic. Yet a simple substitution reveals the ways in which syllogistic thinking lies at the root of profiling:

- The terrorists were Muslim.
- Mohammed is Muslim.
- Therefore, Mohammed is a terrorist.

Clearly, in this example, A is *not* predicated of all C: *not* all Muslims are terrorists. Yet in the historical context of the post-9/11 U.S., interrupting syllogistic thinking becomes less easy: the prevailing attitudes circulating around two *now linked* associations create and perhaps also reward what Sartre calls a "predisposition" to prejudicial thinking. Shifting back to children's apprehension of racial and ethnic categories and the negative attitudes they acquire in that process thus sheds light on the structures underlying stereotypical thought: the faulty deductions at the root of children's use of transdeductive logic are more readily visible than those of adults because theirs represents an imperfect mimicry of how adults assign value to groups. To reiterate: stereotyping is not only a function of learning or absorbing prevailing attitudes from one's environment. It is also a function of cognitive development, psychologically privileging race and ethnicity as inherent properties of people, and, as in this example, syllogistic and faulty transdeductive reasoning.

What is the role of the stereotype in the formation of Asian American identity? In 1972, writers Frank Chin and Jeffrey Paul Chan asserted that the stereotype "operates as a model of behavior. It conditions the mass society's perceptions and expectations. Society is conditioned to accept the given minority only within the bounds of the stereotype. The subject minority is conditioned to reciprocate by becoming the stereotype—live it, talk it, embrace it, measure group and individual worth in its terms and believe it" (Chin and Chan 1972: 66–67). This view does not mince words about the impact of the stereotype on minority subjectivity. But are Asian Americans destined to become the image projected of them? If stereotypes operate as models for behavior, how is the Asian American conditioned to act?

A Serviceable Villain: The Yellow Peril

In his discussion of Asian stock characters generated by Hollywood, Hemant Shah identifies four main stereotypes perpetuated in American film: "'Yellow Peril,' 'Dragon Lady,' 'Charlie Chan,' and 'Lotus Blossom'" (Shah 2003: 1). Robert Lee names six: "the pollutant, the coolie, the deviant, the yellow peril, the model minority, and the gook" (Robert Lee 1999: 8). Yet the array of Asian stereotypes in the U.S. is dizzying. They are ethnic specific: witness the "New Age orientalist" belief in Indian spirituality (Prashad 2000: 59) or the belief that the Hmong are a people who do not have "the same regard for human life that our culture has" (Schein and Thoj 2007: 1070). Racial stereotypes appear at the intersection of differences as in the gendered and class-based image of Asian women being "good with their hands," a representation justifying women's labor in nail salons or technology assembly lines (See M. Kang, L. Kang).

Among the earliest and most durable of Asian stereotypes in the U.S. is the "Yellow Peril," a representation of working-class labor grounded in xenophobia. "Rooted in medieval fears of Genghis Khan and Mongolian invasions of Europe," writes Gina Marchetti, "the yellow peril combines racist terror of alien cultures, sexual anxieties, and the belief that the West will be overpowered and enveloped by the irresistible, dark, occult forces of the East" (Marchetti 1993: 2). However fanciful, this representation had tremendous impact on American immigration policy, which curtailed immigration from China at the end of the nineteenth century and from the rest of Asia in the twentieth. Stereotypes of wanton and "heathen Chinee" and the prodigious and anxiety-producing capacities of the "coolie" worker who could survive on a "bowl of rice and a rat a day," culminated in the Page Act (1875) and the Chinese Exclusion Act (1882). Instigated by nativist labor movements, Yellow Peril imagery contributed to exclusionary legislation targeting other "Asiatics" in turn: Japanese and Koreans in 1907, South Asians in 1917, and Filipinos in 1934 (Ong and Liu 1994). These immigration policies succeeded in keeping Asian American populations in the U.S. deliberately low until reforms in 1965, after which the Yellow Peril took on new iterations.[5]

In the early twentieth century, foreign evil was embodied by British author Sax Rohmer's 1913–1959 pulp novel character, Dr. Fu Manchu.[6] Rohmer's stereotype of the sinister Oriental mastermind spawned any number of garden-variety barbarians in radio, comics, film, television, and now gaming. According to type, they angled for nothing less than world domination; see for example, the Mandarin, Shang-Chi–Master of Kung-fu, and Ming the Merciless. During the Cold War, the 1962 film, *Manchurian Candidate* evoked the hoary stereotype in service of fears of communist sleeper agents undermining America values from within. Increasingly far-fetched iterations of the Yellow Peril were nonetheless based on the same tropes: witness Wonder Woman's nemesis, Egg Fu, a gigantic if easily defeated communist egg. Moreover, in speculative fiction and visual culture, traces of Yellow Peril discourse surface in the Orientalist depiction of any number of dystopian landscapes and bleak futures, from *Blade Runner* to *Serenity*.[7] Around the height of Japan's economic dominance in 1995, David Morley and Kevin Robins coined the term, "techno-orientalism" to convey fears of a future in which the Japanese transcended Western modernity to usher in a technologically advanced world based on cybernetics, robotics, artificial intelligence, and simulation. The vision stoked fears of a "postmodern mutation of human experience" (168), of a culture that is "cold, impersonal and machine-like, an authoritarian culture lacking emotional connection to the rest of the world" (Morley and Robins 1995: 169).

Less fancifully, the twenty-first century version of the Yellow Peril, together with the stereotype of the perpetual foreigner, is cast as a problem of Middle America being overrun by Asian communities. For example, in a misguided attempt at humor, *Time* ran a 2010 piece bemoaning the transformation of Edison, New Jersey, once a white suburban town of the writer's youth, now "a maze of charmless Indian strip malls and housing developments." The piece occasioned biting response from the Indian American community, including one from actor and activist Kal Penn, best known for the *Harold and Kumar* franchise: "Gags about impossibly spicy food? I'd never heard those before! Multiple Gods with multiple arms? Multiple laughs! Recounting racial slurs like 'dot-head'? Oh, Mr. Stein, is too good!"[8] As in the previous two centuries, immigrants continue to be made scapegoats for nativist xenophobia as ethnic stereotypes resurface in service to the same agendas. As Said implies, "barbarians" can take multiple forms: unskilled coolies or skilled, H-1B tech workers.

The ideological work of Yellow Peril representation and its corollary—the Asian as perpetual foreigner—can be somewhat transparent; in contrast, one of the insidious qualities of stereotypes surrounding Asian Americans is that they are situated as being innocently complimentary.

Positive Stereotypes as Racial Microaggressions

There are definitely people who think Asian girls are hot. It's flattering. Why is it offensive? They're not saying we're ugly.

Cited in New York Times Magazine, July 16, 2000, 59

The Asian American woman in the above epigraph discredits the harm of racial stereotypes by asserting that they are not derogatory but complimentary to the group. Whether regarding the beauty of women, work productivity, quality of cuisine, or excessive humility, Asian Americans nevertheless experience these generalizations as racial microaggressions. According to Derald Wing Sue, racial microaggressions are brief, often subtle, everyday forms of racial bias and discrimination that compromise mental health and wellbeing over time. Two microaggressions are specifically "positive" in nature: ascriptions of intelligence or the "model minority" and the "exoticization of women."[9] Unveiling the ways in which praise is experienced as patronizing and evidence of Asian stereotyping, poet Janice Mirikitani ironically questions,

> Do we say thank you?
> When they tell us that they've
> visited Japan
> Hong Kong
> Peking
> Bali
> Guam
> Manila
> several times
> and it's so quaint
> lovely
> polite
> exotic
> hospitable
> interesting
> And when did we arrive?
> Since we speak
> English so well.
>
> *Mirikitani 1987: 24*

The stereotype of the perpetual foreigner emerges here as a form of praise; it becomes a vehicle for loving difference. The seemingly innocent attempt at connection reduces the speaker to the role of Asian representative (pick any country) while rendering this association her primary (or only) feature. The advice offered in the online article, "How Not to be a Dick to your Asian Friend" reacts to this same reduction; one can avoid being a dick, suggests author Clarissa Wei, for one, by abstaining from fetishizing and exoticizing Asian American culture through the compliment.

In 2007, National Public Radio asked, "Are Positive Stereotypes Racist, Too?" challenging the idea that well-intended generalizations somehow evaded the structure and function of the stereotype.[10] Compliments serve the same restrictive function as negative stereotypes by fixing notions of ethnic authenticity and, here, conditioning individuals into conforming to a static, reductive, overdetermined perception of Asianness. More practically, so-called positive assumptions about Asian American educational attainment, for example, serve to justify withholding resources from individuals. On the insidious work of the compliment as prejudicial group perception, Derald Wing Sue notes, "While the intent of the aggressor may be to compliment the Asian American individual by saying that Asians are more successful than other people of color, the negating message is that Asians do not experience racism—denying their experiential reality of bias and discrimination" (Sue et al. 2007:76). The "denial of racial reality" is a form of racial microaggression.

An early iteration of what would emerge as the stereotype of Asian Americans as the "model minority" appears in a 1933 study in which white, male Princeton students were asked to assign traits to ethnic, racial, and national groups. Japanese were most often labeled "intelligent" and "industrious" (ironically, also the top descriptors that they assigned themselves as Americans).[11] Documenting the shift from negative to "positive" stereotypes of Asians in the U.S., by 1970, Stanley Sue and Harry H. L. Kitano found that "the Oriental image is 'whiter than white'"; Asian Americans were thought to be "patient, clean, courteous, and Americanized" and successful "by virtue of their hard work, thrift, family cohesion, and obedience" (Sue and Kitano 1973: 87).[12]

Yet the image of Asian Americans as the "model minority" is not intrinsically "about" Asian Americans; positive generalizations regarding one group often explicitly or implicitly targeting another. First, domestic racial representation has international dimensions. For example, Cindy I-Fen Cheng situates postwar press reports on the civil rights gains of Chinese Americans as Cold War rhetoric: the successes of "model" Chinese American citizens intended to highlight the limited opportunities of overseas Chinese living under communism. Second, Asian American racialization relies upon the racialization of other groups, in particular, of African Americans. Emphasizing the comparative nature of racialization, according to Robert Lee, the first use of the term, "model minority" in the mainstream American press in 1966 came shortly after the 1965 Watts Riots and labor secretary Daniel Patrick Moynihan's *Report on the Black Family* that pathologized single parent households.[13] Resisting the "racist contract" of definitional comparison, Vjijay Prashad wrote *The Karma of Brown Folk* with the explicit desire to challenge the logic that compels immigrants from India and Pakistan to accept "being positioned in such a way that they are seen as superior to blacks" (Prashad 2000: xi). Asian American activists likewise invoked racial comparison in order to identify the terms of their own racialization through the trope of slavery: "Orientals," asserted Alan Nishio in 1969, "act as the 'well-fed' houseboys of the Establishment, defending the plantation from the 'lowly' field slaves" (Nishio 1969: n. p.).

Revealing the ways in which racial expectation conditions behavior, Stacey Lee found that Asian American high school students embraced the stereotype "motivated by the fact that the characterization of Asian Americans as model minorities seems positive and even flattering when compared with the stereotypes of other racial minorities" (S. Lee 2009:12). Yet complicity establishes a fixed and limited criterion for authenticity. Ambiguously confirming or challenging the model minority stereotype, researchers found that faculty members were significantly *less* likely to respond or respond favorably to emails from fictional prospective graduate students with Indian or Chinese names than those with Caucasian names.[14] This finding is consistent with the overall bias against women and racial minorities in accessing gateway institutions such as universities; researchers concluded that "students of Asian descent experience particularly pronounced discrimination challenging stereotypes of Asians as 'model minorities'" (28). Yet the impact of the stereotype plays an ambiguous role here: does a professor's refusal to respond indicate negative bias against Asian students as less worthy of faculty time *or* is assistance withheld based on the stereotype of Asian self-reliance? In either case, the so-called positive stereotype of the model minority serves to highlight the fetishistic structure of Asian American racial representation by revealing that racist love and racist hate do not function oppositionally, but in tandem.[15]

Overdetermining Culture: Stereotypes vs. Social Categories

What is the line between the useful generalization and the limiting stereotype? The tension between the two is suggested by Chandra Talpade Mohanty's careful reading of the ways in which Western feminist scholarship on global economic development appears to reproduce a stereotype of Third World women. In this academic literature, she writes,

> [The] average third-world woman leads an essentially truncated life based on her feminine gender (read: sexually constrained) and being "third-world" (read: ignorant, poor, uneducated, tradition-bound, religious, domesticated, family-oriented, victimized, etc.). This, I suggest, is in contrast to the (implicit) self-representation of western women as educated, modern, as having control over their own bodies and sexualities, and the "freedom" to make their own decisions.
>
> *Mohanty 1988: 65*

As Mohanty implies, Western feminist scholarship may stereotype Third World women in ways that serve the purposes of Western feminist self-definition. As in Said's "barbarians," "we" have what "they" lack, should have, and themselves desire. Certainly, these broad strokes do not reflect the complex lived experience of "Third-World" women, nor does the designation itself exist until called into being by way of contrast. But does dismissing such portrayals as stereotypical devalue group characterization on behalf of women who might indeed need education, control over their own bodies and sexualities, or the freedom to make their own decisions? Here, the seemingly reductive and therefore controversial collective characterization is a precondition of naming and solving a problem on behalf of an imagined community. I will return to this example in a moment; more specific to Asian American group characterization, the line between cultural generalization and stereotyping is likewise blurred in the most and least innocent of venues: children's television programming.

Premiering in 2007, Nickelodeon's *Ni Hao, Kai-lan* features a Mandarin- and English-speaking Chinese American cartoon character and her animal friends. *Ni Hao, Kai-lan* self-styles as having a curriculum focused not only on affirming bilingualism, but biculturalism. Intending to promote multicultural understanding for the pre-school set beyond superficial ethnic markers—food, festivals, names—the program celebrates "growing up in an intergenerational family, having friends from diverse backgrounds, and 'habits of the heart' that are Chinese American."[16] On Nickelodeon's website, such "habits" are defined as follows:

> Mind-body connection: Typically, television portrays excitement as the good emotion to feel. In many Chinese-American communities, the good thing to feel is often calmness and contentment. Feeling excited and feeling calm can both be happy feelings, but they differ in how aroused the body is.
>
> Perspective-taking: In many Chinese and other East Asian families, children are encouraged to take the perspective of others to maintain harmony in relationships with other people.
>
> Being a good member of the group: *Ni Hao, Kai-lan* also emphasizes the Chinese and Chinese American value of being a good member of a group.

To rephrase the famous question posed in Maxine Hong Kingston's novel, *The Woman Warrior*, what here is Chinese and what is the stereotype? What does it mean to portray these modes of being and interaction as "Chinese" or "Chinese American"? At first glance, it may seem that such characterizations trade in clichés about the differences between East and West: one can be both happy and calm (like the Chinese); one can put others first (like the Chinese). Chinese Americans may very well exhibit these values and communication styles or they may very well exhibit none of them: after all, the Chinese in the U.S. are not immune to self-interest, competitiveness ... or, for that matter, passion.

But while one might decry beliefs underlying the cartoon as reinforcing stereotypes about Asian Americans, nevertheless, the perspective here *also* appears in seemingly progressive academic studies on the psychology of biculturalism. For example, in order to ascertain why Asian American college students might seek or eschew mental health support systems, Bryan Kim et. al. developed an "Asian values scale" in order to assess degrees of Asian American enculturation (adherence to Asian culture) among college-age students. The scale is based on questions that reveal levels of the students' "avoidance of family shame, collectivism, conformity to norms, deference to authority, emotional self-control, family recognition through achievement, filial piety, hierarchical relationships, and humility" (Cited in Kim and Omizo 2003: 346).[17] What distinguishes this list from the *Kai-lan* example? At one level, they are fairly similar in content and both assume an unmarked norm based on individualism, competiveness, and freedom of emotional expression that are all invisibly coded as "Western" or American. Both aspire to illuminate differing communication styles or values. Unlike their contextualization on Nickelodeon, in the academic example, traits ascribed to ethnicity are not value free; rather, they prevent individuals from seeking mental health support systems. While naming the traits may indeed be necessary to developing Asian American psychology and collective understanding as the basis for action, they are cast as problematic forms of passivity and anxiety that inadvertently pathologize ethnic socialization and inhibit rather than provide access to support systems.

On the difference between the essentializing gesture and the valuable collective assessment, the stereotype and the meaningful generalization, sociologist Allan G. Johnson writes,

> Although people often object to generalizations as if they were stereotypes, there is an important difference between the terms: a generalization does not apply to individuals, only to collections of individuals such as social categories. That black men are more likely than whites to commit violent crimes does not mean that all, most, or even many black men do so. Anyone who *uses the generalization as a stereotype*, however, will tend to assume just that about any and all black men they encounter.
>
> Johnson 2000: n.p. [emphasis mine]

At stake is not the generalization, but its over-application; it becomes "stereotypical" in its blanket use in regard to individuals. I would also point out, especially given the hot-button topic of race, how likely it is that these *social* categorizations might be taken to be immutable traits that become linked to causality. As in the examples of children's use of transdeductive reasoning, the risk is that the finding can be twisted into the belief that men are violent *because of* their blackness. Class becomes irrelevant; data on criminality based on who is more likely to be arrested or convicted for violent crime is overlooked. The problem lies not with generalization per se, but its selective use; racial and ethnic difference becomes overdetermined.[18]

Racial stereotyping also results from assuming a causal link between *culture* and individual behavior, a link that is overdetermined for Asians in the U.S. This overemphasis was a cause of controversy surrounding the 2011 book, *Battle Hymn of the Tiger Mother* in which Amy Chua argued that "Chinese" parenting based on discipline was superior to permissive "American" parenting. Exposing Chua's faulty bait-and-switch logic, legal theorist Patricia Williams asked why Chua "assign[s] her neurosis to her Chinese-ness rather than to her aspirational American upper-middle-class-ness" (Williams 2011: n.p.). Williams' question highlights Chua's mis-attribution: tough love is represented as an Asian cultural practice rather than an outgrowth of

American middle-class competitiveness and helicopter parenting.[19] Stereotypical belief about Asians in the U.S. becomes reinforced by the desire to see differences emerge along cultural rather than class lines. To return to Mohanty's critique of Western feminist scholarship as reinforcing stereotypical belief in the prefeminist Third World woman, the problem may lie not with the image per se, but in its attribution. Naming aspects of culture—religious fundamentalism, patriarchy, or family structure—as the sources of stressors in the lives of women potentially reinforces the stereotype, which obfuscates economic stressors linked to the uneven allocation of resources and lack of infrastructural development: access to clean water, education, medical care, micro-lending.

For example, one stereotype of Asian American women is that they are oppressed within their families by overbearing, traditional fathers. In the context of Asian American Studies, feminist scholars are wary of deriving simple cultural explanations for any number of pressures that Asian American women face—suicide, self-harm, domestic abuse, negative self-image, or educational barriers. Rather, they view struggles surrounding the gender role to be symptoms of multiple structural issues, whether poverty, racial trauma, forced migration, or the loss of citizenship protections.[20] The group portrait of Asian American women in sociological studies establishes a broader, systemic framework in which ethnic culture appears as merely one analytic. Key to parsing the distinction between the useful social categorization and the stereotype is the notion of reduction, particularly in portrayals that construct pathologies as if they were inherent to ethnic cultural practices and socialization. Allan Johnson makes an important point in stating that what distinguishes the stereotype from the generalization is that the stereotype is consistently and erroneously applied to individuals. When the individual is Asian American, the generalization is likely to take on cultural overtones, individual behavior given an ethnic explanation. As discussed earlier, insofar as they are seen to be, in Hirschfeld's words, "inalienable aspects of a person's being," race and ethnicity are psychologically privileged over class, education, morphology, temperament or any number of attributes that connect and divide people. For Asians in the U.S., these are projected to be irreducible differences.

Complicated Routes of Desire: The Stereotype and Racialized Subjectivity

How can theories of racial stereotyping make space for more complex notions of Asian American spectatorship? For good reason, we tend to think of perpetrators of stereotypes as holding all the cards against those being (mis)represented. Yet American Indian art critic Nancy Mithlo asks, "Why do we tend to regard the subjects of the gaze (those minority cultures so often depicted in one-dimensional type casts) as solely passive recipients of negative naming rather than as active constructors of symbolic icons?" (Mithlo 2008: 16). In her work on contemporary indigenous artists who reinvent the image of the Indian princess or warrior, she allows space for the stereotype in native self-fashioning. Similarly, in *Double Agency: Acts of Impersonation in Asian American Literature and Culture*, Tina Chen takes seriously the role of the stereotype in subject formation, suggesting that Asian American identity emerges through contestations over authenticity and inauthenticity, "reality" and the stereotypes that elicit Asian American resistance and allegiance. Jessica Hagedorn's defiantly titled novel, *Dogeaters*, evokes a derogatory slur for Filipinos head-on. But as art critic Michael D. Harris questions regarding contemporary African American art repurposing stereotypical images like Aunt Jemima, "Is it really possible to appropriate racist images and terms and drain them of their poison?" (Harris 2003: 190). Nguyen Tan Hoang's short film, *Forever Bottom* (1999) attempts to do so via parody. He takes on the stereotype of Asian male emasculation by forcing the viewer to assume the perspective of the anally receptive, promiscuous gay Asian male "bottom."[21] The film's overblown, comic exaggeration asks its audience to claim ownership of the racial/sexual stereotype, but his parody does not preclude his taking pleasure in it. The "*imperfectly* performed act," notes Tina Chen, "marks its operation as social criticism" (Chen 2005: 63).

Filmmaker Wayne Yung likewise raises opened-ended questions about stereotyping, self-conception, and pleasure. *My German Boyfriend* (2004) explores the cross-cultural fantasies that enable racial fetishism. Perhaps controversially, he situates these as mutual. His protagonist, played by himself, naïvely longs for an arty, cosmopolitan, politically minded German partner only to be confronted with German dates who likewise expect him to play to type, the "Oriental" as spiritual, hypersexual, or cheap. *My German Boyfriend* skewers the desires of the Rice King without exempting its Canadian Asian narrator from his own cultural pretensions. Yet Yung's film situates stereotypes not simply as shallow illusions but as fantasies that serve as sources of personal eroticism. As I have suggested elsewhere, the use of stereotypes as a source of sexual fantasy complicates the activist's view of race fetishism (Bow 2014). That is, the stereotype exists not merely as faulty content, but a desiring structure.

In the post-Civil Rights era, Asian Americans may well express ambivalence about the influence that retrograde stereotypes still retain. In his strangely anachronistic, yet touching memoir, *Who Am I?: An Autobiography of Emotion, Mind, and Spirit*, Yi-Fu Tuan, the father of Humanist Geography, delivers a seemingly unequivocal answer when "mistaken" for a Chinese laundryman. In order to facilitate his fieldwork in Panama, he pulls some strings to requisition a jeep from the U.S. Navy. The employee in charge of the carpool is reluctant to release the vehicle to someone not employed by the base, but solves the problem by coming up with a suitable category of work for Tuan's identification card: "laundryman." Tuan recounts,

> I tell this story now to show, once again, that given the confidence that comes naturally to people of a certain class, and especially given the actual experiences of privilege as my father's son, racial slurs and ethnic stereotyping—laundryman!—have *no power to sting*. They seldom occur, in any case. And when they do, I see them as ethnographic curiosities, sources of amusement, incidents that I might serve up during a conversational lull—or, for that matter, in my autobiography.
>
> *Tuan 1999: 28 [emphasis mine]*

The encounter leaves him, a worldly, educated, upper-class Chinese man, with his self-esteem intact. Class privilege, Tuan suggests, inoculates him from the negative associations of his group: the stereotype of working-class labor in the nineteenth century U.S. presumably bears no resemblance to him and has no influence over his self-conception. And yet the story raises these complications: the U.S. image of the Chinese laundryman had the tenacity to follow him around the world; who has the privilege to disavow it? Who exactly is the story meant to amuse? More tellingly, if the encounter leaves no mark, has no power to sting, why continue to recount it? As in Gene Yang's *American Born Chinese*, no matter how we distance ourselves from him, cousin Chin-Kee, the personification of Asian stereotypes, always pays an unexpected visit.

Conclusion

In Philip Kan Gotanda's 1989 *Yankee Dawg You Die*, two Asian American actors struggle over the limited roles available to Asian actors. At the end of the play, the protagonist cries out to both implied casting directors and the (white) audience, "Why can't you see me as I really am?" The answer is, of course, that racial stereotypes continue to cloud our vision. Identifying and challenging racial stereotypes thus remain important aspects of Asian American activism. As Yang asserts, defending his retrograde creation, Chin-Kee, "In order for us to defeat our enemy, he must first be made visible" ("Gene Yang, Origins of *ABC*," 2006, n.p.).

But the notion that Asian stereotypes will meet a timely death when replaced with more accurate images of Asian Americans is naïve. As Said writes, "One ought never to assume that the structure of Orientalism is nothing more than a structure of lies or of myths which, where the truth about them to be told, would simply blow away" (6). The work of activist groups that monitor offensive portrayals of Asian Americans, such as Media Action Network for Asian Americans (MANAA) and the Asian Pacific American Media Coalition, is politically necessary. But fighting against stereotyping should not be caught in the trap of defending authenticity, which, as Lori Kido Lopez notes, risks reifying "a monolithic, 'mainstream' Asian America" (Lopez 2016: 196).[22] Rather, it means critically examining all ideologically invested representation. The stereotype is merely one form of visual or discursive rhetoric that has material effects in legislating how "Asian America" becomes legible.[23]

The importance of taking a closer look at racial stereotyping may lie in the very reason it is dismissed as a serious topic of scholarly inquiry: the stereotype's exaggeration announces its ficticity and therefore its seemingly transparent relationship to power. Yet critic Homi Bhabha suggests that stereotyping is inherently ambivalent, it "vacillates between what is always 'in place', already known, and something that must be anxiously repeated . . . as if the essential duplicity of the Asiatic or the bestial sexual licence of the African that needs no proof, can never really, in discourse, be proved" (Bhabha 1994: 66). Stereotyping is not merely a display of control over others, but a sign of uneasiness surrounding a loss of authority. Shifting away from stereotypes as false content reveals their foundation: a desiring structure beset by an anxiety about racial difference that cannot be allayed. This is why stereotyping as *process* of discursive repetition will not necessarily disappear with the emergence of more "accurate" or positive images of any group: unveiling a truth obfuscated by misrepresentation is never what is really at stake in battling stereotyping.

There is good news: contrary to popular belief, as children grow older, their racial-ethnic biases lessen (Aboud 1988). This suggests that negative attitudes about out-groups expressed by children under age seven do not necessarily reflect prejudices naively absorbed from environment. Rather, categorizing people reflects a stage of cognitive ability, a developmental process that is ongoing. "In their search for coherence, people often suppress individual variations to support group generalizations," notes psychologist Patricia Ramsey. "This phenomenon is particularly true for children because they *can focus only on one attribute at a time*" (Ramsey 1987: 68 [emphasis mine]). Looking at children's understanding of race illuminates the processes by which adults assign racial meaning and pushes stereotyping into the abstract realm of classification or, as *Sesame Street* puts it, "One of these things is not like the others." A form of classifying via a single aspect of thingness, stereotyping does in fact reveal itself to be a form of conceptual laziness: unlike children, adults *can* focus on more than one attribute at a time. We also have the cognitive ability to interrupt the faulty transdeductive reasoning that lies at the heart of racial stereotyping.

In contemporary Asian American Studies, investigations into the stereotype seem somewhat passé. Jennifer Ann Ho suggests that "Asian American studies developed out of a desire for ambiguity, as a way to allow Asians in America to be multiply interpreted and to be read in a richer, more complex manner that moved beyond caricature and stereotype" (Ho 2015: 14). Indeed, engaging caricature and stereotypes as objects of study risks a lack of complexity if the end result is seen only as moralizing (they're wrong) or stating what is self-evident (we all know they're wrong). While it remains an activist gesture to expose the stereotype as "damaged knowledge," unpacking the relationship between the Orientalist image and Asian American identity is perhaps not as straightforward as it first appears. Given advances in the field, it is no longer enough, for example, to expose 1930s screen siren Anna May Wong as perpetuating Dragon

Lady or Lotus Blossom stereotypes in Hollywood. In Anne Cheng's work, Wong is the occasion for a meditation on glamour and surface; in Shirley Jennifer Lim's, she is a "transnational symbol of cosmopolitan femininity" (S. Lim 2012: 2); in Darrell Hamamoto's, Anna May Wong appears in a dual register, both groundbreaking starlet and an aging woman struggling to maintain her dignity. In the silent photograph on the 1924 Certificate of Identity once required of all Chinese resident aliens, she is listed simply as "actress". Which of these depictions is the "stereotype" and which is "real"? Asian American Studies shows that what is at stake is not drawing a distinction between the two, but understanding the desiring, economic, and cognitive structures underlying stereotyping. Racial representation, stereotypical or no, informs the national imaginary and, as fundamentally if uncomfortably, how we imagine ourselves.

Notes

1 Cited on "Gene Yang, Origins of ABC." Web. August 11, 2006. www.firstsecondbooks.com/uncategorized/gene_yang_origi_2/. Accessed October 12, 2016.
2 See, for example, Bascara; Galang; Imada; and Trask for discussions of stereotypes justifying U.S. imperialism.
3 For a discussion of Japanese and Japanese American representation, see Takaki; Creef; and Weglyn.
4 Psychologist Francis Aboud suggests that prejudice in children is "not simply a miniature version of adult prejudice" but should be seen as a reflection of children's age-related abilities (ix). In ascertaining prejudice, "there must be an unfavourable evaluation of a person, elicited by his/her ethnic group membership, and based on an underlying organized predisposition" (4). This adult-oriented definition of prejudice may not be entirely applicable to children because the ability to generalize with consistency requires "cognitive capabilities that are beyond those of a child under 7 years of age" (Aboud, 8).
5 On early iterations of Yellow Peril discourse, see Robert Lee; Tchen and Yeats; Ignacio et al.; Hayot; and Saxton.
6 For more specific discussions of Fu Manchu, see Chen; and Ma.
7 See Hayot for a discussion of the coolie's association with dystopia in nineteenth-century American literature; for contemporary iterations of the Yellow Peril in film and popular culture, see Park; and Morley and Robins.
8 Kal Penn, "The 'Hilarious' Xenophobia of *Time*'s Joel Stein." July 2, 2010. Web. www.huffingtonpost.com/kal-penn/the-hilarious-xenophobia_b_634264.html. Penn responds to Joel Stein's, "My Own Private India: How the Jersey town named for Thomas Edison became home to the all-American Guindian," July 05, 2010. Web. http://content.time.com/time/magazine/article/0,9171,1999416,00.html. Accessed June 4, 2015.
9 To these, Sue later added the subtheme, "immasculinity of Asian American men" (Ong, A. et al., 2013, 190). Other racial microaggressions pathologize Asian cultural values and communication styles (D. Sue, et al., 2007).
10 Farai Chideya, "Are Positive Stereotypes Racist Too?" NPR, October 29, 2007. Web. www.npr.org/templates/story/story.php?storyId=15734426. Accessed October 12, 2016.
11 In contrast, the Chinese were deemed "superstitious" and "sly" (Katz and Braly, 280).
12 For a full account of the origins of the "model minority" stereotype, see Ellen D. Wu (2013). For overviews of the model minority stereotype, see Osajima; Robert Lee; S. Lee, 2009.
13 Echoing the anxious repetition underlying the stereotype, versions of the Asian American as model minority surface every decade: *Time*'s "The New Whiz Kids" (1987); Malcolm Gladwell's *Outliers: The Story of Success* (2008); and Amy Chua and Jeb Rubenfeld's *The Triple Package: How Three Unlikely Traits Explain the Rise and Fall of Cultural Groups in America* (2014).
14 Katherine Milkman, et al. found that faculty "ignored requests from women and minorities at a higher rate than requests from Caucasian males, particularly in higher-paying disciplines and private institutions", (2). Katherine L. Milkman, Modupe Akinola, and Dolly Chugh, "What Happens Before?: A Field Experiment Exploring How Pay and Representation Differentially Shape Bias on the Pathway into Organizations," Working Paper, *Social Science Research Network*, April 23, 2014. Accessed June 2, 2014. http://papers.ssrn.com/sol3/papers.cfm?abstract_id=2063742.

15 The structure of racist hatred as the flipside to racist love became abundantly apparent as businessman Donald Trump sought the Republican presidential nomination in 2015. Seeking to endear himself to a white electorate, he depicted Mexican immigrants as criminals, drug dealers, and rapists. A year later on *Cinco de Mayo*, he tweeted, "I love Hispanics!" along with a photo of himself eating a taco bowl.
16 *Ni Hao, Kai-lan*'s creator, Karen Chau, is Chinese American; her protagonist takes her Chinese name. Cited on "*Ni Hao, Kai-lan*'s Curriculum": www.nickjr.com/ni-hao-kai-lan/about-ni-hao-kai-lan/ni-hao-kai-lan-curriculum_ap.html.
17 See B.S. Kim, D.R. Atkinson and P.H. Yang, "The Asian values scale: Development, factor analysis, validation, and reliability," *Journal of Counseling Psychology* 46 (1999): 342–352. Their sample includes respondents across Asian ethnicities: Asian Indian, Cambodian, Chinese, Filipino, Japanese, Korean, Laotian, Thai, Vietnamese, and multi-ethnic Asian college students of varying generations.
18 A particularly egregious example of cultural overdetermination comes to mind here: Malcolm Gladwell's Outliers in which he theorizes that Korean deference to authority contributes to plane crashes. That is, according to Gladwell, co-pilots failed to alert pilots to potential flight dangers because they did not want to breach cultural etiquette by challenging a superior. Of course, this ignores the fact that Korean-piloted airplanes take off and land without crashing every day. In this sense, Gladwell's attempt at cultural theory seems less about highlighting real flight risks and more about reconsolidating Asia's irreducible difference from the West.
19 Given the backlash to her book, Chua backpedalled by claiming that individuals of other ethnicities could also be "Chinese mothers." Ironically, controversy surrounding Chua's book was not based on her assertions of Asian stereotypes, but her reverse ranking: "Asian parenting" as *superior* to "American parenting."
20 I discuss this at some length in the introduction to *Asian American Feminisms*. [Vol. I. London: Routledge, 2012. 1–16].
21 On the stereotype of Asian male emasculation, see Eng; Fung; and E. Lim.
22 Kido Lopez identifies an important blind spot in Asian American media activism centered on policing "negative" images: "Adhering to a straightforward condemnation of all things stereotypical can leave a group like MANAA unequipped to deal with satire and comic portrayals . . . that might actually help communicate its message about social injustice", (60).
23 Establishing a discursive approach, Ella Shohat and Robert Stam caution against positing stereotypes as fantasies against some notion of authenticity: "Characters are not seen as unitary essences, as actor-character amalgams too easily fantasized as flesh-and-blood entities existing somewhere 'behind' the diegesis, but rather as fictive-discursive constructs", (215).

Bibliography

Aboud, Frances. *Children and Prejudice*. New York: Basil Blackwell, 1988.
Bascara, Victor. *Model Minority Imperialism*. Minneapolis, MN: University of Minnesota Press, 2006.
Bhabha, Homi K. *The Location of Culture*. London: Routledge, 1994.
Bow, Leslie. "Fetish." In *A Companion to Asian American Literature and Culture*, Ed. Rachel Lee. New York: Routledge, 2014. 122–131.
Chen, Tina. *Double Agency: Acts of Impersonation in Asian American Literature and Culture*. Palo Alto, CA: Stanford University Press, 2005.
Cheng, Anne Anlin. "Shine: On Race, Glamour, and the Modern." *PMLA* 126.4 (October 2011): 1022–1041.
Cheng, Cindy I-Fen. *Citizens from Asian America: Democracy and Race During the Cold War*. New York: New York University Press, 2013.
Chin, Frank and Jeffrey Paul Chan. "Racist Love." In *Seeing Through Shuck*, Ed. Richard Kostelanetz. New York: Ballantine, 1972. 65–79.
Creef, Elena Tajima. *Imaging Japanese America: The Visual Construction of Citizenship, Nation, and the Body*. New York: New York University Press, 2004.
Eng, David L. *Racial Castration: Managing Masculinity in Asian America*. Durham, NC: Duke University Press, 2001.
Fanon, Frantz. *Black Skin, White Masks*. Trans. Charles Lam Markmann. New York: Grove Weidenfeld, 1991 [1952].

Fung, Richard. "Looking for my Penis: The Eroticized Asian in Gay Video Porn." In *The Gender and Media Reader*, Ed. M.C. Kearney. New York: Routledge, 2012 [1991]. 380–387.
Galang, M. Evelina. Ed. *Screaming Monkeys: Critiques of Asian American Images*. Minneapolis, MN: Coffee House Press, 2003.
Gotanda, Philip Kan. *Yankee Dawg You Die*. New York: Dramatists Play Service, 1991.
Hagedorn, Jessica. *Dogeaters*. New York: Pantheon, 1990.
Hamamoto, Darrell Y. *Monitored Peril: Asian Americans and the Politics of TV Representation*. Minneapolis, MN: University of Minnesota Press, 1994.
Harris, Michael D. *Colored Pictures: Race and Visual Representation*. Chapel Hill, NC: University of North Carolina Press, 2003.
Hayot, Eric. "Chinese Bodies, Chinese Futures," *Representations* 99. 1 (Summer 2007): 99–129.
Hirschfeld, Lawrence A. Acquiring Social Categories: Cognitive Development and Anthropological Wisdom." *Man* 23.4 (1988): 611–638.
———. "Do Children Have a Theory of Race?" *Cognition* 54 (1995): 209–252.
Ho, Jennifer Ann. *Racial Ambiguity in Asian American Culture*. New Brunswick: Rutgers University Press, 2015.
Ignacio, Abe, Enrique de la Cruz, Jorge Emmanuel, and Helen Torbio. *The Forbidden Book: The Philippine–American War in Political Cartoons*. Ann Arbor, MI: T'Boli, 2004.
Imada, Adria L. *Aloha America: Hulu Circuits Through the U.S. Empire*. Durham, NC: Duke University Press, 2012.
Johnson, Allan G. "Stereotype." *Blackwell Dictionary of Sociology*. Hoboken, NJ: Blackwell, 2000.
Kang, Laura. "Si(gh)ting Asian/American Women as Transnational Labor." *Positions: East Asia Cultures Critique* 5.2 (Fall 1997): 403–437.
Kang, Miliann. "The Managed Hand: The Commercialization of Bodies and Emotions in Korean Immigrant-Owned Nail Salons." *Gender and Society* 17.6 (December 2003): 820–839.
Katz, Daniel and Kenneth Braly. "Racial Stereotypes in One Hundred College Students." *Journal of Abnormal and Social Psychology* 28 (1933): 280–290.
Kim, Bryan S.K. and Michael M. Omizo. "Asian Cultural Values, attitudes toward Seeking Professional Psychological Help, and Willingness to See a Counselor." *Counseling Psychologist* 31 (2003): 343–360.
Lee, Richard. "Asian American Stereotypes." March 29, 2013. Web. www.aapaonline.org/2013/03/29/asian-american-stereotypes/. Accessed October 12, 2016.
Lee, Robert G. *Orientals: Asian Americans in Popular Culture*. Berkeley, CA: University of California Press, 1999.
Lee, Stacey J. "The Road to College: Hmong Women's Pursuit of Higher Education." *Harvard Educational Review* 67.4 (1997): 803–827.
———. *Unraveling the "Model Minority" Stereotype: Listening to Asian American Youth*, 2nd ed. New York: Teachers College Press, 2009.
Lim, Eng-Beng. *Brown Boys and Rice Queens: Spellbinding Performance in the Asias*. New York: New York University Press, 2014.
Lim, Shirley Jennifer. "'Speaking German Like Nobody's Business': Anna May Wong, Walter Benjamin, and the Possibilities of Asian American Cosmopolitanism." *Journal of Transnational American Studies* 4.1 (2012): 1–17.
Lopez, Lori Kido. *Asian American Media Activism*. New York: New York University Press, 2016.
Lye, Colleen. *America's Asia: Racial Form and American Literature, 1893–1945*. Princeton, NJ: Princeton University Press, 2005.
Ma, Sheng-Mei. *The Deathly Embrace: Orientalism and Asian American Identity*. Minneapolis, MN: University of Minnesota Press, 2000.
Marchetti, Gina. *Romance and the "Yellow Peril": Race, Sex, and Discursive Strategies in Hollywood Fiction*. Philadelphia, PA: Temple University Press, 1993.
Mirikitani, Janice. *Shedding Silence*. Berkeley, CA: Celestial Arts, 1987.
Mithlo, Nancy Marie. *Our Indian Princess: Subverting the Stereotype*. Santa Fe, CA: School for Advanced Research, 2008.
Mohanty, Chandra Talpade. "Under Western Eyes: Feminist Scholarship and Colonial Discourses." *Feminist Review* 30 (Autumn 1988): 61–88.
Morley, David and Kevin Robins. *Spaces of Identity: Global Media, Electronic Landscapes and Cultural Boundaries*. London: Routledge, 1995.

Morrison, Toni. *Playing in the Dark: Whiteness and the Literary Imagination*. Cambridge, MA: Harvard University Press, 1992.

Nguyen, T.H. *Forever Bottom. Nguyen Tan Hoang, Videos: 1999–2002*, DVD, Kimchi Chige Productions, Philadelphia, PA, 2006.

Nishio, Alan. "The Oriental as a 'Middleman Minority.'" *Gidra* (May 1969). n.p.

Ong, Anthony D., Anthony L. Burrow, Thomas E. Fuller-Rowell, Nicole M. Ja Derald, and Wing Sue. "Racial Microaggressions and Daily Well-Being Among Asian Americans." *Journal of Counseling Psychology* 60.2 (2013): 188–199.

Ong, Paul and John M. Liu. "U.S. Immigration Policies and Asian Migration." In *The New Asian Immigration in Los Angeles and Global Restructuring*, Eds. Paul Ong, Edna Bonacich, and Lucie Cheng. Philadelphia, PA: Temple, University Press, 1994. 45–73.

Osajima, Keith. "Asian Americans as the Model Minority: An Analysis of the Popular Press Image in the 1960s and 1980s." In *Reflections on Shattered Windows: Promises and Prospects for Asian American Studies*, Ed. Okihiro, Hune, Hansen and Liu. Pullman, WA: Washington State University Press, 1988. 165–174.

Park, Jane. *Yellow Future: Oriental Style in Hollywood Cinema*. Minneapolis, MN: University of Minnesota Press, 2010.

Prashad, Vijay. *The Karma of Brown Folk*. Minneapolis, MN: University of Minnesota Press, 2000.

Ramsey, Patricia G. "Young Children's Thinking About Ethnic Differences." In *Children's Ethnic Socialization: Pluralism and Development*, Ed. Jean S. Phinney and Mary Jane Rotherman. Newbury Park, CA: Sage, 1987. 56–72.

Said, Edward W. *Orientalism*. New York: Random House, 1978.

Sartre, Jean-Paul. *Anti-Semite and Jew*. New York: Schocken, 1970 [1946].

Saxton, Alexander. *The Indispensable Enemy: Labor and the Anti-Chinese Movement in California*. Berkeley, CA: University of California Press, 1995 [1971].

Schein, Louisa and Ma-Megn Thoj. "Occult Racism: The Masking of Race in the Hmong Hunter Incident: A Dialogue between Anthropologist Louisa Schein and Filmmaker/Activist Va-Mcgn Thoj." *American Quarterly* 59.4 (December 2007): 1051–1095.

Seuss, Dr. *The Sneetches and Other Stories*. New York: Random House, 1961.

Shah, Hemant. "'Asian Culture' and Asian American Identities in the Television and Film Industries of the United States." *Studies in Media & Information Literacy Education* 3.3 (August 2003): 1–10.

Shohat, Ella and Robert Stam. *Unthinking Eurocentrism: Multiculturalism and the Media*. London: Routledge, 1994.

Sue, Derald Wing, Jennifer Bucceri, et al. "Racial Microaggressions and the Asian American Experience." *Cultural Diversity and Ethnic Minority Psychology* 13.1 (2007): 72–81.

Sue, Stanley and Harry H.L. Kitano. "Stereotypes as a Measure of Success." *Journal of Social Issues* 29.2 (1973): 83–98.

Takaki, Ronald. *Strangers from a Different Shore: A History of Asian Americans*. New York: Penguin, 1989.

Tchen, John Kuo Wei and Dylan Yeats, Eds. *Yellow Peril!: An Archive of Anti-Asian Fear*. London: Verso, 2014.

Trask, Haunani-Kay. *From A Native Daughter: Colonialism and Sovereignty in Hawai'i*. Monroe, ME: Common Courage Press, 1993.

Tuan, Yi-Fu. *Who Am I? An Autobiography of Emotion, Mind, and Spirit*. Madison, WI: University of Wisconsin Press, 1999.

Weglyn, Michi. *Years of Infamy: The Untold Story of America's Concentration Camps*. New York: William Morrow, 1976.

Wei, Clarissa. "How Not to be a Dick to your Asian Friend." Web. July 7 2013. www.xojane.com/relationships/how-not-to-be-a-dick-to-your-asian-friend. Accessed July 13, 2014.

Williams, Patricia. "The Tiger Mama Syndrome." *Nation*. 21 Feb. 2011. Web. www.thenation.com/article/158285/tiger-mama-syndrome. Accessed July 7, 2014.

Wu, Ellen D., *The Color of Success: Asian Americans and the Origins of the Model Minority*. Princeton, NJ: Princeton University Press, 2013.

Yang, Gene Luen. *American Born Chinese*. New York: First Second, 2006.

Yung, Wayne, Dir. *My German Boyfriend*. Ricecake Productions, Toronto, VHS, 2004. 18 min.

Zizek, Slavoj. *The Sublime Object of Ideology*. London: Verso, 1989.

2

ON THE ASIAN AMERICAN QUESTION

Joshua Chambers-Letson

The Racial Bourgeoisie

In April of 1990, Mari Matsuda took the podium at a fund-raising banquet for the Asian Law Caucus (ALC). ALC is a progressive, grassroots group of lawyers committed to serving the most vulnerable members of the Asian American community. At the time, Matsuda was an unsurprising choice for the keynote. She was emerging as a central figure in what was coming to be known as the critical race theory [CRT] movement and she would later go on to become the first Asian American woman to receive tenure at a U.S. law school at UCLA in 1998. However, by her own admission her address was an "unconventional fund-raiser talk" that moved "beyond the platitudes of fund-raiser formalism [in order to] talk of something that has been bothering me and that I need your help on" (1996, 150, 149). Barely a moment into her speech, Matsuda turned to an unlikely source of inspiration, paraphrasing Karl Marx's characterization of the nineteenth-century bourgeoisie as an economic class "who were deeply confused about their self-interests . . . emulat[ing] the manners and ideology of the big-time capitalists . . . the 'wannabes' of capitalism. Struggling for riches, often failing, confused about the reason why, the economic wannabes go to their graves thinking that the big hit is right around the corner" (150). Noting that Marx limited his thinking to economic class, Matsuda pointedly asked, "Is there a racial equivalent of the economic bourgeoisie?" before answering, "I fear there may be and I fear it may be us."

To make her case, Matsuda historicized the economic success experienced by some Asian immigrants and their descendants. These successes, she argued, are often repackaged and returned to Asian Americans in the form of the model minority myth. On the one hand, Matsuda was concerned that the dominant culture's deployment of the model minority myth exploits narratives of Asian American success to deny the systemic subordination, disenfranchisement, and elision of Asian Americans. As she argued, it is through the framing of Asian Americans as a model minority that the successes of some "are used [by the dominant culture] to erase our [community's] problems and to disavow any responsibility for them" (152). On the other hand, because the model minority myth has always been an anti-black, anti-Native American, and anti-Latino fantasy fostered by the interests of white supremacy, it positions Asian Americans squarely between the white ruling class and other racialized groups. Framing her address as "a plea to Asian Americans to think about the ways in which our communities are particularly susceptible to playing the worst version of the racial bourgeoisie role" (150), Matsuda asked Asian Americans to defy the lure of identification with the ruling class. If Asian Americans are shuttled between the privilege of belonging (as the model minority) and continued experiences of exclusion and subordination, she called upon us to insist that "we will not be used" to forward the ideology of the dominant culture. The irony of Matsuda's performance is clear: this is a scene in which a then untenured, radical, woman of color feminist addresses a room full of the economic bourgeoisie (lawyers and members of the business community) in order to warn them that they were at risk of becoming *like* the bourgeoisie (i.e. a "*racial* bourgeoisie").

Matsuda knew what she was doing. One does not invoke the Marxian critique of the bourgeoisie without being perfectly aware that, despite the term's waning popularity, it remains applicable to the very class of people comprising her audience. And though she may have rhetorically softened the blow by describing Marx's figuration of the economic bourgeoisie as a nineteenth-century, European formation, she does more than enough work in the speech to show how the term continues to be relevant to the economic and racial cast of characters of the late twentieth-century U.S. Thus, as much as Matsuda's performance was an insurgent act, it was also an earnest and auto-critical plea for "successful" members of the Asian American community to leverage our contingently privileged positions to work against the interests of the dominant culture. Of course, one is unlikely to succeed in convincing members of the ruling class to work against the system that makes their existence as a class possible.

I begin with this extended description of Matsuda's performance at the ACL fundraiser to introduce a critical exploration of similar tensions and contradictions within the critical race theory movement. Just over a quarter-century after the commencement of the CRT movement, I believe it is important to explore CRT's limits for those of us who, inspired by CRT, remain committed to the struggle for racial and economic justice. I understand CRT to be a radical legal movement that seeks to bring about greater conditions of racial and economic justice through a dual movement of legal critique and strategic utilization of the law.

In this chapter, I ask how the paradox of Matsuda's performance—which asks the bourgeoisie to betray their own class interests by making a break with their interpellation *as* bourgeoisie— is significant of an internal contradiction within the CRT movement. CRT is founded upon a turn to the law and the discourse of civil rights. Throughout this chapter, I argue that the law functions as an apparatus that assures the maintenance of the dominant order through the reproduction of dominant social relations. As Karl Marx and Fredrich Engels famously accused the ruling class of the nineteenth century, "Your jurisprudence is but the will of your class made into a law for all" (487). Law transforms the will of the ruling class into a disciplinary, regulative, and universal norm (see: Lemons and Chambers-Letson 2014). Within capitalism, the law plays a critical function in securing the capitalist relations of production by protecting the regime of private property. As Marxist philosopher Louis Althusser writes, "All law, since it is in the last instance the law of *commodity* relations . . . is by essence . . . inegalitarian and bourgeois" (2014, 61). U.S. law, written by and on behalf of white, propertied men, meets the burden of this indictment. Race slavery, the subordination of women, and the dispossession and genocide of native peoples, for example, were not anathema to the legal order established by the U.S. Constitution so much as the U.S. Constitution was designed to protect and support these very practices (see: Lyons and Mohawk 1992; Irons 1999; Marshall 2001). The turn to the law for emancipation from exploitation and domination, then, poses critical problems when law may itself serve as the scaffolding and reproductive engine of structural injustice in the U.S.

Taking up Matsuda's question about what role Asian Americans might play in the struggle for racial and economic justice, this chapter playfully appropriates the title of one of Marx's seminal early writings ("On the Jewish Question") to focus "on the Asian American question." Assuming that in the U.S. race and class are inextricable from each other, yet not entirely commensurable with each other, this chapter explores whether, in spite of its significant and radical potential to facilitate greater conditions for racial and economic justice, CRT is a project that remains limited to what Marx describes as "*civic, political* emancipation" (1978, 26). The problem with political emancipation, for Marx, is that it atomizes the subject into an "*independent and egoistic* individual," without casting off the structural conditions that continue to produce her subordination, exploitation, and alienation. As we shall see, political emancipation relies upon the regime of law and civil rights. These formations ultimately reify, reproduce, and secure the rule of the dominant culture. As such, the following critique of CRT is not meant as an Oedipal attack on an intellectual tradition that continues to be a promising and radical tool in the struggle against racism, so much as it is an attempt to think the potentiality of CRT alongside its limits.

Critical Race Theory: An Incomplete Genealogy

One could proffer a series of genealogies to the CRT movement. As Kimberlé Crenshaw, Neil Gotanda, Gary Peller, and Kendall Thomas wrote in their introduction to the seminal anthology of CRT writing, CRT emerged from the seeming successes *and* failures of the civil rights movement: "However compelling the liberal vision of achieving racial justice through legal reform overseen by a sympathetic judiciary may have been in the sixties and early seventies, the breakdown of the national consensus for the use of law as an instrument for racial redistribution rendered the vision far less capable of appearing even merely pragmatic" (1995, xvii). This breakdown resulted in "rearguard attacks on the limited victories" of the civil rights era as U.S. law was increasingly returned to its role as a structural support for a racially stratified capitalist state that masquerades as a free and egalitarian democracy.

Richard Delgado and Jean Stefancic narrate the origins of CRT similarly: "Realizing that new theories and strategies were needed to combat the subtler forms of racism that were gaining ground, early writers such as Derrick Bell, Alan Freeman, and Richard Delgado . . . put their minds to the task" (2001, 4). Delgado and Stefancic note that the movement was consolidated as such when "the group held its first conference at a convent outside Madison, Wisconsin, in the summer of 1989," but noticeably disappear the contributions of women of color from the movement's origin story.

In a preface to her published remarks from this conference, Matsuda (1996, 47) provides an expanded account of the movement's genesis:

> Professor Kimberlé Williams Crenshaw began calling what radical law professors of color were doing "critical race theory" when she organized a retreat at a Spartan, convent in the summer of 1989. It was "critical" both because we criticized and because we respected and drew on the tradition of postmodern critical thought then popular with left intellectuals. It was "race" theory because we were, both by personal circumstance and through our understanding of history, convinced that racism and the construction of race were central to an understanding of American law and politics. As legal theory, critical race theory uncovers racist structures within the legal system and asks how and whether law is a means to attain justice.

In this important passage Matsuda emphasizes Crenshaw's critical role in the formation of the movement, offering an antidote to Delgado and Stefancic's inadvertent centering of male scholars in CRT's history. It also provides a concise definition of CRT as a legally grounded, critical enterprise that interrogates and critiques the centrality of racism to the nation and its laws.

CRT scholars and legal practitioners drew inspiration from a series of contemporary intellectual movements: critical legal studies, radical legal feminism, and continental theory (including postmodern and poststructural theory). Critical legal studies emerged from the legal realist movement of the early twentieth century. As summarized by Wendy Brown and Janet Halley, legal realists forwarded the "point that law is politics by other means" (2002, 19). Legal realists sought to undo the dominant insistence that there is a distinction between law as a technical, rational discourse and the discourses of power, politics, and morality. Building upon this tradition, critical legal theorists employed the often-competing lessons of Marxism and deconstruction to expand the critique of the law as an ideological force that shapes and maintains dominant power structures. They offered substantive critiques of liberalism while pointing to the inescapable legal indeterminacy caused by interpretive (and thus political) gaps that accompany juristic decision and the application of the law (see: Kennedy 2002). For critical legal scholars influenced by Marxism, law is a technology for the reproduction of the relations of production under capitalism. For those rooted in the tradition of deconstruction, critical legal theory is a means for analyzing how it is that legal discourse is mobilized to signify meaning as it produces material effects in the world (see: Derrida 1989–1990). Drawing on both schools of thought, radical legal feminism performs a structural analysis of patriarchy in order to theorize the systemic and historical elements that result in the social construction of patriarchy alongside the subordination and oppression of women (see, e.g.: MacKinnon 1979, Cornell 1999).

Inspired by and departing from these traditions, critical race theorists explore the structural production of race and racism in and by U.S. law. They demonstrate the centrality of racial formation to U.S. American politics, law, and social culture and respond to what Cornel West describes as "the relative silence of legal radicals—namely critical legal studies writers—who 'deconstructed' liberalism, yet seldom addressed the role of deep-seated racism in American life" (1995, xi). Recognizing the key role that the law plays in the construction of race, critical race theorists have produced an influential body of literature that forwards a series of important contentions regarding the social construction of race in the U.S. For example, scholars such as Derrick Bell were able to show how seeming victories for people of color (famously symbolized by the landmark ruling *Brown v. Board of Education*) are often structured by and conditional upon the convergence of the economic interests of the white ruling class and the nation-state (1995). Some, like Ian Haney-Lopez, mapped the production of "white" as a salient and privileged category in and through U.S. law (1996). Crenshaw demonstrated the differential effects of the intersection of seemingly discrete social formations—such as race and gender—arguing for broader coalitions across race, class, and gender (1995). Finally, others, including Matsuda, Patricia Williams and Robert S. Chang, demonstrated how legal discourse assumes/produces a neutral, universal subject that is in fact provincial and particular (white, landed, male). Doing so, they agitated for the inclusion of personal narrative and legal storytelling that would not only disrupt and displace this universal subject, but also open up legal discourse to the marginalized and minoritized voices and perspectives previously silenced by and in the law (Williams 1991, Matsuda 1995, Chang 1999, 61–75). CRT authors advanced structural theories of how law supports racist ideology, from the avowedly discriminatory regime of Jim Crow to the performance of microaggressions and other seemingly undetectable forms of racial discrimination in the sphere of everyday life. In turn, CRT developed effective, practical tools for challenging the law as it does so.

What if He's *Not* All Right? Critical Asian American Legal Theory

The condensed and cursory genealogy I have thus far provided runs the risk of eliding critical components, lines of flight, and points of divergence that occur under the umbrella of what we are calling critical race theory. By narrating the movement thus, I in no way intend to offer a comprehensive definition of CRT so much as I want to tease out some of the critical perspectives and contributions commonly associated with CRT. Indeed, the movement's emphasis on critique opened the movement itself to a series of auto-critical maneuvers that would expand the range of thought contained within it.

Asian Americanist legal critics, such as Robert S. Chang (2004), argued that the movement itself needed to rethink the black–white axis that structured much of the early work in the field. This was not because the black–white axis is not critical to racial formation in the U.S., but instead because the near exclusive focus on this axis obscures other, comparative forms of racialization that structure racial reality across the racial spectrum. Arguing that "one problem . . . with critical race theory is that while it has made the powerful claim that race matters, it has yet to show how different races matter differently" (1999, 46), Chang asserts that "one of the tasks of Asian American legal studies is to break the silence that surrounds our [Asian Americans] oppression" (60). But while Chang's approach insists on the importance of antiracist coalitions, his analysis focuses largely on the points of connection and structural similarities between Asian Americans and other racialized groups (especially African Americans and Latinos). Less attention is given to the Asian American question posed earlier by Matsuda: what are we to do with the cases in which Asian Americans serve as agents of the dominant ideology and, thus, contribute to the ongoing subordination and exploitation of other minoritarian subjects?

As an example of the failure of dominant strands of CRT to include Asian American perspectives, Chang gestures to a then recently published dossier on the Los Angeles Uprising of 1992 in a prominent legal journal. In his analysis of the dossier, Chang rightly notes that the journal's contributors failed to take seriously the violence against ethnic Korean shopowners. During what is known in the Korean American community as *Sa-i-Gu* (referring to the dates of the rebellion), an estimated $400 million dollars in damage was inflicted upon Korean-owned businesses in LA's Koreatown. As Chang notes, the "omission [of Korean voices from the special issue] foreclosed the possibility of reaching a greater understanding for the existence of racial tensions, how they have been fostered by legal decisions, and what might be done to bridge the differences" (2004, 60). Chang's book valiantly attempts to think through the problem of how to build this bridge.

In a critical passage, Chang offers a reading of a famous scene in Spike Lee's *Do the Right Thing*, presenting the scene as a portrait of what such a bridge might look like. In this scene, a "largely black and Latina/Latino crowd gathered in front of [a] Korean immigrant's store" (1999, 131) with the express intent to destroy it. Chang offers a nuanced reading of the scene that traces the uneasy affinities and points of solidarity between Sonny (Steve Park), the Korean shop owner, and the black residents of the Brooklyn neighborhood where his store is located. While Chang acknowledges the incommensurable nature of the characters' relationships to each other, in the end he celebrates the transcendence of these differences with a description of the scene's resolution. Sonny expresses a cross-racial identification when he declares to the black crowd, "I no white! I black! You, me, same!" Ultimately, the character Coconut Sid (Frankie Faison) defuses the racially charged rage towards Sonny by declaring, "The Korean is all right, he's all right." To this, Chang romantically muses, "We need more moments like this" (132).

While I am compelled by much of Chang's argument, I fear that he is too quick to subsume Asian Americans to a place of racial equivalence with other racialized groups (as signified by being "all right"). Doing so, he does not place enough sustained critical pressure on the role that Asian Americans sometimes play in brokering and maintaining the racial and economic subordination of other groups. Is it possible that the rage directed towards Sonny is not solely determined by anti-Asian animus, but is also an expression of class rage? Might the tragic scapegoating of Korean merchants during *Sa-i-Gu* be heard as an attempt to express rage towards the overlapping conditions of racial and economic hierarchy produced within racial capitalism? If this is true, any hope for forging a productive racial affinity across race can only be effective after an honest accounting of the relations of economic privilege and exploitation that divide differently racialized groups from each other.

Put thus, it is not incidental that the rage in this paradigmatic scene from *Do the Right Thing* (or during *Sa-i-Gu*, for that matter) was directed towards Korean *businesses*. Sonny is a character that serves a duly representative role: certainly he can be understood as representing Korean immigrants (and by extension Asian Americans), but he is also a representative of the class of small merchants that Marx described as the petite bourgeoisie. As a lower order of capitalists, the petite bourgeoisie may be closer in many ways to the working poor than to the upper middle class (*haute* bourgeoisie) or the wealthy capitalist classes. But the petite bourgeoisie's economic interests are determined and forwarded by bourgeois economic ideology, often resulting in their adherence to and defense of dominant economic and racial ideology.

The tragedy of *Sa-i-Gu* was compounded by the fact that the capitalist mode of production in the U.S. often ties class to race and immigration status (Lowe 1996, 1–36; Hong 2006). Because of this, one of the only viable ways for racialized immigrants to survive and often provide for their family is to adopt capitalist ideology and join the ranks of the petite bourgeoisie. Before *Sa-i-Gu*, it was the convergence of racism and capitalism that produced a situation in which Korean business owners, themselves exploited by the capitalist mode of production and subject to U.S. American racism, took on a role as the dominant culture's middle-men in the ongoing exploitation and subordination of other racialized subjects. As Korean merchants increased their presence in largely poor, black South Central Los Angeles neighborhoods, this racialized merchant class became the front line representing capitalist industry. Such stores based their profits (however modest) on the exploitation of largely Latino/a and Asian immigrant labor, unpaid and gendered domestic labor (figured in Lee's film by way of Kim (Ginny Yang), Sonny's wife), as well as the necessary consumption of an often poor, working-class, black customer base. During *Sa-i-Gu*, Korean businesses throughout the Los Angeles region became scapegoats for the exploitative conditions wrought by the capitalist relations of production. This surge of violence was as much an effect of structurally fostered anti-Asian racism as it was a response to the shopowners' status as visible and accessible members of the petite bourgeoisie. To be clear, my intention is not to blame the victims of *Sa-i-Gu*, but instead to cast light on the complicated matrix of race and class hierarchies that provided the context in which the violence of the event erupted.

As the case of *Sa-i-Gu* suggests, if Asian Americans want to produce the mode of racial affinity that Chang desires, we must do more than critique the acts of racism, domination, and exploitation perpetuated against us and other groups. When we find ourselves in a position of relative racial and economic privilege, we must be willing to force a break with the very ruling ideology that affords us this position of privilege. Only by criticizing and moving away from our role in the exploitation of others can we find an affinity with others. This is an impossibly difficult thing to demand, as represented by a fictional account of the uprising in Paul Beatty's novel *The White Boy Shuffle* (Beatty 1996). In a key passage, Ms. Kim, a biracial Black-Korean storeowner, burns down her own shop during *Sa-i-Gu* in an act of solidarity with members of the uprising (133). Satirical though it may be, Ms. Kim's performance of solidarity with the members of her community involved in the uprising, over those of the merchant class to which she also belongs, is significant of the difficult choices to be made in the forging of cross-racial affinity.

Reflecting this challenge, Matsuda's work offers an expanded account of class as she thinks the struggle for racial justice in relation to the history of class struggle. At first, Matsuda's address to the ALC *pretends* to place the question of class to the side, as she relegates Marx's concern with class to "nineteenth-century Europe." But then she pivots: "Living in twentieth-century America, in the land where racism found a home, I am thinking about race" (150). Here, race and class seem rhetorically divided from each other, separated as they are by a century and an ocean. But I understand this to be a pretense because the remainder of Matsuda's analysis goes to great lengths to situate the history of Asian American racialization within the history of class struggle.

Matsuda paints a portrait of racial capitalism's exploitation of the surplus labor population produced by the first waves of Chinese and Japanese immigrants during the nineteenth and early twentieth centuries. She also describes the way capital deployed racism in order to pit differently racialized laborers against each other. To make this case, she argues that Asian immigrants and Asian Americans became a kind of symbolic scapegoat for working-class rage at the decaying and exploitative labor conditions wrought by capitalism:

> From out of this decay come a rage looking for a scapegoat, and a traditional American scapegoat is the Oriental Menace ... From the Workingman's Party that organized white laborers around an anti-Chinese campaign in California in 1877, to the World War II internment fueled by resentment of the success of Issei farmers, to the murder of Vincent Chin, and to the terrorizing of Korean merchants in ghetto communities today, there is an unbroken line of poor and working Americans turning their anger and frustration into hatred of Asian Americans.
>
> *Matsuda (1996, 154)*

The rage is just, she contends. It is the direction of this rage towards Asian Americans that is the problem: "Every time this happens, the real villains—the corporations and politicians who put profits before human needs—are allowed to go about their business free from public scrutiny, and the anger that could go to organizing for positive social change goes instead to Asian bashing." Systemic racism becomes a tool of the ruling class as it fosters division amongst the oppressed classes at the ground level. In turn, the oppressed direct their rage towards each other, rather than towards the structural conditions and members of the ruling class who are responsible for the exploitation and domination of the oppressed.

Isn't this part of the problem represented by Sonny or Ms. Kim? Racial capitalism produces conditions that often yoke racialized and immigrant subjects to a class position that forces their entry into the petite bourgeoisie at the expense and exploitation of other racialized minorities. How, then, can we produce a form of political affinity across race if we do not simultaneously undertake the dismantling of the economic relations productive of racially differentiated exploitation and subordination? Do we not need a more complete program for emancipation, which would free us both from the collusive abstractions of race and class? And can CRT, committed as it is to the law, achieve this end? It is at this point that we must return to the question of political emancipation. Doing so, we can explore the limits of the CRT project, and the difficulty CRT has in breaking with the dominant legal ideology, which serves as both its object of critique and its instrument for change.

Joshua Chambers-Letson

Against Political Emancipation, or That One Time Patricia Williams Couldn't Get into Benetton

The law, though a central locus for class struggle, is ultimately an apparatus that serves, protects, and effects the reproduction of the dominant order. As a discourse of and committed to the law, I submit that CRT can only lead to forms of political emancipation. Put differently, because the law is a state apparatus that reproduces and reifies the ruling ideology, complete emancipation ultimately requires emancipation from the law itself. CRT is unable or unwilling to do this. To set up and defend this claim, let us return briefly to Marx's theorization of political emancipation.

For Marx, political emancipation reduces the subject to a civil order determined by bourgeois interests by relying upon the law, and civil rights in particular, to achieve its end. Civil rights, or the rights of citizens (or "man"), protect the subject's universal right to "equality, liberty, security, property" (42). But in the end this regime of rights affects the individuation and privatization of social life and the protection of private property above all else. Marx argues that within a bourgeois legal order, liberty is constructed as the "right to do everything which does not harm others . . . [and] is not founded upon the relations between man and man, but rather upon the separation of man from man"; property, in turn, "is the right of self interest . . . form[ing] the basis of civil society"; equality becomes an empty signifier with "no political significance" as it is "only the equal right to liberty as defined above; namely that every man is equally regarded as a self-sufficient monad"; and so finally security, which protects the integrity and private property of these "self-sufficient monads," becomes "the *assurance* of its egoism" (42–43). Political emancipation, which is achieved through the assertion of civil rights, effects the further alienation of mankind from itself because the "so-called *rights of man* . . . are simply the rights of a member of civil society, that is, of egoistic man, of man separated from other men and from the community" (42).

I should note, here, that the Marx we are working with is still very much a Marx under the influence of Hegel (see: Struik 1964, 31–39, Althusser 1990, Berardi 2009, 35–41). He still understands the world as perfecting itself through a historical process. As such, the young Marx yearns for the impossibility of a transcendent and universal "humankind," achieved through the abolition of alienation from human experience. In spite of the lingering imprint of idealist humanism upon his thought, the young Marx still offers us an effective critique of civil rights discourse and, by extension, the project of political emancipation. In short, while he concedes that political emancipation can assure the liberation of *some* individuals through the law, he insists that political emancipation ultimately leaves in place, reifies, and contributes to the expansion of the legal technologies that reproduce and effect the continued domination and exploitation of many others.

Let us think this problem in relationship to the question of CRT. It's not that critical race theorists have a naïve conception of the law. In Matsuda's essay on "Critical Race Theory," for example, she proffers a nearly Marxian definition of the law as "an instrument of political power used to privilege ruling elites" (1996, 52). The problem, however, is that law is not merely a tool that is "used" by the ruling class. This is because, as I have argued, law is a key state apparatus that contributes heavily to the reproduction of the relations of production within capitalism (see also: Althusser 2014, 57–69). Law is not merely a tool "used to privilege" the ruling class, it is a central apparatus for the reproduction of class relations as such.

Matsuda argues that there is another element to the law, however, rooted in the optimistic possibility of change through legal means: "The struggle against racism is historically a struggle against and within law. The hard-won victories of that struggle demonstrate the duality of law:

law as subordination and law as liberation" (1996, 52). If I am placing pressure on CRT's engagement with law, I must emphasize that I am not refuting the deployment of legal means in the service of a struggle for radical transformation. What I object to is the formulation of the law as a source of *liberation*. There is a radical difference between reform and emancipation and that difference demands to be parsed.

Certainly, law has always been used as a locus of class struggle and social transformation. As Althusser (2014, 112–113) observes in his description of nineteenth- and twentieth-century class struggle, for example:

> The possibility, for the party of the working class, to intervene in revolutionary (non-reformist) fashion in the 'play' of the system of the . . . [dominant culture/ideology], rests on the possibility of *circumventing* the law *even while respecting it* . . . [I]t is a question . . . of invoking the constitutional law recognized by the bourgeoisie itself so as to make it produce effects of agitation and propaganda favouring overt struggle against the bourgeoisie's politics.

For Althusser, a revolutionary utilization of or negotiation with the law must always presuppose the law's ultimate *circumvention*.

Althusser's position echoes that of Marxist revolutionary Rosa Luxemburg, who argued at the turn of the twentieth century that the struggle for emancipation must only engage in legal reform insofar as it presupposes a revolutionary end (Luxemburg 2004, 157). To mistake legal reform *as* an emancipatory end is to abandon the cause altogether:

> He who pronounces himself in favor of the method of legal reforms in place of and as opposed to the conquest of political power and social revolution does not really choose a more tranquil, surer and slower road to the same goal. He chooses a different goal. Instead of taking a stand for the establishment of a new social order, he takes a stands for surface modification of the old order. [original italics]

For both Althusser and Luxemburg, law can only *intervene* in the sets of relations produced by and reproductive of the dominant classes. Ultimately, reformist efforts cannot sublimate, transcend, or overcome the exploitative and unjust conditions wrought by the dominant culture because of the law's critical role in reproducing and securing dominant social (and property) relations. Thus, while law may function as a *locus* of emancipatory struggle, it cannot achieve emancipation as such. In order to be emancipated from the limits of the "old order" (which is secured and reproduced by law), we must ultimately be emancipated from the law itself.

Considered thus, my worry is that CRT affords too great a *respect* for the law while placing too little emphasis on *circumventing* it. Indeed, as Matsuda asserts, in CRT law is *the* privileged site for liberation: "A just world is one that heals the wounded among us, that brings back the lost and the wasted, that elevates all human beings to their highest potential. The only way to do this is through a substantive conception of rights" (1996, 53). But now the "only way" to emancipate oneself is to subject oneself to the regime of rights that, as we observed vis-à-vis Marx, is precisely that which forecloses emancipation *from* the exploitative conditions of racial capitalism. In spite of its radical intent, CRT runs the risk of being trapped within the ideology of the ruling class. It inadvertently effects the reproduction of the ruling ideology, by way of its adherence to a discourse of rights, rather than achieving emancipation from it.

To expand this argument, let's turn to another example in the form of a famous passage from Patricia Williams' groundbreaking volume *The Alchemy of Race and Rights* (1991). Before I begin, I want to explain the tone of the following critique. Williams' book is a classic text of the CRT movement and remains one of the most incisive, nuanced, and necessary meditations on the relationship between race, law, and life in the U.S. I will perform a rather unflinching critique of a passage from the book for two reasons. First, as the reader will see, the *scene* of the passage is paradigmatically bourgeois (in the classical sense). My interrogation of this scene is *not* meant to single Williams out, so much as I intend for it to function as a form of autocritique. Both Williams and I share the relative (though at times tenuous and contingent) economic privilege bestowed upon middle-class academics of color. Second, I turn a critical edge to this passage largely because Williams' book is characterized by a genius so strong that it will have no difficulty weathering the harshness of my engagement with it.

In an important chapter, Williams tells a story that she has called upon throughout her career in order to illustrate the experience of racial microaggression and to evidence the lived effects of racial discrimination (44–51). While Christmas shopping in NY's Soho neighborhood, which was at that time becoming increasingly affluent, Williams passes a Benetton store. She sees a sweater in the window and attempts to enter the store to buy it for her mother. Equipped with a buzzer, a young, white employee in the store dismissively denies Williams entrance. In the face of an overt act of racial discrimination, Williams justifiably flies into a self-described "rage" (45–46).

Through the story, Williams illustrates how the experiences of discrimination are embedded into the daily life of people of color. She also recounts how law school audiences and law journal editors have responded to the story: they objected to and censored her use of personal narrative as well as her insistence that race functioned as a determining factor in the event. Williams' chapter thus deploys the story to document the ground-level experience of discrimination. It also teaches a critically important lesson regarding the presumed *neutrality* of legal discourse as it is commonly used to render racism and structural discrimination invisible.

At the same time, the narrative perfectly demonstrates the way in which critical race theory, as a discourse rooted in bourgeois legal ideology, runs the risk of reproducing and affirming the dominant ideology as such. After all, in the story Williams isn't excluded from just any store, she is excluded from Benetton. That is, she is excluded from a then trendy, upscale, and elite (which is to say economically exclusive) fashion emporium. Indeed, Williams explicitly identifies the negation of middle-class privileges, which in this case includes the ability to bestow the "gift" of her consumption, as one of the injuries produced by the event: "In this weird ontological imbalance, I realized that buying something in that store was like bestowing a gift, the gift of my commerce, the lucre of my patronage. In the wake of my outrage, I wanted to take back the gift of appreciation that my peering in the window must have appeared to be" (45). It is not only Williams' abstract liberty that is negated, here, because liberty is reduced to her right, as a privileged member of the middle class, to enter into the free market as a free and unrestrained consumer.

If the buzzer system is predicated upon the racist logic that excludes Williams because she was black, the economic system that makes high-end retail stores possible regularly presupposes the exploitation and exclusion of the poor and working class altogether. The political emancipation of Williams from the effects of systemic racism may allow for her to shop in upscale boutiques by protecting her *right* to enter and consume a store's luxury items, a right that largely exists because of her elite economic status. But it most certainly won't provide this right for everyone. It won't provide it for the poor, who can't afford the store's commodities in the first place. It also won't provide it for those who labor to produce luxury commodities at often depressed wages. And it most certainly won't provide access for the over 1,100 workers who died on 24 April 2013 in the collapse of the poorly maintained Rana Plaza factory in Bangladesh: a source for some of Benneton's production (Greenhouse 2013).

By protecting the regime of private property and capitalist relations of production, the law protects and makes possible these examples of exploitation and exclusion. Yet, like Matsuda, Williams (164–165) remains committed to the legal discourse of rights as a source of emancipatory transformation:

> The task for Critical Legal Studies, then, is not to discard rights but to see through or past them so that they reflect a larger definition of privacy and property: so that privacy is turned from exclusion based on self-regard into regard for another's fragile, mysterious autonomy; and so that property regains its ancient connotation of being a reflection of the universal self. The task is to expand private property rights into a concept of civil rights, into the right to expect civility from others.

We need to hold to the most radical and important provision of Williams' assessment, which theorizes a revolutionary inversion of the concepts of privacy and property. But we also need to go one step farther. Williams teaches us that we must "see through or past" the legal discourse of rights, but insists that we should not discard them in the process. In turn, I would suggest that it is precisely by "seeing through or past them" that we would come to sublimate and transcend the concept of civil rights altogether.

Where Matsuda argues that a just world—in which all wounds are healed and the lost are returned to us—can only come about through the expansion of civil rights in general, Williams suggests that it is the reformation and expansion of the conjoined rights to privacy and property, in particular, that offers our best hope of living with each other. As I have argued vis-à-vis Marx, civil rights ultimately produce the privatization, individuation, and reduction of the singular being to her status as a "civil" (consuming) subject. Above all other things, law and civil rights protect the regime of private property, which presupposes conditions of alienation and exploitation. By valorizing and committing itself to the law, CRT contents itself with political emancipation, and forecloses the possibility of general emancipation.

Conclusion

To be clear, my argument is not that CRT is limited to a project of political emancipation because it focuses *too much* on race. Rather, I am arguing that CRT relies too much upon the law, limiting CRT's ability to effectively overturn the systemic conditions productive of race/racism and class/exploitation. Because of its commitment to the law and civil rights, at its best CRT may only be able to produce political emancipation from some of the effects of racism. At its worst, it inadvertently facilitates the expansion and reification of the dominant ordering of the world in which the production of race and class are mutually implicated.

In writing this, I do not mean to dismiss or discount the contributions of the CRT movement. On the contrary, I believe the work of the authors I have discussed should be *essential* reading for all of us committed to the project of emancipation. But as much as we must study the extraordinary contributions of the CRT movement, we must also read against its limits. The promise of the CRT movement lies in its radicality: its willingness to work within the structure of law to destroy some of the legal technologies that make racism a lived reality. Its weakness is its commitment to the law and civil rights as ends unto themselves. In the end, emancipation will require freedom *from* the law as we know it, insofar as law serves, *in the last instance,* to reproduce the *inegalitarian and bourgeois* ideology of racial capitalism.

If we are to take seriously Matsuda's call for Asian Americans to resist the lure of serving as the racial bourgeoisie, we must be willing to critique the bourgeois tendencies that underpin the CRT movement. We must continue to learn from CRT's capacity to imagine radical strategies geared towards emancipation from racism, while remembering that there will be no emancipation until we are *all* freed from related and systemic forms of racial and economic exploitation, subordination, and domination. A vision of a just world is not one in which the elite among us have access to Benetton, where some of us attain security for our private property, or where some achieve freedom from the experience of other people's racism without changing the conditions that produce racism in the first place. In the end, these are the best outcomes afforded by legal or political emancipation. It is not enough for the relatively privileged few to take refuge in the precarious oasis of security and private accumulation, protected as it is by a wall of civil rights. What we must struggle for is a world in which we are all free from the dominant ideology, which necessarily entails freedom from the subjectifying discourses and effects of the law itself.

Bibliography

Althusser, Louis. 1990. "On the Young Marx" in *For Marx*, Translated by Ben Brewster, 49–86. London and New York: Verso.

Althusser, Louis. 2014. *On the Reproduction of Capitalism*. Translated by G.M. Goshgarian. London and New York: Verso.

Beatty, Paul. 1996. *The White Boy Shuffle*. Boston, MA: Houghton Mifflin.

Bell, Jr., Derrick A. 1995. "*Brown v. Board of Education* and the Interest Convergence Dilemma" in *Critical Race Theory: The Key Writings that Formed the Movement*, edited by Kimberlé Crenshaw, Neil Gotanda, Gary Peller, and Kendall Thomas, 20–29. New York: Norton.

Berardi, Franco "Bifo". 2009. *The Soul at Work: From Alienation to Autonomy*. Los Angeles, CA: Semiotext(e).

Brown, Wendy, and Janet E. Halley. 2002. "Introduction" in *Left Legalism/Left Critique*, edited by Wendy Brown and Janet E. Halley, 1–37. Durham, NC: Duke University Press.

Chang, Robert. 2004. "Why We Need a Critical Asian American Legal Studies" in *Asian American Studies: A Reader*, edited by Jean Yu-Wen Shen Wu and Min Song, 364–378. New Brunswick, NJ and London: Rutgers University Press.

Chang, Robert S. 1999. *Disoriented: Asian Americans, Law, and the Nation-State*. New York: New York University Press.

Cornell, Drucilla. 1999. *Beyond Accommodation: Ethical Feminism, Deconstruction, and the Law*. New ed. Lanham, MD: Rowman & Littlefield Publishers.

Crenshaw, Kimberlé. 1995. "Mapping the Margins: Intersectionality, Identity Politics, and Violence Against Women of Color" in *Critical Race Theory: The Key Writings that Formed the Movement*, edited by Kimberlé Crenshaw, Neil Gotanda, Gary Peller and Kendall Thomas, 357–383. New York: New Press.

Crenshaw, Kimberlé, Neil Gotanda, Gary Peller, and Kendall Thomas. 1995. "Introduction" in *Critical Race Theory: The Key Writings that Formed the Movement*, edited by Kimberlé Crenshaw, Neil Gotanda, Gary Peller and Kendall Thomas, xiii-xxxii. New York: New Press.

Delgado, Richard, and Jean Stefancic. 2001. *Critical Race Theory: An Introduction*. New York: NYU Press.

Derrida, Jacques. 1989–1990. "Force of Law: The 'Mystical Foundation of Authority'." *Cardozo Law Review* 11: 920–1045

Greenhouse, Steven. 2013. "Retailers are Pressed on Safety at Factories." *The New York Times*, May 10, B1. Accessed August 12, 2014. http://www.nytimes.com/2013/05/11/business/global/clothing-retailers-pressed-on-bangladesh-factory-safety.html?pagewanted=all&_r=0.

Haney-Lopez, Ian. 1996. *White by Law: The Legal Construction of Race*. New York: NYU Press.

Hong, Grace Kyungwon. 2006. *The Ruptures of American Capital: Women of Color Feminism and the Culture of Immigrant Labor*. Minneapolis: University of Minnesota Press.

Irons, Peter H. 1999. *A People's History of the Supreme Court*. New York: Viking.

Kennedy, Duncan. 2002. "The Critique of Rights" in *Left Legalism/Left Critique*, edited by Wendy Brown and Janet E. Halley, 178–228. Durham, NC: Duke.

Lemons, Katherine, and Joshua Chambers-Letson. 2014. "Rule of Law: Sharia Panic and the Us Constitution in The House of Representatives." *Cultural Studies* 28, no. 5–6: 1048–77.

Lowe, Lisa. 1996. *Immigrant Acts: On Asian American Cultural Politics*. Durham, NC: Duke University Press.

Luxemburg, Rosa. 2004 [1899]. "Social Reform or Revolution." In *The Rosa Luxemburg Reader*, edited by Peter Hudis and Kevin B. Anderson, 128–67. New York: Monthly Review Books.

Lyons, Oren R., and John Mohawk. 1992. *Exiled in the Land of the Free: Democracy, Indian Nations, and the U.S. Constitution*. Santa Fe, N.M.: Clear Light Publishers.

MacKinnon, Catharine A. 1979. *Sexual Harassment of Working Women: A Case of Sex Discrimination*. New Haven, CT: Yale University Press.

Marshall, Thurgood. 2001. "Reflections on the Bicentennial of the United States Constitution." In *Thurgood Marshall: His Speeches, Writings, Arguments, Opinions, and Reminiscences*, edited by Mark V. Tushnet, 281–85. Chicago, IL: Lawrence Hill Books.

Marx, Karl. 1978. "On the Jewish Question." in *The Marx-Engels Reader*, edited by Robert C. Tucker, 26–52. New York: Norton.

Marx, Karl, and Friedrich Engels. 1978. "Manifesto of the Communist Party" in *The Marx-Engels Reader*, edited by Robert C. Tucker, 469–501. New York: Norton.

Matsuda, Mari J. 1995. "Looking to the Bottom: Critical Legal Studies and Reparations" in *Critical Race Theory: The Key Writings that Formed the Movement*, edited by Kimberlé Crenshaw, Neil Gotanda, Gary Peller and Kendall Thomas, 63–79. New York: Norton.

Matsuda, Mari J. 1996. *Where Is Your Body? And Other Essays on Race, Gender, and the Law*. Boston, MA: Beacon Press.

Struik, Dirk J. 1964. "Introduction." in *The Economic and Philosophic Manuscripts of 1844*, Karl Marx, edited by Dirk J. Struik, 9–60. New York: International Publishes.

West, Cornel. 1995. "Foreword." in *Critical Race Theory: The Key Writings that Formed the Movement*, edited by Kimberlé Crenshaw, Neil Gotanda, Gary Peller and Kendall Thomas, xi-xii. New York: New Press.

Williams, Patricia J. 1991. *The Alchemy of Race and Rights: Diary of a Law Professor*. Cambridge, MA: Harvard University Press.

3
POSTCOLONIALISM AND ASIAN AMERICAN STUDIES

Erin Suzuki

What does it mean to think of Asian America as a postcolonial formation? At first glance, the use of the term "postcolonial" appears to be at odds with the concept of "Asian America." While the former describes the social and cultural dynamics of a group formerly subjected to direct colonization by another nation-state, the latter refers primarily to a group of ethnically diverse communities situated within the boundary of the United States. Upon closer examination, however, the distinctions between these two categories grow less clear-cut. For example, it would be difficult to discuss the experience of Filipino-Americans without addressing the role of U.S. colonial rule in the Philippines. Likewise, the experiences of several other Asian American communities—particularly those coming from Japan, Korea, and Vietnam—have also been shaped by their home countries' engagement in the colonial (and postcolonial) wars that shifted the balance of power across the Asia-Pacific throughout the twentieth century. As a social and cultural assemblage that operates both inside and outside of the domestic sphere, Asian America has been just as powerfully shaped by postcolonial dynamics and global politics as it has been by the domestic policies that have policed Asian bodies and communities within the territorial boundaries of the United States.

Postcolonial studies and Asian American studies share an interest in analyzing and critiquing the historical and cultural dynamics that have emerged from global legacies of colonialism and imperialism. These legacies include the formation of racial hierarchies, the emergence (and contestations) of cultural nationalisms, and the transnational social, political, and economic forces that drive—and are driven by—diasporic communities around the world. This chapter will focus on these key sites of intersection between Asian American and postcolonial studies in order to illustrate how Asian Americanist criticism and scholarship articulates important connections between nineteenth- and twentieth-century histories of imperialism in Asia and the Pacific and contemporary global flows of capital, commodities, and communities that have become simultaneously *de*national and *trans*national in scope. I begin with a brief discussion of the development of the idea of the postcolonial in Asian American studies, then focus on two historical case studies—the Philippines and Hawai'i—where (post)colonial and Asian American concerns directly intersect. The essay then turns to explore the ways that these colonial and postcolonial concerns extend into critiques of contemporary *neo*colonial projects in the U.S., Asia, and the Pacific, where economic and cultural pressures have mostly come to replace direct colonial administration and/or military intervention. In this context, conceptualizing Asian America in postcolonial terms not only acknowledges the transnational dimensions of Asian communities within the U.S.; it also charts the shifting political, cultural, and economic relationships between the U.S. and the nations of Asia and the Pacific.

Cultural Nationalism and the Decolonizing World

The emergence of Asian American studies in the U.S. academy coincided with a period that also saw the widespread decolonization of former Western colonies and territories in Africa, Asia, and Oceania. Indeed, much of the anticolonial and cultural nationalist rhetoric that had accompanied the struggles for independence in those newly postcolonial states was absorbed into the language and iconography of minority struggle within the U.S. The 1968 student strikes at the University of California, Berkeley and San Francisco State University that ultimately led to the establishment of ethnic studies departments across the U.S. were organized by a coalition called the "Third World Liberation Front" or TWLF, an association whose very name invoked a connection between minority struggles within the U.S. and anticolonial or postcolonial movements abroad. Some students and radical protestors took their inspiration from Mao and the Chinese Communists' stance against Western imperialism, while others drew strong connections between the colonialist assumptions underlying U.S. involvement in the Vietnam War (1960–1975) and the racist laws and stereotypes that had conditioned the experiences of Asians in America.[1]

Despite this lively engagement with decolonization abroad, this radical first wave of Asian American studies has been largely characterized as a movement that sought to combat racial injustice in the United States by articulating a domestic cultural nationalism focused on reclaiming or redefining America through the lens of Asian American experience.[2] This mode of Asian American cultural nationalism—exemplified by the manifesto set forth by Frank Chin, Jeffery Paul Chan, and Lawrence Fusao Inada in the editors' introduction to *Aiiieeeee! An Anthology of Asian American Writers* (1974)—argued for the creation of a specifically Asian *American* canon that sought to revive the historical, material, and cultural contributions of Asians in America and strenuously resisted the persistent stereotyping of Asian Americans as a feminized, Oriental "other."[3] While the cultural nationalist rhetoric used by the *Aiiieeeee!* editors performed the important work of pushing back against racist representations of Asian Americans and helped to make the social struggles of Asian American communities legible in the context of U.S. history and policy, scholars would later note the ways that the *Aiiieeeee!* group's focus on the recuperation of Asian American masculinity in particular obscured, dismissed, or rejected the claims made by Asian American feminist writers. By the 1990s, when cultural nationalist paradigms had been largely replaced by a focus on the "hybridity, heterogeneity, and multiplicity" (Lowe 1991) of an Asian America reshaped by waves of post-1965 immigration, many critics would point out the limitations of the *Aiiieeeee!* editors' persistently domestic focus on "claiming America" (Wong, 3), and how it problematically aligned Asian America with U.S. nationalism at the expense of engaging with the transnational flows shaping the modern Asian American communities. Yet Malini Johar Schueller (2004) cautions against an overly "developmentalist" (Schueller, 172) narrative that envisions early Asian American cultural nationalism purely as a precursor to, or foil for, a broader postcolonial or internationalist outlook. Rather than setting these earlier cultural nationalist concerns in opposition to contemporary postcolonial methodologies, Schueller posits that thinking about Asian America through a postcolonial lens requires forging "a methodological linkage with the beginnings of the Asian American movement" (173) that would establish a sense of continuity between the antiracist rhetoric of the cultural nationalists and the anti-imperialist attitude of postcolonial scholarship.

Some areas where Asian Americanist scholarship has already begun to productively articulate some of these "methodological linkage(s)" between domestic racisms and postcolonial dynamics include research on the Philippines, Guam, and Hawai'i—all current and former sites of direct U.S. colonialism. Along with Puerto Rico, the Philippines and Guam were ceded to the United States following the Spanish–American War in 1898; while Hawai'i, whose monarch had been overthrown in a coup led by American plantation owners five years prior, was annexed as a U.S. territory through an act of Congress later that same year. As the first overseas territories claimed for the United States, the annexation of these Pacific territories in particular marked an evolution in America's imperial ambitions, as well as an important shift from older models of colonialism to a "modern" form of imperial influence primarily focused on markets and economies, rather than territorial gains.[4] John Eperjesi (2004) observes that the pro-imperialist rhetoric of the period was already more explicitly focused on economic motivations: while the highly vocal American Anti-Imperialist League sought to "reconnect the question of imperialism to matters of governmentality" (10) by addressing the conflict between the U.S.'s 'commitments to democracy and self-determination and its actions abroad—particularly regarding the U.S.'s 'role in suppressing Philippine independence during the Philippine–American war (1899–1902) that immediately followed American annexation—these questions of political morality "could not keep pace with the economic theories that were gaining prominence at the time" (11), which explicitly posited expansionism as a way of extending commercial interests.

In the United States, racialized representations of Asians and Pacific Islanders emerged alongside this nascent form of economic imperialism. The resulting "Asiatic racial form," as Colleen Lye (2009) has called it, is a flexible and paradoxical construction that speaks to both the economic promise and social anxieties engendered by America's ongoing involvement in the Asia-Pacific. From the late nineteenth through the twentieth century, Asian bodies came to be racialized in the U.S. as both a foreign, threatening "yellow peril" *and* an easily assimilable "model minority," representing on the one hand, an object to be studied, restricted, and subordinated, and on the other, an ideal subject for the liberal multiculturalism that would be the hallmark of an economic mode of imperialism, seeking to incorporate or co-opt other nations as participants within a broader capitalist hegemony. This apparent paradox has continued to affect not only Asians and Pacific Islanders located within the United States but also informed shifting attitudes and policies toward Asian nations, where (for example) the recent rise of "Asian Tiger" nations like Japan, Taiwan, and Korea has been perceived simultaneously as an economic threat *and* as a role model for emerging neoliberal economies around the world.

Drawing a connection between these paradoxes of modern racial discourse and the historical moment of emergent American empire, Victor Bascara (2006) notes how the ambivalent rhetoric surrounding the annexation of the Philippines, Guam, Puerto Rico, and Hawai'i in 1898 anticipates—through its invocation of what Bascara calls "model minority imperialism"—the selectively inclusive multiculturalist discourse of a later era. Bascara points out that the administration of these territories was initially framed as a "burden" (31) reluctantly taken on by the United States following the liberation of these territories from their former colonial (or, in the case of Hawai'i, monarchical) rule. For example, in a reflection on the annexation of the Philippines, President William McKinley describes the islands as having "dropped into our laps," dismissing out of hand the possibility of Filipino independence and framing American occupation as a Christian duty "to educate the Filipinos, and uplift and civilize and Christianize them, and by God's grace do the very best we could by them."[5] This statement is characteristic of the way that the U.S., like other Western colonial powers during the period, was able to represent its imperial ambitions not simply as a bid for territorial rule—like its previous colonizer, Spain— but rather as part of its duty to "educate" and "civilize" the Filipino. However, it also deftly linked the idea of *liberation* from an oppressive colonial or monarchical power with assimilation to U.S. cultural and economic hegemony. This twin directive not only to *civilize* (that is, to overcome the "anarchy" and savagery that McKinley and his contemporaries saw as inherent in the Filipino subject) but to productively *assimilate* Filipinos into subjects that would participate in the American project of liberty and democracy—without, however, necessarily granting them equal citizenship rights—both conditioned and anticipated the double-bind of Asian American and Pacific Islander experience through the twentieth and twenty-first centuries.

From the period of colonization to the present day, Asian American and Pacific Island artistic and critical responses to this imperial rhetoric have focused on uncovering these discursive contradictions and their ongoing legacies, as well as suggesting ways to reform or subvert these structures. As an example, Filipina-American author Jessica Hagedorn's novel *Dogeaters* (1990) uses McKinley's reflections on America's "duty" toward the Philippines as an epigraph—but in the context of the dysfunctional post-war, postcolonial Philippine state where the novel is set, the hypocrisy of the sentiment and the damaging historical legacies of McKinley's imperialist attitude are made abundantly clear.[6] Set in the 1950s, *Dogeaters* explores the continuing effects of the Philippines' economic and cultural dependence on the United States on the nominally postcolonial state of the Philippines. Yet this dependence is not based, as McKinley would have it, on the inherent unsuitability of Filipinos and Filipinas for self-government; rather, it has been shaped partly by the racialized social hierarchies set in place during the nation's colonial past, as well as by the ongoing complicity of the U.S. in maintaining the corrupt Marcos regime.[7] However, juxtaposing passages by McKinley, Spanish colonial explorers, and anthropologists alongside clips from local gossip columns, news articles, and the voices of Rio and Joey, the novel's young Filipina and Filipino narrators, Hagedorn's novel not only highlights the paradoxes of colonial discourse but also allows her Filipina/o characters the ability to speak for themselves, and create their own ways of understanding, navigating, and revising this complicated legacy. In this way, Hagedorn's novel celebrates an oppositional mode of hybridity—one that does not conform to Progressive-era stereotypes of Filipinos as "little brown brothers" to be educated into U.S. civilization, but actively adapts, ironizes, and creatively reuses the materials and discourses of U.S. colonialism to express a diverse and historically complex Filipina/o identity.

Asian American and Pacific Islander writers and critics who have focused on Hawai'i and Guam—two Pacific states which, unlike the Philippines, remain under direct U.S. administration today—have highlighted the many discrepancies between the rhetoric of liberal democracy and the material conditions engendered by their status as strategic sites for U.S. military projects and transpacific economic networks. Direct responses to U.S. imperial project began as early as 1898, when the former Hawaiian monarch, Queen Lili'uokalani, published *Hawaii's Story by Hawaii's Queen*. In this book, Lili'uokalani outlined her case that the kingdom had been unlawfully seized by a minority group of American plantation owners. She appealed directly to the United States Congress to reject the treaty proposed by the provisional Republic of Hawai'i, contrasting the "autocratic" (371) behavior of the annexationists with the founding principles of the U.S., and warning that a vote for annexation would mean "nothing less than a departure from the established policy of [the United States], and an ominous change in its foreign relations" (370). While the annexation of Hawai'i as a territory of the U.S. was ultimately ratified by both Congress and President McKinley, Lili'uokalani's protest would resonate with later Hawaiian writers, critics, and activists who continue to call upon the United States government to honor the spirit of democracy and the right to self-determination by granting Hawai'i its independence.

In recent years, the spirit of Lili'uokalani's protest has been extended by a number of contemporary academics and authors who have continued to call for Hawaiian independence. In her influential book *From A Native Daughter* (1993), Native Hawaiian author and critic

Haunani-Kay Trask highlights the social and ecological damages that over a century of American colonization have wrought upon Native communities and lands, focusing particularly on the ecological damage created by industrial agriculture; the creation of economic dependence through the development of tourist and military infrastructure in the islands; and the cultural damage wrought by a colonial education that suppressed and devalued indigenous languages and cultures. Writing in response to these crises, Trask frames her call for de-occupation and self-determination as an explicitly postcolonial project. Drawing inspiration from the work of critics like Frantz Fanon and Ngugi wa Thiong'o, as well as Black Power figures like Malcolm X, Trask posits that the first necessary step toward self-determination and political independence begins by refusing to accept the "intellectual colonization" (Trask, 115) fostered first by the Christianizing rhetoric of the American missionaries who arrived in Hawai'i in the nineteenth century, then supplemented by a colonial education system that, through the first half twentieth century, privileged U.S. cultural values over Native ones.

Trask's call for de-occupation has some intriguing points of overlap with the kind of Asian American cultural nationalism expressed by Chin and the *Aiiieeeee!* group. Like Trask, Chin's writing was inspired by the writings of the Black Power movement—which itself drew inspiration from Fanon and other anticolonial intellectuals—and both were highly critical of the way that Western educational systems and the teachings of Christianity in particular were deployed to implicitly posit the inferiority of non-Western peoples and cultures.[8] Trask would also—like Chin—come under fire from critics who accused her of cultural nationalism, arguing that she did not take into account the full complexity of contemporary Hawai'i's hybrid and increasingly transnational local culture.[9]

While these counter-critiques are necessary for highlighting the limitations of both arguments, I would argue that Chin's and Trask's manifestos both stake out the ongoing importance of the principle of *resistance* in the context of rhetorically postracial modes of imperialism. In the second half of this chapter, I will use the case of Hawai'i as an entry point into a discussion of how contemporary Asian American and Pacific Islander critics have navigated a path that combines a rigorous anti-imperial and anti-racist (as distinct from and opposed to *post*-racial)[10] critique with the interests of an increasingly hybridized, diasporic, and diverse Asian American and Pacific Islander community. These critiques apply not only to direct and indirect U.S. imperial projects, but also to the neoliberal economic policies that have emerged alongside the rise of industrialized and industrializing Asian nations like Japan, Taiwan, South Korea, India, and China. Within this broader global context it is difficult to disentangle the study of transpacific flows of peoples, cultures, and capital from critiques of the state-driven policies that are responsible for driving those migrations.

(Post)colonialism and Post-Racial America

Hawai'i has often been portrayed, in both the national press and local public opinion, as a particularly successful example of a multicultural state. From the late nineteenth century through to the present day, widespread immigration from China, Japan, Korea, the Philippines, Micronesia, and many other Pacific states has created a predominantly multicultural and diasporic Asian and Pacific Islander population. In both popular culture and scholarly literature, the complex history of immigration in Hawai'i has frequently been narrated as a practice of multicultural accommodation and assimilation: as each new wave of immigrants arrives in the islands, they are met first with resistance and hardship, then ultimately incorporated into a polyglot "local" culture.[11] Shelly Sang-Hee Lee and Richard Baldoz (2008) trace these "melting-pot" narratives back to theories put forth in the 1920s and 30s by sociologists trained at the University of Chicago, who saw in Hawai'i a "racial laboratory" (88) where they could pursue ethnographic research on interracial relations. Noting the relative lack of race prejudice in everyday interaction between whites, Hawaiians, and Asians in Hawai'i—particularly in contrast to the violent race riots and anti-Asian demonstrations that had broken out in California and the West Coast— the Chicago School sociologists attributed this harmony partly to what they perceived as Native Hawaiians' openness to interracial marriage (96), and partly to the influence of the American missionaries, which the sociologists saw as encouraging "a more civil and inclusive set of social relations" (97). Yet despite these celebratory pronouncements of interracial harmony, those outside observations often overlooked extant ethnic and racial hierarchies and prejudices created by the entrenchment of the plantation system in Hawai'i. Caucasians—who were plantation owners and managers—enjoyed the greatest social status, while Asians and Hawaiians, who often worked as laborers, were generally perceived as racial inferiors.[12] By contrast, the Chicago School's focus on miscegenation assumed that racial *hybridity* necessarily led to social *equality*— a kind of social equality, moreover, that they saw as being primarily fostered and promoted by a specifically Western/Christian, rather than Asian or Native cultural philosophy. As a result, the concept of the "melting-pot" or multicultural state as framed by the Chicago School worked to promote the assimilation of Asian immigrant and Native populations into the ideology of the liberal nation-state.

Just as the rhetoric of "education" and "civilization" worked to frame Filipinos as fledgling American subjects rather than a colonized population at the turn of the century, the construction of Hawai'i as a multicultural state cast Asian and Pacific Islanders as participant-subjects in a progressively post-racial U.S. national project. Yet it is important to note that this narrative of inclusive multiculturalism developed alongside Hawai'i's shift from the agricultural, plantation-based economy of the early twentieth century to an economy based primarily on tourism and U.S. military infrastructure. From the 1920s through the 1950s, Asian immigrant communities in Hawai'i—Japanese and Chinese Americans in particular—were able to gain increased economic mobility and opportunity through pan-ethnic labor organizing, military service, and increased access to higher education. While this mobility certainly operated as a testament to the achievements of the individual actors/activists and the progressive ideologies of liberal multiculturalism, it was also a response to the shifting economic and geopolitical conditions of the twentieth century. Hawai'i's strategic geographical position—halfway between North America and Asia—was one of the primary reasons that the U.S. found it to be an attractive candidate for annexation, and following the Japanese attack on Pearl Harbor and the U.S. entry into World War II, the islands became a critical center for U.S. military efforts in Asia and the Pacific. This military escalation continued through the Cold War years, and Hawai'i's official entry into statehood in 1959 confirmed its centrality to the spread of American economic and military power in the Pacific. The same period saw the emergence of the tourist industry in Hawai'i, which was to replace the plantation as the primary driver of the Hawaiian economy.[13] Vernadette Vicuna Gonzalez argues that the simultaneous rise of the tourist industry and the military-industrial complex in Hawai'i (and the Philippines) is not coincidental: in the Pacific, tourism both depends upon and camouflages the imperial projects that military power enables and supports. Tourism is a practice of "mobility and consumption" (4) enabled by a free flow of consumer and financial capital, while militarism is the mechanism that both secures these pathways and opens up new markets for this capital to flow through. While the military is associated with war and force, tourism masks these negative qualities with an image of pleasure, mobility, and choice; however, as Gonzalez (2013) and others have pointed out, they are inextricably intertwined: militarization paves the way for tourism while tourism keeps the militarized infrastructure that undergirds the flow of transnational capital hidden away.

The emergence of the U.S. military and tourist economies as major drivers of the postwar Hawaiian economy aided the socioeconomic rise of Asian Americans—particularly Japanese Americans—into positions of power in Hawai'i. Many Japanese Americans who had enlisted to serve in the military later attended college on the G.I. Bill and entered into business and politics, becoming an important part of the Democratic "machine" that would become the dominant political power in the years following statehood.[14] In turn, many of those leaders supported the military industry as a way to promote increased mobility and opportunity for Asian American and Pacific Islander communities in Hawai'i.[15] Yet these opportunities also worked to align these communities with the broader global spread of U.S. influence into the Pacific and Asia, as Hawai'i would become a strategic command site for wars waged in Korea and Vietnam. Ironically, as the Cold War progressed, the progressive movement toward racial equality within the state itself became connected to the exercise of U.S. imperial power abroad, not only in terms of direct Asian American and Pacific Islander participation in the U.S. military-industrial complex, but also in terms of the marketing of Hawai'i—and by extension, the United States itself—as a multicultural "paradise," an exemplar not only of natural beauty but also with inter-ethnic harmony achievable under a capitalist democracy. Such representations reprised the colonial stereotypes of the Pacific Islands as an exotic paradise[16] for a neoimperial economy that presented the islands as sites of diversity, mobility, and consumption.

While many Asian Americans in Hawai'i accepted the benefits of postwar liberalization, others remained critical of this incorporation into a national narrative. Stephen Sumida (1991) and Jonathan Okamura (2008) have sought to complicate this progressive multiculturalist narrative by drawing attention to the inter-ethnic tensions and conflicts that have persisted and developed over this shift from the plantation era to a modern global economy. Okamura argues that, much like it did in the plantation era, ethnicity continues to operate as a "regulating principle of the socioeconomic status system" (43), pointing out that while Japanese, Chinese, and Korean American communities have thrived in Hawai'i's postwar economy, other ethnically marked groups, such as Native Hawaiians, Filipino Americans, and Samoan Americans, suffer from more restricted economic and social mobility, based both on preexisting conditions of colonization (particularly in the case of Native Hawaiians) and on negative social stereotypes (in the case of Filipino and Samoan Americans—both communities that have come from formerly colonized nations). Several Hawai'i-born Asian American writers and poets—including Gary Pak and Lois-Ann Yamanaka, among others—have explored these tensions between ethnic groups in their work, while attempting to remain attentive to the ways that they have been conditioned by Hawai'i's colonial relationship to the "mainland" United States.

Other scholars, including Dean Saranillio (2013) and Candace Fujikane and Okamura (2008), have pushed this critique further by pointing out how progressive narratives of "local" multiculturalism have worked to obscure and subvert Native Hawaiian calls for decolonization, making local Asian American and nonindigenous Pacific Islander communities essentially complicit in the project of U.S. settler colonialism.[17] In this reading, the postcolonial diaspora of communities from nations that were formerly colonized or occupied by the United States—including Korea, Japan, Micronesia, and the Philippines—ironically re-enter the United States as participants in the very imperial project that had caused their displacement.

This critique could be extended to Asian American communities on the continental U.S. as well. Just as Asian Americans in Hawai'i gained *social* mobility through their relationship to U.S. military power and by becoming active participants in establishing a multicultural state based on settler colonialism, Susan Koshy notes that the increased *economic* mobility of a diverse range of Asian American communities throughout the United States—particularly the cohorts of middle-class and professional immigrants from South Asia, Japan, Korea, and China that emigrated to the U.S. after 1968—allowed Asian Americans to participate more broadly in discourses of "whiteness as power" (186). Certainly, by the 1960s and 70s, the mobilization of Asian Americans as symbol and harbinger of settler colonialism and progressive post-racial politics was typical not only of the long-established and demographically dominant Asian American communities in Hawai'i, but also of Asian American communities both new and old throughout the continental United States. Koshy (2001) points out that in the years following the emergence of the anti-racist coalitions like the TWLF in the 1960s, changes in U.S. legal policies—particularly regarding "immigration, affirmative action, [and] welfare reform" (155)—worked to reposition the interests of various ethnic communities against one another, and often in alignment with the interests of the white majority. Koshy emphasizes the interconnection between these domestic policies and the demands of an increasingly globalizing economy when she points out that "changed demographics, class stratification [and] new immigration" driven by the transnationalization of labor and capital has

> produced the rearticulation of whiteness as colorblindness . . . this new discourse of race projects a simulacrum of inclusiveness even as it advances a political culture of market individualism that has legitimized the gutting of [U.S. domestic] social services to disadvantaged minorities in the name of the necessities of the global economy.
> *Koshy (155–156)*

In other words, "whiteness" becomes attached not exclusively to race but expands to include economic privilege (hence its "colorblindness"); yet the ability to lay claim to this "whiteness as power" is dependent upon the adoption of an ethos of possessive individualism that tends to benefit people who are already upwardly mobile at the cost of communities that have very little economic and social capital to begin with. This concept of "whiteness as power" works not only to split upwardly mobile Asian Americans from coalitional politics with other ethnic American minority groups, but also fractures the concept of a collective Asian American identity along class lines from within.

These new fractures can be seen in the shifting demographic patterns of Asian immigration to the U.S. after 1965, which also indicate the ways in which postcolonial and transnational projects have continued to shape the contradictory racialization (or perhaps the "post-racialization") of contemporary Asian America. The changes in immigration laws enacted in 1965 allowed for increased immigration of students and members of the professional classes on one hand, and refugees and asylum-seekers on the other. While the cosmopolitan mobility of the former group is due in part to their increased access to capital—including those who benefited from economic structures that emerged out of postwar decolonization in Asia and the subsequent proxy wars in Korea and Vietnam—the transnational movements of the latter are shaped by their *lack* of access to security and capital: they are the people who had been victimized by those same events. Moreover, while the professional classes of Asian Americans may appear to have access to a certain degree of "whiteness"—that is, their economic privilege grants them a certain degree of social mobility—Anna Joo Kim (2014) points out that many working-class Asian American immigrants often continue to live and work in ethnic enclaves, as they are often excluded from "mainstream sectors of the economy" (227) due to linguistic and educational barriers, or questionable citizenship status. Kim argues that these enclave economies offer a flexible labor market that provides opportunities for a mixture of formal and informal (under-the-table) employment, creating an "adaptive, energized, and dynamic economy" (232) that goes unrecognized and unleveraged by local and state governments precisely because it is both "informal" and ethnically marked.

In short, while the flexible citizenship of cosmopolitan Asian American professionals allows them the luxury of a certain degree of unmarked "whiteness," the flexible labor market of the transnational Asian American working class often relegates them to being marked as "ethnic" and thus outside of the mainstream. Yet ironically, the success of both groups—in "mainstream" and "enclave" economies, respectively—has also been deployed in service of the expansion of U.S. hegemony beyond American borders. Asian American critics have recently explored the ways that the experiences of communities of diasporic Asian immigrants (Cheng 2013), refugees (Nguyen 2012), and adoptees (Choy 2013) have been mobilized to articulate discourses of liberal democracy, "freedom," and individual subjectivity not only to support a narrative of universal, "post-racial" opportunity *within* the domestic space of the U.S., but also to promote the virtues of liberal multiculturalism and democratic citizenship abroad. The ability of transnational Asian American individuals to succeed and/or assimilate *within* the domestic space of the nation is then used to support the universal applicability of U.S. ideologies and policies abroad.

In this context, the ambivalent racial rhetoric that alternately framed Asians as inscrutable foreigners or as privileged post-racial subjects within the boundaries of the U.S. also came to apply to American perceptions of and relationships with the primarily East Asian nations that began to emerge as economic powers in the second half of the twentieth century, particularly Japan, South Korea, and Taiwan. On the one hand, these democratic nation-states were seen as strong political and economic allies for the U.S. abroad; unlike their counterparts in North Korea and China, they had adopted the capitalist ethos of U.S. imperialism—in this way, they were selectively included in the American imperium. (In fact, the rise of several of these Asian economies was strongly intertwined with U.S. interventions during the Cold War: Japan's economic resurgence following the destruction of World War II was partly due to their role as a supplier for U.S. deployments in Korea;[18] likewise, South Korea's economy had received a boost from their role as a base for the U.S. army during the Vietnam War.) On the other hand, especially as the Japanese economy began to boom in the 1980s, these Asian nations were increasingly perceived as an economic threat: the specter of militant Japanese colonialism and imperialism from World War II was replaced by the specter of a new form of economic aggression.[19]

At the center of U.S. anxiety about East Asia's growing neocolonial economic influence in the region were concerns about the consequences of the latest stage of economic imperialism, which increasingly tends toward *trans*national, rather than national, networks of interest. As Michael Hardt and Antonio Negri (2001) have observed, this modern form of "Empire" is characterized by a "*decentered* and *deterritorializing* apparatus of rule that progressively incorporates the entire global realm within its open, expanding frontiers" (xii, italics in original). While the language of "incorporation" and "expanding frontiers" reflects the strategies of U.S. imperial projects in the Philippines and Hawai'i, Hardt and Negri argue that in this mode of Empire, "*the United States . . . and indeed no nation-state can today, form the center of an imperialist project*" (xiv, italics in original). This shift from a state-based imperialism to capital-based "Empire" is reflected in the "Pacific Rim" discourse that emerged in the 1970s and 80s. Chris Connery (1994) points out that while the concept of the Pacific Rim as a geopolitical bloc emerged out of Cold War competition, it did not focus on the U.S. alone: rather, it conceived of itself as an "interpenetrating complex of interrelationships with no center: neither the center of a hegemonic power nor the imagined fulcrum of a 'balance of power'" (32). Yet a transpacific economy that focuses on the "interrelationship" of U.S. and Asian powers coexists with anxiety over the erosion of state power in the light of these increasingly transnational networks. This diminishment of state power is a concern not only for the U.S.—where nativist responses to Asian business and investment, for example, led to anti-Japanese sentiment in the 1980s (and continue to fuel anti-Chinese sentiment today)—but increasingly for a number of Asian nations as well. Laura Kang (2012) points out the role that transnational organizations had played in the lead-up to and aftermath of the 1997–1998 Asian Financial Crisis in South Korea: first, as a condition of joining the Organization for Economic Co-operation and Development (OECD), a major international world trade organization, in 1993 South Korea was pressured into "greater financial liberalization *against* the opposition of its own Council of Economic Advisors ... loosening restrictions on both foreign borrowing by Korean banks and the movement of foreign capital investments into and out of the country" (416). This shift in economic policy, introduced by U.S. pressure, spurred on borrowing and lending on a massive scale that would lead to the financial crisis as it would play out in South Korea a few years later. Yet in the aftermath of the crisis, the IMF doubled down on the neoliberal policies that had created the groundwork for the crisis to begin with by making deregulation a condition for nations looking to borrow money for "bailout" loans: these conditions included "privatizing public enterprises, lifting trade restrictions, opening up capital markets, and cutting public expenditures" (422), further loosening national control over the national economy. Yet while Kang characterizes this intervention as "an important episode in the history of U.S. empire in Asia" (413), it's important to note that these types of economic reforms were also working to erode state protections and public services in the U.S. as well: certainly, as Koshy observed above, the same focus on servicing the needs of a global economy has also effectively "legitimized the gutting of social services to disadvantaged minorities" within the United States. While the concept of "Empire" may have become increasingly postracial and postnational in scope, its negative effects are still disproportionately visited on impoverished and often racialized subjects in the U.S.—including Asian American and Pacific Islander communities without significant access to consumer capital.

Situated at the intersection of the U.S.'s domestic and foreign policies, Asian American scholars, authors, and activists have used their position to both reflect back upon America's transformation into a colonial power at the end of the nineteenth century, as well as to chart its shift from a colonial to a neoimperial power over the course of the twentieth. Looking back to the American annexation of the Philippines, Guam, and Hawai'i in 1898 through the destructive Pacific wars of the twentieth century and the financial booms and busts that rocked transpacific economies in the 1990s, over the past twenty-five years, Asian American studies has contributed to postcolonial and transnational scholarship by tracing the entanglement of U.S. imperial projects, Asian and Pacific Islander nationalisms, and the flow of peoples, cultures, and capital between Asia and the Americas. Such work not only serves to expand, extend, or "de-center" the scope of inquiry for Asian American studies; it also continues to highlight potential sites of shared concern between domestic and diasporic Asian American communities, as well as between these communities and the broader postcolonial—and decolonizing—world.

Notes

1 See Sau-Ling C. Wong, "Denationalism Reconsidered," 3.
2 While Wong points out the transnational roots of Asian American studies, she also states that "the Asian American cultural nationalist project ... was characterized by a cluster of domestic emphases, and the subsequent development of this project did involve a certain ossification of identity politics," and notes that "Early Asian American cultural criticism was spearheaded by American-born and -raised, Anglophone, mostly male Asians; it featured certain premises—anti-Orientalism, valorization of working-class ethnic enclaves, 'claiming America'—that explicitly or implicitly discourage, if not preclude, critical attention on things Asian" (3). Similarly, Viet Nguyen and Tina Chen (2000) note that one of the dominant assumptions shaping Asian American studies in its first thirty years is the

need to "claim America" (3), an assumption that operated to privilege the longer-established Chinese and Japanese American communities while obscuring the "postcolonial perspective[s]" (3) that focus on "the experiences of other nations whose histories have helped to generate the flows of culture and capital—or whose histories have been generated from them" (3).

3   See Jeffery Chan, et al., *Aiiieeeee! An Anthology of Asian American Writers*, 3–36.
4   This shift in conceptions of both America-as-empire and American-style imperialism has been a critical site not only for Asian Americanist scholars in particular but also several of the "new Americanist" critics who have been interested in questions of empire and expansionism in American studies, most notably Amy Kaplan and Donald Pease (1994) John Carlos Rowe (2000).
5   James Rusling, "Interview with President William McKinley." *The Christian Advocate*, January 22, 1903, 17.
6   McKinley's text also appears in the theatrical version of *Dogeaters*, which was adapted for the stage by Jessica Hagedorn and first performed at the Public Theater in New York City in 2001.
7   Postwar legislation like the Military Bases Agreement (1947) and the Bell Trade Act (1948) granted much-needed funds for postwar reconstruction to the Philippines in return for a long lease on military bases in the region and preferential trade partnerships that effectively worked to make Filipinos American consumers—the conditions of the Trade Act made it cheaper to purchase American-imported goods than locally-produced ones. In later years, the Marcos regime's ongoing support for continued U.S. military presence in the islands meant that America largely turned a blind eye to the corruption and abuses in his government—and following his defeat in the "People Power" revolution in 1986, the U.S. military flew the Marcoses out of the country and relocated them in Hawai'i. For more on the postcolonial legacies of the U.S., see San Juan Jr. (2000).
8   In their essay on "Racist Love" (1972) Frank Chin and Jeffery Paul Chan argue that the kind of "love" espoused by Christianity is "a bigoted love that has imprisoned the Chinese-American sensibility" (69) by getting them to "internaliz[e] the white supremacist Gospel of Christian missionaries [and look] on themselves as failures, instead of victims of racism" (71).
9   For a detailed description of the cultural nationalist/cultural constructionist debate between Trask and anthropologist Joyce Linnekin, see Jeffrey Tobin's article on "Cultural Construction" (1995).
10 In making this distinction between "anti-racist" and "postracial," I follow Jodi Melamed (2011) in noting the difference between what she calls *official* or *liberal* antiracisms—which include discourses "of reform, of color blindness, of diversity in a postracial world" that attempt to "explai[n] (away) the inequalities of a still-racialized capitalism" (9)—versus the "*race radicalism*" (47) that focuses on the ways that racialization continues to occur under new regimes of market capital.
11 James Michener's perennially bestselling novel *Hawaii* (1959), published in the same year as statehood, is perhaps one of the best fictional examples of this melting-pot narrative. More recently, Ellen Wu notes how Hawai'i's petition to become the site of Barack Obama's Presidential Library has continued to emphasize the "racial paradise myth" as a central strategy for articulating Hawai'i's importance to the ideals of the Obama presidency and the modern U.S. (Wu 2015)
12 For a description of the racial hierarchies on Hawai'i plantations, see Takaki (1983); for more on their ongoing legacies in contemporary Hawai'i, see Okamura (2008) and Fujikane and Okamura (2008).
13 Currently, the tourist industry is responsible for just over 20% of Hawai'i's GSP (Gross State Product), while military spending represents the second-largest source of income, accounting for 18% of the state's GSP in 2009. By contrast, agriculture has consistently accounted for only around 3–4% of the state's GSP since the 1990s.
14 See Fujikane and Okamura, 23.
15 For example, U.S. senator Daniel Inouye, who represented Hawai'i in Congress from statehood until his death in 2012, was a decorated war veteran and Medal of Honor recipient; as a legislator, he also supported the development of military infrastructure in Hawai'i as a way to boost the local economy.
16 Borrowing from the Saidian notion of "Orientalism," Paul Lyons describes this discourse of exotification "American Pacificism," noting how the Western representations of the Pacific dating back to the nineteenth century continue to impinge upon contemporary neocolonial imaginings of the Pacific Islands and its peoples (Lyons 2005).
17 See Fujikane and Okamura (2008), and Saranillio (2013).
18 See Shigematsu and Camacho (2010), xix.

19 In their chapter on "Techno-Orientalism" David Morley and Kevin Robins note the "Japan Panic" that characterized U.S. attitudes toward Japan during the 1980s and 1990s as Japanese companies began to invest heavily in traditionally Western and American enterprises—including the film industry (Sony Pictures), the automobile industry, and real estate—leading to a "fear that Japanese investors are 'buying into America's soul'" (150).

References

Bascara, Victor. 2006. *Model-Minority Imperialism*. Minneapolis, MN: University of Minnesota Press.

Chan, Jeffery Paul, Frank Chin, Lawson Fusao Inada, Eds. 1974. *Aiiieeeee! An Anthology of Asian American Writers*. Washington, DC: Howard University Press.

Cheng, Cindy I-Fen. 2013. *Citizens of Asian America: Democracy and Race During the Cold War*. New York: NYU Press.

Chin, Frank and Jeffery Paul Chan. 1972. "Racist Love." In *Seeing Through Shuck*, edited by Richard Kostelanetz. 65–79. New York: Ballantine.

Choy, Catherine Ceniza. 2013. *Global Families: A History of Asian International Adoption in America*. New York: NYU Press.

Connery, Christopher L. 1994. "Pacific Rim Discourse: the US Global Imaginary in the Late Cold War Years." B*oundary 2* 21. 30–56.

Eperjesi, John. 2004. *The Imperialist Imaginary: Visions of Asia and the Pacific in American Culture*. Hanover: Dartmouth College Press.

Fujikane, Candace, and Jonathan Y. Okamura, Eds. 2008. *Asian Settler Colonialism: From Local Governance to the Habits of Everyday Life in Hawai'i*. Honolulu: University of Hawaii Press.

Fujikane, Candace. 2000. "Sweeping Racism under the Rug of 'Censorship': The Controversy over Lois-Ann Yamanaka's Blu's Hanging." *Amerasia Journal* 26.2: 159–194.

Gonzalez, Vernadette Vicuña. 2013. *Securing Paradise: Tourism and Militarism in Hawai'i and the Philippines*. Durham, NC: Duke University Press.

Hagedorn, Jessica. 1990. *Dogeaters*. New York: Pantheon Books.

Hardt, Michael, and Antonio Negri. 2001. *Empire*. Cambridge, MA: Harvard University Press.

Kang, Laura Hyun Yi. 2012. "The Uses of Asianization: Figuring Crises, 1997–98 and 2007–?" *American Quarterly* 64.3: 411–436.

Kaplan, Amy and Donald Pease, Eds. 1994. *Cultures of United States Imperialism*. Durham, NC: Duke University Press.

Kim, Anna Joo. 2014. "Informality at Work: Immigrant Employment and Flexible Jobs in Los Angeles." In *The Nation and Its Peoples: Citizens, Denizens, Migrants*, Eds. John S.W. Park and Shannon Gleeson. 223–249. New York: Routledge.

Koshy, Susan. 2001. "Morphing Race Into Ethnicity: Asian Americans and Critical Transformations of Whiteness." B*oundary 2* 28.1: 153–194.

Kwon, Brenda. 1999. *Beyond Ke'eaumoku: Koreans, Nationalism, and Local Culture in Hawai'i*. New York: Routledge.

Lee, Shelley Sang-Hee and Richard Baldoz. 2008. "A Fascinating Interracial Experiment Station: Remapping the Orient/ Occident Divide in Territorial Hawaii." *American Studies Journal* 49.3: 87–109.

Lili'uokalani. 1964. *Hawaii's Story by Hawaii's Queen*. New York: Tuttle.

Lowe, Lisa. 1991. "Heterogeneity, Hybridity, Multiplicity: Marking Asian American Differences." *Diaspora: A Journal of Transnational Studies* 1.1: 24–44.

———. 1996. *Immigrant Acts: on Asian American Cultural Politics*. Durham, NC: Duke University Press.

Lye, Colleen. 2009. *America's Asia: Racial Form and American Literature, 1893–1945*. Princeton, NJ: Princeton University Press.

Lyons, Paul. 2005. *American Pacificism: Oceania in the US imagination*. New York: Routledge.

Melamed, Jodi. 2011. *Represent and Destroy: Rationalizing Violence in the New Racial Capitalism*. Minneapolis, MN: University of Minnesota Press.

Morley, David, and Kevin Robins. 2002. *Spaces of Identity: Global Media, Electronic Landscapes and Cultural Boundaries*. New York: Routledge.

Nguyen, Mimi Thi. 2012. *The Gift of Freedom: War, Debt, and Other Refugee Passages*. Durham, NC: Duke University Press.

Nguyen, Viet and Tina Chen. 2000. "Editors' Introduction to Postcolonial Asian America." *Jouvert* 4: 1–11.

Okamura, Jonathan. 2008. *Ethnicity and Inequality in Hawai'i*. Philadelphia, PA: Temple University Press.

Rowe, John Carlos. 2000. *Literary Culture and US Imperialism: From the Revolution to World War II*. New York: Oxford University Press.

San Juan Jr, Epifanio. 2000. *After Postcolonialism: Remapping Philippines-United States Confrontations*. Rowman & Littlefield.

Saranillio, Dean Itsuji. 2013. "Why Asian Settler Colonialism Matters: A Thought Piece On Critiques, Debates, and Indigenous Difference." *Settler Colonial Studies* 3.3–4: 280–294.

Schueller, Malini Johar. 2004. "Claiming Postcolonial America: The Hybrid Asian-American Performances of Tseng Kwong Chi." In *Asian North American Identities: Beyond the Hyphen*, Eds. Eleanor Rose Ty and Donald Goellnicht. 170–186. Bloomington, IN: Indiana University Press.

Shewry, Teresa. 2011. "In Search of Changed Climates: Water, Weather, and Sociality in Gary Pak's 'Language of the Geckos'." *Interventions* 13.4: 627–639.

Shigematsu, Setsu and Keith Camacho, Eds. 2010. *Militarized Currents: Toward a Decolonized Future in Asia and the Pacific*. Minneapolis, MN: University of Minnesota Press.

Sumida, Stephen H. 1991. *And the View from the Shore: Literary Traditions of Hawai'i*. Seattle, WA: University of Washington Press

Takaki, Ronald T. 1983. *Pau hana: Plantation life and labor in Hawaii, 1835–1920*. Honolulu, HI: University of Hawaii Press.

Tobin, Jeffrey. 1995. "Cultural Construction and Native Nationalism: Report From the Hawaiian Front." In *Asia/Pacific as Space of Cultural Production*, Eds. Rob Wilson and Arif Dirlik. 111–133. Durham, NC: Duke University Press.

Trask, Haunani-Kay. 1993. *From A Native Daughter: Colonialism and Sovereignty in Hawai'i*. Honolulu, HI: University of Hawai'i Press.

Wong, Sau-Ling C. 1995. "Denationalization Reconsidered: Asian American Cultural Criticism at a Crossroads." *Amerasia Journal* 21.1: 1–27.

Wu, Ellen. 2015. "Hawaii as 'Racial Paradise'? Bid for Obama Library Invokes a Complex Past." *NPR*, January 15. Accessed January 16, 2015. www.npr.org/blogs/codeswitch/2015/01/15/377197729/hawaii-as-racial-paradise-bid-for-obama-library-invokes-a-complex-past.

4

DIASPORA AS FRAME AND OBJECT OF ANALYSIS IN ASIAN AMERICAN STUDIES

Martin Joseph Ponce

Diaspora is a Greek word that refers to the scattering of a people from an originary location to other places. According to the *Oxford English Dictionary*, its component parts *dia-* (through, over, or across) and *speirein* (to scatter or to sow) combine to denote dispersal and movement. Robin Cohen explains that for the ancient Greeks, "the expression was used to describe the colonization of Asia Minor and the Mediterranean in the Archaic period (800–600 BC)" but has since "acquired a more sinister and brutal meaning" for "Jews, Africans, Palestinians and Armenians," signifying "a collective trauma, a banishment, where one dreamed of home but lived in exile."[1] Brent Hayes Edwards writes that the term "was used to translate a relatively wide number of Hebrew words in the Septuagint [the Greek translation of the Hebrew Torah], including words relating both to scattering and to exile." Drawing on the work of Hellenic period scholars, he reminds us, however, that "the Greek word [diaspora] never translates the important Hebrew words for exile (such as *galut* and *golah*)." The condition of exile, within the Jewish intellectual tradition, is reserved for the anguished experience of homelessness and uprootedness that results from "the loss of that 'homeland' with the destruction of the Second Temple in 70 C.E."[2]

Given the close association of diaspora with Jewish history, some scholars have considered the Jewish diaspora the "ideal type" against which prior and subsequent diasporas may be measured and have sought to outline characteristic aspects based on that model, such as forced ejection from a homeland, dispersal to two or more locales, maintenance of a collective memory about the homeland, forging of connections with scattered co-ethnics, feelings of alienation in the new location that provoke renewed investment in the homeland, and an abiding longing to reconstruct and return to the homeland.[3] Others have questioned this typological approach for implying "that groups become identified as more or less diasporic," as James Clifford remarks, and that diasporas are historically static: "at different times in their history, societies may wax and wane in diasporism, depending on changing possibilities—obstacles, openings, antagonisms, and connections—in their host countries and transnationally."[4] The descriptive "check-list" take on diaspora can lead to prescriptive essentialisms that dictate how diasporic individuals *ought* to feel and act in order to count as "members" of a diaspora, thereby prioritizing the (real or imagined) homeland as the primary locus of affective, political, and economic investment, while devaluing what Clifford refers to as "the lateral axes of diaspora. [. . .] The centering of diasporas around an axis of origin and return overrides the specific local interactions (identifications and ruptures, both constructive and defensive) necessary for the maintenance of diasporic social forms."[5]

Even this brief sketch shows that the kinds of social movements and collectivities that "diaspora" has been used to describe are far from homogenous, oscillating from migration, colonization, and settlement to catastrophic dispossession, dispersal, and wandering. In his overview of past and present diasporas, Cohen distinguishes among victim, labor, imperial, trade, and cultural diasporas, while recognizing that there are inevitable overlaps among them. Not surprisingly, when invoked in the contemporary moment—a period marked by economic globalization, the recalcitrance and transcendence of the inter-state political system, immense disparities in the distribution of wealth, high-speed communicative technologies, and global transfers and transportations of capital, commodities, ideas, cultural forms, and people—the question of whether modern diasporas (should) refer to voluntary or involuntary movement, an aspiration toward social integration or a condition of imposed exile, remains open to debate.

In Asian American studies, diaspora has been deployed in a variety of disciplines in the humanities, arts, and social sciences since the late 1980s to denote the migration of Asians to the Americas from the nineteenth century to the present—though some scholars date the arrival of Chinese and Filipinos in Latin America to the sixteenth and seventeenth centuries, respectively. Although it has by no means superseded proximate terms such as sojourner, immigrant, exile, expatriate, and refugee, diaspora has come into increasing usage in Asian Americanist scholarship, paralleling its proliferation in other ethnic and cultural studies fields. Perhaps most emphatically, diasporic approaches seek to account for the movements of Asians around the world and their transnational connections with their ancestral homelands and co-ethnics in other locations. By exploring their global orientations, activities, and relationships, diasporic frameworks decenter the United States as the privileged frame of analysis and revise the one-directional, teleological immigration narrative of "Asian America": from Asia to America, from racial persecution and class exploitation to cultural assimilation (or hybridity) and "model minority" success, from xenophobic alienation to social acceptance. At its most basic, diaspora opens up the geographic purview of Asian migrations to their global itineraries and recognizes that the U.S. is but one point of destination (whether temporary or permanent) among other possibilities—even as U.S. colonial, imperial, economic, and cultural forces deeply influence how Asians view America as a desirable (or undesirable) place to inhabit and how they have come to hold those perceptions.

In her touchstone 1995 essay, "Denationalization Reconsidered: Asian American Cultural Criticism at a Theoretical Crossroads," Sau-ling Wong notes that the shift from "a domestic perspective that stresses the status of Asian Americans as an ethnic/racial minority within the national boundaries of the United States" to a "diasporic perspective [that] emphasizes Asian Americans as one element in the global scattering of peoples of Asian origin" has occurred within the broader frame of what she terms "denationalization"—intellectual and political projects that have challenged the U.S.-centered, pan-ethnic, "cultural nationalist concerns" that focus primarily on race and ethnicity.[6] Not only has the field sought to account for what Lisa Lowe famously described as the "heterogeneity, hybridity, and multiplicity"[7] of Asian American identities, cultural forms, and social embeddedness; it has also seen an increasing "permeability [...] between Asian Americans and 'Asian Asians'" as well as "between Asian American studies and Asian studies" (1).

The shifts from "identity politics" that stressed "cultural nationalism and American nativity" to "heterogeneity and diaspora,"[8] to cite King-Kok Cheung, have been driven by both academic currents (e.g., feminist, queer, and cultural studies critiques of racial essentialism and national ethnocentrism) and socio-historical conditions. With respect to the latter, Wong, like many others, attributes the opening up of the category of "Asian American" as the locus of self-nominalization, political identification, and academic institutionalization to demographic changes in the wake of the 1965 Naturalization and Immigration Act that has radically diversified the Asian American population, especially along lines of ethnicity (national origin), generationality, and class, thanks to U.S. immigration laws' preferences for skilled professionals and family reunification. These demographic changes, resulting from both internal and external factors (the Civil Rights and Third World movements, anti-communist Cold War imperatives, and the restructuring of the global economy), have taken place concomitantly, as Wong writes, with "the ascendency of Asia as an economic power of global impact, the coalescence of the Pacific Rim as a geoeconomic entity, and the circulation of Asian transnational capital" (5).[9]

Even as she acknowledges the epistemic, demographic, and economic forces destabilizing the disciplinary parameters and political aims of Asian American studies, Wong nonetheless cautions that embracing transnational and diasporic perspectives can lead to teleological "master narratives" of theoretical sophistication (from "the narrow-minded, essentialist 1960s and 1970s" to "the more enlightened, deconstructivist and internationalist 1980s" [12]), a neglect of class privilege when discussing "travel and transnational mobility" (15), and an inattention to generational status when "diasporic" is merely "deployed as a proxy for 'first generation'" (i.e., "immigrant") that then erases the experiences of "American-born generations" (16). But the most significant peril of the diasporic "paradigm shift," according to Wong, is that the "denationalizing" trends will erode the very category of "Asian American" by de-emphasizing the significance of Asian racialization in the U.S. as a site of social oppression and communal resistance. Arguing that "the term *diaspora* attains a global sweep precisely because it has an essentialist core" (17), she warns that

> the loosely held and fluctuating collectivity called "Asian Americans" will dissolve back into its descent-defined constituents as soon as one leaves American national borders behind. Thus one might study the Chinese diaspora, or the Indian diaspora, and so on. A shared origin, even if it has to be traced a long way back, is constitutive in each case: there is an implicit appeal to common interests which motivates the grouping in the first place. (Indeed, the appeal is often to patriotism for the "motherland" or "fatherland.")
>
> Wong (17)

In this conception, diaspora complicates one of the founding impulses of Asian American studies as the academic and epistemic wing of the Asian American movement of the 1960s and 70s, namely, the impulse to challenge orientalist stereotypes of Asian Americans as perpetual foreigners by asserting the rights, responsibilities, and privileges of political and cultural citizenship in the United States. Insofar as diaspora assumes and summons a homeland elsewhere—however imagined, idealized, or criticized—that exerts a gravitational pull on its scattered people, framing Asians in America as segments of ethnonational diasporas would seem to foreground, even prioritize, relationships with their respective homelands and co-ethnics over their situated racialization and political commitments in the United States. In short, diasporic approaches may threaten the coalitional, pan-ethnic rubric of "Asian American," fracturing what Lowe referred to in 1996 as "the hard-earned unity that has been achieved in the last thirty years of Asian American politics."[10] Wong thus argues for a politicized practice of "claiming America" that focuses on "establishing the Asian American presence in the context of the United States' national cultural legacy and contemporary cultural production" (16).

While some scholars have challenged Wong's characterization of "denationalization" and its intellectual and political implications,[11] others have echoed her concerns regarding diaspora's "essentialist conceptual core" (17) and its consequences for Asian American political communitybuilding. Arif Dirlik has analogously traced the historical shifts that have led to conceptualizing

Asian America as an entity "rooted in U.S. history" to being located "on a metaphorical Rim constituted by diasporas and the movement of individuals."[12] Diasporic orientations, asserts Dirlik, may induce "contemporary Asian American populations [to] identify with their societies of origin," making them "once again vulnerable, in their relationships to one another, to replicating the divisions and conflicts that beset Asian societies," and to "distancing themselves from their immediate environments in the United States, especially in their relationships with other minority groups" (42). These inter-Asian conflicts and interracial distancings enable the dominant culture not only to "pit different diasporic populations against one another" but also to construe Asian American populations as, yet again, "foreigners in the context of everyday life" (47). Dirlik thus argues for a place-based politics that confronts "mutual suspicion and racial division" (47), builds solidarities with other minority groups, and seeks "common social and cultural bonds" that facilitate coexistence across differences (48). Indeed, the Japanese American internment makes spectacularly evident that fears regarding the xenophobic collapsing of "Asian" and "Asian American" are far from unfounded. As Kandice Chuh points out, "the conversion of the threat of Japanese empire into Japanese (American) racial difference by governmental and legal apparatuses of U.S. nationalism" occurred through "a 'transnationalization' of Japaneseness."[13] According to this "transnational" logic, internment became "necessary to contain that threat," and Japanese American became "a concretized identity" marked "as ineffably inassimilable, alien, enemy" (69).

While Dirlik and Chuh discuss the potential dangers of diaspora and transnationalism from the viewpoint of a hegemonic United States, Ien Ang critically examines diasporic essentialism from the viewpoint of the homeland. Contending with presumptions about homeland authenticity and purity within a Chinese context, she suggests that "'China' is presented as the cultural/geographical core" which thus places "westernized overseas Chinese" into "a humble position, even a position of shame and inadequacy over her own 'impurity'. In this situation the overseas Chinese is in a no-win situation: she is either 'too Chinese' or 'not Chinese enough.'"[14]

Despite the potential pitfalls of re-fragmenting "Asian America" by reinforcing ethnic particularity and transnational "race" consciousness, of being regarded as foreign and exterior to the U.S. nation for preserving transnational links, or of being perceived as culturally inauthentic by the standards of the homeland, diasporic frameworks continue to remain useful in Asian Americanist scholarship.[15] Sympathetic to Wong's critique, King-Kok Cheung acknowledges the "competing impulses of claiming America and maintaining ties with Asia" but simultaneously "believe[s] that we can both 'claim America'—assert and manifest the historical and cultural presence of Asians in North America—and use our transnational consciousness to critique the polity, whether of an Asian country, Canada, the United States, or Asian America."[16] The practice of "critique" in Cheung's formulation is worth stressing, since "patriotism" (contra Wong) is not the only affective attitude suffusing diasporic connections to the homeland.

Although Asian American studies scholarship and political activism concerned with international issues predates the mid-1990s, the proliferation of studies of Asian diasporas since then has been a striking development in the field. As Wong predicted, much of this research does, in fact, focus on "descent-defined" or ethnic-specific social formations—though not necessarily in exclusive, self-contained ways. Since it is impossible here to survey in detail the wide-ranging scholarship on "Asian diasporas," the following sections outline several uses of diaspora in Asian/Asian American studies: mappings of historical and contemporary ethnic-specific and comparative diasporas; explorations of transnational interactions between Asians in the U.S. and their homelands as well as diasporic artistic and expressive practices and imaginaries; and feminist and queer critiques of normative ideas about gender and sexuality in diasporic frames.

I close with a reflection on the institutional, intellectual, and political implications of adopting diaspora as an organizing principle in the field, suggesting that we cannot abandon altogether the *American* in Asian American studies at this present juncture of ongoing U.S. imperialism.

Mapping Asian Diasporas across Time and Space

Diasporic, transnational, and postcolonial frameworks became prominent in Asian American studies in the last decades of the twentieth century—coincident with the phase of "late" capitalism marked by post-Fordist modes of production run by transnational corporations, global financial markets, and high-speed travel and electronic communication networks—but this is not to suggest that these frameworks are appropriate for studying only migrations and movements of the contemporary period. While the magnitude, speed, and breadth of global Asian migrations may have accelerated in the era of contemporary globalization, it is important to recall that diasporas have histories, however directly or tenuously linked to the present. Taking issue with the conflation of transnationalism with the conditions of late capitalism, Laura Hyun Yi Kang writes "that even before technological advances in travel and communication and the late twentieth century economic developments of certain Asian nation-states, transnational diasporic linkages were constructed and actively sustained."[17] In short, "diasporic linkages" are not new social phenomena, though the infrastructural mechanisms for maintaining and elaborating such connections may have changed dramatically over time.

In historical terms, then, some scholars have distinguished between "old" and "new" Asian diasporas. In a 2005 special issue of the *Journal of Asian American Studies* on transnational history, Erika Lee calls for a hemispheric approach that would "draw and build upon existing scholarship on Asians in Canada and in Latin America and the Caribbean, taking into account both the unique contours separating—and the similarities connecting—the multiple histories."[18] Lee specifically examines "the global dynamics of Orientalism: the ways in which Asian migrants were racialized as dangerous and unassimilable foreigners around the world during the late nineteenth- and early twentieth-centuries," tracing the circulation of anti-Chinese discourses across U.S., Canadian, and Mexican borders (237). There is, in fact, a great deal of research on overseas Chinese laborers in Latin America (especially, Mexico, Cuba, Peru, and Panama) and the U.S. South from the seventeenth century forward. Indentured laborers from China and India were also recruited to work in the British West Indian plantation system from the nineteenth to the early twentieth centuries as alternatives to, and later substitutions for, African slaves during the age of emancipation. These migrations to the Americas and the Caribbean were parts of broader movements of Chinese to Southeast Asia, Australia, New Zealand, the Pacific Islands, and Mauritius, and of Indians to other parts of South Asia, Southeast Asia, Mauritius, Madagascar, Fiji, South Africa, and East Africa.[19] Japanese migration to South America, especially Brazil, during the early twentieth century as well as Japanese-Brazilian return migration to Japan in the latter half of the century has also generated significant scholarly interest.[20]

Despite historical differences, scholarship on more recent Asian diasporas has continued to focus on similar themes elucidated in studies of the "old" diasporas: the imperial and economic forces that lead to emigration, the shifting immigration policies of the receiving countries, the context-specific processes of racialization, the gendered and raced dimensions of the international division of labor constructed by these movements and policies, and even the distinction between enslaved and free labor. Rhacel Salazar Parreñas and Lok C. D. Siu suggest that "[i]f the labor migrations of the Chinese and Indians to the New World characterize mid-nineteenth-century globalization, then the transnational dispersal of Filipino laborers may very well epitomize late-twentieth-century globalization."[21] Parreñas' own research on the "dislocations" experienced by Filipina domestic workers in Los Angeles and Rome, their practices of global community formation, and their tense and often conflicted relationships with their "transnational families" in the Philippines represents notable instances of this work.[22] While the Filipina domestic worker, as "the symbol of the diaspora of Filipino contract workers,"[23] has been the focus of much scholarly—as well as Philippine state—attention, it is important to recognize that the Filipino labor diaspora consists of both women and men employed in all sorts of occupations from construction work and seafaring to "entertaining" and nursing.[24] It is equally important to attend to the Philippine state discourses, bureaucracies, and processes—pre-migration training and certification programs, overseas embassies and consulates, international market and immigration policy research, documentary processing of work visas, policy reforms for protecting workers' rights abroad, and nationalist messages promoting overseas laborers as "national heroes"—that have facilitated this massive explosion of global Filipino workers, as Robyn Rodriguez has documented.[25]

To the extent that the figure of the Filipina domestic worker emblematizes the gendered and classed vulnerabilities of both the female laboring body and the Philippine nation-state's global reputation abroad, the figure of the "multiple-passport holder" and other "Chinese cosmopolitans" examined by Aihwa Ong may symbolize the other side of the class chasm, an "elite transnationalism" impelled by practices of "flexible citizenship" whereby subjects "respond fluidly and opportunistically to changing political-economic conditions" in "their quest to accumulate capital and social prestige in the global arena."[26]

Diasporic Nationalisms and Expressive Practices

Much of the research that utilizes a diasporic framework in Asian American studies focuses on Asian Americans' relationships with the United States and their country of national origin. While some scholars would regard these binational approaches as "transnational" rather than "diasporic" since the subjects being examined "maintain relations only to the home and host societies and do not share a connection or history with compatriots living in other locales,"[27] this strict definition of diaspora would exclude a significant dynamic of the diasporic condition alluded to above: the tensions between perceiving migrants as overseas extensions of the homeland and as locally situated subjects. Nowhere is this binational dynamic more evident than in analyses of diasporic or "long-distance" nationalisms. These political dispositions and practices reflect and complicate Sau-ling Wong's claim that diasporic links are affectively motivated by "patriotism for the 'motherland' or 'fatherland'" (17). The "appeal" can be issued by the homeland under colonial duress to its compatriots abroad, or by those "in diaspora" exhorting each other to participate in the (re)building of the homeland.

These dynamics extend across colonial and postcolonial eras, and the political stances and goals of these movements are often multivalent, making claims on and contributions to both the Asian homeland and the United States. Examples during the early part of the twentieth century include national liberation causes: Filipino statesmen in Washington, D.C., pressing for Philippine independence from U.S. colonial rule;[28] Indian radical activists in California and the Pacific Northwest agitating for independence from British colonial rule and for an end to the racial global order;[29] and Koreans in the United States and Hawai'i seeking U.S. aid for independence from Japanese colonial rule.[30] Japanese imperialism itself exercised its power not only on colonial subjects but also on its migrant population abroad, seeking to conscript Issei and Nissei into projects of "eastward expansionism."[31] Examples of transnational politics during the latter half of the twentieth century mix "patriotic" affect with political critique of communist nationalisms and post-independence dictatorships: Chinese Americans' anti-communist affiliation with the exiled Nationalist Party in Taiwan and qualified incorporation into the Cold War U.S. state after the 1949 Revolution;[32] Filipino Americans' anti-Marcos activism that criticized the authoritarian regime (1972–1986) for its human rights abuses, corruption, and widespread immiseration, while also lobbying the U.S. government to terminate financial and military aid to the dictatorship;[33] and Vietnamese Americans' shifting attitudes yet enduring ambivalence toward the Vietnamese state following the fall/liberation of Saigon in 1975 and the economic modernization project of Đổi Mới in 1986.[34]

Given the complex social, political, and economic conditions that produce mass dispersals in the first place, it should not be surprising that most affective orientations to the homeland are far from unalloyed expressions of "patriotism." While idealized "imaginary homelands," as novelist Salman Rushdie memorably called them, can certainly be found among diasporic populations of all political stripes, nostalgia for lost origins as consolation for displacement, racism, and xenophobia is invariably fused with condemnation for having had to leave at all. Of course, the status of the homeland—as colonized, expansionist, authoritarian, or "illegitimately" ruled—largely determines how diasporic individuals and communities are impacted by and interact with it. Even without embracing the notion that life in the host country is the diametrical opposite of, and thus "better" than, the homeland, such ambivalence can nonetheless transmute into resentment and rage—particularly when the political circumstances that led to departure continue to persist without alleviation. These examples thus reveal the complex affective and material conditions and uneven relations of geopolitical power that subtend diasporic dynamics of long-distance nation-building, state coercion of populations abroad, and "domestic" political activism.

Historical and social science work has generated a wealth of knowledge of Asian diasporas, but cultural studies scholarship analyzing an array of expressive practices has also been central to theorizing and enacting diaspora frameworks. While "diaspora" may merely refer to creative work produced outside the homeland, marking it *as* diasporic, rather than ethnic, placing it within an outernational frame. Such framings can have multiple aims: to account for cultural production by artists living in several locations beyond the homeland; to track how representational practices roam across national boundaries and construct "diasporic imaginaries"; to examine how expressive practices speak to and address multiple readerships and constitute diasporic public cultures; to explore how various cultural artifacts circulate within and beyond national borders and ethnic diasporas and how those artifacts are taken up and reworked into new forms; and to consider how artists, writers, singers, performers, publishers, producers, directors, and the like collaborate across national borders to produce artworks that cannot be designated as originating in a single nation-state. Investigating a wide range of genres and media (literature, film, television, video, music, performance, photography, painting, internet technologies), this interdisciplinary body of scholarship demonstrates that diasporic Asians and their descendants have not only carved out new lifeworlds and habitations, but have also created, participated, and intervened in local and global artworlds.[35]

The Gender and Sexual Politics of Diaspora

Whether social science or arts and humanities based, studies of Asian diasporas frequently contend with the politics of gender and sexuality since those categories accrue freighted meanings in transnational contexts. The term diaspora itself contains important gender and sexual implications. The Greek verb *speirein* is etymologically linked to the Latin *spora* and the English *spore* and connotes the scattering and sowing of seeds. Although spores are agents of nonsexual reproduction, the word is connected to the masculine gamete *sperm*, thus giving rise to the notion of diaspora as a process of dissemination. Such gendered horticultural metaphors of reproduction embedded within diaspora have provoked feminist and queer studies scholars to interrogate its heteronormative underpinnings, particularly regarding issues of familial descent (patrilineality and patrimony), gender normativity ("proper" modes of femininity and masculinity), sexual normativity (married, monogamous, procreative, heterosexual relationships), and ethnonational reproduction and cross-generational transmission of culture.

Queer diasporic critique in Asian American studies has taken up two broad lines of inquiry. The first provides a queer critique of the gender and sexual politics of nation and diaspora. While many feminist and queer postcolonial critics have noted the ways that nations are often imagined through metaphors of the family (e.g., motherland, fatherland, the nation-as-family) and how women are cast to symbolize the nation (whether as the besieged figure to be protected and defended, the oppressed/occupied figure to be rescued and redeemed, or the maternal preserver and transmitter of cultural tradition), diasporas, too, can impose normalizing ideas about gender and sexuality—most commonly through appeals to national authenticity. In Gayatri Gopinath's formulation, "queering" diaspora operates "by unmasking and undercutting its dependence on a genealogical, implicitly heteronormative reproductive logic," thus enabling a recuperation of "those desires, practices, and subjectivities that are rendered impossible and unimaginable within conventional diasporic and nationalist imaginaries."[36] David L. Eng has also sought to disrupt the heteronormativities of diaspora by seeking to reconceptualize "diaspora not in conventional terms of ethnic dispersion, filiation, and biological traceability, but rather in terms of queerness, affiliation, and social contingency."[37]

The reverse procedure of generating diasporic critiques of queerness has also been necessary to make queer "more supple in relation to questions of race, colonialism, migration and globalization."[38] Closely connected to the field of queer of color critique (research focusing on the complex interplay between race and sexuality within gendered, classed, capitalist, national, and transnational contexts), queer diasporic critique challenges the hegemony of white, Eurocentric queer theory not so much by adding "race" to the picture but by exploring the ways that colonial and national modes of racialization are inextricable from processes of non-normative gendering and sexualizing. In Asian American history, one need only think of such stock figures as the Chinese prostitute (subject to immigration restriction through the Page Law in 1875), the lascivious Chinaman, the hypersexual Filipino predator, the dragon lady, the lotus blossom, or the gaysian bottom to recognize this intertwining of race, gender, and sexuality.

On the one hand, then, queer diasporic critique interrogates the circulation of these images, the forms of cultural production (literature, drama, visual culture) that sustain them, and the social infrastructures (military "camptowns," international sex tourism, human trafficking, mail/internet-order brides) that they both reinforce and give rise to. These critiques also illuminate the unstable meanings of sexual identity categories themselves, examining how non-normative figures in both Asian and non-Asian countries negotiate their relationships to and self-understandings of global discourses and practices of "gay" life and politics—indeed, sometimes recurring to and reinventing local terms (such as the Filipino *bakla* or the Indonesian *waria*, *tom*, and *dee*) to mark such differences from Western norms. As Martin F. Manalansan argues in his ethnography, "Filipino immigrant gay men are not passively assimilating into a mature or self-realized state of gay modernity, but rather are contesting the boundaries of gay identity and rearticulating its modern contours," in part by "actively recuperat[ing] the bakla as a way to assert a particular kind of modernity."[39]

On the other hand, queer diasporic critique endeavors to provide more nuanced (less racist) accounts of alternative forms of queer desire and intimacy, those found and forged not only abroad but also in the domestic space of the home and the homeland. To equate the homeland in the global south only with tradition and convention, as scholars like Gopinath and Jasbir K. Puar have argued, can misleadingly render the global north as the space of gender and sexual liberation, free from the accursed conditions of patriarchy, domestic violence, and sexual repression that allegedly prevail in the global south. Puar coins the term "homonationalism" to denote the ways that certain "U.S. national gays and queers" (prototypically white, middle-class, Protestant, patriotic, and in some cases reproductive) are differentiated from "racial and sexual others" that remain exterior to the national imaginary, thus "foregrounding a collusion between homosexuality and American nationalism that is generated both by national rhetorics of patriotic inclusion and by gay and queer subjects themselves."[40] For Puar, the queer Muslim/Arab/South Asian terrorist (often conflated in the United States' confused racial-geographic imaginary after 9/11/2001) is one such figure that must be demonized and expelled for the upstanding American gay and lesbian to be enfolded into the nation. This sense of sexual exceptionalism—America as tolerant and accepting of its (good) LGBTQ citizens—operates transnationally to castigate other areas of the world that appear to be less welcoming of sexual minorities, deeming those societies backward and un-modern.

Institutionalizing "Diaspora" in Asian American Studies

As this overview reveals, one of the most significant interventions of diaspora is that it compels scholars to focus analytical and political attention on more than one location (nation, region, city) at once. The U.S. ethnic frame limits its purview to issues of *im*-migration, racialization, and labor exploitation and the concomitant fight for civil rights, racial-ethnic representation and recognition, and formal equality before the law, thereby appealing to America's putative democratic institutions and calling for inclusionary citizenship. Such nation-based critiques may expose the fundamental contradictions between American ideals and actual practice, but the appeals simultaneously reinstate those myths, as if they did not operate precisely as the alibis for violence, hierarchization, marginalization, and exploitation both domestically and abroad. This is especially true in transnational contexts where appeals to the "perfectibility" of the U.S. union (the reconciliation of rhetoric and reality) reinscribe notions of U.S. exceptionalism vis-à-vis other, especially "Third World" or "non-western" countries. At the same time, the homeland can insinuate itself as the ground of authentic cultural identity, thereby rendering the diaspora derivative and its subjects all the more susceptible to interpellative calls to rebuild, rejoin, revisit, and return to the homeland as a (long-distance) patriotic duty. Diasporic analyses, in contrast to both of these scenarios, foreground the ways that subjects, texts, and cultural practices are not only situated between these poles but also do multiple kinds of economic, artistic, affective work for and against the country of residence and departure.

To return to Sau-ling Wong's apprehensions regarding the potential for diasporic perspectives to downplay the significance of the U.S. racial arena and thereby fracture the pan-ethnic rubric of "Asian America," it is true that the multivalent positionings of diasporic subjects may be seen to detract from local concerns (from a U.S.-centered viewpoint) or transnational imperatives (from a homeland-centered viewpoint), making them appear to harbor "divided loyalties," but these are not preordained outcomes. The fear that involvement with politics in the homeland and other global locations leads to disinterest in U.S.-based politics is predicated on a kind of hydraulic notion of social energy, as though orienting oneself abroad siphons off material and emotional resources away from local interests. But neither the practice nor analysis of diaspora necessarily results in such conclusions. Whether examining social formations, political activities, or cultural production, diasporic frameworks can illuminate how subjects are multiply oriented and multiply engaged, negotiating their relationships with several entities and social formations at once. There is no guarantee either that focusing attention on the "domestic" space of the U.S. and its racializing tactics will prevent the rubric of "Asian America" from disintegrating. Plenty of research has focused on specific Asian American ethnicities that is U.S.- or locally based, but that work has not been accused of fragmenting Asian American studies. (In fact, there are limits to "interethnic" approaches as well, such as the flattening out of differences *within* ethnic groups, and the impossibility of "covering" every possible Asian ethnicity within a single study).

The implications of incorporating diasporic approaches within Asian American studies are not only intellectual and political but also institutional and pragmatic. The relationship between Asian studies (with its origins in Cold War-era area studies methodologies of generating knowledge of "other" cultures to further U.S. geopolitical interests) and Asian American studies (with its origins in 1960s-era social movements and student activism that contested the U.S. state's oppression of racialized minorities) has historically been tense. And yet, despite their distinctive histories, both fields bear the marks of institutionalization as neoliberal appeasement and containment. As Kandice Chuh and Karen Shimakawa write, "Like area studies, ethnic studies is materially supported by corporate and state investments; its institutionalization in the university system ensures that resistance will always be complemented with complicity."[41] Though Asian American studies practitioners have had to define the field not only as a legitimate domain of interdisciplinary inquiry vis-à-vis more established disciplines, but also as precisely *not* Asian studies since its entry into the U.S. academy in the late 1960s and 70s, a number of scholars have nonetheless called for greater rapport between the two fields. More than two decades ago, Sucheta Mazumdar argued against "arbitrarily isolating the immigrants' history and culture of the homeland under the rubric of Asian Studies, and focusing only on his or her existence after arrival in the United States" in Asian American studies, and argued for "a new paradigm which contextualizes the history of Asian Americans within the twentieth-century global history of imperialism, of colonialism, and of capitalism."[42]

While others have considered in further detail the differences between the two fields in terms of intellectual genealogies, institutional support, and academic downsizing (e.g., the collapsing of departments and programs into a single "Asian and Asian American Studies" unit), it is worth gesturing toward models of diasporic analysis that can account for cross-ethnic and cross-racial connections, given Wong's and Dirlik's reservations on this score. As Edwards argues, "there is never a 'first,' single dispersion of a single people, but instead a complex historical overlay of a variety of kinds of population movement, narrated and imbued with value in different ways and to different ends." Rather than view "the movement of groups" as "discrete or self-contained," he suggests focusing "on the ways in which those movements always intersect, leading to exchange, assimilation, expropriation, coalition, or dissension. This is to say that any study of diaspora is also a study of 'overlapping diasporas.'"[43] Parreñas and Siu echo this critique of "self-contained" diasporas by calling for both "ethnic-specific/geographically dispersed and place-specific/comparative ethnic research."[44] In addition to the growing field of Afro-Asian studies,[45] one notable example of a place-specific approach to overlapping diasporas is put forth by Lisa Lowe in "The Intimacies of Four Continents," a conceptual analytic for examining how "the emergence of modern [European] liberal humanism" was predicated on "a modern racialized division of labor" resulting from the interactions among Europeans, Natives, Asians, Africans, and Americans in the colonial Caribbean during the nineteenth century.[46]

The methodological, institutional, material, and political implications of these Asian diasporic and comparative race frameworks are several. First, opening up the analytical frame to include Asia means confronting what Parreñas and Siu call "inter-Asian strife in past and present" contexts, including, but not limited to, Japanese colonialism in East and Southeast Asia during the first half of the twentieth century, as well as the "political and economic inequities" that structure the relations and flows of people, commodities, and power among Asian nations in the post-war period.[47] Recognition of these conflicts and asymmetries obviously ramifies in sensitive ways, since the field can no longer rely on the homogenizing forces of U.S. racism and orientalism to secure its political grounding in pan-ethnic resistance to oppression. Second, diasporic approaches often require "multi-sited" research, which necessitates rethinking graduate education, professional training, and travel funding opportunities. If transnational history, for example, is meant to "[p]rovide substantial focus on the stories and historical contexts in Asia as well as in the Americas," then this approach "presumes non-English language training and multinational archival research."[48]

Finally, while the precarious existence of many Asian American studies departments and programs makes cross-unit and cross-field collaborations a necessity, it is nonetheless necessary in our current moment to hold on to both "Asian" and "American" in the field's name.[49] The first guards against an erasure of Asian specificities within comparative ethnic studies formations. The second is not so much to delimit inquiry to the territorial space of the United States, but to keep a critical eye trained on "America" in its international and imperial dimensions. Here we come full circle and re-encounter one of diaspora's original Greek meanings of colonization and settlement. As Edwards notes, diaspora "opens up new avenues of inquiry into the history of U.S. imperialism, not just in relation to its attendant dispersal of military, labor, diplomatic, and administrative populations, but also because of the ways in which transnational population movements in the Americas, especially those involving groups of those considered 'others' in the U.S. nation-state, necessarily take shape in the shadow of U.S. globe-straddling ambitions."[50] Indeed, certain areas within Asian American studies—particularly research focused on Filipinos, Vietnamese, Cambodians, Indians, and Pakistanis, as well as Pacific Islanders and Arab Americans—have been galvanized and become more visible precisely due to the "turn to empire" in Asian American and American studies. Thus, if there is a political justification for maintaining the "American" part of Asian American studies, it lies not so much in appealing to the "Americanness" of Asian Americans in the face of racial and xenophobic discrimination, but in continuing to contest the imperial myths of U.S. exceptionalism that make such appeals for inclusion appealing in the first place.

Notes

1 Robin Cohen, *Global Diasporas: An Introduction* (Seattle, WA: University of Washington Press, 1997), 2, ix.
2 Brent Hayes Edwards, "Diaspora," in *Keywords for American Cultural Studies*, Ed. Bruce Burgett and Glenn Hendler (New York: New York University Press, 2007), 82.
3 William Safran, "Diasporas in Modern Societies: Myths of Homeland and Return," *Diaspora* 1, no. 1 (1991): 83. See also Cohen, *Global Diasporas*, 26.
4 James Clifford, *Routes: Travel and Translation in the Late Twentieth Century* (Cambridge, MA: Harvard University Press, 1997), 249.
5 Clifford, *Routes*, 269. For an informative collection of essays on diaspora, see Jana Evans Braziel and Anita Mannur, Eds., *Theorizing Diaspora: A Reader* (Malden, MA: Blackwell, 2003).
6 Sau-ling C. Wong, "Denationalization Reconsidered: Asian American Cultural Criticism at a Theoretical Crossroads," *Amerasia Journal* 21, no. 1–2 (1995): 2, 1.
7 Lisa Lowe, *Immigrant Acts: On Asian American Cultural Politics* (Durham, NC: Duke University Press, 1996), 67. Significantly, Lowe's chapter was originally published in the inaugural issue of the journal *Diaspora*. See Lisa Lowe, "Heterogeneity, Hybridity, Multiplicity: Marking Asian American Differences," *Diaspora* 1, no. 1 (1991): 24–44.
8 King-Kok Cheung, "Re-Viewing Asian American Literary Studies," in *An Interethnic Companion to Asian American Literature*, Ed. King-Kok Cheung (Cambridge: Cambridge University Press, 1997), 1.

9 On these legal, economic, and political transformations, see Arif Dirlik, Ed., *What Is in a Rim? Critical Perspectives on the Pacific Region Idea* (Lanham, MD: Rowman & Littlefield, 1998); Lowe, "Work, Immigration, Gender: Asian 'American' Women," in *Immigrant Acts*, 154–73; and Paul Ong, Edna Bonacich, and Lucie Cheng, Eds., *The New Asian Immigration in Los Angeles and Global Restructuring* (Philadelphia, PA: Temple University Press, 1994).

10 Lowe, *Immigrant Acts*, 83.

11 See, for instance, Susan Koshy, "The Fiction of Asian American Literature," *Yale Journal of Criticism* 9 (1996): 340–2. Wong refers to, but does not rebut, some of those critiques and summarizes several subsequent studies that take up transnational and diasporic frameworks in the introduction added to the article for its publication in *Postcolonial Theory and the United States: Race, Ethnicity, and Literature*, Ed. Amritjit Singh and Peter Schmidt (Jackson, MS: University Press of Mississippi, 2000), 122–48.

12 Arif Dirlik, "Asians on the Rim: Transnational Capital and Local Community in the Making of Contemporary Asian America," in *Across the Pacific: Asian Americans and Globalization*, Ed. Evelyn Hu-DeHart (Philadelphia, PA: Temple University Press, 1999), 41.

13 Kandice Chuh, *Imagine Otherwise: On Asian Americanist Critique* (Durham, NC: Duke University Press, 2003), 59.

14 Ien Ang, *On Not Speaking Chinese: Living between Asia and the West* (London: Routledge, 2001), 32.

15 See also Wanni W. Anderson and Robert G. Lee, Eds., *Displacements and Diasporas: Asians in the Americas* (New Brunswick: Rutgers University Press, 2005); Robbie B. H. Goh and Shawn Wong, Eds., *Asian Diasporas: Cultures, Identities, Representations* (Hong Kong: Hong Kong University Press, 2004).

16 Cheung, "Re-Viewing," 7, 9.

17 Laura Hyun Yi Kang, "Conjuring 'Comfort Women': Mediated Affiliations and Disciplined Subjects in Korean/American Transnationality," *Journal of Asian American Studies* 6, no. 1 (2003): 38.

18 Erika Lee, "Orientalisms in the Americas: A Hemispheric Approach to Asian American History," *Journal of Asian American Studies* 8, no. 3 (2005): 236.

19 Evelyn Hu-DeHart's pathbreaking work on Chinese and other Asians in Latin America deserves special mention here. See her "Coolies, Shopkeepers, Pioneers: The Chinese of Mexico and Peru, 1849–1930," *Amerasia Journal* 15, no. 2 (1989): 91–116; "From Area Studies to Ethnic Studies: The Study of the Chinese Diaspora in Latin America," in *Asian Americans: Comparative and Global Perspectives*, Eds. Shirley Hune, Hyung-chan Kim, Stephen S. Fugita, and Amy Ling (Pullman, WA: Washington State University Press, 1991), 5–16; "Immigrants to a Developing Society: The Chinese in Northern Mexico, 1875–1932," *Journal of Arizona History* 21 (1980): 49–86; "Latin America in Asia-Pacific Perspective," in Dirlik, *What Is in a Rim?*, 251–82; "Race Construction and Race Relations: Chinese and Blacks in 19th Century Cuba," in *The Chinese Diaspora: Selected Essays, Volume II*, Eds. Ling-chi Wang and Gungwu Wang (Singapore: Times Academic Press, 1998), 78–85; "Racism and Anti-Chinese Persecution in Sonora, Mexico, 1876–1932," *Amerasia Journal* 9 (1982): 1–28. As Sucheta Mazumdar points out, "Numerous scholars in Asian Studies have long been interested in studying migration and diasporas. Chinese diaspora studies have probably attracted more researchers than some of the other fields." Sucheta Mazumdar, "Asian American Studies and Asian Studies: Rethinking Roots," in *Asian Americans: Comparative and Global Perspectives*, Eds. Shirley Hune, Hyung-chan Kim, Stephen S. Fugita, and Amy Ling (Pullman, WA: Washington State University Press, 1991), 37. A selection of research on Chinese and Indian migrant workers and indentured laborers during this period includes Moon-Ho Jung, *Coolies and Cane: Race, Labor, and Sugar in the Age of Emancipation* (Baltimore, MD: Johns Hopkins University Press, 2006); Walton Look Lai, *Indentured Labor, Caribbean Sugar: Chinese and Indian Migrants to the British West Indies, 1838–1918* (Baltimore, MD: Johns Hopkins University Press, 1993); Kale Madhavi, *Fragments of Empire: Capital, Slavery and Indian Indentured Labor Migration in the British Caribbean* (Philadelphia, PA: University of Pennsylvania Press, 1998); and Adam McKeown, *Chinese Migrant Networks and Cultural Change: Peru, Chicago, Hawaii, 1900–1936* (Chicago, IL: University of Chicago Press, 2001). For important transnational and diasporic analyses of Chinese in the U.S. and Panama, see Madeline Yuan-yin Hsu, *Dreaming of Gold, Dreaming of Home: Transnationalism and Migration between the United States and South China, 1882–1943* (Stanford, CA: Stanford University Press, 2000); and Lok C. D. Siu, *Memories of a Future Home: Diasporic Citizenship of Chinese in Panama* (Stanford, CA: Stanford University Press, 2005).

20 See, among others, Jeffrey Lesser, *A Discontented Diaspora: Japanese Brazilians and the Meanings of Ethnic Militancy, 1960–1980* (Durham, NC: Duke University Press, 2007); Jeffrey Lesser, Ed., *Searching for Home Abroad: Japanese Brazilians and Transnationalism* (Durham, NC: Duke University Press, 2003);

Stewart Lone, *The Japanese Community in Brazil, 1908–1940: Between Samurai and Carnival* (New York: Palgrave, 2001); Joshua Hotaka Roth, *Brokered Homeland: Japanese Brazilian Migrants in Japan* (Ithaca, NY: Cornell University Press, 2002); and Takeyuki Tsuda, *Strangers in the Ethnic Homeland: Japanese Brazilian Return Migration in Transnational Perspective* (New York: Columbia University Press, 2003). Recent anthologies have considered Japanese lives and practices not only in South America but also in North America, Europe, and other parts of Asia. See Nobuko Adachi, Ed., *Japanese and Nikkei at Home and Abroad: Negotiating Identities in a Global World* (Amherst, NY: Cambria Press, 2010); Nobuko Adachi, Ed., *Japanese Diasporas: Unsung Pasts, Conflicting Presents, and Uncertain Futures* (New York: Routledge, 2006); and Lane Ryo Hirabayashi, Akemi Kikumura-Yano, and James A. Hirabayashi, Eds., *New Worlds, New Lives: Globalization and People of Japanese Descent in the Americas and from Latin America in Japan* (Stanford: Stanford University Press, 2002).

21 Rhacel Salazar Parreñas and Lok C. D. Siu, "Introduction: Asian Diasporas—New Conceptions, New Frameworks," in *Asian Diasporas: New Formations, New Conceptions*, Eds. Rhacel Salazar Parreñas and Lok C. D. Siu (Stanford, CA: Stanford University Press, 2007), 21.

22 Rhacel Salazar Parreñas, *Servants of Globalization: Women, Migration and Domestic Work* (Stanford: Stanford University Press, 2001); and *Children of Global Migration: Transnational Families and Gendered Woes* (Stanford, CA: Stanford University Press, 2005).

23 Neferti Xina M. Tadiar, *Fantasy-Production: Sexual Economies and Other Philippine Consequences for the New World Order* (Hong Kong: Hong Kong University Press, 2003), 114.

24 See, among others, Catherine Ceniza Choy, *Empire of Care: Nursing and Migration in Filipino American History* (Durham, NC: Duke University Press, 2003); Kale Bantigue Fajardo, *Filipino Crosscurrents: Oceanographies of Seafaring, Masculinities, and Globalization* (Minneapolis, MN: University of Minnesota Press, 2011); Steven C. McKay, "Filipino Sea Men: Identity and Masculinity in a Global Labor Niche," in Parreñas and Siu, *Asian Diasporas*, 63–83; and Rhacel Salazar Parreñas, *Illicit Flirtations: Labor, Migration, and Sex Trafficking in Tokyo* (Stanford, CA: Stanford University Press, 2011).

25 Robyn Magalit Rodriguez, *Migrants for Export: How the Philippine State Brokers Labor to the World* (Minneapolis, MN: University of Minnesota Press, 2010). See also Anna Romina Guevarra, *Marketing Dreams, Manufacturing Heroes: The Transnational Labor Brokering of Filipino Workers* (New Brunswick: Rutgers University Press, 2010).

26 Aihwa Ong, *Flexible Citizenship: The Cultural Politics of Transnationality* (Durham, NC: Duke University Press, 1999), 2, 24, 6.

27 Parreñas and Siu, "Introduction: Asian Diasporas," 7. The question of how to delimit the parameters of diaspora so that not every individual living outside her or his ancestral place of origin is construed as "diasporic" persists as an ongoing point of debate. See, for example, Khachig Tölölyan, "Rethinking Diaspora(s): Stateless Power in the Transnational Moment," *Diaspora* 5, no. 1 (1996): 3–36.

28 See Bernardita Reyes Churchill, *The Philippine Independence Missions to the United States, 1919–1934* (Manila: National Historical Institute, 1983); Martin Joseph Ponce, *Beyond the Nation: Diasporic Filipino Literature and Queer Reading* (New York: New York University Press, 2012), 29–57.

29 See Seema Sohi, *Echoes of Mutiny: Race, Surveillance, and Indian Anticolonialism in North America* (Oxford: Oxford University Press, 2014).

30 See Richard S. Kim, *The Quest for Statehood: Korean Immigrant Nationalism and U.S. Sovereignty, 1905–1945* (Oxford: Oxford University Press, 2011); and Lili M. Kim, "Redefining the Boundaries of Traditional Gender Roles: Korean Picture Brides, Pioneer Korean Immigrant Women, and Their Benevolent Nationalism in Hawai'i," in *Asian/Pacific Islander Women: A Historical Anthology*, Eds. Shirley Hune and Gail M. Nomura (New York: New York University Press, 2003), 106–19.

31 Eiichiro Azuma, *Between Two Empires: Race, History, and Transnationalism in Japanese America* (Oxford: Oxford University Press, 2005), 10.

32 See Ellen D. Wu, "'America's Chinese': Anti-Communism, Citizenship, and Cultural Diplomacy during the Cold War," *Pacific Historical Review* 77, no. 3 (2008): 391–422.

33 See, most recently, Catherine Ceniza Choy, "Towards Trans-Pacific Social Justice: Women and Protest in Filipino American History," *Journal of Asian American Studies* 8, no. 3 (2005): 293–307; Augusto Espiritu, "Journeys of Discovery and Difference: Transnational Politics and the Union of Democratic Filipinos," in *The Transnational Politics of Asian Americans*, ed. Christian Collet and Pei-te Lien (Philadelphia, PA: Temple University Press, 2009), 38–55; and Benito M. Vergara, Jr., *Pinoy Capital: The Filipino Nation in Daly City* (Philadelphia, PA: Temple University Press, 2009), 109–33.

34 See Hiroko Furuya and Christian Collet, "Contested Nation: Vietnam and the Emergence of Saigon Nationalism in the United States," in Collet and Lien, *Transnational Politics of Asian Americans*, 56–73; and Kieu-Linh Valverde, *Transnationalizing Viet Nam: Community, Culture, and Politics in the Diaspora* (Philadelphia, PA: Temple University Press, 2012).

35 A sampling of this work includes Denise Cruz, *Transpacific Femininities: The Making of the Modern Filipina* (Durham, NC: Duke University Press, 2012); Lan Duong, *Treacherous Subjects: Gender, Culture, and Trans-Vietnamese Feminism* (Philadelphia, PA: Temple University Press, 2012); Gayatri Gopinath, *Impossible Desires: Queer Diasporas and South Asian Public Cultures* (Durham, NC: Duke University Press, 2005); Emily Noelle Ignacio, *Building Diaspora: Filipino Cultural Community Formation on the Internet* (New Brunswick: Rutgers University Press, 2005); Nhi T. Lieu, *The American Dream in Vietnamese* (Minneapolis, MN: University of Minnesota Press, 2011); Anita Mannur, *Culinary Fictions: Food in South Asian Diasporic Culture* (Philadelphia, PA: Temple University Press, 2010); Vijay Mishra, *The Literature of the Indian Diaspora: Theorizing the Diasporic Imaginary* (London: Routledge, 2007); Mariam Pirbhai, *Mythologies of Migration, Vocabularies of Indenture: Novels of the South Asian Diaspora in Africa, the Caribbean, and Asia-Pacific* (Toronto: University of Toronto Press, 2009); Ponce, *Beyond the Nation*; Sonia Ryang, *Writing Selves in Diaspora: Ethnography of Autobiographics of Korean Women in Japan and the United States* (Lanham, MD: Lexington Books, 2008); Cathy J. Schlund-Vials, *War, Genocide, and Justice: Cambodian American Memory Work* (Minneapolis, MN: University of Minnesota Press, 2012); Sandhya Shukla, *India Abroad: Diasporic Cultures of Postwar America and England* (Princeton, NJ: Princeton University Press, 2003); Valverde, *Transnationalizing Viet Nam*; and Su Zheng, *Claiming Diaspora: Music, Transnationalism, and Cultural Politics in Asian/Chinese America* (Oxford: Oxford University Press, 2010).

36 Gopinath, *Impossible Desires*, 10, 11.

37 David L. Eng, "Transnational Adoption and Queer Diasporas," *Social Text* 76; 21, no. 3 (2003): 7.

38 Gopinath, *Impossible Desires*, 11.

39 Martin F. Manalansan, IV, *Global Divas: Filipino Gay Men in the Diaspora* (Durham, NC: Duke University Press, 2003), x.

40 Jasbir K. Puar, *Terrorist Assemblages: Homonationalism in Queer Times* (Durham, NC: Duke University Press, 2007), 39.

41 Kandice Chuh and Karen Shimakawa, "Introduction: Mapping Studies in the Asian Diaspora," in *Orientations: Mapping Studies in the Asian Diaspora*, Eds. Kandice Chuh and Karen Shimakawa (Durham: Duke University Press, 2001), 9.

42 Mazumdar, "Asian American Studies and Asian Studies," 41.

43 Edwards, "Diaspora," 82, 83.

44 Parreñas and Siu, "Introduction: Asian Diasporas," 6.

45 See, for instance, Fred Ho and Bill V. Mullen, eds., *Afro Asia: Revolutionary Political and Cultural Connections between African Americans and Asian Americans* (Durham, NC: Duke University Press, 2008); Helen Heran Jun, *Race for Citizenship: Black Orientalism and Asian Uplift from Pre-Emancipation to Neoliberal America* (New York: New York University Press, 2011); Julia H. Lee, *Interracial Encounters: Reciprocal Representations in African and Asian American Literatures, 1896–1937* (New York: New York University Press, 2011); Vijay Prashad, *Everybody was Kung Fu Fighting: Afro-Asian Connections and the Myth of Cultural Purity* (Boston, MA: Beacon Press, 2001); and Heike Raphael-Hernandez and Shannon Steen, Eds., *AfroAsian Encounters: Culture, History, Politics* (New York: New York University Press, 2006).

46 Lisa Lowe, "The Intimacies of Four Continents," in *Haunted by Empire: Geographies of Intimacy in North American History*, Ed. Ann Laura Stoler (Durham, NC: Duke University Press, 2006), 193, 192.

47 Parreñas and Siu, "Introduction: Asian Diasporas," 16.

48 Erika Lee and Naoko Shibusawa, "What is Transnational Asian American History? Recent Trends and Challenges," *Journal of Asian American Studies* 8, no. 3 (2005): x.

49 Here I am responding to Evelyn Hu-DeHart's question, "in doing transnational history, do we need to examine the ethnocentrism of the term, 'Asian American Studies' for the field, privileging as it does America at the expense of other reference points?" See her "Concluding Commentary: On Migration, Diasporas and Transnationalism in Asian American History," *Journal of Asian American Studies* 8, no. 3 (2005): 312. For a critical reflection on the "Asian" part of "Asian diasporas," see David Palumbo-Liu, "Asian Diasporas, and Yet . . . ," in Parreñas and Siu, *Asian Diasporas*, 279–84.

50 Edwards, "Diaspora," 85.

References

Adachi, Nobuko, Ed. *Japanese and Nikkei at Home and Abroad: Negotiating Identities in a Global World.* Amherst, NY: Cambria Press, 2010.

———, Ed., *Japanese Diasporas: Unsung Pasts, Conflicting Presents, and Uncertain Futures.* New York: Routledge, 2006.

Anderson, Wanni W., and Robert G. Lee, Eds. *Displacements and Diasporas: Asians in the Americas.* New Brunswick: Rutgers University Press, 2005.

Ang, Ien. *On Not Speaking Chinese: Living between Asia and the West.* London: Routledge, 2001.

Azuma, Eiichiro. *Between Two Empires: Race, History, and Transnationalism in Japanese America.* Oxford: Oxford University Press, 2005.

Braziel, Jana Evans, and Anita Mannur, Eds. *Theorizing Diaspora: A Reader.* Malden, MA: Blackwell, 2003.

Cheung, King-Kok. "Re-Viewing Asian American Literary Studies." In *An Interethnic Companion to Asian American Literature.* Ed. King-Kok Cheung. Cambridge: Cambridge University Press, 1997. 1–36.

Choy, Catherine Ceniza. *Empire of Care: Nursing and Migration in Filipino American History.* Durham: Duke University Press, 2003.

———. "Towards Trans-Pacific Social Justice: Women and Protest in Filipino American History." *Journal of Asian American Studies* 8.3 (2005): 293–307.

Chuh, Kandice. *Imagine Otherwise: On Asian Americanist Critique.* Durham, NC: Duke University Press, 2003.

Chuh, Kandice, and Karen Shimakawa. "Introduction: Mapping Studies in the Asian Diaspora." In *Orientations: Mapping Studies in the Asian Diaspora.* Eds. Kandice Chuh and Karen Shimakawa. Durham, NC: Duke University Press, 2001. 1–21.

Churchill, Bernardita Reyes. *The Philippine Independence Missions to the United States, 1919–1934.* Manila: National Historical Institute, 1983.

Clifford, James. *Routes: Travel and Translation in the Late Twentieth Century.* Cambridge, MA: Harvard University Press, 1997.

Cohen, Robin. *Global Diasporas: An Introduction.* Seattle, WA: University of Washington Press, 1997.

Cruz, Denise. *Transpacific Femininities: The Making of the Modern Filipina.* Durham, NC: Duke University Press, 2012.

Dirlik, Arif. "Asians on the Rim: Transnational Capital and Local Community in the Making of Contemporary Asian America." In *Across the Pacific: Asian Americans and Globalization.* Ed. Evelyn Hu-DeHart. Philadelphia, PA: Temple University Press, 1999. 29-60.

Dirlik, Arif, Ed. *What Is in a Rim? Critical Perspectives on the Pacific Region Idea.* Lanham, MD: Rowman & Littlefield, 1998.

Duong, Lan. *Treacherous Subjects: Gender, Culture, and Trans-Vietnamese Feminism.* Philadelphia, PA: Temple University Press, 2012.

Edwards, Brent Hayes. "Diaspora." In *Keywords for American Cultural Studies.* Eds. Bruce Burgett and Glenn Hendler. New York: New York University Press, 2007. 81–84.

Eng, David L. "Transnational Adoption and Queer Diasporas." *Social Text* 76, 21.3 (2003): 1–37.

Espiritu, Augusto. "Journeys of Discovery and Difference: Transnational Politics and the Union of Democratic Filipinos." In *The Transnational Politics of Asian Americans.* Eds. Christian Collet and Pei-te Lien. Philadelphia, PA: Temple University Press, 2009. 38–55.

Fajardo, Kale Bantigue. *Filipino Crosscurrents: Oceanographies of Seafaring, Masculinities, and Globalization.* Minneapolis, MN: University of Minnesota Press, 2011.

Furuya, Hiroko, and Christian Collet. "Contested Nation: Vietnam and the Emergence of Saigon Nationalism in the United States." *The Transnational Politics of Asian Americans.* Eds. Christian Collet and Pei-te Lien. Philadelphia, PA: Temple University Press, 2009. 56–73.

Goh, Robbie B. H., and Shawn Wong, Eds. *Asian Diasporas: Cultures, Identities, Representations.* Hong Kong: Hong Kong University Press, 2004.

Gopinath, Gayatri. *Impossible Desires: Queer Diasporas and South Asian Public Cultures.* Durham, NC: Duke University Press, 2005.

Guevarra, Anna Romina. *Marketing Dreams, Manufacturing Heroes: The Transnational Labor Brokering of Filipino Workers.* New Brunswick: Rutgers University Press, 2010.

Hirabayashi, Lane Ryo, Akemi Kikumura-Yano, and James A. Hirabayashi, Eds. *New Worlds, New Lives: Globalization and People of Japanese Descent in the Americas and from Latin America in Japan*. Stanford, CA: Stanford University Press, 2002.

Ho, Fred, and Bill V. Mullen, Eds. *Afro Asia: Revolutionary Political and Cultural Connections between African Americans and Asian Americans*. Durham, NC: Duke University Press, 2008.

Hsu, Madeline Yuan-yin. *Dreaming of Gold, Dreaming of Home: Transnationalism and Migration between the United States and South China, 1882–1943*. Stanford, CA: Stanford University Press, 2000.

Hu-DeHart, Evelyn. "Immigrants to a Developing Society: The Chinese in Northern Mexico, 1875–1932." *Journal of Arizona History* 21 (1980): 49–86.

———. "Racism and Anti-Chinese Persecution in Sonora, Mexico, 1876–1932." *Amerasia Journal* 9 (1982): 1–28.

———. "Coolies, Shopkeepers, Pioneers: The Chinese of Mexico and Peru, 1849–1930." In *Amerasia Journal* 15.2 (1989): 91–116.

———. "From Area Studies to Ethnic Studies: The Study of the Chinese Diaspora in Latin America." In *Asian Americans: Comparative and Global Perspectives*. Eds. Shirley Hune, Hyung-chan Kim, Stephen S. Fugita, and Amy Ling. Pullman: Washington State University Press, 1991. 5–16.

———. "Latin America in Asia-Pacific Perspective." In *What Is in a Rim? Critical Perspectives on the Pacific Region Idea*. Ed. Arif Dirlik. Lanham: Rowman & Littlefield, 1998. 251–282.

———. "Race Construction and Race Relations: Chinese and Blacks in 19th Century Cuba." In *The Chinese Diaspora: Selected Essays, Volume II*. Ed. Ling-chi Wang and Gungwu Wang. Singapore: Times Academic Press, 1998. 78–85.

———. "Concluding Commentary: On Migration, Diasporas and Transnationalism in Asian American History." *Journal of Asian American Studies* 8.3 (2005): 309–312.

Ignacio, Emily Noelle. *Building Diaspora: Filipino Cultural Community Formation on the Internet*. New Brunswick: Rutgers University Press, 2005.

Jun, Helen Heran. *Race for Citizenship: Black Orientalism and Asian Uplift from Pre-Emancipation to Neoliberal America*. New York: New York University Press, 2011.

Jung, Moon-Ho. *Coolies and Cane: Race, Labor, and Sugar in the Age of Emancipation*. Baltimore, MD: Johns Hopkins University Press, 2006.

Kang, Laura Hyun Yi. "Conjuring 'Comfort Women': Mediated Affiliations and Disciplined Subjects in Korean/American Transnationality." *Journal of Asian American Studies* 6.1 (2003): 25–55.

Kim, Lili M. "Redefining the Boundaries of Traditional Gender Roles: Korean Picture Brides, Pioneer Korean Immigrant Women, and Their Benevolent Nationalism in Hawai'i." In *Asian/Pacific Islander Women: A Historical Anthology*. Eds. Shirley Hune and Gail M. Nomura. New York: New York University Press, 2003. 106–119.

Kim, Richard S. *The Quest for Statehood: Korean Immigrant Nationalism and U.S. Sovereignty, 1905–1945*. Oxford: Oxford University Press, 2011.

Koshy, Susan. "The Fiction of Asian American Literature." *Yale Journal of Criticism* 9 (1996): 315–346.

Lai, Walton Look. *Indentured Labor, Caribbean Sugar: Chinese and Indian Migrants to the British West Indies, 1838–1918*. Baltimore, MD: Johns Hopkins University Press, 1993.

Lee, Erika. "Orientalisms in the Americas: A Hemispheric Approach to Asian American History." *Journal of Asian American Studies* 8.3 (2005): 235–256.

Lee, Erika, and Naoko Shibusawa. "What is Transnational Asian American History? Recent Trends and Challenges." *Journal of Asian American Studies* 8.3 (2005): vii–xvii.

Lee, Julia H. *Interracial Encounters: Reciprocal Representations in African and Asian American Literatures, 1896–1937*. New York: New York University Press, 2011.

Lesser, Jeffrey. *A Discontented Diaspora: Japanese Brazilians and the Meanings of Ethnic Militancy, 1960–1980*. Durham, NC: Duke University Press, 2007.

———, Ed. *Searching for Home Abroad: Japanese Brazilians and Transnationalism*. Durham, NC: Duke University Press, 2003.

Lieu, Nhi T. *The American Dream in Vietnamese*. Minneapolis, MN: University of Minnesota Press, 2011.

Lone, Stewart. *The Japanese Community in Brazil, 1908–1940: Between Samurai and Carnival*. New York: Palgrave, 2001.

Lowe, Lisa. "Heterogeneity, Hybridity, Multiplicity: Marking Asian American Differences." *Diaspora* 1.1 (1991): 24–44.

———. *Immigrant Acts: On Asian American Cultural Politics*. Durham, NC: Duke University Press, 1996.

———. "The Intimacies of Four Continents." In *Haunted by Empire: Geographies of Intimacy in North American History*. Ed. Ann Laura Stoler. Durham, NC: Duke University Press, 2006. 191–212.

Madhavi, Kale. *Fragments of Empire: Capital, Slavery and Indian Indentured Labor Migration in the British Caribbean*. Philadelphia, PA: University of Pennsylvania Press, 1998.

Manalansan, Martin F., IV. *Global Divas: Filipino Gay Men in the Diaspora*. Durham, NC: Duke University Press, 2003.

Mannur, Anita. *Culinary Fictions: Food in South Asian Diasporic Culture*. Philadelphia, PA: Temple University Press, 2010.

Mazumdar, Sucheta. "Asian American Studies and Asian Studies: Rethinking Roots." In *Asian Americans: Comparative and Global Perspectives*. Eds. Shirley Hune, Hyung-chan Kim, Stephen S. Fugita, and Amy Ling. Pullman, WA: Washington State University Press, 1991. 29–44.

McKay, Steven C. "Filipino Sea Men: Identity and Masculinity in a Global Labor Niche." In *Asian Diasporas: New Formations, New Conceptions*. Eds. Rhacel Salazar Parreñas and Lok C. D. Siu. Stanford, CA: Stanford University Press, 2007. 63–83.

McKeown, Adam. *Chinese Migrant Networks and Cultural Change: Peru, Chicago, Hawaii, 1900-1936*. Chicago, IL: University of Chicago Press, 2001.

Mishra, Vijay. *The Literature of the Indian Diaspora: Theorizing the Diasporic Imaginary*. London: Routledge, 2007.

Ong, Aihwa. *Flexible Citizenship: The Cultural Politics of Transnationality*. Durham, NC: Duke University Press, 1999.

Ong, Paul, Edna Bonacich, and Lucie Cheng, Eds. *The New Asian Immigration in Los Angeles and Global Restructuring*. Philadelphia, PA: Temple University Press, 1994.

Palumbo-Liu, David "Asan Diasporas, and Yet . . ." In *Asian Diasporas New Formations, New Conceptions*. Eds. Rhacel S. Parreñas and Lok C. D. Siu. Stanford, CA: Stanford University Press, 2007. 279–284.

Parreñas, Rhacel Salazar. *Servants of Globalization: Women, Migration and Domestic Work*. Stanford, CA: Stanford University Press, 2001.

———. *Children of Global Migration: Transnational Families and Gendered Woes*. Stanford, CA: Stanford University Press, 2005.

———. *Illicit Flirtations: Labor, Migration, and Sex Trafficking in Tokyo*. Stanford, CA: Stanford University Press, 2011.

Parreñas, Rhacel Salazar, and Lok C. D. Siu. "Introduction: Asian Diasporas—New Conceptions, New Frameworks." In *Asian Diasporas: New Formations, New Conceptions*. Eds. Rhacel Salazar Parreñas and Lok C. D. Siu. Stanford, CA: Stanford University Press, 2007. 1–27.

Pirbhai, Mariam. *Mythologies of Migration, Vocabularies of Indenture: Novels of the South Asian Diaspora in Africa, the Caribbean, and Asia-Pacific*. Toronto: University of Toronto Press, 2009.

Ponce, Martin Joseph. *Beyond the Nation: Diasporic Filipino Literature and Queer Reading*. New York: New York University Press, 2012.

Prashad, Vijay. *Everybody was Kung Fu Fighting: Afro-Asian Connections and the Myth of Cultural Purity*. Boston, MA: Beacon Press, 2001.

Puar, Jasbir K. *Terrorist Assemblages: Homonationalism in Queer Times*. Durham, NC: Duke University Press, 2007.

Raphael-Hernandez, Heike, and Shannon Steen, Eds. *AfroAsian Encounters*: Culture, History, Politics. New York: New York University Press, 2006.

Rodriguez, Robyn Magalit. *Migrants for Export: How the Philippine State Brokers Labor to the World*. Minneapolis, MN: University of Minnesota Press, 2010.

Roth, Joshua Hotaka. *Brokered Homeland: Japanese Brazilian Migrants in Japan*. Ithaca, NY: Cornell University Press, 2002.

Ryang, Sonia. *Writing Selves in Diaspora: Ethnography of Autobiographics of Korean Women in Japan and the United States*. Lanham, MD: Lexington Books, 2008.

Safran, William. "Diasporas in Modern Societies: Myths of Homeland and Return." *Diaspora* 1.1 (1991): 83–99.

Schlund-Vials, Cathy J. *War, Genocide, and Justice: Cambodian American Memory Work*. Minneapolis, MN: University of Minnesota Press, 2012.

Shukla, Sandhya. *India Abroad: Diasporic Cultures of Postwar America and England*. Princeton, NJ: Princeton University Press, 2003.

Siu, Lok C. D. *Memories of a Future Home: Diasporic Citizenship of Chinese in Panama*. Stanford, CA: Stanford University Press, 2005.

Sohi, Seema. *Echoes of Mutiny: Race, Surveillance, and Indian Anticolonialism in North America*. Oxford: Oxford University Press, 2014.

Tadiar, Neferti Xina M. *Fantasy-Production: Sexual Economies and Other Philippine Consequences for the New World Order*. Hong Kong: Hong Kong University Press, 2003.

Tölölyan, Khachig. "Rethinking Diaspora(s): Stateless Power in the Transnational Moment." *Diaspora* 5.1 (1996): 3–36.

Tsuda, Takeyuki. *Strangers in the Ethnic Homeland: Japanese Brazilian Return Migration in Transnational Perspective*. New York: Columbia University Press, 2003.

Valverde, Kieu-Linh. *Transnationalizing Viet Nam: Community, Culture, and Politics in the Diaspora*. Philadelphia, PA: Temple University Press, 2012.

Vergara, Benito M., Jr. *Pinoy Capital: The Filipino Nation in Daly City*. Philadelphia, PA: Temple University Press, 2009.

Wong, Sau-ling C. "Denationalization Reconsidered: Asian American Cultural Criticism at a Theoretical Crossroads." *Amerasia Journal* 21.1–2 (1995): 1–27.

———. "Denationalization Reconsidered: Asian American Cultural Criticism at a Theoretical Crossroads." In *Postcolonial Theory and the United States: Race, Ethnicity, and Literature*. Eds. Amritjit Singh and Peter Schmidt. Jackson, MS: University Press of Mississippi, 2000. 122–148.

Wu, Ellen D. "'America's Chinese': Anti-Communism, Citizenship, and Cultural Diplomacy during the Cold War." *Pacific Historical Review* 77.3 (2008): 391–422.

Zheng, Su. *Claiming Diaspora: Music, Transnationalism, and Cultural Politics in Asian/Chinese America*. Oxford: Oxford University Press, 2010.

5

AMERICAN ANTIPODES

Anna Kazumi Stahl's *Flores de un solo* día[1]

Michelle Har Kim

Thirtysomething Aimée Leverier, introspective and laconic heroine of Anna Kazumi Stahl's acclaimed *Flores de un solo día* (*Flowers of a Single Day*) is a *porteña*, a denizen of the port metropolis of Buenos Aires. The novel introduces us to an ordinary day in her life, one remarkably, perhaps even beautifully, organized by routine. Parsed by the well-oiled certitudes of her well-managed work schedule and family responsibilities, Aimée's hours appear to glide by in a eurythmic grace. But today, her predictable calm is intruded upon by an unexpected letter from what seems like the other side of the world. Addressed to Aimée, it has been mailed from somewhere in North America, New Orleans to be exact, another "end" of the Americas. The document's English is acutely foreign to Aimée's ear and to her mundane Spanish-language universe. Trudging through it, she unsuspectingly awakens a buried memories of a voice—her own—speaking in a halting, rusty, and confusing English from what seems like miles away. It is a language new and unknown, yet old and familiar. Aimée begrudgingly starts to decipher the letter's news about the enigmatic Louisianian inheritance, which will soon prompt Aimée to embark on a journey toward the truth about her family and its mysterious American crossings.

As it withholds the crux of *Flores*' fascinating storyline, this essay grapples with its interrogation of one's relation to language, and with the option of understanding Asian American literatures as a field of overlapping spheres of language that may, or indeed may not, transverse the globe. Is it possible to read Asian American literatures in ways that do *not* axiomatically presume one's most intimate or beloved language to be a "first language" or "native tongue," which is also to say, *the* master tongue that is able to plunge a speaker back into an utterly "immediate relation to language"?[2] Doesn't one's most intimate or proficient language, rather than one's first or earliest-acquired tongue, operate like a mother tongue, in its ability to engage feelings of intimacy and beliefs in comprehension, or perhaps even of plenitude? Alternatively, if we were to take the replete familiarity of the native tongue as a regulative idea or cognitive tool[3]—a "fantasy of communion,"[4] as the comparatist Naoki Sakai puts it—then what lines of flight, or fertile confusions, would this incite for the literary field at hand?

Castellano, a common term for the Spanish language in the Hispanophone (i.e., Spanish-speaking) world, is not only a non-native tongue for Aimée. It is also a non-native language for her creator, Anna Kazumi Stahl, who began to learn *castellano* as a graduate student of Comparative Literature. Like her *norteamericana* protagonist, Stahl also hails from Louisiana, a place whose U.S. state boundaries demarcate, just as much as its political mappings belie, a discrete area of known linguistic richness. Published in 2002, *Flores* was nominated for the Venezuela-based Rómulo Gallegos International Novel Prize for books written in *castellano*, garnering praise not only for its Argentinean and Spanish editions, but also for its translated lives in French and Italian.[5] A non-Anglophone[6] text (underscored by the ongoing absence of an English-language translation), *Flores* unravels the entwined worlds of Aimée and her mother Hanako, once unwitting transplants from New Orleans to Buenos Aires. The incidental detail, or perhaps elemental fact, of Stahl's Japanese heritage would perhaps depict the novel as a decidedly Asian American text; more importantly, from Aimée's Louisianian investigations to Hanako's terrified flashbacks (in Buenos Aires) of World War II Japan, *Flores* invokes Asian diasporic life at distinct "ends" of the Americas—a dauntingly plural and space whose referent is neither the United States nor Canada. If, rather, "'America' names the entire hemisphere from the Yukon to Patagonia,"[7] *Flores*, along with other non-Anglophone texts, offers a variegated node of exploration for hemispheric or global constellations within Asian American literatures. The classically North American and Anglophone bounds of the field stand to be muddled by reckonings not only with diametrical or "other" Americas (e.g., "South America" or "The Caribbean" with respect to the United States), but also with the entirety of "the Americas" as a unwieldy, difficult, and unmanageable object; an antipodal Other.[8]

That *Flores* is a Latin American or Argentinean novel originally written in *castellano* stages it as a welcome text for Asian American literatures' increasingly hemispheric arena. Yet I would like to try to deflect the notion that it is an emblematic Asian American text simply *because it is not written in English*. This motive alone would presume the novel's narrative equivalence to other Asian American Anglophone texts. It would also overlook the literary field's overweening Anglophone compasses, along with the intimate symbioses of cultural and national imaginaries with language per se. The mundane natures of Anglophone dominance, exceptionalism, and blindness—let's refer to this as *Anglophonicity*—Work together to shape our reading desires, and certainly how we read. The self-evidence of the English language, its "natural" scope, accessibility, and perceived unity as monadic, schematize the "English-speaking worlds" of Canada, the United States, and the Caribbean, as part and parcel of a North America that is obviously (and from an over-simplified linguistic standpoint, arbitrarily) divided by political and national bounds. Asian Canadian literatures are thus easily assimilated as a correspondent cosmopolitical reflection of U.S. Asian American literatures, despite the persistence of Asian Canadian literatures as an anomalous and "uneasy component of [U.S.] Asian American literature at large."[9]

Anglophonicity works to elide these kinds of stubborn points of transnational comparison. Take, for example, the popular affirmation of Joy Kogawa's *Obasan* as a canonical text for Asian American literatures. Often discussed in the U.S. classroom as an emblematic narrative of Japanese internment broadly, the unremarkable and generally unnoticed authority of Anglophonicity and of the presumable mimetic transparency of English—the idea of "ethnic literatures . . . as transparent, self-evident expressions"[10]—promotes the Canadian novel as a North American internment story par excellence. This emblematic status tends to eclipse *Obasan*'s lines of flight toward other comparative reckonings—not only with respect to historiographies of Japanese and other ethnic confinements beyond formal American borders,[11] but also regarding how literary narratives and other aesthetic objects are assigned value.

Anglophonicity and the Homolingual

Despite its established themes of migrancy, empire, and transnationality, the field of Asian American literatures continues to bear an axiomatic relationship with Anglophonicity. Referring both to the predominant use of English and to cultures symbiotic with this predominance,

Anglophonicity identifies the otherwise unremarkable "nature" of what is difficult to see, perhaps for English and non-English readers alike: the powerfully inconspicuous authority of English—its obvious accessibility, formal quantifiability, and scope—with respect to Asian American literary critique and production. That English is the natural lingua franca for Asian American literatures generally does not draw much attention to itself; it is an axiom that thus manages and glosses over the persistence of fissures and inconsistencies within a ostensibly unified English. Under anglophonicity's rubric, tropes of imperfect or "broken" English (generally undergirded by mastery of an Asian native language), creolizations of English (Hawai'ian pidgin, for example), and the refusal or inability to speak English, are casually tucked away as variations upon a common Anglophone tongue. Anglophonicity operates as a regulative idea in the business of de-prioritizing reckonings with Ying Chen's Québécois-language writings, for example, as possible nodes of Asian American literary inquiry.

The notion that texts across (and thus, curiously, *despite*) the Asian Americas harbor an equivalence irrespective of language, is a decidedly homolingual claim.[12] Along these lines, even if Asian American texts are written and read in different languages, they are bound by a unique ethnic ethos; the fact of ethnicity allows Asian Americans to "see eye to eye" and figuratively "speak the same language" in a shared homolingual communion. If the language of Asian American works can be trumped by an ethnic "transcendence,"[13] then their varying positionalities and axes with respect to language[14]—by way of writer(s), reader(s), or textual persona(e)—are just as nonchalantly swept under the rug. Transcendent Asian American equivalence presumes that any language ought to be congruent and exchangeable with any other, in standardizations that occlude the unpredictable potencies of language and literary constellation. (Constellations, as far as we know, can only be seen from particular points on the earth, during certain times, and under conditions that honor the human eye.) Indeed, when languages are fundamentally equivalent, they seem to capably measure and map a unified sphere of linguistically discrete spaces[15] where, say, "the Lusophone world" and "non-Hmong speakers," alongside their corresponding national spaces and ethnic certitudes, jigsaw seamlessly into an "abstractly idealized . . . international world."[16] To be clear, this essay is not a call toward eliminating such categorical assertions; they are necessary for many reasons. Rather, I encourage a vigilance with regard to habituated homolingualisms, well-worn correspondences between *the* world and *an* internally unified *us*. Are *we* necessarily and always in the business of sharing one common world? Are there not moments in which *our* community is keenly palpable, however ephemerally, due, rather, to imminent "differences and failure in communication"?[17]

The concept of *schema*, as "unconscious coding" or "diagrammatic representation,"[18] may help grapple with such habituated labelings as historically and culturally bound. "Asian American" and "Asian American literatures" crucially emerge, as many critics have discussed, from a specific web of social movements and understandings of equal treatment, protection, and equivalence of individuals with respect to the law. I hope to encourage skepticism toward Asian American literatures' classical schema as an equitable sphere in which discrete Asian American literatures assimilate into an overarching Asian American corpus. And yet why is it so compelling to organize a syllabus in this way, with emblems of equivalence that represent Cambodian American literature, Chinese Canadian literature, and so on, and where "Asian American" and "Asian Canadian" literatures cleanly subdivide in ways that return to re-present national bounds? The classical model nicely accommodates different languages—until a reader is faced by a text's mooring within and cultivation by the language(s) that both engender and inhabit reading and writing. To put it simply, "if you change how people talk, that changes how they think. If people learn another language, they inadvertently also learn a new way of looking at the world. When bilingual people switch from one language to another, they start thinking differently, too."[19] To idealize languages as isometric bodies is to totalize them and to ignore their organicity and flux. Like the texts written "in" them, languages are not as readily exchangeable as they appear. To posit that each sentence in Language A is clinically mappable to a unique sentence in Language B, is to render extraneous the inflections, hesitations, pronunciations, cacophony, temperatures, energies, and smells that are vital to any moment or experience, linguistic or otherwise. The list is infinite; to be wary about this unending fallout—to be wary about the vitality of scaffoldings and shards that do not translate easily (or at all) from one sphere to another—is to be wary of the homolingual. (We might even call this vigilance a heterolingualism.)

How might we avoid emblematizing *Flores* as a Hispanophone or Latin American representative par excellence for Asian American literatures? Is it possible to delve into its "American" *castellano* without presuming its Asian American essence? Might we read the novel, rather, as a text that explicitly grapples with language's unexpected intensities, as free to be included in a range of constellatory schemas? In her Argentinean Spanish, Aimée identifies her native language as "casteghiano," her inflected rendition of "castellano" (which, in my gringa alliteration, also could be "castezhjiano"). We note this fertile fissure within a presumably consistent Spanish, especially as we find ourselves *translating* between the sphere of Aimée's local inflection and that of standard *castellano*. Her manner of speaking could be traditionally described as a *rioplatense* dialect; a subset of official, or vehicular, *castellano*. What do we make of this powerful relegation, of *Flores*' local register to the non-standard and minor? Is our heroine's drawl, if you will, mappable to an English-language equivalent, or is it (un)translatable in certain ways? I list these questions to scrape the surface of certain fissures—between local and global, for example, and the relation between language and one's place within a plural "America"—incommensurabilities that Asian American Anglophonicity *no ve* (i.e., "cannot see"), and to allude to the imperfections, impurities, and inevitably missed meanings that flourish in any language, whether modern or "dead."

Aimée's American Antipodes

Let's return to Aimée's apartment in downtown Buenos Aires. On the ninth floor, her apartment number reads 9°B—"noveno be" in Spanish—an iteration of "no ve, no ve" ("cannot see, cannot see");[20] it is a blindness that does not migrate well into English. As she has done without fail on every Monday and Thursday in the past, Aimée drives her pickup through the city and heads to Buenos Aires' Almagro market. There she greets her favorite wholesaler and begins to choose an assortment of budding flowers and cuttings to restock her store, *Hanako—Floral Arrangements—Traditional and Ikebana*. The shop is named after Aimée's mother, who is adept at *ikebana*, the Japanese art of flower arrangement through which plants are composed to capture the "intensity of a moment," or a singular emotion.[21] By sunrise Aimée is hoisting her wares into the apartment elevator; as her husband Fernando spreads out his morning paper, Hanako and Aimée are, like clockwork, nearly finished with breakfast, and ready for the day's retail orders and arrangements.

What's best for Hanako, as Aimée knows so well, is to be surrounded by predictable structures and stable routines. Terrified of the hazardous world outside, Hanako restricts herself to the apartment's perimeter. It is only within these cozy walls where she is most comfortable and able to help her family and engage in her extraordinary floral work. Hanako is deaf, unable to use "regular" words or standardized signs. In a distinct rhythm, and apart from her arrangements for the shop, she designs a new array of flowers each day for her family. The rage in various city circles, Hanako's arrangements are casually enjoyed each day by Aimée and Fernando. On some days more than others, they can even sense the flowers' extralingual ardor. Today, however, a mystery presents itself. No flowers are to be found on the living room table. In their stead sits an ominous letter waiting to be read in English, a language that will always remain stubbornly foreign for Aimée. Attempting to slog through its uninvited English legalese, she finds it easier to translate it into *castellano*, bit by bit.

> Aimée traduce siguiendo la línea del tipeo con el dedo sobre el papel. Ha perdido la costumbre con el inglés, y de a momentos tarda en recordar ciertas palabras o en descifrar el orden de las frases, por lo que primero le resulta confuso todo, hasta que de pronto, el sentido se esclarece como una foto en el líquido del revelado. Igual no es tan dificultosa la tarea. Es el mensaje mismo del que resulta enigmático. Se quedan en silencio, pensándolo . . . Por algún motivo, el asunto la abruma, ser enfrentada de golpe con esa historia tan lejana. Tan irrecuperable. Sí, recuerda nombres y caras, hasta tonos de voz, perfumes. El problema es el mismo que le generó leer el inglés de la carta: siente que reconoce las palabras, pero el significado es escurridizo y se le escapa. Revisa algunas de ellas—*we duly notify, the express agreement, the holder, the owner, not by marriage or blood relation*— y de repente, como un rayo, se le aparece una vocecita en la mente que dice: "*I am eight, and I . . . this is my . . . her name is . . . just for a little . . . because then . . . to take us back to . . .*". ¿Es ésa su propia voz? ¿De cuándo? ¿A quién está diciendo todo eso?[22]

> Aimée translates as she follows the typed line with her finger across the paper. She's forgotten the twists and turns of English, and is slow at moments in remembering certain words or decoding the order of phrases, which is why at first everything is utterly confusing, until suddenly, the meaning becomes clear like a photograph in developing liquid. The task isn't so hard. It's the message itself that remains a mystery. She remains silent, thinking about it . . . For some reason, the issue overwhelms her, to be faced all of a sudden with this history from so long ago. So irrecuperable. Yes, she remembers names and faces, even the timbres of voices, smells. It's the same problem that she has reading the letter's English: she feels that she recognizes the words, but their meaning is elusive and slips away. She looks again at some—*we duly notify, the express agreement, the holder, the owner, not by marriage or blood relation*—and suddenly, like a ray of light, a little voice in her mind says: "*I am eight, and I . . . this is my . . . her name is . . . just for a little . . . because then . . . to take us back to . . .*". Is that really her voice? From when? And to whom is she speaking?

The document proclaims that Aimée has inherited a small Louisiana estate from a long-estranged relative, a grandmother, who has died in New Orleans. Ostensibly great news, the knowledge jars Aimée's collectedness. She is dislocated and discomfited by an intense *desarraigo*: an uprooting, estrangement or alienation, perhaps with twinges of uncanniness; a term that may also invoke the strident displacement of being reminded that you are non-native, or foreign, to a particular place. *The* world for Aimée begins to shrink into *a* world, a mere bubble within a foam of Others. Yet Aimée's life feels conspicuously bloated from its sudden shifts in scale, as if her individual twists and turns were magnified. Immediately she insists upon her rightful place *here* in Buenos Aires, "in *her* kitchen, with *her* cup of hot chocolate and *her* radio turned on . . . in *her* proper place there are no 'surprises' of this kind, capable of transporting her to the other side of the world."[23] Arrogation of the local, along with Aimée's insistence that all things around her are indisputably her objects, further scrambles her sense of feeling at home.

Aimée deliberately shapes her mouth to the typed words that announce her unanticipated inheritance. As if learning something, she murmurs the English word for *heredero*—"heir." Uncannily, it sounds like "air." Fernando asks his wife what she's talking about. Nothing, Aimée responds, floored by a bizarre awareness.

> Murmura la palabra 'heredero' in inglés que suena como la que dice 'aire': '*Heir. Air.*'"
> —¿Qué?—[Fernando] levanta la cabeza de nuevo para preguntar—: ¿Qué dijiste?
> —No, nada.—Responde con lentitud, con la boca torpe.[24]

> Aimée murmurs the word "*heir*" in English; it sounds like the word "*air*": "Heir. Air."
> "Huh?" Fernando lifts his head up again to ask: "What did you say?"
> "No, nothing," she responds slowly, lethargically.

The sonic sameness of "air" and "heir" is nearly a shrill hail, an unexpected familiarity that sparks both a cleavage and a stretching-out of Aimée's cozy world of control. That she is an *heir* crops up from thin *air*; her plßace is intruded upon by the irrevocable otherness of property, blood, and patria. Aimée's sudden knowledge of other lives and other histories appears not only to enlarge her world, but also to increase the force of its gravity. We might describe this as a distinctly modern feeling. Like a blastula thrown into airy foreground, our heroine's space will begin to bubble, however begrudgingly, with enmeshed narrative flashbacks, interruptions, and startling facts about her North American family, history, and geography. The air gains an alarming heft for our unwitting *heir*, as if in this era of war and environmental depletion, atmosphere and oxygen can no longer be our mere granted objects; these vital entities now hold our human reins and allow us to live precariously with others.[25] With this experience of homonymic weirdness, Aimée begins to hear herself as a young girl babbling in another language. In bewildered self-engagement, she listens to herself *as if she were another*, one split into both native and foreigner, as fragments of an Other childhood invade without warning. Aimée translates her own strange warbling, an example of how "humans are always foreigners vis-à-vis language, and in this sense languages can only be 'foreign' languages."[26] Compelled by such difficult engagements and incomplete translations, Aimée reluctantly decides to "return" to Louisiana for once and for all, to piece together the blurred reasons that once transported her and Hanako from Louisiana all the way to Buenos Aires, to the antipodes of an American world. In Aimée's personal age of exploration, she will come face to face with a New World simultaneously old and anterior, a topsy-turvy place where the inverted seasons, "the smell of another sun and another river," and the upside-down foreignness of "the gestures, the courtesy, the clothes and the rhythm of speech" at the antipodes are dizzying.[27]

An Introduction to Antipodal Confusions

Derived from the Greek "against the foot,"[28] *antipodes* can denote a pair of diametrical locales upon the earth, or a point on the globe diametrically opposite to where we are. Integral to it is the notion of place in human geography as a tripartite term that denotes one's earthly coordinates, "the locus of individual and group identity[,] and the scale of everyday life."[29] Antipodes may also refer to people, denizens of locales "who dwell directly opposite to each other on the globe, so that the soles of their feet are . . . planted against each other."[30] Our antipodes can thus be our utter human inversion, just as Rochester imagines his perfect mate not as Bertha Mason, but as the "antipodes of the Creole."[31] Like Bertha to Jane Eyre, our antipodes are our topsy-turvy Others whose threats of confusion and invasion from a distance cordon the comfortable security of home. For early modern worlds of European expansion, a priori world pictures managed how new worlds were articulated and schematized.[32] Dark swans and nefarious creatures with immense feet that shaded the sun, for example, compartmentalized the outlandish unknown by underscoring the secure uprightness of home. One had to steer clear of *Terra Australis Ignota*—Australia, "the unknown land"—the dark place below the equator, a sunless underworld that crawled with inconceivable creatures. Threats of the ominously new were tamed by inversions, doublings, and displacements.

Looking liberally yet thematically across a set of eclectic literary moments, we find that Aimée is by no means alone in her antipodal confusion. The following excerpts briefly reveal like reckonings and anxious suspicions about foreign encroachments from the ends of the world; I would classify them as Asian American texts, due to their antipodal relevance to the enlarging field at hand, and to their historical and sociopolitical vectors that traverse both Asia and the Americas. Jesuit missionary José de Acosta, responding to a text written over a millennium earlier by the early Christian author Caecilius Lactantius,[33] invokes an antipodal map in his *The Natural and Moral History of the Indies* of 1590. The idea of a round Earth was completely ridiculous for Lactantius, who, in an outburst not unlike Aimée's, rails against simpletons who would consider the possibility of world space populated with utterly foreign Others. Impossible, says Lactantius, for one

> to believe there were a people or nation marching with their feete upwards, and their heades downwards, and that things which are placed here of one fort, are in that other part hanging topsie turvie: that trees and corne growe downwards, and that raine, snow and haile, fall from the earth upward . . . The imagination and conceit which some have had, supposing the heaven[s?] to be round, hath bene the cause to invent these Antipodes hanging in the aire.[34]

Looking across the equator toward his ideological antipodes, Father Acosta is foot-against-foot with his early Christian predecessor. "[N]o matter what he says," he muses, with early modern hindsight, "we who live nowadays in the part of the world that is the opposite of Asia is its antipode, as the cosmographers tell us, how that we do not walk hanging upside down."[35]

Writing in the nineteenth century, U.S. Unitarian minister Arthur May Knapp fiercely battles the specter of his own *desarraigo*, incited by the eccentricity of Japan. Knapp insists that Japanese people are impossibly mysterious with "hopeless contradictions and paradoxes . . . about whom anything could be said, and everything would be true, [and] no adjective . . . would be wholly out of place in a description of their mental and moral characteristics."[36] He shares a virtual plane with the right-side-up Lactantius. Under his virtually flat earth of evenly knowable and "legally demarcated territory,"[37] Knapp compulsively eliminates all antipodal confusion.

> Inversion is the confirmed and ineradicable habit of the far Oriental. It characterizes, not only the general mode as well as every detail of his outward life, but also his intellectual and moral being. It is not simply that his ways and thoughts differ from ours. They are the total reversal of ours. In our childhood we were accustomed to picture the inhabitants of the antipodes as standing upon their heads. We were so far right in our imaginings that that is really the only thing the far Oriental does not do in inversion of our ways . . . That bent is carried so far as to become a somersault.[38]

With a frontiersman's claim to his rightful North American place, Knapp clings to the homolingual. Failing to translate Japan's otherness with any American clarity, Knapp dismisses it as irrelevant for his sphere.

Certainly there are antipodal thinkers that allow for relative openness, despite the risks of parting with a comfortably predictable compass. If you were to travel around and around the entire world, observes Plato, you would "repeatedly take a position at your own antipodes."[39]

This allowance is echoed in the work of Lisbon-born Father Luís Frois, contemporary and fellow Jesuit of José Acosta. Frois tries his best to translate aspects of Japanese life for European readers in his various writings about life in the Asian empire. The following lines are from the early comparatist's collection of over 600 aphorisms on Japanese and European cultural manners, originally written in Portuguese. We can refer to it as the *Tratado*, a truncation of the lengthy *Treatise containing in very succinct and abbreviated form some contrasts and differences in the customs of the people of Europe and this province of Japan*.[40]

> We give our respect by taking off our hats; the Japanese do this by taking off their shoes.
> We eat with our hands; from a young age, Japanese men and women eat with two sticks.
> We sit on chairs to eat with legs extended; they on tatamis or the floor with legs crossed.
> We mount a horse with the left foot; the Japanese with the right.
> We write with twenty two letters; they in 48 cana and infinite characters . . .[41]

The *Tratado* places Japan at the other end of a recognizable European world, through pairings that invite us to observe, as well as extrapolate, commonalities between mutually foreign cultures. Insofar as Frois' descriptive observations try to abstain from explanatory presumptions, they also convey a peculiar vigilance, a heterolingual openness toward potential intelligibility between strangers. As if to compensate for the *Tratado*'s extreme mirroring and ethnographic privilege, the text's final chapter, "Various and extraordinary things that do not fit neatly in the preceding chapters,"[42] provides a virtual margin for Frois' stray observations, thus acknowledging the limits of his formulaic approach.

From his vantage of intimacy from within Japan, a place where the Jesuit missionary lived for over thirty years,[43] which antipodes would Frois call home? Does his *Tratado* of aphorisms reveal that he just as at home in Japan as he is, say, in Portugal or Europe? Does Frois envision his home as a sublime combination of both worlds? Or is he rather uprooted in both, and truly at home in neither? Were Frois to claim one place as his singular home, his dizzying comparisons irreparably recalibrate both antipodes. Neither place may ever offer a grounding stability for Frois; neither may be as compelling or fecund without its Other. How different are Frois' world reckonings from our own grapplings of Asian American texts with which we are generally familiar, narratives that engage with the idea, however minor, of Asian homeland in the face of a newfangled North American home? A premiere trope of Asian American literatures has been the theme of nostalgia for, rejection of, or reconciliation (however blighted) between the specter of an immigrant past and normative national present.

Is this the case for both Frois and Aimée? Whereas Frois' "true" home remains a mystery, Aimée's is soon to become apparent. Our final detour is through *Flores*' virtual prequel, a short piece written by Stahl for the Argentinean *La nación*. Celebrating Buenos Aires' immigrant history, the newspaper's 2004 Christmas supplement features a set of autobiographical vignettes by *porteños* of various immigrant and ethnic backgrounds. In "Mi primera navidad en la Argentina"[44] ("My First Christmas in Argentina"), Stahl fondly recalls Christmas as a U.S. student in Buenos Aires, both awed and displaced by the South American heat in December. In the story, Stahl's Spanish instructor joins her and two other *norteamericano* students for a Christmas meal. Donned in shorts and a Santa Claus cap, the instructor arrives with a piping hot turkey—and a VCR recording of falling snow. "And that is how we had our first inverted Christmas," Stahl writes, depicting a bipolar Christmas in a world that no longer revolves around one center. The sensation of feeling both so close to home and yet "indeterminably *distant*"[45] is a static produced by antipodal overlappings.

> [Aimée] mira otra vez el cuadrado sombrío del televisor. Hay una insinuación de brillo en la pantalla. Al lado está el mueble más bajo, con los estantes. Aimée hace memoria: ¿qué hay en el primer estante? Videos. *Africa mía, Alice, Buenos días, Vietnam, Caro diario, Casablanca* . . . Y arriba está la carta. Recordar la carta le despierta otra sensación, no tan neutra. Desata una cadena espontánea de contradicciones, de movimientos entre las ansias y la resistencia, y otra vez está incómoda.[46]

> [Aimée] looks again at the somber frame of the television. There's a mild glow on the screen. Beside it there's that low cabinet, with shelves. Aimée thinks: What's on that first shelf? Videos. *My Africa, Alice, Good Morning, Vietnam, Dear Diary, Casablanca* . . . And the letter just above. The memory of the letter awakens another sensation, not so neutral. It opens up a spontaneous chain of contradictions, of movements between anxieties and resistance, and she's uneasy yet again.

Like the fateful letter's English that punctures Aimée's *castellano*, the old tapes begin to map an uncanny globe of foreign spaces, releasing fractious memories that threaten Aimée's peace like a *parasite* ("static interference" in French[47]). The television's glow above Aimée's letter, with the rigorously forgotten videotapes beside it, create the imminent static of a Pandora's box or a "Trojan Horse introduced into the heart of the domestic fortress that we call 'home.'"[48] American static, then, sets the stage for Aimée's "return" to Louisiana. Once in New Orleans, Aimée must concatenate the haphazard flashes of what seems to be the past of another. She repeatedly reorients herself amidst "abrupt movements, changes of scenery, looks, faces, voices, things to consider: it was like being trapped in a crazed projector flashing its regular slides but completely out of order and at full speed ahead."[49] In a confusing world stretched open to accommodate her North American self, Aimée's northward "homecoming" is, at best, an ambivalent one.

A Style That Double-Worlds

Will Aimée ultimately embrace Louisiana as her original home? Will she relinquish her newly non-native *castellano* and reclaim English as her "mother tongue"? Alluding to these questions, *Flores* narrates a curious and persistent split between northern and southern worlds. It is as if a clean break between Southern Cone and the U.S. South, and between Spanish and English, is crucial to Aimée's peace of mind. As Aimée "learns Spanish," notes one critic, "she forgets English; they do not overlap."[50] "Rarely is a novel so clearly divided into two halves," observes another critic,[51] claiming that *Flores* shifts too hard between two competing worlds. The first half of the novel is "serene, unfolding bit by bit, creating a solid world of routines that is nibbled at by a mystery. The second is a typical 'inheritance' novel . . . In the Argentinean half, the facts square up in a commendable literary flow. The 'American' half, however, falls into a near excess of best-selling stories . . .[52] (Stahl's generous translation: "that I should have written one book, rather than two."[53]) The novel's structural rift "invades the use of language. A better edition would have pared off errors like the characters who *muelen los dientes*" (an awkward rendition of "they grind their teeth"), "instead of *rechinarlos*," (i.e., the properly grammatical translation).[54] Is this to say that Stahl, as a "transplant to Argentina, daughter of a Japanese mother and an American father,"[55] can claim mastery of neither standard nor colloquial *castellano*?

When *Flores* introduces us to Aimée's antipodal employees, nemeses Javier Nakamura (a *sansei* porteño) and Ariel Lambaré (a blond self-appointed connoisseur of all things Japanese), we can nearly hear Javier gnash his teeth as Ariel waxes poetic about Japan, Buddhism, haiku, and meditation; "Javier *se muele* los dientes cuando Ariel se explaya sobre esos temas" ("Javier gnashes his teeth when Ariel goes on and on about these topics").[56] Fascinatingly, Stahl's *castellano* "errs" in this particular scene that itself interrogates the homolingual correspondence between ethnicity and the putatively ethnic object. Rather than argue for Stahl's mastery of Spanish, however, I would describe *Flores*' style here as one revealing an urgency that is "necessary, indispensable, magnified"—pregnant with estrangements and extra-lingustic alienations "vibrating within it."[57] In a heightened awareness of style and language per se, Stahl's agrammatical usage underscores the vigilance, and heterolingualism, of *Flores*.

> Aimée se levanta muy temprano. Está oscuro todavía, pero se mueve a ciegas en la casa, con la seguridad de quien está habituado al lugar. Saldrá a la calle y volverá antes de que la luz asome por las ventanas de Junín. Usa la entrada de servicio, en el fondo del departamento, y baja por el ascensor que no tiene espejo. La luz es fuerte y hace resaltar los colores: Aimée tiene pelo largo, castaño claro, que lleva suelto, a veces ajustándolo atrás con hilo o un lápiz para trabajar o cocinar. Como es invierno, lleva una campera verde, una polera blanca y un enterito de jean, con botas de goma negras. Es una mujer pequeña y delgada, pero ágil, casi atlética en sus movimientos. Tiene unos treinta y cinco años, y más que linda, tiene algo especial, un mínimo misterio en su cara que llama la atención. De facciones delicadas y mirada franca, confunde al que trate de adivinarle el origen: tiene los ojos de un marrón tan claro que asemeja la miel y rasgados como los de un gato. Se le ve un aire oriental, pero no se puede definir. Por eso, muchas veces, los otros se quedan mirándola, cosa que fastidia a Aimée; su personalidad hace que prefiera el trabajo a la seducción.[58]

I have tried various times, yet always fail, to adequately render this passage into English. In a style that is halting but smooth, mundane but pointed, the above excerpt limns a morning's everyday quality (Aimée is one "habituado al lugar") with subtle anticipations of the future tense (e.g., "saldrá," "volverá"). Despite this morning's sharp lucidity, it echoes so many others. The routine of Aimée's life is emphasized in a fresh prose described as "quintessentially *porteño*" and simultaneously "limpid . . . with a dry rhythm that at moments feels strange."[59] As with the style of Franz Kafka, in which "secure aesthetic distance is undermined,"[60] Stahl's sparseness halts and stays the reader, drawing attention to its own over-clarity. *Flores*' syntax conveys an anticipation, a watchful nearsightedness vis-à-vis to *castellano rioplatense*—"el único que conozco" ("the only kind I know").[61]

HanEchoes

As we approach the novel's conclusion, another narrative begins to emerge. It is of Hanako's "coming to voice." Plagued by an agoraphobia that stems from "the bombings she witnessed as a girl in Japan during the Second World War,"[62] Hanako relies on the keen stability of home as a "universe familiar and predictable."[63] Hanako and Aimée, who often shadow each other in a form antipodal to formal language, live in a precarious peace that "mother and daughter (though they often seemed to switch places) created in the face of it all from a place of indivisibility, each sustaining the other through a balance of opposing natures."[64] This twinness underscores Aimée's early blindness toward Hanako's history. When Aimée finds Phillipe Chalmette in New Orleans, the elderly architect and old family friend can only profess adoration for Hanako. As he remembers the tragic wartime events that led to the union of Aimée's parents, Hanako's transversal story begins to emerge. "[S]he's not sick or stupid," proclaims a yet-smitten Chalmette, "she's of another universe."[65]

Doctors diagnose Hanako's impairment as a failure to produce language. "This neurological disorder, from infancy in this case," they explain, "excludes that kind of cognition: the patient cannot comprehend linear time, cannot connect effects with their causes, and can neither comprehend nor compose syntax. She cannot."[66] Yet Hanako expresses herself through *ikebana* (derived from the Japanese *ikeru*, "to arrange" or to be "alive", and *hana*, "flower"). In arrangements that each betray a "connected order or system of things" via the "harmonious adjustment of parts or elements,"[67] Hanako's syntax is able to communicate "certain experience" and utterances of "complicity."[68]

> Se concentra en un solo elemento que será central—dos calas gemelas, una rama de naranjo, flores de cerezo—y lo contempla desde una quietud alerta, como si buscara algo, casi como en una comunicación que prescindiera de lenguaje y de señas, que escapara a la percepción de los individuos comunes (como son, por ejemplo, los médicos). Luego, en algún momento, empieza el movimiento, y es un intercambio: Hanako da a las flores forma, altura y aire, definición; y recibe de ellas color y calidez o frialdad, la curva o el ángulo severo, y de esa sociedad a la larga lo que emerge es una expresión, la sugerencia (casi más completa de lo que podría hacerse por medio de las palabras) de un sentimiento, una postura o actitud.[69]

> She concentrates on a single element as a center—two twin lilies, an orange branch, cherry blossoms—and contemplates it with an alert stillness, as if looking for something, almost as if by a communication that ignored language and signs, one that could escape the notice of regular people (like doctors, for instance). Then, at some point, she movement begins, and it's an exchange: Hanako gives the flowers form, height and air, definition; and she receives from them their color, heat and coolness, the curve or hard angle, and from this communion ultimately emerges an expression, a suggestion (nearly more complete than that which can be said through words) of a feeling, stance or attitude.

The "materially intense expression"[70] of Hanako's *ikebana* is a vernacular, a non-traditional and non-standardized language within the fissures of medical diagnoses and dominant language. "Deceptively simple" ("Engañosamente sencillas"[71]), the poetry of evanescent flowers is laden with sensations of sight, touch, rhythm and smell, affective materialities that fail to be fully conveyed by formal language.

On the phone with Aimée in Louisiana, Fernando describes Hanako's surprising arrangement to Aimée over the phone. This one, he explains, comes with a supplement: an ink illustration.

> Lo hizo Hanako . . . es sencillito, por supuesto, pero lo hizo sola con tinta china, creo, o con un marcador grueso, sobre una hoja del papel madera que tienen ahí para envolver las *Flores*, ¿viste? Bueno, en una hoja de esas puso una casa, con una puertita y dos ventanas, y está como sobre el agua, quiero decir, está sobre unos pilares metidos dentro del agua, em, como en el Tigre, ¿entendés como es? . . .
> —¿Qué casa será?
> —¿Eh?—responde Fernando un incredulidad—. ¿Qué decís? Vaya a saber, de una revista, de la tele. Parece sólo un dibujo, Aimée, un adorno para las *Flores* del día.[72]

Hanako did it . . . it's simple, of course, but she did it with black ink I think, or a thick marker, on a piece of the brown paper that you guys use to wrap flowers, you know? Anyway, on one of those sheets she drew a house, with a little door and two windows, and it's as if it's on the water, I mean, on some columns that go into the water, uh, like on the Tigre Delta, you know? . . .

"Which house could it be?"

"Huh?" Fernando responds, incredulous. "What do you mean? Who knows, it's from a magazine, or from TV. It's just a drawing, Aimée, an ornament for today's flowers."

Delighted but unaware of what Hanako's depiction represents, Fernando faxes it to Aimée's hotel in New Orleans. Meticulously examining the mechanical reproduction, Aimée can make out a house that looks like those of Argentina's "el Tigre," or the Tigre Delta. And yet, Hanako's drawing looks remarkably like the unique houses in the old fishing community of nearby Delacroix. Fernando and Aimée attempt to translate this citation within Hanako's grammar of flowers. It is the key to the revelation of Aimée's inheritance.

Aimée's Antipodal Home

Al contrario de empezar asuntos, desea *cerrarlos*, y poder *por eso* volver a su vida como ha sido y es. No espera que cambie, sino que se complete con esta parte que faltaba o, mejor dicho, habiendo hecho las preguntas que faltaban hacer. Por más que sea confuso, es mejor que no reconocerse en nada, vivir en un olvido que ni se sabe lo que es, *suspendida en el aire*.[73]

She has no desire to pursue any further matters, on the contrary, she wants to *finish them off*, so she can *finally* get back to life as it is and has been. She doesn't want anything to change, just to recover this missing piece, in other words, to have asked the questions that she needs to ask. As confusing as it all is, it's still better not to live in a void, in an oblivion where you don't even know what you are, *suspended in the air*.

Whatever happens here in Louisiana, Aimée reminds herself, it can't change anything too dramatically. And for sure, it is better than not having traveled here at all; to have remained, like Lactantius, on an impossibly flat earth. Having inspected the New Orleans estate that is soon to be hers, Aimée trudges on toward the ultimate chapter of her North American journey. Equipped with her fax of Hanako's sketch, she drives over to Delacroix. Somewhat haphazardly, she begins to ask around about a home that once belonged to her grandfather Francisco Oleary.

A young man introduces himself. "Mi nombre es . . . Ramón Méndez," he says. "Pero *no hablo español*."[74] A coincidence that once again reflects Aimée back to herself, in a certain antipodal "paradox": Ramón is an ethnic outsider "at home" among these Delacroix Islands, a native non-native who bears but traces of an official, "authentic" tongue. It is until this very moment that Aimée has been an outsider to the area, wary in this odd country of her own origin. Steps away from shoving open the front door of her grandfather's old home, she is startled in the street by an unforeseen sublimity. Aimée is warmly greeted by Ramón's uncle, Evaristo, who introduces himself and begins to chat with her in Spanish.

En medio de la frase en español, dice "Delacroi" de la misma forma que en inglés. Aimée escucha el acento particular, entre gallego y caribeño, y se relaja. En realidad, le causa una sensación más visceral que lingüística, una impresión como podría ser la que da la lluvia en primavera, o las gardenias con rocío, las azucenas en el papel perfumado, la sábana fresca después de un baño caliente. Es *su* idioma, y no tiene que esforzarse más.[75]

In the middle of a sentence in Spanish, he says "Delacroi" in English. Upon hearing that peculiar accent, somewhere between Galician and Caribbean, she relaxes. Actually, it creates more a visceral sensation than linguistic, an impression like that of spring rain, or dewy gardenias, white lilies wrapped in scented paper, fresh sheets after a hot bath. It is *her* language, and doesn't need to exert herself any longer.

Aimée's acute comfort in hearing "her language" in unfamiliar North American country is a homecoming—one that is nothing like her imminent flight back to Buenos Aires, nor her unenthusiastic "return" to New Orleans. With these friendly strangers, Aimée unwittingly shares a language that is neither English nor *castellano*, but "an accenting of the word, an inflection,"[76] a map of the imprecise yet cozy edges of language without tethers to a singular location. This fleeting moment of community is also radically different from that within Aimée's apartment 9ºB, where literal words are often trumped by flowers, touches, and silences. No matter that Evaristo's accent is not a *porteño* one. It is the peculiarity of his minor modulations, and Ramón's "no hablo español"—a blend of local English from here, and a Spanish from elsewhere—that disarm Aimée and make her feel, cozily and imprecisely, at home.

Hardly able to wait to finish all legal proceedings and get back on the plane, our heroine has no desire whatsoever to remain in the United States. Ecstatic to be en route toward her family, she only wants to escape the oppressive heat of the U.S. South, and return to the mild winter in Argentina. Aimée's sphere has been both shaken and enriched by antipodal static. And yet, as she acknowledges her ineluctably provisional grasp of the world, she renews her partiality toward Buenos Aires as her beloved home. Bouts with antipodal otherness have still left her with no "access to an aerial view from which the entirety can be grasped instantaneously";[77] but for the first time in ages, Aimée is laughing—"the only person laughing in the plane, at 10,000 meters above . . . and what is that? . . . Is it Venezuela? Or Brazil, Paraguay?"[78] Is our Louisianian *porteña* giggling at the dissolution of national boundaries from her bird's-eye view? Or at her own projection of pan-American homolingualism? Back at the apartment, Aimée conveys her news to Hanako through gifts, gestures, and other approximations of literal language. She feels a bizarrely fresh sensation of having truly come home, "of *feeling* at home, as if she's finally planted her feet on the ground.[79] Diametrical American estrangements have led Aimée to see her *porteña* life as central, not to *the* world, but to *a* mere world, one of her own heterolingual and homely vantage.

Notes

1 Anna Kazumi Stahl, *Flores de un solo día* (Buenos Aires: Seix Barral, 2002). Stahl's novel and various other Spanish-language texts discussed in this essay are unavailable in English at the time of this publication. I have included my own translations here, and apologize for overlooked errors. I take advantage of this note to thank an incomplete set of friends without whose care this essay would have been further garbled: Gabriel Giorgi, David Lloyd, Anna Kazumi Stahl, Akira Mizuta Lippit, Viet Thanh Nguyen, Nigel Hatton, Jeehyun Lim, Isabela Seong Leong Quintana, Sabeena Setia, Cindy I-Fen Cheng, and Roberto Ignacio Díaz.
2 Naoki Sakai, "Nationality and the Politics of the 'Mother Tongue,'" in *Deconstructing Nationality*, Ed. Naoki Sakai, Cornell East Asia Series 124 (Ithaca, NY: East Asia Program, Cornell University, 2005), 18.

3   A "regulative idea" is a concept that establishes a principal cognitive order for human ideas, as described in Kant's *Critique of Pure Reason*. It provides for crucial points of inquiry in Naoki Sakai's various discussions about translation and the apparent unity of single languages.
4   Sakai, "Nationality and the Politics of the 'Mother Tongue,'" 18.
5   *Fleurs d'un jour* (Paris: Seuil, 2005); *Fiori di un solo giorno* (Palermo: Sellerio Editore Palermo, 2004).
6   *Anglophone* refers to the particular use of the English language and/or to places where English is formally or predominantly spoken; it can also denote an English-speaking person.
7   Kirsten Silva Gruesz, "America," in *Keywords for American Cultural Studies*, Ed. Bruce Burgett and Glenn Hendler (New York: New York University Press, 2007), 17.
8   J. Hillis Miller's discussion of Otherness is helpful here: a presence "of the 'completely other' that inhabits even the most familiar and apparently 'same,' for example my sense of myself or of my neighbor or my beloved, the 'alter ego' within my own home or culture, or my sense of my own culture as such, or my sense of literary and philosophical works that belong to my own culture. Those are, I claim, other to themselves, as well as to 'me.'" Joseph Hillis Miller, *Others* (Princeton, NJ: Princeton University Press, 2001), 1.
9   Guiyou Huang, Introduction to *Asian-American Poets: A Bio-Bibliographical Critical Sourcebook*, Ed. Guiyou Huang (Westport, CT: Greenwood Press, 2002), 8.
10 Kandice Chuh, *Imagine Otherwise: On Asian Americanist Critique* (Durham, NC: Duke University Press, 2003), 232.
11 Greg Robinson introduced me to the aptness of the term "comparative confinements" in his book *A Tragedy of Democracy: Japanese Confinement in North America* (New York: Columbia University Press, 2009).
12 I take the term *homolingual* from the work of comparatist Naoki Saki.
13 "[B]oth imperialism and nationalism seek to occlude troublesome and inassimilable manifestations of difference by positing a transcendent realm of essential identity." David Lloyd, *Nationalism and Minor Literature: James Clarence Mangan and the Emergence of Irish Cultural Nationalism* (Berkeley, CA: University of California Press, 1987), x.
14 Naoki Sakai, "How Do We Count a Language? Translation and Discontinuity," *Translation Studies* 2, no. 1 (2008): 75.
15 Naoki Sakai, "Translation," *Theory, Culture & Society* 23, no. 2–3 (May 1, 2006): 72.
16 Naoki Sakai observes that a "modern schema of co-figuration" allows us to "comprehend the unity of natural language as an ethno-linguistic unity." Sakai, "How Do We Count a Language?" 72–3.
17 Sakai, "Translation," 75.
18 "Schema, n.," *OED Online*. This definition cites Kant: "Any one of certain forms or rules of the 'productive imagination' through which the understanding is able to apply its 'categories' to the manifold of sense-perception in the process of realizing knowledge or experience."
19 Lera Boroditsky, "Lost in Translation," *Wall Street Journal*, July 23, 2010.
20 Gustavo Geirola, "Chinos y japoneses en américa latina: Karen Tei Yamashita, Cristina García y Anna Kazumi Stahl," *Chasqui* 34, no. 2 (Nov. 1, 2005): 113–30.
21 "Los arreglos *ikebana* expresan un estado de ánimo, una emoción." Stahl, *Flores de un solo día*, 18.
22 Ibid., 71–72.
23 Ibid., 72.
24 Ibid., 73.
25 "Life and breath under the open skies can no longer mean what they once did[.]" Peter Sloterdijk, *Temblores de aire: en las fuentes del terror*, trans. Germán Cano (Valencia: Pre-Textos, 2003), 141. This is my translation of the Spanish-language edition.
26 Sakai, "Nationality and the Politics of the 'Mother Tongue,'" 18.
27 Stahl, *Flores de un solo día*, 331, 165.
28 "Antipodes, n.," *OED Online*.
29 Noel Castree, "Place: Connections and Boundaries in an Interdependent World," in *Key Concepts in Geography*, Eds. Nicholas Clifford, Sarah L. Holloway, Stephen P. Rice, and Gill Valentine (Los Angeles, CA: SAGE Publications, 2009), 153.
30 "Antipodes, n." *OED Online*.
31 Charlotte Bronte, *Jane Eyre*, Thrift Study Edition (Mineola, NY: Dover Publications, 2011), 291.

32 David Fausett, *Images of the Antipodes in the Eighteenth Century: A Study in Stereotyping*, Cross/Cultures 18 (Amsterdam, GA: Rodopi, 1995), vii.
33 Caecilius Firmianus Lactantius is believed to have lived from *c.*250–*c.*325 CE. Anthony Bowen and Peter Gamsey, Introduction to *Divine Institutes* by Caecilius Lactantius, trans. Anthony Bowen and Peter Gamsey, vol. 40, Translated Texts for Historians (Liverpool, UK: Liverpool University Press, 2003), 1.
34 José de Acosta, *The Naturall and Morall Historie of the East and West Indies Intreating of the Remarkable Things of Heaven, of the Elements, Mettalls, Plants and Beasts Which Are Proper to That Country: Together with the Manners, Ceremonies, Lawes, Governments, and Warres of the Indians. Written in Spanish by the R.F. Ioseph Acosta, and Translated into English by E.G.*, trans. Edward Grimeston (London: Printed by Val: Sims for Edward Blount and William Aspley, 1604), 22.
35 José de Acosta, *Natural and Moral History of the Indies*, Ed. Jane E. Mangan, trans. Frances Lopez-Morillas, annotated edition (Durham, NC: Duke University Press Books, 2002), 30.
36 Arthur May Knapp, *Feudal and Modern Japan* (London: Duckworth and Co., 1898), 136.
37 Benedict Anderson, *Imagined Communities: Reflections on the Origin and Spread of Nationalism* (Verso, 1993), 26; Wai Chee Dimock, "Literature for the Planet," *PMLA* 116, no. 1 (Jan. 1, 2001): 175.
38 Knapp, *Feudal and Modern Japan*, 137–8.
39 Plato, *Timaeus*, trans. Donald J. Zeyl (Indianapolis, IN: Hackett Publishing, 2000), 56.
40 Daniel T. Reff, "Critical Introduction: The *Tratado*, the Jesuits, and the Governance of Souls," in *The First European Description of Japan, 1585: A Critical English-Language Edition of Striking Contrasts in the Customs of Europe and Japan by Luis Frois, S.J.*, by Luis Frois, S.J., Eds. Robin D. Gill, Daniel T. Reff, and Richard K. Danford, Japan Anthropology Workshop Series (London; New York: Routledge, 2014), 3.
41 I translated these excerpts from the abridged Spanish edition: Luís Frois, *Tratado sobre las contradicciones y diferencias de costumbres entre los europeos y japoneses* (Salamanca: Universidad de Salamanca, 2003), 38, 73, 74, 88, 97; see also Robin Gill and Luís Frois, *Topsy-Turvy 1585: A Translation and Explication of Luis Frois S.J.'s Tratado (treatise) Listing 611 Ways Europeans & Japanese Are Contrary*, trans. Robin Gill (Key Biscayne, FL: Paraverse Press, 2004); Luis Frois, S.J., *The First European Description of Japan, 1585: A Critical English-Language Edition of Striking Contrasts in the Customs of Europe and Japan by Luis Frois, S.J.*, Eds. and trans. Richard K. Danford, Robin Gill, and Daniel T. Reff, Japan Anthropology Workshop Series (London; New York: Routledge, 2014); for those interested in a recent edition of the original; see also *EuropaJapão: um diálogo civilizacional no século XVI: tratado em que se contêm muito sucinta e abreviadamente algumas contradições e diferenças de costumes entre a gente de Europa e esta província de Japão (. . .)* (Lisboa: Comissão Nacional para as Comemorações dos Descobrimentos Portugueses, 1993); Luís Fróis, *Tratado das contradições e diferenças de costumes entra a Europa e o Japão* (Macau: Instituto Português do Oriente, 2001).
42 Frois, S.J., *The First European Description of Japan, 1585: A Critical English-Language Edition of Striking Contrasts in the Customs of Europe and Japan by Luis Frois, S.J.* vii, 244.
43 Michael Cooper, Review of *Historia de Japam* by Luís Frois, *Monumenta Nipponica* 34, no. 1 (April 1, 1979): 120.
44 Anna Kazumi Stahl, "Mi primera navidad en la Argentina," *La Nación*, Dec. 19, 2004, sec. revista, www.lanacion.com.ar/663415-mi-primera-navidad-en-la-argentina.
45 Samuel Weber, *Mass Mediauras: Form, Technics, Media*, ed. Alan Cholodenko (Stanford, CA: Stanford University Press, 1996), 124.
46 Stahl, *Flores de un solo día*, 76.
47 Weber, *Mass Mediauras: Form, Technics, Media*.
48 Ibid., 122.
49 Stahl, *Flores de un solo día*, 322.
50 "A medida que aprende español, va olvidando el inglés: no los acumula." Martín Kohan, "La encarnadura de los recuerdos," *Clarin.com*, January 11, 2003.
51 "Pocas veces una novela está tan claramente dividida en dos mitades." Elvio E. Gandolfo, "Las raíces del presente," review of *Flores de un solo día* by Anna Kazumi Stahl, *Noticias*, December 7, 2002.
52 "No solo [un] viaje separa las dos mitades," he adds. "La primera es serena, se despliega poco a poco, crea un mundo sólido de rutinas, carcomido por un misterio. La segunda es una típica novela 'de herencia' . . . En la mitad argentina, los hechos se insertan en un flujo literario muy logrado.

La 'americana', por momentos parece al borde de caer en el exceso anecdótico del best seller, aunque sea 'de qualité . . .'" Gandolfo, "Las raíces del presente."
53 I interviewed Anna Kazumi Stahl at her apartment in Buenos Aires, in July 2006.
54 "Instalada en la Argentina, hija de madre japonesa y padre norteamericano . . . el riesgo que corre en la estructura del libro también invade el use del lenguaje. Una mejor edición hubiera limado las palabras erróneas, como los personajes que *muelen los dientes* en vez de *rechinarlos*." Gandolfo, "Las raíces del presente."
55 Ibid.
56 Stahl, *Flores de un solo día*, 44
57 Gilles Deleuze and Felix Guattari, *Kafka: Toward a Minor Literature* (Minneapolis, MN: University of Minnesota Press, 1986), 17.
58 Stahl, *Flores de un solo día*, 11.
59 "Una prosa limpida, de ritmo seco y por momentos extraño." Pedro B. Rey, "La sintaxis del silencio," *La Nación*, December 8, 2002.
60 Theodor W. Adorno, *Aesthetic Theory*, trans. Robert Hullot-Kentor, *Theory and History of Literature* (Minneapolis, MN: University of Minnesota Press, 1997), 339.
61 Rey, "La sintaxis del silencio."
62 Stahl, *Flores de un solo día*, 16.
63 Ibid.
64 "Madre e hija (aunque muchas veces parecían invertirse los roles) hicieron frente a todo desde su indivisibilidad, cada una el sostén de la otra a través de un equilibrio de naturalezas opuestas." Stahl, *Flores de un solo día*, 11.
65 Ibid., 294.
66 Ibid., 115–16.
67 Stahl, *Flores de un solo día*, 116.
68 Ibid.
69 Ibid.
70 Deleuze and Guattari, *Kafka*, 19.
71 Stahl, *Flores de un solo día*, 116.
72 Ibid., 255.
73 Ibid. My emphasis on "*suspendida en el aire*," and its uncanny echo of the language of Lactantius.
74 Stahl, *Flores de un solo día*, 303.
75 Ibid.
76 Deleuze and Guattari, *Kafka*, 21.
77 Sakai, "How Do We Count a Language?" 75.
78 Stahl, *Flores de un solo día*, 325
79 Ibid.

References

Acosta, José de. *Natural and Moral History of the Indies*. Edited by Jane E. Mangan. Translated by Frances Lopez-Morillas. Annotated edition. Durham, NC: Duke University Press, 2002.

———. *The Naturall and Morall Historie of the East and West Indies Intreating of the Remarkable Things of Heaven, of the Elements, Mettalls, Plants and Beasts Which Are Proper to That Country: Together with the Manners, Ceremonies, Lawes, Governments, and Warres of the Indians. Written in Spanish by the R.F. Ioseph Acosta, and Translated into English by E.G.* Translated by Edward Grimeston. London: Printed by Val: Sims for Edward Blount and William Aspley, 1604. http://gateway.proquest.com/openurl?ctx_ver=Z39.88-2003&res_id=xri:eebo&rft_val_fmt=&rft_id=xri:eebo:image:494 (accessed October 14, 2016).

Adorno, Theodor W. *Aesthetic Theory*. Translated by Robert Hullot-Kentor. Vol. 88. Theory and History of Literature. Minneapolis, MN: University of Minnesota Press, 1997.

Anderson, Benedict. *Imagined Communities: Reflections on the Origin and Spread of Nationalism*. London: Verso, 1993.

Boroditsky, Lera. "Lost in Translation." *Wall Street Journal*, July 23, 2010, sec. Life and Style. www.wsj.com/articles/SB10001424052748703467304575383131592767868. 9 (accessed October 14, 2016).

Bowen, Anthony, and Peter Garnsey. "Introduction." In *Divine Institutes*, by Caecilius Firmianus Lactantius, 1–54, 1st ed. Translated Texts for Historians. Liverpool, UK: Liverpool University Press, 2003. https://books.google.com/books?id=GuRdq6PE3UYC (accessed October 14, 2016).

Bronte, Charlotte. *Jane Eyre*. Thrift Study Edition. Mineola, NY: Dover Publications, 2011.

Chuh, Kandice. *Imagine Otherwise: On Asian Americanist Critique*. Durham, NC: Duke University Press, 2003.

Cooper, Michael. "Review of *Historia de Japam*", by Luís Froís. *Monumenta Nipponica* 34, no. 1 (April 1, 1979): 119–121. doi:10.2307/2384287.

Deleuze, Gilles, and Felix Guattari. *Kafka: Toward a Minor Literature*. Minneapolis, MN: University of Minnesota Press, 1986.

Dimock, Wai Chee. "Literature for the Planet." *PMLA* 116, no. 1 (January 1, 2001): 173–188.

Durá, Nicolás Sánchez. Prologue to *Temblores de aire: en las fuentes del terror*, 9–33. Translated by Germán Cano. Valencia: Pre-Textos, 2003.

Fausett, David. *Images of the Antipodes in the Eighteenth Century: A Study in Stereotyping*. Cross/Cultures 18. Amsterdam; Atlanta, GA: Rodopi, 1995.

Frois, Luís. *Topsy-Turvy 1585*. Translated by Robin D. Gill. Key Biscayne, FL: Paraverse Press, 2004.

———. *Tratado sobre las contradicciones y diferencias de costumbres entre los europeos y japoneses*. Salamanca: Universidad de Salamanca, 2003.

———. *The First European Description of Japan, 1585: A Critical English-Language Edition of Striking Contrasts in the Customs of Europe and Japan by Luis Frois, S.J.* Edited, translated, and annotated by Richard K. Danford, Robin Gill, and Daniel T. Reff. Japan Anthropology Workshop Series. London; New York: Routledge, 2014.

——— and Robin Gill. *Topsy-Turvy 1585: A Translation and Explication of Luis Frois S.J.'s Tratado (treatise) Listing 611 Ways Europeans & Japanese Are Contrary*. Translated by Robin Gill. Key Biscayne, FL: Paraverse Press, 2004.

Gandolfo, Elvio E. "Review of *Las raíces del presente (Reseña de* Flores de un solo día*)*, by Anna Kazumi Stahl." *Noticias*, December 7, 2002.

Geirola, Gustavo. "Chinos y japoneses en américa latina: Karen Tei Yamashita, Cristina García y Anna Kazumi Stahl." *Chasqui* 34, no. 2 (November 1, 2005): 113–130. doi:10.2307/29741975.

Gruesz, Kirsten Silva. "America." In *Keywords for American Cultural Studies*, edited by Bruce Burgett and Glenn Hendler, 16–22. New York: NYU Press, 2007.

Holloway, Sarah L., Stephen P. Rice, Gill Valentine, and Noel Castree, Eds. "Place: Connections and Boundaries in an Interdependent World." In *Key Concepts in Geography*, 165–185. Los Angeles, CA: SAGE Publications, 2003.

Knapp, Arthur May. *Feudal and Modern Japan*. London: Duckworth and Co., 1898. http://archive.org/details/feudalmodernjapa00knap (accessed October 14, 2016).

Kohan, Martín. "La encarnadura de los recuerdos." *Clarin.com*, January 11, 2003. http://edant.clarin.com/suplementos/cultura/2003/01/11/u-00410.htm (accessed October 14, 2016).

Lloyd, David. *Nationalism and Minor Literature: James Clarence Mangan and the Emergence of Irish Cultural Nationalism*. Los Angeles, CA: University of California Press, 1987.

Miller, Joseph Hillis. "Introduction." In *Others*, 1–4. Princeton, NJ: Princeton University Press, 2001.

Plato. *Timaeus*. Translated by Donald J. Zeyl. Indianapolis, IN: Hackett Publishing, 2000.

Reff, Daniel T. "Critical Introduction: The *Tratado*, the Jesuits, and the Governance of Souls." In *The First European Description of Japan, 1585: A Critical English-Language Edition of Striking Contrasts in the Customs of Europe and Japan by Luis Frois, S.J.*, by Luis Frois, S.J., 1–32. edited by Robin D. Gill, Daniel T. Reff, and Richard K. Danford. Japan Anthropology Workshop Series. London; New York: Routledge, 2014.

Rey, Pedro B. "La sintaxis del silencio." *La Nación*, December 8, 2002. www.lanacion.com.ar/nota.asp?nota_id=456407 (accessed October 14, 2016).

Robinson, Greg. *A Tragedy of Democracy: Japanese Confinement in North America*. New York: Columbia University Press, 2009.

Sakai, Naoki. "How Do We Count a Language? Translation and Discontinuity." *Translation Studies* 2, no. 1 (2008): 71–88. doi:10.1080/14781700802496266.

———. *Translation and Subjectivity: On "Japan" and Cultural Nationalism*. Minneapolis, MN: University of Minnesota Press, 1997.

———. "The Microphysics of Comparison: Towards the Dislocation of the West." *Transversal (European Institute for Progressive Cultural Policies Multilingual Webjournal)*, a communality that cannot speak: europe in translation (June 2013). http://transversal.at/transversal/0613/sakai1/en (accessed October 14, 2016).

Sakai, Naoki. "Nationality and the Politics of the 'Mother Tongue.'" In *Deconstructing Nationality*, edited by Naoki Sakai, 1–38. Cornell East Asia Series 124. Ithaca, NY: East Asia Program, Cornell University, 2005.

———. "Translation." *Theory, Culture & Society* 23, no. 2–3 (May 1, 2006): 71–78.

Sloterdijk, Peter. *Bubbles: Spheres Volume I: Microspherology*. Translated by Wieland Hoban. Los Angeles, CA: Semiotext(e), 2011.

———. *Temblores de aire: en las fuentes del terror*. Translated by Germán Cano. Valencia: Pre-Textos, 2003.

Stahl, Anna Kazumi. *Flores de un solo día*. Buenos Aires: Seix Barral, 2002.

———. "Mi primera navidad en la Argentina." *La Nación*. December 19, 2004, sec. suplemento revista. www.lanacion.com.ar/663415-mi-primera-navidad-en-la-argentina (accessed October 14, 2016).

Weber, Samuel. *Mass Mediauras: Form, Technics, Media*. Edited by Alan Cholodenko. Stanford, CA: Stanford University Press, 1996.

PART TWO

War, Colonization, and U.S. Imperialism

6
THE VIETNAM WAR AND THE "GOOD REFUGEE"

Yen Le Espiritu

At this moment of reinvigorated U.S. imperialism and globalized militarization, it is important to interrogate a new public recollection of the U.S. war in Vietnam. As a "controversial, morally questionable and unsuccessful"[1] war, the Vietnam War has the potential to upset the well-worn narrative of "rescue and liberation" and refocus attention on the troubling record of U.S. military aggression. Having lost the Vietnam War, the United States had no "liberated" country or people to showcase; and as such, the Vietnam War appears to offer an antidote to the "rescue and liberation" myths and memories. Yet, as I will show, in the absence of a liberated Vietnam and people, the U.S. government, academy, and media have produced a substitute: the freed and reformed Vietnamese refugees. In this chapter, I first show how the narrative of the "good refugee," deployed by refugee studies scholars, mainstream U.S. media, and Vietnamese Americans themselves, has been key in enabling the United States to turn the Vietnam War into a "good war." I then flip the script and argue that what appears to be an act of economic assimilation on the part of the Vietnamese—an act of moving beyond the war—is in actuality an index of the ongoing costs of war, not only for the refugees but also for their children.

The Production of the "Good Refugee": Social Sciences – the Desperate-Turned-Successful Refugees

As a people fleeing from the only war that the United States had lost, Vietnamese have been subject to intense scholarly interest—an "overdocumented" population when compared to other U.S. immigrant groups. Indeed, the 1975 cohort, as state-sponsored refugees, may be the most studied arrival cohort in U.S. immigration history.[2] The federal government, in collaboration with social scientists, initiated a series of needs assessment surveys to generate knowledge on what was widely touted as a "refugee resettlement crisis." Viewing the Vietnamese as coming from "a society so markedly different from that of America," government officials and scholars alike regarded the accumulation of data on Vietnamese economic and sociocultural adaptation essential to "protect[ing] the interests of the American public."[3] Other substantial data sets on Vietnamese refugee adaptation followed: from the Bureau of Social Science Research Survey; the Institute for Social Research Survey; the NICHD-funded survey; and other government records, including the 1980 Census.[4] Constituting the primary data sources on

Vietnamese from the mid-1970s and throughout the 1980s, these large-scale surveys, which cumulatively produce the Vietnamese in the United States as a *problem* to be solved, define and conceptually underpin future studies of Vietnamese in the United States.

More qualitative studies on the social and cultural dynamics of Vietnamese adaptation followed.[5] Prescribing assimilation as the solution to the refugee resettlement crisis, these studies impose a generalized narrative of immigration on Vietnamese refugees, thereby reducing the specificities of their flight to a conventional story of ethnic assimilation.[6] The assimilation narrative produces Vietnamese as docile subjects who enthusiastically and uncritically embrace and live the "American Dream." Christine Finnan's 1981 study of the occupational assimilation of Vietnamese in Santa Clara County provides an example. In Finnan's account, the oft-exploitative electronics industry becomes a "symbol of opportunity" in which Vietnamese technicians "are eager to work as many hours of overtime as possible."[7] Even while praising the hard-working and enterprising Vietnamese, Finnan discursively distances them from normative American workers by reporting that "occupations that may seem undesirable to *us* may be perfectly suited to [the refugees'] current needs" and that Vietnamese become technicians "because they are patient and can memorize things easily."[8] Finnan also contends that Vietnamese, even those who were the elite in Vietnam, prefer working as electronics technicians in the United States to working in Vietnam "because there is more potential for advancement here."[9] In the same way, Caplan and colleagues optimistically characterize Vietnamese economic pursuits as "conspicuously successful," even while reporting that the overwhelming majority (71 percent) held "low-level, low-paying, dead-end jobs" and that slightly more than half (55 percent) were employed in the periphery rather than in the core economic sector.[10] Together, these studies present the United States as self-evidently *the* land of opportunity, which then allow the authors to conclude that even when Vietnamese are underemployed and barely eking out a living, they are still better off in the United States than if they had remained in Vietnam. This ahistorical juxtaposition of opportunities in Vietnam and in the United States naturalizes the great economic disparity between the two countries, depicting the two economies as unconnected rather than mutually constituted. This historical revisionism in turn allows the United States to remake itself into the magnanimous rescuers, never mind its role in producing this exodus in the first place.

In the early 1980s, scholars, along with the mass media and policymakers, began to depict the newly arrived Vietnamese as the desperate-turned-successful; that is, as the newest "model minority." *The Boat People and Achievement in America* was among the first and most influential texts to recount the economic and educational success of Southeast Asian refugees who came to the United States during the 1970s.[11] The authors were particularly effusive about the "legendary" academic accomplishments of Vietnamese refugees' children. In a later case study of Vietnamese youth in New Orleans, Min Zhou and Carl Bankston claim that students who have strong adherence to traditional family values, strong commitment to a work ethic, and a high degree of personal involvement in the ethnic community tend disproportionally to receive high grades, to have definite college plans, and to score high on academic orientation.[12] Cumulatively, these studies suggest that Vietnamese rely on their "core cultural values" to gain access to the opportunities readily available in the United States. This "good refugee" narrative naturalizes America's riches and produces a powerful narrative of America(ns) generously and successfully caring for Vietnam's "runaways." As such, it powerfully remakes the case for U.S. war in Vietnam: that the war, no matter the costs, was ultimately necessary, moral, and successful.

Newspaper Media: Liberated and Grateful Refugees

Many American Studies scholars have detailed how the recuperation of the Vietnam veterans has been central to the ongoing renovation of U.S. mythic innocence.[13] I add to this discussion by showing how popular narratives of *Vietnamese refugees* have also been deployed to rescue the Vietnam War for Americans. In this section, I examine the U.S. media commemoration of the 25th anniversary of the Fall of Saigon, noting that the majority of the articles focus on the refugees' purported rags-to-riches accomplishments, and on their "fanatical" anti-Communist stance. I selected the 25th anniversary because of its symbolic significance as a milestone—an occasion for the retelling, reenacting, and reimagining of the war a quarter of a century later.[14] The 25th anniversary is also noteworthy because it took place at the height of the U.S. final recovery from the Vietnam Syndrome and the full restoration of its global power. By 2000, the U.S. had won the Cold War and the Persian Gulf War; and Vietnam (and also China) had begun to "open up" to the West. With these military and economic "successes," the United States appeared to have left behind the Vietnam Syndrome as it confidently reasserted its world power, calling for a "New World Order" under its management.[15] The analysis that follows is based on a total of 112 articles. About half came from three major U.S. newspapers: the *Los Angeles Times*, *New York Times*, and the *Washington Post*. I also included three California newspapers from communities with the highest concentration of Vietnamese Americans: the *Orange County Register*, *San Diego Union Tribune*, and *San Jose Mercury News;* and three from the nation's leading weeklies, *Time Magazine* and *Newsweek*. Finally, twelve articles came from various internet sources.

"We're Very, Very Happy. We Love America"[16]

The refugee success story is deceptively simple. Its bare structure—flight, adjustment, and assimilation—is evident in this typical sample: "Over the years, desperate to flee communism, 1 million refugees have streamed into America . . . Most, after a period of adjustment, have been succeeding in business and a wide range of professions, while their children assimilate at a dizzying pace."[17] Like other "rescue" narratives, most refugee stories inevitably follow the common formula of the "before" and "after" photographs—a staple since Victorian times to visually depict the oft-complete transformation of the socially stigmatized (the "before") into the socially recognized (the "after") primarily due to white benevolent intervention.[18]

Most refugee stories discursively feature a "before" (shot) of the refugees languishing in backward and destitute Vietnam, and an "after" (shot) of them flourishing in cosmopolitan and affluent United States. Often, the description of the "before" draws upon established and naturalized notions of Third World poverty, hunger, or need, with the soon-to-be-rescued Vietnamese living in decidedly premodern conditions; and the "after" relying on accepted knowledge of U.S. democracy and freedom, with the now-assimilated refugees touting access to private property and economic mobility. An example from a story entitled "The Boat People":[19]

> **Before**: Born in 1976, Tran grew up in rural villages off the coast in the south, living in thatched huts. While she romped barefoot in mud puddles and made bracelets from palm leaves, her parents were trying to find ways to get to the United States.
> **After**: She thrived in her new world. After only two years in a Sunnyvale elementary school, she was earning straight A's. She chose the University of California-Berkeley over Yale so she could be close to her parents. Married last year, she is now director of marketing at a local San Jose company. She weaves her shiny black Mercedes through traffic . . .

The transformation brought about by life in the United States is unmistakable: from the "thatched huts" of her rural village, Tran has transformed into a successful professional woman, with a black Mercedes to boot. Lest the reader miss Tran's "makeover" depicted by the "before" and "after" [shots], reporter Arnett deployed another trope: the "would have been"—a postulation of how different the refugees' life and life chances would have been had they stayed in Vietnam:

> **Would-Have-Been**: If they stayed in Vietnam, they knew, their daughter's life would not be much different from their own. At 8, Tran had never stepped inside a school. She didn't know how to read. She didn't even know how to add two plus two. In America, . . . things would be better.[20]

In many ways, the "would-have-beens" are the most powerful in communicating the allures of the United States because they assume the form of a testimonial—a looking back from individuals who have tasted life on the "other side." They are powerful because they make the case that *this* life—of education, opportunities, and social mobility—would be unimaginable in Vietnam, and thus could only be had *here* in the United States. Most often, these "would-have-beens" are mere speculation, as in the following statement attributed to a Vietnamese man who "owns a $419,000 home and a metal-coating business, and drives a Mercedes-Benz": "If I were still in Vietnam, I wouldn't have the business . . . My children would not have succeeded. They would be working in the rice paddies.[21] This statement is mere speculation because of course, there could be no tangible evidence of what his life would have been like had he stayed. The fact that these uncorroborated statements graced so many of the refugee stories testifies to the journalists' confidence in the readers' ability to fill in the "evidence" with their learned cultural knowledge about the differential quality of life in the United States and Vietnam.

On rare occasions, the "would-have-been" stories are fleshed out with lurid "evidence" of life in Vietnam. In a four-page spread in the *Los Angeles Times Magazine*, reporters Scott Gold and Mai Tran tracked the divergent lives of a divided family, juxtaposing the relatively comfortable lifestyle of the father, mother, and three younger children in the United States against the squalid existence of the two older children left behind in Vietnam.[22] Five years into their new lives in the United States, the Trans were reportedly "now nestled in Southern California suburbia," their life "a mosaic of frozen pizzas, skateboards and well-kept lawns." Against this image of orderliness and abundance, the reporters stressed the "hand-to-mouth lives" of those "left behind": "They have never ridden in an airplane, stayed in a hotel or eaten chocolate. They do not have a car or TV"; "the family's address is Alley 116, and the home is a mishmash of corrugated tin and plywood . . . The home's shower doubles as the dishwasher, but at least the family has running water and electricity, unlike many in Vietnam"; and "the older children left behind make about a dollar a day. At times, they cannot afford salt, much less meat . . . His tiny 5-year-old daughter has a persistent cough. Her front teeth are black, and no one is sure why." The reporters also projected that divergent lives begot divergent futures by contrasting the bright prospect of the American-raised teenager who "wants to be a pediatrician" to the already-doomed future of the granddaughter in Vietnam who "probably won't finish middle school."

In the following segment, the article's "would-have-been" trope is unambiguous:

> CONTRASTING ROUTINES: Daughter Be Ba Tran . . . can earn 50 cents a day by doing other families' laundry. The plank she walks on behind her home serves as a bridge over a polluted creek. Children sometimes play there, and the fat rats don't

bother to scurry out of the way when people pass by. On the other side of the world, her sister, Kieu Tien Tran, 17, returns to her parents' modest two-bedroom apartment in Stanton with a load of family laundry.

The message is clear: But for the opportunity provided by being "on the other side of the world," Kieu Tien Tran's life *would have been* as miserable as that of Be Ba Tran; she would have had to do other families' laundry instead of her own, walking over "polluted creek[s]" instead of "well-kept lawns."

The overrepresentation of "rags-to-riches" refugee stories is misleading since the economic status of many Vietnamese Americans is characterized by unstable, minimum-wage employment, welfare dependency, and participation in the informal economy.[23] To be sure, some news reports feature both successful and unsuccessful refugees. In "Three Roads from Vietnam," reporters Philip Pan and Phuong Ly tracked the lives of three friends who were fellow military academy graduates and officers in the South Vietnamese Air Force: Xuan Pham, Hai Van Chu, and Giau Nguyen.[24] Once peers, their lives in the United States have diverged considerably, with Pham now a prosperous research engineer, Chu a comfortable computer programmer, and Nguyen a struggling dishwasher. Although the story is purportedly about the men's divergent lives in the United States, the authors said little about how U.S. conditions have affected the men's life chances. Instead, the story is about *luck*: the lucky Pham who "had the opportunity to escape the country" on the day Saigon fell and Chu who left relatively soon after; and the unlucky Nguyen who endured twenty years in Vietnam before he could "get out." The reporters attributed the men's divergent lives solely to their fate on April 30, 1975: "Today, their lives continue to be influenced by what transpired *on a single day*, by the happenstance that determined who made it out and who didn't." Once again, the point is simple: only by "mak[ing] it out" could Vietnamese partake in the good life. By reducing Vietnamese's life chances to "circumstances on a single day," the reporters "skipped over" the long war that preceded that "single day" and discounted the power structures that continue to constrain the life chances of even the "lucky" ones who made it to the United States.

"All I Ever Wanted . . . Was Freedom":[25] Vietnamese in "The Land of The Free"

On the 25th anniversary of the Fall of Saigon, reporters assured American readers that all Vietnamese refugees ever wanted was *freedom*, and that this freedom could be found only in the United States. This rhetoric of liberation and emancipation, so crucial for U.S. world domination since World War II, was what transformed the Vietnamese from "enemies" to "liberated" (from foes to lovers of freedom), and the United States from "war aggressor" to "freedom protector." By treating the United States as self-evidently "*the* Democratic nation par excellence,"[26] reporters (re)deployed a racial lexicon that produced Vietnam as a global region to which freedom is a foreign principle, and the United States as that to which freedom is an indigenous property.[27] For instance, a *Los Angeles Times* article stated that Vietnamese refugees have a "love and hate relationship" with freedom: while the refugees "treasure the freedoms of their new home" and are "amazed by the freedom they see [here]," they also "have less tolerance for . . . freedom than the average American population" because "they came from a country that didn't have freedom."[28]

Constituted as existing on the other side of Freedom, Vietnamese could only be incorporated into modern subjecthood as the *good refugee*; that is, only when they reject the purported anti-democratic, anti-capitalist (and thus anti-free), communist Vietnam and embrace the "free world."

Otherwise absent in U.S. public discussions on Vietnam, Vietnamese refugees become most visible and intelligible to Americans as anti-communist witnesses, testifying to the communist Vietnamese government's atrocities and failings. Repeatedly, we read accounts of Vietnamese boycotting Vietnam-produced books, magazines, videos, and television broadcasts, waving American flags while shouting anti-Communist slogans, denouncing human rights violations committed by the "corrupt" and "heartless rulers of Vietnam," and plotting the overthrow of the communist government.[29] As discussed earlier, in the post-Cold War and especially post-9/11 era, the refugees' reliance on old Cold War rhetoric to *remember* their history alongside that of U.S. nationalist history has become increasingly futile.

Most often, news reporters deploy the anti-communist trope to valorize capitalism, equating "freedom" with economic access and choice, upward social mobility, and free enterprise. As U.S. Rep. Dana Rohrabacher (R-CA-45) opined in a press release on the 25th anniversary, "The compelling difference between [Vietnamese American] success and the poverty and underdevelopment in their homeland is democracy and freedom."[30] By many news accounts, Vietnamese refugees who "arrived in the United States with little more than the shirts on their back" are "living the American dream, a dream unimaginable 25 years ago."[31] This narrative of opportunities bolsters the myth of "private property as fundamental to human development" and promotes "freemarket/capitalist and procedural notions" of freedom, citizenship, and Democracy, rather than the more radicalized social transformations.[32] As John Fiske suggests, a standard way of marking the difference between capitalist and communist societies is through the language of commodities. According to this capitalist myth, consumer choice promotes individual "freedom," enabling individuals to have control over their social relations and their points of entry into the social order.[33] This narrative is evident in commentator Karnow's glowing assessment of post-Vietnam United States: The United States has emerged from the war "as the world's sole superpower, inspiring people everywhere to clamor for free enterprise, consumer products, the unbridled flow of information and, above all, a greater measure of democracy."[34] It is this collapsing of capitalism into freedom and democracy that discursively distances "the free world" from "communism" and more recently from "terrorism;" and it is this alleged distance that justifies continued militaristic intervention in the service of defending and bestowing freedom. It is no wonder that President Bush regularly evokes past war "successes" and the rhetoric of freedom to sanctify U.S. military conduct in the Middle East: "The United States has adopted a new policy, a forward strategy of freedom in the Middle East. This strategy requires the same persistence and energy and idealism we have shown before. And it will yield the same results."[35]

Private Grief and Public Achievements: The Postwar Generation

While the media and scholars often hold up Vietnamese, especially the second generation, as an example of the quintessential American immigrant success story, the socioeconomic conditions in which most Vietnamese children found themselves have been greatly insecure, "comparable only to those encountered by children of the most underprivileged native minority group."[36] In 1990, the poverty rate of the Vietnamese in the United States stood at 25 percent, down from 28 percent in 1980 but still substantially higher than the national average of 12 percent.[37] According to the 2010 census, the proportion of Vietnamese families living below the poverty line had dipped to 12 percent but was still higher than the national average of 10 percent.[38] Focusing on the postwar generation, this section argues that Vietnamese attempts at prosperity are often valiant, if not always successful, efforts to manage and compensate for the personal and material losses incurred by their families during and after the war.

The information in this section came primarily from in-depth tape-recorded interviews that my then-research assistant, Thuy Vo Dang, and I conducted with 60 Vietnamese Americans—30 men and 30 women—in Southern California between 2005 and 2010.[39] The majority of the respondents (57 percent) were born between 1981 and 1985; 26 percent between 1975 and 1980; and 17 percent between 1986 and 1990. Over half of the respondents (55 percent) were born in Vietnam; 38 percent in the United States; and 7 percent in a refugee camp. The majority reported that they grew up in economically struggling households: 91 percent of the respondents' parents held non-professional jobs such as gardener, custodian, construction worker, and manual laborer for men; and manicurist, seamstress, housecleaner, and child or elderly caretaker for women. A number of respondents reported that their parents did "random" or "odd" jobs or that they were "jack of all trades." Several unemployed fathers stayed home and took care of their children while their wives worked. And yet, at the time of the interviews, 95 percent of the respondents were in college or had earned a college degree.

For the majority of the interviewees, economic insecurities haunt their home life. The young Vietnamese Americans in my study depicted migration to the United States as a move toward economic instability, replete with unstable, minimum-wage employment, lack of health insurance, and welfare dependency. The downward spiral was especially bitter for formerly well-to-do refugees and their families. Liên Ngô, who came to the United States in 1982 at the age of ten, stated that her childhood ended abruptly when she witnessed her father's humiliating downward mobility:

> My dad, he was really wealthy in Vietnam, and he supported all of his thirteen brothers and sisters. Well, when he came over here and got a mechanic job, the mechanics discriminated against him. They thought that he didn't know anything so they gave him the janitor's job of cleaning the shop. My mom told me that . . . when she saw him cleaning the mechanics shop, she just started crying in the car. So that made me cry too. He was the boss and now he came over to America and he's a janitor.

Growing up, many of my respondents were hyper-aware of and anxious about their dire economic circumstances. Take Lan Hoàng's case, for example. Since coming to the United States as a boat refugee in 1983, Lan's monolingual father has toiled as a janitor for a hotel, a school, and a supermarket; he also had a second job delivering pizza. Their chronic poverty crushed her father's spirit: "When my dad gets really drunk, he gets so emotional and he starts talking about his life, about what he accomplished and not accomplished, coming to America. Mostly what we hear is that he feels like he works so hard but he gets nowhere. He compares us to other people like people who have houses and everything and we don't have anything and we live paycheck by paycheck." Lan's mother contributed to the family's meager income by working as an electronic assembler, even when working with a microscope made her physically sick: "It can make you nauseous. And so she'd like throw up and she'd come home and tell my dad. And my dad just said, 'Well, you can't throw up all the time because if you keep doing that they won't let you work there.'"

It is true that downward mobility and economic insecurity is an immigrant story, and not a refugee-specific one. However, our interviewees invariably trace their family's economic hardship back to war-related events, and not to migration. For Erin Duong, learning about the war helped her to understand her parents better:

> I think early on I recognized that my stories, my family, my culture are different. How much so, how abnormal or how unnatural these things were, I didn't really fully grasp

until I was much more mature. Probably not until I got to college and then I started to fully understand that this doesn't happen to everyone. I mean my family, they were refugees and they came from a country that was ravaged by war and their lives were endangered. There were broken families and my dad was born in 1950 and the country was at war in 1954 and then until 1975. So all of his life basically, there was war and that he had to grow up in. So it wasn't until I started to understand the context of what my family came from and when they were raised, that I began to understand their perspective and why they came here. And why they are so harsh on me and wanting me to excel and take advantage of the opportunities that I have. So it's a long process of understanding.

Many interviewees felt deeply and personally responsible for realizing their parents' dream of "making it" in the United States. Their sense of responsibility was palpable: it had cost their parents too much to get here; it was their responsibility to fulfill their parents' dream of family success via intergenerational mobility. Below are some examples of this sentiment:

I compare my life to what my parents had to go through. It's amazing, what they had to go through and the life that they built, from nothing to everything that they have given us. I don't think a lot of people my age have to think about that stuff. They don't think about what their parents did and how hard they worked. That's part of the reason why I try to work hard to make my parents proud. It's because I think about all they've given me. Just to make them happy everyday for them to look at their children and know that *they* made a difference.

Ngiêp Ngô

When the Communists came, there were no opportunities. There was nothing for my dad to do. When he talks about how he grew up, there is a certain mentality that he has which is that there is a whole generation of young men like him whose futures were just wasted. He lived almost twenty years under Communist rule, and no one could be an intellectual. There was just no room for that, and I think that he really regretted it. It was a waste. My dad came here in his late forties and he had to catch up with the rest. And he'd had a really hard time. So he kept telling me and my brother that you need to go to school, graduate, work, and have a great life. I feel that they came here for our future and so now it's up to us to make it happen.

Thao Hô

I think that the only reason why I intended to be pre-med was because of my parents and what they went through. I thought that this was the only way that I would be able to repay them.

Hiên Duong

In recent years, scholars have begun to explore how marginalized groups, and not only elites, use money and consumption to raise or secure their social standing. As Alex Kotlowitz reports, it is primarily as consumers—as "purchasers of the talisman of success"—that poor black youth claim social membership to the larger U.S. society.[40] In her insightful study of children of Asian immigrant entrepreneurs, Lisa Sun-Hee Park likewise shows that it is through conspicuous consumption that young Asian Americans attempt to claim their, and by extension their parents', social citizenship, or belonging as Americans.[41] In other words, college and career choices are less, or not only, a sign of Vietnamese assimilation and social acceptance, and more of a complex and strategic response to their and their parents' forcible and "differential inclusion" into U.S. society. Having grown up in dire poverty, young Vietnamese Americans, like Lan Hoàng, knew that they needed to make money: "I was like who says money is not everything? Money is everything, you know. If you get sick and need to go to the doctor, how do you go to the doctor? Money, you know. The food you eat and the clothes you wear, you need money. And so if someone says money isn't everything, they're wrong. *Money is everything.*" For the majority of the young people whom I interviewed, their investment in success and money is meant to improve the lot and status of their families, and not only or primarily about the pursuit of personal achievements. This investment in intergenerational economic mobility is much more than a reflection of "Vietnamese core cultural values": their alleged strong work ethic, high regard for education, and family values.[42] Rather, it exhibits the poignant and complex ways in which Vietnamese refugees and their children use public achievements to address the lingering costs of war, to manage intimacy, to negotiate family tensions, and to assure their social position and dignity in the racially and economically stratified United States.

No matter their resolve, living for their parents—for their dreams—exacts a lot of personal costs. Some interviewees related that their childhood years were spent working alongside their parents to help improve the family's economic situation:

> I helped out my mom with the sewing jobs. I've done that ever since we came when I was in fourth grade up until high school. So yeah, I remember a lot of things, like how we would stay up until five or six in the morning to make the deadline. Probably one of the reasons why she did that is so that she can stay home and take care of the family. With the sewing job, she can do it anytime. It's funny because whenever I go to sleep, I would hear the machine and the noise. So when we quit, which was pretty recent since it was only a few years ago, I still keep on hearing the noise. I would still hear it, until I left for college and I was away from the machine. That's when I stopped hearing it.

For many others, their financial obligation to their parents influenced their job and other economic decisions. As Vân Nguyen recounted:

> My brother and sister worked as young as they could when they were fourteen. So did I. We did different jobs like work in the supermarkets and at flea markets. My brother is the oldest and when he came [to the United States], he was fifteen. He had a hard time adjusting. He went to a community college. He's very smart, but he somehow felt isolated. So he joined the US Navy when he was nineteen . . . My sister stayed and went to a state university and graduated with a business degree. With this business degree, she works enough to make money to support my parents. We recently bought a house which was split evenly between my brother and my sister. My brother is paying more just because he's in the military and he has more of the federal income . . . My brother recently tried to get out of the military because your contract ends every four years and you renew it every four years. So we are all trying to get him to leave, but he feels an obligation. He said that if he comes back now, then how will he find a stable income to pay the mortgage. So he feels a deep financial obligation. We told him that we will work together as a family and figure something out. Financially, it is always a family decision. We don't really think about who that house will go to or whose name that house will go under. It's a family house and we will do whatever to support it.

The pressure to contribute to the family economic wellbeing has at times led to unwise and desperate undertakings such as gambling. As Hieu Truong related:

> My parents had random jobs. They didn't speak English. My mom sewed clothes for a couple of years. My dad helped her and then did other random jobs including being a gardener, working at McDonalds, and being a home caretaker. Then my older brother was really smart so he was taking classes, but then he realized that the family needed more money. He was in college at that time, so he just said that he would take a year off to make some money and then he would go back to school. But he didn't. He went into gambling mode, but I think it was out of good motivation. He really wanted to help out the family. My other brother went into gambling mode too, so it was really bad. The stress just affected us in all different ways. All of us have good intentions to help out the family. But we were all helpless in a way.

In this section, I have offered an alternative explanation for the postwar generation's seeming drive to succeed: what appears to be an act of economic assimilation is in actuality an indicator of the ongoing costs of war. When asked what Americans should know about the Vietnam War, many respondents offered this answer: that the war did not end in 1975. As Hieu Truong exclaimed: "For my family, [the war] never really ended. People said it ended, but it still went on even after the takeover." Many interviewees insisted that Americans pay attention to "not only what happened during the war but also what happened after the war," and "to know about the people and what happened to them when they came here." In the end, for these young Vietnamese Americans, when they consider the Vietnam War, they think most about what had happened to their family after they came to the United States. This is the part of the war that they knew most intimately and shared most freely. Their insistence that we pay heed to family life is an important reminder that wars affect not only the realms of politics and economics, but also "people's intimate social ecologies."[43] As such, the domains of the intimate—in this case, Vietnamese family life—constitute a key site to register the lingering costs of war that often have been designated as over and done with in the public realm.

Conclusion

Situating Vietnamese refugees within the long durée of U.S. military colonialism in Asia, I have argued that the refugees, as the widely publicized objects of U.S. rescue fantasies, have ironically become the featured evidence of the appropriateness and even necessity of U.S. war in Vietnam. The iconic images of desperate and frantic Vietnamese, wailing with pain, grief, and terror as they scrambled to escape "communist Vietnam" at any costs, have visually and discursively transformed the Vietnamese from a people battered by decades of U.S. warfare in Vietnam to those persecuted by the Vietnamese communist government and rescued by the United States.[44] In short, Vietnamese refugees, whose war sufferings remain unmentionable and unmourned in most U.S. public discussions of Vietnam,[45] have ironically become the featured evidence of the appropriateness of U.S. actions in Vietnam: that the war, no matter the cost, was ultimately necessary, just, and successful. For the postwar generation, the war has become a shifting specter that explains or explains away past transgressions, family tensions, and/or economic instabilities; and a constant motivator that pushes them to assuage private grief with public achievements. The postwar generation's practice of looking to their present conditions in order to understand their parents' past corroborates one of the strongest and most enduring premises of Walter Benjamin's conception of history: the belief that it is not history that enables us to understand the present but, conversely, the present that enables us to understand the past.[46] This conception of history suggests that there is no way to close off new understandings of the Vietnam War, even for the postwar generation(s); and that it is precisely through the domains of the everyday that people remember, forge, and transform a past that has been long suppressed.

Notes

1. Wagner-Pacifici and Schwartz, 1991: 381.
2. Ruben Rumbaut, "Vietnamese, Laotian, and Cambodian Americans," in *Contemporary Asian America: A Multidisciplinary Reader*, Eds. Min Zhou and James Gatewood (New York and London: New York University Press, 2000), 180.
3. Bruce Dunning 1989, "Vietnamese in America: The Adaptation of the 1975–1979 Arrivals" in *Refugees as Immigrants: Cambodians, Laotians, and Vietnamese in America*, Ed. David W. Haines (Totowa, NJ: Rowman and Littlefield), 55.
4. David W. Haines, "Introduction" in *Refugees as Immigrants: Cambodians, Laotians, and Vietnamese in America*, Ed. David W. Haines (Totowa, NJ: Rowman and Littlefield, 1989), 14–23.
5. For example, Kenneth Skinner and G. Hendricks, "The Shaping of Ethnic Self-Identity Among Indochinese Refugees," *Journal of Ethnic Studies* 7, no. 3 (1979): 25–41; Paul Starr and Alden Roberts, "Community Structure and Vietnamese Refugee Adaptation: The Significance of Context," *International Migration Review* 16 (1985): 595–613; and Nathan Caplan, John K. Whitmore, and Quang L. Bui, *The Boat People and Achievement in America: A Study of Family Life, Hard Work, and Cultural Values* (Ann Arbor, MI: University of Michigan Press, 1989).
6. Developed during the peak years of mass immigration from Europe at the turn of the twentieth century, this narrative predicts that with each succeeding generation, US ethnic groups will improve their economic status and become progressively more similar to the "majority culture." See for example, W. Lloyd Warner and Leo Srole, *The Social System of American Ethnic Groups* (New Haven, CT: Yale University Press, 1945), 294–295; Robert Park, *Race and Culture* (Glencoe, IL: Free Press, 1950). While no longer bound by a simplistic assimilationist paradigm, the narrative of immigration has remained "America-centric," with an overwhelming emphasis on the process of becoming American.
7. Christine Finnan, "Occupational Assimilation of Refugees," *International Migration Review*, 15, no. 1 (1981): 300–301; see also Nathan Caplan, John K. Whitmore, and Marcella H. Choy, *The Boat People and Achievement in America : A Study of Family Life, Hard Work, and Cultural Values* (Ann Arbor, MI: University of Michigan Press, 1989); Ruben Rumbaut and John Weeks, "Fertility and Adaptation: Indochinese Refugees in the United States," *International Migration Review* 20, no. 2 (1986): 428–466; Reginald Baker and David North, *The 1975 Refugees: Their First Five Years in America* (Washington, DC; New TransCentury Foundation, 1984); Robert Gardner, Bryant Robey, and Peter Smith, "Asian Americans: Growth, Change, and Diversity," *Population Bulletin* 40, no. 4 (1985).
8. Finnan, "Occupational Assimilation of Refugees," 309, 299, emphasis added.
9. Ibid., 300.
10. Caplan et al., *The Boat People*, 56.
11. Ibid., 136.
12. Min Zhou and Carl L. Bankston III, *Growing Up American: How Vietnamese Children Adapt to Life in the United States,* (New York: Russell Sage, 1998).
13. Sturken 1997; Rowe 1989; Nguyen 2002.
14. In 2000, the Gallup poll found that while 70 percent of Americans knew that the United States had lost the Vietnam War, nearly one in five believed incorrectly that U.S. troops had fought on the side of North Vietnam. Underscoring the generational disconnect, Americans over the age of 30 were more able than younger respondents to place the United States correctly on the side of South Vietnam. www.sad17.k12.me.us/teachers/bburns/com/documents/ttc/gallup_poll_on_vietnam.htm. Accessed May 10, 2016.
15. President George Bush first enunciated his vision of the "New World Order" in a speech before a joint session of Congress in September 1990, and then in a State of the Union address in January 1991.
16. McCombs 2000: F1.
17. Karnow 2000.

18 Wexler 1992: 9–38.
19 Arnett 2000.
20 Arnett 2000. Other examples of "would-have-been" stories: Nguyen, Nam Hoang 2000a and 2000b; Curnutte 2000.
21 Curnutte 2000.
22 Gold and Tran 2000b.
23 Gold and Kibria 1993; Ong and Umemoto 1994. See also the following newspaper story: Arax, 1987.
24 Pan and Ly 2000.
25 Gold and Tran 2000a.
26 Alexander and Mohanty 1997: xxx.
27 Silva 2005.
28 Tran 2000.
29 Martelle and Tran 2000; "Protestors Urge Boycott" 2000; Harris 2000; Hong 2000; Truong 2000.
30 "House Passes Resolution Remembering the Fall of Saigon." Press release. www.house.gov/royce/vietnamfall.p.htm, posted June 19, 2001.
31 "House Passes;" Curnutte 2000; Mangaliman 2000.
32 Alexander and Mohanty 1997: xxix, xxxiii.
33 Fiske 2000: 324.
34 Karnow 2000.
35 White House 2003.
36 Zhou 2001: 194.
37 Zhou 2001: 193.
38 U.S. Census 2010. In 2011, poverty level is defined by the federal government for a family of four with income under $22,350 a year.
39 We interviewed Vietnamese Americans in these counties: San Diego, Riverside, Orange, and Los Angeles. I thank the following transcribers: Maya Espiritu; Evyn Espiritu; Niko Arranz; Mimosa Tonnu; Hao Tam; and Sally Le.
40 Kotlowitz 2000: 257.
41 Park 2005.
42 Zhou and Bankston 1998.
43 Stoler 2006: xi.
44 In a study of the representation of Southeast Asian refugees in academic and popular discourse, Thomas DuBois notes a fascination in particular with refugee escape narratives, with "the events belonging to the escape itself . . . presented in minute detail" while the events preceding or following the escape "are narratively telescoped into mere hints or allusion" (DuBois 1993: 5). Popular oral history collections that detail the refugees' traumatic escape, all done in the name of "helping" the refugees to "express themselves in their own terms," further reinscribe the refugees as only victims in the U.S. imaginary. See Freeman 1989: 10.
45 Nguyen-Vo 2005.
46 Benjamin 1973.

References

Arax, Mark. 1987. "Refugees Called Victims and Perpetrators of Fraud." *Los Angeles Times*, February 10.
Arnett, Elsa. 2000. "The Boat People." *San Jose Mercury News*, 23 April.
Baker, Reginald and David North. 1984. *The 1975 Refugees: Their First Five Years in America*. Washington, DC: New TransCentury Foundation.
Benjamin, Walter. 1973. "Theses on the Philosophy of History." In *Illuminations*, edited by Hannah Arendt. Fontana/Collins. 245–255.
Caplan, Nathan, John K. Whitmore, and Quang L. Bui. 1989. *The Boat People and Achievement in America: A Study of Family Life, Hard Work, and Cultural Values*. Ann Arbor, MI: University of Michigan Press.
Caplan, Nathan, Marcella H. Choy, and John K. Whitmore. 1991. *Children of the Boat People: A Study of Educational Success*. Ann Arbor, MI: University of Michigan Press.
Curnutte, Mark. 2000. "Victories Follow a Lost War: Many Vietnamese Have Built Successful Tristate Lives." *The Cincinnati Enquirer* 30 April.

DuBois, Thomas A. 1993. "Constructions Construed: The Representation of Southeast Asian Refugees in Academic, Popular, and Adolescent Discourse." *Amerasia Journal* 19: 1–25.

Dunning, Bruce. 1989. "Vietnamese in America: The Adaptation of the 1975–1979 Arrivals." In *Refugees as Immigrants: Cambodians, Laotians, and Vietnamese in America*, edited by David W. Haines. Totowa, NJ: Rowman and Littlefield. 55–85.

Finnan, Christine. 1981. "Occupational Assimilation of Refugees." *International Migration Review* 15: 300–301.

Fiske, John. 2000. "Shopping for Pleasure: Malls, Power, and Resistance." In *Consumer Reader*, edited by Juliet B. Schor and Douglas B. Holt. New York: The New Press. 306–328.

Freeman, James. 1989. *Hearts of Sorrow: Vietnamese American Lives*. Stanford, CA: Stanford University Press.

Gardner, Robert, Bryant Robey, and Peter Smith. 1985. "Asian Americans: Growth, Change, and Diversity." *Population Bulletin* 40.

Gold, Scott and Mai Tran. 2000a. "Vietnam Refugees Finally Find Home." *Los Angeles Times* 24 April: A1+.

Gold, Scott and Mai Tran. 2000b. "The Echo of War." *Los Angeles Times Magazine* 30 April: 10+.

Gold, Steve and Nazli Kibria. 1993. "Vietnamese Refugees and Blocked Mobility." *Asian and Pacific Migration Review* 2: 27–56.

Haines, David W. 1989. *Refugees as immigrants: Cambodians, Laotians, and Vietnamese in America*. Lanham, MD: Rowman & Littlefield.

Harris, Bonnie. 2000. "Ceremony to Remember Fall of Saigon Stirs Powerful Emotions." *Los Angeles Times* 1 May: B5.

Hong, Binh Ha. 2000. "Scars of Vietnam Drive Hunger Strike." *Orange County Register* 1 May: 7.

Karnow, Stanley. 2000. "Vietnam: 25 Years After the Fall." *San Jose Mercury News* 23 April.

Kotlowitz, Alex. 2000. "False Connections." In *The Consumer Society Reader*. Center for 21st Century Studies/University of Wisconsin-Milwaukee. 253.

McCombs, Phil. 2000. "The Haunting." *Washington Post* 30 April: F1.

Mangaliman, Jessie. 2000. "Vietnamese Shine in the Lone Star State." *San Jose Mercury News* 29 April.

Martelle, Scott and Mai Tran. 2000. "Vietnam TV Broadcasts Anger Emigres." *Los Angeles Times* 27 April: A1+.

Nguyen, Nam Hoang. 2000a. "Pilot Waited for his Moment." *San Jose Mercury News* 23 April.

Nguyen, Nam Hoang. 2000b. "Former Military Surgeon Feels San Jose is Now Home." *San Jose Mercury News* 23 April.

Nguyen, Viet Thanh. 2002. *Race and Resistance: Literature and Politics in Asian America*. Oxford: Oxford University Press.

Nguyen-Vo, Thu Huong. 2005. "Forking Paths: How Shall We Mourn the Dead?" *Amerasia Journal* 31: 157–175.

Ong, Paul and Karen Umemoto. 1994. "Life and Work in the Inner-City." In *The State of Asian Pacific America: Economic Diversity, Issues, and Policies*, edited by Paul Ong. Los Angeles: LEAP Asian Pacific American Public Policy Institute and University of California at Los Angeles, Asian American Studies. 87–112.

Pan, Philip P. and Phuong Ly. 2000. "3 Roads From Vietnam." *Washington Post* 30 April.

Park, Lisa Sun-Hee. 2005. *Consuming Citizenship: Children of Asian Immigrant Entrepreneurs*. Stanford, CA: Stanford University Press.

Park, Robert. 1950. *Race and Culture*. Glencoe, IL: Free Press.

"Protestors Urge Boycott of Vietnamese Media." 2000. *Los Angeles Times* 30 April: B3.

Rowe, John Carlos. 1989. "Eyewitness: Doumentary Styles in the American Representations of Vietnam." In *The Vietnam War and American Culture* edited by John Carlos Rowe and Rick Berg. New York: Columbia University Press. 148–174.

Rumbaut, Ruben. 2000. "Vietnamese, Laotian, and Cambodian Americans." In *Contemporary Asian America: A Multidisciplinary Reader*, edited by Min Zhou and James Gatewood. New York and London: New York University Press. 175–206.

Rumbaut, Ruben, and John Weeks. 1986. "Fertility and Adaptation: Indochinese Refugees in the United States." *International Migration Review* 20: 428–466.

Silva, Denise Ferreira da. 2005. "A Tale of Two Cities: Saigon, Fallujah and the Ethical Boundaries of Empire." *Amerasia Journal* 31: 121–134.

Skinner, Kenneth and G. Hendricks. 1979. "The Shaping of Ethnic Self-Identity Among Indochinese Refugees." *Journal of Ethnic Studies* 7: 25–41.

Starr, Paul and Alden Roberts. 1985. "Community Structure and Vietnamese Refugee Adaptation: The Significance of Context." *International Migration Review* 16: 595–613.

Stoler, Ann Laura. 2006. "Preface." In *Haunted by Empire: Geographies of Intimacy in North American History*, edited by Ann Laura Stoler. Durham, NC: Duke University Press. xi–xiii.

Sturken, Marita. 1997. *Tangled Memories: The Vietnam War, the AIDS Epidemic, and the Politics of Remembering*. Berkeley, CA: University of California Press.

Tran, Mai. 2000. "Poll Finds Paradox Among Vietnamese in Orange County." *Los Angeles Times*, 20 April: B5.

Truong, Noelle. 2000. "The Time's Not Right for Reconciliation." *Orange County Register* 14 May: 4.

Wagner-Pacifici, Robin, and Barry Schwartz. 1991. "The Vietnam Veterans Memorial: Commemorating a Difficult Past." *The American Journal of Sociology* 97: 376–420.

Warner, W. Lloyd and Leo Srole. 1945. *The Social System of American Ethnic Groups*. New Haven, CT: Yale University Press.

Wexler, Laura. 1992. "Tender Violence: Literary Eavesdropping, Domestic Fiction, and Educational Reform." In *The Culture of Sentiment: Race, Gender, and Sentimentality in Nineteenth-Century America*, edited by Shirley Samuels. New York and Oxford: Oxford University Press. 9–38.

Zhou, Min and Carl L. Bankston III. 1998. *Growing Up American: How Vietnamese Children Adapt to Life in the United States*. New York: Russell Sage.

7

REFUGEE MEMORYSCAPE
The Rhetoric of Hmong Refugee Writing

Chong A. Moua

In a letter addressed to Father Yves Bertrais and his Hmong cultural center staff, Shoua Yang (Suav Yaj) asked for a book on Hmong wedding rituals and an audiocassette of Hmong poetry songs.[1] He went on to explain that he wanted the audiocassette of poetry songs because "mother and father have now left for Laos and this has saddened me so I would like to listen to it [the audiocassette]."[2] In addition to asking for books and the audiocassette, at the end of the letter, he also requested one more thing from the cultural center:

> And please help send this message to mother and father and all the younger brothers who have successfully interviewed and gone back to Laos . . . that we, your son and daughter-in-law, who are living at the Napho refugee camp are doing well (noj qab nyob zoo).[3]

Shoua Yang's letter, written in 1995 from Ban Napho refugee camp in Thailand, is one of the thousands of letters that Hmong people from all over the diaspora wrote to Father Bertrais, his cultural center in French Guiana, his radio program, and mission in Thailand. While the majority of the letters were basic requests for books on Hmong history and culture and primers to learn to read and write in the Hmong language, interspersed throughout are letters like Shoua Yang's. Letters like Shoua Yang's, written mostly in the Hmong language using the Hmong Romanized Popular Alphabet (RPA) script, show how displaced Hmong refugees used writing to move between and reconnect across borders in attempts to reconcile the fractures that had been caused by the fallout of their involvement on behalf of the U.S. in the Secret War in Laos during the Southeast Asian War.

These letters are one facet of the refugee archive in which Hmong refugee figures and their writing are evidence of the U.S. imperialism in Southeast Asia. The refugee archive makes significant intervention in both form and content by centering the refugee figure as a site of critical analysis as well as an embodied category that produces knowledge.[4] In reading not only what Hmong refugees wrote but also how they wrote, this essay examines the expressions of displacement brought on by the U.S.'s failed military efforts to contain communism in Southeast Asia, in particular the Secret War in Laos. What these particular displaced histories transmit is Hmong refugees' desire to reconnect and maintain familial ties at a historical moment when the Hmong diaspora experienced further fracturing as a result of the Secret War. At the same time, these letters also simultaneously revealed a desire for more literacy among Hmong refugees. Letters like Shoua Yang's contained a message to be relayed to a relative or family member as well as a request for more language primers and books to read.

Refugee Memoryscape

By analyzing the letters written from Hmong refugees in Thailand between 1978 and 1999, this essay explores how refugee practices of memory or remembrance, like that of writing letters, are useful archival sites to look for the traces of U.S. imperialism in Southeast Asia that are not represented in any popular national narrative.[5] Father Yves Bertrais and the large collection of letters he and his mission collected are important to conceptualizing the Hmong refugee memoryscape.[6] Father Bertrais is especially significant in regards to the written Hmong language because he played a central role in developing the script popularly used in the present day to write and communicate in the Hmong language, as well as working to help spread Hmong literacy.[7] The script known as the Hmong RPA was a collaborative effort between Father Bertrais, two Protestant missionaries, William Smalley and G. Linwood Barney, and two Hmong assistants, Ya Ying and Tho Hu, in Laos in 1953.[8] The completion of the Hmong RPA enabled Father Bertrais to begin promoting the use of the script through missionary work and the printing of both religious and cultural publications in the Hmong language. These included Hmong language learning materials, such as primers, but also religious publications about Christianity. However, the majority consisted of publications about Hmong culture and traditions, like folktales and marriage and funeral rituals. The significance of Father Bertrais, the cultural center he established in 1977 in French Guiana, the Hmong radio program he created in 1994, and the Good Shepherd Mission founded in Thailand in 1999, is that it created a place, a cultural space, for the emergence of a Hmong refugee public memory in two senses: one, it allowed Hmong refugees to create memory as a collective body or as a "public" and two, it made possible the visible manifestation of memory in the sense of rendering a memory, or a history, public.[9]

The landscape on which refugee memory interacts with global forces is part of the larger cultural complex of the global memoryscape. In theorizing memory as movement along a global landscape, Kendall R. Phillips and G. Mitchell Reyes contend that memories and memory practices disrupt and contest other, older forms of remembrance and ways of conceptualizing the past that are largely framed in terms of national and local practices. The disruption, in turn, enables new memories and practices of remembrance to emerge that provide more nuanced modes of knowledge production to critique people and their processes of connection and disconnection from nations.[10] As the part of the refugee archive concerned with the reproduction and dissemination of memory, the refugee memoryscape brings into focus the imperialist encounters between nation-states that violently disconnect people from their geographic locations and consequently turn them into refugee subjects. This cultural scape, however, is not just characterized by violence and ruptures, but is also a site of recuperation, resistance, and knowledge production. With this framework in mind, this essay relies on the ideal of refugee memoryscape to open up a space to analyze the way Hmong refugees have remembered and talked about their trauma.

Rhetoric of Hmong Refugee Writing

Writing is a relatively new dimension of the Hmong refugee memoryscape, existing in popular form since only the late 1950s. History, genealogy, and cultural and ritual knowledge between generations in Hmong society have traditionally been passed down through oral traditions.[11]

The absence of a writing culture and written texts have led some scholars to use labels such as illiterate, non-literate, or preliterate to describe Hmong culture and society. The significance of Hmong refugee letter writing exceeds the narrow frames of prescriptive words that only focus on writing as an acquired skill instead of an historical event. Hmong refugee literacy was a product of the chaotic environment that witnessed American imperialism attempting to bolster a declining French empire and against the backdrop of Laotian civil war and decolonization. Examining how the convergence of these overlapping contexts promoted and complicated Hmong refugee literacy embodies John Duffy's argument that literacy, defined as the ability to read and write at a basic level, is better theorized as a rhetorical process of development.[12] In treating the context and environment in which people learn to read and write as "rhetoric(s)," literacy becomes a method of employing the written language to contest, re-create, and re-imagine the past.[13]

Qhua Meeb Vaj's undated book request, written on a half sheet of lined paper and addressed to no one in particular, shows the complex terrain of Hmong refugee memoryscape.[14] The ordinariness of Qhua Meeb Vaj's letter betrays what it reveals about the rhetoric of Hmong refugee writing.

1 Ntawv zaj tshoob, 3 phau	1 Book of wedding rituals, 3 books
2 ntawv khawv [kwv] tx[h]iaj 2 phau	2 Book of Hmong poetry songs, 2 books
3 cov ntawv hauv paug 3 phau	3 Book about beginnings, 3 books
4 ntawv ອງກົດ–look at the life-	4 English book, Look at the Life
5 thov ib li npas. kuv cov tub ntaus pob	5 One ball. My sons like to play ball.
thov koj pab kom tau raws li kuv thov no	I hope you will be able to help me with what I have requested.
sau npe qhua meeb vaj (tshav kuam vaj) 12ດ-10 ຫາແສວ ຈວ ແມວ ວວ	Signed qhua meeb vaj (tshav kuam vaj)

His letter made requests that were not unusual of Hmong refugees writing to Father Bertrais and his staff. He used this opportunity to ask for multiple copies of several books, including a Christian religious text and a book in English, as well as for a ball for his sons to play with. It is, however, the manner in which Qhua Meeb wrote his letter that underscores how the rhetoric of Hmong refugee writing contains traces of the conditions and interconnected imperial encounters that rendered Hmong into refugees. Qhua Meeb's simple book request contains a complex and layered history of Hmong engagement and involvement with multiple rhetorics that enabled Hmong literacy. His strategic usage and blending of Hmong RPA, Lao, and English within the letter contests the charge of Hmong being "preliterate." Instead, it shows a Hmong man with the knowledge of at least three writing systems. Even though Qhua Meeb may not have been equally fluent in all three languages, he was proficient enough to know how to use them to communicate effectively his request for books and a toy for his sons.[15]

In the 1950s, Hmong slowly began to acquire literacy primarily through three specific contexts: village schools established by the Laotian government, service in the Hmong military, and encounters with Christian missionaries.[16] Prior to that, formal educational opportunities for the Hmong in Laos were virtually nonexistent. Even though the French established a secular education system in Laos in 1917, it was not until 1939, at the continued request of Hmong leaders, that the first school was built for Hmong students in Nong Het in Xieng Khouang province.[17]

Educational opportunities expanded as schools were built in Hmong-populated areas in Xieng Khouang. These schools, however, remained part of the larger colonial structure because the primary language of instruction remained Laotian. While Qhua Meeb most likely learned the Lao language at such a school, it was probably not until the refugee camp period that he would learn English and Hmong RPA as missionary groups and religious organizations made up a large number of volunteers helping to resettle Hmong refugees.[18] Hmong refugees writing to Father Bertrais reflected a complex history of literacy and engagement with different colonial and dominant societies and writing systems by using multiple languages in their correspondences.

Hmong Writing Memory as Refugee Archive

In addition to documenting a history of encounters with colonial states, Hmong refugee writing in the immediate post-1975 period also revealed its consequences in the displaced reality of splintered Hmong lives. Moreover, this particular set of letters to Father Bertrais and his cultural center and staff would establish the emergence of a refugee archive that's made only possible because of Hmong involvement with imperial contests in Southeast Asia. Yeng Hang's (Ham Yeeb) 1978 letter from Ban Vinai Refugee Camp was a multi-literate letter addressed specifically to Father Bertrais. In his letter, Yeng Hang recounted the time when he and Father Bertrais had sought refuge together in the mountains with other Hmong villagers in 1960 during the war when the Vietnamese had invaded where they were living in northern Laos. He and Father Bertrais became separated because he left Laos early for Thailand. Yeng Hang went on to ask for help in resettling to France. He asked Father Bertrais to

> help ติดต่อ (contact) and เจ้าหน้าที (officials) who used to come around to register people to go to Thailand. See if they can help me and my family go to France because we [his family] live in poverty and have suffered in many ways living here in Thailand.[19]

At the end of his letter, Yeng writes his address as:

Hang Yeng
Camp Refugies Hmong Ban Vinai
P.O. Box 31, Pakchom, Loei
Centre 1, Quartier 2, Maîson 1
Thailand

Yeng's usage of Thai words throughout his letter and the presence of the French language reveal that refugee memoryscapes, and refugee histories, are littered with evidence of their encounters with host and hostile states.

Nus Thoj Yaj also documented Hmong refugees' contained and marginalized experiences in the refugee camps. His letter reveals that since 1994, the officials at Ban Napho Detention Center have consistently mistreated them, using various tactics to coerce the Hmong refugees to agree to repatriate back to Laos. Nus Thoj lamented:

> Because we [the Hmong] do not have a country to live in, we live in their land [Thailand] and so when we sew a piece of embroidery, it seems as if we have killed someone [and] we get punished, and detained to be sent back to Laos. And if we sew a Hmong shirt or pair of pants to wear, we are also punished and asked to pay

3,000–4,000 Baht. If we don't have it [the money] we get taken away and locked up until we agree to go back to Laos.[20]

In linking the suffering of Hmong in refugee camps to the fact that the Hmong are stateless, without a homeland country, Nus Thoj underscores the territorial reality of the refugee status. For the Hmong, it is the historical lack of a homeland, and for most other refugees, the loss of the homeland, through war and military conflicts, that detach the refugee from the nation. The nature of this forced severance, argues Khatharya Um, shapes the liminal diasporic identity of Southeast Asians, and I would add of refugees, in that the place of their being is not necessarily, and certainly not singularly, the place of their belonging.[21]

In the absence of a state, homeland, or originary territory, the Hmong place of belonging is that of the family and kin. The letters that sought to use Father Bertrais and the cultural center, and the Hmong language radio program he created in 1994 as a vehicle to send messages to family members across distances demonstrate how Hmong refugees have used the landscape of the refugee memoryscape to construct and maintain a sense of familial belonging across space. The globalizing force of war disrupted the locality of Hmong life, but also created new ways for Hmong articulation and engagement with one another by spurring the interactions that would bring the technologies of writing, printing, mail delivery, and radio within the realm of the Hmong. The specificity of name and place in the letters that sought to (re)connect with loved ones shows how it is at the level of family that the Hmong attempt to recuperate from the losses of war and forced displacement. Suav Yaj's letter, which appeared at the beginning of this essay, specifically stated that the message that he and his wife were doing well be sent to his parents by the name of Tooj Tuam Yaj, who lives in the city of Nambaak in Luangprabang province, in Laos. The sender of the message, he added, is "your son, Suav Yaj, who lives in the Ban Napho refugee camp."[22]

In similar fashion, Pao Choua Chang (Pob Tsuas Tsab) requested the message, "We, the sons and uncles are faring well in Thailand except that we miss you all very much," be sent to their aunt and uncle by the name of Chong Yee Her and another aunt by the name of Maiv Suas, living in Samneua, Laos.[23] This pattern of family names and places establishes a specific lineage so that the message would not get lost or mistaken when transmitted in other publications or over the radio waves. In this way, Hmong refugees used writing to communicate and connect across increasing geographic distances. Rather than simple communications, these letters are attempts to maintain familial connection despite the separation. The writing of family names and places in the letters, coupled with the way that it gets recited and disseminated by Father Bertrais's radio program and publications, establishes family as the site and method of recuperation.

Letters like the one from Koua Chang Thung Sai expressed a deep desire to establish familial and kin relations across and despite national boundaries. Koua Chang Thung Sai, in Chiang Rai, Thailand wrote to Father Bertrais in April of 1988 looking for family and relatives despite being an orphan. In an attempt to find family through writing to Father Bertrais, Koua Chang wrote:

> The life of being an orphan on this earth is extremely sad. It has been difficult since being displaced without land or a place [to live] to Thailand . . . I am 20 years old and do not yet have a wife . . . Below, I will recount a little bit of my history for you. A long time ago, when my grandparents lived in China, they were named Zoo Kim Tsawb. [Another set of grandparents] one was named Nyiaj Xab Tsab, the second was named Moos Theeb. The one that left [China] to live on the border of Laos and

China was named Txoov Kaub Tsab. Then [they] moved to Moos Nab and then to Phuaj Moos where they had my father Txhiaj Kawb Tsab. They have all since passed. My father died after they moved to Naj Keem in Laos. After my father died, [I] moved to Thailand where I first lived in Huab Xais and then moved to Toos Xai in the province of Chiang Rai. If I have any relatives out there, please write to find me. Please help love and care for me as [being an orphan] I am extremely impoverished. I pray daily so that I may have the opportunity to be with you all.[24]

To ensure that he would find his closest relatives, from the same lineage within the Chang clan, Koua Chang also described the burial practices of his family on the back of the letter before signing off with his name. He wrote that "in the past, our gravesites have been in the style of the Chinese but at the moment, we have changed to Hmong style gravesites."[25] For Koua Chang, displacement entailed losing his home and his entire family. When writing to Father Bertrais, he chose to use the opportunity to look for family members to recuperate the losses he had suffered as a result of the war. By providing a detailed history of his family's lineage down to the detail of rituals such as burial practices, Khoua Chang sought reconciliation of his displaced status through the means of recovery and reconnection at the kin level.[26] Despite having attachments to neither family, land, nor nation, the orphaned refugee uses writing to connect with other Hmong refugees as kin through the refugee memoryscape.

The Silence of Hmong Refugee Women Writing

Letters from Hmong refugee women to Father Bertrais and his staff were few from 1978 to 1999. The convergence of the imperial wars for control and dominance between France, Laos, and the U.S. in Southeast Asia and traditional Hmong society negatively impacted the literacy development of Hmong women. Hmong access to education has historically been limited and inconsistent due to lack of government investment and political instability brought on by the competing forces of French and American imperialism and Laotian decolonization. Before the French arrived in the late nineteenth century, institutionalized education in Laos came in the form of traditional pagoda schools operated in tandem with Buddhist temples. French-sponsored schools began to appear in the first decade of the twentieth century in provincial towns and elsewhere and were taught by trained, secular-teachers.[27] Despite a 1917 French law that decreed the opening of a primary school in every village, mass education was not the goal of the indigenous Lao elite or the French colonialists.[28] The French did not invest as much in building an educational infrastructure in Laos as they did elsewhere in French Indochina, as they were only interested in building up a small corps of Lao civil servants for administrative purposes.[29] The Lao elite received a French education in Hanoi, Saigon, or France and French schools were only established in the big cities with the main purpose of serving the French students whose parents were part of the French administration.[30]

It was not until after Laos gained independence from France that Hmong educational prospects improved. Access to education and literacy increased for the Hmong because of their alliance with the U.S. during the Secret War in Laos. At the behest of Hmong leaders like General Vang Pao and aid from programs like the U.S. Agency for International Development (USAID), a development entity of the U.S. government, schools for Hmong children were built as well as teacher training schools.[31] However, the prospect of widespread educational access that the war and alliance with the U.S. had brought was short-lived. The military alliance between the Hmong and the CIA, however, proved to be an unstable backdrop for the hopes of increasing Hmong access to education. This debilitating effect created a "literacy paradox" in which "more Hmong students were exposed to education than ever before, yet the result was not the advent of widespread literacy but instead destruction," resulting in the abandonment of village schools, the devastation of villages, and the deaths of tens of thousands of Hmong men, women, and children.[32]

Education for Hmong women remained minimal, even after the proliferation of schools in the 1960s. In the 1920s and 1930s, heads of various Hmong clans began sending their sons and male relatives to French elementary schools.[33] The numbers, however, remained small as the schools were too selective and too expensive for Hmong families.[34] Sending sons and male relatives to school reflected gendered norms within Hmong patriarchal society. Even though Patricia Symonds writes that "women and men hold complementary roles in the biological, social, and cosmological process of birth," she continues by stating that Hmong women as well as men ultimately view that "maleness is Hmong."[35] Despite women and men having complementary roles in the birth process, it is through the male that the lineage and patriline continue from generation to generation. Hmong society would continue to live on without Hmong women but "Hmongness" would cease to exist if all Hmong men were to die.[36] According to Pranee Liamputtong Rice's study of Hmong women and reproduction practices, "gender inequality [within Hmong society] begins at birth with the burial of the placenta." The boys' placentas are buried at the most important part of the house, namely by the middle post where the spirit of the clan resides, while girls' placentas are buried under the birth bed, signifying the inferior status of Hmong women.[37] It is only in the afterlife that the male and female, and in turn, Hmong men and women, become equal.[38]

Elite and wealthy Hmong families who sent their sons to school rarely bestowed the same opportunity on their daughters.[39] The small number of Hmong women who were educated were so through attending missionary boarding schools or were recruited to be trained as nurses during the 1960s and 1970s.[40] And even when elite Hmong families began to send their daughters to school in the 1970s, the percentage of literate Hmong women made up less than one percent of the entire Hmong population in Laos.[41]

Of the letters that reached Father Bertrais and his staff from Hmong refugees in Thailand from 1978 to 1999, only four were from Hmong women. One letter was a response to a survey that Father Bertrais's mission sent out via their publication *Liaj Luv Chaw Tsaws* (The Nest of Swallows and Sparrowhawks) to their readers.[42] Mai Houa Xiong's October 1999 letter expressed gratitude for the books she had received. Moreover, Mai Houa revealed that

> I have taught my younger brothers how to read from the book of how to learn Hmong poetry songs. In regards to the two books of Hmong poetry songs and the book of folklores, they have kept me company. When I am free and have nothing to do, I read from it and it helps relieve my worries.[43]

The informal teaching of Hmong RPA within households and villages that Mai Houa Xiong referenced was a common way in which literacy spread. Many who wrote to Father Bertrais and his staff asked for multiple copies of the books on Hmong folklore and the language learning primers in order to share with family or friends or to replace those that families and friends had taken.

Speaking to the gendered contours of the rhetoric of Hmong refugee writing are the letters of Nplas Vaj and Mos Lis. Nplas Vaj's undated letter was addressed specifically to a female staff member, Maiv Nrhoob Vaj, whom the letter writer thanked for sending her letters and books. In particular, Nplas Vaj wanted to thank the staff member because younger sister, I have been learning from the two books [that you sent] up until today. Please read this letter that I wrote you slowly and carefully. If there are any mistakes please let me know because I have never held a pencil before. And this is my first time writing a letter and I'm not very good so please excuse any mistakes.[44]

Nplas Vaj's letter was the first instance of her entrance into the Hmong refugee memoryscape through writing. What is unclear or unwritten in Nplas Vaj's letter is how she has managed to request the books from which she learned how to read and write. Insight as to how Nplas Vaj came to possess literacy in Hmong RPA may be gleaned from Mos Lis' September 9, 1998 letter. Sent from Khek Noi, Thailand, Mos Lis' letter looks like a typical book request. She asked for five books, three of which were Hmong folklore books, volumes one through three. Her address on the label is written in Thai.[45] It is, however, the signing of her name, "Mos Lis," that further shows another dimension of Hmong refugee writing. The signature of "Mos Lis" at the end of the letter was markedly different from the handwriting of the rest of the letter. The signature "Mos Lis," rather, resembled more of the handwriting of a beginner, the ink lines dark and heavy from taking her time and being careful. The shapes of the letters of the signature were also uneven in size, mixing upper and lower case letters together. Clearly not written by her, Mos Lis' letter makes it evident that her literacy development is in the early stages of the process and that this letter was likely written by a male family member or relative. What they do point to is that within the rhetoric of Hmong refugee writing, Hmong women's experiences and voices are textually silenced. Colonialism and Hmong involvement within the various contests for control over the former region of Indochina have suppressed the literacy development of Hmong refugee women. If the Hmong alliance with the U.S. was a paradox that eliminated the possibility of widespread literacy for the Hmong within Southeast Asia, this paradox has been doubly felt by Hmong women.

Conclusion: Family as Expression of Sovereignty

On the margins of an August 1999 letter, Phauj Ntxhais, a staff member at Father Bertrais's Good Shepherd Mission, noted that she had already broadcast the message that Phauj Maiv Vwj requested help to disseminate during the August 19, 1999 announcements, just eight days after receiving the letter. Phauj Maiv Vwj wanted to urge her three cousins in Laos to write because she and her children, who are faring well in Thailand, miss and think of the cousins often.[46] The recurring theme of a desire to (re)establish family and kin relationships reinforces that it is the form of the family through which Hmong refugees attempt to express sovereignty. The letters examined in this essay treat the search for family and kin in the post-Secret War period as a simultaneous expression of statelessness and sovereignty. Hmong refugee letters articulated statelessness as beyond geographical displacement to include separation of families, adding more nuance to the historical statelessness of the Hmong. That Hmong refugees requested books and language materials in order to gain more literacy in the same letter as using literacy to reconnect with family provides significant insight on different ways to think about the nation and the boundaries of the nation. In using family and kin as the method to challenge the violent disruption of colonialism and war, Hmong refugees demonstrate a contestation of state power, both national and imperial, through the formation of an extra-territorial sovereignty. By using literacy and writing to not only document but reconnect families against the backdrop of forced displacement, Hmong refugees rebuild a Hmong nation through familial networks articulating a stateless sovereignty outside the bounds of any nation, land, or territory.

Notes

1. I would like to thank Dr. Geraldo Cadava and my colleagues Ashley Barnes-Gilbert, Brendon George, Rachel Gross, Ariana Horn, and Jillian Jacklin for their comments and fruitful discussion on an earlier version of this essay which I then presented at the 2014 Annual Conference of the Organization for American Historians.

    I also wish to thank Larry Ashmun for his help in the proof reading and translation of Lao and Thai words found in the letters.

    In this essay, when the authors of the letters have provided a Romanized version of their Hmong name, I will use that spelling of their name as the primary while supplying their Hmong name in parentheses. Otherwise, I will use their Hmong names as they are written in Hmong Romanized Popular Alphabet (RPA).

    Additionally, all the letters analyzed in this essay were written mainly in the Hmong language using the Hmong RPA script. Any quote or information taken from the letters has been translated into English and all translations are mine unless noted otherwise.

2. Shoua Yang (Suav Yaj), October 5, 1995, Bertrais Collection, Box 11, Folder 35, Department of Special Collections, Memorial Library, University of Wisconsin-Madison.

3. Ibid.

4. Ma Vang theorizes that the "refugee archive" is where the refugee figure is the trace of the collision of the archives about and by refugee. More importantly, Vang emphasizes that the refugee archive situates Hmong *displaced histories* as a site of historical analysis crucial to tracing knowledge transmission and production outside of the official record. Not only is the Hmong refugee figure a site of critical analysis but it is also an embodied category that produces knowledge. For more, see Ma Vang, "Displaced Histories: Refugee Critique and the Politics of Hmong American Remembering" (PhD diss., University of California, San Diego, 2012), 6, 2.

5. The period from 1978 to 1999 encompasses the era of the refugee camps that first opened in Thailand after 1975 by the Royal Thai Government to deal with the massive overflow of displaced peoples and refugees created by the end of the Southeast Asian War and the civil wars in Laos and Cambodia.

6. Not all of the letters were addressed to Father Bertrais. Some of them were specifically addressed to particular staff members of the cultural center, radio program, or mission. In cases where a specific person was not named, the letters were addressed generally to the cultural center, the mission, or the radio program. Of the 49 folders of letters from Thailand that I read, there were two folders of letters which had no clear indication as to when they were written by the author or received by the missionary staff.

7. For a brief biography of Father Yves Bertrais's life and missionary work with the Hmong, see Philippe Chanson, "Le père Yves Bertrais des Oblats de Marie Immaculeé (1921–2007)," in *Histoire Missions Chrétiennes*, vol. 4, no. 4 (2007): 183–191. www.cairn.info/zen.php?ID_ARTICLE=HMC_004_0183 (accessed June 1, 2014). Also see Xia Vue Yang, "Fr. Yves Bertrais," http://aumonerie.hmong.free.fr/TP_Nyiaj_Pov/PereBertraisBiography.pdf (accessed June 1, 2014). For a discussion of how Father Bertrais's work with the Hmong and publication efforts blended missionary work and anthropology, see Violet Thor, "Father Yves Bertrais: O.M.I.: The Good Shepherd and Anthropologist" (M.A. thesis, University of Wisconsin-Madison, WI, 2013).

8. By the time Father Bertrais, G. Linwood Barney, and William Smalley met in Luang Prabang, Laos in 1952, Bertrais and Barney had each created his own script as a result of their missionary work living with the Hmong. Bertrais's script was based on the White Hmong dialect while Barney's was based on the Green Hmong dialect. Smalley, on the other hand, did not know the Hmong language but was a specialist in linguistics and phonetics and his expertise helped merge the two systems that Bertrais and Barney had created into a singular, more standardized version. For more on the creation of the Hmong RPA script, see Yves Bertrais, "How the 'Hmong R.P.A.' Was Created and Has Spread from 1953 to 1991." The original article was written in Hmong in three successive issues of the "Liaj Luv Chaw Tsaws" Bulletin that Bertrais's Hmong cultural center printed and circulated.

9. For a discussion of the meanings and usage of "public memory" see *Framing Public Memory* by Kendall R. Phillips, (Tuscaloosa, AL: University of Alabama Press, 2004).

10. Kendall R. Phillips and G. Mitchell Reyes, Introduction to *Global Memoryscapes: Contesting Remembrance in a Transnational Age*, Eds. Kendall R. Phillips and G. Mitchell Reyes (Tuscaloosa, AL: University of Alabama Press, 2011), 2, 13, 8. Phillips and Reyes borrow from cultural theorist Arjun Appadurai's

conception of globalization. According to Appadurai, globalization is the movements of people and ideas across a complex and varied global landscape. In a similar fashion, Phillips and Reyes envision the movement of *memory* along the same global landscape. For Appadurai, the global landscape is composed of a group of shifting and often conflicting cultural "scapes." To this framework of cultural "scapes" Phillips and Reyes add the "global memoryscape." For more on Appadurai's concept of globalization as a process of encounters between different cultural "scapes" see Arjun Appadurai, "Disjuncture and Difference in the Global Culture Economy," in *The Phantom Public Sphere*, ed. Bruce Robbins (Minneapolis, MN: University of Minnesota Press, 1993): 269–295.

11 For more on Hmong oral traditions and practices see Yer J. Thao, *The Mong Oral Tradition: Cultural Memory in the Absence of Written Language* (Jefferson, NC: McFarland & Company, Inc., Publishers, 2006). Thao interviewed 13 Mong elders about their lives in the highland of Laos and the role that oral traditions played. From the life stories of the elders, Thao details how oral traditions are central to Hmong identity and maintenance of Hmong culture and ritual knowledge. Thao, however, also highlights that resettlement to the U.S. has brought the Hmong into contact with a literate society and forms of formal education that present challenges to the continuance of oral traditions within Hmong society.

12 John Duffy's work on Hmong American writing and literacy argues that labels like "preliterate" are inadequate and devalue the cultures to which they are applied and obscure the historical processes through which literacy is promoted or suppressed. See John M. Duffy, *Writing from these Roots: Literacy in a Hmong-American Community*, (Honolulu, HA: University of Hawaii Press, 2007), 19. He defines "literacy" as the ability to read and write at the primary school level or above. Thus "literate" then is the possession of the skills to perform these acts. And "literacy development" refers to the gradual accumulation of these skills over time. In this essay, I use these terms as Duffy has defined them. See *Writing from these Roots*, 7.

13 Ibid., 15, 18. Here Duffy also offers a more detailed definition of "rhetorics" as the ways in which institutions, groups, or individuals use language (and other symbols) for the purpose of shaping conceptions of reality.

14 Qhua Meeb Vaj, No Date, Bertrais Collection, Box 11, Folder 27, Department of Special Collections, Memorial Library, University of Wisconsin-Madison, WI.

15 Duffy contends that individuals like Qhua Meeb Vaj show how the Hmong have experienced diverse forms of literacy in multiple languages over the last century. Moreover, that the Hmong have long been aware of writing systems of the more politically powerful societies around them—that of the Chinese, Vietnamese, Lao, and the Thai. More than just awareness of writing systems, the Hmong also have multiple versions of folk stories about the loss of a Hmong writing system or Hmong book in the Hmong oral tradition. See *Writing from these Roots*, 38, 79.

16 Duffy, *Writing from these Roots*, 79.

17 Yang Dao, "Comments on Educational Policies for the Hmong People of Laos," (Laos: USAID/EDU, 1973), 3. These comments were extracted and translated from Yang Dao's doctoral thesis, "Les Difficultés du Développement Économiques et Social des Populations Hmong du Laos," for informational purposes by the Education Division of USAID/Laos. The content came from the following original pages 163–165, 188–193, 252, 256.

18 Father Bertrais writes that it was in the refugee camp period that young Hmong people had the opportunity to study Lao, Thai, English, French, Chinese, and Hmong RPA. He also notes that after a few years of Hmong people residing in refugee camps, thousands knew the RPA writing system. See Yves Bertrais, "How the 'Hmong R.P.A.' Was Created and Has Spread from 1953 to 1991."

19 Ham Yeeb (Hang Yeng), February 20, 1978, Bertrais Collection, Box 11, Folder 27, Department of Special Collections, Memorial Library, University of Wisconsin-Madison, WI.

20 Yaj Nus Thoj, February 20, 1995, Bertrais Collection, Box 11, Folder 33, Department of Special Collections, Memorial Library, University of Wisconsin-Madison, WI. Ban Napho Detention Center was initially conceived of as a holding place for those who would be repatriated back to Laos. However, eventually, the Thai government allowed some groups to apply for resettlement.

21 Khatharya Um, "Exiled Memory: History, Identity, and Remembering in Southeast Asia and Southeast Asian Diaspora," *Positions* 20:3 (Summer 2012): 836.

22 Shoua Yang (Suav Yaj), May 10, 1995, Bertrais Collection, Box 11, Folder 35, Department of Special Collections, Memorial Library, University of Wisconsin-Madison, WI.

23 Pao Choua Chang (Pob Tsuas Tsab), No Date, Bertrais Collection, Box 11, Folder 25, Department of Special Collections, Memorial Library, University of Wisconsin-Madison, WI.
24 Koua Chang Thung Sai (Kuam Tsab Toos Xais), Received date April 28, 1988, Bertrais Collection, Box 11, Folder 30, Department of Special Collections, Memorial Library, University of Wisconsin-Madison, WI.
25 Ibid.
26 In her study of the Hmong RPA and Hmong Pahawh scripts, MaiGer Moua argues that Hmong refugees in the U.S. have used literacy for political and competing ethno-national purposes. She writes that literate proponents of both the Hmong RPA and Pahawh used the scripts to construct nation in cultural specific terms, disrupt western portrayals of Hmong as illiterate, and to negotiate the process of becoming American. See MaiGer Moua, "Contesting Literacy: Hmong in the United States and Expressions of Statelessness, 1975–2010" (Master's thesis, University of Wisconsin-Madison, WI, 2011). What is significant about Moua's work is that it shows how literacy is not always a stabilizing or unifying tool. While this essay focuses on how Hmong literacy has been used to express the trauma and reconstruction of statelessness, MaiGer Moua's work reveals how literacy also exposes the many fractures caused by statelessness.
27 Meyer Weinberg, *Asian-American Education: Historical Background and Current Realities*, (Mahwah, NJ: Lawrence Erlbaum Associates, Inc., 1997), 176.
28 Ibid., 177.
29 Richard Noonan, "Education in the Lao People's Democratic Republic: Confluence of History and Vision," in *Education in South-East Asia*, Eds. Colin Brock and Lorraine Pe Symaco, (Oxford: Symposium Books, 2011), 71. Noonan writes that in fact the education system in all of French Indochina was managed from Hanoi.
30 Ibid., 73.
31 Duffy, *Writing from these Roots*, 74; Douglas Chuedoua Vue, "The Three Eras of Hmong Educational History in Laos: French Colonial, Laotian Independence, and USAID, 1917-1975," (Ph.D. diss., Capella University, 2008), 26–29.
32 Duffy, *Writing from these Roots*, 77. Edgar "Pop" Buell was the director of USAID, and he together with other Hmong leaders like Moua Lia, built schools for Hmong children. See Weinberg, *Asian-American Education*, 186; Vue, "The Three Eras of Hmong Educational History," for more on Moua Lia's role in expanding educational opportunities for the Hmong in Laos during the 1960s. Moua Lia eventually became the superintendent of the schools in the Xieng Khouang province in Laos. Vue sees the expansion of education during the 1960s period as existing within what he calls the "USAID Era (1961–1975)."
33 Weinberg, *Asian-American Education*, 185.
34 Vue, "The Three Eras of Hmong Educational History," 26.
35 Patricia V. Symonds, *Calling in the Soul: Gender and the Cycle of Life in a Hmong Village* (Seattle, WA: University of Washington Press, 2004), 5, 8.
36 Ibid., 8.
37 Pranee Liamputtong Rice, *Hmong Women and Reproduction* (Westport, CT: Bergin & Garvey, 2000), 26.
38 Symonds, *Calling in the Soul*, 10.
39 Historian Mai Na M. Lee argues that education, especially literacy in a foreign or colonial language, was important to achieving political leadership and legitimacy for the Hmong during the French colonial era. The success of Touby Lyfoung, a well-known Hmong leader, and his family was largely attributed to their ability to be literate in not only Hmong but also Lao and French. While Touby and his brothers were sent far away to school, his sister, Mao Song Lyfoung, was "kept at home like other women of her time" and thus "remained non-literate all her life." See Mai Na M. Lee, "The Dream of the Hmong Kingdom: Resistance, Collaboration, and Legitimacy Under French Colonialism, 1893–1955," (Ph.D. diss., University of Wisconsin-Madison, WI, 2005), 6, 265–272, 208.
40 Dia Cha, "Women in the Hmong Diaspora," in *Diversity in Diaspora: Hmong Americans in the Twenty-first Century*, Eds. Mark Edward Pfeifer, Monica Chiu, and Kou Yang, (Honolulu, HA: University of Hawaii Press, 2013), 170.
41 Ibid., 171.
42 Mao Lee Her (Mos Lig Hawj), Received October 1, 1999, Bertrais Collection, Box 11, Folder 48, Department of Special Collections, Memorial Library, University of Wisconsin-Madison, WI.

43 Mai Houa Xiong, October 12, 1999, Bertrais Collection, Box 11, Folder 49, Department of Special Collections, Memorial Library, University of Wisconsin-Madison, WI.
44 Nplas Vaj, No Date, Bertrais Collection, Box 11, Folder 25, Department of Special Collections, Memorial Library, University of Wisconsin-Madison, WI.
45 Mos Lis, September 20, 1998, Bertrais Collection, Box 11, Folder 43, Department of Special Collections, Memorial Library, University of Wisconsin-Madison, WI.
46 Phauj Maiv Vwj/Neng Vang, August 4, 1999, Bertrais Collection, Box 11, Folder 45, Department of Special Collections, Memorial Library, University of Wisconsin-Madison. I list both Phauj Maiv Vwj (who we know is female because the Hmong word "phauj" means "aunt") and Neng Vang (typically, but not always, this English spelling of the Hmong name "Neng" refers to a male) as possible authors because it is unclear as to who wrote the letter. Phauj Maiv Vwj is the name that signed off at the end of the letter; however, Neng Vang is the name listed on the return address on the envelope. It is entirely possible that Phauj Maiv Vwj wrote the letter but put Neng Vang as the return address because he is the head of the household she lives with.

References

Appadurai, Arjun. "Disjuncture and Difference in the Global Culture Economy." In *The Phantom Public Sphere*, edited by Bruce Robbins, 269–295. Minneapolis, MN: University of Minnesota Press, 1993.
Bertrais, Yves. "How the 'Hmong R.P.A.' Was Created and Has Spread from 1953 to 1991." N.D.
Cha, Dia. "Women in the Hmong Diaspora." In *Diversity in Diaspora: Hmong Americans in the Twenty-first Century*, edited by Mark Edward Pfeifer, Monica Chiu, and Kou Yang, 165–187. Honolulu, HI: University of Hawaii Press, 2013.
Chanson, Philippe. "Le père Yves Bertrais des Oblats de Marie Immaculeé (1921–2007)." *Histoire et Missions Chrétiennes* 4, no. 4 (2007): 183–191. Accessed June 1, 2014. www.cairn.info/zen.php?ID_ARTICLE=HMC_004_0183.
Duffy, John M. *Writing from these Roots: Literacy in a Hmong-American Community*. Honolulu, HI: University of Hawaii Press, 2007.
Moua, MaiGer. "Contesting Literacy: Hmong in the United States and Expressions of Statelessness." MA thesis, University of Wisconsin-Madison, 2011.
Phillips, Kendall R. *Framing Public Memory*. Tuscaloosa, AL: University of Alabama Press, 2004.
Rice, Pranee Liamputtong. *Hmong Women and Reproduction*. Westport, CT: Bergin & Garvey, 2000.
Symonds, Patricia V. *Calling in the Soul: Gender and the Cycle of Life in a Hmong Village*. Seattle: University of Washington Press, 2004.
Thao, Yer J. *The Mong Oral Tradition: Cultural Memory in the Absence of Written Language*. Jefferson, NC: McFarland, 2006.
Thor, Violet. "Father Yves Bertrais: O.M.I.: The Good Shepherd and Anthropologist." MA thesis, University of Wisconsin-Madison, 2013.
Um, Khatharya. "Exiled Memory: History, Identity, and Remembering in Southeast Asia and Southeast Asian Diaspora." *positions* 20, no. 3 (Summer 2012): 831–850.
Vang, Ma. "Displaced Histories: Refugee Critique and the Politics of Hmong American Remembering." PhD diss., University of California-San Diego, 2012.
Vue, Douglas Chuedoua. "The Three Eras of Hmong Educational History in Laos: French Colonial, Laotian Independence, and USAID, 1917–1975." PhD diss., Capella University, 2008.
Weinberg, Meyer. *Asian-American Education: Historical Background and Current Realities*. Mahwah, NJ: Lawrence Erlbaum Associates, Inc., 1997.
Yang, Dao. "Comments on Educational Policies for the Hmong people of Laos." Translated by Rebecca Weldon for Education Division of USAID/Laos. 1973. Original from Yang Dao, "Les difficultés du développement économiques et social des populations Hmong du Laos." PhD diss., Université de Paris, 1972. Pages 163–165, 188–193, 252, 256.
Yang, Xia Vue. "Fr. Yves Bertrais." Accessed June 1, 2014. http://aumonerie.hmong.free.fr/TP_Nyiaj_Pov/PereBertraisBiography.pdf.

8

PROSECUTING THE KHMER ROUGE

Cambodian American Memory Work

Cathy J. Schlund-Vials

To destroy you is no loss, to preserve you is no gain.
> Khmer Rouge slogan, *Pol Pot's Little Red Book:*
> *The Sayings of Angkar*[1]

It [life under the Khmer Rouge] was a slow death. People were walking skeletons; their eyes so deeply sunken into their sockets that I couldn't tell who was who. Everyday I saw dead bodies wrapped in blankets taken away to be thrown in the river, fed to the fish, or left behind bushes of bamboo to rot.
> Seng Ty, *The Years of Zero: Coming of Age Under the*
> *Khmer Rouge (2013): 67–68.*

By the time Pol Pot took the capital Phnom Penh. / His military has reached over thirty thousands. / They emptied cities, bomb banks, and cleared out prisons./ Separated families, eliminated private property, and outlaw religions. / There was no warning shot, what's told was never twice. /It was total chaos, they destroy all aspects of social and cultural life . . . It's about POWER, TERRITORY, and RICE, /And of course that comes with a hefty price./ Whenever there's WAR, there's always sacrifice, /And it's usually the innocent who lose their life . . .
> praCh (Prach Ly), "Power, Territory, and Rice,"
> *Dalama: The Lost Chapter*, 2003.

Thirteen days before the American War in Vietnam (1959–1975) came to a dramatic close with the April 30, 1975 "Fall of Saigon," the Khmer Rouge (a.k.a. "Red Cambodians") marched triumphantly into Cambodia's capital, Phnom Penh. Dressed in black uniforms, draped in red checkered *kramas*, and armed with Chinese-issue AK-47s, the Khmer Rouge entered the Southeast Asian municipality atop Soviet army tanks, in battered military jeeps, and on rubber-sandaled foot.[2] The April 17, 1975 arrival of Khmer Rouge troops tactically coincided with the nation's New Year observances; incontrovertibly, their presence in the Cambodian urban hub signaled profound "in country" political shifts. Initially, the Khmer Rouge appeared to be harbingers of a much-anticipated peace: Loudspeakers accompanied soldiers as they made their way through Phnom Penh's major thoroughfares and marketplaces, blaring promises of armistice, assurances of reconciliation, and guarantees that U.S. intervention in the region and civil war had come to an end.

To briefly recapitulate, in the face of an overt and internationally recognized neutral position vis-à-vis the American War in Vietnam, Cambodia (like its Southeast Asian neighbors, Thailand and Laos) became an undeniable *realpolitik* front in the conflict.[3] Guided by the politically vexed assumption in Washington that Cambodia contained supply stops and way stations on the Ho Chi Minh Trail, the Richard M. Nixon administration covertly supported the euphemistically named "Operation Menu" (1969–1970) and "Operation Freedom Deal" (1970–1973) campaigns, which involved recurrent and controversial B-52 bombings of the nation's rural areas.[4] As historian Ben Kiernan persuasively summarizes, by 1973, "half a million tons of U.S. bombs had killed over 100,000 peasants and devastated the countryside.[5] Encompassing almost half of Cambodia's eastern landmass, the quantity of munitions tonnage used during both campaigns was the equivalent of five Hiroshima bombings and surpassed the total amount deployed during the entirety of the American Pacific campaign throughout World War II.[6]

Such catastrophic policy interventions, along with the concomitant installation of the right-wing Lon Nol government (in 1970), destabilized an already tenuous political situation, thrusting the Southeast Asian country into a bloody civil war between anti-communist and communist forces. Subsequently, by the time the Khmer Rouge assumed control of Phnom Penh, the city had witnessed a mass influx of Cambodians warily seeking refuge from the war-torn landscape. Roughly two million people (25 percent of the nation's population), faced with the wholesale destruction of their homes and militarized annihilation of their livelihoods, relocated from rural areas to Cambodia's cities; in Phnom Penh alone, the city's population ballooned from 600,000 in 1970 to almost two million by 1975.[7] Situated perpendicular to this bellicose milieu, many of the capital city's denizens cheered the arrival of the Khmer Rouge on the understandable presupposition that their victory represented an unambiguous conclusion to war. Others, less certain as to what exactly lay in store, sat anxiously in their homes awaiting radio updates from "Voice of America" broadcasts. Soldiers of the now-defeated Lon Nol government abandoned their green uniforms and attempted to blend into civilian crowds; still others tried to continue their lives "as usual" by heading out to market and going to work.

Yet, as the hours, days, weeks, and months that followed the April 1975 takeover of Phnom Penh would appallingly make clear, there would be no return to "normalcy." Nor would the nation experience anything resembling a lasting peace. Consumed with an overwhelming desire to enact a classless, agricultural revolution "by any means necessary," the Khmer Rouge (a.k.a. *Angkar*, or "the organization") systemically emptied Cambodia's cities (often at gunpoint) and renamed the nation "Democratic Kampuchea."[8] Key to the regime's revolutionary mission was forcibly turning the country back to "year zero," which its leadership (particularly "Brother Number One" Saloth Sar—a.k.a. Pol Pot—and "Brother Number Two," Nuon Chea, the Khmer Rouge's chief ideologue) emphatically characterized and absolutely imagined as a time *before* so-castigated Western influence.[9] To that end, as Kiernan observes and Khmer American rapper praCh confirms (in the introductory epigraph), *Angkar* abruptly dismantled and violently deconstructed all facets of Cambodian economic, political, social, and cultural life. Formal education was outlawed, Western medicine (namely basic antibiotics such as penicillin) banned, and property ownership forbidden. Currency was eliminated, Theravada Buddhism (the nation's majority religion) was proscribed; familial names (such as *Mak* and *Pa*) were prohibited and classless nomenclature (e.g., "comrade" and "cadre") privileged; children were separated from parents; husbands and wives were forced to live and work apart.[10]

From the outset, the Democratic Kampuchean government targeted pre-revolutionary institutions, which operated as built emblems of pre-Khmer Rouge infrastructure and memory:

following suit, Cambodia's national bank was destroyed; its state-supported library emptied and converted into a pigsty; Buddhist temples were raided and religious relics shattered; the country's public history museum was similarly looted and its roof left to rot. Such offensives against Khmer tradition and the previous regime were by no means limited to economic institutions, knowledge repositories, and heritage sites. Rather, the Khmer Rouge also waged fatal assaults against those who embodied the past via profession, education, and affiliation. Lon Nol officials, officers, and soldiers were summarily executed, along with others deemed "enemies of the people," including civil servants, university students, engineers, doctors, lawyers, monks, and teachers. As the Khmer Rouge continued its reign of terror, those slated for "smashing" (to access *Angkar*'s ominous terminology) were expanded to include the Cham (ethnic Cambodian Muslims), Khmer Khrom (ethnic Cambodians living in southern Vietnam), ex-patriots (who were fellow leftists), Khmer court musicians, classically trained royal dancers, and allegedly disloyal Khmer Rouge cadres.[11] As large-scale dam projects faltered and rice crops failed, the nation descended into mass starvation and wide-ranging famine; those incapable of laboring in Cambodia's rice fields (particularly "new people" from the cities, the sick, the very young, and the elderly) were, as the above-placed Khmer Rouge saying makes clear, distressingly disposable.

Unquestionably, such a disregard for human life was not limited to state-authorized dictate; instead, it was apparent immediately after the regime's deposal. When the Vietnamese ostensibly "liberated" the country on January 7, 1979, an estimated 1.7 million Cambodians (roughly 21–25 percent of the extant population) had perished due to disease, starvation, forced labor, torture, and execution. For those outside Cambodia, this period is devastatingly known as the "Killing Fields" era; for those in the country, it is evocatively referred to as "Pol Pot time." Notwithstanding the relatively short duration of the regime—three years, eight months, and twenty days—its impacts were unassailably ruinous and long-lasting. Following Democratic Kampuchea's 1979 dissolution, approximately 65 percent of the population was female, underscoring the disproportionate number of men killed due to their pre-revolutionary positions as professionals within a traditional gendered labor economy. Three-quarters of Cambodia's teachers died or fled the country; nine judges remained in country; out of an estimated 550 doctors, only forty-eight survived; 90 percent of Khmer court musicians and dancers were dead. In the weeks, months, and years following the political end of Democratic Kampuchea and the concomitant ousting of the Khmer Rouge, an estimated 510,000 Cambodians fled to neighboring Thailand; another 100,000 sought refuge in close-by Vietnam.[12] Between 1980 and 1985, almost 150,000 Cambodians came to the United States, facilitated by the congressional passage of the 1980 Refugee Act. To date, more than 287,000 individuals of Khmer descent live in the United States, making it home to the largest population of Cambodians living outside Southeast Asia in the world.[13]

This particular history of war, genocide, and migration ineludibly undergirds the present-day experiences of first- and 1.5-generation Cambodian Americans, whose harrowing journeys from Cambodia's Killing Fields to the United States foreground a particular mode of refugee subjectivity.[14] Such traumatized personhood, as the opening passage by Seng Ty accentuates, is incontrovertibly constrained by history, undeniably preoccupied with mortality, and necessarily dominated by bereavement. The degree to which Cambodian American cultural producers such as Ty and praCh engage the Killing Fields past is made more urgent when set against a backdrop of overwhelming juridical non-reconciliation. To date, notwithstanding the passage of almost four decades since the Democratic Kampuchean regime drew to a pugnacious close, only three Khmer Rouge officials—Kaing Guek Eav (a.k.a. "Comrade Duch," the head warden of the notorious Tuol Sleng Prison), Nuon Chea ("Brother Number Two"), and Khieu

Samphan (former Democratic Kampuchean Prime Minister)—have been successfully tried and sentenced for crimes against humanity and war crimes.[15] As the title of this chapter suggests, to comprehend the current state of Cambodian American studies (generally) and Khmer American cultural production (specifically) then, one must attend to not only the histories which brought Cambodian refugees "into being"; one must simultaneously account for the ways in which recollections about "Pol Pot time" make discernible a transnational mode of "memory work."[16]

Such remembrance-oriented labor, which in the absence of state-authorized justice assumes a prosecutorial register vis-à-vis the Khmer Rouge and negotiates multiple sites of forgetting, correspondingly demarcates the contemporary parameters of an identifiable Cambodian American selfhood.[17] To contexualize the juridical investments at the forefront of Cambodian American memory work, I briefly recount the ways in which such labor militates against strategic amnesias in the country of origin (Cambodia) and the nation of settlement (the United States) about the Killing Fields era. I simultaneously consider the present-day machinations of the contemporary U.N./Khmer Rouge Tribunal (officially known as the "Extraordinary Chambers in the Courts of Cambodia"), which—despite multinational support and the expenditure of almost $173 million—has substantively failed in its mission to facilitate prosecutions and provide reparations for regime victims.[18] Set against such non-reparative belatedness, I conclude with a critical overview of Khmer American cultural productions about the Killing Fields era—inclusive of Seng Ty's recently published memoir, *The Years of Zero: Coming of Age Under the Khmer Rouge* (2013) and praCh's hip-hop *Dalama* trilogy (2000, 2003, and 2016)—to highlight the juridical, political, and commemorative stakes of contemporary Cambodian American memory work.[19]

Genocide Justice and Juridical Belatedness: The U.N./ Khmer Rouge Tribunal

On December 29, 1998, Cambodian Prime Minister Hun Sen, having just met with members of his newly assembled cabinet, responded to recent reports concerning upper-level Khmer Rouge defections (namely the aforementioned Chea and Khieu Samphan, former Democratic Kampuchean Prime Minister). These high-profile "about-faces" substantively signaled the political end of the Khmer Rouge, which had maintained an active—albeit waning—presence throughout the 1980s and early 1990s (predominantly in nation's uppermost northwestern Pailin province). To reiterate, the regime's demise began with its 1979 overthrow by Vietnamese forces, which ushered the start of the decade-long Vietnamese-occupied People's Republic of Kampuchea era (1979–1989). It was further cemented in 1993 when, after United Nations transitional intervention (1991–1993), the Cambodian monarchy was restored; this royal reestablishment precipitated the surrender of thousands of Khmer Rouge guerrillas—on condition of parliamentary pardon—the following year. In 1996, as Hun Sen's Cambodian People's Party gained control of the country via a successful though controversial coup d'état, Ieng Sary (former Khmer Rouge Foreign Minister and Deputy Leader) switched alliances, defected, and was legislatively exonerated. As significant, on April 15, 1998, "Brother Number One" Pol Pot died peacefully in his sleep while under house arrest.

In an indiscriminate effort to reconcile—once and for all—Cambodia's catastrophic past, Hun Sen, a former Khmer Rouge commander himself, stressed that those heretofore affiliated with the Democratic Kampuchean era should be "welcomed with bouquets of flowers, not with prison and handcuffs," repeating a position he conveyed by way of champagne toast delivered four days prior (December 25) at a dinner held in his palatial Phnom Penh residence.[20] Hun

Sen further clarified his conciliatory stance to reporters, recommending that Cambodians "should dig a hole and bury the past and look ahead to the twenty-first century with a clean slate."[21] Pointedly, the prime minister's insistence on reconciliation through forgetting—demonstrated through governmental pardon and based on the absolution of direct culpability—operated in direct contradiction to international efforts, which at the time were focused on prosecuting Khmer Rouge leaders for crimes against humanity.

To concisely summarize, whereas the Cambodian head of state formerly supported such tribunal efforts, Hun Sen's view (as evidenced by his "blank slate" characterization) dramatically shifted following this latest dissolution of Khmer Rouge leadership. Indeed, when subsequently questioned about the possibility of a tribunal, Hun Sen averred:

> In Cambodia we know how to heal ourselves using our own medicines . . . If we try mixing in foreign medicine it will not cure Cambodian diseases . . . The interests of the nation and the people do not require a trial or conflicts among ourselves, but national reconciliation.[22]

Sen's polemical juxtaposition of "foreign medicine," "Cambodian diseases," and "national reconciliation" inadvertently yet poignantly brings to light a consistent set of governmental, political, and juridical obstacles which continue to undermine state-sanctioned efforts to "put to rest" the nation's genocidal past.[23] Set within a longue durée context of Cold War politics, the limits of present-day human rights law, and ongoing allegations of corruption vis-à-vis the current U.N./Khmer Rouge Tribunal, justice has, quite profoundly, yet to be served in Cambodia.

To wit, while the 1979 Vietnamese invasion of Cambodia effectively ended Khmer Rouge control, the nation (then the People's Republic of Kampuchea) was not recognized as legitimate by the United Nations; in fact, the state's leadership was dismissed in favor of the Khmer Rouge, who were accepted as Cambodia's rightful governing entity.[24] Such non-recognition is in part attributable to a post-1975 U.S. foreign policy which supported the Khmer Rouge via humanitarian aid and multilateral acknowledgement as per an anti-Vietnamese government strategy (1979–1989). Shifting from the political to the juridical realm, this international disavowal was analogously applied to the Vietnamese-supported prosecution of deposed Khmer Rouge leaders. Expressly, in August 1979, the state-authorized People's Revolutionary Tribunal tried Pol Pot and Ieng Sary in absentia for crimes of genocide, which at the time began with the allegation that three million Cambodians perished during the Khmer Rouge era.[25] Dismissed by the United Nations as a "show trial," the tribunal—which took place over a breakneck two-week period—found both Khmer Rouge defendants guilty. Admittedly, the tribunal did not adhere to the tenets of international law insofar as the defense attorneys argued for a guilty verdict and neither defendant was present.[26] Nevertheless, the tribunal did amass a total of 995 pages of witness testimony, which included consistent accounts of systemic torture, organized mass killing, and willful regime neglect (particularly with regard to disease and famine).[27]

Whereas preliminary attempts to try Khmer Rouge officials for crimes against humanity failed due to extenuating Cold War politics, the very charge of genocide vis-à-vis the regime proved equally obstructive. To elucidate, the Khmer Rouge—which, with the exception of the Cham and Vietnamese Cambodians—did not exclusively target one ethnic, racial, religious, or national group; correspondingly, some in the international community have questioned whether what happened during the Democratic Kampuchean era fulfills the current definition of genocide. According to Article II of the 1948 United Nations Convention on the Prevention and Punishment of the Crime of Genocide, "genocide" means any of the following acts committed with intent to destroy, in whole or in part, a national, ethnical, racial, or religious groups, such as: (a) Killing members of the group; (b) Causing serious bodily or mental harm to members of the group; (c) Deliberately inflicting on the group conditions of life calculated to bring about its physical destruction in whole or in part; (d) Imposing measures intended to prevent births within a group; and (e) Forcibly transferring children of the group to another group.

Subsequently labeled by scholars and historians as an "autogenocide," the prosecution of state-sanctioned violence in Cambodia was from the beginning complicated by an inadequate, non-legally binding label. It was not until 1991 that the United Nations began to refer to the Killing Fields period as one marked by genocidal policies. After a seemingly endless back-and-forth between Prime Minister Hun Sen and the United Nations, the hybrid U.N./Khmer Rouge Tribunal was formed in 2003, its judges confirmed in 2006, and heard opening arguments on February 17, 2009 for "Case 001" involving abovementioned Kaing Guek Eav.[28] Currently, the U.N./Khmer Rouge Tribunal (at the moment tasked with trying the regime's senior leadership) has—not without disagreement and with much consternation—indicted defendants for crimes against humanity along with charges of genocide.

Delimited with regard to temporality (April 17, 1975–January 6, 1979), constrained by perpetrator definition (e.g., "senior leaders of Democratic Kampuchea" and "those believed to be most responsible for grave violations of national and international law"), hampered by past declarations to "bury the past," and troubled by the fact former Khmer Rouge still inhabit high-level positions of governmental power, the U.N./Khmer Rouge Tribunal has been overshadowed by claims that it operates as a "masquerade" of justice.[29] On one level, this characterization of "masquerade"—suggestive of false pretense and indicative of obfuscation—pivots on juridical belatedness, particularly with regard to former high-ranking Khmer Rouge officials.[30] As a point of reiterated reference, the regime's leader, Pol Pot, passed away in 1998; General Ta Mok (a.k.a. "The Butcher"), who oversaw the regime's military, likewise died with little incident in 2006. Of the four defendants originally charged with genocide (as per the parameters of "Case 002," a two-part case which issued its first verdict on August 7, 2014), one has died in custody (Sary); another has been deemed mentally incompetent and released due to an Alzheimer's diagnosis (Ieng Thirith, former Khmer Rouge Social Minister). Only two Khmer Rouge leaders—Chea (who is presently 87 years old) and Samphan (aged 83)—remain in custody; while both have been found guilty of crimes against humanity, they are still facing additional genocide charges. The advanced age of the defendants has not surprisingly contributed to an overwhelming sense that justice—as defined by the bounds of international law—will remain upsettingly elusive and distressingly open-ended.

On another level, this bleak characterization of juridical failure is fixed to structural amnesias and preemptive omissions (with regard to temporality, history, and politics). For example, the tribunal's prosecutorial timeline fails to accommodate for the historical registers of the regime (which undeniably extend before and after its official three-year, eight-month, twenty-day reign). This strict historicization similarly disremembers the international politics which brought the Khmer Rouge "into being," particularly the aforementioned illegal U.S. bombings of the Cambodian countryside, China's sustained support of the regime (as its primary financial and ideological apparatus), and its post-1979 support by the United Nations.[31] Moreover, the emphasis on senior leaders tactically forgets the role of lower-level cadres and other Khmer Rouge perpetrators.[32] Alternatively, such critical assessments about the hybrid U.N./Khmer Rouge Tribunal are made even clearer when compared to the indictments pursued in other human rights tribunals and in light of constant allegations of corruption. Whereas the Extraordinary Chambers in the Courts of Cambodia have issued a total of five indictments, 177 were pursued during the Nuremberg Trials (1946–1949); 95 for the Rwandan Genocide (1993); and 22 for the Serra Leon Civil War (1991–2002). Last, but certainly not least, despite the almost $200 million spent on bringing former Khmer Rouge leaders to justice, tribunal employees (particularly Cambodians) have not been paid, its judges have faced bribe allegations, and the Victims Support Section (VSS)—tasked with representing survivors via reparation — continues to struggle with adequate funding and consistent leadership.[33] Set against this dizzying, problematical backdrop, as Cambodian American survivor and juridical activist Theary C. Seng critically characterizes, "this is no longer a legitimate court. It's a sham. It does such a disservice to Cambodian victims and international justice in general."[34]

Prosecution, Remembrance, and Commemoration: Cambodian American Memory Work

Whereas internationally sanctioned tribunals and state-authorized courts have, to varying ends and divergent means, *failed* to reconcile Cambodia's genocidal past via prosecution, meditation, and reparation, Cambodian American cultural production potently engenders alternative modes for and practices of justice. Situated within the context of such juridical failure, Khmer American cultural production makes salient a justice-oriented agenda that from the outset emerges from a commemorative desire to articulate the experiences of those lost during the Democratic Kampuchean era. Such commemoration accretes significance given that no nationally sanctioned memorial exists for those who perished during the regime. Characterized by testimonial accounts of the genocide and its aftermath, based on familial stories of survival, and fixed to a diasporic 1.5 generation, Cambodian American memory work represents a multivalent archive constitutive of Cambodian history, Khmer/American culture, and refugee subjectivity. From memoir to documentary film, from hip-hop to staged performance, Cambodian American cultural producers strategically access legible forms of testimony within the United States—hearkening back to modes found in 19th-century slave narratives and American autobiography—to generate both a literal and an imagined space of justice in Cambodia while living in the United States.

Such Cambodian American memory work is evident in Khmer American singer/songwriter Bochan Huy, who currently resides in Oakland, California. Born in Phnom Penh during the Khmer Rouge era, Huy and her family eventually migrated to the United States, where they lived in numerous places (New York, Ohio, and Colorado) before settling in California. Huy's father was previously a singer in Cambodia; he continued his career in the United States. Since the age of nine, Huy performed alongside her father until he passed away after a long struggle with cancer. A self-described 1.5-generation Cambodian American, Huy's music is marked by a fusion of seemingly disconnected styles; expressly, her oeuvre is marked by a layering of traditional Khmer beats, acoustic instrumentation, contemporary R&B, and electronica. Guided by her parents' stories of life before, during, and after the Khmer Rouge regime, Huy's lyrics consistently stress not only survival but resilience in the face of state-authorized mass violence. These registers are at the forefront of Huy's 2011 single, "Chnam Oun 16" ("I'm 16 Years Old"), a remix of Ros Sereysothea's Cambodian rock classic (which served as the title song for the 1973 Cambodian film bearing the same name). Named "the Golden Voice of the Royal Capital" (*Preach Reich Theany Somlang Meas*) by Prince Norodom Sihanouk, Sereysothea was a prime target for a regime intent on eliminating Western influence and pre-revolutionary artists; though the exact circumstances of her death remain a mystery, she did perish during the Killing Fields era.

Whereas Sereysothea's original version is a playful teenage love song, Huy's rendition focuses its attention on the Killing Fields era and its aftermath. Blending Khmer and English lyrics, Huy's "Chnam Oun 16" is both intergenerational and transnational in scope. In the digital video that accompanied the single's release, "Chnam Oun 16" begins with a shot of a three orange banners atop an overgrown stone structure; this initial scene is juxtaposed with black and white images from Tuol Sleng Prison, contemporaneous film footage of Khmer Rouge officials, and documentary shots of labor camps. These somber images are juxtaposed with the bright colors of women dressed as traditional Cambodian *apsara* dancers; Huy, likewise dressed, initially sings the opening lines of the song in Khmer. She then shifts to English for the chorus, stressing: "They tried to stop us—they tried, they tried—they tried to rob us—they tried, they tried—like an *apsara*—I survived—we survived." These collocations, between genocidal history and present-day resilience, presage the video's depiction of 1.5-generation Cambodian Americans, who—dressed as S-21 prisoners—look directly at the camera and at times mouth the remaining lyrics, which layer Huy's vocals with those of emcee Raashan Ahmad (of Crown City Rockers).

On the one hand, Huy's use of Khmer Rouge footage, S-21 photographs, pre-Khmer Rouge artist (Sereysothea), and traditional Khmer dress (via the figure of the royal court *apsara* dancer provocatively recollects—by way of direct allegation and undeniable culpability—the profound losses endured by the majority of Cambodians and Cambodian Americans during the Killing Fields era. Indeed, Huy's tactical assemblage in "Chnam Oun 16," which rescripts a well-known love song into a contemplative, post-genocide ballad—assumes a juridical register in its repeated insistence that the regime attempted to "stop" and "rob" multiple facets of Khmer sociocultural identity (specifically with regard to the arts). On the other hand, Huy's utilization of hip-hop (as an identifiable U.S. mode) and the inclusion of other Cambodian Americans as silent victims-turned-voiced agitators renders discernible a transnationally inflected resistance rooted in not only remembering the past but also maintaining a collective, agentic subjectivity in the present. Such collectivity is apparent in the closing moments of the video, which showcases Cambodian refugees (of all ages), assembled in a mass vigil, holding portraits of family members who were either lost in the regime or who had passed away.

Hence, to be "Cambodian American" post-genocide necessarily embodies an identity formed by way of catastrophic collisions with U.S. Cold War foreign policy, traumatically shaped by Khmer Rouge totalitarianism, and problematically fixed to post-Vietnam War humanitarianism. Read within and outside essentialized narratives of "refuge" and "asylum," which often assume a clear divide between traumatic past and reconciled present, Cambodian American selfhood—to draw upon Lisa Lowe's multilayered characterization of Asian Americanist critique—"tirelessly reckons" with the collateral damages embedded in the American War in Vietnam (e.g., the bombing of the Cambodian countryside) and the un-reconciled human rights abuses connected to the Democratic Kampuchean era.[35] Such indefatigable negotiation of Cambodia's killing fields, wherein Khmer American cultural producers rehearse, restage, and remember "Pol Pot time," foregrounds an identifiable Cambodian American critique which brings into focus genocide, human rights, and civil rights. Correspondingly, Cambodian American memory work begins with and converges on the realities of large-scale human loss, forced relocation, and involuntary settlement. These ruptured modalities cohere with Khatharya Um's evocative question: "As the bodies move, where does the memory lie?"[36]

Um's interrogation of refugee remembrance, predicated on the literal, political, and cultural movement of bodies from country of origin to nation of settlement, encapsulates the scope of diasporic Cambodian American cultural production. Since 1999, Cambodian American authorship has largely taken testimonial form, evident in works such as Molyda Szymusiak's

(Buth Keo's) *The Stones Cry Out: A Cambodian Childhood, 1975–1980* (1999); Chanrithy Him's *When Broken Glass Floats: Growing Up Under the Khmer Rouge* (2000); Vatey Seng's *The Price We Paid: A Life Experience in the Khmer Rouge Regime* (2005); Ronnie Yimsut's *Facing the Khmer Rouge: A Cambodian Journey* (2000); Loung Ung's three-part autobiographical project: *First They Killed My Father: A Daughter of Cambodia Remembers* (2000), *Lucky Child: A Daughter of Cambodia Unites with the Sister She Left Behind* (2010), and *Lulu in the Sky: A Daughter of Cambodia Finds Love, Healing, and Double Happiness* (2012); Theary Seng's *Daughter of the Killing Fields* (2005); Oni Vitandham's *On the Wings of a White Horse: A Cambodian Princess's Story of Surviving the Khmer Rouge Genocide* (2006); Nawuth Keat's *Alive in the Killing Fields: Surviving the Khmer Rouge Genocide* (2009); previously mentioned Seng Ty's *The Years of Zero*; and Vaddey Ratner's *In the Shadow of the Banyan* (2012), which represents the first book-length Cambodian American-authored fictionalized account of the Cambodian genocide. Shifting from memoir to film and hip-hop, Khmer American rapper praCh's above-discussed *Dalama* series (which includes samples from traditional Khmer music and features lyrics taken from family interviews) and Socheata Poeuv's *New Year Baby* (2006) analogously detail the legacies of the Khmer Rouge via a focus on parental stories of survival.

Notwithstanding differences with regard to genre (e.g., film, literature, and music) and distinctions with regard to identity (particularly with regard to gender and class), such productions consistently recollect, in tactical Janus-faced fashion, a pre-revolutionary and post-revolutionary Cambodia which produces an identifiable Cold War cartography (inclusive of U.S. bombings of the Cambodian countryside and civil war) and reconstructs a Democratic Kampuchean imaginary. Moreover, such work unswervingly highlights a post-genocide subjectivity (wherein Cambodian refugees are transformed into Cambodian Americans) while agitating for juridical action (particularly with regard to commemorating those lost and critiquing the non-prosecution of Khmer Rouge perpetrators). For the most part, ordered chronologically, such works, as Teri Shaffer Yamada significantly notes, utilize an identifiable "autobiographical chronotype" composed of three time periods: before April 1975 (pre-revolutionary Cambodia), 1975–1979 (Democratic Kampuchea), and after 1979 (wherein protagonists flee the Vietnamese-occupied People's Republic of Kampuchea for Thai refugee camps).[37] Taken together, Cambodian American cultural production time and again accesses this "before, during, and after" Khmer Rouge continuum in a manner that militates against the strict and unavoidably limited contours of the tribunal. In the process, Cambodian American memory work instantiates new sites for genocide justice by directly remembering those lost, actively naming those responsible, and highlighting the specific histories which brought regime and refugee into being.

For these reasons, and in conclusion, the desire to combat such historical amnesias in the face of genocide is of paramount significance in Cambodian American Killing Fields narratives. In his introduction to *Children of Cambodia's Killing Fields* (1999), survivor Dith Pran provocatively argues:

> It is important for me that a new generation of Cambodians and Cambodian Americans become active and tell the world what happened to them and their families under the Khmer Rouge. I want them never to forget the faces of their relatives and friends who were killed during that time. The dead are crying out for justice. Their voices must be heard. It is the responsibility of survivors to speak out for those who are unable to speak, in order that genocide and holocaust will never happen again in this world.[38]

Pran's declaration to "never forget the faces of their relatives and friends" directly challenges individual and communal impulses to disremember the tragic realities of the Khmer Rouge era.

As significant, Pran's desire that "a new generation of Cambodians and Cambodian Americans become active" by "tell[ing] the world what happened" underscores a testimonial programme fixed to intergenerational juridical protest. This collective impulse—to fully represent and juridically interrogate the Cambodian experience between 1975 and 1979—powerfully situates Cambodian American memory work within the rubric of collective (and collected) articulation.

Notes

1 See Locard, Henri, *Pol Pot's Little Red Book: The Sayings of Angkar*. Chiang Mai, Thailand: Silkworm Books, 2004, 210.
2 An oft-used description vis-à-vis the Khmer Rouge takeover involves the soldiers' shoes; in particular, witnesses emphasize that their sandals were constructed from discarded tire material.
3 Despite "contained" nomenclature, the American War in Vietnam involved multiple Southeast Asian, East Asian, and Pacific Rim sites: planes were loaded and fueled on U.S. military installations in Guam, the Philippines, and Thailand. Between 1953 and 1975, the United States (via the Central Intelligence Agency) waged a secret war in Laos (which involved the communist Pathet Lao and anti-communist Royal Lao government).
4 Protests against the illegal bombings in Cambodia and Southeast Asia took center stage in 1970, with the infamous Kent State shooting on May 4. Prior to the protests, President Nixon repeatedly denied large-scale military involvement in Cambodia.
5 See Kiernan, Ben, "Recovering History and Justice in Cambodia." *Comparativ 14* (2004), 78.
6 While Cambodia's countryside was quiet, neighboring Laos would bear the brunt of these B-52 missions. Expressly, 85 percent of the nation was subject to cluster bomb attacks, making Laos the most bombed country in the world.
7 See Shawcross, William, *Sideshow: Kissinger, Nixon and the Destruction of Cambodia*. (New York: Simon and Schuster, 1979), 222.
8 A useful but admittedly incomplete analogy involves China's "Great Proletarian Cultural Revolution" (1966–1976), which sought to compulsorily remove perceived capitalist and traditionalist elements via forced relocations of individuals to re-education camps and centers.
9 See Schlund-Vials, Cathy J., *War, Genocide, and Justice: Cambodian American Memory Work* (Minneapolis, MN: 2012).
10 Consistent with the Democratic Kampuchean vision of an agricultural utopia, rural peasants were valued by the regime and cast as "base people." Congruent with on the Khmer Rouge's disavowal of political, social, and cultural memory, children became ideal citizens due to the fact that, with regard to the previous state order, they remembered the least. Encouraged to report on their parents' pre-revolutionary pasts, children were quickly promoted as cadres and assumed military positions.
11 The identification of such "enemies of the people" grew exponentially as tensions between the Socialist Republic of Vietnam and Democratic Kampuchea increased; previously limited to border and maritime skirmishes (1975–1977), the Cambodian-Vietnamese War entered full swing with the 1977 invasion of Vietnam by Khmer Rouge troops as per a perceived anti-Vietnamese expansionist campaign. The war, along with drought, drained the country's already limited resources; faced with international conflict, the Khmer Rouge proceeded to turn inward and purge purported traitors from their ranks. Tuol Sleng Prison in Phnom Penh (a.k.a. S-21) was one of 186 Khmer Rouge detention centers; those imprisoned were forced to sign confessions of disloyalty (e.g., affiliations with the CIA and the KGB) and list names.
12 See Southeast Asian Resource Center (SEARAC), "Removing Refugees." www.searac.org/sites/default/fils/2010%20 Cambodia%20Report_Fina.pdf, accessed March 3, 2014.
13 Ibid. Within the United States, Long Beach, California is home to the largest Cambodian/Cambodian American population; an estimated 50,000 reside in the West Coast port city. Lowell, Massachusetts is the second largest Cambodian American hub with approximately 25,000–30,000.
14 "1.5-generation" refers to those individuals who were children during the Killing Fields era or born in refugee camps soon after the dissolution of the Khmer Rouge regime in 1979.
15 Duch's verdict was delivered on July 26, 2010 as per "Case 001" of the Extraordinary Chambers in the Courts of Cambodia. Of the almost 20,000 inmates interned at S-21, approximately 200 survived.

On August 7, 2014, under the auspices of "Case 002/01," Chea and Samphan were convicted and received life sentences for crimes against humanity during the Khmer Rouge era. Chea and Samphan are currently facing crimes of genocide under the rubric of Case 002/02; Case 002 was divided to delineate between crimes against humanity and crimes of genocide.

16 See Schlund-Vials, Cathy J., *War, Genocide, and Justice: Cambodian American Memory Work* (Minneapolis, MN: 2012).
17 Ibid.
18 See "Cambodia Races Death, Dwindling Resources on Khmer Rouge War Crimes," *Voice of America*. 23 October 2013. www.voacambodia.com/content/cambodia-races-death-dwindling-resources-on-khmer-rouge-war-crimes/1775314.html, accessed July 2, 2014.
19 This notion of "memory work" deliberately accesses James Young's conceptualization vis-à-vis the efficacy of memorials. Focused on Holocaust memorials, Young maintains that the effectiveness of such a structure is not the degree to which it commemorates those who have been lost; rather, it is the extent to which the memorial instantiates debates and engenders further contemplation. See *The Texture of Memory: Holocaust Memorials and Meaning* (New Haven, CT: Yale UP, 1993).
20 See Mydans, Seth. "Cambodian Leader Resists Punishing the Khmer Rouge." *New York Times*. 29 December 1998. www.nytimes.com/1998/12/29/world/cambodian-leader-resists-punishing-top-khmer-rouge.html, accessed June 12, 2014.
21 Ibid.
22 Ibid.
23 I have previously characterized such strategic forgetting vis-à-vis the notion of "the Cambodian syndrome." Suggestive of a forgetting that is transnationally-inflected with regard to the Killing Fields era, I maintain that the "Cambodian syndrome" revises the "Vietnam syndrome" in a manner that legitimizes contemporary US and Cambodian governmental power. See *War, Genocide, and Justice: Cambodian American Memory Work* (2012).
24 See Widyono, Benny, *Dancing in the Shadows: Sihanouk, the Khmer Rouge, and the United Nations in Cambodia*. New York: Rowman and Littlefield Publishers, 2007.
25 This particular number—three million—was mentioned in Sydney Schanberg's "The Death and Life of Dith Pran," which appeared in 1980 *New York Times Magazine* cover story; this was the source text for Roland Joffé's *The Killing Fields* (1984). Pran is credited with using the term "killing fields" to characterize the Khmer Rouge regime.
26 See Maguire, Peter, *Facing Death in Cambodia*. New York: Columbia University Press, 2005.
27 Ibid. These witness accounts, which were originally ignored by the international community, have proved foundational for the current U.N./Khmer Rouge Tribunal.
28 On April 30, 1994, President William Jefferson Clinton signed into law the "Cambodian Genocide Justice Act" (22 US.C. 2656). "Consistent with international law," the act established that it was "the policy of the United States to support efforts to bring to justice members of the Khmer Rouge for their crimes against humanity committed in Cambodia between April 17, 1975 and January 7, 1979." Uncannily, the Cambodian Genocide Justice Act was passed as human rights tragedy in Rwanda was in full swing. This act in part funded the formation of the Documentation Center of Cambodia which presently provides most of the prosecutorial evidence in the current U.N./Khmer Rouge Tribunal. The current tribunal represents a hybrid formation that pairs international lawyers/judges and Cambodian lawyers/judges; it likewise considers international law concomitant with 1956 Cambodian Penal Code. While this formation assuages Hun Sen's original statement about "foreign" and "domestic" solutions, it is also a construction born out of necessity given that so few Cambodian judges and lawyers survived the Killing Fields era.
29 It should be noted that the court's charge was and remains two-fold: the court is tasked with the responsibility of trying Khmer Rouge officials while simultaneously determining what it terms "symbolic reparation" (which can take the form of genocide museums, educational centers, and memorials). In the case involving Duch, those whose family members perished at the prison (civil parties) were afforded a public apology (that was posted online) along with a list of names (also published online). Duch originally received a verdict of 19 years (due to the time he served while in custody). Both verdict and reparation proved controversial: Duch could feasibly survive his imprisonment; the majority of Cambodians at the time had limited internet access. The S-21 warden appealed the verdict; he would, as of 2012, receive a life sentence. To date, no plans for symbolic reparation have been confirmed.

30 This notion of "masquerade" vis-à-vis present-day tribunal politics and contemporary Cambodian American cultural production is further explored in an essay I have authored in Christine Sylvester's edited collection, *Masquerades of War* (Routledge 2015).
31 Robert Eap's work with regard to "arrested temporality" and the tribunal in his recently filed dissertation is especially illuminating. See "Contested Commemorations: Violence and Memory in Cambodia" (PhD diss., University of Southern California, CA, 2014).
32 This slippage between "victim" and "perpetrator" is particularly relevant to recent analyses of the oft-accessed "S-21" photographs (which have troublingly been referred to as "mug shots"). The images have largely circulated via a narrative of wholesale victimhood. Nevertheless, as Alex Hinton has recently reminded, what remains outside the dominant frame is the fact that 70 percent of those photographed and imprisoned were lower-level Khmer Rouge cadres who may have at one point occupied the role of perpetrators in their respective districts.
33 In 2010, Michael Karnavas (the defense attorney for Ieng Sary), accused Judge Nil Nonn, the President of the ECCC's Trial Chamber, of corruption via a very public bribe allegation. See O'Toole, James. "KRT Judge Accused of Taking Bribes" 19 September 2010. www.phnompenhpost.com/national/krt-judge-accused-taking-bribes, accessed May 4, 2014. Such allegations of corruption have persisted throughout the tribunal.
34 Quoted in Campbell, Charlie, "Cambodia's Khmer Rouge Trials are a Shocking Failure," 13 February 2014. http://time.com/6997/cambodias-khmer-rouge-trials-are-a-shocking-failure/, accessed May 13, 2014. Seng's criticism of the court was by no means limited to in-state politics; in November 2012, Seng organized a protest in conjunction with President Barack Obama's visit to Cambodia as per the auspices of the ASEAN meeting. This marked the first time that a sitting U.S. president had visited the Southeast Asian country. Seng and other activists called on the president to publicly apologize for the U.S. bombings of the Cambodian countryside during Nixon's administration; they also asked that China's role as a primary supporter for the Khmer Rouge be recognized. See "Protests Greet Obama's Visit to Cambodia." http://latitude.blogs.nytimes.com/2012/11/20/protests-greet-obamas-visit-to-cambodia/.
35 Lowe, Lisa, *Immigrant Acts: On Asian American Cultural Politics*. Durham, NC; Duke University Press, 1996.
36 Um, Khatharya, "Exiled Memory: history, Identity and Remembering in the Southeast Asian Diaspora." Southeast Asians in the Diaspora conference, University of Illinois, Urbana-Champaign, April 16, 2008.
37 As Yamada further notes, Cambodian American memoir in particular "signifies a painful testimony of culture genocide and dislocation, as it recenters the perimeters of American identity to an international application of American values in the form of global human right ... [its] form and content act synergistically to frame an ideological perspective reflective of a hybrid Cambodian American identity, unique to the Cambodian American experience" (144). See "Cambodian American Autobiography" in *Form and Transformation in Asian American Literature*. Zhou Xiaojing and Samina Najimi (editors). Seattle, WA: University of Washington Press, 2005.
38 Pran, Dith (Ed.). *Children of Cambodia's Killing Fields: Memoirs of Survivors*. (with Kim DePaul). New Haven, CT: Yale University Press, 1999, x.

References

"Cambodia Races Death, Dwindling Resources on Khmer Rouge War Crimes," *Voice of America*. October 23, 2013. www.voacambodia.com/content/cambodia-races-death-dwindling-resources-on-khmer-rouge-war-crimes/1775314.html (accessed October 14, 2016).

Kiernan, Ben. "Recovering History and Justice in Cambodia." *Comparativ* 14 (5-6): 76-85 (2004).

Locard, Henri. *Pol Pot's Little Red Book: The Sayings of Angkar*. Chiang Mai, Thailand: Silkworm Books, 2004.

Lowe, Lisa. *Immigrant Acts: On Asian American Cultural Politics*. Durham, NC: Duke University Press, 1996.

Maguire, Peter. *Facing Death in Cambodia*. New York: Columbia University Press, 2005.

Mydans, Seth. "Cambodian Leader Resists Punishing the Khmer Rouge." *New York Times*. December 29, 1998. www.nytimes.com/1998/12/29/world/cambodian-leader-resists-punishing-top-khmer-rouge.html (accessed October 14, 2016).

Pran, Dith. Ed. *Children of Cambodia's Killing Fields: Memoirs of Survivors.* (with Kim DePaul). New Haven, CT: Yale University Press, 1999.

Schlund-Vials, Cathy J. *War, Genocide, and Justice: Cambodian American Memory Work.* Minneapolis, MN: University of Minnesota Press, 2012.

Shawcross, William. *Sideshow: Kissinger, Nixon and the Destruction of Cambodia.* New York: Simon and Schuster, 1979.

Southeast Asian Resource Center (SEARAC). "Removing Refugees." www.searac.org/sites/default/fils/2010%20 Cambodia%20Report_Fina.pdf (accessed March 3, 2014).

Widyono, Benny. *Dancing in the Shadows: Sihanouk, the Khmer Rouge, and the United Nations in Cambodia.* New York: Rowman and Littlefield Publishers, 2007.

Yamada, Teri Shaffer. "Cambodian American Autobiography" in *Form and Transformation in Asian American Literature.* Zhou Xiaojing and Samina Najimi (editors), 144-167. Seattle, WA: University of Washington Press, 2005.

Young, James. *The Texture of Memory: Holocaust Memorials and Meaning.* New Haven, CT: Yale University Press, 1993.

9
ASIAN SETTLER COLONIALISM'S HISTORIES

Bianca Kai Isaki

In 2000, a special issue of *Amerasia* journal, "Whose Vision? Asian Settler Colonialism in Hawai'i" first took "Asian settler colonialism" (ASC) as an object of critical scholarly inquiry (Fujikane and Okamura 2000). ASC describes futures of past practices of land theft and political control through which descendants of nineteenth- and early twentieth-century Asian migrant laborers moved into middle-class American-ness in Hawai'i. It concerns the complicity, and resistance, but mostly complicity, of Asian settlers in the colonization of Hawai'i. Asian American studies, however, with its historical focus on the alliances between U.S. racial minorities and immigrants in civil rights struggles, offered a limited frame within which to approach Asian settlers' beleaguered relationship to Hawaiians' indigeneity.[1] (Fujikane 2005, 174). Since the Hawaiian "renaissance" of the 1970s, Hawaiians have reasserted their history of colonial resistance and unrelinquished national sovereign independence (Kanahele 1982, 25). Hawaiian sovereignty struggles have also pushed Asian settlers to answer for our participation in strategies of displacement through which Hawaiian nationality was made to not matter. *Amerasia* contributor, Haunani-Kay Trask wrote:

> Asians and haole [whites] have been thrown into a cauldron of defensive actions by our nationalist struggle. Either they must justify their continued benefit from Hawaiian subjugation, thus serving as support for that subjugation, or they must repudiate American hegemony and work with the Hawaiian nationalist movement.
>
> Trask (2000, 20)

As Hawaiians reassert their histories, Asian settlers must newly account for who we have been in Hawai'i. The usual story of Asian settlers is one of suffering and resistance to haole (white) planter elites, American-becoming through military service, struggles to upgrade second-class U.S. citizenship, and a defanging incorporation into settler state apparatuses. This story tracks a timeline of citizenly maturation and political exhaustion. Whereas working-class Asian settlers have been at the fore of labor and anti-development struggles, the present relative quiescence of an ascendant Asian settler middle class reads as the silence of those who have got their own by working *with* the contradictions of a U.S. capitalist democracy.

My work places a bet with postcolonial and queer studies scholars who call on a corporeal conception and practice of time to address "time [as] always several and any historical moment correspondingly consists of many[.]" (Freeman 2005, 58) citing (Bhabha 1994, 1–18). "[T]he indigenous challenge to Asian American claims to America[,]" Fujikane writes, "incites the most profound of Asian American anxieties." (Fujikane 2005, 83). Much must be made of this anxiety because it is an affective transit that carries history through corporeal structures. This chapter thus approaches ASC as a historical object; a critical intervention; and an affective structure. Part one accounts for histories that set up Asian settlers as colonial agents. Part two critiques the ASC studies' interventions for lacking a historical theory of decolonial agency. Part three assesses intersections between ASC studies and Hawaiian histories of decolonial resistance.

History

Asian settlement begins with nearly 300,000 labor migrants who came to Hawai'i's plantations on both sides of the turn of the nineteenth century. In 1888, my great, great-grandmother, arrived to work on Kaua'i's plantations in 1888.[2]

In 1848, the "Great Māhele" instituted a private property regime that secured lands for plantations. These plantations thirsted for labor, especially after the 1875 Reciprocity Treaty, which removed tariffs on Hawaiian sugar sold to U.S. markets in exchange for U.S. naval rights to Ke Awalau o Pu'uloa (Pearl Harbor).[3] Multiple agreements between the Hawaiian Kingdom and private commercial agents facilitated the in-migration of Asian plantation laborers. The Hawaiian Sugar Planters' Association (1895) was a central organ of the "Big Five"[4] corporations, an interlocking coterie of business interests that dominated Hawai'i's political economy.

In 1893, under the auspices of the U.S. military, white planters and their political allies overthrew the last monarch of the Kingdom of Hawai'i, Queen Lili'uokalani. Engineers of the overthrow then formed the Republic of Hawai'i, which lasted from 1894 until 1900, when Hawai'i was formally reorganized as a U.S. Territorial government under the U.S. Organic Act. In 1898, and against Hawaiians' petitions, the U.S. annexed Hawai'i via, not a treaty, but a congressional joint resolution (Silva 1998).

Until the early 1930s, the dominant Republican Party harbored a tenuous alliance between haole and a politically active community of Hawaiians, who outnumbered haole voters by more than three to one (Stannard 2005, 69). Asian laborers were disqualified from voting through discriminatory statutes such as the Territorial 1903 Citizenship Labor Act, and the Republican party allied around anxieties that a growing "alien" Asian voting bloc would come to control Hawai'i.[5] By the late 1920s, these anxieties were realized as Territory-born Asians increasingly took on the features of a settler community—marrying, having children, seeking employment away from the isolated rural plantations, and voting.

During the 1930s–1950s, working-class Hawaiians and Asian settlers found common cause in labor unionization and anti-racism. In the 1930 *Massie* case, white naval officers lynched a Hawaiian man accused of raping an officer's wife. Local Asian and Hawaiian communities protested the Territorial government's refusal to punish the lynchers specifically, and white racism more generally. During World War II, Hawai'i labor unions placed a moratorium on strikes to support U.S. war interests. At the same time, U.S. martial law froze plantation workers' wages and restricted their occupational mobility, allowing a predominantly haole workforce from the U.S. continent to obtain work in Hawai'i's more lucrative wartime defense industry.[6] By the war's end, Hawai'i was ripe for labor union activity.

The 1946 "sugar strike" inaugurated a new era of labor power and antiracism in Hawai'i. Labor unions pushed for progressive state welfare, centralized funding for public education, abortion rights, non-discriminatory housing statutes, and equal opportunity employment (Stannard 2005, 421–422). Also in the post-World War II period, Hawaiians found themselves increasingly replaced by Asian settlers in state government and civil service positions.[7] Returning Asian settler World War II servicemen received GI Bill-funded higher education and entered professional employment. In 1954, middle-class Asian settler democrats displaced historically dominant haole and Hawaiian Republicans in a "Democratic Revolution."Hawai'i's 1954 democratic legislators were disproportionately Japanese (67%), attorneys (63%), and veterans from either the majority-Japanese American 442nd or 100th battalions during WWII (39%) (Cooper and Daws 1985, 42–43). Girded by a rhetoric of "racially egalitarian power sharing," these legislators collaborated with a likewise racially mixed entrepreneurial class of land developers and financiers (Trask 2000, 3). With "their hands on the levers of control by which government approved or disapproved much that had to do with development," these politicians were well positioned to exploit elected office to capitalize on tourism and military associated economic expansion (Cooper and Daws 1985, 46). From 1954 through the 1980s, they consolidated the power structure from economic and political opportunities that is most identified with ASC (Cooper and Daws 1985, 3–7). Hawai'i statehood, which was imposed through a 1959 referendum that failed to identify independence as an option in violation of international law, was key to this consolidation[8] (Kauanui 2005, 4).

Asian settler incorporation into Hawai'i's settler colonial government was a race- and class-striated process: working-class Asian settlers and Hawaiians, allied against evictions from their agricultural and traditional lands by land *hui* (groups) composed of the same Asian settler officials and developers. These communities were united by an identification with local lifestyles and a collective sense that having worked to build Hawai'i meant deserving to determine its future.

Through the 1980s, Asian settlers continued to dominate Hawai'i's civil service and government. Asian settlers' shift from subjection to white settler colonialism into shareholders of that system buoyed an "illusion" of modern Hawai'i's multiracial harmony. This illusion excises class struggle from local identity and is reproduced in, especially tourist industry, accounts of Hawai'i's racial difference (Okamura 1994).

In part, this illusion is accomplished by resetting the historical referent of Hawai'i's social formation to plantation-era in-migration of Asians, Portuguese, and Chicano laborers, as opposed to the 1893 Overthrow of the Hawaiian Kingdom—a timeline that facilitates the (mis)recognition of Hawaiians as ethnic Americans. Ascendant discourses of Hawai'i's hard-working multicultural society offered the syntax for the Hawai'i Immigrant Heritage Preservation Center (HIHPC) to assert: "Hawai'i is a land of immigrants, beginning with the first Polynesian settlers" (Odo and Sinoto 1985, 11). Recently, HIHPC's collection formed the basis for a new exhibit in the Bishop Museum in Honolulu, a trust legacy of Hawaiian *ali'i* Bernice Pauahi Bishop. Curators again exhibited a history of Hawai'i that "assumes that Native Hawaiians are simply another racial or immigrant group that has passed out of prominence to make way for the successes of current (read immigrant) communities as part of an American multicultural democracy" (King 2014, 50, 56).

Excising differences between Hawaiian indigeneity and nonwhite immigrants accomplishes a settler community by, amongst other things, eliding an "other" history of settler complicity with Hawaiian dispossession (Kosasa and Tomita 2000, viii). Critical approaches to ASC refract historical struggles for citizenship and racial equality into what they have meant to Hawaiian sovereign self-determination and entitlements to "ceded" lands.[9] ASC studies thus underlines what Hawaiian (and other) political theorists have been saying: demands for Native sovereignty are not structurally coherent with the identity predicates of U.S. liberal politics (Sai 2004, Kauanui 2008).

ASC studies thus pushes for a politics of being *supporters* of Hawaiians' self-determination. In this view, Asian settlers support Hawaiians by keeping their own community in check (Fujikane and Okamura 2008, 30), "leaving a space for the Hawaiian nation to reconstitute itself" (Kosasa 2004, viii–ix) and treading thinly on territory that shades towards Hawaiian self-determination. This putatively hands-off approach is expressed as a temporal orientation that tends to bring with it a set of presumptions about the constitution of community, oppression, and historicity that may stymie its intentions to shore up Hawaiian sovereignty. The problem is that unless allying with Hawaiians can approach multiple struggles of the multiple "selves" of Hawaiian self-determination—the move to be "on the side of Hawaiians" becomes dogmatic. It limits address to intersecting operations of imperialism and fails to account for changing relationships between Asian settlers and Hawaiian sovereignty.

Office of Hawaiian Affairs trustee, Manu Boyd once observed, "our islands were transformed from subsistence crops to plantations where cheap immigrant labor generated profits for non-native businessmen . . . But we Hawaiians, perhaps one of the most ethnically and culturally diverse populations on earth, are still here" (Boyd 1998). A robust analysis of ASC can account for the pejorative anti-Asian valences in Boyd's use of "cheap" to describe labor immigrants (which some contend are endemic to ASC studies (Takagi 2004, 284 and Sharma and Wright 2008)) and his invocation of a liberal, ethnically, and racially diverse Hawaiian nation. The answer is not merely that ASC does not exist, but that ASC studies must situate itself amidst the trajectories of other projects that approach the multiple economic, gendered, affective, and political dimensions of Hawaiian dispossession.

Intervention

On May 23, 2009, the Japanese Cultural Center of Hawai'i (JCCH) hosted a public forum in Honolulu. Speakers included contributors to *Asian Settler Colonialism: From Local Governance to the Habits of Everyday Life* (UH Press, 2008). The event's flier read:

> The Japanese in Hawai'i have fought long and hard for civil rights, but at this time, we need to rethink who we are and where we are going. Hawaiians have a unique political status as the indigenous peoples of Hawai'i, and at this critical moment in history, they are fighting for their lands and nation. As settlers, Japanese and other Asian communities need to discuss what our responsibilities to Hawaiians are.

This announcement phrases the present as a crisis configured by the social justice of Hawaiian self-determination (Trask, Franklin, and Lyons 2004, Fujikane and Okamura 2008). In this moment, critical attentions previously oriented by race, ethnicity, and class culminate towards Asian settlers getting right with Hawaiian independence. Constellating the present as a historical crisis frames Asian settler histories *as* political projects. This begs the question of why Asian settler colonial complicity did not constitute a crisis before. And, insofar as it did, what prevented it from being seen that way?

Such questions give rise to criticisms of ASC as ahistorical (McGregor 2009). Settler colonialism, some argue, is a historical arrival from "white" nations and the "Asian settler" constitutes historical revisionism motivated by, amongst other things, neo-racism (Sharma 2010, 108; Takagi 2004; Luangphinith 2006). ASC scholars respond that racial migrants can be complicit with settler colonialism and note how indigenous identifications are distinct from racisms (Saranillio 2013; Wolfe 2013, 265).

The problem of "ahistoricity" is better understood as arising from the ways ASC studies calls forth its critical object. The capacity to organize a collective subject across time does not make the Asian settler subject ahistorical because that capacity is itself organized historically.

Put otherwise, ASC studies is a method of decolonizing history. Decolonizing history does not happen only by identifying ready-made resistant subjects that we then reclaim as part of an unwritten heritage of Asian settler decolonization. Decolonization entails sorting out structures that reproduce allegiances to colonial systems, "which we must acknowledge in order to act" (Spivak 1999, 370, n79). These structures produce Asian settlers as colonial agents who "inherit the power to represent or enact settler colonialism." (Morgensen 2011, 20).

Historical agency is not localized within individual failings or attempts to get right with history. An Asian settler *decolonizing* subject differentiated only by a belief in justice[10] remains ensnarled within liberal models of enlightened subjectivity. To wit, settlers who support decolonization know more, know better, or have greater moral agency than their non-supportive settler counterparts. While decolonizing struggles are a kind of awareness-raising project, a decolonizing pedagogy does not work by approaching political difference as a gap in someone else's knowledge. ASC studies needs a fuller account of the historical formations to which ASC studies owes its impetus toward intervention.

Approaching Asian settler complicity as a structural condition importantly avoids a too-thin characterological inquiry that founders on adjudicating between "good" and "bad" settlers.[11] That Asian plantation workers, for instance, "unknowingly became a part" of settler colonialism, does not disavow their presence to a part of it (Fujikane and Okamura 2008, 20). Certainly, nineteenth- and early twentieth-century economic migrants to Hawai'i's plantations are poor candidates for an analysis of Asian settler historical agency.[12] They had little access to structures of governance and many were dependent on husbands and fathers for social and economic identities. While by no means politically quiescent,[13] these economic migrants carried the "burden of transnationality"—a struggle for basic civil rights in the adopted country (Spivak 1996, 252). The burden of settler colonial agency more properly falls to descendents who acquired cultural literacy, formal citizenship, and professionalized inroads into power structures of the colonial state. This distinction is implicit in ASC studies' identification of Asian settler decolonization with dismantling power structures that condition colonial privileges that have accrued to us.

How we feel about who we have been is conditioned by histories we can and do claim, such as being part of a family or having worked on a plantation. Trask criticizes Asian, and particularly Japanese, settlers who "like to harken back to the oppressions of the plantation era, although few Japanese in Hawai'i today actually worked on the plantations during the Territory (1900–1959)." (Trask 2000, 4). She indicts Asian settler "false nostalgia" because it collapses a claim to oppression by proxy into "the resilience of settler ideology which facilitates and justifies non-Native hegemony: 'immigrants' who have struggled so hard and for so long *deserve* political and economic supremacy" (Trask 2000, 4). Asian settler invocations of plantation pasts operate these discourses as metrics of belonging. Belonging in these ways presumes problematic, un-inevitable equations between family ties, plantation labor, and a meritocratic claim to literal and political space in a contemporary Hawai'i (Kinsohita 2002, 9). Parsing pasts from the ways they are taken up to validate middle-class enfranchisement is one way of historicizing ASC's emergence as a critical object of study.

While unity happens in adversity, a unity claimed on the basis of adversity-*overcome* should raise questions about the political function of that unit. The recursive passage links Hawai'i's liberal histories of overcoming plantation oppression and a contemporary Asian settler colonial power structure. This structure is organized by affect. Affect bridges the gap between sensuous experience and the naming of that sensation within a context in which naming feelings enacts a commentary on one's sociopolitical orientation. When, and for whom, are structural injustices things that are felt? Through what affective calculus do past experiences of suffering become the glue that holds us together? We are looking at memory, feelings, and histories as political contexts in which sensations and experiences get attached to the kinds of people who can have them.

Being "set up" by history is a deeply unsatisfying way of having a self. Histories do not only make us; we become agents through the histories we can and do claim. Agency happens not only in acts of opposition, but in intimate spaces of colonization, such as enacting Trask's "false nostalgia." Colonial nostalgia requires a capacity to synthesize a relationship to something outside of experience—such as a parent's past life. Living in a horizon set out by the plantation story, post-plantation subjects configure authorship from a repeatable mode of asserting who one "really is" (Foucault 1972) and the "pleasure" of recounting plantation pasts linked to "the self-confirmation one receives by repeating the dynamics of an affective scene" (Berlant 2008, 14). These moments of authorship in post-plantation worker-memories identify agency. But it is a kind of agency bound up with familial ties and claims to being a subject of economic injustice that get amplified into a colonial holding pattern. This occurs despite other purposes of plantation remembrances, such as a diasporic's desire to have finally found a home (Luangphinith 2006, 57). Asian settler claims to belonging to Hawai'i are never out of the orbit of Hawaiian struggles for land and self-determination, because "imperialism has forced settlers and arrivants [nonwhite non-Natives] to cathect the space of the native as their home" (Byrd 2014b, xxxix). Settler feelings can thus function as placeholders. They can hold a colonial order in place. This way of displacing wrongdoing, or at least keeping it at a distance, cites contrition as our new difference from the past authors of injustice—the effect of which is to reconfirm the justice of colonial authority as itself a resource for trumping a violent colonial past.

Limits

A present overwhelmed by settler colonial predations absorbs forms of struggle and resistance into its orbit, even the ones that, historically, worked outside of rubrics of indigeneity. I caution that a call for self-reflection in a present grasped too tightly may tend towards a telos that finds from the past only "lessons learned." In our focus on exigency, we may fail to attend to "the rich residues and layerings of past time in the present moment, the complex interplay and disjuncture of the old and the new" (Felski 2002, 27).

The need for this better account of ASC studies' interventions was signaled in a kerfuffle following the JCCH forum in April 2009. Candace Fujikane wrote that 1970s struggles for ethnic studies at the University of Hawai'i were dominated by local Asians who had "no perception that Hawaiians have their own struggle" (Fujikane 2009).

To backtrack a bit, Hawai'i's ethnic studies program was born amidst protests against U.S. imperialism in Vietnam, the demolition of family farms by suburban tract developers, and a racist refusal to value local community, as well as a growing awareness of a need for education and histories that would sustain these communities (Witeck 1999). A poster for a 1976 Ethnic Studies rally stated: "We working people of Hawai'i cultivate the land and harvest the sea. We build every home, harbor, airport and industry. Through the centuries we've fought loss of lands, evictions, low pay, unemployment, and unsafe working conditions. Yes, we working people struggled for and built Hawai'i" (Aoudé 1999, x). "Ethnicity" itself is a misnomer for Hawaiians' sovereign political status; and the failure to foreground the difference Hawaiian sovereignty makes has, historically, abetted the formation of a, sometimes problematic, local identity (Aoudé 1999, x). As discussed above, "local" identity was a crucial touchstone for 1960–1970s alliances of working-class Asian settlers and Hawaiians against land development and military occupation, but it has since been used to gloss fundamental fractures in the society assembled by and for settler colonialism, particularly in the state's management of ethnic difference as liberal multicultural diversity. Slippages within the "local" are present in the 1970s ethnic studies slogan, "we built Hawai'i", insofar as it tenses a meritocratic index against indigenous claims that "Hawai'i was stolen from us[.]"(Trask 1987). ASC theorists critiqued this slogan as failing to articulate how Hawaiians' political status as Kingdom of Hawai'i citizens, indigenous peoples, or Natives, positions Asians as settlers (Fujikane and Okamura 2008, 4).

McGregor had much to say about this ASC critique. ASC is "ahistorical" (McGregor 2009). McGregor elucidated her statement in a response to Fujikane's interview. Even if the ethnic studies model was not explicitly built around Hawaiian national claims, McGregor pointed out, Hawaiians innovated that model, authored the slogan, "Our history, our way" (which Fujikane had mistakenly attributed to Asian settlers), and used it to expand the scope of Hawaiian history, politics and community. McGregor framed ethnic studies within a legacy initiated and carried out by Hawaiians, amongst others: "We [Ethnic Studies advocates] empowered our students with a history of resistance, from the maka'āinana of Ka'ū who killed abusive chiefs; to the killing of Captain Cook; the taking of the Fair American; the rebellion of Chief Kekuaokalani and Chiefess Manono; the 1845 petitions against Ka Māhele; the Wilcox Rebellion; the Hui Aloha 'Āina; the 1895 Restoration; and Hawaiian longshoremen who founded the [International Longshore and Warehouse Workers Union (ILWU)]. Moreover, we got involved, with our students, in Kalama Valley, Waiahole-Waikāne, He'eia Kea, Waimānalo, Niumalu Nawiliwili and Kaho'olawe community struggles" (McGregor 2009).

It matters that Hawaiians built Hawai'i. They initiated plantation labor unionization, supported liberal politics and led labor resistance movements. And, in a history of our decolonizing present, it matters that the discourses, alliances, and cultures engendered through these resistant unities continue to undergird protests against militarization, land development driven evictions, as well as struggles for ethnic studies, racial equality and Hawaiian sovereignty.

"Honoring past struggles" must mean refusing to relegate their interventions to the past—because it is not the case that these struggles have only come before us. They may be unfinished rather than fatally disrepaired for decolonization. The problem lies with assuming that past resistance movements have already had their moment and become irrelevant in an exhausted present. We need to revisit the notion that it worked to resist this way then, but conditions have changed and these tactics need to be rehabilitated, discarded, or opposed for new complicities with colonial capitalist hegemonies.

Forward movement from a time when vicious plantation lunas abused indentured plantation laborers, nonwhites could not vote, and whites-only histories celebrated Hawai'i's American-becoming, must be approached with Fujikane's canny caution, "[h]onoring the struggles of those who came before us, however, also means resisting the impulse to claim only their histories of oppression and resistance" (Fujikane and Okamura 2008, 7). Futures that proliferated from pasts of resistance and oppression consist also in corrupt cronyism within a multiracial government, the U.S. imposition of statehood onto Hawai'i, and a "militourist" economy deeply entrenched in Hawaiian lands (Teaiwa 1999). We need, therefore, to recognize how a critical (present) moment constellates a politics around a sense that a crisis has not been addressed before.

Mimi Nguyen pointed to a parallel problem in feminism's tendency to "corral . . . certain critical feminist inquiries . . . as belonging to a particular historical moment, as uttered (for example) in the pedagogical sentiment, 'Theirs was an important intervention during a period of crisis, and we learned our lessons thusly and thereafter'" (Nguyen 2009). She was talking about projects like the 1980s black feminist Combahee River Collective or second-wave feminisms that, rendered into historically bound interventions, are effectively denied a copresence in contemporary political life. It is as if their imperatives to intersect race, class, sexuality, disability, and gender are *not* unfinished projects in our present as well.[14] Nguyen's observations advise against a hasty periodizing of Hawai'i's ethnic studies' interventions as merely "bright spots" in an otherwise shady ASC history. Historical, extant engagements with projects of Hawaiian self-determination in the context of a multiracial Hawai'i are theoretically frameworked away by focusing too finely on the presumption that self-determination means an exclusive focus on indigenous decolonization.

McGregor's letter concludes: "labeling Asian immigrant workers and their descendants as colonial 'settlers' is ahistorical, narrow-minded, lacking in class analysis, and too simplistic to explain our complicated islands' society." What McGregor means by "ahistorical" is not an absence of references to the past, but a failure to see how history's actors, Hawaiians in particular, used discourses and institutions in ways that exceed what their categories might predict for them. Even if Ethnic Studies nominally modeled Hawaiian-ness as an ethnicity, it nonetheless acted as a vehicle for expressions of Hawaiian self-determination, political imagination, and cultural communities. So, what if, when the Ethnic Studies collective in Hawai'i called for "Our History, Our Way"—they were claiming history for a distinctively Hawaiian model of multiethnicity? What if in 1935, when Hawaiian labor unionizer, Harry Kamoku, said he wanted to empower workers, this was also a way of saying that he wanted to secure Hawai'i's autonomy from Euro-American colonial capitalists (Beechert 1985)? In other words, how are class and ethnicity already languages of Hawaiian decolonization, albeit in ways that do not call out their aims as such?

The methodological question thus concerns how to engage ASC in a history that is not a history of indigenous colonization only. The move to split settlers, Asian or otherwise, from Hawaiian sovereignty struggles denies the ways a local identity, amongst other social justice projects accomplished varied names and through unexpected alliances, has been politically useful to Hawaiians. Jackie Lasky points out, the "continual production and reproduction of Waiahole-Waikāne [antidevelopment community struggles] as a Local, multiethnic, working-class community has prevented a larger critique being levied against . . . the dispossess[ion of] Hawaiians of land" (Lasky 2009, 1), yet the same local identity enabled articulations of longstanding antimonies between working-class Hawaiian and settler tenant farmers against Hawaiian landowners (Nakata 1999). Undergirding Waiahole-Waikāne community claims, whether as local tenants or Hawaiian landowners, has been a larger aim of preserving traditional Hawaiian cultural practices, taro farming in particular. This is Hawaiian class politics that, because of the stakes of its struggles, do not organize under the rubric of Hawaiian self-determination while being a constitutive part of that process.

Seen this way, Hawaiian self-determination is engaged in subjects, imaginations, discourses, and struggles that sometimes took form in the collective resistance to Big Five employers through ILWU unionization, local farmers' anti-eviction struggles, as well as the explicitly Hawaiian Protect Kahoʻolawe ʻOhana. This has implications for the call for Asian settlers to support Hawaiian sovereignty. What if "standing behind" Hawaiian self-determination means to stand behind a plethora of resistance projects whose futures remain worked-toward in a critical colonial present? How might critical theories of indigeneity archive inheritances from struggles that might, or more usually, might not have, announced their aims in terms of self-determination, land rights, and nation? It is not the case, for instance, that civil rights struggles against Japanese internment had no relationship to Hawaiian self-determination—although the language of civil rights is an impoverished way of talking about that relationship. Asking these questions does not mean subsuming Hawaiian sovereignty as an adjunct to antiracist and class-based struggle. Rather the inquiries call attention to the political value of theorizing indigenous pasts not explicitly organized around sovereignty, nation or Native identity as *also* enactments of Hawaiian self-determination.

Chickasaw scholar, Jodi Byrd, observes U.S. colonization "functions not so much as a binary between settlers and natives, but through a series of recognitions and misrecognitions that coerce settlers, *arrivants,* and natives into service as proxies, agents, and at times beneficiaries, however undesired and unwanted, of the processes that have stripped land, lives, and nations away from the indigenous peoples who have always been here" (Byrd 2014b, 175). Parsing ASC studies' model of political agency into serial (mis)recognitions would better respond to McGregor's concern that what is historical about subjecthood is getting left behind. Her concern is with an ASC studies that constellates decolonization in a present that is complexly layered with pasts in which neither Hawaiian self-determination nor ASC were already gathered together under those names. The rush to reconstellate pasts of who we have been to Hawaiian dispossession is to quickly put a name on clusters of affiliations, struggles and relation that have not yet called in their cards. Rather than approaching ASC as a roster of wrongdoings, we should attend to the situated, actual events through which Asian settlers invest, and are invested, in U.S. colonialism.

This call to ground ASC studies in "history" is also part of the scholarly turn towards operations of power within the quotidian, the affective, and the corporeal—". . . the point where power reaches into the very grain of individuals, touches their bodies and inserts itself into their actions and attitudes, their discourses, learning processes and everyday lives" (Foucault 1980, 39). ASC, in partnership with U.S. colonialism operates on the quotidian to "continually reorient the world into ambivalent and improvisatory patternings that realign one's relationality into maintaining and replicating colonialism's modes of dominance" (Byrd 2014a, 615). It is not enough to insist on historical material as evidence because we need also to recognize colonialism as patterns, events, non-events, and affects. ASC studies must step up to settler colonialism's methods with an embodied practice of decolonial historiography that allows Hawai'i "a sense of belonging to a discourse world that only partly exists yet" (Berlant and Warner 1995, 344). This posture is appropriate to an independent process of Hawaiian self-governance that proliferates scenarios of futures that cannot be known so much as oriented-towards (Byrd 2014a, 614). Such non-knowledge means ASC studies must not only support Hawaiian sovereignty, to inventory the critical vocabularies of past and other struggles that, instead of coming to a cauldron-borne focus, command us to recognize an expansive Hawaiian project of self-determination and over a diffuse time that can harbor its necessarily multitudinous projects of decolonization.

Notes

1 In Hawai'i, "Hawaiian" does not indicate a resident of Hawai'i, but Native Hawaiians exclusively—those whose ancestors inhabited the Hawaiian island chain prior to 1778. HAW. REV. STAT. § 10H-3. This chapter refers to Hawaiians out of recognition for the space from which it is written.
2 Motoyo Ogawa was born in Anahola, Kauai in 1888. She gave birth to my grandmother, Edith Fujimoto, in Honolulu in 1920. I am a fifth-generation Asian settler in Hawai'i.
3 Between 1870 and 1930, the total acreage under cultivation increased from 8,500 to 251,544 acres (Beechert 1985, 178).
4 The "Big Five" major commercial interests in Hawai'i were: American Factors (AmFac), Alexander and Baldwin, Theo. H. Davies, Castle and Cooke, and C. Brewer.
5 Michael J. Shapiro has addressed the manipulation of voting qualifications to disenable "Asiatic" political enfranchisement; see 'Shapiro 2002, Burgess and Dole 1936'. For more discussion of anti-Asian sentiment in Hawai'i; see Okihiro 1991.
6 Martial law was declared in the Territory after the bombing of Pearl Harbor in 1941. For plantation laborers, martial law specifically meant 1) their wages were frozen, 2) they could not change jobs without permission from their employer, 3) if they lost their civilian employment, they would have to accept military jobs, 4) absenteeism was punishable by fines up to $200 or imprisonment up to two months,

5) Labor contracts were suspended, 6) plantation workers could be "borrowed" by the army, who would pay the planters $0.21/hour for each worker they loaned out. Planters are reported to have received about $6 million dollars for workers and equipment loaned out in this way.

7 Private-sector employment in mid-twentieth century Hawai'i was mostly controlled by haoles who refused to hire Asians. By contrast, discrimination in hiring for government jobs and territorial civil service was made illegal by the federal Ramspeck Act of 1940. Together, these factors resulted in a disproportionate influx of middle class Asians, especially Japanese, into Hawai'i government and civil service jobs; see Haas 1998, 42-43.

8 Designated a non-self governing territory by the United Nations in 1946, Hawai'i was entitled to a plebiscite under the U.N. General Assembly Resolution 742 in which integration (statehood) would have been one choice amongst others: free association, commonwealth, or independence (Trask 2000, 19).

9 In 1898, 1.4 million acres of lands were "ceded" to the U.S. federal government upon annexation and then to the State of Hawai'i in 1959, when Hawai'i became an American state (by a process that violated international law) (Kauanui 2005, 4). Another 180,000 acres is currently held in trust by the State of Hawai'i Department of Hawaiian Homelands (Trask 1987, 151).

10 Eric Yamamoto's suggestion that Japanese Americans affirm reparations for "other groups' wounds" (African Americans' and Hawaiians') also positions them as intending-agents in ways that I unpack here (Yamamoto 1998, 17).

11 Jean-Paul Sartre, *Le Colonialisme est un systéme*, (1956).

12 Commodity export of sugar and pineapple drove Hawai'i's settler colonial economy in the late nineteenth through the mid-twentieth century. Whereas twenty sugar plantations were in operation in 1875, sixty-three existed in 1880. Under the Reciprocity Treaty of 1875, plantation owners could export their sugar to the U.S. tariff-free. Also, the passage of the 1850 U.S. Master and Servants Act stepped up sugar planter lobbying efforts to meet "island labor shortages" by providing for foreign contract labor (mostly Japanese) to be brought to Hawai'i. After an initial proliferation of small agricultural operations, plantations increased consolidation and capital investment. By 1957 only twenty-seven plantations existed, but the average land acreage size increased 20-fold and physical capital investment per plantation increased almost 28-fold (Mollett 1961, 28).

13 Early labor organization amongst Asian migrant communities prioritized race. For instance, organizers of a Japanese plantation strike in 1909 were not themselves plantation workers, but rather merchants, newspaper editors and clerks, who founded the Higher Wage Association (Kotani 1985, 39–41).

14 This phrase is reproduced from Christina Hanhardt's talk, "'We Are Not Trash': Safety, Quality-of-Life Policing, and the Contested Development of Queer Urban Space" Levis Faculty Center, University of Illinois, Urbana-Champaign: April 30, 2009.

References

Aoudé, Ibrahim G. 1999. "Introduction to the ethnic studies story: the political economic environment." *Social Process in Hawai'i* 39: xv–xxxvi.

Beechert, Edward D. 1985. *Working in Hawaii: A Labor History*. Honolulu, HI: University of Hawaii Press.

Berlant, Lauren. 2008. *The Female Complaint: The Unfinished Business of Sentimentality in American Culture*. Durham, NC and London: Duke University Press.

Berlant, Lauren, and Michael Warner. 1995. "What does queer theory teach us about X?" *PMLA* 110 (3): 343–379.

Boyd, Manu. 1998. "Sugar came and went, but we're still here." *Wai ola o OHA* 15 (6): 4.

Burgess, John W., and Sanford B. Dole. 1936. "Documents: Letters of Sanford B. Dole and John W. Burgess." *The Pacific Historical Review*: 71–75.

Bhabha, Homi. 1994. *The Location of Culture*. New York: Routledge.

Byrd, Jodi. 2014a. "A Return to the South." *American Quarterly* 66 (3): 609–620.

Byrd, Jodi A. 2014b. "Arriving on a different shore: US empire at its horizons." *College Literature: A Journal of Critical Literary Studies* 41 (1): 174–181.

Cooper, George, and Gavan Daws. 1985. *Land and Power in Hawaii: The Democratic Years*. Honolulu, HI: Benchmark Books, Inc.

Felski, Rita. 2002. "Telling time in feminist theory." *Tulsa Studies in Women's Literature* 21 (1): 32–38.
Foucault, Michel. 1972. *The Archeology Of Knowledge And The Discourse On Language*. Translated by A.M. Sheridan Smith. New York: Pantheon Books.
Foucault, Michel. 1980. *Power/Knowledge: Selected Interviews And Other Writings, 1972–1977*. Translated by Colin Gordon. Edited by Colin Gordon. New York: Pantheon Books.
Fujikane, Candace. 2005. "Foregrounding native nationalisms: a critique of antinationalist sentiment in Asian American studies." In *Asian American Studies After Critical Mass*, edited by Kent A. Ono, 73–97. Malden, MA: Blackwell.
Fujikane, Candace, and Jonathan Okamura, Eds. 2000. *Whose Vision? Asian Settler Colonialism in Hawai'i*. Edited by Russell C. Leong. Vol. 26, *Amerasia*. Los Angeles, CA: Asian American Studies Center Press.
Fujikane, Candace, and Jonathan Okamura, Eds. 2008. *Asian Settler Colonialism: From Local Governance to the Habits of Everyday Life*. Honolulu, HI: UH Press.
Freeman, Elizabeth. 2005. "Time binds, or erotohistoriography." *Social Text* 23 (3-4):57–68.
Haas, Michael, Ed. 1998. *Multicultural Hawai'i: The Fabric of a Multiethnic Society*. New York and London: Taylor and Francis.
Kauanui, J. Kehaulani. 2005. "Precarious positions: Native Hawaiians and US federal recognition." *The Contemporary Pacific* 17 (1): 1–27.
Kauanui, J. Kehaulani. 2008. "Colonialism in equality: Hawaiian sovereignty and the question of U.S. civil rights." *South Atlantic Quarterly* 107 (4): 635–650.
Kanahele, G. S. 1982. "The new Hawaiians." *Social Process in Hawai'i* 29: 21–31.
King, Lisa. 2014. "Competition, complicity, and (potential) alliance: Native Hawaiian and Asian immigrant narratives at the Bishop Museum." *College Literature: A Journal of Critical Literary Studies* 41 (1): 40–65.
Kinsohita, Gaku. 2002. "Telling our roots in the sugar plantation: collective identities of Japanese American elderly in Puna, Hawai'i." *Social Process in Hawai'i* 41: 1–20.
Kosasa, Eiko. 2004. "Predatory Politics: U.S. imperialism, settler hegemony, and the Japanese in Hawai'i." PhD, Political Science, University of Hawai'i at Manoa.
Kosasa, Karen K., and Stan Tomita. 2000. "Whose vision, 2000." *Amerasia Journal* 26 (2): xii–xiv.
Kotani, Roland. 1985. *The Japanese of Hawaii: A Century of Struggle, The Official Program Booklet of the Oahu Kanyaku Imin Centennial Committee*. Honolulu, HI: The Hawaii Hochi.
Lasky, Jackie. 2009. "The limits of multiculturalism in Hawai`i." The Association of Asian American Studies Honolulu, Hawai`i, April 24, 2009.
Luangphinith, Seri. 2006. "Homeward bound: settler aesthetics in Hawai'i's literature." *Texas Studies in Literature and Language* 48 (1): 54–79.
McGregor, Davianna Pōmaika'i. 2009. "Settling the record straight." *Honolulu Weekly*, May 13–19, 2009, 3.
Mollett, J.A. 1961. "Capital in Hawaiian sugar: its formation and relation to labor and output, 1870–1957." *Agricultural Economics Bulletin* 21.
Morgensen, Scott Lauria. 2011. *Spaces Between Us: Queer Settler Colonialism and Indigenous Decolonization*. Minneapolis, MN: University of Minnesota Press.
Nakata, Bob. 1999. "The struggles of the Waiahole-Waikane community association." In *The Ethnic Studies story: politics and social movements in Hawai'i*, edited by Ibrahim G. Aoudé, 60–73. Honolulu.
Nguyen, Mimi. 2009. "Feminist futures roundtable." *Feminist Futures*, Urbana, IL, May 8, 2009.
Okamura, Jonathan. 1994. "The illusion of paradise: privileging multiculturalism in Hawai'i." In *Making Majorities: Composing the Nation in Japan, China, Korea, Fiji, Malaysia, Turkey and the United States*, edited by D.C. Gladney. Palo Alto, CA: Stanford UP.
Okihiro, Gary Y. 1991. *Cane Fires: The Anti-Japanese Movement in Hawaii, 1865–1945*. Edited by Sucheng Chan, *Asian American History and Culture*. Philadelphia, PA: Temple UP.
Odo, Franklin, and Kazuko Sinoto. 1985. *A Pictorial History of the Japanese in Hawai'i*. Honolulu, HI: Bishop Museum Press.
Sai, David Keanu. 2004. "American occupation of the Hawaiian state: a century unchecked." *Hawaiian Journal of Law & Politics* 1 (Summer): 46–81.
Saranillio, Dean Itsuji. 2013. "Why Asian settler colonialism matters: a thought piece on critiques, debates, and Indigenous difference." *Settler Colonial Studies* 3 (3–4): 280–294.
Seeto, Margot. 2009. "Critical Transformations: Q and A with Candace Fujikane." April 22. *Honolulu Weekly* (Honolulu, HI).

Silva, Noenoe K. 1998. "Kanaka Maoli Resstance to Annexation." *ÿÖiwi: A Native Hawaiian Journal* I: 40–80.

Shapiro, Michael J. 2002. "Social science, geophilosophy and inequality." *International Studies Review* 4 (2): 25–46.

Sharma, Nandita. 2010. "Asian settler colonialism: from local governance to the habits of everyday Life in Hawai, edited by Candace Fujikane and Jonathan Y. Okamura." *Hawaiian Journal of History* 44: 107–110.

Sharma, Nandita, and Cynthia Wright. 2008. "Decolonizing resistances, challenging colonial states." *Social Justice* 35 (3): 93–111.

Spivak, Gayatri Chakravorty. 1996. "Diasporas old and new: women in the transnational world." *Textual Practice* 10 (2): 245–269.

Spivak, Gayatri Chakravorty. 1999. *A Critique of Postcolonial Reason: Toward A History of the Vanishing Present*. Cambridge, MA: Harvard UP.

Stannard, David E. 2005. *Honor Killing: How The Infamous "Massie Affair" Transformed Hawai'i*. New York: Viking Press.

Takagi, Dana. 2004. "Faith, race and nationalism." *Journal of Asian American Studies* 7 (3): 271–288.

Teaiwa, Teresia. 1999. "Reading Gaugin's Noa Noa with Hau'ofa's Nederends: 'militourism,' feminism and the 'Polynesian' body." In *Inside Out: Theorising Pacific Literature*, edited by Vilsoni Hereniko and Rob Wilson, 249–264. Colorado: Rowman and Littlefield.

Trask, Haunani-Kay. 1987. "The birth of the modern Hawaiian movement: Kalama Valley, O'ahu." *The Hawaiian Journal of History* 21: 126–153.

Trask, Haunani-Kay. 2000. "Settlers of color and "immigrant" hegemony: "locals in Hawai'i." *Amerasia Journal* 26 (2): 1–26.

Trask, Haunani-Kay, Cynthia Franklin, and Laura E. Lyons. 2004. "Land, leadership, and nation: Hauani-Kay Trask on the testimonial uses of life writing in Hawai'i." *Biography* 27 (1): 222–249.

Witeck, John J. 1999. "The rise of ethnic studies at the University of Hawai'i: anti-war, student and early community struggles." *Social Process in Hawai'i* 39: 10–18.

Wolfe, Patrick. 2013. "Recuperating binarism: a heretical introduction." *Settler Colonial Studies Journal* 3 (3-4): 257–279.

Yamamoto, Eric K. 1998. "Racial reparations: Japanese American redress and African American claims." *Boston Third World Law Journal* 19 (477): 1–26.

10

THE STRANGE CAREER OF THE FILIPINO "NATIONAL": EMPIRE, CITIZENSHIP, AND RACIAL STATECRAFT

Rick Baldoz

The United States' bid for an overseas empire during the late nineteenth century greatly enlarged its territorial jurisdiction, and in doing so, raised some urgent questions about the shifting boundary lines of the national polity. The annexation of the Philippines attracted a disproportionate amount of attention in public debates surrounding the projection of U.S. sovereignty beyond its continental borders. Proponents of extraterritorial expansion believed that the acquisition of the Philippines would bolster the nation's commercial and geo-political interests in Asia and elevate the standing of the United States vis-à-vis European powers. Opponents of extraterritorial expansion voiced concerns about a range of issues, including the political and the logistical costs associated with long-distance colonial rule and Filipino demands for national self-determination.

Uncertainty regarding the political status of newly acquired Filipino subjects also generated significant controversy. Anti-imperialists in Congress warned that the act of territorial annexation would trigger the collective naturalization of the native inhabitants of the Philippines. They pointed to the historical precedent of granting American citizenship to the inhabitants of territories annexed during the continental expansion of the United States earlier in the nineteenth century. The prospect of extending U.S. citizenship rights to the 8–9 million residents of the Philippines gave many lawmakers pause, insofar as the people who inhabited the territory were deemed to be of suspect racial pedigree. Imperialist leaders dismissed these concerns citing the political subordination of Native Americans as an exemplar of territorial incorporation decoupled from citizenship.

The United States' formal annexation of the Philippines in 1899 did little to clarify the status of Filipinos regarding their place in the American polity, though congressional leaders asserted "plenary authority" to determine the socio-legal standing of recently acquired colonial wards, which also included Puerto Ricans. Imperial statesmen made clear their desire to dissever the political futures of the two territories so that potential statehood or U.S. citizenship rights for Puerto Rico did not carry over to the Philippines. Congress ratified separate organic acts declaring the Puerto Ricans and Filipinos to be "citizens of Puerto Rico" and "citizens of the Philippine

Islands" respectively. What it meant to be a "citizen" of a colonial dependency, rather than a sovereign state was unclear, though these legislative enactments affirmed that these populations were not citizens of the United States.[1]

The U.S. Supreme Court in a series of decisions known as *The Insular Cases* weighed in on the issue, affirming that the act of territorial annexation did not automatically trigger the collective naturalization of the inhabitants of these domains. At the same time the justices declared that the inhabitants of overseas colonies held a special status vis-à-vis the American polity since they were under the administrative jurisdiction of the United States. Consequently, Filipinos and Puerto Ricans occupied a shadowy space between alienage and citizenship giving rise to a new species of political subject popularly known as the *U.S. national*. Questions remained, however, regarding where newly minted nationals fitted into the administrative machinery of the state since this was an anomalous socio-legal classification without any clearly defined constitutional parameters.

This new political designation raised more questions than answers. What rights and obligations did Filipinos have vis-à-vis the United States as subjects of its sovereignty? Were Filipinos who immigrated to the metropole eligible for naturalized citizenship in the "mother country"? Did racially targeted legal proscriptions such as *alien land laws* apply to Filipinos, who were technically speaking, not aliens? Were these newly minted nationals subject to wartime conscription into the U.S. military to demonstrate their allegiance to imperial state? The answers to these questions proved contentious and generated significant controversy on both sides of the Philippine–American divide. The failure to clearly define the socio-legal standing of newly acquired subjects underscores the ad hoc and fragmentary nature of the U.S. imperium. The makeshift character of American colonial policy had some unexpected consequences as Filipino immigrants exploited the uncertainty about their socio-legal status to challenge boundaries of exclusion and demonstrated an uncanny ability to circumvent and/or subvert the racial checkpoints in American society.

This essay takes as its starting point the fact that nation-states claim a monopoly on legitimate movement across and within their borders and that nation-states are intended to be bounded, mutually exclusive communities that exercise sovereignty over both the external (territorial borders) and internal (citizenship) boundaries of the national polity. Recent scholarship has highlighted the ways in which citizenship policy has functioned as an instrument of social closure wielded by entrenched population groups who seek to monopolize valuable public goods by excluding rival claimants who compete for scarce societal resources. This essay examines how Filipinos' unique status as colonial migrants complicated conventional efforts to effect social closure and in doing so, reveals the contingent and contested nature of racial and national boundaries during the age of American empire.[2]

Debates over the political consequences of U.S. imperium reflected escalating tensions between expansionist and restrictionist political blocs in the federal government whose ideological programs ran at cross-purposes. On one side were the expansionists who favored the enlargement of the territorial jurisdiction of the United States in an effort to bolster America's geopolitical standing, especially when it came to securing a foothold in Asia and the Caribbean Basin. In addition to opening up new opportunities for resource extraction in Southeast Asia, key American business interests viewed the Philippines as a potential source of cheap, migrant manpower embracing the global circulation of colonial labor as a constituent feature of racial capitalism.

The push to expand the United States' global sphere of influence, however, ran up against powerful political countercurrents in American society, evinced by the powerful nativist lobby who tapped into popular anxieties about unrestricted immigration and racial conflict. Nativist sentiment gathered momentum during the late nineteenth and early twentieth centuries, and Congress passed a series of legislative measures aimed at shoring up immigration and naturalization controls in the United States as part of a larger effort to preserve the Anglo-Saxon character of the national community. The procurement of overseas colonies at the turn of the twentieth century brought tensions between expansionist and restrictionist camps to a head as American statesmen worked to resolve the civic status of millions of new subjects now living under the U.S. flag.

The key dilemma facing policymakers pivoted on the question of how to enlarge the geographic borders of the imperial state, without necessarily expanding the boundaries of national citizenship. Fashioning a policy that would absorb the territory of the Philippines into the U.S. administrative jurisdiction without simultaneously incorporating Filipinos into the nation's body-politic proved to be a challenge due in large part to the ad hoc character of the American colonial system. Although the United States had a long history of domestic territorial conquest, the seizure of overseas possessions raised a new set of questions about the boundary lines of the American polity, which now extended across the globe. While the Supreme Court had rejected the claim that Filipinos had been collectively naturalized resulting from territorial annexation, it made no determination regarding whether or not they were individually eligible for naturalization if they applied for citizenship through regular channels while living in the United States. Federal officials acknowledged that American nationals held some sort of special status vis-à-vis the U.S. since they were under its administrative sovereignty and because Filipinos "owed permanent allegiance to the United States." The issue was not of pressing concern in the years immediately following annexation, since the Filipino population residing in the metropole was negligible. Labor demands in the burgeoning agribusiness sectors in Hawaii and the West Coast during the early decades of the twentieth century, however, set large-scale Filipino emigration to the United States into motion.[3]

The emergence of the transpacific imperial zone as a major commercial hub in the world economy during the early twentieth century spurred large-scale movement of people back and forth between metropole and colony. The right to travel freely across and within the borders of the United States was one of the few explicit privileges accorded to American nationals. This fact soon caught the attention of agribusiness concerns in Hawaii, Alaska and the West Coast looking to secure new channels of labor after the enactment of restrictive federal policies barring the entry of immigrant workers from China and Japan. Representatives from Hawaii's sugar industry were the first to enlist Filipinos to meet labor needs in the islands during the first decade of the twentieth century. Business leaders initially greeted the influx of Filipinos with enthusiasm, believing that centuries of colonial subordination made the newcomers well suited for hierarchical command-and-control structure of the plantation system. That the arrival of Filipinos might also be used to offset the growing militancy of Japanese workers in Hawaii was an added bonus. Filipinos were particularly disadvantaged in Hawaii because they worked under onerous labor contracts negotiated between sugar industry representatives and American colonial officials in the Philippines. Though "alien contract labor" had been banned in the U.S. during the late nineteenth century as unduly exploitative, Filipino migrant workers were exempted from this protection since they were not aliens.

By the early 1920s Filipinos grew increasingly restive about punishing working and living conditions on the plantations, finding common cause with Japanese co-workers seeking improvements in wages, housing and medical services. Filipinos soon built a reputation for labor militancy in the islands, orchestrating a wave of crippling strikes that provoked a violent response from business elites seeking to stifle increasingly sophisticated union campaigns. Close ties between the sugar industry and the local political apparatus (police, legislature, courts) proved difficult to overcome and labor activists operated under constant threat of arrest and blacklist for their organizing activities.[4]

Class subordination and political turmoil in Hawaii alongside heavy demand for migrant labor on the West Coast during the 1920s spurred many Filipinos to depart the islands for new opportunities in the heart of the metropole. As the number of Filipinos living in the United States grew, so too did concerns about their integration into the social and economic fabric of the United States. Efforts to contain and discipline the Filipino population through traditional methods such as legal prohibitions on family formation (e.g., anti-miscegenation laws), property rights, and restrictions on labor market mobility were often ineffective since the newcomers did not fit neatly into the preexisting system of administrative classification. The socio-cultural climate on the United States mainland, which unlike Hawaii featured a large white majority population, brought questions of race, citizenship, and empire to the foreground of the Filipino experience.

The rise of the transpacific west (Hawaii, Alaska, West Coast) as a global economic hub was fueled by agribusiness, an industry dependent on the steady availability of inexpensive seasonal labor. Federal restrictions curbing the entry of Chinese and Japanese immigrants alongside grower ambivalence about the long-term viability of Mexican migrants led employers to turn to Filipinos to fill labor demands in the region's booming agricultural sector. Though key members of the business community embraced the arrival of Filipinos on the West Coast during the 1920s, their presence also generated controversy. Anxiety surrounding the newcomers' disregard for traditional racial checkpoints in American society was a primary source of concern. Moreover, their anomalous political status provided openings for Filipinos to challenge the array of legal exclusions implemented to subordinate Asian immigrants in the United States. Filipinos' public defiance of the color line, alongside their growing reputation for labor militancy prompted nativists to condemn the newcomers as an unassimilable population who threatened American institutions. The contentious politics surrounding the status of Filipinos in the U.S. was not easily resolved. Nativists pressed the federal government to restrict immigration from the Philippines beginning in the 1920s, but Congress was hesitant to take action noting that such a policy would flout international convention that allowed colonial subjects unimpeded entry to the "mother country."

Uncertainty over Filipinos' civic status in the United States spurred a series of legal battles to determine their location in the American racial order. On one side of this conflict were officials at the federal, state, and local levels who policed the nation's patchwork system of racial stratification. On the other side were Filipinos who challenged discriminatory laws often using the government's own bureaucratic machinery against itself. They drew on the language of benevolent empire to contest their exclusion from the national community, citing their compulsory allegiance to the United States and challenging the legitimacy of race as a criterion of citizenship or participation in America's democratic institutions. In addition, their outlier ethnological designation as "Malays" placed them outside the preexisting system of racial boundaries, forcing state officials to recalibrate the color line. For instance, Filipinos challenged anti-miscegenation statutes prohibiting intermarriage between whites and Asians, cleverly arguing that state laws barring unions between whites and Mongolians (the ethnological term for East Asians) did not apply to them since they were popularly classified as "Malays." While Filipinos did successfully contest some discriminatory measures, these were often provisional victories as gatekeepers fashioned new, more refined methods, to sustain the racial hierarchy.[5]

Although Filipinos, as colonial subjects, were afforded unimpeded entry to the United States, their standing vis-à-vis the boundaries of American polity remained ambiguous in the early years of colonial rule. This issue took on new urgency once Filipinos began applying for naturalized citizenship in the early decades of the twentieth century. By the early twentieth century the racial disqualification of Asian immigrants from naturalized citizenship in the U.S. was a matter of settled law. These rulings, however, had not anticipated the unique situation of colonial migrants settling in the "mother country." The key question taken up by the courts addressed the role that Filipinos' colonial attachment to the United States played in determining their socio-legal standing in the national community.

Initial efforts to resolve this issue revealed the unanticipated dilemmas occasioned by extraterritorial expansion as American lawmakers worked to integrate colonial subjects into the imperial polity. Early twentieth-century naturalization law in the United States established administrative procedures for aliens to become citizens. Federal policy, however, provided no procedure to naturalize non-alien immigrants subject to U.S. sovereignty. In effect, this meant that a Filipino could not even technically apply for citizenship because there was no box on the application form for a U.S. national to check. A second bureaucratic obstacle involved the so-called first papers requirement of the naturalization application. The first papers provision entailed a two-step process—the first part was the "declaration of intent" (to become a citizen) and the second part required that the applicant "renounce allegiance" to his or her former sovereign. This of course was illogical since it would require Filipinos to renounce allegiance to their former sovereign—*the United States*—to become a citizen.[6]

Congress amended U.S. naturalization law in 1906 seemingly to address this administrative conundrum. The 1906 Naturalization Act made eligible for citizenship "*all persons*, not citizens who owe permanent allegiance to the United States." The intent of the legislation to make nationals eligible seemed clear since no other class of people fit into this category of non-citizens owing allegiance to the U.S. The issue, however, was far from resolved revealing the stubborn persistence of racial ideology in determining the boundaries of inclusion and exclusion in the national polity. A series of test cases in 1910s and 1920s addressing the admissibility of Filipino nationals produced contradictory results. Some courts ruled that Filipinos were indeed eligible for citizenship, citing their unique political attachment to the U.S., especially the fact that they "owed allegiance" to the imperial state. The prevailing opinion (that would eventually be upheld by higher court), however, declared them disqualified on racial grounds, citing Section 2169 of the U.S. Revised Statutes which limited naturalization eligibility to free white persons and persons of African descent.

While the federal courts had ruled that Asian immigrants were racially ineligible for U.S. citizenship, Filipinos argued that their status as American nationals exempted them from this disqualification. Moreover, the fact that U.S. colonial authorities had specifically mandated that white Americans were eligible for "Philippine citizenship" in the archipelago if they so desired led Filipinos to assume that they would be granted reciprocal rights in the metropole. Most of the early test cases involved Filipinos serving in the U.S. Navy, who filed their naturalization papers while stationed at military bases in the continental United States. A key argument advanced by these petitioners asserted their eligibility based on special provisions enacted by Congress offering expedited citizenship to aliens who had served honorably in the U.S. military. This claim was especially compelling during the World War I era, when American officials lauded military service as the ultimate expression of patriotic fidelity to the nation. Another tactic was employed by mestizo (mixed race) appellants who cited their partial white ancestry to test the definitional boundaries of whiteness as a criterion of exclusion. In fact, many petitioners employed both arguments since American military commanders favored mestizo recruits, believing them to be of superior racial stock to full-blooded Filipinos.

While the particulars of the Filipino test cases varied, they all examined the statutory implications of the 1906 Immigration Act, which was adopted to address the precarious status of newly acquired colonial wards. The core issue taken up by the courts was the Congressional intent behind the 1906 Act's expansion of naturalization eligibility to include "all persons, not citizens who owe permanent allegiance to the United States." While the law's intent to make U.S. nationals like Filipinos, Puerto Ricans, and Guamanians eligible for citizenship seemed unambiguous, the specter of race loomed large as the issue worked its way through the federal courts. The key point of contention was whether fitness for citizenship should be determined by the civic attributes of individual applicants or whether racial selection would remain the core principle regulating admission to the national community.

Two cases illustrate the divergent interpretations regarding Filipinos' political status in the United States. In the first, Francisco Mallari applied for naturalization in a Massachusetts District Court in 1916. Mr. Mallari was a U.S. Navy veteran who was in the process of re-enlisting based on the recommendation of his commanding officer. The case hinged on the court's interpretation of Section 30 of the 1906 Naturalization Act, asking whether its inclusive language contained therein superseded the racially restrictive prerequisites established in the Section 2169 of the U.S. Revised Statutes. The judge in the Mallari case noted that the 1906 Act had authorized "the admission to citizenship of *all persons* not citizens, who owe permanent allegiance to the United States." By highlighting the phrase "all persons," the court accentuated the broadness of the statutory language as explicitly including native residents of U.S. colonial possessions. Judge Morton's opinion addressed the salience of racial bars to citizenship established in Section 2169, but situated his analysis against the historical backdrop of extra-territorial expansion and the acquisition of colonial subjects. The court stressed that congressional debates surrounding the passage of the 1906 Naturalization Act had explicitly referenced the predicament of the Filipinos and Puerto Ricans and the judge cited statements made by other federal agencies, including the U.S. Attorney General and the State Department suggesting that American nationals were indeed eligible for naturalization resulting from the Act.

The court's ruling stressed the disadvantaged status of Filipinos as neither citizens, nor aliens in the United States. This questionable classification meant that this particular group of American nationals were "more unfavorably treated by our laws" than aliens from foreign nations. In Judge Morton's estimation, it would be impolitic for the U.S. to place the same racial limitations on residents of its dependencies that it placed on aliens from foreign countries. Mr. Mallari's petition was eventually denied on a technicality, unrelated to race, but the court's interpretation that Filipinos were exempt from racial limitations was noteworthy.[7]

The question of whether Filipinos were subject to racially restrictive citizenship laws received a very different interpretation later that same year. This petition was heard in the Southern District Court in 1916 in New York State and involved another Navy veteran, Ricardo Lampitoe. Lampitoe's legal filing cited his European ancestry (Spanish father/Filipina mother) as well as his military service as qualifying grounds for naturalization. His naturalization application was dismissed in a curt, three-sentence opinion rendered by celebrated American jurist, Billings "Learned" Hand, who declared that the petitioner fell within the exclusionary legal precedent established in earlier case law disqualifying Asian immigrants from U.S. citizenship. For Judge Hand, the racial bases of American nationality law were sacrosanct and rendered all other issues, including Filipinos' political attachment to the U.S. moot. The Court summarily rejected Lampitoe's claim to whiteness as absurd. Judge Hand allowed that an appellant's partial white ancestry might warrant consideration in certain instances, but only if they met an unspecified blood quantum. While the judge didn't enumerate what that necessary threshold of white blood was, he declared that it had not been met in Lampitoe's case because, "where the Malay blood predominates it would be a perversion of language to say that the descendant is a 'white person.' Certainly any white ancestor, no matter how remote, does not make all his descendants white."

Judge Hand glossed over the fact that it was Lampitoe's father, not some "remote" ancestor who was the source of his European extraction. Lampitoe, like many other mestizo petitioners, was denied citizenship on arbitrary determinations about the boundaries of white racial identification. Because the category "white" was never precisely defined, legal authorities were granted a wide berth to determine who was included or excluded from this classification. In this case, Judge Hand relied on a biological definition, suggesting that the prevalence of "Malay blood" overshadowed Mr. Lampitoe's claims to whiteness. The court's ruling made reference to neither the petitioner's honorable military service nor Filipinos' unique status as U.S. colonial subjects, which Judge Hand determined had no bearing on one's qualification for citizenship. Subsequent decisions would follow a similar logic rejecting the claim that the 1906 Act had made Filipinos eligible for U.S. citizenship. Ultimately, the courts averred that the statutory phrase "all persons, not citizens who owe permanent allegiance to the United States" used in the 1906 Act has not explicitly nullified the racial prerequisites established in Section 2169 of the Revised Statutes and therefore applied only to Filipinos of the "white" or "black" races. By this twisted logic native residents of the Philippines had indeed been made eligible under the 1906 Act unless they were Filipino.[8]

The divergent interpretations rendered by the federal courts in the Mallari and Lampitoe cases highlight how fitness for citizenship ultimately pivoted on the question of whether membership in the national community should be determined by group based on ascriptive criteria (race, national origin) or by the civic attributes (political attachment, military service) of individual petitioners. Modifications to U.S. naturalization policy resulting from the United States involvement in World War I led to a temporary expansion of the boundaries of national membership. Not surprisingly, definitions of citizenship emphasizing patriotic sacrifice and national fidelity took on increasing significance during this time. The federal government launched a series of public campaigns aimed at strengthening links between wartime service and national obligation to mobilize support for the war effort. In support of the war effort, Congress enacted legislation allowing expedited citizenship for aliens who enlisted in the U.S. armed forces. Efforts to recruit noncitizens into the military took on particular urgency during the World War I period, when one out of every six draft-age men in the United States was a non-citizen. While these efforts were primarily aimed at European immigrants, Filipino servicemen demanded the same benefits for their patriotic war efforts.

Filipinos had long contended that their compulsory allegiance to the United States entitled them to special consideration with regard to American naturalization law—though this argument had gained little traction. The war, however, provided an opportunity to demonstrate their unalloyed allegiance to the United States through martial sacrifice. The 1914 Naturalization Act was one of the early legislative initiatives implemented to entice "alien" enlistees with the reward of citizenship, but the statutory language did not explicitly address the status of Filipinos who were not technically classified as "aliens." Congress passed another amended naturalization bill in 1918, which offered expedited citizenship to "any alien" who served in the U.S. armed forces during the war. Importantly, the 1918 Act included a provision permitting Filipinos who had served "in this present war" to petition for naturalization.

The 1918 Act provided a very narrow expansion of the boundaries of national community. Only Filipinos who had rendered the requisite military service in the U.S. armed forces during the war would be eligible for citizenship, while all other persons of Filipino descent remained disqualified "based on color or race." The manpower needs of the wartime state led the federal government to temporarily ease some of its restrictions against the naturalization of non-citizen soldiers of Asian descent. After some initial confusion about the scope of the law, naturalization courts across the nation and in the territory of Hawaii started granting citizenship to soldiers of

Asian descent with the approval of the Bureau of Immigration and Naturalization. Nativists, however, quickly regrouped after the war ended and began contesting the legality of the naturalization certificates granted to Asian American veterans. A series of legal challenges filed during the interwar period tested just how far the boundaries of the national polity had been expanded during the war and whether the racial limitations on citizenship imposed by Section 2169 had in fact been superseded by the 1918 Act. While Asian American activists hoped that their wartime sacrifices might lead U.S. lawmakers to revise racial barriers to citizenship, exclusionary provisions remained in place. The decisions handed down by the Supreme Court in the *Ozawa* and *Thind* cases in 1922 and 1923, respectively, reaffirmed that Asians remained racially disqualified from naturalized citizenship though neither case directly took up the issue of whether Asian veterans had correctly been granted citizenship under the 1918 Act.

It was not until 1925 that the Supreme Court finally took up the issue of the eligibility of Asian veterans in the case of *Hidemitsu Toyota v. United States*. The case involved a Japanese immigrant, Hidemitsu Toyota, who applied for naturalization after serving ten years in the U.S. Coast Guard. Though the case involved a Japanese applicant, the Court also weighed in on the status of Filipinos, primarily to distinguish their situation from that of other persons of Asian descent. The justices opined that Asian veterans, including Toyota, had not been made eligible for citizenship under the 1918 Naturalization Act, because that law did not explicitly rescind the racial prerequisites established in Section 2169 of the Revised Statutes. The Court did acknowledge that the status of Filipinos needed to be dealt with separately because of their compulsory allegiance to the United States. The Court concluded that Filipino servicemen fell under the purview of the 1918 Act, thus making them eligible for citizenship regardless of race as long as they met the prescribed military obligations. The justices emphasized that their ruling did not overturn the racial barriers to citizenship enshrined in Section 2169; it simply created a narrow exemption for noncitizen nationals who had served in the U.S. armed forces during wartime. The Court's opinion stressed that "it has long been the national policy to maintain the distinction of color and race, [and] radical change is not lightly to be deemed to have been intended . . . As Filipinos are not aliens and owe allegiance to the United States, there are strong reasons for relaxing as to them the restrictions, which do not exist in favor of aliens who are barred because of their color and race."

The Supreme Court's decision in *Toyota* reaffirmed the exclusionary character of the U.S. polity affirming that persons of Asian descent were still disqualified from naturalized citizenship. This decision thwarted the efforts of Asian veterans to assert an alternative definition of national membership based on civic criteria such as military service. At the same time the Court acknowledged the unique status of Filipinos in the American polity and affirmed the eligibility of individuals who met the prescribed qualifications laid out in the 1918 Act. The *Toyota* case provided an important, though somewhat incongruous ruling on the civic status of Filipinos, declaring the racial boundaries of citizenship to be simultaneously permeable (for war veterans) yet inviolable for all others. The federal courts did affirm, however, that Filipinos held a special status in the American polity inasmuch as they "owed allegiance" to the United States and were subject to its sovereignty. The ruling was an acknowledgement that non-citizen nationals were fractional members of national community whose rights and obligations vis-à-vis the U.S. would be determined on an ad hoc basis.[9]

One of the few clearly defined rights granted to Filipino nationals was the right to travel to the metropole without restriction. They were treated, legally speaking, the same as citizens when it came to entering and exiting the United States. The influx of Filipinos during the interwar period spurred a new cycle of nativist mobilization aimed at stemming what they called the "third Asiatic invasion." Nativists ratcheted up their rhetoric characterizing Filipinos as a problem population that posed a grave threat to the American social order. They alleged that the federal state had failed to protect the white citizenry from Filipinos, who "stole" their jobs, brazenly pursued young white women, and displayed a troubling affinity for radical labor politics. Nativist spokesmen propagated alarmist messages about interracial sex, labor competition, and political subversion to galvanize public support for Filipino exclusion. Federal officials, however, remained lukewarm to the idea of barring the nation's doors to its own colonial subjects, fearing that such a policy would undermine America's self-proclaimed image as a benevolent imperial sovereign. Congress's failure to act on the so-called Filipino problem prompted Western nativists to take ownership of the issue seizing the mantle of popular direct action to reclaim their communities from the putative invaders. A dramatic uptick in extralegal actions such as vigilante campaigns and mass expulsions aimed to make life intolerable for Filipinos. Nativist leaders exploited the outbreak of racial discord that swept across the West Coast blaming the persecuted Filipino community for the turmoil, claiming that they brought the reprisals on themselves with their open defiance of racial and class conventions. Movement partisans cast the violence as regrettable, but inevitable response to shortsighted government policies that allowed Filipino immigrants to flood into the country and to openly subvert the color line. Nativist arguments were couched in the aggrieved discourse of white racial victimhood, a rhetorical strategy that both explained and justified vigilante action, suggesting that such campaigns were carried out in "self-defense" by besieged communities who had been abandoned by the federal state.[10]

Popular support for Filipino exclusion on the West Coast did not translate readily into policy change at the national level. Legislation aimed at barring the entry of Filipinos into the United States repeatedly stalled in Congress despite the unyielding efforts of nativists. The main obstacle was that Congressional leaders worried about the diplomatic consequences of barring Filipinos from the "mother country" while they were still living under the U.S. flag. It was not until nativist leaders switched tactics in the mid 1930s and began pressing for Philippine independence that they made headway. Exclusionists entered into a makeshift political alliance with Filipino nationalists, and the Midwestern agricultural lobby (e.g., dairy and sugar beet interests), worried about competition from cheap Philippine imports, were also pushing for Philippine independence. Filipino exclusion was eventually achieved through the back door, by way of a proviso attached to the Tydings–McDuffie Act in 1934 that established a framework for Philippine independence after a ten-year probationary period. Though independence would not come into effect for ten years, a restrictive quota of 50 per annum went into effect immediately upon passage of the bill. That the quota of 50 per year was lower than even the despised Japanese offered a good barometer of the intensity of anti-Filipino animus in the 1930s. One important takeaway from the campaign behind the passage of Tydings–McDuffie Act was that it was as much about the United States seeking its *independence from* the Philippines as it was about supporting national self-determination for the Filipino people.[11]

Though happy about the passage of an exclusion measure, nativist spokesmen quickly realized that a ban on future immigration from the Philippines did not really solve the "Filipino problem" since it did nothing to address the population already living in the U.S. Nativist leaders pivoted quickly and began pressing Congress to pass a repatriation bill aimed at sending Filipinos back to the islands. One stumbling block to the passage of such legislation was the powerful Western agribusiness lobby, which had also opposed the earlier exclusion campaigns due to their reliance on Filipino and Mexican labor. Western farm operators' support for Filipinos, however, began to crumble by the mid 1930s as the social and economic costs of employing them escalated. The growing political militancy of Filipino workers who orchestrated a series of large-scale strikes attracted sensational media attention on the West Coast. As a result, local officials warned that many Filipino workers had become increasingly militant and difficult to control. In response, Congress passed the first in a series of repatriation bills in 1935 which offered Filipinos free one-way passage back to the Philippines if the prospective repatriate signed a contract promising never to return to the United States. Filipino community leaders denounced the measure as a "disguised form of deportation" and few ever participated in the program.

Except for the new restrictions on immigration to the metropole, the status of Filipino nationals during the Commonwealth period (1934–1946) did not actually differ much from their standing during the colonial era. The outbreak of global war during the late 1930s and early 1940s, however, brought the imperial relationship between the U.S. and the Philippines back into the spotlight. Filipinos, as stipulated in the Tydings–McDuffie Act, retained their classification as American nationals during the Commonwealth period and consequently, they still "retained permanent allegiance" to the United States. Moreover, a provision in the Act authorized the President of the United States to conscript "all military organized by the Philippine government" to serve under the U.S. military command at his discretion.[12]

In many ways the socio-legal status of Filipinos became even more precarious once both countries were drawn into World War II. The federal government passed a series of emergency measures in the leadup to the war in an effort to shore up the borders of the wartime state and mobilize manpower for the Allied military operations. Over the course of the war, they were subject to a series of confounding edicts from the federal government regarding their standing. For certain wartime measures, Filipinos were classified as "aliens," but they were categorized as "citizens" or "nationals" when it came to other federal statutes. Wartime schizophrenia about the status of Filipinos in the U.S. polity echoed previous disputes over their eligibility for citizenship, landholding, and occupational rights. It also served as a reminder that Filipinos remained under the sovereignty of the United States even as the two countries moved inexorably toward political severance. During the late 1930s and early 1940s American authorities declared Filipinos to be U.S. citizens under the Neutrality Act of 1939, suspect aliens under the Alien Registration Act of 1940, and non-citizen nationals under the Nationality Act of 1940. The bizarre notion that one could be simultaneously be legally classified as a citizen, an alien, and national created an unprecedented situation under American law. Despite the arbitrary way in which U.S. officials adjudicated the status of Filipinos there was an underlying logic at work. When it came to exacting maximum loyalty and military service from Filipinos, U.S. authorities considered them to be citizens, with the requisite obligation to defend the nation and provide military service to the state during war. When it came to the state's reciprocal obligation to extend the full spectrum of civic rights to Filipinos or to provide for their social welfare as full members of the national community, they were classed as aliens or nationals, with a limited claim to the rights and protections guaranteed to citizens by the federal government.[13]

Questions surrounding Filipinos' status vis-à-vis the Selective Service Act of 1940 highlight how this administrative imperiousness played out on the ground. The Selective Service Act established a wartime draft in the leadup to America's entry into the World War II. The Act decreed it the "duty of every male citizen . . . and every male alien residing in the United States" between the ages of eighteen and thirty-six to register for the military draft. Interestingly, Filipino nationals residing in the United States were initially left outside the statutory scope of the 1940 Selective Service Act. This oversight had some unexpected consequences: After the Japanese attacks on Pearl Harbor and the Philippines a few hours apart in December 1941, domestic war mobilization shifted into high gear. Filipinos in the U.S. like many others were swept up in the patriotic fervor of the period and showed up in droves at recruiting stations on the West Coast to enlist. To their surprise, they were turned away because there was no administrative box on the selective service forms for nationals to check. Moreover, the enlistment forms required non-citizen enlistees to "renounce allegiance" to their former sovereign, which for Filipinos would meant renouncing the United States.

Strangely just a few months before, on July 26, 1941 President Roosevelt had issued Executive Order 81 conscripting 150,000–200,000 Filipinos in the Philippine Army under the U.S. military command. This created a somewhat bizarre situation whereby Filipinos living in the United States could not join American armed forces due to their status as U.S. nationals yet Filipinos in the Philippines were conscripted en masse into the U.S. armed forces because they were nationals. While the Selective Service Act would later be amended to allow Filipinos to enlist, the confusion surrounding their initial attempts to enlist underscores the arbitrary character of Filipinos' political status during the Commonwealth period.

Filipino leaders embraced the Allied cause despite their resentment over their callous treatment before and during the war, and exploited their patriotic exploits to launch their own version of the Double-V campaign demanding rights and recognition as a reward for the service to the wartime state. Though they did win some notable political concessions during the war—most notably the granting of national independence and the removal of racial bars disqualifying Filipinos from American citizenship, these victories were bittersweet as the United States quickly reneged on promises of veteran's benefits and citizenship rights for Filipino soldiers who served under the U.S. command during the war.[14]

The inauguration of Philippine independence at the conclusion of the war in 1946 brought the strange career of the Filipino national to an abrupt end. U.S. officials moved quickly to scrub all traces of this longstanding political attachment, especially as it pertained to lingering obligations to former Filipino nationals who had been conscripted into the U.S. armed forces. Wartime pledges of access to full U.S. military benefits, postwar healthcare, and citizenship rights were rescinded as congressional leaders claimed that the United States no longer held any obligations to Filipinos now that they had been granted national independence. While the formal colonial relationship between the U.S. and the Philippines concluded in 1946, the specter of the Filipino national would continue to reverberate in the ensuing decades as the legacies of militarism, veterans' benefits, and political interference remained contentious issues tying the two countries together.

Notes

1 R. Baldoz and C. Ayala, "The Bordering of America: Colonialism and Citizenship in the Philippines and Puerto Rico," *Centro* 25(1) (2013): 76–105. C. Duffy Burnett, (2009). "Empire and the Transformation of Citizenship" in *Colonial Crucible: Empire in the Making of the Modern American State*, Eds. Alfred W. McCoy and Francisco A. Scarano. (Madison, WI: University of Wisconsin Press) 332–341; G. Neuman and T. Brown-Nagin, *Reconsidering the Insular Cases: The Past and Future of American Empire* (Cambridge, MA: Harvard University Press, 2015).

2 R. Smith, *Civic Ideals: Conflicting Visions of Citizenship in U.S. History* (New Haven, CT: Yale University Press, 1997); R. Waldinger and T. Soehl, (2013) "The Political Sociology of International Migration: Borders. Boundaries, Rights, and Politics" in Eds. S. Gold and S. Nawyn, *Routledge International Handbook of Migration,* New York: Routledge 334–344; L. Bosniak, *The Alien and the Citizen: Dilemmas of Contemporary Membership* (Princeton, NJ: Princeton University Press, 2006).

3 R. Baldoz, *The Third Asiatic Invasion, Empire and Migration in Filipino America, 1898–1946*, (New York: NYU Press, 2011); M. Ngai, *Impossible Subjects: Illegal Aliens and the Making of Modern America*, (Princeton, NJ: Princeton University Press, 2004).

4 E. Beechert, *Working in Hawaii: A Labor History*, (Honolulu: University of Hawaii Press, 1985); R. Baldoz, "Comrade Carlos Bulosan: U.S. State Surveillance and the Cold War Suppression of Filipino Radicals" *Asia-Pacific Journal* 11(3) (2014): 1–18.

5 R. Baldoz, *The Third Asiatic Invasion*, 70–76, 90–110; M. Koessler, "Subject, Citizen, National, and Permanent Allegiance," *Yale Law Review* 56 (1946): 60–67.

6 Ibid., 75–86.
7 In re *Mallari*, 239 F. 416; See also *Bautista*, 245 F. at 765–766.
8 In re *Lampitoe* 232 F. 382; See also *Rallos* 241 F. 687.
9 *Toyota v. United States*, 268 U.S. 402.
10 R. Baldoz, *The Third Asiatic Invasion*, 140–165; M. Ngai, *Impossible Subjects*, 110–126.
11 R. Baldoz, *The Third Asiatic Invasion*, 156–192.
12 Ibid., 194–220. See also A. Fabros, "The Fight for Equality in the U.S. Armed Forces in World War II by Uncle Sam's Colored Soldiers," *Filipino American National Historical Society Journal* 4 (1996): 46; J. Wingo, "The First Filipino Regiment," *Asia and the Americas* 42 (6) (1942): 562–564. F. Golay, *Face of Empire: United States–Philippines Relations* (Manila: Ateneo de Manila University Press, 1998).
13 R. Baldoz, *The Third Asiatic Invasion*, 196–225.
14 Ibid., 203–209.

References

Baldoz, Rick. and Ayala, Cesar. "The Bordering of America: Colonialism and Citizenship in the Philippines and Puerto Rico," *CENTRO* 25, no. 1 (2013): 76–105.

Baldoz, Rick. "Comrade Carlos Bulosan: U.S. State Surveillance and the Cold War Suppression of Filipino Radicals," *Asia-Pacific Journal* 11, no. 3 (2014): 1–18

Baldoz, Rick. *The Third Asiatic Invasion: Empire and Migration in Filipino America 1898-1946*. New York: New York University Press, 2011.

Beechert, Edward. *Working in Hawaii: A Labor History*. Honolulu, HI: University of Hawaii Press, 1985.

Bosniak, Linda. *The Alien and the Citizen: Dilemmas of Contemporary Membership*. Princeton, NJ: Princeton University Press, 2006.

Burnett, Christina Duffy. "Empire and the Transformation of Citizenship." In *Colonial Crucible: Empire in the Making of the Modern American State*, Eds. Alfred W. McCoy and Francisco A. Scarano, 332–341. Madison, WI: University of Wisconsin Press, 2009.

Fabros, Alex. "The Fight for Equality in the U.S. Armed Forces in World War II by Uncle Sam's Colored Soldiers," *Filipino American National Historical Society Journal,* 4 (1996): 42–48.

Golay, Frank. *Face of Empire: United States–Philippines Relations*. Manila: Ateneo de Manila University Press, 1998.

Koessler, Maximillian. "Subject, Citizen, National, and Permanent Allegiance," *Yale Law Review* 56, (1946): 60–67.

Neuman Gerald and Tomiko Brown-Nagin, *Reconsidering the Insular Cases: The Past and Future of American Empire*. Cambridge MA: Harvard University Press, 2015.

Ngai, Mae. *Impossible Subjects: Illegal Aliens and the Making of Modern America*. Princeton, NJ: Princeton University Press, 2004.

Smith, Rogers. *Civic Ideals: Conflicting Ideals of Citizenship in U.S. History*. New Haven, CT: Yale University Press, 1997.

Waldinger, Roger and Thomas Soehl. "The Political Sociology of International Migration: Borders. Boundaries, Rights, and Politics." In *Routledge International Handbook of Migration*, Eds. S. Gold and S. Nawyn, 334–344. New York: Routledge, 2013.

Wingo, James "The First Filipino Regiment," *Asia and the Americas,* 42 no. 6 (1942): 562–564.

11

THE ARAB AMERICAN EXPERIENCE: FROM INVISIBILITY TO HEIGHTENED VISIBILITY

Louise Cainkar

The social history of Arab Americans is different from that of most other ethnic or national origin groups in the U.S., whether white or nonwhite. Early in the 20th century, Arab Americans as a group largely benefited from the social inclusion and perquisites that accrued to marginal whiteness. Defined as Caucasian [the original peoples of Europe, North Africa, and the Middle East] and said to share in the culture and history of the West, intermittent attempts to exclude them from the structural benefits accruing to whiteness were usually successfully challenged. Yet as the U.S. government increasingly engaged in global ventures of power after World War II, popular movements within the Arab world became obstacles to its and its allies' aspirations for unfettered dominance. In order to justify U.S. ambitions and actions in the region, the U.S. government, mainstream U.S. media, and interested U.S. parties undertook extensive efforts to define Arabs as a problem for the West: they were a monolithic, fanatic, and uncivilized people who did not share Western values. Resistance to Western colonialism, domination, and oppression was [re-]framed as an inherent cultural proclivity to violence. As dominant social constructions of who they were changed, so did the social status and position of Arab Americans in the American racial hierarchy. By 2002 Arab Americans had become the least favored among American ethnic and religious groups, even less than Muslims, as measured by the Bogardus scale of social distance.[1] Over a span of time, Arab American experiences and their treatment by actors in government, mainstream social institutions, and the American public came to mirror the historic experiences of people of color. Indeed, these days one must often describe Arab American experiences and South Asian American experiences jointly, because in many ways their fates have aligned, especially in the case of South Asian Muslims and Sikhs.

This chapter traces both the divergent history of Arab Americans and the social processes through which their history moved toward convergence with Asian Americans. It argues that empire has tied these trajectories together, for if European colonialism invented the historic definitions of race and racial hierarchies that defined early U.S. policies towards Asian Americans, African Americans, Native Americans, and Latinos, the rise of the U.S. as a global superpower invented the Arab as being first, and foremost, a problem for the West. Through the repeated propagation of essentializing stereotypes and tropes, Arabs became racialized as nonwhite, losing rights to individuality, difference, freedom, justice, and safety that accrue to that status.

While some think that the 9/11 attacks brought about negative views and treatment of Arab Americans, the process of stereotyping and stigmatizing Arab Americans long preceded these attacks. Yet for reasons explained below, these features of the Arab American experience remained invisible to most Americans, including to scholars; lack of concern and solidarity allowed them to further deteriorate. Because these negative views pre-existed the 9/11 attacks, they paved the way for a majority of Americans to hold Arab Americans [and Muslim Americans and often South Asian Americans] collectively responsible for them. The act of holding an entire group responsible for the actions of a few exposes a racialized response. Racism causes all members of a group to be held responsible for something; the "something" does not happen first. What happens first is an understanding that all members of a certain group can be viewed as the same, that they have limited internal variation in values, beliefs, or points of view. Just as the Pearl Harbor bombing did not cause anti-Japanese racism and the subsequent internment of Japanese Americans, rather, pre-existing racism against Japanese Americans provided popular support for the idea that all Japanese in the western U.S. should be interred because they posed a threat to the U.S. Similarly, the "Asiatic Barred Zone" was created out of an understanding that all persons from the area so demarcated shared traits that were unwelcome in the U.S. In mainstream United States culture, misdeeds by individuals or small groups perceived as nonwhite are usually represented as the products of that group's deviant culture; when it comes to whites, reprehensible acts perpetrated by an individual or group are represented as the actions of outliers, the mentally ill or other deviants to white culture. Thus, the actions of 19 persons on 9/11 who were not Arab Americans nor known to Arab Americans brought about official and public responses that created "homeland insecurity" for all Arab Americans.[2]

The Early Arab American Experience (1880s–1960s)

Arabs began migrating to the U.S. in significant numbers, mainly from western Asia, after 1880. Between 1880 and 1924 some 95,000 Arabs migrated to the United States, largely from the Ottoman-ruled province of "Greater Syria" (present-day Syria, Lebanon, Jordan, and Palestine/Israel), with smaller numbers migrating from Yemen and Iraq, as well as Morocco and Egypt in North Africa.[3] While males initially dominated "Syrian" migration, as it came to be called, by 1920 females were dominant, signally both family reunification and independent female migration.[4] These male and female migrants settled mostly on the East Coast and in the Midwest, but also moved to the South. While many Arab immigrants worked in manufacturing, particularly in the auto and related industries, and some established or labored in small textile or canning factories, Arab immigrants also developed a specialized niche in trade, whether as long-distance linen and dry goods peddlers in the countryside, short-range urban peddlers, or small-scale urban shopkeepers.[5] Arab American wholesalers, mainly located in the New York "mother colony," were key suppliers of these traders, who were mostly men but also included women.

While scholars have demonstrated that Arab Americans encountered racialized treatment and discrimination during their early years in the U.S.,[6] and surely more accounts will be uncovered by ongoing research, they nonetheless as a group had far greater levels of freedom of movement, residential choice, access to education, financial mobility, and civic inclusion than contemporaneous Asian Americans, African Americans, Latinos, and Native Americans. During this early period, Arab Americans established a significant number of social, cultural, and religious institutions, such as churches, mosques, social clubs, newspapers, and literary magazines, as well as homeland-oriented philanthropic and political organizations.[7] They were largely not denied immigration visas, nor were they pressured to live in urban ghettoes. Their social lives were often interwoven with members of other groups considered white.[8] Indeed, U.S. Census data show that the children of these Arab immigrants had high rates of marriage with Irish and German Americans.[9] Like European groups immigrating in large numbers at the time—southern and eastern Europeans and Jews—they faced the pressures of nativism as well as exclusions and barriers imposed by established whites, but on a collective level their access to resources for social mobility was higher than that of members of groups considered nonwhite.

Local power brokers contested the whiteness of Arab Americans at some times and in some places, as historian Gualtieri has shown in a number of studies.[10] Between 1910 and 1924, in places such as Detroit, Buffalo, Cincinnati, St. Louis, and parts of Georgia and South Carolina, local court clerks and judges challenged Arab applications for naturalization on the basis that they were not white as "commonly understood" or "intended by U.S. law."[11] At the time, local court clerks made decisions about applications for naturalization on a case-by-case basis, using their own sense of who was white to determine eligibility, since the federal government had been unclear as to which standards applied to determinations of race. Decisions to deny Arab naturalization applications were challenged in the courts and judges ruled in varying ways; some argued that the "common man's" understanding of whiteness excluded Arabs, even if they were officially considered Caucasian. Although the Arab region was largely excluded from the 1917 "Asiatic Barred Zone," it included some parts of modern day Saudi Arabia, Somalia, and Yemen. The inclusion of parts of Yemen provided ammunition for those who opposed Yemeni naturalization on the basis of race. These matters were settled for a while when federal appellate judges court ruled in the case of *Dow v U.S.*, 1915, that George Dow, a "Syrian," was eligible for naturalization because "generally received opinion" supported the idea that people from the part of Asia that included Syria were white persons.

Congress instituted immigration quotas in the 1920s, mainly aimed at limiting the migration of southern and eastern Europeans (and Arabs), groups considered by established whites as racially inferior, yet marginally white.[12] Arabs continued to migrate to the U.S. after this time, but in much smaller numbers. Yet challenges to Arab whiteness were still being brought, as the 1940 case of Majid Ramsay Sharif shows. Sharif appealed the denial of his immigrant visa on the basis that he was not white to the Bureau of Immigration Appeals [BIA]. The BIA ruled in 1941 that Sharif was white, and used a government brief submitted in the 1923 Supreme Court case *U.S. v. Thind* to support its decision. The BIA declared that Arabs were white because "so much of the Near East has contributed to, and was assimilable with, the development of Western Civilization of Greece and Rome" and "that it was not intended, either in 1790 . . . or certainly in 1940 . . . that Arabians be excluded from the group of 'white persons.'[13] Thus, as Smith has demonstrated, based on historical and civilizational arguments, the BIA argued that "whiteness" was associated with Western civilization and that Western civilization included the Arab world.[14] As the birthplace of Christianity, ruling differently might have challenged Jesus' customary portrayal in dominant American culture as a white man.

The period between 1920 and 1965 is, to date, the least studied of Arab American history. Arab American historiography renders this period as one of the second generation's economic success and social mobility, with low migration and considerable transnational movement.[15] New but relatively small migrations had commenced of [less than 2000] Palestinian refugees after 1948, spouses of Arab immigrants who had served in WWII, Arab students in pursuit of higher education, and professionals. The achievements of Arab American entrepreneurs and actors are highlighted in the literature covering this period, and in line with the trend of many other U.S. ethnic groups, World War II heroes are celebrated in a show of loyalty.[16] By most accounts,

Arab Americans had become a largely middle-class, well-educated group whose path to full membership in the American dominant group and whiteness was proceeding well. The removal of the Asiatic Barred Zone in 1952 had little impact on Arab migration.

Much, however, had changed in the Arab world during this period. Following World War I, European imperialism controlled most of the lands of the former Ottoman Empire, creating nation states, establishing boundaries, and installing monarchs in its favor. The Republic of Lebanon was established in 1943 under French hegemony, creating a Christian dominant nation in part of Syria, and the Jewish State of Israel was created in areas under British hegemony; hundreds of thousands of Palestinians were expelled to make way. Pan-Arabism as an anti-imperialist ideology of Arab strength and unity grew in popularity; in some places it was strong enough to overthrow European installed rulers. Pan-Arabism also challenged Israel's right to exist as a Jewish-ruled state built on the eviction of the native inhabitants of Palestine.

1965–2001: US Empire and Constructing the Arab Other

The U.S. immigration policy overhaul codified in the 1965 Immigration Act—the removal of country quotas, introduction of family reunification preferences, and expansion of immigrant visas for persons with skills needed in the United States—brought about major changes in the character of migration to the United States. Now a growing superpower, U.S. policymakers had determined that limiting the migration of persons based on racial criteria was untenable for an aspiring global leader. With these changes, and in light of global economics, over time the majority of new immigrants came no longer from Europe but from Asia, Latin America, and Africa. Migration from the Arab world increased markedly after these policy changes. Between 1965 and 2000 more than 630,000 Arabs immigrated to the United States.[17] Most Arab immigrants entered the U.S. under family reunification preferences although a significant proportion of some groups, such as Egyptians, entered on professional visas. More recent decades have witnessed large numbers of refugee admissions from Iraq, Somalia, and the Sudan. Palestinians, the largest refugee population in the world for much of the second half of the 20th century, have been ineligible for U.S. refugee status since the early 1960s. The Arab American Institute currently estimates that there are some 3.5 million Americans of Arab descent, based on the American Community Survey and its own research.[18]

At the same time as the Arab population the U.S. grew, the "common understanding" of the earlier era, that the Arab world and the West had a shared history and civilization, was being steadily dismantled. While southern and eastern Europeans who had earlier experienced limiting immigration quotas were being absorbed into "whiteness," Arab Americans were being moved symbolically in the opposite direction by an increasing array of negative portrayals that represented them as monolithic, inherently different from whites, and inferior in culture to the civilized West. These negative social constructions of Arabs and the Arab world became dominant in American culture starting in the late 1960s. They suited the foreign policy objectives of a rising U.S. global power and especially efforts to build broad American popular support for the State of Israel. The 1967 Israeli invasion and military occupation of the rest of Palestine, as well as parts of Egypt and Lebanon, was portrayed in the U.S. media as something with which Americans should identify and share elation. It was hailed as a victory of the civilized over the barbaric, of "us" over "them." Arabs were portrayed as incompetent, undeveloped, and morally undeserving of controlling their own destiny, while Israelis were portrayed as forward-moving people just like "us."[19] This binary narrative, which has been elaborated and used consistently in the American media ever since, contributed to the racial formation of Arabs, and later Muslims, as nonwhites.

Referring to 1967 as a "watershed" year in Arab American history, political scientist Suleiman reported that Arab Americans were "shocked and traumatized by the 1967 war" and in particular, "how greatly one-sided and pro-Israeli the American communications media were in reporting on the Middle East."[20] Arab Americans reported stingingly negative portrayals of Arabs as backwards, defeated, and primordial in newspapers and on televisions sets across the nation, during the course of the war and persistently thereafter.[21] Anthropologist Shryock concluded, "Arab Americans were forced to rethink their identities in response to U.S. government policies and American media representations. The latter were negative, biased against Arabs and Muslims, and profoundly alienating.[22] According to Awad, "The shock for Arab Americans was not so much the defeat . . . but the way it was received in the West and especially the United States, where strong derogatory racial overtones in the media toward the Arab contributed significantly, for the first time, to a growing political and ethnic awareness in the Arab American community."[23]

The 1967 Arab–Israeli war ignited an "Arab American awakening" according to anthropologist Naber.[24] Political scientist Jamal observed that: "the racialization of Muslims and Arabs stems from the consistent deployment of an "us" versus "them" mentality, excessively propped up for the justification of military campaigns in the Arab world.[25] If whiteness is determined not only by phenotype [skin color, facial structure, hair] but also by notions of a shared culture, history, and values, then Arabs became unambiguously nonwhite when the narrative was rewritten to sever historical ties between white America and "them." The U.S. social climate became so hostile to Arabs that Arab Americans founded several major organizations during this time to combat the growing racism, including The American Arab Anti-Discrimination Committee, The Association of Arab American University Graduates, The National Association of Arab Americans, and later, The Arab American Institute.

A flow of anti-Arab films and television talk shows continued throughout the 1970s, augmented by racialized media coverage of the 1973 Arab oil embargo, the Abscam FBI congressional sting operation [where FBI agents posed as wealthy Arabs], and increasing federal government scrutiny of Arab American activists.[26] In 1977, prominent sociologist Seymour Martin Lipset reported that public opinion polls showed American attitudes towards Arabs were "close to racist."[27] The renowned Palestinian American scholar Edward Said published his 1978 masterpiece *Orientalism*, a study driven in part by his wanting to understand how it was that the depictions of Arabs he observed in the U.S. bore no relationship to the reality of the Arab World he knew. *Orientalism* meticulously detailed the ways in which European imperial powers defined and described their colonial subjects, indeed wrote their histories in ways that demean them while celebrating the superiority of the colonial master's history and culture. Now, Orientalism defined the dominant American representation of Arab history and culture, and American empire was its author. Yet American studies scholar Salaita has pointed out that "anti-Arab racism" is a more useful term than Orientalism because it situates Arab American experiences in the specific context of American traditions:

> Orientalism is not entirely appropriate when we consider the effects of stereotyping and bigotry on Arab Americans, who . . . need to be located in a particular tradition of which they have been a partial inheritor. That tradition, uniquely American, includes the internment of Japanese Americans during WWII, institutionalized anti-Semitism until the 1960s, and a peculiarly durable xenophobia spanning decades.[28]

Arab Americans had been fully transformed into a cultural "other" by the 1980s. In addition to being represented negatively in films and on American television, its talk shows and news programs, they were described in dehumanizing ways in school textbooks and classroom teaching, in encyclopedias and thesauruses, and were degraded in other venues of culture, such as Halloween costumes, video games [shoot an Arab] and t-shirts [smoke a camel]. The following quote from an article published in the popular science *Omni* magazine entitled "The Importance of Hugging" by Howard Bloom provides a flavor of the discourses that characterized the time.[29] In it, Bloom offers a cultural explanation for "Arab brutality" [or is it Muslim?, note the conflation] and called Arabs a "walking time bomb."

> Could the denial of warmth lie behind Arab brutality? Could these keepers of Islamic flame be suffering from a lack of hugging? . . . In much of Arab society the cold and even brutal approach to children has still not stopped. Public warmth between men and women is considered a sin. And the Arab adult, stripped of intimacy and thrust into a life of cold isolation, has become a walking time bomb. An entire people may have turned barbaric for the simple lack of a hug.[30]

Anyone visiting the Arab world would in fact observe that children receive incredible amounts of physical affection. Yet the invention of the Arab as problem seemed to have no limits in American culture, even when such depictions would be condemned as racist if used to describe any other group. All of these colonial-type efforts to write Arab history for the Arabs were intended to convey a simple message: Arabs were a people who held different values from everyone else, but most significantly, from "us." They were from a barbaric, backwards civilization that shared no history with the civilized West: they did not respect freedom, human life, women, or children. And most importantly, they were all the same, whether rich, poor, Christian, Muslim, educated, illiterate, Palestinian, Egyptian, Iraqi, Saudi, male, female, young, or old.

On a political level, Arab Americans were treated like leprosy, a deadly contagion, throughout the 1980s and 1990s, which only increased their voicelessness and social and political exclusion. Candidates for political office frequently returned Arab American campaign contributions on the premise that they tainted their candidacy, and made sure to notify the press that they had done so.[31] Federal government agencies, often with local police cooperation, spied on Arab American activists and student organizers, labeling them as [and sometimes charging them with being] supporters of terrorism.[32] Arab Americans were routinely excluded from coalitions of activists and policy makers because their presence was thought to "poison" a group's credibility, except among a few progressive Left circles.[33] Arab American women scholars were shouted down by feminists at scholarly meetings, unable to present their research papers while being accused of endorsing misogyny.[34] As a doctoral candidate and burgeoning scholar of Arab Americans, some department faculty members claimed that I was studying terrorists, while my mentor, Professor Janet Abu-Lughod, said that I would never get a university job in the United States. All of these actions combined rendered Arab American experiences, issues, history, activism, and scholarship "invisible" to the majority of the U.S. population. When you are invisible, no one cares about what is happening to you. This principle applied equally to Arab Americans and to Arabs overseas, and that was the point.

It was said during these times that Arabs were the only group who could be openly portrayed as barbaric, caricatured as animals, publicly slandered in the mainstream media, and ridiculed at work and school without negative reprisal. Yet since Arabs were not officially a minority group—their racialization having occurred at a different time than that of historic minority groups [derived not from Manifest Destiny but American Empire]—they were not on the government's post-civil rights movement list of disadvantaged racial and ethnic minority groups (1977,

OMB Directive 15). This meant in practice that they had limited access to the nation's primary civil rights coalitions and no formal venues for reporting incidents, launching complaints, and demanding redress, since they were still officially white. Official government recognition of racial discrimination had inaugurated many positive changes in American society, yet it also set in motion an organizational stasis. Although there was growing understanding of the socially constructed nature of race, there was no room at the table for new "racial" claimants.[35] Arab Americans were largely excluded from organized discussions of racism and racial discrimination, and they were absent from the content of multi-cultural education, tolerance trainings, and textbook treatments of American racial and ethnic groups.[36]

Institutional exclusion had its parallel in everyday social relations and Arab Americans experienced multiple forms of institutional and individual prejudice, discrimination, and harassment.[37] They were denied jobs, called "sand niggers," asked if they were carrying bombs, and questioned about the actions of Arabs living in a wide range of locations, under the assumption that all Arabs think alike. Arab American experiences were not monitored for discrimination except by Arab American organizations, which stood virtually alone in challenging powerful mainstream institutions. American culture scholar Saliba argued that while Arab Americans were the victims of racist policies, their experiences were rendered "invisible" by dominant discourses about race.[38] Their legal classification as Caucasian, moreover, placed a cover "over discriminatory and racist practices" and disempowered Arab Americans. That status also denied them affirmative action benefits. In 1977 Egyptian Mostafa Hefny filed suit against the U.S. government for denying him benefits and opportunities available to minorities by classifying him as white when he was clearly Black.

Following the 1979 Iranian revolution, Muslims were increasingly characterized by the very same stereotypes as Arabs and often conflated with them, a pattern that intensified in the 1990s. Bloom's quote above is only one of many such examples of conflation. When social constructions about inherent violence were nearly seamlessly extended to Muslims, Arabs and Muslims came to be viewed together in an undifferentiated way by many Americans, often under the rubric "Middle Easterners" and associated with a phenotype [brown skinned], mode of dress [modest, head coverings, beard], written script, and type of name. Here again we see the strong relationship between stereotypes and foreign policy: as challenges to Western hegemony in the Arab world and beyond came increasingly from Islamist activists and decreasingly from nationalists, the stereotypes were nearly seamlessly shifted from one collectivity to the other, or applied to both at the same time. So Muslims were also portrayed as a group that potentially threatened American culture itself, in particular its core values of democracy and personal liberty. Despite organized protests and attempts to counter these representations, both Arab Americans and Muslim Americans lacked the power to have much impact; after all, being negatively racialized and being powerless are highly correlated.

Broadened stereotyping began stitching all "brown people" together, and Asian Americans and sometimes Latinos were increasingly the victims of hate crimes intended for Arabs and Muslims.[39] The first major wave of anti-Arab hate crimes focused on Arab American organizations and their allies. Six violent incidents occurred between 1979 and 1985 which historian Orfalea says are traceable to the Jewish Defense League, an extremist group. These included: firebombing the offices of Palestinian rights and activist clergy organizations (1979), planting bombs outside the apartments of students of Palestinian origin at Arizona State University (1982), setting fire to a Lebanese restaurant (1985), planting bombs at the Boston and Washington offices of the American-Arab Anti-Discrimination Committee [ADC] (1985), and the bombing murder of the director of the American-Arab Anti-Discrimination Committee's West Coast director (1985).[40]

The character of hate crimes changed after the U.S. government stepped up its direct military engagement in the Arab world. When the U.S. military attacked Libya in 1986, among the many documented incidents were vandalization of Arab American businesses in Dearborn, Michigan and the beatings of five Arab students at Syracuse University by persons shouting anti-Arab slogans.[41] During the 1990–1991 Gulf War, the ADC documented 158 violent hate crimes against Arab Americans and persons assumed to be Arab Americans. These included "four acts involving a bomb, five arsons, two shooting incidents, and twelve acts of physical assault.[42] Orfalea points out that these statistics do not include actions like disc jockeys spewing anti-Arab slogans and t-shirts showing an Arab in the cross hairs of a rifle that read "I'd fly 10,000 miles to smoke [military jargon for blast] a camel."[43] Following the 1995 Oklahoma City bombing, perpetrated by a white, Christian man, ADC recorded 150 hate crimes against Arab Americans and the Council on American Islamic Relations recorded 222 incidents of harassment of Muslim Americans.

The Post-9/11 period: Heightened Visibility and the War on Terror

There is no doubt that it all got worse for Arab Americans and Muslim Americans in the years that followed the 9/11 attacks—a historical period that cannot be easily summarized.[44] On September 11, 2001 all of this prior stereotyping, stigmatization, disempowerment, and exclusion crystallized into a multifaceted attack on Arab Americans, Muslim Americans, and others perceived to be members of these groups. Arab and Muslim Americans were held collectively responsible by agencies of the U.S. government and much of the American public for the violent attacks on the World Trade Center and Pentagon. After all, pre-existing social constructions had configured them as people who were inherently violent and who would readily conduct and/or approve of this type of attack. Absent this pre-existing framework for interpreting the 9/11 attacks, it is unlikely that millions of brown-skinned Americans would have been held accountable for the actions of 19 people they had never met. It is important to point out in this context that other contemporaneous mass murders in the U.S., such as the Oklahoma City bombings, the Columbine, Virginia Tech, Sandy Hook, Aurora, and Oak Creek Sikh Temple shootings, did not evoke a similar response charging collective culpability.

The racialized attachment of physical and other attributes to the American public's concept of Arab, and its conflation with notions of Middle Easterners and Muslims, meant that persons who simply appeared to be members of these groups were held responsible. To speak accurately about the post-9/11 era and the "war on terror" one had to use the term "Arabs, Muslims, and persons assumed to be Arabs and Muslims" to describe the victims of hate crimes, verbal assaults, discrimination, and the subjects of government surveillance and interview policies. Whether traveling, driving, working, walking through neighborhoods or sitting in their homes, Arabs in America—citizens and non-citizens—and persons assumed to be them, became subject to heightened scrutiny. They were greeted with stares, spitting, hate graffiti, finger signs, arsons, and assaults that were not aimed at distinct individuals but at persons generally perceived to be members of the suspect group because of their looks, names, or mode of dress. In most cases, the "persons assumed to be Arab Muslims" were South Asians, so encapsulated because of their brown skin and/or their mode of dress. For example, Sikhs reported more than 300 attacks in the first months following 9/11. Balbir Singh Sodhi, a Sikh American, was the first person murdered in a post-9/11 hate crime.[45] South Asian Leaders of Tomorrow reported 645 "bias incidents and hate crimes" in the first seven days following the attacks.[46]

Government Policies

The Bush Administration and the mainstream media conveyed a strong message that terrorists were hiding in American communities just waiting to attack, provoking fear in the hearts of Americans and casting a heavy air of suspicion on Arab Americans, Muslim Americans, and those presumed to be members of these groups. Attorney General Ashcroft made statements that were clear in their directives: "The federal government cannot fight this reign of terror alone. Every American must help us defend our nation against this enemy" (October 25, 2001).[47] The message was that Arabs and Muslims in the United States should be closely observed and their seemingly normal activities should be treated as suspect. Within a week of the attacks, the Department of Justice received 96,000 anonymous "tips" from members of the American public (Ashcroft September 18, 2001) and within a few weeks nearly 1000 persons had been arrested and held in incommunicado detention by the federal government. In the words of the Attorney General:

> Within days of the September 11 attacks, we launched this anti-terrorism offensive to prevent new attacks on our homeland. To date, our anti-terrorism offensive has arrested or detained nearly 1,000 individuals as part of the September 11 terrorism investigation. Those who violated the law remain in custody. Taking suspected terrorists in violation of the law off the streets and keeping them locked up is our clear strategy to prevent terrorism within our borders.[48]

Such statements led the public to believe that the government was doing a good job and stoked public fears that terrorists were everywhere. The "suspected terrorists" Attorney General Ashcroft referred to were in fact overwhelmingly Arab and South Asian men questioned on the basis of their looks or on reports of suspicion, and who were unable to prove on the spot that their presence in the United States was legal. They were thus presumed to be "in violation of the law." Human Rights Watch found that even members of these "suspect groups" (including U.S. citizens) who volunteered to help the federal authorities ended up in indefinite, incommunicado detention. Once arrested, detainees were largely unable to obtain release from prison until a host of government agencies proved that they were not terrorists, a very lengthy process, after which visa violators were deported.[49] In the end, none of these detainees were charged with support for terrorism even though they were held in solitary confinement, and sometimes abused, for months while under investigation.[50]

While President George W. Bush made public statements condemning hate crimes and opposing profiling, members of his administration simultaneously developed policies that relied on profiling.[51] The federal government launched 37 known national security initiatives in the first two years after the 9/11 attacks: 25 of them either explicitly or implicitly targeted Arabs, South Asians, and Muslims living in the United States.[52] These measures included mass arrests, secret and indefinite detentions, prolonged detention of "material witnesses," closed hearings and use of secret evidence, government eavesdropping on attorney–client conversations, FBI home and work visits, wiretapping, seizures of property, removals of aliens with technical visa violations, freezing the assets of charities, and mandatory special registration. Mandatory holds were placed on all non-immigrant visa applications submitted by men aged 18–45 from 26 countries, most of them Arab and South Asian. Thousands of persons planning to enter the U.S. for study, work, training, meetings, and health care were denied access. Profiling at U.S. airports, including special security checks and removal from airplanes, sharply reduced the willingness of Arabs, Muslims, and South Asians to fly.

Special registration was a program launched by the Department of Justice, Immigration and Naturalization Service (INS; now Department of Homeland Security) on September 11,

2002.[53] It required males from certain countries who entered the U.S. on temporary visas prior to October 1, 2002 to report to designated INS offices for fingerprinting, photographing, and questioning. The persons targeted were from: Afghanistan, Algeria, Bahrain, Bangladesh, Egypt, Eritrea, Indonesia, Iran, Iraq, Jordan, Kuwait, Lebanon, Libya, Morocco, North Korea, Oman, Pakistan, Qatar, Saudi Arabia, Somalia, the Sudan, Syria, Tunisia, United Arab Emirates, and Yemen. The purpose of the program was to facilitate the "monitoring" of aliens "in the interest of national security.[54] The INS produced flyers to advertise the call-in program, which had THIS NOTICE IS FOR YOU splayed across the top, eerily reminiscent of the notices posted for Japanese living in the western U.S. during WWII. After 83,000 call-in interviews, the government ended the program in May 2003.[55] More than 13,000 men were slated for removal from the United States as a result of the program, none charged with connections to terrorism.[56] These removals, and the hundreds of pre-special registration removals ["absconders initiative"], meant that more Arabs, Muslims, and South Asians (none accused of terrorist connections) were deported from the United States than the number of foreign nationals deported for their political beliefs following the infamous 1919 Palmer Raids.[57]

Very conservatively, at least 100,000 Arabs, Muslims, and South Asians living in the United States personally experienced one of these government measures.[58] A former FBI Special Agent in Charge of Counterterrorism cited much larger numbers. He said, after "about 1/2 million interviews . . . I'm not aware, and I know 9/11 about as well as anybody in the FBI knows 9/11 . . . of any single person . . . who had they stepped forward could have provided a clue to help us get out in front of this."[59] FBI interviews were reported to be particularly stigmatizing as onlooking neighbors and co-workers interpreted them to signify guilt. Yet, it was the near 100 percent rate of false positives that created extensive anxiety among Arabs, Muslims, and South Asians in the U.S., producing an understanding that really anything goes. If it were true that terrorists were lurking inside Arab and Muslim American communities, the government's strategies were counterproductive to finding them because they instilled in all community members a deep fear of government agents.[60] In its 2005 report Witness to Abuse, Human Rights Watch concluded that needless incarcerations "aggravated distrust towards the government in Muslim communities in the United States that have been repeatedly targeted by sweeping, ill-advised, and at times illegal post-September 11 investigation, arrest, and detention policies."[61]

Despite these extraordinary efforts of the U.S. government, few terrorists posing a threat to the United States were uncovered. Not a single person was convicted of a terrorist crime out of more than 80,000 special registrations, 5,000 preventive detentions, and tens of thousands of FBI interviews, activities referred to by legal scholar David Cole as the "most aggressive national campaign of ethnic profiling since World War II."[62] Criminal indictments in "terrorism-related" cases fared slightly better: more than 400 post-9/11 indictments produced some 200 convictions, very few of which, however, were for terrorism.[63] The Syracuse-based Transactional Records Access Clearinghouse found that the median sentence handed down in cases the Justice Department identified as "terrorism-related" was 14 days.[64] New York University's Center on Law and Security found upon review of "terror-related" cases that there were "almost no convictions on charges reflecting dangerous crimes."[65]

Even after the National Commission on the 9/11 attacks concluded that there was no evidence of American Arab or Muslim participation in or knowledge of the 9/11 attacks, collective policies continued.[66] The greatest source of discrimination against Arabs and Muslims during this period was the U.S. government, mostly the Department of Justice and the Immigration and Naturalization Service (INS), which later became the Department of Homeland Security. Cainkar's extensive post-9/11 study found that fear of government far outweighed any other fears among Arab Muslim Americans.[67] During the period of research, a substantial number of

Arab Muslim Americans expressed worry that they might be rounded up and sent to internment camps by agents of the American government (especially should another attack occur, an event over which they had no control), and believed that the American government had the power and mass media influence to auger popular support for such an action. Their sense of "homeland insecurity" was driven less by the public's behavior than by the government's.[68] Many blamed the U.S. government and its sweeping and unfocused actions in their communities for encouraging anti-Arab and anti-Muslim sentiments and attacks.

Hate Crimes

The safety of Arabs, Muslims, and persons perceived to be one of them on the American streets was fragile for a few years after the 9/11 attacks, as this period was also characterized by a large number of hate crimes and extensive harassment. Quantification of these crimes often proved to be difficult, however, due to counting mechanisms based on racial categories; hate crimes against Arabs lacked a coding category. Risk of death was highest in the first few weeks after the attacks. As noted above, the first murder victim after 9/11 was a Sikh man shot on September 15, 2001. The same perpetrator shot at a Lebanese-American gas station clerk and riddled an Afghani home with bullets.[69] Later that day an Egyptian Copt was murdered, and on October 2 a Yemeni man was murdered, both murders occurring in stores in California. On October 15 a Somali Muslim died of head wounds after being attacked in Minneapolis.

Over time hate acts driven by cues of phenotype and dress were more likely to take the form of assault, harassment, and vandalism. Harassment occurred at schools, in the workplace, at shopping malls, and at airports.[70] There were countless reports nationwide of teachers in the classroom calling Arabs, Muslims, and Palestinians terrorists, or asking Arab American and Muslim American students to explain the 9/11 attacks to their classmates. Dozens of persons reported being removed from airplanes simply for looking suspicious or making employees or passengers feel uncomfortable. Repeated incidents of removal caused ADC and the American Civil Liberties Union (ACLU) to file lawsuits against United Airlines, Continental, and American Airlines; ACLU filed a similar separate suit against Northwest Airlines. Also reported were persons fired from their jobs. Attacks on restaurants, businesses, and religious institutions were fairly common across the nation. Spray-painted slogans such as "Kill All Arabs Now" or "Arabs go Home" were found in various locations across the country.[71]

In Chicago, more than 100 hate crimes against Arabs and Muslims, as well as persons mistaken for them, were reported to the Chicago Commission on Human Relations by the end of December 2001. On September 12, the largest predominantly Arab mosque in the Chicago metropolitan area was surrounded by a mob of hundreds of angry whites, some shouting "kill the Arabs," some wielding weapons. Police encouraged Muslims to close the schools affiliated with the mosque until safety could be assured and not to attend Friday prayers at the mosque. The schools were closed for one week, but prayer at the mosque continued. An Assyrian church on the north side and an Arab community organization on the southwest side were damaged by arson in the late fall. The rebuilt community center was again vandalized in March 2002. Muslim women in Chicago repeatedly reported having their head scarves yanked off or being spat at on the street.

Nationwide, ADC reported "over 700 violent incidents targeting Arab Americans, or those perceived to be Arab Americans, Arabs, and Muslims," including several murders, in the first nine weeks after the attacks, and another 165 between January 1 and October 11, 2002.[72] The Council on American-Islamic Relations reported 1,062 incidents of violence, threat, and harassment during the initial onslaught of post-9/11 backlash.[73] Full 2001/2002 reporting-year claims affected 2,242 victims, mostly in incidents of bias-motivated harassment and violence. In its 2004 report, Unpatriotic Acts, the Council on American–Islamic Relations (CAIR) reported a 121 percent rise in all anti-Muslim incidents and a 69 percent rise in reported hate crimes. Although the level of hate crimes and attacks against Arabs, Muslims, and those perceived to be Arab or Muslim sharply decreased after a few months, media monitoring revealed at least one reported hate attack per week across the country for the subsequent two years. What one can say with certainty is that hate crimes against Arab and Muslim Americans and persons perceived to be them, and against their businesses and institutions, did not end in 2001 and continue to this day. Civil rights and advocacy organizations place responsibility for the persistence of these attacks largely on the mass media and on prominent personalities who make public statements that dehumanize Arabs and Muslims.

In addition to coping with government programs and hate crimes, Arabs and Muslims living in the U.S. faced questions over their national loyalty. Reporting on the Detroit area, anthropologist Shryock described a "state of emergency" in which Arab Americans made dramatic efforts to prove to their neighbors that they were loyal Americans. Shryock recounts: "In the days following September 11, Arab Detroit was awash in American flags" on stores, gas stations, churches, and mosques. "Many non-Arab and non-Muslim observers thought it was all for show—some of it was, of course—but this skeptical attitude only proved how hard it was for Arabs and Muslims to be seen as "authentically" American."[74] American studies scholar Salaita described the post-9/11 political experience of Arab Americans as "imperative patriotism." Expressing support for domestic and global Bush Administration policies, including the ill-fated U.S. invasion of Iraq, was required to prove national loyalty, while dissent signaled one as anti-American and a threat.[75]

Social Changes Ensuing from the Post-9/11 "War on Terror"

The global "War on Terror" that commenced on September 11, 2001 remains active at the time of writing (2015). Prisoners lacking charge or trial are still imprisoned by the U.S. government at Guantanamo Bay, and state violence and counter violence continues across parts of the Arab world and South Asia. On the domestic front, government surveillance programs continue [and have expanded].[76] Arab, Muslim, and South Asian Americans still experience prejudice, discrimination, and hate crimes, and their religious institutions continue to face threats.[77] A small, but well-organized and -financed Islamophobia network works to ramp up Americans' fear of Muslims and keep suspicion alive. At the same time, the visibility, activism, and inclusion of Arab, South Asian, and Muslim American organizations has increased significantly when compared to the pre-9/11 era. Mobilizations of Arab, Muslim, and South Asian Americans and their allies have opened places at the table that were long denied. This agency has taken many forms, from civil rights advocacy, to activism for a unique census category, to unapologetic campaigns for Palestine, and everything in between. Race and ethnic studies scholars no longer sideline or exclude the experiences of Arabs, Muslims, and South Asians and there has been greater agreement among Arab Americans to actively challenge their official status as whites. American culture scholar Alsultaney noted the development of slightly more complex Arab/Muslim characters in American television dramas since 9/11. No longer only bad, they can also be good, as long as they stand up against the terrorists among them. Unfortunately, Alsultaney says, these plot scenarios do not challenge the purported relationship between Arabs and Muslims and terrorism.[78] Alsultaney also argues that the war on terror "temporarily reconfigured" American racism; in the debates that emerged over whether or not profiling Arabs and Muslims was acceptable practice, the racism faced by other groups was back-burnered while they were temporarily embraced by whiteness.

Conclusion

Arab Americans are no longer invisible. It took the excesses of their treatment following the 9/11 attacks to wake up a nation to the racism they had faced for decades. While Arab Americans largely benefited from their official status as Caucasians in the first half of the 20th century, these benefits became vestiges when the U.S. rose to global superpower status. After this point, Arabs and later Muslims were configured as a problem for American interests and became subject to the same type of essentializing, stereotyping, and writing of history that had long characterized European colonialism. Yet their highly negative American experiences remained invisible for decades due to a range of exclusions. They were silenced by those who benefitted politically and economically from the negative portrayals, sidelined by groups seeking to avoid their "taint," and unnoticed by activists and scholars who assumed that race was a fixed notion. Despite a different American historical timeline, Arab American experiences of exclusion have now merged with those of South Asians, Asians more generally, and other people of color in the U.S.

Notes

1 Parillo, V. and Donoghue, C., "Updating the Bogardus Vincent Social Distance Studies: A New National Survey," *The Social Science Journal* 42 (2005): 2 257–271. doi:10.10r16/j.soscij.2005.03.011. Page 264: Arabs ranked last among 30 groups.
2 Louise Cainkar, *Homeland Insecurity: The Arab American and Muslim American Experience after 9/11*. New York: Russell Sage Press, 2009.
3 Louise Cainkar, "Coping with Culture, Change, and Alienation: The Life Experiences of Palestinian Women in the United States" (PhD diss, Northwestern University, 1988). Between 1916–1919 cross-Atlantic travel was limited by war and more than 90 percent of Arab immigrants, mainly of "Greater Syrian" origin, came to the U.S. from other countries in the Americas.
4 Louise Cainkar, "Coping with Culture, Change, and Alienation: The Life Experiences of Palestinian Women in the United States" (Northwestern University, 1988). For an analysis of women's migration see Sarah Gualtieri, *Between Arab and White: Race and Ethnicity in the Early Syrian American Diaspora* (Oakland, CA: University of California Press, 2009).
5 Gualtieri, *Between Arab and White*. Alixa Naff, *Becoming American: The early Arab immigrant experience* (Carbondale & Edwardsville, IL: Southern Illinois University Press, 1985). Eric Hooglund, Ed., *Crossing the Waters: Arabic-Speaking Immigrants to the United States before 1940* (Washington, DC: Smithsonian Institution Press, 1987). James Zogby, Ed. *Taking Root: Bearing Fruit—the Arab American Experience* (Washington, DC: American-Arab Anti-Discrimination Committee Research Institute, 1984). Eric Hooglund, Ed. *Taking Root: Arab-American Community Studies* (Washington, DC: ADC Research Institute, 1985).
6 Sarah Gualtieri, "Strange fruit? Syrian immigrants, extralegal violence and racial formation in the Jim Crow South," *Arab Studies Quarterly,* 26 (2004): 63–85. Sarah Gualtieri, *Between Arab and White*.
7 The latter have been subject to less study in the Arab American Studies literature. See Hani Bawardi, *The Making of Arab Americans: From Syrian Nationalism to Us Citizenship* (Austin, TX: University of Texas Press, 2014).
8 Elizabeth Boosahda, *Arab-American Faces and Voices: The Origins of an Immigrant Community* (Austin, TX: University of Texas Press, 2003). Also see note 5.
9 Cainkar, "Coping with Culture, Change, and Alienation: The Live Experiences of Palestinian Women in the United States."
10 Sarah Gualtieri, ""Strange Fruit? Syrian Immigrants, Extralegal Violence and Racial Formation in the Jim Crow South," *Arab Studies Quarterly* 26, no. 3 (2004). Gualtieri, *Between Arab and White*.
11 Marian Smith, "Race, Nationality, and Reality: INS Administration of Racial Provisions in US Immigration and Nationality Law since 1898. Parts 1, 2, & 3" *Prologue* 34, no. 2 (2002).
12 For a delineation of a hierarchy of whites, see: Madison Grant, *The Passing of the Great Race; or, the Racial Basis of European History* (New York: C. Scribner, 1916).

13 INS Instruction No. 168, Central Office view on the racial qualifications for entry and naturalization with respect to persons of the Arabian race, September 9, 1943.
14 Smith, "Race, Nationality, and Reality: INS Administration of Racial Provisions in US Immigration and Nationality Law since 1898. Parts 1, 2, & 3."
15 Gregory Orfalea, *The Arab Americans: A History* (Northampton, MA: Interlink Publishing Group, 2006).
16 Orfalea, *The Arab Americans*.
17 Louise Cainkar, ""Immigrants from the Arab World" in John Koval, Michael Bennett, et al., Eds., *The New Chicago*. (Philadelphia, PA: Temple University Press), 182–196.
18 Arab American Institute. www.aaiusa.org/demographics.
19 From a settler colonial perspective, the "just like us" similarity goes well beyond the narrative.
20 Michael W. Suleiman, Ed. *Arabs in America: Building a New Future* (Philadelphia, PA: Temple University Press, 1999), 10.
21 Author interviews with founding members of the Association of Arab American University Graduates: Ibrahim Abu-Lughod, Sofia and Hassan Haddad; Ghada Talhami; and Elaine Hagopian.
22 Andrew J. Shryock, "The Moral Analogies of Race: Arab American Identity, Color Politics, and the Limits of Racialized Citizenship," in *Race and Arab Americans before and after 9/11: From Invisible Citizens to Visible Subjects*, Ed. Amaney and Nadine Naber Jamal (Syracuse, NY: Syracuse University Press, 2008), 94.
23 Gary Awad, "The Arab Americans: An Invisible Minority Awakened," *The News Circle/Arab-American Affairs Magazine*, March 1981, 31
24 Amaney A. Jamal and Nadine Christine Naber, *Race and Arab Americans before and after 9/11: From Invisible Citizens to Visible Subjects*, 1st ed., Arab American Writing. (Syracuse, NY: Syracuse University Press, 2008); Nadine Naber, "Arab Americans and U.S. Racial Formations," in *Race and Arab Americans before and after September 11th*, Eds. Amaney Jamal and Nadine Naber (Syracuse, NY: Syracuse University Press, 2008), 33.
25 Amaney Jamal, "Civil Liberties and the Otherization of Arab and Muslim Americans," in *Race and Arab Americans before and after 9/11: From Invisible Citizens to Visible Subjects*, Eds. Amaney Jamal and Nadine Naber (Syracuse, NY: Syracuse University Press, 2008), 119
26 On scrutiny of Arab American activists, see M. Cherif Bassiouni, Ed. *The Civil Rights of Arab-Americans: The Special Measures* (North Dartmouth, MA: Arab-American University Graduates, 1974). On film portrayals, see Jack Shaheen, *Reel Bad Arabs: How Hollywood Vilifies a People* (New York 2001). On television programs, see Jack Shaheen *The TV Arab* (Bowling Green, OH: Bowling Green State Press, 1984).
27 Seymour M. Lipset, and William Schneider, "Carter Vs. Israel: What the Polls Reveal," *Commentary* 64, no. 5 (1977).
28 Steven Salaita, "Ethnic Identity and Imperative Patriotism: Arab-Americans before and after 9/11," *College Literature* 32, no. 2 (2005); *Anti-Arab Racism in the USA: Where It Comes from and What It Means for Politics Today* (London: Pluto Press, 2006), 14.
29 Howard Bloom, "The Importance of Hugging," *Omni*, 1989.
30 Ibid.
31 James J. Zogby and Helen Hatab Samhan, "Special Report: Arab-Baiting in the 1986 Elections," *Washington Report on Middle East Affairs*, February 1987.
32 Susan Akram and Kevin R. Johnson, "Race and Civil Rights Pre-September 11, 2001: The Targeting of Arabs and Muslims," in *Civil Rights in Peril: The Targeting of Arabs and Muslims*, Ed. Elaine C. Hagopian (Chicago, IL: Haymarket, 2004).
33 Author's field notes.
34 Rabab Abdulhadi, Evelyn Alsultany, and Nadine Christine Naber, *Arab & Arab American Feminisms: Gender, Violence, & Belonging*, 1st ed., Gender, Culture and Politics in the Middle East. (Syracuse, NY: Syracuse University Press, 2011).
35 Space was extended, for example, to women, gays, and the disabled, and because they were not a "racial" group, to Muslims.
36 Louise Cainkar, "The Treatment of Arabs and Muslims in Race and Ethnic Studies Textbooks," in *American Sociological Association* (Atlanta, GA: 2002).
37 For an explanation of why Arab Americans and Muslim Americans show relatively high levels of education and income despite this racialization, see Louise Cainkar, "The Social Construction of Difference and the Arab American Experience," *Journal of American Ethnic History* 25, no. 2–3 (2006).

38 Therese Saliba, "Resisting Invisibility," in *Arabs in America: Building a New Future* (Philadelphia, PA: Temple University Press, 1999), 309.
39 The largest group of American Muslims is Asian [not Arab], followed by African Americans. Globally, the countries with the largest Muslim populations are in South and South East Asia: Indonesia, Pakistan, India, and Bangladesh.
40 Orfalea, *The Arab Americans: A History*.
41 Human Rights Watch, 2002. "We Are Not The Enemy" Hate Crimes Against Arabs, Muslims, and Those Perceived to be Arab or Muslim after September 11 [New York].
42 Orfalea, *The Arab Americans: A History*, 277.
43 Ibid., 284.
44 For a fuller account, see Louise Cainkar, *Homeland Insecurity: The Arab American and Muslim American Experience after 9/11*. (New York: Russell Sage Press, 2009).
45 www.huffingtonpost.com/2012/08/07/history-of-hate-crimes-against-sikhs-since-911_n_1751841.html (accessed October 15, 2016).
46 South Asian Leaders of Tomorrow, *American Backlash: Terrorists Bring War Home in More Ways Than One* (Washington, DC: September 28, 2001).
47 Attorney General John Ashcroft, "Prepared Remarks for the Us Mayors Conference," (Office of International Information Programs, U.S. Dept. of State, 2001).
48 Attorney General John Ashcroft. Prepared Remarks for the US Mayors Conference October 25, 2001. Distributed by the Office of International Information Programs, U.S. Department of State. Web site: http://usinfo.state.gov. Accessed June 7, 2007.
49 David Cole, *Enemy Aliens* (New York: The New Press, 2003). Human Rights Watch, "Presumption of Guilt: Human Rights Abuses of Post-September 11 Detainees," (New York, 2002); "Witness to Abuse: Human Rights Abuses under the Material Witness Law since September 11," (New York, 2005).
50 Human Rights Watch, "Presumption of Guilt: Human Rights Abuses of Post-September 11 Detainees"; "Witness to Abuse: Human Rights Abuses under the Material Witness Law since September 11." Human Rights Watch (2005) *Witness to Abuse*. (New York).
51 Human Rights Watch, *Presumption of Guilt: Human Rights Abuses of Post-September 11 Detainees* (New York, August 2002); American Civil Liberties Union, *Safe and Free in Times of Crisis* (Washington, DC: August 2002); Reporters Committee for Freedom of the Press, *Homefront Confidential* (Arlington, VA: April 2002); Dan Eggen and Susan Schmidt, "Secret Court Rebuffs Ashcroft; Justice Department Chided on Misinformation," *Washington Post* (Washington, DC), August 23, 2002.
52 Fred Tsao, and Rhoda Rae Gutierrez, "Losing Ground," (Chicago, IL: Illinois Coalitition for Immigrant and Refugee Rights, 2003).
53 For extensive details on special registration, see Cainkar, *Homeland Insecurity: The Arab American and Muslim American Experience after 9/11*.
54 INS Memo (undated) HQINS 70/28 from Johnny Williams, Executive Associate Commissioner, Office of Field Operations.
55 Another 127,694 persons were registered at their Port of Entry. June 7, 2003.
56 Richard Swarms "More than 13,000 May Face Deportation" *New York Times* June 7, 2003.
57 556 foreign nationals were deported during the Palmer Raids. Alex Gourevitch "Detention Disorder" *The American Prospect* January 31, 2003.
58 My estimate of at least 100,000 was derived as follows: Nearly 83,000 persons living in the US underwent special registration. It can be safely assumed that at least 20,000 more Arabs and Muslims nationwide were affected by one or more of the other post-9/11 national security initiatives, such as FBI interviews, wiretapping, or detention.
59 Michael E. Rolince. Excerpt from speech made at the 2005 MPAC Convention 12/17/05 at Long Beach Convention Center, CA during Workshop 2B: Muslim-Law Enforcement Partnership. The audio file can be accessed at www.mpac.org/multimedia/audio. This remark is found at the question and answers section at the end of the recording.) Accessed on June 10, 2007.
60 Louise Cainkar, "US Muslim Leaders and Activists Evaluate Post 9/11 Domestic Security Policies," In Social Science Research Council, Program on Global Security and Cooperation; Reframing the Challenge of Migration and Security, 2004.
61 Human Rights Watch, "Witness to Abuse: Human Rights Abuses under the Material Witness Law since September 11", 6.

62 David Cole, "Are We Safer?," *New York Review of Books* 53, no. 4 (2006), 17.
63 Dan Eggen, and Julie Tate, "U.S. Campaign Produces Few Convictions on Terrorism Charges," *The Washington Post*, June 12 2005.
64 "Criminal Terrorism Enforcement since the 9/11/01 Attacks," (New York City: The Transactional Records Access Clearinghouse, 2003).
65 "Terrorist Trials: A Report Card," (Transactional Records Access Clearinghouse, 2005).
66 *National Commission on Terrorist Attacks Upon the United States.*, (Washington, DC: US Government Printing Office, 2004).
67 Cainkar, *Homeland Insecurity: The Arab American and Muslim American Experience after 9/11*.
68 Interviews with Arab American Christians produced the same findings, because post 9/11 US government policies targeted Arab Christians as well as Muslims.
69 Orfalea, *The Arab Americans: A History*, 304.
70 ADC. "Report on Hate Crimes and Discrimination Against Arab Americans: The Post-September 11 Backlash - September 11, 2001 to October 11, 2002." Washington, DC: ADC Research Institute, 2003. ADC. "Post-9/11 Report on Hate Crimes and Discrimination." Washington, DC: ADC Research Institute, 2002.
71 Orfalea, *The Arab Americans: A History*, 304–305.
72 "Post-9/11 Report on Hate Crimes and Discrimination," (Washington, DC: ADC Research Institute, 2002), 7.
73 *The Status of Muslim Civil Rights in the United States: Unpatriotic Acts*, (Washington, DC: Council on American-Islamic Relations, 2004).
74 Andrew J. Shryock, "New Images of Arab Detroit: Seeing Otherness and Identity through the Lens Of September 11," *American Anthropologist* 104, no. 3 (2002), 917–918.
75 Salaita, "Ethnic Identity and Imperative Patriotism: Arab-Americans before and after 9/11."
76 *The Guardian*, "Edward Snowden," www.theguardian.com/us-news/edward-snowden.
77 See, for example, the websites of South Asian Americans Leading Together, http://saalt.org/policy-change/post-9-11-backlash/ (accessed October 15, 2016) for comprehensive reporting.
78 Evelyn Alsultany, *Arabs and Muslims in the Media Race and Representation after 9/11*, New York: New York University Press, 2012.

References

Abdulhadi, Rabab, Evelyn Alsultany, and Nadine Christine Naber. *Arab & Arab American Feminisms : Gender, Violence, & Belonging*. Gender, Culture and Politics in the Middle East. 1st ed. Syracuse, NY: Syracuse University Press, 2011.
ADC (American-Arab Anti-Discrimination Committee. "Post-9/11 Report on Hate Crimes and Discrimination." Washington, DC: ADC Research Institute, 2002.
ADC. "Report on Hate Crimes and Discrimination Against Arab Americans: The Post-September 11 Backlash - September 11, 2001 to October 11, 2002." Washington, DC: ADC Research Institute, 2003.
Akram, Susan, and Kevin R. Johnson. "Race and Civil Rights Pre-September 11, 2001: The Targeting of Arabs and Muslims." In *Civil Rights in Peril: The Targeting of Arabs and Muslims*, edited by Elaine C. Hagopian. Chicago, IL: Haymarket, 2004.
Alsultany, Evelyn. *Arabs and Muslims in the Media Race and Representation after 9/11*. New York: New York University Press, 2012.
Ashcroft, Attorney General John. "Prepared Remarks for the Us Mayors Conference." Office of International Information Programs, U.S. Dept. of State, 2001.
Awad, Gary. "The Arab Americans: An Invisible Minority Awakened." *The News Circle/Arab-American Affairs Magazine*, March 1981, 31–32..
Bassiouni, M. Cherif, Ed. *The Civil Rights of Arab-Americans: The Special Measures*. North Dartmouth, MA: Arab-American University Graduates, 1974.
Bawardi, Hani. *The Making of Arab Americans: From Syrian Nationalism to Us Citizenship*. Austin, TX: University of Texas Press, 2014.
Bloom, Howard. "The Importance of Hugging." *Omni*, 1989, 30–31.

Boosahda, Elizabeth. *Arab-American Faces and Voices: The Origins of an Immigrant Community*. Austin, TX: University of Texas Press, 2003.

Cainkar, Louise. "Coping with Culture, Change, and Alienation: The Life Experiences of Palestinian Women in the United States." Northwestern University, 1988.

———. "The Treatment of Arabs and Muslims in Race and Ethnic Studies Textbooks." In *American Sociological Association*. Atlanta, Georgia, 2002.

———. "US Muslim Leaders and Activists Evaluate Post 9/11 Domestic Security Policies." In Social Science Research Council, Program on Global Security and Cooperation; Reframing the Challenge of Migration and Security, 2004.

———. "Immigrants from the Arab World" In *The New Chicago*, edited by Michael Bennett John Koval, et al. , 182–196. Philadelphia, PA: Temple University Press, 2006.

———. "The Social Construction of Difference and the Arab American Experience." *Journal of American Ethnic History* 25, no. 2–3 (2006): 243–278.

———. *Homeland Insecurity: The Arab American and Muslim American Experience after 9/11*. New York: Russell Sage Press, 2009.

Cole, David. *Enemy Aliens*. New York: The New Press, 2003.

———. "Are We Safer?". *New York Review of Books* 53, no. 4 (2006).

"Criminal Terrorism Enforcement since the 9/11/01 Attacks." New York City: The Transactional Records Access Clearinghouse, 2003.

Eggen, Dan, and Julie Tate. "U.S. Campaign Produces Few Convictions on Terrorism Charges." *The Washington Post*, June 12, 2005.

Grant, Madison. *The Passing of the Great Race; or, the Racial Basis of European History*. New York: C. Scribner, 1916.

Gualtieri, Sarah. "Strange Fruit? Syrian Immigrants, Extralegal Violence and Racial Formation in the Jim Crow South." *Arab Studies Quarterly* 26, no. 3 (2004): 63–85.

———. *Between Arab and White: Race and Ethnicity in the Early Syrian American Diaspora*. Oakland, CA: University of California Press, 2009.

Guardian, The. "Edward Snowden." *The Guardian*, www.theguardian.com/us-news/edward-snowden (accessed October 15, 2016).

Hooglund, Eric, Ed., *Taking Root: Arab-American Community Studies*, vol. 2. Washington, DC: ADC Research Institute, 1985.

———. Ed. Crossing the Waters: Arabic-Speaking Immigrants to the United States before 1940. (Washington, DC: Smithsonian Institution Press, 1987.

Human Rights Watch. "We Are Not The Enemy" Hate Crimes Against Arabs, Muslims, and Those Perceived to be Arab or Muslim after September 11 [New York], 2002.

Human Rights Watch. "Presumption of Guilt: Human Rights Abuses of Post-September 11 Detainees." New York, 2002.

———. "Witness to Abuse: Human Rights Abuses under the Material Witness Law since September 11." New York, 2005.

Jamal, Amaney. "Civil Liberties and the Otherization of Arab and Muslim Americans." In *Race and Arab Americans before and after 9/11: From Invisible Citizens to Visible Subjects*, edited by Amaney Jamal and Nadine Naber, 114–130. Syracuse, NY: Syracuse University Press, 2008.

Jamal, Amaney A., and Nadine Christine Naber. *Race and Arab Americans before and after 9/11 : From Invisible Citizens to Visible Subjects*. Arab American Writing. 1st ed. Syracuse, NY: Syracuse University Press, 2008.

Lipset, Seymour M., and William Schneider. "Carter Vs. Israel: What the Polls Reveal." *Commentary* 64, no. 5 (1977): 22.

Naber, Nadine. "Arab Americans and U.S. Racial Formations." In *Race and Arab Americans before and after September 11th*, edited by Amaney Jamal and Nadine Naber, 1–45. Syracuse, NY: Syracuse University Press, 2008.

Naff, Alixa. *Becoming American: The early Arab immigrant experience* (Carbondale & Edwardsville, IL: Southern Illinois University Press, 1985).

National Commission on Terrorist Attacks Upon the United States. Washington, DC: US Government Printing Office, 2004.

Orfalea, Gregory. *The Arab Americans: A History*. Northampton, MA: Interlink Publishing Group, 2006.

Parillo, V. and Donoghue, C., "Updating the Bogardus Vincent Social Distance Studies: A New National Survey," *The Social Science Journal* 42 (2005): 2 257–271. doi:10.10r16/j.soscij.2005.03.011.

Salaita, Steven. *Anti-Arab Racism in the USA: Where It Comes from and What It Means for Politics Today*. London: Pluto Press, 2006.

———. "Ethnic Identity and Imperative Patriotism: Arab-Americans before and after 9/11." *College Literature* 32, no. 2 (2005): 146–168.

Saliba, Therese. "Resisting Invisibility." In *Arabs in America: Building a New Future*, 304–319. Philadelphia, PA: Temple University Press, 1999.

Shaheen, Jack. *Reel Bad Arabs: How Hollywood Vilifies a People*. New York: Olive Branch Press, 2001.

———. *The TV Arab*. Bowling Green, OH: Bowling Green State Press, 1984.

Shryock, Andrew J. "New Images of Arab Detroit: Seeing Otherness and Identity through the Lens of September 11." *American Anthropologist* 104, no. 3 (2002): 917–922.

———. "The Moral Analogies of Race: Arab American Identity, Color Politics, and the Limits of Racialized Citizenship." In *Race and Arab Americans before and after 9/11: From Invisible Citizens to Visible Subjects*, edited by Amaney and Nadine Naber Jamal, 81–113. Syracuse, NY: Syracuse University Press, 2008.

Smith, Marian. "Race, Nationality, and Reality: INS Administration of Racial Provisions in US Immigration and Nationality Law since 1898. Parts 1, 2, & 3." *Prologue* 34, no. 2 (2002).

South Asian Leaders of Tomorrow, *American Backlash: Terrorists Bring War Home in More Ways Than One* (Washington, DC: September 28, 2001).

Suleiman, Michael W., Ed. *Arabs in America: Building a New Future*. Philadelphia, PA: Temple University Press, 1999.

Swarms, Richard. "More than 13,000 May Face Deportation" *New York Times* June 7, 2003.

"Terrorist Trials: A Report Card." Transactional Records Access Clearinghouse, 2005.

The Status of Muslim Civil Rights in the United States: Unpatriotic Acts. Washington, DC: Council on American-Islamic Relations, 2004.

Tsao, Fred, and Rhoda Rae Gutierrez. "Losing Ground." Chicago, IL: Illinois Coalition for Immigrant and Refugee Rights, 2003.

Zogby, James, Ed. *Taking Root: Bearing Fruit—the Arab American Experience*. Washington, DC: American-Arab Anti-Discrimination Committee Research Institute, 1984.

Zogby, James J., and Helen Hatab Samhan. "Special Report: Arab-Baiting in the 1986 Elections." *Washington Report on Middle East Affairs*, February 1987, 5–6.

PART THREE

Globalization, Global Restructuring, and the Question of National Belongings

12
POPULAR MUSIC, GLOBALIZATION, AND ASIAN/AMERICA

Christine Bacareza Balance

Globalization and Asian American are two important concepts in popular and academic literature indicative of long-established relations, attachments, and encounters. As a term, globalization did not appear in public and intellectual discourses until the mid-20th century. Yet, everyday "notions and images of 'the global' and the 'globe'" have been popular from early in that same century, as the modern media and communications industries were becoming acutely aware of their own globalizing networks serving mass audiences.[1] At the turn of the 20th century, popular music technologies, such as the phonograph and radio, directly served the purposes of U.S. and European wars and colonialism overseas, through anthropological recordings and the dissemination of Western pop music and culture.[2] These earlier "world music" recordings of traditional/folklore music from around the globe set the stage for live performances in the U.S., such as the Chop Suey and hula circuits of performance.[3]

Thus, as Stuart Hall has argued, our historical and contemporary "global culture" is a media-driven construct. Film and television have been principal agents of cultural globalization, with popular music occupying its own special place. As David Held has noted,

> Pop music is, without doubt, one of (if not "the") great "globalizers." Dependent on neither written nor spoken language, and locking into the universal human need for rhythm and melody, pop music is now, literally, "everywhere." The market is dominated by American pop music, followed by British, and has been closely allied since the mid-1950s to youth subculture. Pop music is the archetypal product of Western capitalism and the search is always on for novel musical sounds, styles, and promotable "stars." Black, ethnic music and street music is repackaged to appeal to a wider audience and "world music" occupies only a small share of the market (Robinson et al., 1991) compared to Western pop.[4]

In this formulation, pop music's globalizing power and ubiquitous presence is due both to its non-semantic form as well as its fulfillment of an innate and "universal human need." Closely tied to an ever-changing youth culture and its consistent need to find the new and latest "sounds, styles, and 'promotable' stars," catering to the "tastes" of a "wider" (read, mainstream) audience, the commodities of popular music typify "Western capitalism" and certain versions of "Western pop" culture. NOTE: This formulation more commonly functions under the sign/concept of "cultural imperialism," that is, a top-down construct of U.S. popular music's relationship to the rest of the world.

Yet, globalization operates on different scales (local/regional/national/global) as too does "Asian America" simultaneously work on the levels of the domestic (national) and global (transnational).[5] Both these key terms evoke various social processes—political, cultural, economic, ecological—and the meanings assigned to them. And, just like culture itself, these processes and meanings have always operated in a two-way and even multi-directional traffic that works against cultural imperialism's hegemonic approach. Conceived by student and community activists in the 1960s, the term "Asian American" referred to a social, cultural, and political movement, an alternative network that overcame traditional boundaries of nation and ethnicity in the service of shared political visions and culture. Since that time, the politics and meaning of Asian American have transformed, accounting for changes brought on by post-1965 immigration, such as the increasing numbers of professional/technically skilled laborers as well as wartime/reunification immigrants; the rise of Asian "Tiger economies," "Asian cool" culture and Asian American creative class by the late 1990s; and the turn of the 21st century development of digital technologies and social media.[6] Before the 1960s, Asians in the U.S. identified more with their own ethnicity/nationality and less with a pan-ethnic marker. However, with the more expansive terms of Asian/American and Asian America, scholars have had the opportunity to research earlier events and encounters from the vantage point of narrating a long history of U.S.–Asia relations.

Thus, just as globalization is an ongoing process, rather than a static condition, so too do the borders and the meanings of Asian/America move and shift. More specifically, rather than conceiving of a prescriptive (generic) category like "Asian American music," studies of popular music in Asian America argue that it is more useful to think instead of, what Deborah Wong terms, "Asian Americans making music."[7] Armed with this performative approach, by asking what popular music *does*, these scholars have had to take on the historical realities and aftermath of Asian/American, described by David Palumbo-Liu, as the moments when the two terms' entangled meanings emerged in discourse as contrasts and juxtapositions between "Asia" and "America." For Palumbo-Liu, these moments materialize in the "forever-foreign" and "model minority," two discursive terms that have and continue to plague Asians in America, at different points over the last century.[8]

Rather than completely resist or assimilate to these discourses, various scholars have addressed these terms' social, cultural, and political implications while still paying detailed attention to the actual and everyday manner in which popular music is produced, distributed, and consumed in Asian America. An expansive term meant to connote the places, practices, and discourses, both based in the U.S. and Asia and generated by their long history of relations, Asian America has provided these writers with the unique intellectual challenge of remaining committed to cultural and geographical specificity while also not losing sight of interconnections, interdependencies, and knotted histories.

Globalization is nothing "new." Instead, it is the ways and manners in which life has expanded and sped up that have otherwise shifted over the years. For example, as media technologies and distribution platforms transformed and grew (from live performance, to phonographs, to radio and film, to broadcast television, to cassette tapes and CDs, to today's Internet and other digital forms), so too did popular music transform and grow. However, each new form of pop music did not simply and completely subsume the previous form or platform. Instead, as Henry Jenkins has noted, each form simply transformed, retaining qualities of previous mediums. And, in today's media-saturated world, all forms of pop music continue to exist (even if obsolete during a certain time).[9]

This essay analyzes the analytics of globalization, popular music, and Asian/Asian American, in tandem, and delineates how various scholarly works have helped ground these connections in material histories. For the purposes of this essay, I define globalization as a set of processes, structures, and practices that occur at both the macro and micro levels. I have organized my discussion into three historical periods to account for patterns dominant within the fields of global studies, popular musical histories, and Asian American studies.

I. (1850s–1945)

The mid-18th century until the end of World War II is an era broadly characterized by advancements in transportation (global shipping, transcontinental railroad) as well as communication and media technologies (telephone, phonograph, camera/photography). For Asian/America, this era is marked by histories of U.S. and European colonialism throughout Asia, wars in the Asia/Pacific region to signal the beginning of the Pacific Century, and the establishment of legal and economic systems that encouraged and then restricted labor migration from Asian countries. During this historical period, various immigration and exclusion acts (Chinese Exclusion, 1882; Geary Act, 1892; Gentleman's Agreement, 1908; Asiatic Barred Zone, 1917; National Origins system, 1921; Immigration Act, 1924; War Brides Act, 1945), citizenship court cases, national treaties and trade agreements, and colonial and imperial events (Philippines, Hawai'i, and Guam) depended upon while also feeding into nativist sentiments regarding Asian immigration, bodies, and marriage/miscegenation and their attendant and scientific discourses of difference, including eugenics and Social Darwinism.[10]

During this time, international world's fairs, anthropological exhibitions, dime museums, and freak shows dominated the U.S. popular cultural landscape, serving as stages for displaying and performing racial, ethnic, sexual, and gendered difference. Similar to the antebellum era, when vaudeville and minstrelsy set the stage for public displays of distorted cultural representation and African American and other racialized performers, excluded from mainstream venues by de jure segregation, were forced to develop their own chitlin' circuits, certain racialized performers tapped into desires for the modern while others established alternative stages of performance.

"[T]he American cabaret scene arose in the 1910s," dance scholar SanSan Kwan writes, "as vaudeville was on its wane and urban restaurant culture was emerging" (Kwan, 122). By the 1930s and 1940s, Asian American cabaret acts that toured a string of nightclubs across the United States, otherwise known as the Chop Suey Circuit, emerged. Asian American entertainers and performers headlined at so-called "Oriental" clubs such as the Forbidden City in San Francisco (which remained open until 1962) and the China Doll in New York, akin to other "exotic"-themed clubs such as the Copacabana and Cotton Club.[11] In this early 20th-century U.S. "cartography of segregation," both fantastical notions of places such as Asia, China, and Chinatown and real sites, both in the streets and on stage, worked to produce race. Through such productions, "[T]he distinction between Chinese and Chinese American is obliterated" (Kwan, 127–128). These performers from various Asian backgrounds "sang the popular songs and danced the well-known styles of the day" while also performing juggling acts, skits, dance routines, and even striptease numbers.

As the work of Kwan and Krystyn Moon has shown, these early Asian American entertainers "performed 'Asian,' through acts of "faking accents, adopting Chinese-sounding names, and wearing coolie hats."[12] Marketed as Chinese versions of famous white American originals—the "Chinese Frank Sinatra," "Chinese Sophie Tucker," etc.—they also performed whiteface in their ongoing hopes for U.S. cultural citizensip and belonging. The former upheld and reinforced notions of whiteness (by performing its racial Other) while also meeting the demands of a "new fascination for all things Chinese" "spurred on by the U.S. involvement in the Pacific theatre during WWII" (Kwan, 126). Despite their talent, the latter marked that "they never quite achieved full American status" (Kwan, 128–129). As Kwan underscores, "[A] glowing review of Jadin Wong and Li Sun remarks, 'If it were not for their race, they would undoubtedly be headliners in New York's Rainbow Room or some other first-line cabaret' (Morley 1941)" (Kwan, 125). "[N]either 'authentically' Oriental nor 'truly' American," these lives and experiences of these entertainers point to the existence of Asian America in the decades before its "official" emergence with the Asian American movement in the 1960s (Kwan, 130).

During this same time, migrant Filipino musicians also established themselves as performers as well as musical composers and arrangers throughout Asia. Due to direct and sustained contact with Spanish and American colonizers since the mid-16th century, Filipino musicians were trained in Western musical styles and techniques and could play on Western instruments.[13] As Lee Watkins notes, during this time "[T]hey [also] wrote for Chinese instruments and observed Chinese musical aesthetics" (Watkins, 77). Starting in the late 19th century, Filipinos "made their presence felt in the musical scenes of Macau, Shanghai, and Hong Kong" (Watkins, 79). In Macau, Filipinos shared with the Portuguese the rich band culture both nations had acquired due to Spanish influence. Active in Shanghai's entertainment industry since 1881, Filipino musicians were dubbed "foreign piano devils" by the Chinese. By the early twentieth century, they entertained local and ex-pat audiences in China with American jazz music they had learned to "appreciate and perform" in the Philippines (during the U.S. occupation). Drawing from the analytical language and studies of 19th-century U.S. minstrelsy, Watkins likens the migrant Filipino musician in Hong Kong to minstrel performers:

> In Hong Kong, it is the Filipino musician's brown skin, which instantly announces a different reality to that of the host. The Filipino's racial color brings to mind [Eric] Lott's astute interpretation of minstrelsy, for in the case of the Filipino musician in Hong Kong, it too may be argued that he produces a dramatic spectacle based on an overriding investment in the body, and a figural content preoccupied with racial marking and racial transmutation (Lott 1993, 6).
>
> *Watkins (75)*

Through their skin color, migrant Filipino musical performers are marked as visually distinct from that of their audience/host society. At the same time, these musical performers naturalized and racialized their musical talents by both acknowledging their nonwhiteness and aligning with certain connotations of blackness (i.e., the Filipino's natural, inborn talent for dance and music that, according to Filipino musical migrant worker Bing Soledad, "is so natural we can compare ourselves with the colored Americans or Africans. There is music in their bodies. That is what they can say about us" (as quoted in Watkins, 76)). Through such illusory gestures of "passing through musical sound" (specifically, U.S. pop musical sounds), according to Watkins, these Filipino musicians/minstrels had the potential to "invert and mock power relations" (Watkins, 76).

More than simply migrant entertainers, these musicians constitute a particular labor force. "[M]arkets in Asia demand of [migrant Filipino musicians] this repertoire" while Hong Kong employers "consider Filipino musicians an easily exploitable resource from the developing world." These overseas performing artists (OPAs) "are tied in relations with a transnational economy where the music of the other is depended upon for economic prosperity and cross-border mobility" (Watkins, 93). Perceived as both "in *excess*" and yet in possession of "an *exceptional* sense of musicality," the competition for work among these Filipino musicians has increased over the last century (Watkins, 76).

II. (1945–1990s)

The time period between the end of World War II until the late 1990s is marked by transportation innovations such as transpacific flights and the rapid expansion of communication and media technologies from musical LPs/albums and television, singular platforms of distribution, to cassette tapes and VHS, methods of recording and copy/dubbing, all the way to the emergence of a digital era and the Internet, participatory modes that would lend themselves to cross-platform or transmedia distribution. Politically, this period was broadly characterized by the uneasy transition from the "active" world wars of the early 20th century to the (seemingly passive) Cold War and its "hot wars," the rise of postcolonial nations and their Third World resistance movements as well as the ushering in of the neoliberal era. Within the U.S., the increasing awareness of Asian America as both a "domestic and transnational" formation by Asian American and Third World liberation movements in the 1960s and 1970s worked in conjunction and solidarity with overseas postcolonial projects, such as the 1955 Bandung conference, and more local social movements, such as the Black Panthers, Young Lords, and Red Guard (Maeda, 2009). At the same time, immigration legislation (such as the 1965 Immigration Act, Refugee/Relocation Acts after the Vietnam War, and Family Relocation acts of the 1970s and 1980s) not only increased but diversified Asian American communities to include white-collar medical and technology professionals (famously known as the "brain drain"), Southeast Asian refugees, as well as the younger and older family members petitioned by naturalized U.S. citizens under family reunification acts and programs.

One way to characterize the immediate post-World War II era would be in its move from espousing – what Jodi Kim has termed a politics and aesthetics of "containment" to one of protest.[14] Through artistic forms such as musical theater, performance revues, and military base entertainment, Asian/Asian American actors worked within and against narratives, characters and caricatures, and types (such as the model minority)—ones seemingly "good" in their assimilationist nature yet "bad" in the ways they contained and circumscribed race and racialized Asian/Asian American behavior. At the same time, various forms of Asian American musical and political protest—in Asian American jazz, folk rock, and spoken word (Asian Improv Arts, A Grain of Sand, to name a few)— sounded their protest against such assimilationist figures and discourses such as the "model minority," in the various musical idioms, collaborative projects, and performance practices.

Since its emergence in the 19th century, Western musical theatre has been a strong globalizing force, not only through its staging of Orientalist characters, places/backdrops, costuming and dance/musical performances but also through its export of these and other Western cultural values and ideas across the globe. In globalization, juxtaposing images of the West and the rest circulate, making sense and upholding certain structures of power. Against the backdrop of the global Cold War, U.S. musicals, such as *South Pacific* and *Flower Drum Song*, were written, produced, and staged.[15] Through the theatrical form of the musical, Christina Klein has argued, "antagonistic forces" are either "eliminated" or "incorporated":

> musicals, [in turn,] tend to feature a collective hero, usually a couple or a community, in which feminine and familial values dominate. They express their dramatic conflicts as emotion and resolve them by integrating antagonistic characters into a harmonious community, usually through the mechanism of romance. . . . The musical's ideological power, in turn, resides in the way it imagines community: the differences among people that can be transcended, the kinds of bonds that can be forged, and the nature of communities that can be created . . . What the Western [film] imagines as a gunfight, the musical imagines as a dance.
>
> *Klein (192–193)*

Based on a 1957 novel by C.Y. Lee and later adapted into a 1961 musical film, *Flower Drum Song* focuses on the romantic plot of Wang Ta, the American-born Chinese and oldest son of the orthodox Master Wang, who has to choose between the seductive and Americanized club performer, Linda Low, and the shy, traditional immigrant girl, Mei Li. Through this main plot and other subplots and supporting characters, the 1958 musical deals with the generation gap and cultural differences between immigrant Asian parents and Asian Americans. While the novel focuses on Master Wang's narrative (as he flees Communist China in the 1950s and grapples with cultural assimilation through the figure of his son) and paints a grim picture of immigrant life in the U.S., through its songs and characters, *Flower Drum Song* the musical reinforced the emerging narrative of model minority discourse—Asian Americans as docile, hardworking, and politically non-confrontational/assimilationist subjects. For this reason, many Asian American critics have either chided or completely overlooked this musical theatre classic.

Yet, as Klein and other scholars remind us, *Flower Drum Song* "should be read as both a cultural narrative and a social practice," a popular story and an "investment of capital, body of hiring practices, and series of marketing decisions" (Klein, 230). Along with the musical's plot, staging, and songs, critics must also take heed of the principal and starring roles it has and continues to offer Asian and Asian American actors and the ways that, through listing the show's cast members' various Asian countries and U.S. cities/towns of origins, the show's Playbill programs mapped the diverse landscape of Asian America.

Paying critical attention to musical theater's performers and the labors their performing bodies enact is where Lucy San Pablo Burns' study of *Miss Saigon* begins.[16] An updated version of Puccini's 1904 opera *Madama Butterfly*, according to Burns, Alain Boubil and Claude-Michel Schoenberg's 1990s musical "uses the Vietnam War as a backdrop for the greatest love story of all: a mother's selfless love, and the immense sacrifices she makes for her child" (Burns, 108). Yet, while the musical re-enacts "what is often narrated as the most painful chapters of American history," it has drawn more controversy from its history of casting. When it premiered on Broadway in 1989, the musical drew heated criticism from and galvanized members of various Asian American communities into organizing multi-city protests.[17] Initially ignited by the casting of white actor Jonathan Pryce in the role of the Eurasian Engineer, "anti-*Miss Saigon* organizing," both in the U.S. and abroad, broadened its attention to U.S. musical theater's historical practices of yellowface, its staging and viewing of Asian female sexuality, its rehearsal of "the image(s) of the 'oppressed and exploited Third World woman'" and her white male savior, and its figuring in the "imperialist globalization of culture" (Burns, 116–117). Thinking beyond the representational politics of the musical, however, Burns and theater studies scholar Joi Barrios take seriously the larger globalizing forces that set the stage for "the commodification of Filipino performers/laborers in the *Miss Saigon* production," situating them as part of the migrant labor force of Filipino overseas performing artists (OPAs) and "transmigrant entertainment workers" (Joi Barrios as quoted in Burns, 116–117). Such analyses not only bring into relief the histories of U.S. colonial education in the Philippines that make such a labor force possible; they also allow for a more radical consideration of the connections between the U.S. military-government and the Philippines' role in Cold War politics during the time of the Vietnam War.

Often overlooked yet extremely palpable and cultural sites of globalization, military bases have served as unexpected places for the development and distribution of popular music and its cultures across Asia.[18] In 1938, the U.S. owned 14 military bases outside its continental borders. By 1945, that number had ballooned to 30,000 installations, large and small, in approximately 100 countries. According to Catherine Lutz, in 2009, "over 190,000 troops and 115,000 civilian employees are massed in 909 military facilities in 46 countries and territories" (Lutz, 3). As she describes, "The global scale of military basing would remain primarily the twentieth-century outcome of World War II, and with it, the rise to global hegemony of the United States (Blaker 1990: 22)" (Lutz, 10). The increase in U.S. military bases coincides with the nation's three major periods of global ambition (1898, 1945, and 2001) as well as the 20th century as the "Pacific century" of U.S. wars in Asia. This "empire of bases" has often been chided, by cultural imperialist theorists, as one of the most dominant purveyors of U.S. popular culture and music.

Against these simplified theories, Pilyoung Kim and Hyunjoon Shin actually argue that "the U.S. military base, a powerful symbol of American hegemony, turned into an improbable incubator of a fledgling Korean counterculture movement" (Kim and Shin, 203). In their study of Korean *rok*, Kim and Shin note that U.S. military presence in Korea led to the development of camp show acts and the increased professionalism of local Korean musical artists.[19] Not simply musical concerts, these "camp show acts" were "entertainment variety show" performed by *ssyodan* (big band orchestra, singers, comedians, dancers, and other performers). For these artists, musical versatility was crucial as they had to cater to the musical tastes of diverse U.S. military personnel. Over time, combo bands—groups that played purely instrumental music—transformed into vocal groups (or group sounds)—bands that did their own singing. While many of these group sounds began by performing covers of U.S. and Western pop songs, over time, they began to create their own music, "shooting for mainstream respectability" among the larger South Korean listening public. While some might have argued that these group sounds' musical structures were simply "knock-offs" of American and Western pop musical styles, Kim and Shin argue, "What these detractors either did not see or chose to ignore was the intense efforts of leading group sounds to find their own voice and achieve authenticity, the elusive goal of all rock music" (Kim and Shin, 220).

One remarkable example of Korean musical entertainment specifically geared towards U.S. troops in Asia was the girl group known as The Kim Sisters. Composed of two actual sisters (Sook-ja and Ai-ja Kim) and their cousin (Mia Kim), the group's career began when they were children singing for U.S. troops during the Korean War. As Mia Kim recalls in a 2011 interview with *Korea Times*:

> My aunt had an American record that contained two songs, "Ole Buttermilk Sky" and "Candy & Cake." Although we couldn't speak a word of English, we memorized these two songs and sang them to the GI troops along with my aunt. They just loved us. Our pronunciation was bad, but they knew the melody and always said, "More, more, more!" We didn't know more songs, so we kept repeating these two over and over again.[20]

In 1959, the musical act was invited by Las Vegas producer Tom Ball to perform at the Thunderbird Hotel as an Oriental musical revue. That same year, while playing the Stardust Hotel lounge, their big break came when they performed on *The Ed Sullivan Show*. With this national recognition, they returned to perform on the classic TV show a historic 21 more times and continued performing in Las Vegas until the early 1990s. More emerging Korean American pop music and culture scholarship attributes the beginnings of Korean pop's (or K-Pop) cultural history with the story of The Kim Sisters.

III. (1990s–present)

The late 1990s until the present has been characterized by the development of digital technologies (the "digital revolution" and "Internet age") that have advanced, what David Harvey has rightfully described as, the "time-space compression." This time period has also been marked by the rise of social media and networking sites (SNS), ones that have shifted our notion of media's cultural "taste" purveyors and broadened the industry's notions of marketing in order to take seriously fans, niche audiences, and prosumers (producer + consumers). The early 1990s in the U.S. appeared flanked by, what Lisa Lowe termed, nation-state policies of multiculturalism.[21] By the early 21st century, however, as Laura Kang has deftly argued, neoliberalization has fully ushered in the nation-state's new "role" "as an active proponent and protector of private capital and corporate interests"[22] (Kang, 304). This era in Asian/America has also been marked by the faster and broader multidirectional flows of culture aided by new patterns of migration and migrant groups, including helicopter parents, parachute kids, and global elites. These issues of im/migration and im/migrant histories, state-driven cultural exports and market-driven multiculturalism, as well as alternative genealogies of U.S. popular music have put pressure on the generic categories in which Asians and Asian Americans "make" music—hip-hop; various forms of Asian pop; and indie rock, to name a few.

An umbrella term coined in the late 1990s by Chinese journalists to designate the growing popularity of South Korean popular cultural forms throughout Asia, Korean Wave (also known as Hallyu), encompasses Korean dramas (soap operas), popular music, film, and fashion. By 2005, the revenue from overall Hallyu exports totaled $1 billion U.S. dollars, making South Korea one of the top 10 cultural exporters worldwide. Within the K-Pop music industry, three companies dominate—JYP (founded by musician/producer Jin-Young Park), SM Entertainment (founded by musician/mogul/record producer Soo-man Lee), and YG Entertainment (founded by a former member of one of South Korea's most successful boy bands, Seo Taiji & Boys, and record producer, Hyun-Suk Yang). A music industry and musical genre known for its star system, rigorous audition and training processes, slick choreography and audio-visual creativity (as evidenced in its advertising and music videos), K-Pop has not only found audiences/markets within the Asia-Pacific region but has also crossed the Pacific and infiltrated and influenced U.S. audiences and musical artists. K-Pop has made a name for itself as a global musical export through its artists' collaborations with U.S. pop musical artists (such as Missy Elliott, Will.I.Am, and Nicki Minaj), Southern California-based events such as the annual KCON (K-Pop Conference), online platforms such as YouTube and fan websites (allthingskpop.com), as well as the fandom of the *yuhaksaeng* generation—Korean students who study abroad in the U.S.[23]

In their cover performances of Cambodian pop songs, ones prevalent and popular in the years before the Khmer Rouge regime, the U.S.-based indie rock band Dengue Fever "foregrounds a history that has been virtually erased from the historical consciousness of many U.S. audiences.[24] Also known as "Democratic Kampuchea," as Joshua Chambers-Letson writes, this pre-Khmer Rouge era musical culture "came to its zenith in the late Sihanouk (1952–1969) and Lon Nol (1969–1975) years" with "the increased U.S. military presence in neighboring South Vietnam and Thailand in the 1960s" (Chambers-Letson, 269). Through the spread of "affordable radio technology," many local Cambodians "were introduced to rock and roll as well as rhythm and blues on pirated radio waves carrying the voice of America and the U.S. Armed Forces Radio." In their choice to revive a pre-DK catalogue of pop songs, almost 40 years later, Dengue Fever "does not invent a performance practice that destabilizes authenticity; it inherits one." Whereas nostalgia for Cambodian pop songs might render these pieces as traditional, Dengue Fever's members emphasize histories of "exchange and overlap" and "consistently articulated the music's genesis less as linear progression from an origin than as a series of networked exchanges that defy linear temporality or geographic and cultural purity" (Chambers-Letson, 271).

A former underground L.A. hip-hop group turned American pop musical success, the Black Eyed Peas (BEP) are among some of the very few recognizable Asian Americans in mainstream

U.S. pop culture today.[25] With members of African American, Filipino American, Native American, and Latino descent, BEP truly are both a multiracial and multicultural group. Their albums, in turn, provide "smorgasbords of racialized flavors from around the world (i.e. 'bhangra, salsa, New Orleans jazz, and crunk, just to name a few') sandwiched by some uplifting political gesturing . . ." (Devitt, 123). The group therefore offers a kind of pliable, "something for everyone" chicness that, as Rachel Devitt argues, functions as marketing tool. In the particular case of "The Apl Song," a track rapped in Tagalog whose main hook draws from Filipino folk rock group Asin's 1970s anthem, Devitt notes:

> Apl's "version of the ghetto" builds on the verbiage of hip-hop vernaculars to construct a transnational link between a rural province in the Philippines and urban enclaves in the United States that powerfully demonstrates the global scale of the impact of Western imperialism and global capitalism. On the other, it shapes a very particular version of the Philippines, perpetually translating Apl's "homeland" as un-modern, traditional, "real" and articulating a codified vocabulary of authenticity into which Apl can tap.
> *Devitt (124)*

Through its lyrics and music video, the song indexes the U.S. hip-hop group's resistance vernaculars and their "prescriptive effect when the struggle is armed with an over-determined ideology of authenticity that, in turn, can translate as essentialist codifications of ethnicity and class" (Devitt, 123–124). This brand of multiculturalism defines the Peas' marketing niche, both domestically and globally. Yet, despite the cultural and political work performed when one critically listens to "The Apl Song," the group's label (A&M) "showed no signs of supporting the Tagalog tracks or their videos in the United States" (Devitt, 123), while no U.S. mainstream music section or publication mentions the songs in their "laundry list" reviews (Devitt, 118). As a cultural and musical form, hip-hop draws from its origins in "migration and dispersal" and insists upon pastiche, borrowing, sampling, and remixing. However, on the racial and economic battlefields of the U.S. pop music industry, hip-hop still depends upon certain racial, linguistic, class-based, and nationalist essentialisms and archetypes, in order to make money and meaning.

By bringing together the key terms of globalization, Asian/American, and popular music and moving them throughout various periods, this essay reminds us of globalization and Asian/America's histories as well as the central role that arts and culture have played throughout. With its performative approach, this essay recognizes culture, specifically popular music, as not just reflecting but actually constituting social realities. Popular music—in its live, recorded, and shared participatory forms—and its politics have shaped and been shaped by moments of encounter, performing/laboring bodies, and mobile sounds. I end this essay with the hope that as students of popular music, global histories, and Asian/American studies, we listen differently to the stories of the past, the performances on the horizon, and the ways we encounter and record them.

Notes

1 James, Paul and Manfred Steger. "A Genealogy of Globalization: the Career of a Concept." *Globalizations*, 11:4 (September 2014) (Routledge), 422.
2 See Erika Brady's *A Spiral Way: How the Phonograph Changed Ethnography* (University Press of Mississippi, 1999); Jonathan Sterne's *The Audible Past: Cultural Origins of Sound Reproduction* (Duke University Press, 2003); and Dave Tompkins' *How to Wreck a Nice Beach: The Vocoder from World War II to Hip-Hop, The Machine Speaks* (Stop Smiling Press, 2011).

3 Kwan, SanSan. "Performing a Geography of Asian America: the Chop Suey Circuit." *TDR: The Drama Review* (55.1) Spring 2011, 120–136; Imada, Adria. "Hawaiians On Tour: Hula Circuits through the American Empire." *AQ: American Quarterly* (56.1) 2004, 111–149.
4 Held, David, Anthony McGrew, David Goldblatt and Jonathan Perraton. *Global Transformations: Politics, Economics, and Culture.* (Stanford University Press, 1999), 350–353.
5 Maeda, Daryl. *Chains of Babylon: the Rise of Asian America* (University of Minnesota Press, 2009).
6 See Mimi Nguyen and Thuy Linh Tu's introduction to their edited collection, *Alien Encounters: Popular Culture in Asian America* (Duke University Press, 2007).
7 Wong, Deborah. *Speak It Louder: Asian Americans Making Music* (Routledge, 2004).
8 Palumbo-Liu, David. *Asian/American: Historical Crossings of a Racial Frontier* (Stanford University Press, 1999).
9 Jenkins, Henry. *Convergence Culture: Where Old and New Media Collide* (NYU Press, 2006)
10 See Rick Baldoz, *The Third Asiatic Invasion: Migration and Empire in Filipino America, 1898–1945* (NYU Press, 2011); Dawn Bohulano Mabalon, *Little Manila is in the Heart: The Making of the Filipino/a American Community in Stockton, California* (Duke University Press, 2013); Mae Ngai, *Illegal Aliens and the Making of Modern America* (Princeton University Press, 2003); Nayan Shah, *Contagious Divides: Epidemics and Race in San Francisco's Chinatown* (UC Press, 2001).
11 See Arthur Dong's book, *Forbidden City, USA: Chinese American Nightclubs, 1936-1970* (DeepFocus Productions, 2014), and film *Forbidden City, USA* (DeepFocus Productions, 1989) for more on the Chop Suey circuit.
12 Moon, Krystyn. *Yellowface: Creating the Chinese in American Popular Music and Performance, 1850s–1920s* (Rutgers University Press, 2005).
13 Watkins, Lee. "Minstrelsy and Mimesis in the South China Sea: Filipino Migrant Musicians, Chinese Hosts, and the Disciplining of Relations in Hong Kong." *Asian Music* (40.2) Summer/Fall 2009 (University of Texas Press), 72–99.
14 Kim, Jodi. *Ends of Empire: Asian American Critique and the Cold War* (University of Minnesota Press, 2010).
15 Klein, Christina. *Cold War Orientalism: Asia in the Middlebrow Imagination, 1945–1961* (UC Press, 2003).
16 Burns, Lucy San Pablo. *Puro Arte: Filipinos on the Stages of Empire* (NYU Press, 2012).
17 For more on this history, see Yoko Yoshikawa's essay, "The Heat is On Miss Saigon Coaliation: Organizing Across Race and Sexuality," in Karin Aguilar San Juan's edited collection, *The State of Asian America: Activism and Resistance in the 1990s* (South End Press, 1999).
18 Lutz, Catherine, ed. *The Bases of Empire: the Global Struggle Against U.S. Military Posts* (NYU Press, 2009).
19 Kim, Pilyoung and Hyunjoon Shin. "The Birth of 'Rok': Cultural Imperialism, Nationalism, and the Glocalization of Rock Music in South Korea, 1964–1975." *positions* (18.1) (Duke University Press, 2011), 199–230.
20 Teszar, David. "From Seoul to Las Vegas: Story of the Kim Sisters." *Korea Times.* (Sept 21, 2011) (www.koreatimes.co.kr/www/news/special/2011/09/178_95166.html, accessed online June 25, 2016).
21 Lowe, Lisa. *Immigrant Acts: On Asian American Cultural Politics* (Duke University Press, 1996).
22 Kang, Laura. "Late (Global) Capital" in *The Routledge Companion to Asian American and Pacific Islander Literature*, edited by Rachel Lee (Routledge, 2014), 201–314.
23 See essay "Curatorial Conversations/Correspondences", pp. 12–37 in Viet Le and Yong Soon Min's edited exhibition catalogue, *Transpop: Korea Vietnam Remix* (2008).
24 Chambers-Letson, Joshua. "Illegal Immigrant Acts: Dengue Fever and the Racialization of Cambodian America" in *A Race So Different: Performance and Law in Asian America* (NYU Press, 2013).
25 Devitt, Rachel. "Lost in Translation: Filipino Diaspora(s), Postcolonial Hip Hop, and the Problems of Keeping It Real for the 'Contentless' Black Eyed Peas." *Asian Music* (39.1) Winter/Spring 2008 (University of Texas Press, 2011).

References

Brady, Erika. *A Spiral Way: How the Phonograph Changed Ethnography* (University Press of Mississippi, 1999).
Burns, Lucy San Pablo. *Puro Arte: Filipinos on the Stages of Empire* (NYU Press, 2012).

Chambers-Letson, Joshua. "Illegal Immigrant Acts: Dengue Fever and the Racialization of Cambodian America" in *A Race So Different: Performance and Law in Asian America* (NYU Press, 2013).

Devitt, Rachel. "Lost in Translation: Filipino Diaspora(s), Postcolonial Hip Hop, and the Problems of Keeping It Real for the 'Contentless' Black Eyed Peas." *Asian Music* (39.1) Winter/Spring 2008 (University of Texas Press, 2011).

Dong, Arthur. *Forbidden City, USA: Chinese American Nightclubs, 1936–1970* (DeepFocus Productions, 2014). (book)

Dong, Arthur. *Forbidden City, USA* (DeepFocus Productions, 1989). (film)

Held, David, Anthony McGrew, David Goldblatt, Jonathan Perraton. *Global Transformations: Politics, Economics, and Culture.* (Stanford University Press, 1999).

Imada, Adria. "Hawaiians On Tour: Hula Circuits through the American Empire." *AQ: American Quarterly* (56.1) 2004, 111–149.

Jenkins, Henry. *Convergence Culture: Where Old and New Media Collide* (NYU Press, 2006).

James, Paul and Manfred Steger. "A Genealogy of Globalization: the Career of a Concept." *Globalizations*, 11:4 (September 2014).

Kim, Jodi. *Ends of Empire: Asian American Critique and the Cold War* (University of Minnesota Press, 2010).

Kim, Pilyoung and Hyunjoon Shin. "The Birth of 'Rok': Cultural Imperialism, Nationalism, and the Glocalization of Rock Music in South Korea, 1964–1975." *positions* (18.1) (Duke University Press, 2011), 199–230.

Klein, Christina. *Cold War Orientalism: Asia in the Middlebrow Imagination, 1945–1961* (UC Press, 2003).

Kwan, SanSan. "Performing a Geography of Asian America: the Chop Suey Circuit." *TDR: The Drama Review*, 55.1 (Spring 2011), 120–136.

Lowe, Lisa. *Immigrant Acts: On Asian American Cultural Politics* (Duke University Press, 1996).

Lutz, Catherine, Ed. *The Bases of Empire: the Global Struggle Against U.S. Military Posts* (NYU Press, 2009).

Kang, Laura. "Late (Global) Capital" in *The Routledge Companion to Asian American and Pacific Islander Literature*, edited by Rachel Lee (Routledge, 2014), 201–314.

Maeda, Daryl. *Chains of Babylon: the Rise of Asian America* (University of Minnesota Press, 1999).

Moon, Krystyn. *Yellowface: Creating the Chinese in American Popular Music and Performance, 1850s–1920s* (Rutgers University Press, 2005).

Nguyen, Mimi and Thuy Linh Tu, Eds. *Alien Encounters: Popular Culture in Asian America* (Duke University Press, 2007).

Palumbo-Liu, David. *Asian/American: Historical Crossings of a Racial Frontier* (Stanford University Press, 1999).

Sterne, Jonathan. *The Audible Past: Cultural Origins of Sound Reproduction* (Duke University Press, 2003).

Teszar, David. "From Seoul to Las Vegas: Story of the Kim Sisters." *Korea Times*. (Sept 21, 2011) www.koreatimes.co.kr/www/news/special/2011/09/178_95166.html, accessed online June 25, 2016.

Tompkins, Dave. *How to Wreck a Nice Beach: The Vocoder from World War II to Hip-Hop, The Machine Speaks* (Stop Smiling Press, 2011).

Watkins, Lee. "Minstrelsy and Mimesis in the South China Sea: Filipino Migrant Musicians, Chinese Hosts, and the Disciplining of Relations in Hong Kong." *Asian Music* (40.2) Summer/Fall 2009 (University of Texas Press), 72–99.

Wong, Deborah. *Speak It Louder: Asian Americans Making Music* (Routledge, 2004).

Yoshikawa, Yoko. "The Heat is On Miss Saigon Coaliation: Organizing Across Race and Sexuality," in Karin Aguilar San Juan, Ed. *The State of Asian America: Activism and Resistance in the 1990s* (South End Press, 1999).

13

THE SPORTS LOYALTY TEST

Asian Athletes and Asian American Cultural Politics

Rachael Miyung Joo

Yao. Yuna. Ichiro.[1] In the era of contemporary globalization,[2] these sporting figures exist as global icons referenced and recognized by a single name. They are part of a growing number of top-level celebrity athletes of Asian[3] origin in North American and European sports leagues including baseball, golf, basketball, soccer (football), figure skating, and tennis.[4] Throughout the 20th century, organized sport played an important role in Asian American communities (Yep 2009; Franks 2000; Regalado 2013) and some Asian American athletes, like diver Sammy Lee and baseball pitcher Ron Darling, achieved national recognition for their athletic accomplishments.[5] Beginning in the 1990s, Asian athletes who were by and large citizens of Asian nations started to become a regular presence in several major sporting leagues as sports and media industries focused on globalizing their markets. Commercial sports featuring Asian athletes have had a major impact in Asian American communities as seen in the commercial, racial, and national significance of figures such as Filipino boxer Manny Pacquiao and basketball player Yao Ming. The regular presence of Asian athletes in commercial media has played an important role in shaping the racial landscapes of sport and has added to the corpus of images of Asians featured in mainstream media. Through transnational media coverage, global advertising, and digital communications technologies, athletes have emerged as transnational icons that produce deterritorialized nationalisms as they come to stand in for the nation in diaspora (Joo 2000). The increasing visibility of Asian athletes reflects important changes in Asian America, especially in how racial, ethnic, and national differences are represented and shaped by global commercial interests.

Asian athletes have become a common sight in North American sport, not simply because of the development of world-class athletic talent in Asian nations, but also due to the globalization of media markets and the circulation of global commodity-signs (Andrews 1996). With the liberalization of Asian media markets, communications infrastructures now provide lucrative markets for North American commercial sports as Asian populations are perceived as harboring consumers for sporting organizations like Major League Baseball (MLB), the Professional Golf Association (PGA and LPGA), and the National Basketball Association (NBA). Investments are made on Asian athletes who achieve success in Western countries with the assumption that their victories will result in national celebrity status. Riding on the popularity of Yao Ming, the NBA sold media and merchandising rights to Chinese companies and worked to create an institutionalized presence in the country through NBA-sponsored workshops, public engagements, charities, and training institutes (Wang 2004; Houlihan et al. 2010).[6] In nations like South Korea and China, athletic careers have recently become a socially acceptable pursuit as athletic participation presents an opportunity to display family wealth through conspicuous consumption, especially in the capital-intensive sports of golf, figure skating, and tennis. While Asian players have had a significant impact in their countries of origin or ethnic heritage, this chapter focuses primarily on the impact of Asian athletes in Asian America and highlights the contradictory role of global capital in shaping ideas of race and nation in North American sports.

The field of Asian American Studies has traditionally drawn important distinctions between Asian Americans as U.S. citizens and Asians as foreign citizens given the sordid history of discrimination against Asian Americans based on their depictions as perpetual foreigners (Takaki 1998; Ngai 2004). While barriers remain to full incorporation into U.S. national culture (Lowe 1996), Asian Americans are increasingly included in mainstream portraits of multicultural America (Palumbo-Liu 1999). While there are growing numbers of Asian Americans in positions of visibility in media, politics, and the arts, Asian Americans are also caught up in what Thuy Tu (2010) refers to as "transnational intimacies" with Asia. The last two decades have been characterized by increasing transnational connections between Asia and America given the rising number of people who possess multiple citizenships, reside in a number of nations, acquire various educational degrees and work experiences, travel frequently, demonstrate facility with multiple languages, and engage in financial exchanges across the Pacific. Given the frequency and intensity of these transnational connections, distinctions between Asian as foreigner and Asian American as American citizen have grown increasingly blurry. Asian athletes in North American sports also confound the distinction between foreigner and citizen given that they are sponsored by a multinational cadre of advertisers and management interests, travel frequently between Asia and North America, and often reside in homes located in Asia and North America. Clearly, commercial interests benefit from these national ambiguities. Global athletes are elites who demonstrate a "flexible citizenship" that enables them to highlight different aspects of their national and racial identities for commercial gain (Ong 1999). In this chapter, the term Asian athlete references American citizens as well as Asian foreign nationals and relies on broad U.S. census categories of race rather than nationality or ethnicity, sense of acculturation or affiliation, or self-identification. Moreover, the use of the term Asian athlete in this chapter refers to athletes of Asian heritage who have competed in North American commercial sports.

Asian athletes offer emotional pleasures and a sense of new possibilities for Asian American audiences by representing a significant shift in the history of limited characterizations of Asians in mainstream commercial media. The first part of this chapter discusses how Asian athletes both engage and contradict long-held stereotypes based in eugenic theories about Asian physical inferiority and competitive ineptitude. Asian athletes represent physical strength, agility, aggressiveness, and star power within multicultural contexts where athletes of multiple races and nationalities compete. They thrive in a realm of competition ideologically defined by notions of meritocracy and fair play where the best players are said to participate and win due to their sheer athletic talent. Second, Asian athletes demonstrate how ideas of race are circulated within the context of global capitalism. As "Asianness" becomes increasingly commodified (Tu 2010), sport offers an arena for the global marketing of American ideas of race as in the case of Michael Jordan and Tiger Woods who became black global icons (Andrews 2001; Starn 2011). While these players are marketed as representing Asianness across the globe, ethno-national identifications remain salient and arguably even more lucrative. The connections between ethno-nationalisms and Asian athletes are discussed in the final section. Sports function as a powerful context for the iteration of transnational identities and generate ideas of nation that circulate within diasporic communities. Asian athletes raise important questions about how global capital shapes ideas of nation in Asian American communities. The chapter concludes with important questions about future directions for Asian American critique raised by transnational sports.

Sporting Pleasures and Possibilities

In his classic text, *Beyond a Boundary* (1983) originally published in 1963, the anti-colonial intellectual and political activist C.L.R. James offers a powerful account of the role of the sport of cricket in his own personal and political development and in the movement for West Indian independence. He writes, "What do they know of cricket who only cricket know? West Indians crowding to Tests bring with them the whole past history and future hopes of the islands" (1983, 25). Cricket operated as a site where British colonial practices were inculcated and contested. The sport existed as a context for the expression and celebration of the individuality, artistry, and strength of West Indians. Cricket offered an arena where a nation could be envisioned through the community of players and fans that gathered to play and watch the sport; it was where independence could be imagined through a game. James sketches an important framework for detailing the political importance of sport for minority communities and interpreting the paradoxes of sport for subjugated peoples. Rather than a simple connection between sport and politics, sport played a complex and often contradictory role in shaping revolutionary politics.

Asian athletes competing in North America demonstrate the continuing political significance of sport for politically marginalized groups, albeit in contradictory ways and within a contemporary global sporting context overwhelmingly defined by corporate interests. Asian athletes function as powerful symbols of race, gender, and nation which animate Asian American cultural politics as representations have and continue to play a central role in ongoing political and social discrimination against Asians in America (Lee 1999). Athletes defy more than a century of eugenic representations of Asian bodies as naturally weak, small, and diseased (Shah 2001). They challenge notions of Asians as a homogenous group of people who lack individuality and creativity as they distinguish themselves through their unique mastery of their sports and their distinctive characteristics both in and out of competition. Ideas of Asian subservience and docility are contested through players' achievements in strenuously competitive contexts. While stereotypes categorize Asians in a limited number of subordinate social positions, Asian athletes open imaginative possibilities for public visibility and media exposure through their participation in a field where victories, celebrity, and wealth are hailed as the ultimate symbols of success.

While athletes might challenge some enduring stereotypes, they do not transcend entrenched ideologies of race as commercial sports both enable and work through paradoxes of race, gender, and national ideologies. For instance, Asian athletes are often presented as hardworking model minorities in relation to black athletes who are depicted as naturally gifted but lazy, whiny, entitled, or criminal (Leonard and King 2011). The popular rise of Chinese American basketball player Jeremy Lin, for instance, can be understood within the context of the vilification of blackness in the NBA (Leonard 2012). Lin was featured as the model minority whose evangelical Christianity and Ivy-league degree from Harvard University set himself apart from the dominant "hip-hop" culture of a Black league defined by bad attitudes, conspicuous consumption, and disgraceful personal baggage. Lin demonstrated a humility and modesty as he lived on his brother's couch and surprised the NBA establishment and fans who delighted in "discovering" his talents. As scholars like Robert G. Lee (1999) have noted, model minority discourse operates to divide minorities against each other while diverting attention from the structural roots of white supremacy and racial inequality. Rather than seeing inequality as a result of systematic discrimination, the lack of success by racial minorities is blamed on "cultural traits" expressed in racial minorities. Placed in this context, Jeremy Lin, along with his marketing potential in

China and Asia, comes to represent for the NBA establishment the antidote to the exasperating problems of a Black league plagued by negative representations of African American athletes.

Media reports often perpetuate stereotypes of Asian players as indistinguishable, lacking individuality and easily replaceable. Reports on Asian female golfers in the LPGA have referenced their talents as hailing from a robotic approach to the game inculcated through constant and relentless repetitive practice that takes place in worker camp-like conditions (Joo 2012). Criticism has been heaped on Korean golfers for sticking together as a group and speaking in Korean rather than socializing with non-Korean players and fans in English. These stereotypes of Asians as a horde and an impenetrable clique have a history in the distrust against Asians fueled by wars (Ngai 2004) and trade competition and enforced through spatial segregation in spaces such as Chinatowns (Lui 2004). The LPGA was clearly concerned about the large numbers of Korean players entering its ranks as a threat to the white supremacy of the LPGA, and attempted to institute an English language-only policy as a way to lower the number of players from Korea and other Asian nations (Joo 2012). Yet Korean players understand themselves as individuals who worked hard to land their place in the league, and they see their play as unique in terms of their own strengths and challenges. While they may have friends on tour who are Korean, many see other Korean individuals as their fiercest competitors and realize their foremost duty is to win.

Media representations of athletes function to paradoxically challenge some gendered and sexualized stereotypes of Asians while also perpetuating binary depictions of male and female differences. While Asian male athletes challenge ideas of Asian men as effeminate, small, weak, and nerdy, masculine Asian players can be used to celebrate male heterosexual dominance. Athletes like baseball players Hideki Matsui and Shin-Soo Choo present masculine dominance on the baseball field, as tall and heavy-set men with severe facial expressions, confident swaggers, and powerful swings. While athletes like tennis player Michael Chang and baseball player Ichiro Suzuki have been known for their athletic feats despite their relatively small and lithe bodies, athletes like basketball player Yao Ming demonstrate that Asians can present as large, strong, tall, and intimidating competitors (Wang 2004).[7] Rather than exceptional freaks, these large Asian male players are seen as representing the rising competitiveness and size of Asia in general due to economic development and capitalist expansion (Ling 1999).

The athletic accomplishments of Asian females contest stereotypes of Asian women as delicate and servile existing to serve their fathers, husbands, and sons. Asian female athletes have emerged as formidable competitors in a number of sporting contexts. Chinese tennis player Li Na famously poked fun at her husband during her winner's speech at the 2014 Australian Open. Standing with her winner's trophy, she stated: "My husband, you are famous in China . . . you are [sic] nice guy. Also you're so lucky."[8] Her ability to joke with ease and confidence about a non-traditional relationship with her husband was widely hailed as a sign of the growing individualism, independence, confidence, and entrepreneurialism of Chinese women. South Korean figure skater Yuna Kim had a long and successful career despite intense media exposure and national pressure. She publicly expressed a sense of self-confidence and personal conviction rather than deferring to her coach or other sources of authority. She also represented South Korea as part of its Olympic bid committee with high-profile male members including President Lee Myung-bak and a number of CEOs of large corporations. After the 2014 Sochi Olympics, despite her disappointing second-place finish, she stated, "I did all I wanted to do, like I wanted to do it."[9] Her expressions of confidence reflect her individual drive and motivation in the high-stakes arena of international competition.

The extraordinary athletic accomplishments of these women are often overshadowed by the pressure to display hyper-feminine personas for heterosexual men who are imagined as the broadest and most significant sports market (Messner 2002).[10] This overemphasis on the attractive and ultra-feminine female works to exaggerate the differences between male and female competitors (Feder-Kane 2000). As Asian competitors have become a regular and expected presence in the sports of figure skating and golf, some Asian female athletes have worked to strengthen a connection between Asianness and ultra-femininity. In LPGA golf, the imbalance in compensation and exposure for attractive players was clear in the relatively low commercial interest and media coverage for South Korean golfer Inbee Park. Park was the number one player in the world in 2013 and came close to a historic sweep of all four major tournaments in the calendar year, but fell short by failing to win the British Open. She has been publicly chastised for her stout body and her round face, and her compatriots often receive more positive interest and media coverage, including So Yeon Ryu who is known for her cute and bubbly personality and Na Yeon Choi who is hailed for her surprising power despite her pixie-like appearance. Media coverage and advertising contracts for the long-legged and svelte U.S. citizen Michelle Wie have always far exceeded the coverage for other Korean heritage players, even when she was struggling with her play.[11] Clearly, Inbee Park experienced a major "penalty" for not conforming to an ultra-feminine ideal and for lacking an "entertainment" quality that is now expected of top athletes.

While sports may be a context for contesting some of the most enduring racial stereotypes, these changes need to be understood in relation to the other narratives of race, gender, and sexuality that circulate within the commercial sporting realm. Asian athletes function within a multinational and multi-racial field of athletes who are often defined against each other, but usually in the interests of the league. For instance, Asian model minority athletes are often represented as such in an attempt to "discipline" other athletes into behaving in ways that will benefit corporate interests. Asian athletes, like other superstar athletes, are also rewarded for reproducing gender and sexual stereotypes that privilege the gaze of heterosexual viewers, especially men. Therefore, the political function of athletes, while significant, remains limited, constrained within the conservative confines of corporate profit-making.

Commodifying Race through Sport

Asian athletes embody material fantasies of success in an image-oriented, capitalist arena by displaying physical power, competitive success, and conspicuous consumption. In an era of global sports celebrity, these players offer a representation of race that gives Asians and Asian Americans the opportunity to identify with a player that looks "like them" who succeeds in highly exposed and extremely competitive environments. Even while national distinctions remain powerful, athletes like Jeremy Lin and Michelle Wie are marketed to project a global Asianness. The marketing of Asianness facilitated by personality-driven sports coverage promoted by talent agents and image management companies works to maximize the earning potential of athletes. As commercial media attempt to sell the images of these athletes to as many people and places as possible, Asian athletes who compete in the United States project American ideas of race and multiculturalism to markets around the globe.

American sports leagues present themselves as utopian bastions of multiculturalism wherein Asianness is accepted, if not celebrated. The major U.S.-based sporting leagues like MLB, PGA, NFL (National Football League), NHL (National Hockey League), and the NBA boast that they attract the best players in the world. Many Asian baseball players who were considered the best players in their home countries, such as Japanese pitcher Yu Darvish[12] and Korean Hyun Jin Ryu, eventually made the decision to leave their home countries to compete in the MLB. Gold medalist figure skaters Yuna Kim and Yuzuru Hanyu went to Toronto, Canada, to train with Olympian Brian Orser. The migrations of elite athletes to North America seem to confirm ideas of the dominance of the United States and Canada in sport as these athletes "choose" to come to America to compete. The sporting leagues themselves come to stand in for an idealized nation representing America as a place of capitalist opportunity, meritocracy, and tolerance. Bonnie Honig (1998) has stated that the immigrant myth that underpins American nationalism presents the United States as a place that welcomes migrants despite legal restrictions and widespread hostility. With the migration of elite athletes from Asia, American commercial sport is seen as offering opportunities for success that these athletes cannot find in their home countries. With increasing economic inequality and stringent anti-immigrant sentiment in American society writ large, sports remains a domain where migration is praised as representing American ideals of openness, meritocracy, and fairness; it is assumed that participants from anywhere are welcome to come to compete on a "level playing field" as long as they are "playing by our rules."[13]

The immigrant myth centrally depends on the idea that economic opportunity remains boundless and that the American Dream of prosperity can be realized if enough effort is placed into achieving one's goals. The Filipino boxer-cum-politician, Manny Pacquiao embodies this version of the immigrant myth. Journalist Gareth A. Davies proclaims, "In his homeland, or indeed in the United States, Pacquiao has become a modern embodiment of 'The American Dream.'"[14] Any biographical sketch invariably mentions his journey as a very poor boy from a shantytown in the Philippines to multi-millionaire athlete and elected politician. Although the opportunities for success and even the chance to enter the nation are extremely limited for poor migrants from developing nations, athletes like Pacquiao are hailed as examples that the "American Dream" exists in reality—that migrants and the world's poor have the chance at success despite overwhelming odds. These individuals do so through their own strength and skill rather than depending on any government entity and inspire others to strive for success in America and in the global economy.

Asianness can also come to represent a brand of cool, as in the case of Ichiro Suzuki whose long career with the Seattle Mariners came to represent a kind of Pacific Rim "coolness" characteristic of Seattle which has been branded to possess a unique blend of cultural influences from Asia, Native Americans, and white Americans (Klingle 2009). Yet this sense of "cool" is also the source of ambivalence and anxiety for Americans who have difficulty coming to terms with the fact that a Japanese player has been able to demonstrate such dominance in the "American pastime."[15] This idea of Asian cool in sports is similar to the idea of "Asian chic" that Thuy Tu uses to discuss the use of Asian aesthetics in fashion. Tu borrows from the definition of "Asian chic" offered by anthropologists Carla Jones and Anne Marie Leshkowich, who interpret it as a kind of "utopian and euphoric embrace of elements of particular Asian traditions that have now come to stand in for an undifferentiated Asia" (cited in Tu 2010, 101). While Asian chic may seem to demonstrate an embrace of Asianness, Tu points to the limits of incorporation, which can "shore up Americans' sense of difference from and superiority to" cultures from the so-called East (101). Tu writes:

> Asian chic can be understood as a symbolic resolution to the dilemma of global interconnectedness, which has enriched American consumers with a world of goods but has also opened them up to a world of competition. In the face of such inescapable intimacy, it provided a means to reassert distance and distinction, even as such efforts were belied by Americans' everyday lives. Both a diagnosis of and a cure for this cultural anxiety, it structured Asia always as a place out there, an idea to be revered or reviled.
> *(102–103)*

Similarly, in the sporting context, while Asian athletes grant American sports leagues a smug sense of global superiority, Asian athletes also create a sense of anxiety about the future character of North American-based sports given their rising numbers. Although Asian players have made the LPGA into a global brand, there are fears that Korean and other Asian players will come to overwhelm the LPGA as a majority presence and change the proud white traditions of the league. As Tu's analysis suggests, anxieties around "Asianness" are resolved by projecting Asianness as a distant and foreign element, even while American corporations benefit from and are defined by these "transnational intimacies" with Asia.

Therefore, the Asianness of these players operates in contradictory ways. While Asian athletes indicate the global marketability of American multiculturalism and its peculiar brand of Asianess, Asianness also operates to maintain a distinction and distance from "mainstream" American society. Lalaie Ameeriar (2012) has argued that despite hailing itself as a multicultural state, racial difference is incorporated into the Canadian national public on a contingent and partial basis. The usefulness of migrants is largely written onto and projected through the body. Ameeriar argues that the foreignness of Pakistani Canadian women's bodies is aestheticized through smells, fashions, and comportment, and that these markers of difference are treated in contradictory ways; while sensory markers of difference should be hidden in the context of work and in public spaces, these same elements can be commodified for the consumer enjoyment of the white majority in the forms of food and ethnic festivals. Similarly, Asian athletes are expected to play by the same rules as other athletes by attempting to accommodate themselves to American cultural traditions and avoiding such "foreign" gestures such as bowing. On the other hand, Asian athletes should be willing to market their foreignness in the case of Asian nights and in off-season marketing tours in Asia. These contradictions are particularly acute in American commercial sports, which retain a powerful American nationalist bent. Despite the attempts of sporting leagues to market their multinational multiculturalism towards their aims at global expansion, American commercial sports leagues continue to operate as powerful sites for the expression of militarized nationalisms, which becomes intensely apparent in times of war (Silk and Falcous 2005).

Long-Distance Nationalisms and the Sports Loyalty Test

With the assumption that Asian players are received as national heroes in their homelands, sports leagues and their media sponsors have been eager to promote the national identities of individual players. North American sports leagues see national markets in Asia as representing tremendous potential for growth, and these markets are defined by a shared national interest in players competing in the "West." Does the Korean American community feel a sense of connection to the path-breaking Chinese athletes Yao Ming or Li Na? Do Japanese Americans express a sense of devotion to the Korean national heroes golfer Se Ri Pak or the baseball player Chan Ho Park? Did Chinese Americans respond to Ichiro's record-breaking hitting streak? Is Manny Pacquiao popular amongst Asian Americans who are not Filipino American? For sporting leagues and corporations, the answer to these questions is largely irrelevant given that they are reaching for entire national populations beyond the United States.

North American sports feature rosters where an athlete's nationality along with a representative flag is placed next to their names, especially when they are competing in an individual sport like tennis or golf. These national symbols work to convey the international reach of the sporting association while also promoting and explaining foreign national interest in players. Players come to stand in for the nation in diaspora and become sites around which long-distance nationalisms are expressed, as in the case of boxer Manny Pacquiao. His narrative as a traveling boxer who has succeeded all over the world and especially in the West has resonated with a global Filipino community of fans dispersed throughout the world. Given his political success in the Philippines, it is clear that his athletic success abroad was not seen as taking away from his connection to homeland, but in fact, has worked to prove his loyalty to nation in an era of mass labor migration (see Parreñas 2001; Rodriguez 2010).

In a way, the nation-specific appeal of athletes has flipped the code on the "cricket loyalty test" which was detailed in 1990 by a Conservative member of the UK Parliament, Norman Tebbitt. The cricket loyalty test, also known as the "Tebbitt test," was explained as a way of assessing the loyalty of immigrants to the United Kingdom (Hall 1993). If immigrants rooted for the team from their country of heritage in international competitions, it indicated their lack of loyalty to Britain and marked them as undeserving of British citizenship. While the cricket loyalty test was hotly contested when it was announced, it seems that commercial sporting interests are generally uninterested in assessing the loyalty to the United States of either Asian players or their fellow ethnics residing in America. Instead, sporting leagues assume that Asian players and fans maintain a strong sense of connection to their homelands and that the leagues themselves are doing fellow ethnics around the world a favor by offering them a way to engage with their countries of heritage through sport. In a way, commercial sports featuring Asian athletes operate to test loyalty to one's ethnic heritage in a kind of transnational loyalty test.

Theories of deterritorialization and reterritorialization have functioned as important geographic metaphors to understand the power of nationalism within diasporic communities (Gupta and Ferguson 1997; Grewal et al. 1999). While nationalisms are deterritorialized from the geographic space of nation, they are reterritorialized in Asian American communities through the commodities and contests of sport. The expressions of nationalism through commodities are a significant way that subjects in the diaspora interpret and access ideas of homeland (Grewal 2005). Dodgers and Korean/American corporate partners have held Korea Night in Dodger Stadium, featuring Korean pitcher Hyun Jin Ryu along with members of the popular K-Pop girl group, SNSD, whose members are both South Korean and U.S. nationals. Korea Night becomes a way to define a global Koreanness through the shared experience of consuming Korean popular culture. Korean and Korean American fans play an important role in this regard because they act as living evidence of the transnational significance of nation as they wave Korean national flags in an American stadium.[16]

For nations that see the diasporic populations in America as important sources of capital and resources, sustaining a sense of nationalism in these subjects is especially important and sports success in the West is seen as an especially effective way of making this happen. Sports do not simply reflect existing nationalisms, they have the power to produce national sentiment in subjects who had previously little interest in homeland. While some may see their interest in Asian players as simply a consumer preference, the fact that there are both corporate and national pressures to commodify nationalism through sport indicates the political significance of sport. While the primary motive for promoting nationalisms through sport remains capitalistic, sports can also open up opportunities for those in the diaspora to effect change in their countries of heritage. Hines Ward, the professional American football player and winner of the mirror-ball trophy in Dancing with the Stars, garnered national attention in South Korea after he was awarded the Most Valuable Player award in the National Football League. During a visit to his place of birth, he was hailed as a national hero by South Korean leaders, and while the attention he received was clearly an attempt to nationalize his exceptional sporting accomplishments, he used this national spotlight to bring attention to the problems of racism in South Korean society and to effect positive change in the treatment of mixed-race Korean children (Joo 2014).

The convergence of sports and nationalist interests in Asian athletes raises important questions about the role of Asian American communities in producing Asian nationalisms. In the context of sports, diasporic communities demonstrate the existence of nationalism in populations that reside outside the homeland. The assumption that all Chinese root for Yao Ming works to suture the differences between Chinese populations within and outside of the PRC and works to naturalize the connections between Chinese located throughout the world. For diasporic communities, sports operate beyond and even alongside more traditional political, religious, and media productions to locate nation in a consumer entertainment spectacle. Through the fun of a game, athletes help to sustain interest in the homeland and become an important context where political attitudes about nation are shaped.

Conclusion

Given the power of sport to create transnational fan communities, the implications for Asian American community building through sport fandom remain ambiguous at best. Most Asian players in North American commercial sport are foreign nationals and marketed as representatives of their home countries, and this transnational dimension makes it difficult to make broad claims about the significance of Asian athletes for all Asian Americans. Given the transnational dimensions of Asian athletes, discussions of Asian athletes should take into account ethnic, national, and transnational specificities. Yet, transnationality can become the justification for unequal treatment based on the idea that full inclusion as equal and the same is not a goal. Rather, Asianness becomes important only in its marketable difference. For instance, during Yao Ming's tenure with the Rockets, many basketball teams featured Asian nights when the Rockets were in town with events such as "Chinese acrobatics shows and dragon dances" to promote his visit to Asian American audiences or to those who wanted to consume a brand of Asian difference along with his visit.[17] Of course, many Asian Americans were bewildered by these gestures and many recoiled at the fact that fortune cookies were distributed when Yao Ming and the Houston Rockets came to Miami to play the Heat. Yao Ming was able to laugh off the gimmick by pointing out that he had no idea what a fortune cookie was until he came to America, but this association of Chineseness and food as a sign of servitude and difference is not a laughing matter for most Asian Americans.

One way to attempt to avoid the complexity of the transnational condition would be to focus on athletes who are portrayed as fully assimilated, native English speaking, U.S. or Canadian educated, U.S. or Canadian citizens who are at least second-generation American, such as tennis player Michael Chang, basketball player Jeremy Lin, figure skaters Kristi Yamaguchi and Michelle Kwan, American football players Dat Nguyen and Hines Ward, and golfer Michelle Wie. Yet even while some Asian Americans might be marketed as completely "American," their Americanness might be precisely what limits their appeal. For some, there is a contradiction inherent in the idea of an American who is of Asian appearance (Palumbo-Liu 1999) as Asian appearance continues to be associated with foreignness, and this association with foreignness emerges in both overt and subtle ways as in the 1998 MSNBC headline that stated, "American beats out Kwan,"[18] or in the orientalized images of Michelle Wie in Sony ads (Joo 2012, C. 3). Moreover, this Americanness might be seen as a barrier to accessing foreign national markets. In an infographic on the *Houston Press Blog* assessing the relative merits of Jeremy Lin and Yao Ming,[19] the two are compared along a number of categories, including "Family Comes From," "English Skills," and "Ability to help the NBA in the China market." Yao ends up the clear winner in the "Ability to help the NBA in the China market" section, with Lin as a poor substitute. With the retirement of Yao Ming, the NBA has desperately searched for an equivalent Chinese replacement, and until then, Lin will have to suffice.

This attempt to lure Asian fans with Asian Americans as an added bonus places Asian American fans in an ambivalent and even melancholic position of being passed over or taken for granted. While Asian Americans might connect to a foreign player who is attempting to succeed in America, this player may have no interest or desire to remain in America after her or his career is over. As elite athletes who are often national celebrities, they may have no interest or investment in the everyday lives and struggles of people in Asian American communities. Moreover, while Asian Americans might connect to Asian players through a sense of racial recognition as they defy eugenic ideas about physical limits based on race, their investments in these players might also lead to instances of misrecognition of their own fandom. Lakers fans might resent having their lifelong fandom for their team interpreted as support for a fellow Asian American, Jeremy Lin. Some Korean American Dodgers fans resent having their team loyalty reduced to nationalist support for a Korean player and might even avoid attending on Korea Night. Asian American sports fans might resent the ploys of sports marketers that lump all Asian and Asian American fans into a group based on the idea that they will cheer for a fellow ethnic.

Many Asian American sports fans themselves subscribe to the mythologies of "pure" fandom which locates their passion in their love for sport itself because of their own experiences competing in a sport, their own connections with a hometown team, and their intimate knowledge of players regardless of their race. In contrast to the idea of "pure sport," however, sports continue to be arenas for the production of ideas around race and nation that have social consequences. Asian athletes function as a site for projecting and contesting these stereotypes, and athletes can operate as points of recognition and debate for Asian American viewers. When athletes function as contexts for the display of enduring stereotypes, these images can work to affirm suspicions in Asian Americans of actually existing racism—that they are not simply expressing a kind of "racial paranoia" when subject to everyday slights and micro-aggressions based on their physiognomy (Jackson 2008). While Asian American voices have been active in challenging blatant discrimination against Asian and Asian American athletes, they have been largely silent in critiquing the powerful narratives of nationalism that operate within the context of sport. Discourses that take place around sports can offer an important case study for how Asian American critique might remain relevant in an era of transnationalism, as an effective Asian American critique will need to engage the transnational connections that Asian American subjects maintain while also fighting against enduring inequalities of race.

As in the case with West Indian cricket during the British colonial era, Asian athletes can offer Asian Americans a sense of visibility and belonging to the mainstream as equal and significant participants. Since the actual play on the field is unpredictable and broadcast live, sports present spontaneous action that can defy predictions and offer something close to authentic expression. Sports display an interplay of differences by presenting a highly diverse group of players including non-native speakers with varying modes of comportment, physical techniques, facial expressions, social interactions, and fashion sensibilities. This combination of unpredictability and difference enables sport to work in a number of ways that both reinforce and defy dominant racial logics. Asian athletes act as an important part of commercial sporting representations that present a diverse portrait of athletic potential and performance not just for Asian Americans, but for all viewers.

Notes

1 Yao Ming (basketball), Yuna Kim (figure skating), and Ichiro Suzuki (baseball).
2 By contemporary globalization, I refer to the intensification of transnational connectivities facilitated by neoliberal political and legal transformations, technological advances, and human migration within the context of global capitalist hegemony (Appadurai 1996; Harvey 2007).

3 The following chapter focuses primarily on Asian and Asian American athletes with East Asian national origins. Unfortunately, this focus largely excludes important discussions of other Asian American and Pacific Islander groups, including the significance of Pacific Islanders to American football and Southeast Asian competitors in mixed martial arts (MMA). This discussion also does not focus on athletes of mixed race like Tiger Woods and Hines Ward who have themselves been popular national in Thailand and South Korea respectively.
4 This discussion also largely excludes discussions of the history of martial arts (kung fu, taekwondo, etc.) in the United States and the field of mixed martial arts (MMA), which has a considerable and multi-ethnic Asian participation.
5 For a sense of the diverse and varied history of Asian/American athletes, see the anthology titled, *Asian American Sports and Society*, edited by C. Richard King (2014).
6 As Houlihan, Tan, and Green (2010) note, the NBA had attempted to "break in" to the China market earlier, but Yao Ming supercharged its growth.
7 While the realm of male figure skating has been recently dominated by Asian skaters, including 2014 gold medalist Japanese skater Yuzuru Hanyu and Chinese Canadian, Patrick Chan, male figure skating does not register as a popular sport in North America, especially compared to the popularity of "ladies" figure skating. While female figure skaters reproduce notions of ultra-femininity due to their dress and comportment, male skaters are often perceived participating in an effeminate sport (Feder-Kane 2000).
8 "Li Na's brilliant winner's speech – 2014 Australian Open," January 25, 2014, accessed July 14, 2014, www.youtube.com/watch?v=M-uVsj2pJDo.
9 Bryan Arman Graham, "The Sad, Perfect End of Kim Yuna's Figure Skating Reign," *The Atlantic*, February 22, 2014, accessed August 3, 2014, www.theatlantic.com/entertainment/archive/2014/02/the-sad-perfect-end-of-kim-yunas-figure-skating-reign/283986/.
10 Clearly, male consumers are not the only ones interested in sex, yet they remain the primary market for sexualized images of female sports stars. In *Sportsex*, Toby Miller (2001) discusses the dominant role of sexuality in marketing athletes. He argues that sexual marketing is not limited to the male consumer and details the increasing acknowledgment of female and gay consumers who are attracted by sexualized images.
11 Some might argue that this discrepancy is due to the fact that Wie has had a major talent agency promoting her image since she was sixteen, first with the William Morris Agency and then the global talent agency, IMG. Other's might argue that it is her Americanness that explains her popularity. Elena Tajima Creef (2004) writes about how in the coverage of the women's figure skating competition during the Albertville 1992 Winter Olympics juxtaposed Kristi Yamaguchi's Americanness to Midori Ito's foreignness during a period of American anxiety around Japan's economic rise. While Yamaguchi was presented as a svelte, lean and all-American "cheerleader, prom goer, sister of the all-star basketball player, and exclusive dater of white men," (154), Ito was depicted as the "'stout little' rival" (159) with "daikon legs" (160).
12 Darvish has an Iranian father and a Japanese mother, and was raised in Japan. He is a Japanese icon who has lived and worked in Japan most of his life.
13 The schizophrenic treatment of Latinos in MLB baseball demonstrates the contradictory position of this rhetoric of multiculturalism in American sport (Juffer 2002). While migration of Latinos, especially Dominicans, has operated to strengthen the level of competition in the league, there has been immense anxiety around what a Latino-dominated league would do to the popularity of the game (Klein 1991).
14 Gareth A. Davies, "Boxing career precursor to political life as Manny Pacquiao 'bubble' shows no sign of bursting," *The Telegraph*, April 10, 2014, accessed August 4, 2014. www.telegraph.co.uk/sport/othersports/boxing/10758530/Boxing-career-precursor-to-political-life-as-Manny-Pacquiao-bubble-shows-no-sign-of-bursting.html.
15 Ian Casselberry, "Breaking Down the Hall of Fame Legacy Ichiro Suzuki Built in Seattle," *Bleacher Report*, July 24, 2012, accessed August 6, 2014, http://bleacherreport.com/articles/1271160-breaking-down-the-hall-of-fame-legacy-ichiro-suzuki-built-in-seattle.
16 As nationalism has proven to be a great boon for expanding markets in Asia, there is concern as to how to sustain this interest after a national icon has retired. There is hope that nationalism might act as a gateway to fandom for a particular team or a sport. Beyond these assumptions, sporting leagues are working to create infrastructures that will ensure a supply of athletes and fans between Asia and America.

17 Associated Press, "NBA wants to turn Yao Ming admirers into full-fledged fans," April 6, 2004, accessed August 1, 2014, http://sports.espn.go.com/espn/wire?section=nba&id=1775298.
18 Erin Khue Ninh, "Jeremy Lin, Face of America," *ESPN.com*, March 15, 2012, accessed August 11, 2012, http://espn.go.com/espn/commentary/story/_/id/7682770/jeremy-lin-becomes-face-asian-americans.
19 Richard Connelly, "Jeremy Lin vs. Yao Ming: The Breakdown" *Houston Press Blog,* February 21, 2012, accessed August 1, 2014, http://blogs.houstonpress.com/hairballs/2012/02/jeremy_lin_vs_yao_ming_the_bre.php.

References

Ameeriar, Lalaie. "The Sanitized Sensorium." *American Anthropologist* 114, no. 3 (2012): 509–520.

Andrews, David. "The (Trans)National Basketball Association: American Commodity-Sign Culture and Global-Local Conjuncturalism." In *Articulating the Global and the Local*, edited by Ann Cvetkovich and Douglass Kellner, 72–101. Boulder, CO: Westview, 1996.

Andrews, David L., Ed. *Michael Jordan, Inc.: Corporate Sport, Media Culture, and Late Modern America*. Albany, NY: State University of New York, 2001.

Appadurai, Arjun. *Modernity at Large: Cultural Dimensions of Globalization*. Minneapolis, MN: University of Minnesota Press, 1996.

Creef, Elena Tajima. *Imaging Japanese America: The Visual Construction of Citizenship, Nation and the Body*. New York: New York University Press, 2004.

Farred, Grant. *Phantom Calls: Race, Globalization and the Nba*. Chicago, IL: Prickly Paradigm Press, 2006.

Feder-Kane, Abigail. "'A Radiant Smile from the Lovely Lady': Overdetermined Femininity in 'Ladies' Figure Skating." In *Reading Sport: Critical Essays on Power and Representation*, edited by Susan Birrell and Mary G. McDonald, 206–233. Boston, MA: Northeastern University Press, 2000.

Franks, Joel S. *Crossing Sidelines, Crossing Cultures: Sport and Asian Pacific American Cultural Citizenship*. Lanham, MD: University Press of America, 2000.

Grewal, Inderpal. *Transnational America*. Durham, NC: Duke University Press, 2005.

Grewal, Inderpal, Akhil Gupta, and Aiwha Ong. "Introduction: Asian Transnationalities." *Positions: East Asia Cultures And Critique* 7, no. 3 (1999): 653–666.

Gupta, Akhil, and James Ferguson. "Beyond "Culture": Space, Identity, and the Politics of Difference." In *Culture, Power, Place: Explorations in Critical Anthropology*, edited by Akhil Gupta and James Feguson, 33–51. Durham, NC: Duke University Press, 1997.

Hall, Stuart. "Culture, Community, Nation." *Cultural Studies* 7, no. 3 (1993): 349–363.

Harvey, David. *A Brief History of Neoliberalism*. Oxford: Oxford University Press, 2007.

Honig, Bonnie. "Immigrant America? How Foreignness 'Solves' Democracy's Problems." *Social Text 56* 16, no. 3 (1998): 1–27.

Houlihan, Barrie, Tien-Chin Tan, and Mick Green. "Policy Transfer and Learning from the West: Elite Basketball Development in the People's Republic of China." *Journal of Sport and Social Issues* 34, no. 1 (2010): 4–28.

Jackson Jr., John L. *Racial Paranoia: The Unintended Consequences of Political Correctness*. Philadelphia, PA: Basic Civitas, 2008.

James, C.L.R. *Beyond a Boundary*. New York: Pantheon, 1983.

Joo, Rachael Miyung. "(Trans)National Pastimes and Korean American Subjectivities: Reading Chan Ho Park." *Journal for Asian American Studies* 3, no. 3 (2000): 301–328.

———. *Transnational Sport: Gender, Media, and Global Korea*. Durham, NC: Duke University Press, 2012.

———. "Hines Ward." In *Asian Americans: An Encyclopedia of Social, Cultural, and Political History*, edited by Xiaoiian Zhao and Edward Chang, 1187–1188. Santa Barbara, CA: Westview, 2014.

Juffer, Jane. "Who's the Man? Sammy Sosa, Latinos, and Televisual Redefinitions of The "American" Pastime." *Journal of Sport and Social Issues* 26, no. 4 November (2002): 337–359.

King, C. Richard. *Asian American Sports and Society*. New York: Routledge, 2014.

Klein, Alan M. *Sugarball: The American Game, the Dominican Dream*. New Haven, CT: Yale University Press, 1991.

Klingle, Matthew. *Emerald City: An Environmental History of Seattle*. New Haven, CT: Yale University Press, 2009.

Lee, Robert G. *Orientals: Asian Americans in Popular Culture*. Philadelphia, PA: Temple University Press, 1999.

Leonard, David J. *After Artest: The NBA and the Assault on Blackness*. Albany, NY: SUNY Press, 2012.

Leonard, David J. and C. Richard King. *Commodified and Criminalized: New Racism and African Americans in Contemporary Sports*. New York: Rowman and Littlefield, 2011.

Ling, L. H. M. "Sex Machine: Global Hypermasculinity and Images of the Asian Woman in Modernity." *positions: east asia cultures critique* 7, no. 2 (1999): 277–306.

Lowe, Lisa. *Immigrant Acts: On Asian American Cultural Politics*. Durham, NC: Duke, 1996.

Lui, Mary Ting YI. *The Chinatown Trunk Mystery: The Elsie Sigel Murder Case and the Policing of Interracial Sexual Relations in New York City's Chinatown, 1880–1915*. Ithaca: Cornell University Press, 2004.

Messner, Michael. *Taking the Field: Women, Men and Sports*. Minneapolis, MN: Minnesota University Press, 2002.

Miller, Toby. *Sportsex*. Philadelphia, PA: Temple University Press, 2001.

Ngai, Ming. *Impossible Subjects: Illegal Aliens and the Making of Modern America*. Princeton, NJ: Princeton University Press, 2004.

Ong, Aihwa. *Flexible Citizenship: The Cultural Logics of Transnationality*. Durham, NC: Duke, 1999.

Palumbo-Liu, David. *Asian/American: Historical Crossings of a Racial Frontier*. Stanford: Stanford University Press, 1999.

Parrenas, Rhacel Salazar. *Servants of Globalization: Women, Migration, and Domestic Labor*. Stanford, CA: Stanford University Press, 2001.

Regalado, Samuel O. *Nikkei Baseball: Japanese American Players from Immigration and Internment to the Major Leagues*. Urbana, IL: University of Illinois Press, 2013.

Rodriguez, Robyn. *Migrants for Export: How the Philippine State Brokers Labor to the World*. Minneapolis, MN: University of Minnesota Press, 2010.

Shah, Nayan. *Contagious Divides: Epidemics and Race in San Francisco's Chinatown*. Berkeley, CA: University of California Press, 2001.

Silk, Michael, and Mark Falcous. "One Day in September/a Week in February: Mobilizing American (Sporting) Nationalisms." *Sociology of Sport Journal* 22, no. 4 (2005): 447–471.

Starn, Orin. *The Passion of Tiger Woods: An Anthropologist Reports on Golf, Race, and Celebrity*. Durham, NC: Duke University Press, 2011.

Takaki, Ronald. *Strangers from a Different Shore*. Boston, MA: Back Bay, 1998 [1989].

Tu, Thuy Linh Nguyen. *The Beautiful Generation: Asian Americans and the Cultural Economy of Fashion*. Durham, NC: Duke University Press, 2010.

Wagg, Stephen, and David Andrews, eds. *East Plays West: Sport and the Cold War*. New York: Routledge, 2007.

Wang, Chi-ming. "Capitalizing the Big Man: Yao Ming, Asian America, and the China Global." *Inter-Asia Cultural Studies* 5, no. 2 (2004): 263–278.

Yep, Kathleen. *Outside the Paint: When Basketball Ruled at the Chinese Playground*. Philadelphia, PA: Temple University Press, 2009.

14

JEREMY LIN, GLOBAL ASIAN AMERICAN

Timothy Yu

In February 2012, Jeremy Lin—an undrafted backup point guard for the New York Knicks—became an international sensation, rising from obscurity to superstardom as he led a struggling, depleted Knicks team to a seven-game winning streak. "Linsanity" gripped the sports world, as Lin's image vaulted to magazine covers and led sports broadcasts. Of course, central to Lin's story, and his "underdog" status, was the fact that he was the first Asian American to rise to professional basketball stardom in a league dominated by African American and white players.

Much of the discussion of Lin's race employed familiar tropes used to characterize Asian Americans. Most prominent among these was the image of the Asian American as perpetual foreigner, evident in debates over whether Lin was "Chinese" or "Taiwanese" and in discussions of how Lin would help the NBA's marketing efforts in China. Despite Lin's now established fame, such perceptions continue: during a Houston Rockets game against the Milwaukee Bucks in February 2014, one of the Bucks announcers remarked that the American-born Lin was "from the other side of the world."[1]

In some senses, we can see Lin's story, and his stardom, as a case study in the shifting, and increasingly global, identities of Asians in the U.S. His parents are part of the post-1965 wave of immigration that has transformed the demographics and economics of Asian America. His status as an international marketing superstar illuminates the role Asian Americans increasingly find themselves called upon to play in a globalized marketplace. Yet Lin's story also gives us insight into the way the category "Asian American" continues to claim a space within national and global discourses—a lesson often illustrated through Lin's own engagement with, and claiming of, Asian Americanness.

Over the past two decades, the category "Asian American" has come to be understood in increasingly global and transnational terms. Beginning in the early 1990s, scholars in Asian American studies grew increasingly critical of what they viewed as the strongly nationalist orientation of Asian American studies. Elaine Kim's foreword to Shirley Geok-lin Lim and Amy Ling's 1992 collection *Reading the Literatures of Asian America* describes a shift in the field away from a "cultural nationalism" based on a "unitary identity" toward a "cultural pluralism" based on the "multiplicitous identities and experiences of contemporary Asian Americans" (xi–xiv). One of the major factors in this shift, Kim observes, is that "lines between Asian and Asian American, so important in identity formation in earlier times, are increasingly being blurred" (xiii). Travel and communication between the U.S. and Asia, once daunting, "has become easy and inexpensive," meaning that "As material and cultural distances diminish, middle-class Asian American youths can spend the summer in Seoul or Taipei almost the way middle-class American youths of yore went to summer camp" (xiv).

A few critics have sounded a cautionary note in the rush toward transnationalism. Sau-ling C. Wong's "Denationalization Reconsidered: Asian American Cultural Criticism at a Theoretical Crossroads" acknowledges that "permeability has been increasing in the boundaries between Asian Americans and 'Asian Asians,'" leading to what Wong describes as a "diasporic perspective" that stands opposed to the traditional "domestic perspective" of Asian American studies (126–127). Wong's concern is that the embrace of the diasporic perspective may lead to an erosion of the traditional groundwork of Asian American studies, which placed at its center the idea of "claiming America" for Asian immigrants and their descendants: "if claiming America becomes a minor task for Asian American cultural criticism and espousal of denationalization becomes wholesale, certain segments of the Asian American population may be left without a viable discursive space" (137). The diasporic perspective, Wong suggests, may—in a reversal of the earlier tendencies of Asian American studies—privilege the first-generation immigrant over the American-born Asian. Wong also argues that the diasporic perspective poses a threat to the pan-ethnic nature of the category "Asian American," suggesting that "the loosely held and fluctuating collectivity called 'Asian Americans' will dissolve back into its descent defined constituents as soon as one leaves American national borders behind" (138). Asian American studies, in short, might well give way to studies of the Chinese, Filipino, or Korean diaspora.

Indeed, scholarship of the past two decades has increasingly embraced this diasporic perspective, examining Asian Americans in global contexts and as part of communities that reach beyond the national boundaries of the United States. Aihwa Ong's *Flexible Citizenship: The Cultural Logics of Transnationality* offers an alternative to U.S.-centric analyses of Asian Americans through its concept of "flexible citizenship," in which "individuals as well as governments develop a flexible notion of citizenship and sovereignty as strategies to accumulate capital and power" and "the cultural logics of capitalist accumulation, travel, and displacement . . . induce subjects to respond fluidly and opportunistically to changing political-economic conditions" (6). Rather than claiming belonging within a single national context, Ong's transnational subject adopts multiple allegiances, moving through networks that are not contained within national boundaries. For Ong, the Chinese diaspora exemplifies this flexible subjectivity: "For over a century, overseas Chinese have been the forerunners of today's multiply displaced subjects, who are always on the move both mentally and physically" (2).

Ong's primary focus is on those elites who have the ability to take advantage of such flexibilities: "mobile managers, technocrats, and professionals seeking to both circumvent *and* benefit from different nation-state regimes by selecting different cites for investments, work, and family relocation" (112). Among her iconic figures are the "astronaut," the Chinese business executive who lives in constant international transit, and "parachute kids" who "can be dropped off in another country by parents on the trans-Pacific business commute" (19). As such, her work has an ambiguous relationship to the traditional bases of Asian American studies, both in its focus on elites and in its examination of a single ethnic group. Indeed, Ong suggests that the arrival of new, affluent, diasporic Chinese in the U.S. has "reworked the cultural meaning of 'Asian American'" (130) and "upset the ethno-racial hierarchy that has disciplined Asian Americans as a docile minority" (179). She is critical of ongoing Asian American attempts to claim Americanness, arguing that Asian American efforts "to distance themselves from the new transnational publics, although logical within American racial politics . . . ignor[es] the objective reality that a majority of Asian Americans are now linked to transnational family networks" (180); the logic of claiming America is "trapped" within "an American ideology that limits the moral claims to social legitimacy of nonwhites" (180). In short, as Ong somewhat sardonically remarks, the new diasporic perspective "gentrifies Asian American identity" by exchanging minority status in the U.S. for a broader global identification with Asian capital (130).

While Ong attributes such "gentrification" primarily to changing economic and ideological conditions in Asia, scholars who focus on the U.S. context point to the 1965 changes in U.S. immigration law as a major factor in Asian American demographic shifts. Lisa Lowe titles her paradigm-shifting 1996 book *Immigrant Acts* in part as a nod to the passage of the 1965 Immigration Act, whose abolition of national quotas and exclusions created "dramatic shifts" in immigration from Asia, leading to a situation in which "the majority of Asian Americans are at present Asian-born rather than multiple-generation" (7). The rapid growth in Asian immigration post-1965 also led to what Lowe calls an "enormous widening of the definitions of 'Asian American,'" with new growth particularly in South and Southeast Asian populations. Post-1965 Asian immigration was also tilted more strongly than in previous eras toward middle-class professionals, including physicians, engineers, and scientists.[2]

Jeremy Lin's family history fits squarely into this narrative of post-1965 immigration. As the *New York Times* reported in a February 2012 profile titled "Tight-Knit Family Shares Lin's Achievement," Jeremy Lin's father, Lin Gie-Ming, came to the United States from Taiwan as an engineering student in 1977; at Old Dominion University in Virginia, he met Shirley Wu, a computer science student and fellow immigrant from Taiwan. After getting married, both worked as engineers and ultimately settled in Palo Alto, California, where their son Jeremy, with his parents' encouragement, developed into a basketball star.

Much of Jeremy Lin's story from this point is now widely known: despite leading Palo Alto High School to a state championship, Lin received no college scholarship offers. He went to Harvard, where he became a breakout star, yet went undrafted by the NBA. After stints with the Golden State Warriors and Houston Rockets, Lin landed with the New York Knicks as a little-used backup point guard. On February 4, 2012, a depleted roster led Knicks coach Mike D'Antoni to turn to Lin in a game against the New Jersey Nets; Lin responded by scoring 25 points in a 99–92 victory. Lin went on to lead the Knicks to a seven-game winning streak in scorching fashion, highlighted by a 38-point performance against the Los Angeles Lakers.

Lin's unexpected emergence electrified fans, sparking a national, and international, phenomenon that was quickly dubbed "Linsanity." News of Lin's exploits dominated sports media and soon made mainstream news headlines as well. Lin's "underdog" story, as an undrafted, unheralded backup suddenly thrust into the spotlight, was a compelling narrative, but the real story was race: Lin was the first American-born Asian player to achieve NBA stardom. Debate raged over whether Lin had previously been overlooked because of his race, because coaches did not look at an Asian American and see a basketball star. When asked by Charlie Rose on CBS's *60 Minutes* why he thought he had not received any college scholarship offers, Lin replied, "Well, the obvious thing in my mind is that I was Asian American . . . I think that was a barrier." The fault, Lin argued, lay with the "stereotype" that Asian Americans lacked athletic ability. Later on in the same program, NBA commissioner David Stern, asked by Rose if race was a factor in the NBA's failure to draft Lin, said, "I think in the true sense the answer to that is yes." What made Lin a sensation—and a hero to many Asian American fans—was his upending of those stereotypes in his breakout performances.

There's much to say about the phenomenon of "Linsanity," but what I'd like to focus on here is the intersection of race, ethnicity, and nationality in identifying, celebrating, critiquing, and marketing Lin. Lin was widely hailed as a "first," a pioneer, in a league dominated by African American and white players. But what was the nature of Lin's novelty? He was not the first Asian American player in the NBA; Wataru Misaka, a Japanese American point guard, played for the New York Knicks in the 1947–1948 season. Nor was he the first player of Asian descent to become a star; that title would likely belong to Yao Ming, the Chinese center who starred for the Houston Rockets in the 2000s. Lin's "firstness" itself thus became a major site for negotiating not only his identity, but the very category of the Asian American.

For many Asian Americans, Lin's major significance was that he was the first American-born Asian player to have a serious shot at stardom—a status that distinguished him from Yao, a Chinese citizen who did not identify himself as American. We may see in this remnants of the historical emphasis on American-born Asians, as opposed to immigrant Asians, in the cultural-nationalist era of Asian American identity, and in the emphasis on claiming American identity that has been seen by some critics as central to the project of Asian American studies. In mainstream media coverage, however, this distinction took a back seat to the parsing of Lin's ethnicity and of his family's national origins. After some early confusion about how to describe Lin's ethnicity, reporters converged on an awkward phrasing: Lin was "the first American-born player of Chinese or Taiwanese descent" in the NBA.[3] The odd duality in the description of Lin's ethnicity stemmed from a debate over Lin's ancestry: Lin's parents both immigrated to the U.S. from Taiwan, but like most Taiwanese, both trace their ancestry back to mainland China. In the first days of Linsanity, numerous media outlets reported on the "tug-of-war" between fans in China and Taiwan to "claim" Lin. The *Wall Street Journal*'s Paul Mozur and Jenny W. Hsu observed in a February 15, 2012 story that Lin's performance "has led both Chinese and Taiwanese to lay claim to Mr. Lin, opening up a debate in social and traditional media about just who the Harvard graduate represents in Asia." Such debates were generally framed not in terms of U.S. racial politics, but in terms of geopolitics, with journalists and commentators viewing Linsanity as a case study in China–Taiwan relations and rivalry.

The debate over Lin's ancestry is closely linked to another major theme in media coverage of Lin: his ability to help the NBA's marketing efforts in Asia. A Reuters story by Melanie Lee from February 13, 2012 sounds a common note in hailing Lin as a "marketing dream in Asia," presenting him as "a potential candidate to fill the very large shoes left by last year's retirement of Yao Ming," and quoting a tongue-in-cheek online comment characterizing Lin as "America's self-produced, self-sold, fully-customized product for the Chinese market." A *Wall Street Journal* story, "Marketing Jeremy Lin in China," by Josh Chin, quotes David Shoemaker, head of the NBA's China operations, vowing to "do everything possible to work with our partners to capitalize" on Linsanity. Each of Lin's subsequent moves has led to a fresh bout of coverage devoted to his ability to boost NBA business in Asia. Lin's signing by the Houston Rockets, the former team of Yao Ming, was greeted by many commentators as a brilliant marketing move, given the team's existing relationships with Chinese businesses and the Chinese market; in a story from July 2012 titled "Can Jeremy Lin's Appeal in China Really Help Houston's Bottom Line?", *Time* reporter Sean Gregory cites the Rockets' "extensive experience marketing players to the massive, fast-growing Chinese market" as a major reason the team was willing to offer Lin a $25.1 million contract. Lin's overseas marketing potential again came to the fore with his trade to the Lakers in 2014, with a Taiwanese tire company, Maxxis, signing up as a Lakers sponsor within weeks of Lin's signing. When Lin was acquired by the Charlotte Hornets in 2015, his international marketing value to the team was emphasized yet again. CBS Sports reporter Ananth Pandian wrote that Lin's "popularity in Asia has instantly made the Hornets a popular team in countries like China and Taiwan," and a visit by the Hornets to China in October 2015 became a showcase for Lin; asking, "Will 'Linsanity' Erupt Again During Charlotte Hornets' China Visit?", *Charlotte Observer* reporter Rick Bonnell observed that "Chinese basketball fans—estimates say there are more than 300 million of them in this country—have adopted Lin as their own.[4]

Lin has embraced his role as global brand ambassador, touring both China and Taiwan in the off-season and accepting international endorsement deals from a limited number of companies, most notably from Volvo. During the Hornets' 2015 trip to China, Lin undertook his starring role with good humor, remarking to Rick Bonnell that "I feel like in some ways I'm indirectly hosting it" and saying of his teammates, "I just want to share the culture ... I can show them where my grandparents are from." And indeed, we may in some ways see Lin's status as a global marketing phenomenon as an affirmation of the transnational view of Asian Americans espoused by Ong and others. The mobility of Lin's parents—students-turned-technology professionals who were able to gain access to middle-class life in California—seems paralleled by their son's ability to return across the Pacific and to be embraced as "Chinese" or "Taiwanese." Lin is, in this sense, a diasporic star for whom national boundaries are relatively porous, and whose ties to a diasporic concept of Chineseness have become a major economic asset.

Yet what may be of most interest in this context is Lin's own resistance to being cast purely in such diasporic terms. Lin's response to the "Chinese" vs. "Taiwanese" debate has generally been described as diplomatic, with Lin nodding to his heritage in both countries; in a widely quoted interview, Lin remarked, "I'm really proud of being Chinese. I'm really proud of my parents being from Taiwan." Yet Lin generally has not used ethnically specific terms such as "Chinese American" or "Taiwanese American" to describe himself. Instead, he has tended to employ the pan-ethnic term "Asian American," particularly when referring to issues of racism and stereotyping—as in the *60 Minutes* interview, in which Lin attributes his failure to win a college basketball scholarship to the fact "that I was Asian American." The pan-ethnic nature of "Asian American" relegates the debate over Lin's Chinese or Taiwanese ethnicity to the background in favor of a more U.S.-focused discourse of race. Returning again to the Hornets' 2015 China trip, it's striking to note that in his remarks to Bonnell, Lin is never quoted describing himself as "Chinese" or even "Chinese American"; instead, he is only quoted describing himself as "Asian" and "Asian American," and only within the context of discussing racial stereotypes: "When you watch the NBA you don't see a lot of Asian Americans or Asians in general. When you see one, it takes you by surprise, so you don't necessarily think the same thing."

Nor has Lin only invoked "Asian American" in negative contexts. Indeed, Lin's most powerful invocation of "Asian American" has been in his open avowal of the term, most notably in an interview during the 2012 NBA All-Star weekend. As Howard Beck of the *New York Times* reported, Lin responded strongly to sports media descriptions of him as "deceptively quick":

> I'm not sure what's deceptive. But it could be the fact that I'm Asian American. But I think that's fine. It's something that I embrace, and it gives me a chip on my shoulder. But I'm very proud to be Asian American, and I love it.

While a few Asian American celebrities have discussed the challenges of being Asian Americans in Hollywood or elsewhere, it's difficult to think of another famous Asian American openly discussing his pride in, and love for, Asian American identity.

What is the nature of Lin's embrace of Asian Americanness? What does it mean to Lin to be "Asian American," and how that link up with the transnational, diasporic conceptions of the Asian American that increasingly dominate academic discourse? While Lin has not discussed Asian American identity in great detail in his public interviews, it's possible to explore this question through tracing Lin's connection to an Asian American community—a community that increasingly exists and defines itself online.

As reporters and bloggers scoured the Internet for information about the little-known Lin in the early days of Linsanity, a curiosity turned up: Lin's page on Xanga, a blogging and social networking site whose popularity peaked in the early 2000s. The images on the site included a teenage Lin in a series of humorous photos imitating the headband-wearing styles of various NBA players. Most striking from the perspective of an Asian American reader, however, was the screen name Lin had chosen for himself: "ChiNkBaLLa88." In a post for the sports site *Grantland* called "A Question of Identity," Jay Caspian Kang writes that nothing about Lin's early life has excited him as much as this seemingly trivial detail:

> If you stare at the word "ChiNkBaLLa88" for long enough, you begin to see, a bit more clearly, the reason why Linsanity has sparked such an intensity of emotion among Asian Americans. Within that strange, thoroughly American word contraption, a racial slur is fused . . . with a highly racialized, identifiably black swagger . . . When I was 15, I must have come up with at least 200 different nicknames for myself. Each one involved a racial slur and a hip-hop reference.

Kang sees in "ChiNkBaLLa88" a teenage Asian American's attempt to navigate race through a triangulation with African American culture. But it's worth breaking down Lin's chosen moniker even further. Lin's appropriation of the racist slur "chink" is, of course, reminiscent of African American reclaiming of the "n-word," particularly in hip-hop. The reclaiming of "chink" points not to a diasporic Chinese (or Taiwanese) heritage but to a history of U.S. racism. At the same time, the number "88" may point in a different direction; while it likely references Lin's birth year of 1988, it may also allude to the traditional Chinese association of the number eight with good fortune. "ChiNkBaLLa88" is thus a portmanteau that points toward a diasporic heritage, but that just as strongly grounds itself in a U.S. discourse of race and in the language of American racism.

Lin's participation in online culture has continued into his professional basketball career, and has persisted through his stardom. In 2011, while he was still a largely unknown player with the Golden State Warriors, Lin launched a YouTube channel. As Lin told Nina Mandell of *USA Today*,

> When people think Harvard or Asian American or they see my demeanor on the court, they automatically come up with certain preconceptions . . . and I think one thing that was really missing was my off-the-court personality. So a friend had suggested I start making YouTube videos awhile back when I was with Golden State. And after I made my first one I was like "wow this is really fun" and since then we've just been having fun with it.

But from the very start, Lin's YouTube productions have been far from casual, amateur productions. As the media scholar Lori Kido Lopez has observed,[5] many of Lin's videos have been collaborations with Asian American YouTube stars such as KevJumba, Ryan Higa, and Wong Fu Productions. The strong presence of Asian Americans on YouTube—a sharp contrast to their still-poor representation in mainstream media—has been the subject of frequent media comment. In a 2011 article, "For Asian-American Stars, Many Web Fans," the *New York Times*' Austin Considine observes that three of the top 20 most-subscribed channels on YouTube belong to Asian Americans. Ryan Higa, who co-stars in a 2011 video with Lin titled "How to Get into Harvard," currently has over 13 million subscribers to his channel, nigahiga, which was at one time the most-subscribed channel on YouTube. ("How to Get into Harvard" itself has been viewed over five million times.) As Kevin Wu (aka KevJumba) remarks in "For Asian-American Stars," Asian American YouTube stars are part of "a new breed of Asian Americans, and I'm a representative of that." This "new breed" of online Asian Americans tends to be young and American-born, and while their videos cover a wide range of topics, they will often address race frankly (and humorously). In "The Virtuosic Virtuality of Asian American YouTube Stars," Cindy Gao discusses the video "Yellow Fever" by Wong Fu Productions, a satirical take on the always popular and controversial topic of dating between whites and Asians. Gao observes that the Wong Fu sensibility "represent[s] the burgeoning, loosely affiliated community of Asian American YouTube personalities who today occupy top spots in many of YouTube's subscriber and page-view rankings."

Lin's 2014 YouTube video, "Lindorsements," is a collaboration with Wong Fu Productions. It offers a humorous take on Lin's status as a marketing star, placing Lin in a series of parodic commercials, from State Farm (Jeremy Lin with his "twin" Jeremiah) to Dos Equis (Lin as "The Most Linteresting Man in the World"—drinking bubble tea). In a sly but sharp comment on Lin's "overseas" marketing potential, one of the other characters in the video suggests that Lin should "cater to the Asian market because you're Asian. You should do, like, Asian products." The video then cuts to a scene of Lin in a Chinese herb shop, watching silently as an elderly Asian man places roots on a scale against a background of stereotypical music. After a moment, Lin turns with an exasperated glare to the camera and the scene ends, cutting back to another character saying, "No, he shouldn't limit himself."

Given the breathless media promotion of Lin as an avenue of access to the "Asian market," we can see this brief vignette as placing a caution or limit on what it means for Lin to speak to and for the "Asian." The video rejects stereotyped notions of Asian (indeed, Chinese) tradition and authenticity, revealing such notions as clichés that "limit" Lin's identity. Lin's appeal to the "Asian market" cannot be reduced to "catering to the Asian market because you're Asian"; the video characterizes such essentialism as absurd. Lin's extensive off-season travels in China and Taiwan may be seen less as a Chinese/Taiwanese American "returning to his roots" than as an athlete traveling to Asia *as an Asian American*. That a distinction might be made between the "Asian" and the "Asian American" is again suggested by the video itself. While the scene in the herb shop is framed as "Asian" (complete with clichéd music), the first skit, in which Lin is pictured drinking bubble tea, is *not* framed as an "Asian" marketing pitch. Instead, Lin deadpans, "I don't always drink boba, but when I do, I use a buy-one-get-one-free coupon," while flanked by two Asian American actresses—one Filipina American, the other Japanese American. While it may be a bit of a stretch to see this scene as a representation of Asian America, there is little doubt of the sharp contrast to the "Asian marketing" scene. While that scene relies on clichéd signifiers of "traditional" Chinese culture, the "Most Linteresting Man" scene is centered on a contemporary product from Taiwan (bubble tea) that has become widely popular among young Asian Americans of various ethnicities, with a pan-ethnic cast that clearly marks the milieu as an Asian American one, rather than one focused on the the Chinese or Taiwanese diaspora.

As a case study in Asian American identity in a global context, the story of Jeremy Lin enriches and complicates the usual binaries of national vs. transnational, domestic vs. diasporic. The global reach of Lin's stardom, and his promotional tours to Taiwan and China, may make him appear to be an icon of the newly transnational, highly mobile, "gentrified" Asian American identity that Aihwa Ong describes. The debates over his Chinese or Taiwanese ancestry would seem to locate his identity within a diasporic, rather than a national, framework. And his parents' post-1965 immigration story locates Lin within the "new," more heterogenous Asian America explored by Lisa Lowe and others. For many scholars, these tendencies toward the diasporic and transnational present a challenge to traditional definitions of the Asian American and perhaps contribute to the loosening of the category's hold.

But Lin's story shows that the transnational, global, and diasporic can and do coexist with powerful avowals of Asian American identity. Lin's invocations of Asian Americanness, whether in interviews or in YouTube videos, are highly self-conscious ones, aware of larger U.S. racial contexts and drawing coherence from links to Asian American youth communities, particularly online communities. Perhaps most strikingly, documents like the "Lindorsements" video show that an invocation of Asian American identity in a U.S. context can in fact provide a position from which to critique the more reductive or essentialist qualities of diasporic thinking. The transnational economic imperative—the need to appeal to the "Asian market"—is linked to limitation and stereotype, and risks complicity with the notion of the Asian American as perpetual foreigner. It is counterbalanced by a vision of an Asian American community that is young, pan-ethnic, and composed of both cultural consumers *and* producers.

The ultimate point, perhaps, is not to again privilege the domestic over the diasporic in Asian America but to illustrate how, even in an increasingly globalized world, the two are not mutually exclusive, and indeed can coexist in a critical dialectic. Jeremy Lin may have been embraced by the media and marketers as a global personality, but he may be most compelling when understood as a *global Asian American*—a figure whose active participation in and engagement with Asian American communities, and whose implication in US racial hierarchies, can be projected to a worldwide audience.

What might Lin as global Asian American look like? We may catch a glimpse in one of Lin's most recent YouTube videos, "Undercover Trainers," posted in September 2015. In the video, Lin and Taiwanese American actor Vanness Wu masquerade as personal trainers in what appears to be a gym in Taiwan. Lin, wearing a wig, facial hair, and stomach padding, speaks in Chinese throughout the video (which is subtitled in English) in his role as a comically inept and obnoxious trainer who dispenses bad advice to unsuspecting customers. On the surface, the video might appear to be a testament to Lin's smooth acceptance as a global marketing ambassador to the Chinese diaspora. The video is branded by Adidas, is titled in English and Chinese, and is conducted almost entirely in Chinese. Wu, Lin's partner in the video, would seem to be another example of Chinese diasporic fluidity—an American-born Asian who has found success as an actor and singer in Taiwan. But we might also read the video as a reflection on the absurdity of Lin's attempt to "pass" as a native of Taiwan. Lin's Chinese, although fluent, is less idiomatic and more limited in its vocabulary than that of a Taiwan native (in contrast to the smoother and more idiomatic spoken Chinese of Wu). And one comic moment in the video hinges on a linguistic error made by Lin. Wu is exhorting a gym customer to do pull-ups by shouting "I want to do pull-ups!" When it is Lin's turn to repeat the exhortation, however, he garbles the phrase, saying something that sounds more like "I want cake!" The error is played for laughs, with Wu saying to Lin, "You are fat enough and you want to eat more cake." Whether the error is intentional or not, it would seem to play on the viewer's understanding that Lin is not Taiwanese, but rather an Asian American who is *pretending* to be Taiwanese—a fact highlighted by Lin's absurd and not very convincing disguise.

The artificiality of Lin's Taiwanese masquerade is multiply emphasized at the end of the video. After the main action of the video concludes, we shift to a "behind-the-scenes" view that includes an inset showing the elaborate makeup job required for Lin to play his role. When Lin learns that he himself has been pranked during the video—a young woman whom he was "assisting" on the gym floor turns out to be an Olympic medalist—Lin "breaks character," dropping out of Chinese and into English ("She's a gold medalist? Oh, shoot"). Lin again "breaks character" when one of the customers asks "Are you Jeremy Lin?" and Wu pretends to be Jeremy Lin; Lin laughs and turns away, saying in English, "I can't do this anymore!" But perhaps most striking is the "unmasking" that ends the video, when Lin and Wu remove their disguises. For Lin this simply means pulling off his wig and stomach padding, but Wu, it turns out, has been wearing a much more elaborate disguise that includes a glued-on mask. As Wu pulls the mask off, he loudly says "Ow!" and Lin says in English, "Oh, man, that's gross!" Wu then turns to Lin and offers him the mask, saying, in English, "Here, it's for you." This is the only time Lin and Wu speak directly to each other in English, and I would read it as the video's moment of Asian American recognition: Lin and Wu acknowledge each other as fellow Asian Americans who are playing particular roles within the Chinese diaspora, and (briefly) register and laugh at the artificiality of those performances. The briefness of the moment is marked by the fact that Wu immediately turns back toward someone off camera and resumes speaking in Chinese, holding up the mask and saying, "Here, do you want it?"

While I do not mean to claim that Lin's identity as Asian American is his real or "authentic" identity, the video does, I would argue, present Asian Americanness as underlying Lin's (and Wu's) masquerade. But this Asian American "reveal" is only possible when Lin and Wu speak *to each other*, forming a brief moment of Asian American solidarity in what is otherwise a performance oriented toward a public space in Taiwan. Lin's circulation within the Chinese diaspora is one that continues to be sharply marked by Asian American particularity, and in fact his presentation to global, Chinese-speaking audiences tends to highlight, and even draw comic value from, the performative nature of Lin's participation in the Chinese diaspora. By highlighting the artificiality of Lin's masquerade as "Taiwanese," "Undercover Trainers" gives us a possible glimpse of what the position of a global Asian American might look like. What is most critically interesting—and, indeed, most entertaining—in Lin's circulation within the Chinese diaspora, and the Chinese-speaking market, is precisely those ways in which that circulation is *not* smooth, but instead registers Lin's crossing of national boundaries. Although "Undercover Trainers" shows that the Asian American "moments" within Lin's global presentation can be fleeting and often at risk of being lost in the larger imperative to present him as "Chinese," it also, by linking Lin's Asian Americanness to his humor and charisma, shows the way such Asian American moments can be incorporated into the very structure of globally circulating texts.

Notes

1. In an apparent attempt to correct this gaffe, another announcer responded, "By way of Harvard . . ."
2. As Pyong Gap Min notes in "Asian Immigration: History and Trends," a majority of Asian immigrants during the 1960s were from professional or technical occupations, while "Engineers, computer specialists, and other scientists were also overrepresented among Asian immigrants in the 1960s and early 1970s" (18). The 1990 Immigration Act, with its establishment of H-1B temporary worker visas, helped reinforce these preferences for Asian professionals and skilled workers in immigration (20).
3. Some version of this phrase has been used in stories by CNN, ESPN, the *Guardian*, the *Los Angeles Times*, and other sources; it is even used in NBA press releases, including the July 13, 2014 announcement of Lin's trade to the Los Angeles Lakers.
4. It's worth noting that the "perpetual foreigner" stereotype has not entirely disappeared from such coverage, with subtle slips suggesting Lin is really "from" China. Bonnell describes Lin's China visit as a "homecoming," although of course he was not born in China and his parents immigrated from Taiwan. *NBA.com* reporter Scott Howard-Cooper, in "Hornets Get Their Worldwide Moment with China Exhibition," remarks on the "predictable mania of Lin *back in* Asia" (emphasis added).
5. As part of the roundtable "Linsanity: Media, Culture, Masculinity," Association for Asian American Studies Conference, April 18, 2013.

References

Beck, Howard. "Lin's New Challenge: Media Onslaught at All-Star Weekend." *New York Times*, February 24, 2012. Web. 17 October. 2014.

Bonnell, Rick. "Will 'Linsanity' Erupt Again During the Charlotte Hornets' China Visit?" *Charlotte Observer*, October 10, 2015. Web. January 31, 2016.

Borden, Sam, and Keith Bradsher. "Tight-Knit Family Shares Lin's Achivement." *New York Times*, February 25, 2012. Web. October 19, 2014.

Chin, Josh. "Marketing Jeremy Lin in China." *Wall Street Journal*, February 15, 2012. Web. February 19, 2014.

Considine, Austin. "For Asian-American Stars, Many Web Fans." *New York Times*, July 29, 2011. Web. October 19, 2014.

Gao, Cindy. "The Virtuosic Virtuality of Asian American YouTube Stars." *Scholar & Feminist Online* 10.3 (Summer 2012). Barnard Center for Research on Women. Web. October 19, 2014.

Gregory, Sean. "Can Jeremy Lin's Appeal in China Really Help Houston's Bottom Line?" *Time*. July 19, 2012. Web. October 19, 2014.

Hansford, Corey. "Maxxis Signs On as Lakers Sponsor after Jeremy Lin Joins Team." *Lakers Nation*. Medium Large. 15 September. 2014. Web. 15 October. 2014.

"Houston Rockets' Jeremy Lin on Asian Stereotype." *60 Minutes*. CBSNews.com. CBS News. April 5, 2013. Web. September 30, 2014.

Howard-Cooper, Scott. "Hornets Get Their Worldwide Moment with China Exhibition." *NBA.com*. October 10, 2015. Web. January 31, 2016.

Kang, Jay Caspian. "A Question of Identity." *Grantland*. March 20, 2012. Web. October 19, 2014.

"Lakers Acquire Jeremy Lin and Draft Choices in Trade with Rockets." *NBA.com*. NBA Media Ventures. July 14, 2014. October 15, 2014.

Lee, Melaine. "'Linsanity' a Marketing Dream in Asia." *Reuters.com*. Reuters. February 13, 2012. Web. October 15, 2014.

Lim, Shirley Geok-lin and Amy Ling. *Reading the Literatures of Asian America*. Ed. Philadelphia, PA: Temple UP, 1992.

Lin, Jeremy. "Lindorsements." Online video. *YouTube*. YouTube, September 26, 2014. Web. October 19, 2014.

———. "Undercover Trainers." Online video. *YouTube*. YouTube, September 1, 2015. Web. January 31, 2016.

Lowe, Lisa. *Immigrant Acts: On Asian American Cultural Politics*. Durham, NC: Duke UP, 1996.

Mandell, Nina. "Jeremy Lin Is Trying His Best to Be a YouTube Sensation." *USA Today*. September 25, 2014. Web. October 19, 2014.

Min, Pyong Gap. "Asian Immigration: History and Trends." In *Asian Americans: Contemporary Trends and Issues*. 2nd ed. Thousand Oaks, CA: SAGE, 2006. 7–31.

Mozur, Paul, and Jenny W. Hsu. "China, Taiwan Both Lay Claim to Jeremy Lin." *Wall Street Journal*. February 15, 2012. Web. October 15, 2014.

Ong, Aihwa. *Flexible Citizenship: The Cultural Logics of Transnationality*. Durham, NC: Duke UP, 1999.

Pandian, Ananth. "Michael Jordan Calls Jeremy Lin the Hornets 'Biggest Acquisition.'" *CBSSports.com*. October 11, 2015. Web. January 31, 2016.

Wang, Gene. "Jeremy Lin Can Be Inspiration to Chinese Americans." *Washington Post*. February 9, 2012. Web. October 17, 2014.

Wong, Sau-ling C. "Denationalization Reconsidered: Asian American Cultural Criticism at a Theoretical Crossroads." In *Postcolonial Theory and the United States: Race, Ethnicity, and Literature*, Eds. Amritjit Singh and Peter Schmidt. Jackson, MI: University Press of Mississippi, 2000. 122–148.

15

BENEATH EACH LAYER OF CLOTH

Chinese Women in the New York City Garment Industry

Margaret M. Chin

Introduction

This essay is not about the glamorous part of fashion, but is instead about the everyday lives of Chinese women who once made the majority of women's apparel in New York City for close to forty years. During this time, the city had not only the people who designed the clothes—from glamourous wear to ordinary attire—but also the workers who were skilled enough to make them, in particular, Chinese women workers who were the backbone of the industry.

For over a century, immigrants have been vital to the New York City fashion industry. The garment industry has had many incarnations and is always remaking itself, adapting to the changing needs of the city and the immigrants who move there. In 2015, the garment industry is once again remaking itself. While New York City no longer produces garments in great quantities, it is still a thriving center for fashion creativity. Various designers are headquartered there, including those who are immigrants or the sons and daughters of immigrants. For example, Alexander Wang, Jason Wu, Vivienne Tam, and Vera Wang all have their design houses in New York. And while large-scale garment sewing shops are disappearing, small sample shops that create garments for designers in the midtown garment district are still recruiting Chinese and Latino workers in 2015.

A Brief Ethnic History of the Industry

The industry has cycled through many shifts and changes over the years. For example, during the late 1800s men were considered more skilled and sewed the heavier clothing, such as suits and coats, leaving women to sew women's apparel. The industry then became mostly women as the craft became "deskilled" and workers were no longer required to know how to piece together an entire garment.

There have been small shops and large factories, and now once again we have small shops. There have been shops where both the employees and employers were of the same ethnicity. As early as the 1890s, there were Jewish "shops" housed in tenement buildings. The more enterprising of the first Eastern European Jews became contractors and hired members of their families or co-ethnic acquaintances from the old country (Chin 2005a).

By the turn of the century Italian women became increasingly important, as many Jewish women left the industry when homework was outlawed. Jewish employers liked hiring Italian women because they were less sympathetic to unions and were readily available to replace departing workers. Italian women quickly became the second largest group in the garment industry (Green 1997).

Manufacturers were able to recruit and hire workers efficiently because the process of sewing a garment was broken down into separate tasks that required few skills. Production lines were organized into assembly lines that increased the demand for unskilled laborers. The character of the industry changed with this non co-ethnic work force. Employers started to recruit differently, such as in Italian language newspapers, rather than by word of mouth through friends and relatives. Less individualized training was required. Thus, garment shops were able to accommodate increasing numbers of untrained workers, including a number of men who worked side by side with co-ethnic women.

After World War II, shortages of Jewish and Italian workers created opportunities for members of nonwhite ethnic groups. With the change to Fordist production processes and different ways of recruiting workers, members of other groups ventured into the shops. American-born racial minority groups, including blacks, Puerto Ricans, and some Chinese-Americans, started entering the industry. The apparel industry was secure, well paying, for the most part unionized, and often the only industry that would hire members from these groups.

The Chinese became the dominant group, hiring their co-ethnics during the 1970s–1990s, easily tripling the number of factories during that time. However, during the 1990s, Koreans entered the industry as entrepreneurs and quickly opened over 200 shops, hiring Mexicans, Ecuadorians, Dominicans, and the Chinese as their apparel sewers/garment workers. These were not union shops, and they hired a mix of undocumented and documented workers. Many people in the industry did not expect to see co-ethnic Chinese employers and unionized Chinese employees working alongside non co-ethnic Korean-owned garment shops, but there was just enough work for both groups.

In Manhattan's Chinatown today, one would be hard pressed to find even 50 shops. The only ones remaining tend to be of mixed ethnicities and located in the midtown garment district.

The Chinese and the Garment Industry

Native-born Chinese made their first entrance into the garment industry during the 1940s and 1950s, as both sewers and garment shop owners. Few Chinese women that I interviewed said they worked in Jewish- or Italian-owned garment factories, or knew of other Chinese women who did so. In fact, because of the Chinese Exclusion Act (the first immigration law to limit any group based on race), there were very few Chinese women in New York City before World War II. In 1940, there were six Chinese men for every Chinese woman in the city.

However, after World War II many Chinese women entered the U.S. as a result of the War Brides Act of 1945, which permitted the wives of members of the U.S. armed forces to enter the country from 1944–1953. Chinese-American men had served in both segregated and non-segregated units during the war. In the early years, these war brides comprised 82 percent of Chinese immigrants to U.S. There were about 12,000 Chinese women in New York City in 1960, comprising 37 percent of the total Chinese population. A decade later, the Chinese female population grew to 32,000, and by 1980 there were 60,000 Chinese women living in New

York (Zhou 1992). Since most of these women needed to work to supplement the family income, they were a ready labor supply for anyone needing workers.

The first Chinese to own garment factories in lower Manhattan were ambitious. In 1950, the Chinese owned just three or four shops. By the mid-1950s, the number grew to about fifteen garment shops in the Lower East Side and Chinatown. From my own interviews with former Chinese garment workers, the owners were the American-born sons and daughters of Chinese parents who were laundry and grocery shopkeepers. The parents provided funds for some, while others used their G.I. benefits to buy the shops. These early factories were created in an effort to duplicate the success of their Jewish neighbors, and to provide opportunities for American-born Chinese and their new brides entering the country.

There were thirty-five Chinese-owned unionized garment shops in 1965. By 1969, 23 percent of Chinatown residents were working in the garment industry, based on data collected by the Columbia University Study Group (1970). The number of shops grew to 247 by 1975. By 1979, 60 percent of Chinatown residents worked in the garment industry. The proportion of workers kept growing in tandem with increasing Chinese immigration to the U.S. The Chinese owners easily recruited their co-ethnics via word of mouth. And in turn, the women were very willing to take these jobs (Bao 2001). Moreover, those who recruited them into the garment shops were often willing to train a sister, a cousin, or an aunt in the new skill of sewing whole garments in a factory (Chin 2005a). Sewing whole garments allowed these women some flexibility in how they scheduled and balanced their family and work obligations. In many of these factories, the women only got paid for the number of garments completed. Thus, one can choose to sew more or less depending on family needs.

Chinese women saw these jobs not only as a means to earn an income, but also as a way to get health insurance, paid vacation days, sick pay, and other benefits for themselves and their families via the International Ladies' Garment Workers' Union (ILGWU). Chinese men worked mostly in Chinese restaurants that were not unionized and did not provide benefits. Moreover, they were often paid in cash. Since the garment factories paid in a formal manner, the garment workers learned how to handle finances and American banking. Women's income records, bank and checking accounts, and other financial statements easily became the documents that were the backbone of applications to sponsor their relatives coming to the U.S. Moreover, these financial records also allowed many Chinese women to get mortgage credit to buy their first homes (Chin 2005a). Links to banking were an important way for new immigrants to forge connections with American institutions that would assist in their upward mobility.

From the 1960s through the 1990s, Chinese membership in the ILGWU grew despite declines in other locals in New York City. By 1971, Local 23–25, with membership that was mostly Chinese, became the largest affiliate of the ILGWU and remained that way through 1995, until the ILGWU and Amalgamated Clothing and Textile Workers Union (ACTWU) became the Union of Needletrades, Industrial and Textile Employees (UNITE). In 2004, UNITE merged with HERE (Hotel Employees and Restaurant Employees International Union) to become UNITE HERE. Even though Chinese women made up an increasing share of the workforce in New York City since the 1970s, it was not until after the 1982 Chinatown strike that they moved into leadership positions in the ILGWU.

Throughout the 1970s and 1980s, the garment industry remained robust. Because New York had the communication and financial connections that facilitated the marketing of fashion products globally and locally, the city attracted prominent design houses. In addition, New York City had a sizable local population willing to buy such products and plenty of immigrants who could produce them. During the 1980s, Donna Karan, Liz Clairborne, Anne Klein, Eileen Fisher, and many other notable designers and manufacturers made their headquarters in New York. At the industry's peak in the 1980s, Chinatown alone had over 500 shops with more than 25,000 workers.

Chinese Immigration and New York City

Growing Chinese immigration rapidly changed the composition of Chinatown. After the passage of the Hart-Cellar Act in 1965, Chinatown grew tremendously from the 1960s to 2000. The Chinese immigrant stream consistently had people who were both blue collar and also capable of being entrepreneurs. The availability of a low-skilled and mostly female work force, along with capital, managerial skills, and space, allowed more garment shops to open. The combination of entrepreneurial skills and large numbers of low-skilled workers fueled the garment industry. From 1966–1970, an average of 5,000–7,000 Chinese (from China, Hong Kong, and Taiwan) were admitted to New York City each year. The numbers increased even more dramatically after 1970. As Table 15.1 shows, the early growth of the garment factories was fueled by immigration. Not until the mid-1980s do we begin to see a large-scale exodus from the industry because of increased overseas competition.

As the Italian and Jewish communities grew prosperous they moved out of lower Manhattan, thus creating room for new Chinese immigrants. Chinatown more than tripled in size from 1970 to 2000. Families moved into low-rent apartments in tenement buildings as these were vacated by Jews and Italians. From 1990 to 2000, the Chinese started moving into larger rent-stabilized apartments, New York City Housing Authority (NYCHA) apartments in lower Manhattan, and to apartments, single-family homes, and semi-attached houses in Queens and Brooklyn.

In 1970, the area surrounding the core of Chinatown, which included Little Italy and the Lower East Side, consisted of plenty of inexpensive manufacturing or loft spaces that could easily be converted into garment factories. A study by the city reported that even as late as 1980 these spaces cost only $1.50 per square foot, which explains how garment shops could expand and the industry could thrive.

In lower Manhattan, garment shops were in close proximity to the majority of Chinese immigrants, creating a situation where women could walk to work. The number of garment shops expanded along Canal Street and Broadway, reaching into Little Italy along Mulberry and Elizabeth Streets, and extending into the Lower East Side along East Broadway and Allen Street. From the late 1960s to the 1980s, Chinese contractors could purchase a factory of twenty-five sewing machines for as little as $25,000 by making a down payment of about $6,000–$7,000. As a result, the garment industry grew rapidly in Chinatown (Bao 2001, Chin 2005a).

Table 15.1 NYC Chinese Population, 1940–2010

NYC Population	Total	Chinese
1940	7,455,995	12,753
1950	7,891,957	18,327
1960	7,781,984	32,831
1970	7,894,862	69,324
1980	7,071,639	124,372
1990	7,322,564	238,919
2000	8,008,278	361,531
2010	8,175,133	406,463

(US Census Bureau, NYC Department of Planning)

From 1965 to 1975, the number of garment shops grew from 34 to 247; by 1980, the number peaked at over 500 (Bao 2001, 177). By 1983 an estimated $125 million was paid in wages to Chinese garment workers, which meant that Chinatown was one of the city's largest manufacturing areas (Chin 2005a).

Even though garment production in general fell during the 1990s in the U.S. and in New York City, the Chinese garment industry kept producing a substantial portion of all women's apparel for U.S. consumption. And, by extension, these garment shops kept a large portion of garment production in New York and subsequently in the U.S. Moreover, the garment industry had a huge impact on the Chinese community. The $125 million earned by Chinese women went right back into the local economy and fueled a thriving Chinatown.

The Dual-income Family

Anyone walking the streets of Chinatown in the 1960s would not be able to avoid young children and families. As Chinese immigration increased, the Chinese family became the predominant household form in Chinatown, as compared to the earlier male-dominated households. In a 20-year span, the neighborhood expanded and became a haven for families and dual-income earners.

Some of these early families owned Chinese laundries and lived behind or above the business. It was difficult to survive, even with the entire family working in this livelihood. Men usually worked in the front, and the wives and children worked in the back. Slowly, the Chinese laundry started to fall out of favor in the 1950s. Automatic washing machines became very popular after World War II. These machines quickly displaced many Chinese hand laundries. The established Chinese laundries remained, but few families invested in new laundry businesses.

Other than the laundry business, there were limited jobs for Chinese immigrant men who could not speak English well. Some Chinese families found their livelihood in the restaurant business. When Chinese families owned their own restaurants, every single family member worked, including the children. Of course, many other Chinese families tried different businesses in Chinatown, including markets that sold produce, fresh fish, and meat, as well as general grocery stores. Those families with specific skills opened bakeries, jewelry shops, herbal stores, and dried beef stores, among others. Families that owned stores and were entrepreneurial tended to be a little bit better off. By the 1980s the Chinese immigrant stream was bifurcated; some were "Uptown Chinese" who were educated and did not have to work in menial labor, and others were "Downtown Chinese" who worked in restaurants and the garment industry, both as owners and laborers (Kwong 1987).

Much of the Chinese population would sell their labor. The majority of Chinese men who were not self-employed joined the growing restaurant industry. It was very difficult for Chinese men to support their new families on low restaurant wages that were mostly paid in cash. However, there were hardly any other choices for immigrant Chinese men. The types of jobs were so limited that Chinese men have told me that they knew they would be working in the restaurant industry even before they immigrated, if not in New York City, then in a nearby state. But restaurant work clearly did not pay enough to support a family and new immigrants quickly realized that two wage earners were necessary.

Therefore, women in China waiting to immigrate knew that they would be working in the sewing industry; in fact, they knew exactly who they would meet in the U.S. to take them to their first day of work. The employment possibilities for immigrant non-English-speaking Chinese men and women were very limited from the 1950s to the 1990s. Many researchers would say that Chinatown had two pillars, the restaurant and garment industries, by which the entire community earned its income and re-circulated that money back into the community to support ever more services. The size and population of Chinatown grew from the 1960s through the 2000s largely because of the robustness of these two sectors. The number of Chinese ILGWU members grew phenomenally after 1970, in concert with the growth of Chinese immigration. And Local 23–25, with the largest number of Chinese members, became the largest local in the nation.

The 1982 Strike

To the surprise of everyone, Chinese women took to the streets in 1982 to protest working conditions in the garment industry. Over 20,000 Chinese workers, mostly women, attended two rallies in Chinatown to pressure Chinese employers to sign a new union contract (Bao 2001). It was the largest labor strike in Chinatown's history. Moreover, this strike changed the face of the ILGWU. To the surprise of many, women who were leaders of the 1982 strike were offered positions in ILGWU.

Prior to the strike, the New York City garment industry was beginning to face stiff competition from out-of-state non-union production as well as imports. Manufacturers who did not want to unionize moved their operations to the South. Non-unionized workers were a cheaper labor force that allowed manufacturers to hold down labor costs and stay profitable.

Manufacturers held an inordinate amount of power over Chinese garment factory owners because of the way the manufacturers, unions, and workers were tied together. From the very beginning, union organizers—who were mostly non-Chinese—had trouble communicating with and recruiting workers; Chinese workers were barely accessible to union organizers. However, ILGWU organizers were able to convince shop owners that unionization would guarantee them a stable workforce. Thus, many workers became union members without knowing exactly what that was. This didn't matter to the ILGWU, which happily cut a deal with midtown manufacturers and Chinese contractors.

By 1980, Chinese garment shop owners complained that they were only middlemen who barely made any money after paying their workers. Why should they sign a deal with the ILGWU again? The manufacturers were squeezing every cent out of them. Chinese garment shop owners often competed with one another to get any type of contract for sewing work, including from non-union manufacturers at the lowest possible prices. The manufacturers' search for cheaper labor had a huge impact on Chinese factory owners and workers. The union was supposed to guarantee union work for owners and workers, while in return the garment shop owners guaranteed that Chinese women workers would join the union (Bao 2001). But conditions changed so rapidly during the 1980s that manufacturers could no longer promise enough union work for Chinese garment factories. By this time garment work was moving overseas as well as to the southern United States, where labor was cheaper and non-unionized (Bonacich and Appelbaum 2000).

At the same time, rents and utilities rose in the Chinatown area, raising costs for both garment shops owners and workers. The rapid increase in immigration had created a demand for apartments and other real estate in the Chinatown area. To counter the decline of unionized garment work and to increase earnings, garment shop owners took in work from non-union manufacturers, something that the midtown garment shops were already doing. This only created more tension between the union, workers, and garment shop owners. When their union contract was up for renewal in 1982, the workers feared that co-ethnic garment shop owners would not sign it, depriving them of medical coverage, pensions, and other benefits that came with union membership. During the last few months of contract negotiations, workers were mobilized and threw their support to the union instead of garment shop owners. As workers continued to join the union's side, small contractors signed the new contract. But it wasn't until more than 20,000 workers held a one-day strike on July 15, 1982 that all garment shop owners signed the contract.

The 1982 strike was a significant event in the history of Chinese women in New York, as well as in the overall history of Chinatown. Chinese women who were leaders in the strike were recruited to work in the ILGWU and a few rose in the ranks. This was meaningful in that the union started to explicitly recognize the needs of Chinese workers and their families; nevertheless, there was no widespread recruitment of Chinese women workers. Chinese women continued to be excluded from the top leadership positions of Local 23–25, even though they made up the majority of the membership.

"Quick Time" and the Garment Industry

By 1992, imported clothing comprised 60 percent of U.S. retail sales, up from 10 percent in 1984. Yet despite these dire circumstances, New York City still had a significant garment industry, though smaller than in decades past. To sustain itself, the industry reinvented itself by fulfilling "quick time" orders, replenishing popular items quickly so that manufacturers wouldn't have to wait for overseas production and shipment (Waldinger 1986, Chin 2005a). The New York City garment industry was able to hang on by a thread in the 1990s due to the adaptability and flexibility of the industry (Zhou 1992, Lin 1998, Chin 2005a).

By the late 1980s, computer technology was sophisticated enough to determine which items were the most popular in any store for the week, particularly in chain stores like Macy's. Inventory programs could also determine exact sales for the week and approximately how much inventory had to be ordered for the following month. "Quick time" also helped satisfy the demand for trendy items that might be popular only for a short time with customers. Chain stores and manufacturers couldn't afford to send their orders overseas and wait a month or two for their most popular items to be replenished. Moreover, manufacturing a relatively small number of these garments was not a high priority for overseas garment factories. Production schedules might not be able to absorb these new runs of items. For these reasons, a certain amount of local production was necessary to fulfill these quick orders, and Chinese-owned garment shops in New York City fit the bill. Within a matter of days, they could sew the requisite number of garments that were required and have them quickly delivered to stores.

Even in the 1990s, the Chinese still had close to 400 unionized shops and nearly 20,000 workers in Chinatown. They worked alongside and in competition with more than 200 Korean-owned non-union shops that were staffed with 14,000 Mexican, Dominican, and Ecuadorian workers who made smaller refill orders that could be shipped quickly to U.S. retail stores.

The Shop Floor

For the majority of Chinese immigrant women, income from working in the garment shops was crucial for a family's survival. One garment worker told me, "Without the garment industry, I really couldn't imagine how my family would have survived." In Xiaolan Bao's work, she mentions how women praised the work that was given to them.

The majority of women I interviewed during the 1990s all knew that they were going to work in a garment factory even before they left China. Their sisters or aunts or cousins brought them to the shop and asked the shop owners whether they could learn to sew. Since workers sewed a whole garment, a new arrival could practice all day and be paid for that particular piece upon completion. That might have been $20 for the two or three garments she was able to finish that day. She couldn't become a union member until she made the minimum income required by the union.

Not only did the "whole garment rate" training allow new immigrant women to learn a trade, but it also enabled them to balance their work and family lives. Garment jobs allowed women flexible hours. Women could come to work after dropping their children off at school or at childcare. They could buy groceries and run errands during their lunch hours. Some women left work in the afternoon to pick up their children and have dinner, before returning for an hour or two at the end of the day.

Women came to know each other well in the workplace. They arrived at work together and left together. Before the machines started, the women would spend time chatting. While they talked, they unpacked their lunches and placed them by the rice cookers provided by their employers. They set up their stations with bottles of warm tea and candy and other snacks. They gathered bundles of clothing to sew, discussing the techniques required to finish the items quickly. Conversation would turn to kids and spouses over and over again. The factory experience facilitated camaraderie and sociability among workers from China and Hong Kong.

During school holidays there would be numerous kids in the shops. If they didn't want to play with the other kids, they would sometimes help their mothers. If the factory owners' kids were there, they might play together. You would also see kids congregating in the owners' offices, where they ate, played, and did homework.

The Decline of the Chinatown Garment Industry

Following the September 11, 2001 terrorist attacks and the 2008 recession, at least a quarter of Chinatown's workforce became unemployed. The majority of these were Chinese women, who were less protected than their husbands. These women were overly connected to the community, and when disaster and recession hit Chinatown, they felt the impact. The garment industry diminished greatly after 2001 (Chin 2005b). When trucks could not move clothing in and out of Chinatown after the attacks, manufacturers with overseas connections strengthened those ties. It was simpler to have garments sewn overseas.

Chinatown and its garment industry were located just ten blocks (about a half mile) from the World Trade Center. After the attacks, no work, not even quick time work, could be completed for at least three months. As a result, many factories went out of business. With improved computer tracking and project management software, manufacturers realized that overseas production could be time and cost effective. Quick time was not as cost efficient as before. Thus, after 2001, the garment industry deteriorated at an increasingly fast pace. Today, there are few shops left.

As early as 2002, women started to look for jobs outside of the garment industry that offered health, vacation, and pension benefits. Their networks led them to restaurants and small businesses in Chinatown. The jobs they most wanted were as home health attendants, or in the hotel and hospitality service sector. Fortunately, some Chinatown community centers organized training programs for these sectors (Chin 2013).

Nevertheless, Chinese women faced many obstacles as they moved into industries outside of Chinatown. They encountered a wholly different hiring process, where they needed to speak English, fill out job applications, and be interviewed. Second, they had to learn customer service—how to interact with customers, converse with them, and offer assistance. These new industries forced women to rely less on their co-ethnics and more on soft skills that required English and traveling outside of their enclaves. It was a new and different way of working that ultimately had a huge effect on the Chinatown neighborhood (Chin 2013). Today, in 2015, we see a Chinatown with fewer Chinese families. However, the legacy of the garment industry is that it afforded dependable work for several generations of Chinese-Americans. The income they earned helped them buy homes and send children to college, in addition to providing them with a lifetime of friends and a tightly knit community.

References

Asian American Federation of New York 2002a. "Chinatown after September 11: An Economic Impact Study-An Interim Report." New York: April.

———. 2002b. "Chinatown: One Year after September 11: An Economic Impact Study. New York: November.

Bao, Xiaolan 2001. *Holding Up More Than Half the Sky: Chinese Women Garment Workers in New York City, 1948–1992.* Urbana, IL: University of Illinois Press.

Bonacich, Edna and Richard P. Appelbaum 2000. *Behind the Label: Inequality in the Los Angeles Apparel Industry.* Berkeley, CA; Los Angeles, CA; London: University of California Press.

Chin, Margaret M. 2005a. *Sewing Women: Immigrants and the New York City Garment Industry.* New York: Columbia University Press.

Chin, Margaret M. 2005b. "Moving On: Chinese Garment Workers after 9/11." In *Wounded City*, Ed. Nancy Foner. 184–207. New York: Russell Sage Foundation.

Chin, Margaret M. 2013. "Changing Expectations: Economic Downturns and Immigrant Chinese Women in New York City." In *Immigrant Women Workers in the Neoliberal Age.* Eds. Flores-Gonzalez, Guevarra Toro-Morn, Chang. 117–130. Champaign, IL: University of Illinois Press.

Chinatown Study Group. "Chinatown Report: 1969." Columbia University Library. East Asian Stacks.

Green, Nancy L. 1997. *Ready to Work, Ready to Wear: A Century of Industry and Immigrants in Paris and New York.* Durham, NC: Duke University Press.

Kwong, Peter 1987. *The New Chinatown.* New York: Noonday Press.

Lin, Jan 1998. *Reconstructing Chinatown.* Minneapolis, MN: University of Minnesota Press.

Waldinger, Roger 1986. *Through the Eye of the Needle.* New York: New York University Press.

Zhou, Min 1992. *Chinatown: The Socioeconomic potential of an Urban Enclave.* Philadelphia, PA: Temple University Press.

PART FOUR

Representations Within and Across Nations

16

THE GLOBALITY OF AF-PAK

U.S. Empire and the Muslim Problem

Junaid Rana

Af-Pak as No-Body's Land

In this essay, I elaborate the theoretical insights of anti-Muslim racism and the analytical approach of relationality to describe how scholarship in Asian American Studies and related fields addresses the challenge of these terms. I then briefly describe recent shifts in urban spatialization that are intertwined in how the global War on Terror impacts patterns of migration and habitation in the foundational global city of the U.S. settler state, New York City, to provide an example of the racial process of globality. To do so, I draw on the U.S. imperial military term of "Af-Pak" as a geographic descriptor that collapses a number of global terms of raciality that build upon prior forms of colonial warfare under British Empire and the on-going renewal of the imperial Great Game.[1] The term Af-Pak deploys a spatial geography in the scales of the nation-state that functions as a racial common sense of globality. It is a term that names as much as it hides. It refers to the assumptions of militancy mapped for the purposes of strategic containment by the warfare state. And through this sublimated category, the term Af-Pak represents a violence that is continuous in a process of elimination—a euphemism for a site of genocidal warfare. With the implicit narrative of imperial genocide embedded in this term of Af-Pak, what exactly does it signify beyond geographic terms of mapping and identification? And how might this term be useful in thinking through the processes of global racial formation, imperialism, and settler colonialism?

This is not to say that the term Af-Pak is a widespread and commonplace term of use, rather it is a state discourse that represents a global term of raciality that imposes universality. In doing so, it demarcates a relational logic of a *racializing* formation, as opposed to a racial formation, in which anti-Muslim racism is part of a global project of U.S. imperial formation. In the pantheon of U.S. imperial terms configured for the War on Terror, such as those of Guantanamo[2] and Abu Ghraib that refer to military places of non-space and exception, and the congruent corporeal terms of enemy combatant and the figure of the Muslim, an expansive narrative of U.S. empire employs tropes and figures to resolve the problem of the Muslim through racialization, white supremacy, and the logics of settler colonialism. The Muslim problem as the occurrence of anti-Muslim racism and so-called Islamophobia is a symptom of a larger problem—namely the structure of white supremacy as a central organizing principle of modernity. The illegibility of anti-Muslim racism in relationship to white supremacy is an aspect of what makes it so powerful. Take for example the pervasive, violent, and deadly anti-black racism that has emerged in the public spectacle of social media so clearly in the last few years in which the principle of naming and identifying such violence is to comprehend it in the terms of antiracist struggle and to work against it. This visibility presents a coherence that provides for a theory of anti-black racism and antiracist analysis. But what of the forms of racism that are unnamed, unnameable, and even unremarkable? The paradox of anti-Muslim racism in the contemporary moment in contrast is that it is obscured as much as it is rampant and commonplace—a social phenomenon that refers to illegibility and invisibility in a general theory of racism. The contradiction is perhaps even greater than mere invisibility since it is something that is known yet incoherent as racism.

In the decade and a half since September 11, 2001, a number of important revelations have emerged in social theory and critical race scholarship. These insights have been a boon for further intellectual inquiry and an expanded comprehension of the contemporary social landscape. The first of these includes the theorization of the racialization of Muslims and Islam. The conceptual development of anti-Muslim racism has expanded the conceptual repertoire of race and racism in relationship to white supremacy, empire, and war. Although the antagonism against Islam and Muslims is clear as a claim, many still do not accept the overlap of racial and religious signifiers that culminates in what is here described as anti-Muslim racism. In other words, it is more commonly accepted that anti-Muslim sentiment is based on the convergence of religious difference and prejudicial hatred. In many ways the notion of anti-Muslim racism is paradoxical to the late modern racial common sense that typically imagines racism as primarily based on phenotypic difference—a color-based schematic that often hinges on black and white. Yet, as scholars have shown from legal categories to social and political imaginaries, Islam and Muslims have been racialized as "other."[3] This does not only refer to a demographic category of those who identify as Muslim or practice Islam, but the figure of the Muslim that is itself a racialized figure that encompasses multiple racial logics.[4] The racial figure of the Muslim encompasses a broad set of those who are "Muslim-looking" based in national, ethnic, gender, sexuality, racial, and class differentiation. Even those who identify as Muslim in the sense of a faith-based practice, consist of a heterogeneous population that is undoubtedly a multiracial category. The Muslim as a racial figure combines notions of religion as culture in order to make the distinction of religious difference as naturalized in racial difference. In other words, to be a Muslim is to be a racial other in the U.S. racial formation in a religion–culture–race linkage, and as part of an emergent global racial system. To speak of anti-Muslim racism is to point out a paradoxical category of race in which, for example, the discourse of multiculturalism and diversity that understands multiple racial categories as distinct is itself a new feature that is being racialized as an increasingly versatile and malleable category.

As a thought exercise it is worth reflecting on how such categories as Latina/o and Asian American are, for example, made to be racial categories in the lexicon of the U.S. racial formation. Both represent a broad spectrum of raciology in terms of phenotypic difference and geographic area and often represent the contradictions and in-betweenness of the bipolar racial logic of blackness and whiteness. Asian is itself a racial amalgamation that in popular parlance of U.S. racial formation is more commonly associated with East Asia and the histories of U.S. wars abroad including interventions in Korea, Vietnam, and the Pacific, to name a few. But in this imaginary of "Asian" racial formation, where does Asia begin and where does it end? What of West Asia, the Arab and Muslim world? While these geographic and racial cartographies are problematic in their assumptions of social stasis and the cohesion or areas, these logics of place bounded in regional difference are mired in notions of modern rationality and political liberalism that have fundamentally informed the ideological rationales that simultaneously position anti-

Muslim racism in relation to white supremacy. Similarly, anti-Muslim racism is enveloped in a process of racialization that has included anti-Arab racism that is itself imagined through an ambiguous whiteness.[5] Both anti-Arab and anti-Muslim encompass a similar effect in the U.S. racial formation that absorbs populations through the notions of inclusivity and homogeneity.[6] And yet while anti-Arab racism includes Arab Christians, who incidentally make up the majority of the Arab population in the U.S., this is not at all representative of something we might call anti-Christian racism but is distinctly a formation of anti-Muslim racism. It is thus that anti-Muslim racism is more readily linked to an innovation of racial logics that I describe as Muslim racial becoming.[7] This is the invocation of potentials and threats that are summoned by the racialization of the trope of the "terrorist" such that anti-Muslim racism fits a flexible and arbitrary logic of white supremacy.

A second insight of critical race scholarship has been a shift from comparative approaches to relational analysis.[8] Building on the thought of Black feminist theorists such as Hortense Spillers and Sylvia Wynter,[9] the turn toward relationality has had an important impact on how scholars particularly within critical ethnic studies approach their object of analysis. While the debate of comparison has often been mired in approaches of hierarchy and racial differentiation as a narrative of racial suffering and violence, relationality offers a complex shift in analysis. The War on Terror, for example, in a mode of comparison would place degrees of suffering as a historical teleology of "greater than," in which say blackness is the foundational justification of genocide and incapacitation in which the atrocities of the 2003 Abu Ghraib torture scandal draw from the U.S. penal system,[10] and are preoccupied with the genealogical foundations of power relations. In a relational approach, such comparisons shift attention toward examining histories of settler colonialism, white supremacy, and genocide as the concepts that organize such violence and not just as genealogical tools of cause and effect, or that in which a recovery of origins compels a rationale of a primary or first-order oppression. And while it is undeniable that native genocide and anti-blackness are pivotal to understanding the organization and pervasive continuation of racialized terror as a death-principle, as Iyko Day has argued, such comparisons obfuscate the workings of settler colonial racial capitalism that fail to comprehend the racialization of the category of Asian and migrant as part of a necropolitical dimension of war and colonialism.[11] The inability to formulate a complex theorization of racialization only serves to enable the power of white supremacy to reorganize and reproduce itself, and to miss important theoretical and analytical imperatives regarding the concepts of race and racism. Broadly speaking, the complex theorization of the workings of settler colonialism and racial capitalism in a global sense thus speaks to a logic of a terror formation in which state violence is tightly interwoven with subaltern actors in which the terms of colonial, colonized, and anti-colonial continue. Many such archives still remain to be unearthed and examined in terms of not only how domination and oppression have worked from racial capitalism, white supremacy, and settler colonialism, but also the range of solidarities that responded to the longer historical formation of the figure of the Muslim and anti-Muslim racism. For example, the work of Sohail Daulatzai points to the innovative and rich social and cultural histories of Black, Arab, and Muslim radical thought that he has called the "Muslim International."[12] Similarly, in what Seema Sohi has called insurgent modernity, new histories of radicalism in the South Asian diaspora have shown how a range of interactions in the early twentieth century pushed important debates and practices of decolonization and anti-colonialism.[13]

These two productive theorizations of anti-Muslim racism and relationality are useful in setting up the conceptual argument I pursue regarding a recent trajectory in critical thought that draws on the modern form of the nation-state and social structure of racial formation to explain the concept of globality. In a series of recent essays and the book *Toward a Global Idea of Race*, critical race scholar Denise Ferreira da Silva establishes the concept of globality as a way to trace how the nation-state and modernity are central systems and products of racialization.[14] In Silva's conception, the nation-state, rather than being culpable for the particularities of social structure and the violence of racism, is in fact a central and unavoidable part of a *racializing* formation. Thus the promises of freedom, democracy, and development are better understood as globalizing state projects in which the use of force is a coercive power that is both crude and passive. In a more exacting intervention into the philosophical debates of modernity, the notion of globality, in Silva's thought, refers to the horizon of raciality in which violence and dominance are normalized. Put simply, racialization is inescapable in the modern world. Raciality as globality is what makes brute force an unnoticed part of everyday life. It is in this sense that racism rather than being an aberrant form of modernity, encompasses and enables liberal modernity as a process and system that constructs an ethical and historical subject from which the law and the status quo of everyday practices emerge.[15] Through the artifice of modernity, maintained through a teleology based in a hope for a progressive future, Silva argues that the force of racial violence is interconnected with this sense of a global purpose. It is thus that the use of policing and occupying technologies with military training to control urban populations seems as if it were by the design of state social engineering for the "improvement" of society. In an essay with the astute title "No-Bodies," Silva sets a scene to summarize this point:

> The law enforcement tactics in these occupations go beyond ostensive patrolling of streets; they also include shooting from low-flying helicopters, deployment of armoured cars, and use of automatic guns. While the state government provides the basic social services—education, health, etc—to these neighborhoods, its presence is more evident in the military actions, which have become the primary mode of management of the city's economically black and brown territories. During these occupations, *favelas'* residents participate in scenes similar to the war scenes unfolding in Iraq, Afghanistan, Palestine and other corners of the globe. To be sure, the "kill on site/sight" practice of Rio de Janeiro's police does not make one wonder whether Rio's *favelas* are concentration camps or battlefields, but rather prompts consideration of the question of what exactly is the difference between them.[16]

The term "nobodies" speaks to an evisceration of the body and its materiality, and to the notion of anonymity that conveys a lack of importance or recognition of humanity. In this formulation the state in the above passage is imagined as generalizable to multiple conflict zones in the world—most apparently those mired in U.S. imperial wars and the on-going primitive accumulation of settler colonialism. Mid-way through the description, the signs of place and the familiar language of the urban center of Rio de Janeiro (e.g., *favela*) situate the reader. Silva makes quite clear at the outset of this article that the critique of this essay is about military violence and the state occupations of the Brazilian black and brown neighborhoods castigated as "no-bodies." To add to Silva's rumination about whether favelas are concentration camps or battlefields, one can also continue the metaphor of globality to articulate these occupied zones as places of colonial conquest. The logic of force and the enforcement of modernity is one that critics of colonialism have examined through the analytical framework of colonizer and colonized, and the workings of race and culture.[17] The disembodiment of race yields a social and cultural geography, that under the rhetorics of colonialism is to be tamed and disciplined, replacing bodies as an object, with that of the land as object. With the naming of Rio in the passage is a reference to a relational context, a planetary mode of warfare in which the inner city, indeed any inner city, is equated with the tactics and strategies of the police state with the military state, namely, the global War on Terror. Such a relational context of globality matches what Paul Amar has referred to as the shift from neoliberalism to the security state in a context that ties countries such as Brazil to Egypt of the global South.[18] Similarly the idea of how the body and the land are obfuscated under the necropolitical practices of the state draws on Achille Mbembe's instructive examples of apartheid South Africa and occupied Palestine. For Mbembe, these two examples are parallel sites of modern colonial occupation in which land and bodies are subject to territorial fragmentation and the banality of settlement under apartheid regimes that continue to perfect a system of colonial occupation with technical precision designed to separate and seclude.[19]

Following Silva's theorization of globality, it is this fundamental insight constructed in the rhetoric of security and counterinsurgency that I pursue in terms of understanding how the War on Terror appears in a range of conceptual and spatial shifts that depend on the intertwining of raciality and globality. The parallel of "war scenes unfolding in Iraq, Afghanistan, Palestine" implies a metaphoric distance away from the favelas of Rio in the parallel theaters of imperial violence that connect zones of raciality and coloniality. Yet it is also precisely the point of this globality, of racial violence under the machinations of the nation-state, that is the universal arbiter of violence in the Weberian sense, and it is the modular form and process that enable particular systems of violence to perpetuate as if they were normal and quotidian. Even further there is an assumption related to how we understand these variegated places in relationship to those who inhabit (or once inhabited) these geographies. For it is not only the War on Terror that travels and becomes normalized as a state project but people who evade or are ensnared by this trap of raciality. The migrant, the refugee, the other, are the "no-bodies" of racialized globality that are expendable and functional to the logic of modernity. They come from zones, such as Af-Pak, that in the language of occupation and settler colonialism are *terra nullius*, the land of null and void, or more directly "no-body's land," a riff on Silva's title that speaks to an evisceration of people from places through military nomenclature. This relinquishing of sovereign notions of power over the body and the land is precisely what I would argue is a key aspect of racialization of the Muslim as an abstract object, and also a central aspect of how Muslim racial becoming works from which land and body are torn apart.

The Problematic of Af-Pak

Around 2008 the term "Af-Pak" appeared in a media quote provided by Richard Holbrooke to describe the parts of Afghanistan and Pakistan that make up a major frontline in the U.S. War on Terror.[20] Af-Pak was a neologism deployed to imagine a single military theater of operations that expanded upon the British repertoire of colonial terms such as "frontier" to include a more nebulous region in the lexicon of U.S. empire that dubbed it a targeted military zone.[21] Holbrooke, who was later appointed President Obama's Special Representative for Afghanistan and Pakistan, imagined this frontier region of Af-Pak not only in relation to these two countries, but also in relationship to other regional players such as Iran, China, and India. In language that harkens to the importance of the veritable Silk Road as a passageway connecting disparate landscapes divided by rugged terrain, Af-Pak is a theater of war in which the play for resources is part of the new Great Game of creating a veneer of stability through military occupation. The term Af-Pk is embedded in a historical relationship in which an occupied Afghanistan under the War on Terror was imagined by the terms of U.S. political and regional interests that would place the U.S. military client-state of Pakistan as a willing partner.[22] Moon-Kie Jung has usefully conceptualized the United States as not simply a nation-state but an empire-state that operates beyond the territorial boundaries of the nation and must constantly renew its imperial form.[23] In this configuration of the empire-state, Af-Pak is part of an expanding vocabulary that names historical regions important to the continued imperial expansion from the British and Russians, to those of the U.S. that most recently fall under the global War on Terror. Yet this designation is a consequence of already existing disruptions of the boundaries of Afghanistan and Pakistan, in which the actual territorial border is described as porous and defenseless because of the challenges presented by the rough terrain of a mountainous region, that cloaks the multiplicity of the people, cultures, and traditions that inhabit this region. The areas straddling the boundaries of Afghanistan and Pakistan are dominated by a borderland that has historically been represented by the Pashtun ethnic and linguistic group. Afghanistan, torn apart by war for over the last 35 years, has been the object of numerous imperial struggles including the British and Russians at the turn of the twentieth century and the more recent conflict in which the U.S. and other NATO forces have escalated military involvement in the fight against the Taliban, but also in a geostrategic struggle over energy resources most prominently with China and India. Af-Pak in this understanding is an imperial metaphor of a racialized geography that is globalized in the sense I discussed above borrowing from Denise da Silva. And while in some senses the term Af-Pak is about this borderzone, it also signifies a historical conjoining of Afghanistan and Pakistan in the U.S. imperial imagination that is considerably different from, say Indo-Pak, as a reference to India and Pakistan.

In framing the concept of Af-Pak as a term of globality I follow the theoretical insights and developments of new fields such as critical ethnic studies. In many ways the study of South Asia has taken such borderland regions for granted because of the normative dependence on area-studies of the nation-state. As a geopolitical descriptor, Af-Pak has taken on the metaphor of a social and political geography to describe a condition and potential for threat that emanates from such ambiguous and hard-to-define zones and bodies outside of the nation-state. Recent scholarship by Ronak Kapadia and Keith Feldman argues that Af-Pak is a form of global racialization enabled by U.S. imperial cartographies that employ military visuality onto a range of social and political conditions.[24] Out of this emergent scholarship, racialization emerges as a transnational and global narrative. Such a process requires a more sophisticated theoretical understanding. In this seemingly all-encompassing moment of U.S. empire, the possibility of articulating the complex workings of racialization as it is placed on a range of social groups including Arabs, Iranians, Central Asians, South Asians, and Muslims more generally, has the capacity to reframe our understanding of U.S. racial formation in a global framework. The creation of the term Af-Pak is not strictly about a bounded sense of territory or land, but the bodies that are unnamed in this relationship. As a term of military metaphor this reveals something both in terms of globality and raciality as a combining of land with bodies in the imperial logic that informs anti-Muslim racism. Further, land does not travel in the way that people do. The Muslim immigrant is imputed with these ideas of land that also blur race and religion. Notions of modernity and nationality are most certainly about the imagined creations associated with such things as land and blood.[25] For Asian American Studies and the broader approach of ethnic studies, this analytical approach that thinks through regional and global objects of study can be found in comparative and relational research agendas that have become increasingly transnational, intersectional, and interdisciplinary. For example, Native American and indigenous studies, settler colonial studies, and queer of color critique have been central in expanding fields of study in such terms.[26] In the last two decades such critical approaches in scholarship have also witnessed the substantial production and inclusion of a number of geographic areas from South Asia and West Asia within the intellectual and scholarly debate regarding the scope of Asian American Studies within an approach that incorporates critical ethnic studies and the formation of Arab American Studies. It is to the inclusion of these geographic areas that I now turn to examine the overlapping of land and bodies in relationship to raciality, the global, and the notion of Af-Pak.

Arab-Af-Pak-Muslim

Soon after the tragedy of September 11, 2001, the social divisions that separate New York City quickly became the means to enforce hierarchies in the outer boroughs. Pakistanis live all over New York, with large concentrations in Queens, Brooklyn, and the Bronx. And yet large population shifts have occurred in the decade and a half since 9/11.[27] Initially, almost a quarter to half of the residential populations fled from the United States for fear of recrimination and potential detention under the National Security Entry-Exit Registration System of the U.S. government, popularly known as NSEERS, and ultimately potential deportation. As stability returned to these New York neighborhoods in which Pakistanis, Muslims, and other South Asians continued to live, renewal came to many of the commercial areas with a return to steady growth in residential populations.[28] Alongside this regeneration, there was also a diversification of these ethnic neighborhoods. Afghans and ethnic Pashtuns from Pakistan who fled war in their home countries, largely as immigrants rather than the specific state category of refugees, began to appear significantly in the Little Pakistan of Brooklyn. While this pattern represents a complex movement of those from Afghanistan and Pakistan, this is not simply a matter of convenience of connecting to fellow compatriots or co-religionists, but one that reflects a consolidation of ethnic neighborhoods in a post-9/11 framework. Rather than dissipating such neighborhoods, they remain known entities for law enforcement and as gateways of habitation in ethnic enclaves, particularly for those who are constrained by educational attainment and English-language proficiency. Similarly, while such neighborhoods have historically served Pakistani immigrants, increasingly service organizations have begun to also assist Arab immigrants who have moved into these neighborhoods. In other words, Little Pakistan as an ethnic neighborhood has been a receiving area that is defined in terms of class and economic ability, and increasingly in terms of religious classification through the visibility of a Muslim community with places of worship, grocery stores, restaurants, and service organizations that cater to the needs of Islamic cultural and social practice.

Nestled at the southern border of Brooklyn's Prospect Park, the larger and more unruly relative of Manhattan's more famous Central Park, are the neighborhoods Kensington, Flatbush, Midwood, and Ditmas Park that make up Little Pakistan. In this direction are the quieter, lesser known, Pakistani neighborhoods of Brooklyn. Mostly residential, immigrant, and in the nether zone between the hipper parts of Brooklyn and the infamous recreational parts of Coney Island to the south and along the beachfront, they represent an amalgamation of the ambiguity that is inherent in the conceptual apparatus of the term Af-Pak. While there are literally those who hail from Pakistan and Afghanistan living in Brooklyn's Little Pakistan, instead of the exclusive meaning of Af-Pak designated to a spatial zone of geographic territory, here I refer to the way that landscapes are inhabited by people who are racialized through uniformity despite difference. In the distant southwest corner of the Brooklyn borough is the Bayridge neighborhood that is predominantly Arab. And while by car, or even seen from a map, these areas might seem close, from the vantage of public transportation, whether by bus or subway system, the distance between Little Pakistan and Arab Bayridge can end up taking more time to reach than, say, a quick trip into Manhattan. Between these concentrations of ethnic Muslim neighborhoods are a range of immigrant neighborhoods that include older European populations including Russian and Jewish migrations, and more recent Latina/os, Chinese, and others. Scattered throughout these southern neighborhoods are burgeoning ethnic commercial areas with shopping and restaurants that do not cater to tourists but to the working poor who often live and work in the surrounding areas. Amidst this immigrant diversity is a wide array of inhabitants that include those who will go to Little Pakistan or Bayridge for the ethnic stores and restaurants and services that cater to Arabic, Urdu, Bangla, and Hindi speakers. Yet, these areas go even beyond this spectrum. For example, the Black Muslim populations that surround say the commercial strip of Coney Island Avenue of Little Pakistan, and often live in these areas, will often visit these neighborhoods for specific purposes such as performing prayers at local mosques or shopping that might include visiting a halal butcher in Midwood. The interplay of Arab, Afghan, and Pakistani, has become even more apparent in the social services provided by community-based organizations that cater to specifically Muslim needs whether through services for the elderly, English-language training, or youth programs. For local community organizers this shift in the demographic needs is directly attributable to the patterns that have forced immigrants from their home countries because of the ravages of war and economic and social hard-times. The War on Terror has created new social patterns of habitation in the ethnic enclaves of New York's outer boroughs, in which a complex array of Arabs and Afghans come to Little Pakistan seeking aid and help. This creates specific demands on the community service workers who are challenged by single language speakers. Arab immigrants are often referred to organizations in Bayridge that have Arabic language services, whereas Afghans who speak Pashto are easily incorporated into the community that serves Pakistani immigrants. Because ethnic Pashtuns who speak Pashto and are part of this border region between Pakistan and Afghanistan, there is a shared culture and language that facilitates this process. Indeed, Pashtuns are an important component of the Little Pakistan of Brooklyn although their numbers do not reflect the larger ethnic breakdown of Punjabis and Kashmiris who have historically lived in this neighborhood. Significantly, Pashtuns have been arriving in the New York City area for much of the last century as sailors who at times have jumped ship and intermarried among local communities of color.[29]

What this broad description of ethnic Muslim neighborhoods in Brooklyn shows, is the way that Af-Pak as a conceptual descriptor is implicit in the ways that social structure and urban organization is layered. While in some senses this is always the case for immigrant neighborhoods and ethnic enclaves, in this case, what is also clear is that these Muslim communities of these neighborhoods are part of an economic and social assemblage that repeats a false rationale of the racial figure of the Muslim as assimilable into a single category apparent in the logic of Af-Pak. In the ways that immigrants have often been tied to nationalities of home countries, in the case of the Little Pakistan of Brooklyn it also important to point out that a significant number of the inhabitants of this neighborhood are U.S. citizens. Yet they are more easily imagined as "forever foreigners" in the trope of Asian American immigration. Indeed in my own description I have relied on a short-cut to describe "Pakistani" immigrants more in terms of cultural identity rather than nationality. And there is also the equal challenge of the assumption that would have all Pakistanis as Muslims in a narrative of anti-Muslim racism, particularly when this is not the case in Pakistani Brooklyn where a significant Pakistani Christian population exists. And yet the slippage between religion and nationality is often unproblematically assumed in the conflation of Pakistanis-as-Muslims. This problem is at the heart of the difficulty of theorizing racialization as a process and the reliance on nationality as a framework from which to understand the complex shifts in transnational identity.

Whereas scholars of Asian and Arab American Studies have been at the forefront of chronicling the complex ways in which identity is produced and practiced among Arabs, Muslims, and South Asians, in the United States and throughout their diasporas, racialization presents a particular challenge that is still undertheorized. For example, scholarship in South Asian American Studies employs multiracial and comparative frameworks as a fruitful arena to contrast areas, regions, histories, and populations that are analytically separated spatially, temporally, and conceptually. Vijay Prashad's now classic, *The Karma of Brown Folk* posed "desi" as the solidarity term of those belonging to the South Asian homeland and imagined through a shared culture between Indian and Pakistani peoples and cultures.[30] While Prashad challenges readers to craft new ways of being and thinking along lines of radical solidarity, the model of shared culture has a tendency to flatten difference to favor a celebrated India as opposed to the often demonized Pakistan–or for that matter all of the nationalities, regions, cultures, and traditions—that do not fall into this shared culture. This is certainly not Prashad's intention, particularly with the turn to polyculturalism,[31] it is however one of the unfortunate scholarly and activist practices that are difficult to overcome given the language and models to discuss immigration and communities of color. More recently critical work has attempted to bridge these divides that include complex analysis of how social science approaches the study of categories that span from South Asian America to Arab America.[32]

Indeed what is happening in the theaters of the War on Terror in Pakistan and Afghanistan has repercussions in the U.S. From patterns of migration to the increase in refugee populations, to the social and political consequences of military campaigns, in this essay I have sketched how Af-Pak as a term works as an oblique provocation that brings together area studies of South and Central Asia into a dialogue with a critical approach to Asian American Studies and ethnic studies. As scholarship in these fields has shown, the geographies of U.S. imperial formation have also been resisted and responded to through the interconnections of solidarity and intermixture. The racial and imperial cartography of which Af-Pak is now a part is also a way to understand how land and bodies are wrapped into geographies and histories. Af-Pak is a quick and easy term. It renders two different nation-states into a zone of borderlands and buffers—what I called at the outset the literal no-body's land. Yet the notion that these spaces are not meant for anyone is absolutely quite the opposite—from other vantage points they are venerable homelands of peoples with history and an important past that is significant to the contemporary moment. As the expression of Af-Pak signifies, this is also a condition in which the meaning of this zone is about a globality in the War on Terror that defines a process of racialization. As these idioms travel, the insight that is to be gained is to elaborate how terms such as Af-Pak generate racial meanings and targeted populations without seeming to have this purpose.

Notes

1 The Great Game refers to the political and economic struggle that the British and Russian imperial powers fought over Afghanistan and Central Asia in the 19th century. In the late 20th century this was replaced by a war with the Soviet Union and Afghan factions supported and trained by the United States and Pakistan such as the Taliban. The most obvious dog-whistle code word at work with Af-Pak is that of the Taliban and the importance of water, oil, and gas politics. See part 3 "The New Great Game" of Rashid, Ahmed. 2001. *Taliban: Militant Islam, Oil, and Fundamentalism in Central Asia*. New Haven, CT: Yale University Press.
2 Kaplan, Amy. 2006. "Where is Guantanamo?" *American Quarterly* 57 (3): 831–858.
3 Bayoumi, Moustafa. 2006. "Racing Religion." *New Centennial Review* 6 (2): 267–293; Bayoumi, Moustafa. 2015. *This Muslim American Life: Dispatches From the War on Terror*. New York: New York University Press; Jamal, Amaney A., and Nadine Christine Naber. 2008. *Race and Arab Americans Before And After 9/11: From Invisible Citizens to Visible Subjects*. 1st ed. Syracuse, NY: Syracuse University Press; Razack, Sherene. 2007. *Casting Out: The Eviction of Muslims from Western Law And Politics*. Toronto: University of Toronto Press; Salaita, Steven. 2006. *Anti-Arab Racism in the USA: Where It Comes From and What it Means For Politics Today*. London; Ann Arbor, MI: Pluto Press.
4 Rana, Junaid. 2011. *Terrifying Muslims: Race and Labor in the South Asian Diaspora*. Durham, NC: Duke University Press.

5 Gualtieri, Sarah M. A. 2009. *Between Arab and White: Race And Ethnicity in The Early Syrian American diaspora*. Berkeley, CA: University of California Press; op. cit. Salaita 2006.
6 See for example Lowe, Lisa. 1996. *Immigrant Acts: On Asian American Cultural Politics*. Durham, NC: Duke University Press; and Lowe, Lisa. 2015. *The intimacies of four continents*. Durham, NC: Duke University Press.
7 Rana, Junaid. Forthcoming. "The Racial Infrastructure of the Terror-Industrial Complex."
8 Weheliye, Alexander G. 2014. *Habeas viscus: Racializing Assemblages, Biopolitics, and Black Feminist Theories of the Human*. Durham, NC: Duke University Press.
9 Spillers, Hortense J. 2003. *Black, White, and in Color: Essays on American Literature and Culture*. Chicago, IL: University of Chicago Press; Wynter, Sylvia, 2003. "Unsettling the Coloniality of Being/Power/Truth/Freedom: Towards the Human, After Man, Its Overrepresentation—An Argument." *CR: The New Centennial Review* 3 (3): 257–337; McKittrick, Katherine. Ed. 2015. *Sylvia Wynter : On Being Human as Praxis*. Durham, NC: Duke University Press.
10 Sexton, Jared. 2007. "Racial Profiling and the Societies of Control." In *Warfare in the American Homeland: Policing and Prison in a Penal Democracy*. James, Joy. Ed. Durham, NC: Duke University Press.
11 Day, Iyko. 2015. "Being or Nothingness: Indigeneity, Antiblackness, and Settler Colonial Critique". *Critical Ethnic Studies* 1 (2): 102–21.
12 Daulatzai, Sohail. 2012. *Black Star, Crescent Moon: The Muslim International and Black Freedom beyond America*. Minneapolis, MN: University of Minnesota Press. This formation is a rich one that can be ascertained in a range of radical and progressive thought, for example see: Aydin, Cemil. 2007. *The Politics of Anti-Westernism in Asia: Visions of World Order in Pan-Islamic and Pan-Asian Thought, Columbia Studies in International and Global History*. New York: Columbia University Press; and Khuri-Makdisi, Ilham. 2010. *The Eastern Mediterranean and the Making of Global Radicalism, 1860–1914, The California World History Library*. Berkeley, CA: University of California Press.
13 Sohi, Seema. 2014. *Echoes of Mutiny: Race, Surveillance, and Indian Anticolonialism in North America*. Oxford: Oxford University Press. See also Bald, Vivek. 2013. *Bengali Harlem and the Lost Histories of South Asian America*. Cambridge, MA: Harvard University Press; and Ramnath, Maia. 2011. *Haj to Utopia: How the Ghadar Movement Charted Global Radicalism and Attempted to Overthrow the British Empire*, Berkeley, CA: University of California Press.
14 Silva, Denise Ferreira da. 2007. *Toward a Global Idea of Race*. Minneapolis: University of Minnesota Press; Silva, Denise Ferreira da. 2009 "No-Bodies: Law, Raciality, Violence." *Griffith Law Review* 18: 212–236; Silva, Denise Ferreira da. 2013 "To Be Announced: Radical Praxis or Knowing (at) the Limits of Justice." *Social Text*. 31(114): 43–62.
15 Similarly, this domain of ethical and historical formation is the arena in which Sherene Razack argues Muslims are 'cast out' of western law and politics, Razack op.cit., 2007.
16 Silva op.cit., 2009, 213.
17 Fanon, Frantz. 2004 [1965]. *The Wretched of the Earth*. Translated From the French by Richard Philcox; Introductions by Jean-Paul Sartre and Homi K. Bhabha. New York: Grove Press.
18 Amar, Paul. 2013. *The Security Archipelago ; Human-Security States, Sexuality Politics, and the End of Neoliberalism*. Durham, NC: Duke University Press.
19 Mbembe, Achille. 2003. "Necropolitics." *Public Culture* 15: 11–40.
20 Helene Cooper, "Choosing Which War to Fight," *New York Times*, February 24, 2008. The complete quote is as follows: "There is a theater of war, that I would call AfPak, with two fronts—an eastern front and a western front," said Richard Holbrooke, the former United States ambassador to the United Nations and a supporter of Mrs. Clinton's. "I believe that we will look back ten years from now and say that AfPak was even more important to our national security than Iraq."
21 Part of the zone that is considered to be Af-Pak region consists of the formerly named North-West Frontier Province that borders Afghanistan on the Pakistan side. The Province has recently been renamed the Khyber-Pakhtunkhwa Province denoting the two sides of the Pakthun or Pashtun peoples with the Pakistan side demarcated by the Khyber Pass.
22 For more on the recent military pact between the US and Pakistan see Rana, Junaid. 2012 [2014]. "The Desperate U.S.–Pakistan Alliance." In *Dispatches from Pakistan*, edited by Vijay Prashad Qalandar Memon, and Madiha Tahir. New Delhi: LeftWord Books (Republished Minneapolis, MN: University of Minnesota Press).

23 Jung, Moon-Kie. 2015. *Beneath the Surface of White Supremacy: Denaturalizing U.S. Racisms Past and Present*. Stanford, CA: Stanford University Press. See also Cooper, Frederick. 2005. *Colonialism in Question: Theory, Knowledge, History*. Berkeley, CA: University of California Press.

24 Ronak K. Kapadia, "Up in the Air and On the Skin: Wafaa Bilal, Drone Warfare, and the Human Terrain," in *Shifting Borders: America and the Middle East/North Africa*, Ed. Alex Lubin (Beirut: American University of Beirut Press, 2014): 147–163; Ronak K. Kapadia "Up in the Air and On the Skin: Drone Warfare and the Queer Calculus of Pain" in *Critical Ethnic Studies: An Anthology* (Durham, NC: Duke University Press, 2016); Feldman, Keith. 2011. "Empire's Verticality: The Af/Pak Frontier, Visual Culture, and Racialization from Above." *Comparative American Studies* 9 (4): 325–341.

25 On the connection of modernity, liberalism, and racial state formation see Goldberg, David Theo. 2002. *The Racial State*. Cambridge: Blackwell; Goldberg, David Theo. 1993. *Racist Culture: Philosophy and the Politics of Meaning*. Cambridge: Blackwell. The classic study of nationalism is Anderson, Benedict. 1983. *Imagined Communities: Reflections on the Origin and Spread of Nationalism*. London: Verso.

26 Examples of this work include: Barker, Joanne. Ed. 2005. *Sovereignty Matters: Locations of Contestation and Possibility in Indigenous Struggles for Self-Determination*. Lincoln, NE: University of Nebraska Press; Byrd, Jodi A. 2011. *The Transit of Empire: Indigenous Critiques of Colonialism*. Minneapolis, MN: University of Minnesota Press; Gopinath, Gayatri. 2008. "Queer Regions Locating Lesbians in Sancharram." In *A Companion to Lesbian, Gay, Bisexual, Transgender, and Queer Studies*, 341–354. Blackwell Publishing Ltd.; Manalansan IV, Martin F. 2006. "Queer Intersections: Sexuality and Gender in Migration Studies." *International Migration Review* 40 (1): 224–249.

27 "Profile of New York City's Pakistani Americans: 2013 Edition." Asian American Federation Census Information Center. 2013. Available at www.aafederation.org/cic/ethnic.asp. Accessed October 16, 2016.

28 "Demographic Profile of Flatbush, Kensington, and Midwood." Asian American Federation Census Information Center. September 2015. Available at www.aafederation.org/cic/geo.asp. Accessed October 16, 2016.

29 Many of the cases I encountered reflect the history described by Vivek Bald 2013, op. cit.

30 Prashad, Vijay. 2000. *The Karma of Brown Folk*. Minneapolis, MN: University of Minnesota.

31 Prashad, Vijay. 2001. *Everybody was Kung Fu Fighting: Afro-Asian Connections and the Myth of Cultural Purity*. Boston, MA: Beacon Press.

32 Examples relevant to this include: Alsultany, Evelyn. 2012. *Arabs and Muslims in the media: race and representation after 9/11*. New York: New York University Press; Cainkar, Louise. 2009. *Homeland insecurity: the Arab American and Muslim American experience after 9/11*. 1st ed. New York: Russell Sage Foundation; Maira, Sunaina. 2009. *Missing: Youth, Citizenship, and Empire After 9/11*. Durham, NC: Duke University; Maira, Sunaina, and Magid Shihade. 2006. "Meeting Asian/Arab American Studies: Thinking Race, Empire, and Zionism in the U.S." *Journal of Asian American Studies* 9 (2): 117–140; Naber, Nadine Christine. 2012. *Arab America: Gender, Cultural Politics, and Activism*. New York: New York University Press; Rudrappa, Sharmila. 2004. *Ethnic Routes to Becoming American: Indian immigrants and the Cultures of Citizenship*. New Brunswick, NJ: Rutgers University Press; Shankar, Shalini. 2008. *Desi Land: Teen Culture, Class, and Success in Silicon Valley*. Durham, NC: Duke University Press; Visweswaran, Kamala. 2010. *Un/Common Cultures: Racism and the Rearticulation of Cultural Difference*. Durham, NC: Duke University Press.

References

Alsultany, Evelyn. 2012. *Arabs and Muslims in the Media: Race and Representation after 9/11*. New York: New York University Press.

Amar, Paul. 2013. *The Security Archipelago; Human-Security States, Sexuality Politics, and the End of Neoliberalism*. Durham, NC: Duke University Press.

Anderson, Benedict. 1983. *Imagined Communities: Reflections on the Origin and Spread of Nationalism*. London: Verso.

Aydin, Cemil. 2007. *The Politics of Anti-Westernism in Asia: Visions of World Order in Pan-Islamic and Pan-Asian Thought*. New York: Columbia University Press.

Bald, Vivek. 2013. *Bengali Harlem and the Lost Histories of South Asian America*. Cambridge, MA: Harvard University Press.

Barker, Joanne. Ed. 2005. *Sovereignty Matters: Locations of Contestation and Possibility in Indigenous Struggles For Self-Determination*. Lincoln, NE: University of Nebraska Press.
Bayoumi, Moustafa. 2006. "Racing Religion." *New Centennial Review* 6 (2):267–293.
Bayoumi, Moustafa. 2015. *This Muslim American Life: Dispatches From the War on Terror*. New York: New York University Press.
Byrd, Jodi A. 2011. *The Transit of Empire : Indigenous Critiques of Colonialism*, First peoples: new directions. Minneapolis, MN: University of Minnesota Press.
Cainkar, Louise. 2009. *Homeland Insecurity: The Arab American and Muslim American Experience After 9/11*. 1st ed. New York: Russell Sage Foundation.
Cooper, Frederick. 2005. *Colonialism in Question: Theory, Knowledge, History*. Berkeley, CA: University of California Press.
Daulatzai, Sohail. 2012. *Black Star, Crescent Moon: The Muslim International and Black Freedom beyond America*. Minneapolis, MN: University of Minnesota Press.
Day, Iyko. 2015. "Being or Nothingness: Indigeneity, Antiblackness, and Settler Colonial Critique". *Critical Ethnic Studies* 1 (2). 102–121.
Fanon, Frantz. 2004 [1965]. *The Wretched of The Earth*; translated from the French by Richard Philcox; introductions by Jean-Paul Sartre and Homi K. Bhabha. New York: Grove Press.
Feldman, Keith. 2011. "Empire's Verticality: The Af/Pak Frontier, Visual Culture, and Racialization from Above." *Comparative American Studies* 9 (4): 325–341.
Goldberg, David Theo. 1993. *Racist Culture: Philosophy and the Politics of Meaning*. Cambridge: Blackwell.
Goldberg, David Theo. 2002. *The Racial State*. Cambridge: Blackwell.
Gopinath, Gayatri. 2008. "Queer Regions Locating Lesbians in Sancharram." In *A Companion to Lesbian, Gay, Bisexual, Transgender, and Queer Studies*, 341–354. Blackwell Publishing Ltd.
Gualtieri, Sarah M. A. 2009. *Between Arab and White: Race and Ethnicity in the Early Syrian American Diaspora*. Berkeley, CA: University of California Press
Jamal, Amaney A., and Nadine Christine Naber. 2008. *Race and Arab Americans Before and After 9/11: From Invisible Citizens to Visible Subjects*. 1st ed, Arab American writing. Syracuse, NY: Syracuse University Press.
Jung, Moon-Kie. 2015. *Beneath the Surface of White Supremacy: Denaturalizing U.S. Racisms Past and Present*. Stanford, CA: Stanford University Press.
Kapadia, Ronak K. 2014. "Up in the Air and On the Skin: Wafaa Bilal, Drone Warfare, and the Human Terrain." In *Shifting Borders: America and the Middle East/North Africa*, 147–163, Ed. Alex Lubin Beirut: American University of Beirut Press.
Kapadia, Ronak K. 2016. "Up in the Air and On the Skin: Drone Warfare and the Queer Calculus of Pain" in *Critical Ethnic Studies: An Anthology* Durham, NC: Duke University Press.
Kaplan, Amy. 2006. "Where is Guantanamo?" *American Quarterly* 57 (3): 831–858.
Khuri-Makdisi, Ilham. 2010. *The Eastern Mediterranean and the Making of Global Radicalism, 1860–1914*. Berkeley, CA: University of California Press.
Lowe, Lisa. 1996. *Immigrant Acts: On Asian American Cultural Politics*. Durham, NC: Duke University Press.
Lowe, Lisa. 2015. *The Intimacies of Four Continents*. Durham, NC: Duke University Press.
Maira, Sunaina. 2009. *Missing: Youth, Citizenship, and Empire After 9/11*. Durham, NC: Duke University.
Maira, Sunaina, and Magid Shihade. 2006. "Meeting Asian/Arab American Studies: Thinking Race, Empire, and Zionism in the U.S." *Journal of Asian American Studies* 9 (2): 117–140.
Manalansan IV, Martin F. 2006. "Queer Intersections: Sexuality and Gender in Migration Studies." *International Migration Review* 40 (1): 224–249.
Mbembe, Achille. 2003. "Necropolitics." *Public Culture* 15: 11–40.
McKittrick, Katherine. Ed. 2015. *Sylvia Wynter: on Being Human as Praxis*. Durham, NC: Duke University Press.
Naber, Nadine Christine. 2012. *Arab America: Gender, Cultural Politics, and Activism*. New York: New York University Press.
Prashad, Vijay. 2000. *The Karma of Brown Folk*. Minneapolis, MN: University of Minnesota.
Prashad, Vijay. 2001. *Everybody was Kung Fu Fighting: Afro-Asian Connections and the Myth of Cultural Purity*. Boston, MA: Beacon Press.
Ramnath, Maia. 2011. *Haj to Utopia: how the Ghadar movement charted global radicalism and attempted to overthrow the British empire*. Berkeley, CA: University of California Press.

Rana, Junaid. 2011. *Terrifying Muslims: Race and Labor in the South Asian Diaspora*. Durham, NC: Duke University Press.

Rana, Junaid. 2012 [2014]. "The Desperate U.S.–Pakistan Alliance." In *Dispatches from Pakistan*, edited by Vijay Prashad Qalandar Memon, and Madiha Tahir. New Delhi: LeftWord Books (Republished Minneapolis, MN: University of Minnesota Press).

Rana, Junaid. Forthcoming. "The Racial Infrastructure of the Terror-Industrial Complex."

Rashid, Ahmed. 2001. *Taliban: Militant Islam, Oil, and Fundamentalism in Central Asia*. New Haven, CT: Yale University Press.

Razack, Sherene. 2007. *Casting Out: The Eviction of Muslims From Western Law and Politics*. Toronto: University of Toronto Press.

Rudrappa, Sharmila. 2004. *Ethnic Routes to Becoming American: Indian Immigrants and the Cultures of Citizenship*. New Brunswick, NJ: Rutgers University Press.

Salaita, Steven. 2006. *Anti-Arab Racism in the Usa: Where it Comes From and What it Means For Politics Today*. London; Ann Arbor, MI: Pluto Press.

Sexton, Jared. 2007. "Racial Profiling and the Societies of Control." In *Warfare in the American Homeland: Policing and Prison in a Penal Democracy*. James, Joy. Ed. Durham, NC: Duke University Press.

Shankar, Shalini. 2008. *Desi Land: Teen Culture, Class, and Success in Silicon Valley*. Durham, NC: Duke University Press.

Silva, Denise Ferreira da. 2007. *Toward a Global Idea of Race*. Minneapolis, MN: University of Minnesota Press.

Silva, Denise Ferreira da. 2009. "No-Bodies: Law, Raciality, Violence." *Griffith Law Review*. 18: 212–236.

Silva, Denise Ferreira da. 2013. "To Be Announced: Radical Praxis or Knowing (at) the Limits of Justice." Social Text. 31(114): 43–62.

Sohi, Seema. 2014. *Echoes of Mutiny: Race, Surveillance, and Indian Anticolonialism in North America*. Oxford: Oxford University Press.

Spillers, Hortense J. 2003. *Black, White, and in Color: Essays on American Literature and Culture*. Chicago, IL: University of Chicago Press.

Visweswaran, Kamala. 2010. Un/common cultures: racism and the rearticulation of cultural difference. Durham, NC: Duke University Press.

Weheliye, Alexander G. 2014. *Habeas Viscus: Racializing Assemblages, Biopolitics, and Black Feminist Theories of the Human*. Durham, NC: Duke University Press.

Wynter, Sylvia. 2003. "Unsettling the Coloniality of Being/Power/Truth/Freedom: Towards the Human, After Man, Its Overrepresentation-An Argument." *CR: The New Centennial Review*, 3(3) 257–337.

17

THE JAPANESE AMERICAN TRANSNATIONAL GENERATION

Rethinking the Spatial and Conceptual Boundaries of Asian America

Michael Jin

In a special report on April 7, 1939, the Japanese national daily newspaper *Asahi Shimbun* announced a wedding ceremony held the previous night in Tokyo. The article celebrated the international marriage between Yukiko Tajima, a gifted graduate of prestigious women's schools in Tokyo, and Zheng Zihan, a resident scholar at Tokyo's Waseda International Institute and Keio University. Zheng was a son of the then mayor of Mukden, the industrial center of Manchuria. The groom's late grandfather, Zheng Xaoxu, had been the first prime minister of the Japanese puppet state Manchukuo when Manchuria had become an integral part of Japan's colonial empire in Asia in the early 1930s. The *Asahi Shimbun* proudly depicted the matrimony as an event that signified Tokyo as a reigning cosmopolitan center of Asia that had allowed a talented Manchu noble and a modern Japanese woman to pursue a romantic relationship across national borders.[1] The celebratory article on Tajima's wedding was a part of the efforts made by the Japanese press, under the watchful eye of the militarist government that had seized the country's political power by the late 1930s, to curtail the negative international publicity brought on by Japan's aggressive military and foreign policy.

The story of Tajima's marriage to Zheng, however, told another complex aspect of international relations. A daughter of Japanese emigrants, Tajima had been born and raised in California's Central Valley and relocated to Japan with her mother and siblings six years before, in 1933.[2] This highly educated modern Japanese woman thus had turned out to be a young immigrant from the United States. Tajima and her three siblings were far from alone in their unique position as American citizens living abroad. They were part of the Japanese American transnational generation, over 50,000 U.S.-born *Nisei* (second-generation Japanese Americans) that relocated to Japan and Japanese colonies before the Pacific War.[3] Many among these young Japanese Americans were sent to Japan by their first-generation (*Issei*) immigrant parents to acquire a Japanese education. Others, like Tajima, accompanied their Issei parents who returned to Japan or moved to Japanese colonies, such as Korea and Manchuria, when the Great Depression added to many Japanese immigrant families' struggle for survival in the United States during the era of anti-Asian exclusion. Many Nisei also embarked on transpacific journeys to various corners of the expanding Japanese empire in Asia for career opportunities that were difficult to attain in the U.S. due to racial discrimination.

While the story of Tajima's marriage to a young Manchu aristocrat in Japan was unique enough to grace a page in a major newspaper, all of the Nisei who migrated to Japan found themselves in a world that was intimately shaped by Japanese colonialism in Asia-Pacific.[4] Like Tajima, those Nisei educated in the Tokyo area were in a metropole where they interacted with students, workers, and sojourners from all corners of the Japanese empire. Some Nisei migrants and students witnessed and experienced colonies first-hand as they traveled through Korea and Manchuria for educational and employment opportunities or for the pleasure of touring the colonial frontiers.[5]

Despite the presence of a significant number of U.S.-born Nisei in Asia before World War II, these transnational individuals have rarely appeared in the popular narratives of Japanese American history. Although Japanese American history has been one of the most thoroughly researched areas within Asian American studies, the scholarship's dominant domestic framework has kept the multifaceted experiences of the Nisei transnational generation at the margins. The post-WWII Japanese American scholarship's focus on the history of mass incarceration in the American internment camps during World War II and the emphasis on Nisei loyalty to the United States have contributed to the U.S.-centered paradigm that has confined Japanese American history to the interior of the U.S. political and cultural boundaries. In the decades that followed the end of the war, many scholar-activists focusing on the injustice of the internment policy found it difficult to write about the Nisei who lived in Japan and its colonial world during the time of aggressive Japanese imperialism in Asia-Pacific. These scholars feared that inclusion of the Nisei transnational migrants in the master narrative of Japanese American history would create a backlash against the postwar movement for redress and reparations that hinged on the notion of Nisei's loyalty and hundred percent Americanism.[6] It was not until the mid-1990s, after the U.S. government issued an official apology and reparations for the Japanese American internment, that academic presses published memoirs written by these Nisei that offered remarkable complexities in their transnational experiences.[7] However, although recent scholars like Eiichiro Azuma in the United States and Kumei Teruko in Japan have written about the Nisei educated in Japan before WWII based on their important analyses of Japanese-language sources, the history of Nisei migrants in the Japanese Empire largely remains a critical missing link in the Japanese American scholarship.[8]

As Yuji Ichioka has argued, what transpired during the war years "cannot be fully comprehended without an understanding of the historical continuities and discontinuities between the 1930s and 1940s."[9] A closer look at the large contingent of American-born Nisei emigrants and sojourners who moved in multiple directions in the decades that preceded the Pacific War can serve as an important addition to that understanding. These Nisei migrants lived in a world that was actively shaped by volatile international relations between the United States and Japan. The aggressive Japanese colonial expansion in Asia and the anti-Japanese racial hostility in the United States intimately intertwined with their experiences in Japan and Japanese territories. In addition to the 50,000 Nisei migrants who worked and studied in prewar and wartime Japan, there were many young Japanese Americans who visited Japan on a variety of occasions, from visiting their relatives to joining short-term study tours sponsored by various U.S.-based Japanese organizations to experience their parents' homeland. Many of these Nisei returned to the United States with varying impressions and new perspectives on Japanese culture, politics, society, and colonialism. Thus, Nisei's contact with Japan and the movements of Japanese Americans across the Pacific in both directions were common throughout the decade before the war.

In other words, the Nisei transnational experience was a norm rather than the exception in Japanese American history. The presence of 50,000 U.S.-born Nisei in the Japanese Empire necessitates the geographical, temporal, and spatial reconceptualization of the second-generation experience in Asian American studies. Many works of immigration and ethnic studies on second-generation transnationalism have focused on the U.S.-born children of immigrants as groups that are physically and culturally rooted in the United States whose transnational engagement is shaped almost exclusively by their ethnic or diasporic affiliation within the U.S. political borders. On the other hand, the Nisei migrants in the Japanese Empire found themselves at the crossroads of Asian history and Asian American history. They encountered multiple social, linguistic, political, and legal systems, as well as different racial and national ideologies across borders. The history of these "forgotten Nisei" that traversed the Pacific before WWII reveals complex interconnections among U.S. social, political, and cultural history, the history of Japanese colonialism in Asia-Pacific, and the history of migration. Upon relocation to Japan, Nisei migrants of different ages and diverse social backgrounds went through experiences that made them a unique group of American citizens living abroad. I argue that this history of second-generation Asian Americans was not merely an anomaly in Asian American studies; it must be understood in the context of larger, international, and transnational legal, political, and cultural history.

Jim Crow in the American West and the Making of the Japanese American Diaspora

By the time Yukiko Tajima began her studies at Keisen Girls' School in Tokyo in the mid-1930s, Japan's position as a formidable colonial power in Asia-Pacific lured a significant number of Japanese Americans from the United States. According to the Japanese Home Ministry and Foreign Ministry records, the number of U.S.-born Japanese Americans residing in Japan remained consistently at close to 20,000 between the mid-1930s and the eve of Pearl Harbor. Yamashita Soen, a Hiroshima-born journalist who had lived in Hawaii, wrote extensively about Nisei from Hawaii and the U.S. mainland in Japan in the 1930s. Yamashita claimed that as early as 1931, Hiroshima and Yamaguchi, two prefectures that had sent large numbers of emigrants to North America and Hawaii in the late eighteenth and early nineteenth centuries, had more than 20,000 Nisei. Yamashita also believed that by the middle of the 1930s, 40,000 Nisei had arrived in Japan as young children.[10]

The circumstances that compelled a significant number of American-born Nisei to embark on transpacific journeys reveal social realities and racial relations in the United States that affected life decisions in the Japanese American community. Many of the Japanese Americans that relocated to Japan were either infants or young children accompanying their immigrant parents who returned to Japan. In the 1910s and 1920s, anti-Asian and anti-immigrant sentiment in the United States culminated in legal measures that forced many Japanese immigrants in the agricultural and business sectors to rethink their future in America and opt for return migration. Young Nisei eighth-grader Koh Chiba followed his Issei father's return journey to Japan in 1921 after the California Alien Land Law had stripped his family of the right to own or lease property and denied them the opportunity to build a viable economic future in the United States. Chiba's father learned from his correspondents in Japan that Manchuria had emerged as the next destination for Japanese emigrants in search of land and opportunities. Shortly after the family's relocation to Japan in 1921, he managed to secure a job in Manchuria, joining some 150,000 Japanese agricultural settlers in the future colony. After graduating from middle school in Manchuria, Koh Chiba moved to Tokyo to settle permanently in his parents' homeland and live the rest of his life as a Japanese citizen.[11]

Yukiko Tajima also followed her family's return migration to Japan. Yukiko's father, Takayuki Tajima, had left his hometown in Hiroshima Prefecture in 1905 to settle in California, where he would establish himself as the Central Valley's "lettuce king." Within fifteen years after his arrival in the United States, Takayuki Tajima had become the number-one lettuce farmer in San Benito County, transporting as much as sixteen cargo cars of lettuces to New York in the spring of 1920.[12] However, the Alien Land Law and the Great Depression worked in tandem to drive Takayuki out of business by 1931. After his attempt to reestablish his lettuce kingdom in Napa Valley ended in a failure two years later, he committed suicide. Yukiko Tajima had turned sixteen when she accompanied her dejected mother and siblings in their journey to Tokyo in November 1933 to begin a new life in Japan on a small sum of insurance money.[13]

Many among the Japanese immigrants who decided to stay put in the United States despite the hardships sent their young American-born children to be raised by their relatives in Japan. For these Issei parents, this was a sensible economic option especially during the Great Depression. When both the Issei mother and father needed to work, sending at least one child to their relatives in Japan alleviated the cost and labor associated with childcare. This was not a practice unique to Japanese families in the United States, as first-generation Italian immigrants were also known to send their American-born children to Italy to live with relatives during this period.[14]

In the 1920s and 1930s, bilingual and bicultural education became another important reason for many Issei parents to send their children to Japan. As Yuji Ichioka has noted, Issei community leaders in the United States saw transnational education as both an ideological and practical solution to cultivating future leaders of the Japanese American community, as the exclusionist movement in the United States during the 1920s compounded the economic hardships of Japanese immigrant families. The anti-Asian and anti-immigrant sentiment that culminated in the Johnson–Reed Act of 1924, which placed a restrictive quota on the annual number of immigrants and effectively blocked the entrance of new Japanese migrants to the United States, proved to be especially devastating to the image of Japanese immigrants. This new immigration law convinced Issei leaders that as a group of excluded immigrants, they could not effectively fend off the anti-Japanese sentiment on the U.S. West Coast that was only growing stronger. Issei intellectuals such as Abiko Kyutaro vigorously promoted the idea that the future of the Japanese American community and the legacy of Japanese immigration to the United States depended on the second generation, who were American citizens by birth. Immigrant leaders argued that Nisei children should be raised as truly bicultural leaders in order to assume the role of a "bridge of understanding" (*kakehashi*) between Japan and the United States.[15] According to this ideal, Nisei could become truly bicultural only when they had armed themselves with the knowledge and understanding of their parents' homeland. Only then would they be able to communicate effectively with the American public and combat the cultural and political misunderstanding that had caused exclusionist movement against the Japanese in the United States.[16]

Driven by the "bridge of understanding" ideal, Japanese American newspapers, prefectural associations (*kenjinkai*), religious organizations, and other community groups sponsored "Nisei study tours" (*kengakudan*) to Japan from the mid-1920s to early 1940s.[17] These study tours lasted several weeks and gave young Japanese American students opportunities to visit major industrial centers and tourist destinations in Japan. In the 1930s, Nisei study tours included excursions to the Japanese colonies of Korea and Manchuria.[18] Kay Tateishi, a Nisei from Southern California and a future migrant to Japan, visited Tokyo in 1934 on a program sponsored by the Young Buddhist Association. After Tokyo, Tateishi's group toured various cities and towns in Japan, as well as Korea and Manchukuo. While Japanese culture and customs did not impress Tateishi much, he thought Japanese city folks were "more modern" than "humble" Japanese immigrants and their American children in rural California towns.[19]

A growing number of Nisei young adults and teenagers during this period believed that relocation to Japan would offer career opportunities that were difficult to attain in the United States due to institutional racism and anti-Japanese hostility on the U.S. West Coast. Before World War II, even Japanese Americans with college degrees struggled to secure employment outside the Japanese American ethnic community. There was a growing sentiment within the Japanese American community on the U.S. West Coast that Nisei's U.S. citizenship did not guarantee their full acceptance into American society. The immediate and practical concern was that the existing racial hostility and discriminatory social institutions in the U.S. not only affected the lives of first-generation Japanese immigrant parents, but also threatened their U.S.-born children's chance of building desirable careers in business, public service, and professional fields outside the ethnic community.[20] To some Nisei in the U.S., exploring their career options in the expanding Japanese empire seemed like a logical alternative, if they could learn to speak Japanese well enough. The increasing Japanese economic and political might in Asia-Pacific also compelled Issei parents to urge their children to explore opportunities in the potentially lucrative field of international commerce between the U.S. and Japan.[21]

However, while those Nisei migrants with means and abilities did capitalize on the opportunities abroad, many Japanese Americans that relocated to their parents' homeland would find out that establishing a viable career in the Japanese Empire was not as easy as they had hoped. Many Nisei in Japan faced language barriers and had difficulties understanding the nuances of Japanese customs in the business and professional world. A 1939 survey of 400 Japanese Americans in the Tokyo metropolitan area conducted by Nisei students at Keisen Girls' School in Tokyo revealed that the majority of the Nisei respondents in Japan had "continued the same type of work" in retail and agriculture that they had done in the United States before their relocation to Japan.[22] That same year, the Tokyo-based *Japan Times Weekly* warned young Japanese Americans not to be fooled by the false notion that they could automatically find better jobs in Japan.[23] Many of the Japanese Americans who relocated to their parents' homeland with a romantic idea that they would be welcome by the Japanese with open arms would soon come to the realization that despite their purported diasporic identity as Japanese, they were, after all, immigrants in a "host society."

Moreover, many Japanese Americans that had relocated to Japan to escape racial discrimination in the United States found themselves confronting a society with a system of racial ideologies and hierarchy of its own in an expanding colonial world. For example, in Hiroshima, a site of major munitions plants, many Nisei migrants witnessed the plight of conscripted laborers from Korea under the Japanese colonial rule and the vicious social discrimination that these colonial subjects faced. Some Japanese Americans in Japan became fed up with Japanese imperialism in Asia altogether, as well as what they viewed as increasing signs of fascism in Japan. San Francisco native Karl Ichiro Akiya, one of the first Nisei to set foot on Japanese soil, became a labor activist while in Japan and grew resentful of Japanese militarism, so much so that he decided to return to the United States and face the system of racial oppression instead. A lifelong activist and leftist intellectual, Akiya later reflected in an interview, "It was through my experience in Japan that I dedicated my life to the emancipation of all peoples . . . and especially the common people of Japan . . . [because in Japan, I] learned the meaning of fascism and learned to fight against its oppressive measures."[24] Not all Japanese American migrants shared the kind of internationalism that Akiya had developed in Japan. Nevertheless, their exposure to the complex social realities in Japan and its colonial empire shattered many Nisei migrants' romantic ideas about Japan as home in their diasporic consciousness. Disillusioned by the life in Japan, many Nisei migrants returned to the United States before World War II.

Also, in the latter half of the 1930s, Japanese American community groups in the United States began a movement to bring back the young Nisei from Japan. According to the contemporary accounts, many Issei parents nearing retirement age wished the return of their children—especially their sons who had reached adulthood—from Japan to take over the family farms and businesses.[25] Led by the Japanese Association of North America, the *Kibei Undō*— the campaign to encourage Nisei in Japan to return to the U.S.— brought back thousands of Nisei from Japan.[26] By the eve of Pearl Harbor, 10,000–20,000 Japanese Americans returned to the United States from their sojourns in the Japanese Empire and became known as *Kibei* ("returned to America").[27]

Yet, Japanese Americans continued to make transpacific journeys to Japan, some still lured by Japan's colonial success in Asia and others under various personal circumstances. On the eve of Pearl Harbor, despite the heightened U.S.–Japan diplomatic tension, Japan still attracted a few Nisei in the United States who wanted to pursue opportunities in education and employment. However, while the expansion of the Japanese Empire indeed offered these Nisei ideal career opportunities, it also meant that some Nisei migrants now found themselves working as agents of Japanese colonialism. For example, Kazumaro Uyeno, a California native, landed a well-paying position as a press attaché at the Central Broadcasting Station in Changchun, the capital of the Japanese puppet state Manchukuo in northeast China. Others joined the South Manchurian Railroad Company, a key vehicle of Japanese colonial expansion into the Chinese subcontinent since the early twentieth century. Less than two weeks before Pearl Harbor, Hawaiian Nisei Bill Ishikawa started his post at the Japanese Consulate General in Nanjing, China, the city ravaged by a brutal massacre at the hands of the Japanese invaders four years before.[28] When the aggressive Japanese military expansion into Asia compounded the already hostile U.S.–Japan relations, these Japanese American migrants proved to be valuable assets to the Japanese government, media outlets, and some of the leading Japanese corporations that tapped the bilingual Nisei from the United States as spokespersons for the ideal of "Greater East Asia Co-Prosperity Sphere," the motto for the Japanese Empire in the Pacific.

The Japanese government itself took part in recruiting Nisei from North America as potential cultural brokers that could promote positive images of the Japanese Empire. In 1939, the Japanese Ministry of Foreign Affairs established a school called Heishikan in the outskirts of Tokyo that educated these Nisei. Kawai Tatsuo, director of the Ministry's Intelligence Bureau who had served as a consul and first minister in Canada and the United States, carefully devised a plan to place the graduates of Heishikan in positions in public relations at major companies like the Southern Manchurian Railroads on Japan's colonial frontier. Also, the two-year education at Heishikan would offer Nisei graduates employment as English correspondents at the Tokyo-based *Japan Times* and Domei News Agency. The two-year scholarship and opportunities to work for prominent companies and press outlets attracted applications from many Nisei in North America.[29]

Kay Tateishi, who had dropped out of college in 1936 because of financial difficulties, seized the opportunity to compete for a two-year scholarship and a chance to work as a journalist in Japan. A son of strawberry farmers in Southern California, Tateishi saw the education at Heishikan as a way out of the family farm. He later spoke on behalf of the other Nisei students at Heishikan who had little prospect of pursuing respectable careers outside the Japanese American community in the United States in spite of their education and talents:

> We didn't want to toil the earth, work in fruit and vegetable stalls and gasoline stands, handle dirty clothing and laundries, sling hash in cheap restaurants and cafeterias, or slave away as gardeners and domestics.[30]

Sam Masuda, another Southern California Nisei from Garden Grove, also fit the profile of a talented Japanese American stuck in his family farm. Masuda was a gifted debater who won the national speech contest sponsored by the Japanese American Citizens League. He was forced to drop out of high school in 1935 when his father died of illness; he then had to run his struggling family farm and later worked at a fruit and vegetable stand. Masuda nevertheless pushed himself to continue his education at Santa Ana Junior College and, after graduation, applied for the Heishikan scholarship in 1939.[31] In December 1939, Tateishi and Masuda joined the first Heishikan class that included sixteen students, fourteen men and two women, from the U.S. West Coast, Hawaii, and Canada.[32]

The curriculum at Heishikan reflected the program's focus on offering optimal courses that would train students as journalists. The students at Heishikan took classes on the Japanese Constitution, Japanese language, economics, history, geography, stenography, and composition. In addition, they learned to read Chinese characters and Japanese newspapers. Also included in the curriculum was an excursion program that offered students the opportunity to tour various historical and cultural sites throughout Japan, as well as Japan's colonies.[33]

In 1940, Heishikan sent Nisei students to Hokkaido and Sakhlin, the northernmost colonial frontiers of the Japanese Empire. Hokkaido had become a Japanese territory in 1886 and the country's second largest island, where the indigenous Ainu people had once outnumbered Japanese settlers. The vast frontier province presented the students a dramatic contrast to the crowded cities on the main island of Honshu. To California-native George Kyotow and other students in the group, Hokkaido's open scenery looked strikingly similar to that of the American countryside. The spectacular hills and lakes they visited could easily rival the most splendid national parks in North America. In Hokkaido, students also stopped by an Ainu village, where a "Japanized" native man told the history and culture of his "tribe." For Kokuro Nakata from Honolulu, this was not his first encounter with an indigenous people in a colonized land. Yet, seeing the Ainu village stimulated Nakata's curiosity and he was moved by the "simplicity" and "innocence" of the natives of Hokkaido.[34]

On the other hand, Sakhalin, then known as Karafuto Prefecture, did not impress the students as much. Tamaye Tsutsumida's excitement about the opportunity to tour this colonial territory turned into a mild disappointment when she encountered the utterly "desolate" landscape of Sakhalin. Other students thought the climate of Karafuto very disagreeable, as the cold air and perpetual cloudiness added to the island's desolateness. The itinerary on Sakhalin included Shinto shrines, museums, and agricultural settlements that had been established since the island became a Japanese territory in 1905 as a result of Japan's victory over Russia in the Russo-Japanese War. The highlights of the tour included a visit to a fox farm, which supplied fur to Japan and Japanese military posts in Asia. Although most students were anxious to return to Tokyo, Kaoru Furuya from Los Angeles thought the trip was worthwhile. A short visit to the frontier had intrigued him about Sakhalin's future development and he could not wait for a chance to revisit the colony one day.[35]

The varied experiences of Japanese Americans in the Japanese colonial world thus reveal the complex interplay between Japan's expanding colonial empire and the heightened anti-Japanese sentiment and institutional racism in the United States. Whether by choice, circumstance, or coincidence, Japanese Americans who traversed the Pacific before World War II found themselves in a world that was intimately shaped by Japanese colonialism. Moreover, from the enactments of discriminatory immigration and naturalization policies in the U.S. to Japan's colonial expansion in Korea and China to the Pacific War, these Americans of Japanese ancestry found themselves mired in complex and tragic events across multiple regions in Asia-Pacific.

The Nisei Strandees in the Pacific during WWII and Japanese American History

The volatile U.S.–Japan relations in the Pacific made the issues of citizenship, loyalty, and national allegiance ever complicated and elusive for the Japanese American migrants. Many of the Nisei who relocated to Japan on the eve of Pearl Harbor would not manage to return to North America in time and became stranded in Japan when the Pacific War broke out in December 1941. For Japanese American strandees in Japan, the war would forever alter their life plans, goals, and aspirations. Moreover, although their U.S. citizenship did not compel the Japanese government to treat these Nisei as "enemy aliens," many Nisei in Japan nevertheless faced mounting pressure to fulfill their citizenship by blood and demonstrate their allegiance to the Japanese government.

Many of the Nisei Heishikan graduates remained in Tokyo during the Pacific War to serve the Japanese government as short-wave radio monitors that translated broadcast programs from Allied countries, such as Voice of America, All India Radio, and BBC News, that had been intercepted by the Japanese Foreign Ministry's Intelligence Bureau.[36] The role of Japanese Americans in wartime intelligence work for the Japanese government became the basis for the assertion made by some postwar critics of Heishikan that Kawai's brainchild essentially had been a clandestine spy school. For instance, an article published in the monthly news magazine *Gendai* in 1997 claimed that the young Nisei students at Heishikan had been indoctrinated by the Japanese government to serve Japanese colonialism and the war with the Allied Powers.[37]

However, most of the Heishikan graduates after the war dismissed the allegation that monitoring shortwave broadcasts had qualified them as Japanese spies. They even argued that their work for the Japanese government during the war was a way to fulfill their role as the "bridge of understanding" between the U.S. and Japan. They believed that the work of monitoring radio programs from the Allied nations during the war would somehow help ameliorate U.S.–Japan relations by providing the Japanese Foreign Ministry with accurate information from home. Former Heishikan student and Wapato, Washington native Norio Hide wrote to his fellow alumni in November 2006 to stress that his education at Heishikan during the war had strengthened his "international understanding" through his service to both Japan and the United States. Hide emphasized that his belief in the bridge-building ideal and the knowledge of Japan he had gained from the school had allowed him to build a career in the U.S. Department of Defense after the war and enabled him to serve effectively as a liaison between the U.S. and Japanese forces for 47 years.[38]

California-native Peter Sano's journey to Japan adds to the complexity of the Nisei experience in Japan and their citizenship during the Pacific War. Sano left for Japan in the summer of 1939 at the age of fifteen to become a *yoshi*, or an adopted son, of his childless uncle and aunt in Yamanashi Prefecture in central Japan. Sano's adoption into his uncle's household was entirely his parents' decision, but he accepted it without protest and kept no resentment at the prospect of being separated from his family in Imperial Valley. Instead, he wondered how he would learn Japanese, of which he spoke very little, and adjust to new customs and surroundings. Sano managed to learn enough Japanese that summer to enroll in middle school and relocated to Tokyo to attend high school.[39]

A dual citizen, he was eligible for draft into the Japanese military. After the Pacific War broke out, Sano returned to Yamanashi to wait for the draft order. In 1945, he was among the last group of young Japanese men who joined the army and fought in northeast China.[40] Sano was one of the hundreds of Japanese American men who were forced to serve in the Japanese military during World War II.[41] Sano served in the Kwantung Army when the Japanese military was desperately scraping through the final phase of the war. He and other troops of his regiment were trained to carry the last remaining bombs and dive under Soviet tanks. By the time they prepared for the final showdown in August 1945, however, the war had come to an end and the regiment surrendered to the Soviet army. For Sano, the end of the war was the beginning of his three-year ordeal in a Soviet POW camp in Siberia. As a prisoner of war, he was forced to perform heavy labor that included coal mining. Sano was one of over 650,000 Japanese POWs detained in Soviet camps after WWII. Upon his release, Sano was repatriated to Japan in June 1948.[42]

The experiences of Sano and other Nisei soldiers in the Japanese armed forces during WWII illuminate an important gendered dimension of loyalty and citizenship. For many Nisei male dual citizens who were stranded in Japan during the war, the Japanese government's claim of their citizenship forced them to take arms against the Allied Powers. These Nisei's military service under duress cost them their American citizenship and permanently excluded them from the dominant postwar narrative of Japanese American loyalty and Americanism in the United States. After the war, the U.S. government strictly enforced the provisions in Section 401 of the 1940 Nationality Act to take these men's U.S. citizenship away. According to this law, the Japanese Americans who served in the Japanese armed forces during the war had committed the treasonous act of "bearing arms against the United States."[43]

The Japanese Americans who lost their U.S. citizenship as a result of their service in the Japanese military were confronted with the American legal system that once again scrutinized their loyalty after the war. No longer a U.S. citizen, Peter Sano returned to the United States in 1952 as an immigrant and had to apply for naturalization to regain his citizenship. After his return to his country of birth, the former suicide bomber became an architect and a passionate peace activist who participated in anti-Vietnam war demonstrations in the 1960s and 1970s. He also refused to work on any military-related project. Sano continues to speak publicly about his wartime experiences and the danger of military indoctrination.[44]

While more than 110,000 Japanese and Japanese Americans in the United States endured mass incarceration during World War II, the war forced the Nisei in Japan to confront the question of loyalty and citizenship in different ways. However reluctant they might have been about taking up arms against the United States, the Nisei draftees in the Japanese armed forces had little choice but to fulfill their duty as Japanese citizens. More importantly, the Nisei in the Japanese Empire, both soldiers and civilians, were forced to negotiate ways to survive the war in unfamiliar territories, from the firebombed cities in Japan to the battlefronts in the Pacific to the POW camps in Siberia.

The issue of Nisei loyalty and nationalism has had a lasting impact on the public narrative of Japanese American history in the United States. Postwar scholars have grappled with the need to challenge and complicate the meanings and implications of history centered on Nisei Americanism in the context of Japanese American internment. However, a U.S.-centered national narrative that claims the loyalty of Japanese Americans has had little room for the experiences of Japanese American strandees in the Japanese Empire during World War II.

Rethinking the Boundaries of Asian America

The wartime language of loyalty and Americanism suppressed the dynamic celebration, debates, and critiques of the cultural dualism in the Japanese American community.[45] As Eiichiro Azuma notes, the war between the United States and Japan from 1941 to 1945 "culminated in a complete polarization between things Japanese and things American in each warring state." For both Issei and Nisei in the United States, it became no longer possible "to openly fancy Japanese American compatibility or their mediating roles in the Pacific."[46] Such polarizing notions of America and Japan during the war resulted in the general absence of the Nisei transnational generation and their rich, complex, and even tragic experiences in both the United States and Japan.

The history of Nisei transnational migrants demonstrates that Asian American history, immigration history, Asian history, and the history of the American West are intimately interconnected not only within the United States, but also throughout the Pacific Rim. The stories of people who encountered multiple legal and educational systems, racial ideologies, as well as cultural and linguistic barriers can challenge the salience of the linear process of assimilation and Americanization. Further studies on U.S.-born emigrants and trans-migrants in different temporal and spatial contexts will be an important addition to the transnational scholarship bridging ethnic studies and area studies.[47]

The experiences of the Nisei transnational generation in the Pacific reveal that Asian America for the second generation is not merely a place within the United States, but a multiple location in the world in constant transition. The multiplicity and multilocality of Asian America allow us to reconsider nationalities and ethnicities as ideas that are constantly reshaped by historical and political developments in both the U.S. and Asia-Pacific.[48] Japanese American transnational experiences before, during, and after WWII demonstrate a critical intersection of the histories of migration, transnational families and communities, and volatile international relations. The Japanese American diaspora before, during, and after WWII was a process contingent upon complex, unpredictable, and unexpected convergences of multiple social realities across national borders. This process reminds us of the critical need to rethink the spatial and conceptual boundaries of Asian American studies.

Notes

1 "Kyō-a no shinsen kekkonsan," *Asahi Shimbun*, April 7, 1939.
2 Ibid.
3 Paul R. Spickard, *Japanese Americans: The Formation and Transformations of an Ethnic Group* (New York: Twayne Publishers, 1996), 89, 167. See also Robert Lee's introduction to Mary Kimoto Tomita, *Dear Miye: Letters Home from Japan, 1939–1946*, edited by Robert Lee (Stanford, CA: Stanford University Press, 1995), 18–19. and Yuji Ichioka, "Introduction" in Karl G. Yoneda, *Ganbatte: Sixty-Year Struggle of a Kibei Worker* (Los Angeles, CA: Asian American Studies Center, University of California, 1983), xii.
4 There were a few third-generation (*Sansei*) Japanese Americans among the American sojourners of Japanese ancestry in the Japanese empire before World War II. However, the overwhelming majority of Japanese American transnational migrants were Nisei.
5 John Stephan's 1997 study examines the migrants and visitors (Issei and Nisei) from North America to Manchuria in the 1930s. See John Stephan, "Hijacked by Utopia: American Nikkei in Manchuria," *Amerasia Journal* 23:3 (1997).
6 For critiques of the postwar scholarship's emphasis on Japanese American loyalty, see Yuji Ichioka, "The Meaning of Loyalty: The Case of Kazumaro Buddy Uno," *Amerasia Journal* 23, no. 2 (Winter 1997–1998): 45–71; Naoko Shibusawa, "The Artist Belongs to the People: The Odyssey of Taro Yashima," *Journal of Asian American Studies* 9(3) (October 2005): 257–275. For a detailed study on the multiple representations of the history of the Japanese American internment, see Alice Yang Murray, *Historical Memories of the Japanese American Internment and the Struggle for Redress* (Stanford, CA: Stanford University Press, 2008).
7 The earliest works published in English are Jim Yoshida, *The Two Worlds of Jim Yoshida* (New York: William Morrow and Company, 1972) and Karl G. Yoneda, *Ganbatte: Sixty-Year Struggle of a Kibei*

Worker (Los Angeles, CA: Asian American Studies Center, University of California, 1983). Other examples include Mary Kimoto Tomita, *Dear Miye: Letters Home from Japan, 1939–1946*, edited by Robert Lee (Stanford, CA: Stanford University Press, 1995); Minoru Kiyota, *Beyond Loyalty: The Story of a Kibei*, translated by Linda Klepinger Keenan (Honolulu, HI: University of Hawai'i Press, 1997); Iwao Peter Sano, *One Thousand Days in Siberia: The Odyssey of a Japanese American POW* (Lincoln, NE: University of Nebraska Press, 1997). See also the accounts of Frank Hirahata, Sen Nishiyama, Kay Tateishi, and Nobuyo Yamane in *Amerasia Journal* 23:3 (1997).

8 See Chapter Six in Eiichiro Azuma, *Between Two Empires: Race, History, and Transnationalism in Japanese America* (New York: Oxford University Press, 2005); Teruko Kumei, "1930 nendai no kibei undo: amerika kokusekiho to no kanren ni oite," *Imin kenkyu* 30 (1993): 149–162. Kyoko Norma Nozaki, "'Just Like Sunshine, Like Moon (light)': The Life of Matsumi Kanemitsu, a Kibei Artist," *Kyoto Sangyo University Essays Foreign Language and Culture Series* 23 (March 2001): 35–51; Kaoru Yoshimi, "Aru nikkei amerikajin kibei nisei gaka no kojutsu seikatushi," *Nagoya University of Foreign Studies Journal of the School of Contemporary International Studies* 5 (March, 2009): 393–425; Eliko Kosaka, "Caught in Between Okinawa and Hawai'i: 'Kibei' Diaspora in Masao Yamashiro's *The Kibei Nisei*," *Amerasia Journal* 41:1 (2015): 1–14.

9 Yuji Ichioka, "Introduction" in Yuji Ichioka, *Before Internment: Essays in Prewar Japanese American History*, edited by Gordon H. Chang and Eiichiro Azuma (Stanford: Stanford University Press, 2006), 3.

10 Soen Yamashita, *Nikkei shimin no nihon ryugaku jijo* (Tokyo: Bunseisha, 1935), 179–180; Soen Yamashita, *Nichibei wo tsunagu mono* (Tokyo: Bunseisha, 1938), 266.

11 "The Forgotten Nisei," *Pacific Citizen*, December 19–25, 1975.

12 *The Morning Daily Advance* (Hollister, CA), May 19, 1920.

13 *The Evening Free Lance* (Hollister, CA), September 18, 1933.

14 Dino Cinel, *From Italy to San Francisco: The Immigrant Experience* (Stanford, CA: Stanford University Press, 1982), 127. Another study by Cinel on Italian return migrants in the early 1900s suggests that a significant number of U.S.-born Italian Americans migrated to Italy with their return migrant parents. For instance, about 75 percent of the 25,000 foreigners admitted to four major Italian ports in 1906 were U.S. citizens by birth or naturalization. See Dino Cinel, *The National Integration of Italian Return Migration, 1870–1929* (New York: Cambridge University Press, 1991), 107–107.

15 Yuji Ichioka, "Kengakudan: The Origin of Nisei Study Tours of Japan" in *Before Internment: Essays in Prewar Japanese American History*, Eds. Gordan H. Chang and Eiichiro Azuma (Palo Alto, CA: Stanford University Press, 2006), 223–227.

16 Ibid.

17 Ichioka, "Kengakudan," 72–73.

18 John Stephan, "Hijacked by Utopia: American Nikkei in Manchuria," *Amerasia Journal* 23:3 (Winter 1997–1998), 7.

19 Kay Tateishi, "An Atypical Nisei," *Amerasia Journal* 23:3 (Winter 1997–1998), 201.

20 Junichi Takeda, *Zaibei hiroshima kenjinshi* (Los Angeles, CA: Zaibei Hiroshima Kenjinshi Hakkojo, 1929), 43.

21 Yuji Ichioka, "Dai Nisei Mondai: Changing Japanese Immigrant Conceptions of the Second-Generation Problem, 1902–1941" in *Before Internment: Essays in Prewar Japanese American History*, Eds. Gordan H. Chang and Eiichiro Azuma (Palo Alto, CA: Stanford University Press, 2006), 33.

22 Keisen Girls' School, *The Nisei: A study of Their Life in Japan* (Tokyo: Keisen Girls' School, 1939), v, 16–28.

23 *Japan Times Weekly*, October 19, 1939.

24 Karl Akiya in "Why They Volunteered," *Fighting Americans, Too!* 2nd ed., Volunteers for Victory, Topaz, Utah, April 1943, Edward N. Barnhart Papers, Box 49, Folder 6, Japanese American Research Project Collections, University of California, Los Angeles Special Collections.

25 Zaibei Nihonjinkai, *Zaibei nihonjinshi* (San Francisco: Zaibei Nihonjinkai, 1940), 1117–1118; Ichioka, "Dai Nisei Mondai," 35.

26 Nagai Matsuzo, Ed., *Nichibei bunka koshoshi* (Tokyo: Yoyosha, 1952).

27 *Zaibei nihonjinshi* ["History of Japanese in America"] in 1940 reported that 10,000 Nisei returned to the United States from Japan, which left the number of Nisei remaining in Japan to be 20,000: *Zaibei nihonjinshi*, 1117–1118. Brian Hayashi notes that figures suggested by contemporary estimates were probably too low: See Brian Masaru Hayashi, *Democratizing the Enemy: The Japanese American Internment*

(Princeton, NJ: Princeton University Press, 2004), 44–45, 238n11.
28 "Heishikan kiroku," *Heishikan News*, June 5, 1942.
29 *Heishikan News*, August 10, 1940.
30 Tateishi, "An Atypical Nisei," 199, 203.
31 *Heishikan Newsletter*, June 2004.
32 *Heishikan News*, August 10, 1940.
33 "Heishikan no yurai oyobi genjo," *Heishikan News*, August 10, 1940.
34 "Hokkaido, karafuto kengaku ryoko," *Heishikan News*, September 16, 1940.
35 Ibid.
36 Norizane Ikeda, *Hinomaru awa: taibei boryaku hoso monogatari* (Tokyo: Chuo Koronsha, 1979), 11–13.
37 Tetsuro Shimojima, "Gaimusho no hanzai: moteasobareta nikkei choho soshiki 'Heishikan' no higeki," *Gendai* (April 1997), 276–296.
38 *Heishikan Newsletter,* November 2006.
39 Iwao Peter Sano, interviewed by author, Palo Alto, CA, March 12, 2007; Iwao Peter Sano, *One Thousand Days in Siberia: The Odyssey of a Japanese-American POW* (Lincoln, NE: University of Nebraska Press, 1997), 14–24.
40 Iwao Peter Sano, interviewed by author, Palo Alto, CA, March 12, 2007; Sano, *One Thousand Days*, 25.
41 Military records in Japan do not provide information that can be used to determine how many U.S.-born Nisei were conscripted into the Japanese armed forces during World War II. Although Kadoike Hiroshi has speculated that 20,000–30,000 Nisei served on various battlefronts in Asia-Pacific from 1942 to 1945, this estimate is not based on any reliable source: Hiroshi Kadoike, *Nihongun heishi ni natta amerikajin tachi: bokoku to tatakatta nikkei nisei* (Tokyo: Genshu Shuppansha, 2010), 34–35; Hiroshi Kadoike, interviewed by author, Osaka, Japan, August 10, 2010.
42 Sano, *One Thousand Days*, 197; Supreme Commander for the Allied Powers, *Reports of General MacArthur* (Washington, DC: Center for Military History, 1994), 150; William Nimmo, *Behind a Curtain of Silence: Japanese in Soviet Custody, 1945–1956* (Westport, CT: Greenwood Press, 1988).
43 76th Congress, H.R. 9980; Pub. L. 76-853 Stat. 1137, Washington, DC, October 14, 1940.
44 Sano, *One Thousand Days*, 203–204, 208–209; Peter Sano, interview with author, July 12, 2007, Palo Alto, CA; Peter Sano, Guest Lecture, World War II Memories in the United States and Japan from the University of California, Santa Cruz, Santa Cruz, CA, February 15, 2013.
45 See Yuji Ichioka, "A Study in Dualism: James Yoshinori Sakamoto and the Japanese American Courier, 1928–1942" in Ichioka, *Amerasia Journal;* Ichioka, "Dai Nisei Mondai"; Yuji Ichioka, "Japanese Immigrant Nationalism: The Issei and the Sino-Japanese War, 1937–1941." *California History* 69:3 (1990): 260–275.
46 Eiichiro Azuma, *Between Two Empires,* 209.
47 For examples of the works that bridge multiple area studies, ethnic studies, and Asian American history, see Rhacel Salazar Parreñas, *Servants of Globalization: Women, Migration and Domestic Work* (Stanford, CA: Stanford University Press, 2001); Madeleine Yuan-yin Hsu, *Dream of Gold, Dream of Home: Transnationalism and Migration between the United States and South China, 1882-1943* (Stanford, CA: Stanford University Press, 2000); Dorothy Fujita-Rony, *American Workers, Colonial Power: Philippine Seattle and the Transpacific West, 1919-1941* (Berkeley, CA: University of California Press, 2003).
48 Arif Dirlik, "Asians on the Rim: Transnational Capital and Local Community in the Making of Contemporary Asian America," *Amerasia Journal* 22:3 (1996), 13.

References

Asahi Shimbun (Tokyo). 1939

Azuma, Eiichiro. *Between Two Empires: Race History, and Transnationalism in Japanese America*. New York: Oxford University Press, 2005.

———. "'Pioneers of Overseas Japanese Development': Japanese American History and the Making of Expansionist Orthodoxy in Imperial Japan." *Journal of Asian Studies* 67, no. 4 (November 2008): 1187–1226.

Cinel, Dino. *From Italy to San Francisco: The Immigrant Experience*. Stanford, CA: Stanford University Press, 1982.

———. *The National Integration of Italian Return Migration, 1870–1929*. Cambridge: Cambridge University Press, 1991.

Dirlik, Arif. "Asians on the Rim: Transnational Capital and Local Community in the Making of Contemporary Asian America." *Amerasia Journal* 22, no. 3 (1996): 1–24.

Evening Free Lance (Hollister, CA). 1933.

Fighting Americans, Too! (Topaz, UT). 1943.

Fujita-Rony, Dorothy. *American Workers, Colonial Power: Philippine Seattle and the Transpacific West, 1919–1941*. Berkeley, CA: University of California Press, 2003.

Hayashi, Brian Masaru. *Democratizing the Enemy: The Japanese American Internment*. Princeton, NJ: Princeton University Press, 2004.

Heishikan News. 1940–1942.

Heishikan Newsletter. 2004–2006.

Hsu, Madeline Y. *Dream of Gold, Dream of Home: Transnationalism and Migration between the United States and South China, 1882–1943*. Stanford, CA: Stanford University Press, 2000.

Ichioka, Yuji. "A Study of Dualism: James Yoshinori Sakamoto and the Japanese American Courier, 1928–1942." *Amerasia Journal* 13, no. 2 (1986–1987): 49–81.

———. "Japanese Immigrant Nationalism: The Issei and the Sino-Japanese War, 1937–1941." *California History* 69, no. 3 (1990): 260–275.

———. "The Meaning of Loyalty: The Case of Kazumaro Buddy Uno." *Amerasia Journal* 23, no. 3 (Winter 1997–1998): 45–71.

———. *Before Internment: Essays in Prewar Japanese American History*. Edited by Gordon H. Chang and Eiichiro Azuma. Stanford, CA: Stanford University Press, 2005.

Ikeda, Norizane. *Hinomaru awa: taibei boryaku hoso monogatari*. Tokyo: Chuo Koronsha, 1979.

Japan Times Weekly. 1939.

Kadoike, Hiroshi. *Nihongun heishi ni natta amerikajin tachi: bokoku to tatakatta nikkei nisei*. Tokyo: Genshu Shuppansha, 2010.

Keisen Girls' School. *The Nisei: A study of Their Life in Japan*. Tokyo: Keisen Girls' School, 1939.

Kiyota, Minoru. *Beyond Loyalty: The Story of a Kibei*. Translated by Linda Klepinger Keenan. Honolulu, HI: University of Hawaii Press, 1997.

Kosaka, Eliko. "Caught in Between Okinawa and Hawai'i: 'Kibei' Diaspora in Masao Yamashiro's *The Kibei Nisei*." *Amerasia Journal* 41, no. 1 (2015): 1–14.

Kumei, Teruko. "1930 Nendai no kibei undo: amerika kokusekiho to no kanren ni oite." *Imin kenkyu* 30 (1993): 149–162.

———. "Yujo to yuko wo musunde: Heishikan kara rajio presu-e," *Kaigai imin shiryokan kenkyu kiyo* 4 (2009): 1–10.

Morning Daily Advance (Hollister, CA). 1920.

Murray, Alice Yang. *Historical Memories of the Japanese American Internment and the Struggle for Redress*. Stanford, CA: Stanford University Press, 2008.

Nagai, Matsuzo, Ed. *Nichibei bunka koshoshi*. Tokyo: Yoyosha, 1952.

Nimmo, William. *Behind a Curtain of Silence: Japanese in Soviet Custody, 1945–1956*. Westport, CT: Greenwood Press, 1988.

Nozaki, Kyoko Norma. "'Just Like Sunshine, Like Moon (light)': The Life of Matsumi Kanemitsu, a Kibei Artist." *Kyoto Sangyo University Essays Foreign Language and Culture Series* 23 (March 2001): 35–51.

Pacific Citizen. 1975.

Parreñas, Rhacel Salazar. *Servants of Globalization: Women, Migration, and Domestic Work*. Stanford, CA: Stanford University Press, 2001.

Sano, Iwao Peter. *One Thousand Days in Siberia: The Odyssey of a Japanese-American POW*. Lincoln, NE: University of Nebraska Press, 1997.

Shibusawa, Naoko. "The Artist Belongs to the People: The Odyssey of Taro Yashima." *Journal of Asian American Studies* 8, no. 3 (October 2005): 257–275.

Shimojima, Tetsuro, "Gaimusho no hanzai: moteasobareta nikkei choho soshiki 'Heishikan' no higeki." *Gendai* (April 1997), 276–296.

Spickard, Paul R. *Japanese Americans: The Formation and Transformations of an Ethnic Group*. Revised Edition. New Brunswick: Rutgers University Press, 2009.

Stephan, John J. "Hijacked by Utopia: American Nikkei in Manchuria," *Amerasia Journal* 23, no. 3 (1997): 1–42.

Supreme Commander for the Allied Powers. *Reports of General MacArthur*. Washington, DC: Center for Military History, 1994.

Takeda, Junichi. *Zaibei hiroshima kenjinshi*. Los Angeles, CA: Zaibei Hiroshima Kenjinshi Hakkojo, 1929.

Tateishi, Kay. "An Atypical Nisei." *Amerasia Journal* 23, no. 3 (1997): 199–216.

Yamashita, Soen. *Nikkei shimin no nihon ryugaku jijo*. Tokyo: Bunseisha, 1935.

———. *Nichibei wo tsunagu mono*. Tokyo: Bunseisha, 1938.

Yoneda, Karl G. *Ganbatte: Sixty-Year Struggle of a Kibei Worker*. Los Angeles, CA: Asian American Studies Center, University of California, 1983.

Yoshida, Akira, Ed. *Amerika nihonjin imin no ekkyo kyoikushi*. Tokyo: Nihon Tosho Center, 2005.

Yoshida, Jim. *The Two Worlds of Jim Yoshida*. New York: William Morrow and Company, 1972.

Yoshimi, Kaoru. "Aru nikkei amerikajin kibei nisei gaka no kojutsu seikatushi." *Nagoya University of Foreign Studies Journal of the School of Contemporary International Studies* 5 (March, 2009): 393–425.

Zaibei Nihonjinkai. *Zeibei nihonjinshi*. San Francisco, CA: Zeibei Nihonjinkai, 1940.

18
MIGRATION, CITIZENSHIP, AND SEXUALITY IN ASIAN/AMERICA[1]

Yu-Fang Cho

The migrations between Asia and the United States—and also more broadly the Americas—are commonly described as movements of people across geographical spaces to seek opportunities for social mobility or to escape from life-threatening circumstances, presumed to be explainable by push and pull factors in general terms. However, such descriptions and explanations of "why" people move cannot fully account for "how" the unequal power relations between different political and economic entities developed over time have shaped the processes of migration. Scholars of Asian migration to the United States illuminate that these processes are inherently tied to U.S. capitalist and imperialist expansion that required the import and regulation of labor supply from Asia. In the nineteenth to early twentieth centuries, when the U.S. significantly expanded its western territory and military presence in the Asia Pacific, U.S. capital also actively recruited low-wage laborers from Asia.[2] This demand for exploitable labor, however, conflicted with the U.S. nation-state's and mainstream society's desire for racially homogeneous "white" citizenry. As a result, the U.S. government responded to this contradiction through a series of exclusionary laws that prohibited laborers from Asia from naturalizing as citizens, owning agricultural land, and forming family, thereby restricting their participation in political, social, and cultural spheres.[3] During this period of mass migration, racial violence, and imperial conquests, these exclusionary laws solidified whiteness and heterosexuality as key criteria of U.S. citizenship: through the association of prostitution, polygamy, bachelor society, and female-dominant households, prevailing perceptions of the Chinese as morally degenerate and sexually deviant were written into exclusionary laws that governed immigration and marriage. In other words, nineteenth-century U.S. capitalist and imperialist expansion gave rise to the racialization of Asians as perpetual aliens through their exclusion from citizenship and also from heterosexual reproduction. During this period, Asian migrations connected sites across national and geographical borders around the Pacific and the Americas, yet institutions of U.S. nation-state increasingly codified "Asia" as antithetical to what "America" presumably stands for: whiteness, democracy, progress, and moral superiority. "Asia" and "America" thus emerged as mutually exclusive categories of race and knowledge as the anti-Chinese sentiment traveled across U.S. borders both north and south throughout the Americas.[4] In the century that followed and even to this day, such perceptions of race, gender, and sexuality originating in the late nineteenth century have become ingrained in American mainstream consciousness despite the stereotype of Asian Americans as model minorities that developed in the latter half of the twentieth century.

Early Formation of Asian Racialization and Sexualization

As early as the late eighteen century, the settlement of Filipinos in America was recorded; Orientalist cultural production also began to play an important role in shaping U.S. culture and politics.[5] It was not until the mid-nineteenth century that systemic racialization started to take shape in response to the migration of Chinese workers to the U.S. West Coast—the first immigrant group from Asia to settle in large numbers in the Americas—and produced racial stereotypes that persisted in the twentieth century. As part of the global migrations of indentured labor from China and India that connected not only Pacific shores but also the Caribbean and the U.S. South, Chinese coolies were recruited as agricultural and industrial labor in western regions of the United States as well as on sugar plantations in the South and the Caribbean.[6] From these early days, the construction of racial difference was inherently tied to the status of Chinese laborers within the overall colonial strategy of racial management. In the West Indies, the Chinese, recruited upon the abolition of African slavery in the early nineteenth century, were figured as "free": different from Africans yet racialized and indentured. Such figuration of the Chinese played an instrumental role in the establishment of emerging tiered labor structure during the transition from slavery to free labor market and also informed racialized notions of Asian labor in the United States.[7] In the absence of Chinese families, colonial administration's fantasy about its creation and about the virtue of Chinese women sought to establish a racial barrier between colonial whites and enslaved blacks, whereas lower-caste Indian women, who managed to migrate, were framed as licentious and immoral.[8]

In the United States, on the contrary, nineteenth-century racial construction of Chinese workers relied on the popular trope of "yellow slavery" that marked them as unfree and disposable labor in contrast to white free labor. This trope emerged when anti-Chinese sentiment exploded in the 1870s during the recession only a few years after the United States signed the Burlingame Treaty of 1868 with China in order to ensure sufficient supply of labor for the railroad project after the 1867 strike occurred. Figured as "yellow slaves" in the broader discourse of Yellow Peril, the Chinese during this period were viewed as the epitome of sexually deviant unfree labor that threatened white workingmen, their family, and the U.S. nation and empire. In addition to the association of polygamy, racialization of the Chinese entails gender-specific terms. On the one hand, Chinese women were presumed to be prostitutes until proven otherwise and all "enslaved" regardless of their social status.[9] In 1875, the U.S. Congress passed the Page Act, the first race-based immigration act in the U.S. that singled out Chinese, Japanese, and any other "Oriental Prostitutes" for exclusion, even though their number was small and white prostitution was more prevalent.[10] On the other hand, institutions and discourses of emasculation sought to contain the threat that Chinese men were perceived to pose on white women: Chinese men were considered lacking both proper masculinity and respectable domesticity because they were relegated to forms of work conventionally done by women (such as laundry and restaurants), unable to form families due to anti-miscegenation laws and immigration exclusion of Chinese women, and inhabited male-dominated households due to necessity.[11] Such perceptions fed into the racial conflict instigated by Irish workingmen that led to the 1882 Chinese Exclusion Act, which banned both skilled and unskilled laborers and barred them from becoming citizens through naturalization.[12] In 1885, the Foran Act excluded all contract laborers to protect "free white workingmen" by reducing labor competition. Moreover, this act allowed exceptions for family reunion while exclusion laws and anti-miscegenation legislation barred Chinese workers from family formation.[13] Under such conditions, Chinese women's and men's perceived deviation from heterosexual respectable domesticity—which was *created* by U.S. mainstream values, economic interests, and political institutions—paradoxically *became* proof of their unfitness for citizenship and positioned them in conflict with white workingmen, white women, and blacks in their effort at seeking fair wages and equal rights.[14]

In the subsequent years, male laborers from Korea, Japan, India, and the Philippines were recruited and then subjected to exclusion, while Canada, Mexico, Brazil, and Peru also implemented anti-Asian policies targeting the Chinese, Indians, and Japanese at different times.[15] Meanwhile, exclusion from naturalization and citizenship did not only affect the Chinese. The 1907 Marital Expatriation Act stripped citizenship from U.S. women married to foreign nationals ineligible for citizenship, who were predominantly Asian men during this period. In the Cable Act of 1922, the racial criterion of whiteness for reinstating citizenship, which ended white women's dependence on their husbands for their formal citizenship status, reinforced white heterosexuality—and by inference, white heterosexual reproduction—as the norm. Moreover, because most non-citizen Asian women were only allowed to immigrate as dependents of their husbands, the "independence" that white American women gained as a result of this act made it even more difficult for non-citizen Asian women to enter or remain in the United States.[16] During this period, as racial boundaries tightened throughout the Americas, white heterosexuality became institutionalized through immigration exclusion and anti-miscegenation measures in the United States. Meanwhile, U.S. imperial expansionism fueled the inculcation of Christian notions of marriage and "respectable sexuality" among the "heathens," thereby legitimizing the eradication of indigenous kinship systems, prostitution, and polygamy. This was key to the rhetorical construction of the United States as a benevolent, progressive civilizing force, which rationalized genocides, violent colonial extractions of labor and resources, and the establishment of U.S. military prostitution in border zones and the Philippines despite the moral outcry against prostitution.[17]

Cultural Responses to Early Formation

Countering the prevalence of such anti-Asian discourse couched in nationalist and imperialist terms of white heterosexuality, alternative cultural representation and practices emerged to unsettle or contest the effects of the racialization of Asians as immoral, deviant gender and sexual subjects. For example, the works of mixed-race North American writer Sui Sin Far (Edith Maude Eaton) not only portray the possibilities for the Chinese to have a proper domestic life and the challenge of interracial couples, but they also problematize the prevailing gender and sexual stigmatization of the Chinese and expose inherent racial contradictions within U.S. values and laws.[18] Moreover, while fighting racial exclusion through civic and democratic participation, many Indian male migrants in western regions of the United States and Canada also created alternative and homosocial domesticities and nonheteronormative sociality that exceeded conventional kinship lineage and traditional domesticity.[19]

Before the U.S. Immigration and Nationality Act of 1965 abolished national origins quotas and exclusions and brought the exclusion era to an end, immigration legislation prioritized northern European immigration and codified white family as the dominant structure of national reproduction.[20] During the exclusion era, as the presence of Asians within U.S. national borders was severely restricted, cultural media, military institutions, and missionary enterprises became primary sites of interracial encounters that gave rise to popular cultural narratives of race, gender, and sexuality. For example, the character Fu Manchu, who appeared first in the 1910s in a series of novels and became popularized in a variety of media throughout the twentieth century, including films and comics, exemplifies the persistent demonization of Chinese men as evil, cunning, and violent criminals that dramatizes Asian men's imminent threat to white heterosexual reproduction.[21] The imagining of Asian men as violent killers seeking to take women away from white men works in tandem with the popular fantasy of Asian women's persistent romantic yearning for white men. This dual fantasy rationalizes violent exclusion and emasculation of Asian men; meanwhile, it simultaneously displaces and legitimates white men's desire for innocent and submissive Asian women, who are often portrayed as always sexually available for white male consumption but prohibited from consummating their miscegenous love only permitted outside of U.S. territory.

Such Orientalist fantasy about Asian women with numerous variations—from the Lotus Blossom, China dolls, to Geisha girls—can be traced back to the character Madame Butterfly, who first appeared in a French novel in 1887 and was then popularized by Italian composer Giacomo Puccini's opera of the same name throughout the twentieth century. In this popular narrative, the protagonist is a young Japanese woman who kills herself when her American husband, a U.S. naval officer, returns to Japan with his new American wife to take away their mixed-race child after a period of absence. This narrative recasts the nineteenth-century stereotype of Asian women as prostitutes into willing and convenient vehicles of both sexual pleasure and partial reproductive labor for white men.[22] Framing the Asian woman as a disposable bearer of the white man's child, this cultural script denies her the right to the child and excludes her from family formation, legitimizing white men's desire for Asian women while keeping it from undermining the dominant logic of white national and imperial reproduction. While this particular fantasy of submissive Asian women suggests exploitative partial incorporation of their reproductive labor outside of U.S. territory into the new white "American family" without her, the dragon lady stereotype, which appeared in the late 1920s as an aggressive, manipulative, deceitful, and murderous femme fatale, has kept Asian women outside of proper femininity and normative heterosexual reproduction within the U.S. domestic context. This dyad has importantly defined Asian/American femininity to this day and informed the phenomenon of Asian fetish, which has extended beyond heterosexual communities (as implied in the term "rice queen" in interracial LGBTQ discourses) and U.S. borders and, is arguably, also attributed to the far greater number of white–Asian marriages between Asian women and white men than those between Asian men and white women. In Chinese American playwright Henry David Hwang's *M. Butterfly* (1988), such Orientalist fantasies are recast as the liaison between a male French diplomat and a male Chinese spy, loosely based on a real-life event, to critique the effects of such fantasies on both Asian men and Asian women, to reverse unequal power relations between the East and the West through appropriating and subverting gendered racial stereotypes. In doing so, this rewriting of Orientalist scripts also exposes homophobia in Western culture and the vulnerability of white heterosexual masculinity.[23]

Reinforcing the criterion of heterosexual domesticity for U.S. national incorporation, popular stereotypes that developed during the exclusion era also importantly informed and were shaped by the migrations and interracial encounters that came out of U.S. wars in Asia—with the Philippines (1898–1910), against Japan (1941–1945), in Korea (1950–1953), and in Vietnam (1955–1975). At the end of World War II, the 1945 War Brides Act not only allowed Chinese women to come to the United States as brides of Chinese American soldiers, but also enabled U.S. military personnel to bring their children, both natural and adopted—and also their Asian wives after the 1952 McCarren–Walter Act eliminated all racial prerequisites for citizenship—to the United States.[24] In the aftermath of the Korean War, the establishment of state-sponsored sex services in South Korea near U.S. military bases, which still exist today, significantly facilitated the immigration of Korean women as brides of U.S. servicemen and also the transnational adoption of children left behind by their American fathers. This particular interracial formation reiterates the framing of U.S. military violence as paternalistic and humanitarian benevolence that can date back at least to the 1898 Spanish–American War. Moreover, this formation extends the narrative of sacrificial Asian wives in the Madame Butterfly story, wherein the death of the submissive Asian wife overseas makes it possible for prospective incorporation of the Amerasian child into the newly formed heterosexual white U.S. military family. By turning reviled camptown prostitutes into respectable military wives for national incorporation, this formation erases militarized sex work, obscures U.S. military violence, and reinstates male privilege of conferring citizenship.[25] Meanwhile, mainstream narratives about the orphans produced by the Korean War—both Amerasian children left behind by their American fathers and Korean children who lost their parents—support the rhetoric of American benevolence through portraying the American solider as a benevolent father and valorizing the white American family's moral superiority and multicultural sensibility at the expense of the adoptees' well-being and in some cases, naturalize what some critics call the "social death" of Korean mothers.[26] More recently, young girls from Asia have become ideal transnational adoptees to enable predominantly white same-sex couples to claim a class-based, queer version of the nuclear family in the United States. Because proper domesticity based on the structure of the conventional heterosexual family has long been a defining marker of full citizenship in the U.S. context, this new formation of queer family has been viewed by critics as a sign of conformity to mainstream nationalist values, which affirm the U.S. nation-state's absolutely authority to define the terms of and confer individual political rights. This phenomenon is often referred to as homonormativity or queer liberalism, which, as some argue, characterizes the gay marriage movement.[27] From Madame Butterfly, military wives, transnational adoptees, to domestic and care workers, the racialization of Asian women in the twentieth century makes possible their heterogeneous, incremental, and incomplete incorporation into the U.S. national body politics that facilitates both American white heterosexual reproduction and emerging normative queer domesticity.[28]

Contemporary Developments

In the period after WWII, as the U.S. established its dominance in the Asia Pacific region, several concurrent developments ushered in what critics refer to as contemporary globalization, characterized by the increasing speed at which money, people, goods, and information cross national borders. During this period, U.S. corporations significantly expanded their reach overseas by outsourcing manufacturing as U.S. immigration laws were "liberalized" to recruit needed professional and menial labor from Asia and Latin America.[29] Meanwhile, the broad-based civil rights movement of historically marginalized and exploited working people, in coalition with anticolonial struggles throughout the world, exerted pressure on longstanding white dominance that U.S. political, economic, social, and cultural institutions had sought to maintain. Emerging from these formations, the 1965 Immigration and Nationality Act marked a paradigmatic shift in U.S. immigration regulation. Replacing the system of national origins quotas and exclusions with an employment- and skill-based preference that also prioritized heterosexual family relationships with U.S. citizens or residents, this watershed legislation created significant demographic shifts among the Asian American population in the following decades. In the 1990s, not only did Asian-born population became the majority, immigrants from South Vietnam, South Korea, Cambodia, Laos, Thailand, the Philippines, Malaysia, India, and Pakistan diversified the existing group of largely Chinese, Japanese, Korean, and Filipino descent.[30] Contrary to the prohibition of Asian reproduction during the exclusion era, the Act of 1965 made family formation possible and created transnational middle and privileged classes. This significant demographic shift aligned racialized "Asians" closer to American mainstream values, from conventional domesticity to work ethic, and gave rise to the model minority myth. Departing from the Yellow Peril discourse in earlier periods, the model minority discourse has become an instrument of race management that obscures ongoing anti-Asian racism, on the one hand, and disciplines poor blacks and Latinos and rationalizes their de facto disenfranchisement, on the other hand.[31] This discursive shift also complemented the incremental incorporation of different Asian female subjects into the white heterosexual social order discussed above, making the Asian/American woman an increasingly desirable addition to heterosexual domesticity in American imagination—so "naturally" heteronormative that she may even displace the white woman—while Orientalist stereotypes continue to shape the terms of their desirability and incomplete incorporation.[32]

The perceptions of Asian gender and sexual deviance, as important legacies of the exclusion era, also significantly affected LGBTQ Asian/Americans. While Asian transnational adoptees make it possible for many white American queer couples to claim a modern form of respectable domesticity, the persistent white heteronormative logic of national incorporation has rendered bi-national or undocumented LGBTQ Asian/Americans and those seeking political asylum unusually vulnerable to state violence. Before the Supreme Court overturned Section 3 of the Defense of Marriage Act (DOMA) in June 2013, LGBTQ Asian/Americans were barred from many rights attached to heterosexual marriage that were particularly important to migrant people, such as the right to sponsor one's spouse's permanent residence application and the application for a hardship waiver that would allow undocumented immigrants reentry into the United States in order to apply for proper legal status.[33] Before DOMA was overturned, with the increasing heterosexualization of Asian/Americans as well as the growing prevalence and visibility of gay families with transnational adoptees, family reunification principle in immigration laws separated Asian/American LGBTQ communities from both heterosexual Asian/Americans and white American LGBTQ communities along lines of race, class, sexuality, and citizenship.[34]

Despite the liminal spaces that LGBTQ migrant workers of Asian descent occupy within capitalist hetero- and homonormative social order, alternative kinship structures and affective relations that are not based on biological ties have emerged to negotiate and contest the effects of globalization, from alienation and exclusion, to marginalization. For example, *Paper Dolls* (2006), a documentary about Filipino transgender care workers in Israel, portrays the community that they have built far away from their families in the Philippines and the refusal of the demand of racialized affective labor—the demand that they perform the happy, servile, warm-hearted Filipinos—as an important survival strategy.[35] Released during an earlier period of rapid realignment of race, gender, and sexual relations, award-winning film director Ang Lee's *The Wedding Banquet* (1993) foregrounds the relationship between the emerging transnational elite class and working immigrants with the story of a triangular affair among a well-off Taiwanese American man, a white American man, and a poor Chinese woman. The film focuses particularly on the transnational Asian male subject's negotiation between the reproductive demand of traditional Asian patriarchy and the erotic and affective possibility promised by American multicultural sexual modernity symbolized by the interracial Taiwanese American and white American gay couple. At the end of the film, this transnational gay couple are able to attain both an Asian reproductive family and an alternative interracial family by enlisting the reproductive labor of the Chinese woman, who, with a comic twist, ends up bearing the Taiwanese American man's biological child. In this way, the film underscores that access to a reproductive family—be it heteronormative, homonormative, or otherwise—is often overdetermined by one's access to capital as well as by the availability of exploitable and racialized reproductive female labor, especially when social relations are overwhelmingly shaped by forces of globalization that facilitate movements of money, people, and commodities across national borders. In this way, the film alludes to the rise of what critics call "flexible citizens"—a class of wealthy Asians and Asian Americans with multiple passports who travel frequently and extensively across national borders to maximize their accumulation of wealth.[36] As beneficiaries of the rise of Asian economic miracles made possible by the collaboration between U.S.-based transnational capital and authoritarian Asian states to suppress the rights of low-wage Asian workers, the "success" of such a transnational elite class affirms the myth of the American Dream disseminated by U.S. popular media—that the United States is the ultimate site of freedom, social mobility, and reproductive future.

These contemporary narratives actively negotiate U.S.-based LGBTQ discourses—or what some refer to critically as the "global gay discourse." In this context, the United States is commonly figured as the space of sexual and gender liberation, where true self-expression and the creation of queer families are possible; hence, the United States is often posited as the destination that "oppressed" Asian LGBTQ people must be rescued "to"[37]. In contrast, Asia is often figured as the space of violence and death or a site of Western commodification or consumption, as exemplified by the rising industry of sex reassignment surgery in Thailand.[38] Scholarship on sexuality in Asia, however, illuminates that Western conceptions of sexuality—including the aforementioned particular racialization of Asians in the United States—cannot fully capture the fluid and complex taxonomies of gender and sexuality that are contextually distinct, geographically variant, and historically specific.[39] As some argue, contrary to the monolithic representation of Asia as a site of sexual repression and the popular narratives of sexual liberation only possible in the West, alternatives to Western conceptions of sexuality were eradicated with the advent of "sexual modernity" during colonial encounters.

In recent years, the emerging new terrain of transpacific reproductive economy also urges critics to recast such important critiques of U.S.-based LGBTQ discourses in new perspectives. The suppression of wages—coupled with many Asian governments' increasing disregard for the rights and welfare of wage-earning workers, the influx of foreign investment money into the real estate market, and other factors—has made normative family formation for working people in industrialized Asia increasingly unattainable even when the heterosexual family is still posited by the dominant culture as compulsory. While a significant number of women, including mothers, from the Philippines and Indonesia left home to work as domestic workers overseas, many parts of industrialized Asia that witnessed economic miracles in the 1980s are now faced with record-low fertility rates. This new transpacific reproductive economy is characterized by an increasing separation among different subjects with uneven access: (1) Asian/American transnational middle and privileged classes, who embody the promise of hetero-reproductive future; (2) migrant workers, who provide reproductive labor for others while leaving their families behind; and (3) immobile working people and the struggling, shrinking middle class, for both of whom conventional family is increasingly beyond reach.

In response to these new developments, queer theory is being broadened to grasp the uneven and wide-ranging impact of the ways that transnational capitalism has reorganized different people's access to the "promise" of reproductive future.[40] Instead of focusing exclusively on sexually non-normative subjects, critical efforts now also seek to grapple with the plight of heterogeneous Asian/American subjects—LGBTQ and otherwise—who fall outside of the capitalist order of heterosexual reproduction in uneven ways, including those who work to obtain reproductive domesticity (such as private property ownership) and also who are denied access to it and thus become completely redundant and excessive in contemporary capitalist social order.[41] Today, as the cases of hightech workers in East Asia and call center workers, software programmers, human organ donors, and gestational surrogates in India illustrate, exploitable and dispensable Asian labor no longer needs to "migrate" to sustain the reproduction of families—both heteronormative and homonormative—in the United States.[42] Hence, mapping alternative knowledges of struggle requires new analytics that move beyond positing sexuality as an entity with specific content so as to more effectively grapple with the complex and flexible processes of racialization that transnational capitalism has occasioned through wide-ranging reorganization of normative reproduction and non-reproductive lives of disposable workers.

Notes

1. Following Laura Hyun Yi Kang, the use of Asian/America(n) in this chapter seeks to denaturalize "Asia" and "America" as categories of knowledge and their oppositional relations produced by discursive formations. This term foregrounds the shifting meaning of objects of knowledge that are designated as "Asia" or "America" shaped by changing ideological, political economic, and material forces. See Laura Hyun Yi Kang, *Compositional Subjects: Enfiguring Asian/American Women* (Durham, NC: Duke University Press, 2002), 1–28. The use of this term also seeks to underscore the tendency that Asian Americans, regardless of their citizenship status and cultural affiliations, are often racialized as "Asian."
2. See Lisa Lowe, *Immigrant Acts: On Asian American Cultural Politics* (Durham, NC: Duke University Press, 1996): 1–36. Lowe's analysis focuses on the United States from the nineteenth to the twentieth centuries, but can be broadened to understand the transnational development of Chinese exclusion laws in the Americas in the late nineteenth and early twentieth centuries.
3. In nineteenth-century U.S. public discourse, people of Asian descent were identified with specific countries of origin or location (such as China, Japan, the Philippines, etc.) or other terms (such as Oriental, Mongolian, etc.). The concept of "Asians" as a racially distinct group emerged during the exclusion era. In this essay, the term "Asian" is used in the general, contemporary sense for descriptive purposes without disregarding potential anachronism.
4. See Erika Lee, "The 'Yellow Peril' and Asian Exclusion in the Americas," *Pacific Historical Review* 76, no.4 (2007): 537–562. For a discussion of the incorporation of the Chinese into the national imaginary as a way to displace indigenous populations in mid-twentieth-century Mexico, see Martha Chew Sánchez, "Deconstructing the Rhetoric of Mestizaje through the Chinese Presence in Mexico," in *Strange Affinities: The Gender and Sexual Politics of Comparative Racialization* (Durham, NC: Duke University Press, 2011), 215–240. For discussions of the racialization of Chinese in Spanish Cuba, see Kathleen López, "Afro-Asian Alliances: Marriage, Godparent, and Social Status in Late-Nineteenth-Century Cuba," *Afro-Hispanic Review* 27, no.1 (2008): 59–72.
5. The first recorded settlement of Filipinos in America was about their escaping imprisonment aboard Spanish galleons by jumping ship in New Orleans and fleeing into the bayous. See *Screaming Monkeys: Critiques of Asian American Images*, ed. M. Evelina Galang (Minneapolis: Coffee House Press, 2003), 162. For a discussion of the Chinese in U.S. imagination before the first wave of mass migration, see John Kuo Wei Tchen, *New York Before Chinatown: Orientalism and the Shaping of American Culture, 1776–1882* (Baltimore, MD: Johns Hopkins University Press, 2001).
6. See Lee; Henry Yu, "Los Angeles and American Studies in a Pacific World of Migrations," *American Quarterly* 56, no.3 (2004): 537–538, 541; Moon-Ho Jung, *Coolies and Cane: Race, Labor, and Sugar in the Age of Emancipation* (Baltimore, MD: John Hopkins University Press, 2008); Nayan Shah, *Stranger Intimacy: Contesting Race, Sexuality, and the Law in the North American West* (Berkeley, CA: University of California Press, 2011).
7. Moon-Ho Jung argues that racialized notions of Asian labor in the United States first started to emerge in response to the presence of the Chinese on sugar plantations in the American South and the Caribbean instead of that in the gold mines in the American West.
8. Lisa Lowe, "The Intimacies of Four Continents," in *Haunted by Empire: Geographies of Intimacy in North American History*, Ed. Anne Laura Stoler (Durham, NC: Duke University Press, 2006), 198–199.
9. The period's newspaper accounts even portrayed Chinese housewives as sex slaves. See Yu-Fang Cho, *Uncoupling American Empire: Cultural Politics of Deviance and Unequal Differences, 1890–1910* (Albany, NY: SUNY Press, 2013), 77–102.
10. See Judy Yung, *Unbound Feet: A Social History of Chinese Women in San Francisco* (Berkeley, CA: University of California Press, 1995), 31–32.
11. Lisa Lowe, *Immigrant Acts*, 11–12; Nayan Shah, *Contagious Divides: Epidemics and Race in San Francisco's Chinatown* (Berkeley, CA: California University Press, 2001); David L. Eng, *Racial Castration: Managing*

Masculinity in Asian America (Durham, NC: Duke University Press, 2001); Amy Sueyoshi, *Queer Compulsions: Race, Nation, and Sexuality in the Affairs of Yone Noguchi* (Honolulu, HI: University of Hawaii Press, 2012).

12 The exclusionist legislation provided exemptions for Chinese officials, students, teachers, merchants, clergymen, and tourists in the interest of diplomatic and trade relations between China and the United States. See Sucheng Chan, Ed., *Entry Denied: Exclusion and the Chinese Community in America, 1882–1943* (Philadelphia, PA: Temple University Press, 1991), 97; Ronald Takaki, *Iron Cages: Race and Culture in Nineteenth-Century America* (Seattle, WA: University of Washington Press, 1979), 111; and Yung, 22.

13 For the history of U.S. anti-miscegenation laws, see Peggy Pascoe, *What Comes Naturally: Miscegenation Law and the Making of Race in America* (Oxford: Oxford University Press, 2010). For a brief summary, see Susan Koshy, *Sexual Naturalization: Asian Americans and Miscegenation* (Palo Alto, CA: Stanford University Press, 2004), 3–12. For the 1907 Marital Expatriation Act and the 1992 Cable Act, see Leti Volpp, "Divesting Citizenship: On Asian American History and the Loss of Citizenship through Marriage," *UCLA Law Review* 53, no.2 (2005): 403–483. For further details on the Foran Act, see Nancy Cott, *Public Vows: A History of Marriage and the Nation* (Cambridge, MA: Harvard University Press, 2002), 138; Eithne Luibhéid, *Entry Denied: Controlling Sexuality at the Border* (Minneapolis, MN: University of Minnesota Press, 2002), 2.

14 See Cho, *Uncoupling American Empire*, 1–24.

15 In the United States, Asian Indians were excluded in 1917, Koreans and Japanese in 1924, and Filipinos in 1934. See Lowe, *Immigrant Acts*, 7. For anti-Asian measures in the Americas, see Lee, "'Yellow Peril"; her "Orientalisms in the Americas: A Hemispheric Approach to Asian American History," *Journal of Asian American Studies* 8, no.3 (October 2005): 235–256; and Shah, *Stranger Intimacy*.

16 See Volpp, 458.

17 See Laura Briggs, *Reproducing Empire: Race, Sex, Science, and U.S. Imperialism in Puerto Rico* (Berkeley, CA: California University Press, 2002); and Paul L. Kramer, "The Darkness That Enters the Home: The Politics of Prostitution during the Philippine-American War," in Stoler, 366–404.

18 See Cho, *Uncoupling American Empire*, 77–126.

19 See Shah, *Stranger Intimacy*, 16.

20 See Leti Volpp, "The Legal Mapping of U.S. Immigration, 1965–1996," in *Crossing into America: the New Literature of Immigration*, Eds. Louis Mendoza and S. Shankar (New York: The New Press, 2003), 257–269; Mae Ngai, *Impossible Subjects: Illegal Aliens and the Making of Modern America* (Princeton, NJ: Princeton University Press, 2004); Matthew Frye Jacobson, *Whiteness of a Different Color: European Immigrants and the Alchemy of Race* (Cambridge, MA: Harvard University Press, 1998). Chinese exclusion laws were repealed in 1943 as a result of wartime alliances between China and the United States. The 1946 Luce-Celler Bill granted Indian and Filipino immigrants right to naturalize, but small quotas were established. The 1952 McCarren-Walter Act eliminated all racial prerequisites for citizenship, but maintained national origins quotas.

21 For a discussion of different formations of Asian American masculinity in popular culture, see Daryl Joji Maeda, "Trans-Pacific Flows: Globalization and Hybridity in Bruce Lee's Hong Kong Films," *Global Asian American Popular Cultures*, Eds., LeiLani Nishime, and Tasha Oren (New York: NYU Press, 2016).

22 Reproductive labor refers to work performed within the domestic or private sphere that helps to sustain a household.

23 Shin, Andrew. "Projected Bodies in David Henry Hwang's 'M. Butterfly' and 'Golden Gate," *MELUS* 27, no.1 (2002): 177–197.

24 The Asian exclusion act of 1924 still applied to the 1954 War Brides Act.

25 See Ji-Yeon Yuh, *Beyond the Shadow of Camptown: Korean Military Brides in America* (New York: New York University Press, 2004); Grace M. Cho, *Haunting the Korean Diaspora: Shame, Secrecy, and the Forgotten War* (Minneapolis, MN: University of Minnesota Press, 2008); and SooJin Pate, *From Orphan to Adoptee: U.S. Empire and Genealogies of Korean Adoption* (Minneapolis, MN: University of Minnesota Press, 2014). I thank Grace Hong for sharing her insights.

26 See Jodi Kim, "An 'Orphan' with Two Mothers: Transnational and Transracial Adoption, the Cold War, and Contemporary Asian American Cultural Politics," *American Quarterly* 61, no. 4 (2009): 855–880. The term "social death" suggests that the biological mother of the adoptee is rendered "dead"

by political economic and ideological factors even though she is still alive. These factors include political economic circumstances that gave rise to the commodification of adopted children, where the presence, rights, and voices of biological mothers were completely obliterated and rendered illegible and irrelevant.

27 See David Eng, "Transnational Adoption and Queer Diasporas," *Social Text* (Fall 2003) 76, no. 3: 7–8. For his critique of queer liberalism and homonormativity, see *The Feeling of Kinship: Queer Liberalism and the Racialization of Intimacy* (Durham, NC: Duke University Press, 2010). For a history of Asian international adoption in the United States, see Catherine Ceniza Choy, *Global Families: A History of Asian International Adoption in America* (New York: New York University Press, 2013).
28 For accounts of the struggles with racialization, see Kim; Yuh; and Eng, "Transnational Adoption."
29 Even though the 1965 Immigration and Nationality Act can be viewed as a development that embodies the spirit of democracy and equality, in fact it is more of an instrument of racial and labor management that serves U.S. economic interests. See Volpp, "Legal Mapping."
30 Lowe, *Immigrant Acts*, 7.
31 See Robert G. Lee, "The Model Minority as Gook," in his *Orientals: Asian American in Popular Culture*. Philadelphia, PA: Temple University Press, 1999, 180–203.
32 For a discussion of literary representation of Asian women as good wives, see Susan Koshy, *Sexual Naturalization*, 132–186. For the sexualization of Asian women, see Celine Parreñas Shinizu, *The Hypersexuality of Race: Performing Asian/American Women on Screen and Scene* (Durham, NC: Duke University Press, 2007).
33 Section 3 of DOMA defines marriage as a legal union between one man and one woman as husband and wife.
34 For a critique of the heteronormative principle of family reunification and its impact on migrant queers of color, see Chandan Reddy, *Freedom with Violence: Race, Sexuality, and the US State* (Durham, NC: Duke University Press, 2011).
35 Martin F. Manalansan IV, "Servicing the World: Flexible Filipinos and the Unsecured Life," in *Political Emotions*, Eds. Ann Cvetkovich, Janet Staiger, and Ann Reynolds (New York: Routledge, 2010): 215–228.
36 The term "flexible citizenship" was coined by Aihwa Ong. See her *Flexible Citizenship: The Cultural Logics of Transnationality* (Durham, NC: Duke University Press, 2001).
37 Karin Aguilar-San Juan, "Going Home: Enacting Justice in Queer Asian America," in *Q &A: Queer in Asian America*, Eds. David L. Eng and Alice Y. Hom (Philadelphia, PA: Temple University Press, 1998), 25–40.
38 For discussions of the global gay discourse, see Martin F. Manalansan IV, *Global Divas: Filipino Gay May in the Diaspora* (Durham, NC: Duke University Press, 2003); Mark Chiang, "Coming Out into the Global Systems: Postmodern Patriarchies and Transnatinoal Sexualities in *The Wedding Banquet*," in *Q&A: Queer in Asian America*, Eds. David L. Eng and Alice Y. Hom (Philadelphia, PA: Temple University Press, 1998), 374–398. For discussions of Asia as a site of commodification and consumption, see A. Z. Aizura, "Where Health and Beauty Meet: Femininity and Racialisation in Thai Cosmetic Surgery Clinics," *Asian Studies Review* 33, no.3 (2009): 303–317; Dredge Byung'chu Käng, "Kathoey 'In Trend': Emergent Genderscapes, National Anxieties and the Re-Signification of Male-Bodied Effeminacy in Thailand," *Asian Studies Review* 36, no.4 (December 2012): 475–494.
39 Gayatri Gopinath, *Impossible Desires: Queer Diasporas and South Asian Public Cultures* (Durham, NC: Duke University Press, 2005); Petrus Liu, "Why Does Queer Theory Need China?" *positions: east asia cultural critique* 18, no.2 (Fall 2010): 291–320; *Queer Singapore: Illiberal Citizenship and Mediated Cultures*, Eds. Audrey Yue and Jun Zubillaga-Pow (Hong Kong: Hong Kong University Press, 2012); Eng-Beng Lim, *Brown Boys and Rice Queens: Spellbinding Performance in the Asias* (New York: New York University Press, 2013).
40 Grace Kyungwon Hong, "Existentially Surplus: Woman of Color Feminism and the New Crises of Capitalism," *GLQ: A Journal of Lesbian and Gay Studies* 18, no.1 (2012): 87–106; *Death Beyond Disavowal: The Impossible Politics of Difference* (Minneapolis, MN: Minnesota University Press, 2015).
41 Lisa Marie Cacho, *Social Death: Racialized Rightlessness and the Criminalization of the Unprotected* (New York: New York University Press, 2012); Cho, "Nuclear Diffusion: Notes Toward Reimagining Transnational Reproductive Justice." *Amerasia Journal: Asian American/Pacific Islander/Transcultural Societies* 41, no.3 (2015): 2–25.

42 Kalindi Vora, *Life Support: Biocapital and the New History of Outsourced Labor* (Minneapolis, MN: Minnesota University Press, 2015).

References

Aguilar-San Juan, Karin. "Going Home: Enacting Justice in Queer Asian America." In Eng and Hom, 25–40.

Aizura, A. Z. "Where Health and Beauty Meet: Femininity and Racialisation in Thai Cosmetic Surgery Clinics." *Asian Studies Review* 33, no.3 (2009): 303–317.

Briggs, Laura. *Reproducing Empire: Race, Sex, Science, and U.S. Imperialism in Puerto Rico*. Berkeley, CA: California University Press, 2002.

Cacho, Lisa Marie. *Social Death Racialized Rightlessness and the Criminalization of the Unprotected*. New York: New York University Press, 2012.

Chan, Sucheng, Ed. *Entry Denied: Exclusion and the Chinese Community in America, 1882–1943*. Philadelphia, PA: Temple University Press, 1991.

Chiang, Mark. "Coming Out into the Global Systems: Postmodern Patriarchies and Transnational Sexualities in *The Wedding Banquet*." In Eng and Hom, 374–398.

Cho, Grace, M. *Haunting the Korean Diaspora: Shame, Secrecy, and the Forgotten War*. Minneapolis, MN: University of Minnesota Press, 2008.

Cho, Yu-Fang. "Nuclear Diffusion: Notes Toward Reimagining Transnational Reproductive Justice." *Amerasia Journal: Asian American/Pacific Islander/Transcultural Societies* 41.3 (2015): 2–25.

———. *Uncoupling American Empire: Cultural Politics of Deviance and Unequal Differences, 1890–1910*. Albany, NY: SUNY Press, 2013.

Choy, Catherine Ceniza. *Global Families: A History of Asian International Adoption in America*. New York: New York University Press, 2013.

Cott, Nancy. *Public Vows: A History of Marriage and the Nation*. Cambridge, MA: Harvard University Press, 2002.

Eng, David L. *Racial Castration: Managing Masculinity in Asian America*. Durham, NC: Duke University Press, 2001.

———. "Transnational Adoption and Queer Diasporas." *Social Text* (Fall 2003) 76, no. 3: 1–37

———. *The Feeling of Kinship: Queer Liberalism and the Racialization of Intimacy*. Durham, NC: Duke University Press, 2010.

Eng, David L. and Alice Y. Hom, Eds. *Q&A: Queer in Asian America*. Philadelphia, PA: Temple University Press, 1998.

Galang, M. Evelina, Ed. *Screaming Monkeys: Critiques of Asian American Images*. Minneapolis, MN: Coffee House Press, 2003.

Gopinath, Gayatri. *Impossible Desires: Queer Diasporas and South Asian Public Cultures*. Durham, NC: Duke University Press, 2005.

Hong, Grace Kyungwon. *Death Beyond Disavowal: The Impossible Politics of Difference*. Minneapolis, MN: Minnesota University Press, 2015.

———. "Existentially Surplus: Woman of Color Feminism and the New Crises of Capitalism." *GLQ: A Journal of Lesbian and Gay Studies* 18, no.1: (2012): 87–106.

Jacobson, Matthew Frye. *Whiteness of a Different Color: European Immigrants and the Alchemy of Race*. Cambridge, MA: Harvard University Press, 1998.

Jung, Moon-Ho. *Coolies and Cane: Race, Labor, and Sugar in the Age of Emancipation*. Baltimore, MD: John Hopkins University Press, 2008.

Kang, Laura Hyun Yi. *Compositional Subjects: Enfiguring Asian/American Women*. Durham, NC: Duke University Press, 2002.

Käng, Dredge Byung'chu, "Kathoey 'In Trend': Emergent Genderscapes, National Anxieties and the Re-Signification of Male-Bodied Effeminacy in Thailand," *Asian Studies Review* 36 no.4 (December 2012): 475–494.

Kim, Jodi. "An 'Orphan' with Two Mothers: Transnational and Transracial Adoption, the Cold War, and Contemporary Asian American Cultural Politics." *American Quarterly* 61, no. 4 (2009): 855–880.

Koshy, Susan. *Sexual Naturalization: Asian Americans and Miscegenation*. Palo Alto, CA: Stanford University Press, 2004.

Kramer, Paul L. "The Darkness That Enters the Home: The Politics of Prostitution during the Philippine-American War." In Stoler, 366–404.

Lee, Erika. "Orientalisms in the Americas: A Hemispheric Approach to Asian American History." *Journal of Asian American Studies* 8, no.3 (October 2005): 235–256

———. "The 'Yellow Peril' and Asian Exclusion in the Americas." *Pacific Historical Review* 76, no.4 (2007): 537–562.

Lee, Robert G. *Orientals: Asian American in Popular Culture*. Philadelphia, PA: Temple University Press, 1999.

Lim, Eng-Beng. *Brown Boys and Rice Queens: Spellbinding Performance in the Asias*. New York: New York University Press, 2013.

Liu, Petrus. "Why Does Queer Theory Need China?" *Positions: East Asia Cultural Critique* 18, no.2 (Fall 2010): 291–320

Lowe, Lisa. *Immigrant Acts: On Asian American Cultural Politics*. Durham, NC: Duke University Press, 1996.

———. "The Intimacies of Four Continents." In Stoler, 191–212.

López, Kathleen. "Afro-Asian Alliances: Marriage, Godparent, and Social Status in Late-Nineteenth-Century Cuba." *Afro-Hispanic Review* 27, no.1 (2008): 59–72.

Luibhéid, Eithne. *Entry Denied: Controlling Sexuality at the Border*. Minneapolis, MN: Minnesota University Press, 2002.

Maeda, Daryl Joji. "Trans-Pacific Flows: Globalization and Hybridity in Bruce Lee's Hong Kong Films," *Global Asian American Popular Cultures*, Eds. Shilpa Dave, LeiLani Nishime, and Tasha Oren (New York: NYU Press, 2016).

Manalansan, Martin F., IV, *Global Divas: Filipino Gay May in the Diaspora*. Durham, NC: Duke University Press, 2003.

———. "Servicing the World: Flexible Filipinos and the Unsecured Life." In *Political Emotions*, Eds. Ann Cvetkovich, Janet Staiger, and Ann Reynolds, 215–228. New York: Routledge, 2010.

Ngai, Mae. M. *Impossible Subjects: Illegal Aliens and the Making of Modern America*. Princeton, NJ: Princeton University Press, 2004.

Ong, Aihwa. *Flexible Citizenship: The Cultural Logics of Transnationality*. Durham, NC: Duke University Press, 2011.

Pascoe, Peggy. *What Comes Naturally: Miscegenation Law and the Making of Race in America*. Oxford: Oxford University Press, 2010.

Pate, SooJin. *From Orphan to Adoptee: U.S. Empire and Genealogies of Korean Adoption*. Minneapolis, MN: University of Minnesota Press, 2014.

Reddy, Chandan. *Freedom with Violence: Race, Sexuality, and the US State*. Durham, NC: Duke University Press, 2011.

Sánchez, Martha Chew. "Deconstructing the Rhetoric of Mestizaje through the Chinese Presence in Mexico." In *Strange Affinities: The Gender and Sexual Politics of Comparative Racialization*, Ed. Grace Kyungwon Hong and Roderick A. Ferguson, 215–240. Durham, NC: Duke University Press, 2011.

Shah, Nayan. *Contagious Divides: Epidemics and Race in San Francisco's Chinatown*. Berkeley, CA: California University Press, 2001.

———. *Stranger Intimacy: Contesting Race, Sexuality, and the Law in the North American West*. Berkeley, CA: University of California Press, 2011.

Shimizu, Celine Parreñas. *The Hypersexuality of Race: Performing Asian/American Women on Screen and Scene*. Durham, NC: Duke University Press, 2007.

Shin, Andrew. "Projected Bodies in David Henry Hwang's 'M. Butterfly' and 'Golden Gate.'" *MELUS* 27, no.1 (2002): 177–197.

Stoler, Anne Laura, ed. *Haunted by Empire: Geographies of Intimacy in North American History*. Durham, NC: Duke University Press, 2006.

Sueyoshi, Amy. *Queer Compulsions: Race, Nation, and Sexuality in the Affairs of Yone Noguchi*. Honolulu, HI: University of Hawaii Press, 2012.

Takaki, Ronlad. *Iron Cages: Race and Culture in Nineteenth-Century America*. Seattle, WA: University of Washington Press, 1979.

Tchen, John Kuo Wei. *New York Before Chinatown: Orientalism and the Shaping of American Culture, 1776–1882*. Baltimore, MD: Johns Hopkins University Press, 2001.

Volpp, Leti. "The Legal Mapping of U.S. Immigration, 1965–1996." In *Crossing into America: the New Literature of Immigration*, Eds. Louis Mendoza and S. Shankar, 257–260. New York: The New Press, 2003.

———. "Divesting Citizenship: On Asian American History and the Loss of Citizenship through Marriage, *UCLA Law Review* 53, no.2 (2005): 403–83.

Vora, Kalindi. *Life Support: Biocapital and the New History of Outsourced Labor*. Minneapolis, MN: Minnesota University Press, 2015.

Yu, Henry. "Los Angeles and American Studies in a Pacific World of Migrations." *American Quarterly* 56, no.3 (2004): 531–543.

Yue, Audrey and Jun Zubillaga-Pow, Eds. *Queer Singapore: Illiberal Citizenship and Mediated Cultures*. Hong Kong: Hong Kong University Press, 2012.

Yuh, Ji-Yeon. *Beyond the Shadow of Camptown: Korean Military Brides in America*. New York: New York University Press, 2004.

Yung, Judy. *Unbound Feet: A Social History of Chinese Women in San Francisco*. Berkeley, CA: University of California Press, 1995.

19
FROM NOXIOUS QUARTERS TO AFFLUENT ETHNO-BURBS
Race and Space in Asian American History

Shelley Sang-Hee Lee

Introduction

Working from the now commonly accepted idea that race is a social construct with a range of material consequences, recent scholarship on race in America has revealed much about how racial categories are generated, manipulated, and solidified, as well as how they have changed over time. In Asian American studies, and ethnic studies more generally, attention to space has illuminated some of the discussions of race and racial formation. This is not in itself a new focus, as some of the earliest scholars doing research about Asians in America—sociologists affiliated with the University of Chicago—often presented their findings about ethnic and racial difference via spatial mappings and conceptualizations.[1] Going back further, to draw on Edward Said's discussion of the West's construction of the East, Europeans as early as the Greeks during the fourth century BCE linked cultural difference to spatial distance, and few parts of the world, they surmised, were as distinct as the "East" and "West." Subsequently embedded in U.S. culture and thought, these ideas informed how Americans viewed Asia and its people. A task of recent scholars, then, has been to dismantle such assumptions in order to explain how they were—rather than natural, common-sense knowledge about people, space, and geography—the outcome of processes that shored up racial differences and hierarchies.

In the mid-nineteenth century, the presence of thousands of Asian immigrants on U.S. soil challenged a pillar of the East–West imaginary by effectively bringing the "Orient" and "Occident" into close physical proximity. Yet space remained crucial to people's understandings of Asian otherness, and would figure in struggles to reinforce or dismantle racial discrimination. Because for decades Asians' subordination in the United States was achieved via de jure and de facto segregation, their pursuit of mobility often turned on their right to enter and claim otherwise restricted spaces. The following essay describes how through much of Asian American history space has been integral to the construction of race, and further, how the entanglement of race and space shaped contours of Asian American daily life. Fluid and malleable yet subject to contestation and control, space has been a vehicle of racism and exclusion, but it has also been a platform for community building, intergroup relations, and rearticulating the meanings of race and ethnicity.

Containing Racialized Space in the City

Chinatown is perhaps the most iconic locale associated with Asian racialized space in America. From the mid-nineteenth century the mere mention of "Chinatown" evoked mystery and depravity, while prompting the alarm of journalists, moral crusaders, and police. Although Chinatowns and other Asian urban enclaves were usually multiethnic in composition, the perception that they were homogeneous—and thus additionally dangerous and undesirable—quickly took hold and endured. Historians Mary Ting Yi Lui and Nayan Shah have shown how the cognitive and geographic emergence of Chinatown and the racial formation of Chinese in America were part and parcel of the same process.[2] So ingrained was this conflation of race and space by the turn of the twentieth century that the entry of even a small number of Asians in white areas or the occurrence of interracial mixing in minority quarters would trigger social panic that then justified further segregation, surveillance, and isolation. And with greater isolation, outsiders' imaginings about Asian spaces grew more vivid; public health reports and popular writings about San Francisco's Chinatown (with titles like "Horrors of a Mongolian Settlement") noted the "dens, density, and the labyrinth" of the area and, as Nayan Shah explains, "cast Chinatown as a deviant transplantation of the traditional East in the modern Western city."[3]

In San Francisco, since the mid-nineteenth century, municipal officials had tried to regulate residents' behavior and organize space in the name of environmental and public health, and they singled out Chinatown as a particular menace. Although courts usually blocked the use of nuisance laws to racially discriminate against residents, the widespread perception of Chinatown as a noxious place rationalized its surveillance and harassment during major health scares. One case involved a quarantine of Chinatown (and neighboring Japanese areas) in March 1900, ordered after the body of a Chinese man thought to have died of bubonic plague was found in a hotel basement. Although quarantining people in their homes during epidemics was not a new practice, sequestering an entire district was. Officials ordered all white people to leave, disinfected Chinatown, and inoculated its residents, only lifting the quarantine some sixty hours later after people complained about its discriminatory execution and doctors confirmed there had been no plague.[4] Chinatowns elsewhere were similarly targeted, perhaps none faring worse than Honolulu's. In early 1900, following a quarantine of the area during a bubonic plague scare, several new cases of the disease surfaced.[5] But instead of calling a new quarantine and round of disinfection, officials ordered the burning of several buildings, which eventually consumed all of Chinatown and left 4,500 people homeless.[6] After the fire, the disease appeared elsewhere in Honolulu and on other islands, exposing the fallacy of the notion that officials could contain epidemics by controlling racialized bodies and spaces.

While the ineffectiveness of quarantines showed that contagion, race, and space were not so easily collapsible, racial segregation nonetheless remained a feature of urban geographies. Asians who immigrated after the Chinese usually settled in or near Chinatowns because these were the only places where they could live and get needed services. Further reinforcing this settlement pattern were restrictive covenants, zoning laws, white flight, and intimidation campaigns. Because they were usually in or near marginal areas where working-class people and minorities converged, Asian sections tended to also be regarded as taboo. Indeed, this concentrated spatial transgressiveness—signaled further by the presence of establishments like integrated dance halls, brothels, and opium dens—also marked racial difference, continually fascinating and repulsing "respectable" whites.

While the control and containment of Asian spaces accompanied the enforcement of racial boundaries, the occurrence and prospect of interracial mingling, in and outside those spaces, represented alarming threats to racial order. One illustrative episode from New York in 1909 followed the discovery of the body of a young white woman named Elsie Sigel in the trunk of a Chinese man, Leon Ling. Ling had gone missing prior to the discovery, and a set of love letters that Sigel had addressed to him made him a suspect for her murder. Details about their relationship and the search for Ling, which captivated New York and much of the nation, were spun as a cautionary tale about the dangers of modern life, Chinese men, and interracial relations. Sigel had met Ling while teaching at a Chinese Sunday School, a job she held against her parents' wishes, and her biggest mistake, according to journalists, had been treating a Chinese as a social equal, or "white man."[7] Sigel's murder raised concerns about the work of Chinese missions, and led to the closure of some and the expulsion of white women workers from others.[8] The hunt for Ling showed the vulnerability of Chinatown and New York's Asian residents. A number of Asian men—many Japanese—were arrested after being mistaken for the Chinese Ling, and people were subjected to intrusive searches of their homes, workplaces, and neighborhoods by police, reporters, and ordinary citizens.[9]

With all of this said, it bears emphasizing that the meanings of Asian urban enclaves varied, depending on one's position and point of view. Although they were subject to derision and neglect, these spaces also provided vital resources, services, and sanctuary for their residents. To take Seattle's Jackson Street neighborhood as an example, most whites by the 1930s regarded it as the city's ghetto. Arising in the historic "Skid Road" district and known for its high concentration of minorities and transients, Jackson Street also became home to a large share of the city's Asian American population. Residents were keenly aware of how outsiders looked upon them. In 1933, the *Northwest Enterprise*, a local Black newspaper established in 1920, acknowledged that the area was "one of the most abused streets in Seattle," not to mention, "the butt of jokes," and a place "sneeringly referred to by residents of other sections of the city."[10]

Although outsiders did not appreciate it, Jackson Street's residents held a strong connection to and pride in their neighborhood.[11] Chinese American Ken Louie, who had moved to Seattle from New York in 1938, remembered fondly, saying, "In the old days you don't have that many people in Chinatown to start out with. The Japanese people on one side of us, and the Filipino people sort of intermingle with both sides. And you walk down the street, you say hello to everybody."[12] Yoshisada Kawai, who came to the U.S. from Japan in 1918 at the age of sixteen, remembered, "I couldn't help being astounded at the vigorous liveliness of those Japanese who could hardly speak English and yet had brought their businesses to success.[13] A newspaper column in the local ethnic paper, *Japanese-American Courier*, called "Down Main Street" a close-knit Japanese American community against a backdrop of ethnic diversity. A common street scene included Filipino "dandies" in town from the canneries, "swarm[ing] over the sidewalks of Jackson Street and by avenues, nattily attired in the 'latest' balloon pants"; a Hebrew, "wearing a black skull cap and a long flow of beard [standing] in front of his shop"; and a Black man changing a flat tire at the corner of Maynard and King.[14] In another description of Jackson Street's sights and sounds, the column noted, "A wild southern symphony combined with the tenor of a colored jazz singer emanates from a tea shop below the Kin Ka Low Restaurant. A bit of Southern philosophy mixed in with that of the Orient."[15] Such images contributed to a powerful counternarrative to the dismissive characterizations of Jackson Street and showed that the same qualities that marginalized the area for some people made it special to others.

Other scholars have discussed similarly rich social, cultural, and economic lives that flourished in "seedy" enclaves. In Stockton, California, Filipinos entered an already segregated city during the 1920s and settled in one of the only downtown sections (the "Oriental Quarter") that did not exclude racial minorities.[16] From there, the newcomers quickly learned the city's spatial customs. For instance, they could only sit in certain sections in theaters, were banned from entering other businesses, and if they crossed into the wrong side of Main Street—called Stockton's

"Mason Dixon line"—they were vulnerable to police beatings.[17] Learning how to navigate this territory was necessary to survive, but it also solidified Filipinos' status as racial "others." At the same time, with the emergence of Little Manila, they put their own imprint on the urban geography. For example, the tendency of Ilocanos to gather on one side of Lafayette Street and Visayans on the other represented a kind of ethnic mapping that became part of the everyday logic of life in Stockton.[18] And when outsiders attacked Little Manila, they often did so by targeting Filipino community spaces: association buildings, businesses, or public gathering areas. That these incidents then rallied residents to defend their community and its institutions showed the degree to which ethnic solidarity was understood and mapped spatially.

Spatial Precarity and Working-Class Racialization

Factories in the Field, the title of Cary McWilliams's 1935 study of migrant farm workers in California, also lives on in the historical lexicon to denote the system of corporate agriculture in the American West, as well as the laborers indispensable to its growth.[19] In highlighting "factories" and "fields," the phrase also brings attention to spatial considerations in worker experiences and working-class formation. Applying the insights of intersectional theory to underscore the mutually constitutive relationship among social and identity categories—here race and class—the following section discusses how, in Asian American history, the capitalist disciplining of labor, itself a process of racialization, relied on the careful management of space. This management manifested in varied ways, including the careful organization of work camps, the placement of Asian laborers on the most punishing and isolated terrain, and their exclusion from key sites of opportunity. The impact of these tactics was a fundamental precarity in Asian workers' relationship to space, seen in the constant movement among migratory workers as well as a lack of autonomy over space among those more physically rooted.

The agricultural migratory labor circuit illustrates some of the costs of spatial precarity. The physical challenges of migratory labor went beyond exhaustion, as the lack of geographic rootedness could also inhibit family and community formation, as well as labor organizing. A male Korean immigrant who came to America via San Francisco in 1916 recalled meeting a co-ethnic labor contractor days after his arrival. With about twenty co-ethnics, he went to Stockton, where a contractor had arranged jobs for the group on a bean farm. "We were hoeing the bean fields," he remembered, "and when we finished we went to another bean farm for hoeing. It was hard work. Then we went to Dinuba picking grapes. I was flocking with other Koreans, and I went where they went for available farm jobs."[20]

On Hawaii sugar plantations, workers did not so much contend with a lack of physical rootedness as a carefully organized environment that undermined their autonomy over their spatial lives. Over the second half of the nineteenth century, planters had become reliant on Asian labor from China, Japan, the Philippines, and Korea.[21] As part of a divide and conquer strategy that informed the layout of the plantations, laborers were typically placed in ethnically segregated living quarters and worked in gangs with co-ethnics. Planters' desire for a compliant imported labor force led them to start recruiting Chinese during the nineteenth century, and a few decades later, fearing that they had grown too dependent on these workers, they turned to Japanese. As one planter stated, "We lay great stress on the necessity of having our labor mixed. By employing different nationalities, there is less danger of collusion among laborers, and the employers [are able to] secure better discipline."[22] By the end of the first decade of the 1900s, Japanese dominance in the workforce as well as their involvement in labor agitation led employers to look to a new set of imported workers, this time Filipinos.

Planters manipulated workers' ethnic loyalties not merely for the sake of controlling laborers. Because this was also a strategy aimed at maintaining a racial hierarchy that privileged whiteness, it called on the predominantly nonwhite workforce to be continually subject to poor living and working conditions. The quarters that laborers were housed in varied in quality, but were usually overcrowded and dirty.[23] On Aiea plantation, a single "humble shed" housed about fifty bachelors and several married couples, and families lived in rooms measuring six-by-eight feet. The camps at Paia plantation were even more crowded; male laborers lived in warehouse-like buildings with bunks stacked four or five levels high.[24] The class and racial inequalities that these spatial configurations symbolized and upheld were evident in how jobs were distributed: a 1902 survey of 55 plantations found that 83 percent of plantation laborers were Japanese and Chinese, while members of these groups held just 18 percent of superintendent jobs.[25]

While being subject to a perpetual state of dislocation and precariousness exacted a toll, scholars have shown how Asian workers mitigated some of the effects by forming translocal communities and networks, developing new identities, and strengthening ethnic solidarities. For example, some Filipinos on the West Coast during the 1920s and 1930s navigated the geographic challenges of migratory labor by pooling money with co-ethnics to purchase a car to travel from job to job.[26] They also defied the general debasement of migratory labor through the creation of their own hierarchies. While they crisscrossed the American West to work in lumber mills, ranches, farms, canneries and homes, only the heartiest braved the Alaska canneries. Called *Alaskeros*, these men held an esteemed place in the Filipino labor community.

In Hawaii by the early twentieth century, the population's racial and ethnic diversity, originally a strategy of labor control, had various unintended consequences, including the development of a pidgin dialect and the emergence of a mixed-race population. Regarding the former, laborers generally retained the language of their home countries, which was reinforced by the organization of gangs and plantations as well as establishment of language schools and ethnic institutions. However, when working with members of other ethnic groups, they had to learn to communicate across boundaries, which led to the evolution of a plantation dialect called pidgin that incorporated elements of Japanese, Chinese, Portuguese, and other languages. Because it was associated with laborers, it facilitated the formation of a multiethnic working class identity in Hawaii.[27]

As these examples have shown, labor practices that restricted Asian workers' spatial freedom went hand in hand with highly circumscribed possibilities of citizenship. Their encounters with the racialized economy gave rise to an imagined and material world in which their natural place was in the "fields" or "factories" as laborers. During the nineteenth and early twentieth centuries, this idea was even codified through measures like foreign miners taxes, alien land laws, and laundry ordinances, which excluded or onerously regulated Asian immigrants so as to effectively keep them out of spaces—mines, land they own, businesses—in which they could pursue mobility and economic independence.

Freedom and Equality in the Suburbs

As noted above, an aspect of racial disfranchisement among Asians in America was spatial exclusion and precarity, whether this related to property, access, visibility, or the ability to lay down roots. Because of this, the right to enter, control, and own space were key preoccupations in Asian Americans' struggles for mobility and success. By the mid-twentieth century, suburbs were held up as the ideal of the American "good life," and they also became a sanctuary for middle- and working-class whites unhappy with the chaos and nonwhiteness of the city. But the suburbs did not just appeal to white Americans. The same things that drew them—better schools, the promise of home ownership, safety—appealed to people of all backgrounds, and from the mid-twentieth century for many Asian Americans, a new narrative began to unfold, that of spatial inclusion and incorporation.

The desire among people of all groups to live in the suburbs turned these communities into battlegrounds over racial privilege. The whiteness of suburban residential communities had long been protected by the practices of homeowners' associations, real estate companies, and loan institutions. For decades, racially restrictive covenants (ruled unconstitutional in 1948) governed by homeowner associations forbade the selling of property to minorities. The home loan system was also rigged against minorities, as loan officers relied on neighborhood ratings provided by the real estate industry that reserved the highest rating for all-white areas. In Los Angeles, for example, assessors considered Blacks and Asians the most detrimental to home values. These ratings determined whether buyers could obtain FHA insurance, so nonwhite applicants were rejected the most.

For many Asian Americans, a house in the suburbs symbolized a reward to which they felt entitled, especially after World War II, and during the 1950s and 1960s they began to make some inroads. Two key developments worked to their advantage: the changing domestic racial landscape and wartime alliances with Asian countries. The war had helped to herald a new orthodoxy that envisioned America as a multiracial democracy. But things did not always play out so smoothly on the ground with regard to whom white Americans would welcome as their neighbors. Developers still wished to contain the entry of nonwhites, but they also saw Asians as a palatable alternative to Blacks. For example, in Los Angeles the Pacific Investment Company (PIC) offered Japanese Americans the chance to take advantage of FHA financing for first time by granting loans to purchase homes in the Jefferson Park area. Although assessors considered the area undesirable, Japanese Americans nonetheless embraced it, and the FHA realized the profitability in marketing a development to this group. However, even this was too close for comfort to many white residents in nearby West Adams who worried that the entry of Japanese into Jefferson Park would hurt their own home values, so some owners responded by leaving.

Others also faced an uphill battle, but as mentioned above, were aided by the relatively favorable climate toward Asian Americans. In late 1952, Sam Yoshihara, a disabled Nisei veteran who had served in the famed all-Japanese 442nd Infantry Regiment tried to buy a house in San Jose, California, a growing community with defense and military industries. Although several residents of the street circulated a petition to reject Yoshihara, their voices were eclipsed by other residents and a local civic unity group that pushed back to defend him.[28] Citing his military service and fear of negative publicity, Yoshihara's supporters argued that recent developments called for the acceptance of Japanese and other Asians; as one resident said, "my property values aren't as important as my principles."[29] Sufficiently shamed, the residents apologized for the petition and welcomed Yoshihara to the neighborhood.

The movement of Asian Americans into suburban communities was evident in California by 1960, marking a discernible shift in the state's residential landscape. Although many remained in the urban enclaves, the trend, for the rest of the twentieth century, was toward suburbanization. The racial significance of this movement, moreover, was not lost on contemporaries. As one San Francisco real estate broker stated, "Japanese and Chinese are often accepted almost like whites."[30] To be sure, this did not mean Asians did not face any discrimination, whether socially or with regard to obtaining loans, but brokers were increasingly willing to sell to them. In California, Asian American suburbanization was especially pronounced in the San Francisco Bay Area, Los Angeles and Orange counties. In addition to signaling residential mobility, living in the suburbs also gave children access to good schools, which then allowed Asian American residents to make greater inroads in the mainstream economy.

It is no coincidence that Asian Americans' accelerated movement into the suburbs occurred at the same time that the "model minority" image entered the public consciousness. During the 1960s, academic and popular publications extolled Asian American assimilation and integration into mainstream life. Commonly cited in these reports were their low crime rates, strong families, occupational mobility, and homeownership, but a largely unspoken subtext of these celebrations of Asian Americans was African Americans' failure to succeed in a similar fashion. Further, the contrasting spatial imagery of Asian American suburbanites and African American inner city dwellers became a common and powerful marker of racial differentiation from the 1960s on.

Asian American Suburbs and Ethno-burbs

By the late twentieth century, it was evident that Asian Americans' participation in suburban growth, although indicative of changes in the racial landscape and their place within it, was not a sign that they had "become white." The suburbanization of Asian America, which started before 1965, accelerated and broadened as more newcomers entered the United States, and drove the striking transformation of some areas into predominantly nonwhite communities. Nor was the shift toward suburban living an extension of Asian Americans' socioeconomic mobility and the pursuit of the "good life." Many working-class newcomers had no choice but to look to the suburbs, as existing urban ethnic enclaves were wiped out or squeezed due to urban renewal programs that restricted the availability of both housing and jobs. With regard to the Chinese, in emerging inner-ring suburban neighborhoods like Richmond in San Francisco and Flushing, Queens in New York, long-time Chinese Americans increasingly lived alongside newly arrived immigrants. Meanwhile, across the nation, a shrinking percentage of Chinese lived in city centers—in 2000, for example, just 2 percent of those in the Los Angeles metropolitan area lived in Old Chinatown—although they have by and large remained in major metropolitan areas.[31]

Destinations at the edges of metropolitan areas—called ex-burbs and ethno-burbs known for having concentrations of particular ethnic groups—have emerged as vital centers of growing Asian American communities from the 1970s on. To take the example of Monterey Park, California, located in the San Gabriel Valley and nicknamed the "first suburban Chinatown," this community's growth was driven by the arrival of people from Taiwan, Hong Kong, and the PRC. In 1980 Monterey Park became a "majority minority" city where Asians made up 35 percent of the population, and ten years later, they represented 56 percent, with whites making up about 25 percent.[32] Similar transformations occurred elsewhere in the San Gabriel Valley as well as in Orange County, South Bay communities in Northern California, Queens and other New York boroughs, Houston, Texas and Orlando, Florida, as well as locations outside the United States, such as Sydney, Australia and Vancouver, Canada.

Turning again to Monterey Park, its Chinese community emerged from the efforts of Frederic Hsieh, a realtor who had come to the U.S. as a student from Hong Kong in 1963. Arriving in San Gabriel Valley in the early 1970s, he envisioned the area becoming a "modern day mecca" for the "new Chinese," people seeking to move to the United States due to political uncertainty as well as good investment opportunities.[33] Believing that Los Angeles's Chinatown would not appeal to affluent, educated, and skilled newcomers, he bought property in Monterey Park and promoted it as the "Chinese Beverly Hills." By the mid-1970s an influx of young engineers, businessmen, and other professionals were heeding his call. Infusions of Asian capital supplemented the arrival of immigrants, with large numbers of Chinese-owned banks setting up operations over the 1980s. As Wesley Ru, a Monterey Park businessman explained the transformation, "First it was the real estate people, and then trading companies, heavy investors, people that come with hundreds of thousands of dollars in cash."[34]

Like the Chinese in Monterey Park, Filipino Daly City, a suburb south of San Francisco, is a post-1965 phenomenon, but its growth has not been accompanied by the appearance of wealth on the same scale. Known as the "Pinoy capital" of the United States, Daly City is, to many residents "indistinguishable from life 'back home.'"[35] In 1970 it was about 86 percent white, and by 2008 Filipinos represented about 32 percent—or 32,720—of a population that was now majority Asian and foreign born. According to Benito Vergara, proximity to San Francisco was a major factor leading to settlement in Daly City. It was an especially appealing option for upwardly mobile immigrants who wished to become homeowners. After the first few arrivals settled, family sponsorship-based chain migration fueled the rapid growth of Daly City's Filipino population, and it soon became a site of first settlement for large numbers of newcomers. Like many other new Asian suburban enclaves, the Filipino American community in Daly City lacks a clear center and to many outsiders is barely recognizable as a distinct enclave. However, Filipinos can be found congregating in nondescript shopping centers, at events such as Filipino Cultural Nights and evidence of their business presence in Goldilocks restaurants and other establishments.[36]

For many longtime white residents, the transformation of suburban space by Asian bodies, food, culture, and wealth was bewildering, and their complaints echoed urban controversies from over 100 years ago. In Monterey Park, a middle-aged white resident named Howard Fry recalled "an elderly Chinese gentleman riding his bicycle down the street with a satchel slung on one of the handlebars and if he saw anybody in the front yard, he would approach them and ask: 'Would you like to sell your house? I've got the money.'"[37] Beneath the surface, racial resentment simmered among those who felt that this once white, Christian community that had revolved around the Methodist Church and service clubs had changed too much and too quickly. By the late 1970s, land speculation and construction inflated property values and increased rents, giving rise to widespread anti-growth sentiments. In 1978 the city Planning Commission recommended a moratorium on the construction of multiple dwelling units, which Frederic Hsieh protested was discriminatory against Chinese immigrants.[38] Chinese-owned businesses also became targets of resentment, both for their preponderance—by the 1990s, Chinese owned between two-thirds and three-quarters of all business enterprises in Monterey Park—and foreign language signage that transformed the visual landscape.[39] Anxiety about growth and change increasingly manifested as racial and cultural intolerance. Examples included a 1985 petition by to get an Official English initiative on the municipal ballot, and cars displaying bumper stickers reading, "Will the Last American to Leave Monterey Park Please Bring the Flag?"[40] More recently in the early 2000s in West San Gabriel Valley, a controversy over "city branding" pitted Chinese who wished to highlight their contributions to local history and commerce against white leaders who wanted to invoke the more familiar and conventional Spanish/Mexican heritage and legacy. As Wendy Cheng has explained, "In the West SGV, Asian space and Spanish/Mexican space were triangulated vis-à-vis whites: in municipal politics white elites were able to dictate the terms of belonging, often validating the Spanish space as central to the identity of the area (firmly relegated to the past), while continuing to treat Asian space as perpetually foreign."[41]

In light of recent trends in Asian American suburbanization, there are numerous implications to consider with regard to the changing but still critical relationship between race and space. Transnational Asian families, although not a new phenomenon, have increasingly reflected post-1965 immigrants' considerable resources and flexibility. Many Asian investors hoping to make money in the United States immigrated to establish a business, then brought and settled family members in a community like Monterey Park, and commuted back and forth across the Pacific.

Having children born in the United States gave parents an automatic foothold. In other cases, both parents stayed in Asia while children attended school in the United States, and once the children obtained permanent residency, they sponsored their family members.[42] These children have been called "parachute children," a term that describes students—disproportionately Chinese—who came to the United States to attend school while living on their own, having been admitted on F-1 student visas as teenagers or pre-teenagers.[43] These examples exemplify how, in the late twentieth and early twenty-first centuries, technological innovation in travel and communications, as well as accelerated economic globalization, have dramatically opened up the geographic meanings and possibilities of ethnicity and community.

Taking another view, the growth and diversification of suburban areas, especially with regard to the preponderance of nonwhites, compels us to reconsider whether it makes sense to continue to view suburbs as normatively white, middle-class spaces. Returning to the West San Gabriel Valley (SGV), an area that is now 90 percent Latino and Asian, Wendy Cheng notes the emergence of a distinct nonwhite identity among residents. In arguing against dominant generalizations about race and space, she urges for a consideration of regional variants and challenges the notion that nonwhite spaces are inherently underprivileged.[44] With regard to Asian Americans in the western SGV, Cheng finds that home ownership and other class advantages gave them a "racialized privilege" over Latinos, representing a striking evolution in Asian American race and space.[45] This hierarchy would be internalized in settings such as schools. At Alhambra High School, whose student body is like the western SGV, 90 percent Asian and Latino, the former group achieved a higher position in the "socioacademic ladder" due to scholarly achievements. Interethnic resentment, however, was not the only outcome of the SGV's distinct demographics. In the "SGV Dreamgirl" campaign, for example, a local streetwear company produced and marketed a T-shirt depicting a dark-haired and dark-eyed woman, who was described in the website catalog as "your dreamgirl; she's half Asian, half Latina."[46] This kind of celebration of the nonwhite multiracial place-based identity unique to the area illustrated the interethnic melding that played out just as commonly as friction or tension in the SGV.

Conclusion

As discussed above, space has long been integral to the construction of race in Asian American history. Whether it is a neighborhood or street being associated with a particular group, members of that group rallying to protect their community, or minorities being excluded from designated places, configuring, imagining, and mapping space is how people have often given meaning to the world around them. As powerful as spatial approaches have been in mobilizing affinities as well as prejudice, racialized space has always been a material impossibility. Chinatowns, for instance, were never all-Chinese, and attempts to contain spaces—whether in the name of public health, worker discipline, or something else—have fallen short of their goals. But the power of the connection between race and space remains and has rationalized draconian solutions against racial minorities in times of crisis. As discussed above, the facile but nonetheless influential belief in the links between race, space, and contagion underlays turn-of-the-century quarantines of Chinatown, and forty years later, perhaps the most ambitious strategy of racial containment was carried out with the evacuation of Japanese Americans from the West Coast during World War II. Calls to intern Arab Americans in the wake of 9/11 attested to the persistence of the belief that racialized threats can be spatially managed.

The issues at stake in discussions about Asian American race and space evolve as we move further into the twenty-first century. As the tentacles of gentrification—a term loaded with racial and class implications—continue to encroach on Asian urban neighborhoods, residents and business owners—and their cities writ large—will have to reckon with these changes.[47] The significance of virtual spaces, in which Asian Americans like the rest of the population are spending increasing amounts of time with advancing technology, may certainly be relevant. A host of other issues and questions will also factor into how space and race intersect in Asian American life, shaping academic and public discussion alike.

Notes

1 Henry Yu, *Thinking Orientals: Migration, Contact, and Exoticism in Modern America* (New York: Oxford University Press, 2001).
2 Mary Ting Yi Lui, *The Chinatown Trunk Mystery: Murder Miscegenation, and Other Dangerous Encounters in Turn-of-the Century New York City* (Princeton, NJ: Princeton University Press, 2005); Nayan Shah, *Contagious Divides: Epidemics and Race in San Francisco's Chinatown* (Berkeley, CA: University of California Press, 2001).
3 Shah, *Contagious Divides*, 43.
4 Ibid., 132.
5 Ibid., 127.
6 Ibid., 128.
7 Lui, *The Chinatown Trunk Mystery*, 8.
8 Ibid., 15.
9 Ibid., 13.
10 "Jackson Street is Quiet Thoroughfare on Sunday," *Northwest Enterprise*, October 12, 1933.
11 "A Dangerous Corner," *Japanese-American Courier*, May 5, 1928.
12 "Ken Louie," in *Reflections of Seattle's Chinese Americans: The First 100 Years*, ed. Ron Chew (Seattle, WA: University of Washington Press, 1994), 57.
13 Kazuo Ito, *Issei: A History of Japanese Immigrants in North America*, trans. Shinichiro Nakamura and Jean S. Gerard (Seattle, WA: Japanese Community Service, 1973), 803.
14 "Down Main Street," *Japanese-American Courier*, September 29, 1928.
15 "Down Main Street," *Japanese-American Courier*, March, 17, 1928.
16 Dawn Mabalon, *Little Manila is in the Heart: The Making of the Filipina/o Community in Stockton, California* (Durham, NC: Duke University Press, 2013), 113.
17 Ibid., 141.
18 Ibid., 104.
19 Carey McWilliams, *Factories in the Fields: The Story of Migratory Farm Labor in California* (Berkeley, CA: University of California Press, 1935).
20 Ronald Takaki, *Strangers from a Different Shore: A History of Asian Americans* (Boston, MA: Little Brown, 1989), 174.
21 Between 1876 and 1885, 40,000 to 50,000 Chinese arrived to work on Hawaiian plantations. Following them were Japanese, of whom about 180,000 entered between 1886 and 1924, and the third major group of imported laborers came from the Philippines (120,000 from 1907 to 1931). Edna Bonacich, "Asian Labor in the Development of California and Hawaii," from Lucie Cheng and Edna Bonacich, Eds., *Labor Immigration Under Capitalism: Asian Workers in the United States before World War II* (Berkeley, CA: University of California Press, 1983), 179; Evelyn Nakano Glenn, *Unequal Freedom: How Race and Gender Shaped American Citizenship and Labor* (Cambridge, MA: Harvard University Press, 2002), 193.
22 Ronald Takaki, *Pau Hana: Plantation Life and Labor in Hawaii* (Honolulu: University of Hawaii Press, 1983), 24.
23 Ibid., 94.
24 Ibid., 95.
25 Glenn, *Unequal Freedom*, 196.
26 Howard Brett Melendy, *Asians in America: Filipinos, Koreans, and East Indians* (Boston: Twayne Publishers, 1977), 128.
27 Takaki, *Pau Hana*, 118–119.

28 Charlotte Brooks, *Alien Neighbors, Foreign Friends: Asian Americans, Housing, and the Transformation of Urban California* (Chicago, IL: University of Chicago Press, 2009), 206.
29 Ibid.
30 Ibid.
31 Peter Kwong and Dusanka Miscevic, *Chinese America: The Untold Story of America's Oldest New Community* (New York: New Press, 2006), 339.
32 Timothy Fong, *The First Suburban Chinatown: The Remaking of Monterey Park* (Philadelphia: Temple University Press, 1994), 27.
33 Ibid., 29.
34 Ibid., 48.
35 Benito Vergara, *Pinoy Capital: The Filipino Nation in Daly City* (Philadelphia: Temple University Press, 2008), 2.
36 See Ibid., Chapter 2.
37 Fong, *The First Suburban Chinatown*, 38.
38 The recommendation was ultimately rejected. Ibid., 42.
39 Ibid., 44.
40 Ibid., 4.
41 Wendy Cheng, *The Changs Next Door to the Diazes: Remapping Race in Suburban California* (Minneapolis, MN: University of Minnesota Press, 2013), 132.
42 Fong, *The First Suburban Chinatown*, 49.
43 Min Zhou, "'Parachute Kids' in Southern California: The Educational Experience of Chinese Children in Transnational Families," *Educational Policy* 12 (1998): 682–704.
44 Cheng, The Changs Next Door to the Diazes, 10.
45 Ibid., 16.
46 Ibid., 171.
47 One example is controversy over The Line hotel in Koreatown. Although the restaurants and other businesses in the hotel are helmed by Korean Americans, its opening was met with criticisms for encouraging the gentrification of Los Angeles Koreatown. See Daniel Djang, "L.A. Story Spotlight: Roy Choi," *Discover Los Angeles*, March 18, 2014, www.discoverlosangeles.com/blog/la-story-roy-choi (accessed October 17, 2016).

References

Bonacich, Edna. "Asian Labor in the Development of California and Hawaii." In *Labor Immigration Under Capitalism: Asian Workers in the United States before World War II,* edited by Lucie Cheng and Edna Bonacich. Berkeley, CA: University of California Press, 1983. 130–185.
Brooks, Charlotte. *Alien Neighbors, Foreign Friends: Asian Americans, Housing, and the Transformation of Urban California.* Chicago, IL: University of Chicago Press, 2009.
Cheng, Wendy. *The Changs Next Door to the Diazes: Remapping Race in Suburban California.* Minneapolis, MN: University of Minnesota Press, 2013.
"A Dangerous Corner," *Japanese-American Courier,* May 5, 1928.
Djang, Daniel. "L.A. Story Spotlight: Roy Choi." *Discover Los Angeles*, March 18, 2014. www.discoverlosangeles.com/blog/la-story-roy-choi. Accessed October 17, 2016.
"Down Main Street," *Japanese-American Courier,* March 17, 1928.
"Down Main Street," *Japanese-American Courier,* September 29, 1928.
Fong, Timothy. *The First Suburban Chinatown: The Remaking of Monterey Park.* Philadelphia, PA: Temple University Press, 1994.
Glenn, Evelyn Nakano. *Unequal Freedom: How Race and Gender Shaped American Citizenship and Labor.* Cambridge, MA: Harvard University Press, 2002.
Ito, Kazuo. *Issei: A History of Japanese Immigrants in North America,* trans. Shinichiro Nakamura and Jean S. Gerard. Seattle, WA: Japanese Community Service, 1973.
"Jackson Street is Quiet Thoroughfare on Sunday." *Northwest Enterprise,* October 12, 1933.
"Ken Louie." In *Reflections of Seattle's Chinese Americans: The First 100 Years*, edited by Ron Chew. Seattle, WA: University of Washington Press, 1994. 57.

Kwong, Peter and Dusanka Miscevic. *Chinese America: The Untold Story of America's Oldest New Community*. New York: New Press, 2006.

Lui, Mary Ting Yi. *The Chinatown Trunk Mystery: Murder Miscegenation, and Other Dangerous Encounters in Turn-of-the Century New York City*. Princeton, NJ: Princeton University Press, 2005.

Mabalon, Dawn. *Little Manila is in the Heart: The Making of the Filipina/o Community in Stockton, California*. Durham, NC: Duke University Press, 2013.

McWilliams, Carey. *Factories in the Fields: The Story of Migratory Farm Labor in California*. Berkeley, CA: University of California Press, 1935.

Melendy, Howard Brett. *Asians in America: Filipinos, Koreans, and East Indians*. New York: Twayne Publishers, 1977.

Shah, Nayan. *Contagious Divides: Epidemics and Race in San Francisco's Chinatown*. Berkeley, CA: University of California Press, 2001.

Takaki, Ronald. *Strangers from a Different Shore: A History of Asian Americans*. Boston, MA: Little Brown, 1989.

Takaki, Ronald. *Pau Hana: Plantation Life and Labor in Hawaii*. Honolulu, HI: University of Hawaii Press, 1983.

Vergara, Benito. *Pinoy Capital: The Filipino Nation in Daly City*. Philadelphia, PA: Temple University Press, 2008.

Yu, Henry. *Thinking Orientals: Migration, Contact, and Exoticism in Modern America*. New York: Oxford University Press, 2001.

Zhou, Min. "'Parachute Kids' in Southern California: The Educational Experience of Chinese Children in Transnational Families." *Educational Policy* 12 (1998): 682–704.

20
THE INVENTION OF THE MODEL MINORITY

Ellen D. Wu

The metamorphosis of Asians in American society from "yellow perils" to "model minorities" in the mid-twentieth century stands as one of the most arresting racial makeovers in U.S. history. To contemporaries, the rapid evolution from despised Orientals to the country's most exceptional and beloved people of color was so breathtaking that it was literally front-page news: the *New York Times* (1970) declared ethnic Japanese and Chinese "an American success story," having witnessed "the almost total disappearance of discrimination." Remarkably, their "assimilation into the mainstream of American life" was a situation that would have been "unthinkable twenty years ago."[1] How did this happen? And what were the consequences of this transformation—if more image than reality—not only for Asian Americans but also for the nation as a whole?

For more than a generation, Asian American Studies scholars have erroneously located the origins of the "model minority myth" in a pair of magazine articles published in 1966: William Petersen's "Success Story, Japanese American Style" (*New York Times Magazine*) and "Success Story of One Minority Group in U.S." (*US News and World Report*).[2] The conventional account stresses that white conservatives concocted the model minority concept to neutralize Civil Rights/Black Power activists' calls for the fundamental redistribution of wealth and power in American society.

The "model minority myth" was undoubtedly a salient and powerful form of anti-black racism espoused by mainline media in the throes of the racial upheavals of the 1960s. But this explanation is incomplete on number of levels. First, the model minority's beginnings date back to World War II. Second, liberals—not conservatives—were its instigators. Third, the model minority had its roots in the United States' push for global power as much as the African American freedom movement. And fourth, the focus on the mainstream press obscures the crucial role of Asian Americans in representing themselves as model minorities. It is impossible to comprehend the birth of the model minority without paying attention to these indispensable factors.

The model minority, in short, did not appear suddenly in 1966 in the pages of the *New York Times Magazine* and *US News and World Report*. It arose within a much longer and broader historical context.[3] The stereotype's invention was the unanticipated outcome of a series of intersecting political, social, and cultural imperatives—both domestic and international—that drove the pronounced reconfiguration of America's racial order between World War II and the Vietnam era.

Since the mid-twentieth century, white Americans had deemed so-called "Orientals" *definitively not-white*, unassimilable aliens unfit for membership in the nation. They had systematically shut out "Asiatic" persons from all types of civic participation through such measures as bars to naturalization and the franchise, occupational discrimination, residential and school segregation, anti-miscegenation legislation and customs, lynching, and terrorism. Popular representations of "Orientals" as rat-eating, opium smoking, sexually depraved, untrustworthy sub-humans provided the racial logic that justified Exclusion. Asian Americans tried mightily to reverse their degradation by claiming cultural compatibility with middle-class Anglo-Saxon Protestants. But they were unsuccessful until World War II.

Asian Americans' luck changed when the United States took up arms against the Axis powers. As the nation fought in the name of democracy against Nazis and fascists—and, soon thereafter, the Communist Soviets and Chinese—blatant white supremacy became a diplomatic liability. Such hypocrisy endangered the country's ambitions to become a geopolitical powerhouse. The United States could not claim to be the leader of the free world without attending to its race problems at home. So Americans had a strong incentive and convincing reason to reconsider the social standing of ethnic Asians in their midst. Given these circumstances, liberals moved to undo the regime of Asian Exclusion—the legal framework and web of social practices (akin to Jim Crow in the South) that had relegated Asians outside the boundaries of the national community.[4]

Yet dismantling Asian Exclusion also posed a problem for the nation. Under the old system, the status of Asian immigrants and their descendants was very clear: they were permanent foreigners with no hope of equality with whites. But when the global exigencies of the 1940s and 1950s rendered Exclusion indefensible, Asian Americans' social standing was no longer certain. The terms of their *inclusion* into the nation needed to be determined. A host of stakeholders—including some Asian Americans themselves—resolved this dilemma by the mid-1960s by coining a new image and position for Asians in the national racial order. Together, they christened Asian Americans the "model minority"— a racial group distinct from the white majority but lauded as well-assimilated, upwardly mobile, politically nonthreatening, and *definitively not-black*.

Taking this bigger picture into account in tracing the origins of the model minority myth yields big payoffs for Asian American Studies and kindred fields. It allows for a deeper and more nuanced understanding of Asian American and U.S. history more generally in the decades after World War II by illuminating the lasting impacts of international affairs on domestic racial change, and vice versa. U.S. engagement in the Asia/Pacific region was a critical engine of the making of the model minority. Asian Americans' fortunes were tied directly to the national identity politics of World War II and the Cold War. Very importantly, liberal whites moved to assimilate—rather than marginalize—ethnic Asians *because* of their putative foreignness.[5] They did so in order to help legitimate the global expansion of U.S. power, arguing that treating Asians more kindly at home would strengthen America's ties abroad.[6] For Asian Americans, becoming *assimilating Others* (persons acknowledged as capable of acting like white Americans while remaining racially distinct from them) in turn was a key stepping stone to emerging as definitively not-black model minorities.

The broader historical context also highlights the ways in which mid-twentieth-century race making (the work of creating racial categories, living within them, altering them, and even obliterating them[7]) was very much a relational process. What it meant to be Asian American or the model minority was profoundly shaped by understandings of blackness and whiteness in this period. At the same time, the era's definitions of blackness and whiteness cannot be fully grasped without taking Asian Americans into account.

Yet other interdependencies also mattered. The invention of the model minority reveals that those came to the fore at various moments, including internal divisions *within* ethnic groups ("loyal" vs "disloyal" Japanese Americans, Communist vs anti-Communist Chinese Americans), assumptions about Mexican American zoot suiters in the early 1940s, and contrasts between Native Hawaiians, haole (whites), and Asians in postwar Hawai'i. The fashioning of Asians into model minorities in the post-Exclusion decades, therefore, happened through a constellation of historically contingent comparisons with "other" Asians, African Americans, whites, Latinos, and indigenous peoples.[8]

Critically, Asian Americans were at the very heart of the process of becoming the model minority, even if the outcome was largely an unintended one. The significance of this cannot be stressed enough. In some ways, it has served the purposes of Asian American Studies to downplay the role of Asian Americans in creating the model minority myth. Acknowledging that history would seem to undercut the very important project of interracial solidarity among peoples of color, but admitting to Asian American complicity in maintaining the denigration of blackness that anchors model minority ideology is more analytically and ethically honest. Moreover, uncovering this involvement actually *helps* to overthrow the tyranny of the model minority by highlighting the *political* diversity of Asian America, past and present. If one of the thorniest problems with the model minority is that it flattens variations among those thrown together under the rubric, a history that zooms in on the various strategies and actions Asian Americans took to deal with racism in American life actually "unflattens" those differences. Rather, Asian Americans have not only worked to create the model minority stereotype but have also been at the forefront of laboring to destroy it in the decades since its inception.

Assimilating Others: Japanese America

Global conflicts profoundly altered the social standing of Japanese and Chinese Americans, the two largest ethnic-Asian populations and the ones that figured most prominently in the public eye at midcentury. World War II, the Cold War, and the Korean War framed the concurrent evolution of both from despicable strangers to "American success stories."

Divergences between U.S.–Japan and U.S.–China relations in the 1940s and 1950s resulted in major differences in their respective trajectories. For ethnic Japanese, the Pacific War between the United States and Japan led not only to their imprisonment by the federal government, but also their reconfiguration as loyal, patriotic Americans as proven by their military heroism. This, in turn, became the basis for the standard assessment that Japanese Americans were distinct from—and superior to—African Americans, a view that coalesced by the mid-1960s. In contrast, representations of ethnic Chinese as unlike *and* better than blacks emphasized anti-communism, good behavior, and family values.

But a key parallel laid the groundwork for the simultaneous emergence of Japanese and Chinese Americans as definitively not-black model minorities after World War II. This was the political philosophy known as racial liberalism, the growing belief that the country's racial diversity could best be managed by assimilating and integrating minorities into the white middle class. Beginning in the 1940s, liberal political leaders and intellectuals endorsed the use of state intervention to orchestrate the social engineering necessary to achieve civil rights and equality of citizenship for nonwhites.[9]

Japanese American internment (1942–1945) was without question the very nadir of Asian Exclusion. The federal government's incarceration of some 120,000 Nikkei as an (unproven) fifth column for Japan entailed a spectacular denial of civil liberties. In authorizing, executing, and defending the constitutionality of mass imprisonment, the state effectively classified each and every Nikkei (ethnic Japanese) in the United States as "enemy aliens."[10]

Yet internment also marked the beginnings of Asian *inclusion* by serving as the vehicle through which Japanese Americans were recast into assimilating Others. Liberals—including the officials of the War Relocation Authority (WRA), the federal agency charged with operating the camps—saw in internment an opportunity and a necessity to assimilate Japanese Americans into the mainstream. To the WRA's administrators, it also presented an unparalleled promise for refashioning ethnic Japanese into model American citizens via state-engineered cultural and structural assimilation. Internee life was designed with this goal in mind. Camp schools curricula, for instance, prioritized English language instruction and the inculcation of American values, while camp "community councils" trained inmates in the arts of domestic governance.[11]

The WRA also laid out two pipelines to re-entry into American life and fortifying Nikkeis' station in the national polity. The first of these was postinternment migration throughout the United States, or "resettlement." For state authorities, resettlement seemed the perfect test case for racial liberalism's incipient solution to America's race problems. The federal government planned to scatter Japanese Americans around the country so that they might disappear into the white middle class instead of returning to their West Coast farms and Little Tokyos. The WRA unambiguously stressed total assimilation to potential resettlers. Prisoners who wanted to leave the camps had to promise federal officials that they would only speak English in public, avoid associating with large groups of Nikkei, and conform to polite standards of decorum. (The last point was particularly aimed at Nisei zoot suiters whose conspicuous comportment—suggesting an explicit kinship with Mexican Americans and African Americans—especially troubled resettlement coordinators.)[12]

The results of resettlement were mixed. Internees greeted the plans with tepid enthusiasm. In all, only 36,000 prisoners—less than one third of the total number—took part in the resettlement program before the end of the war, starting anew in locations throughout the Midwest, the Atlantic seaboard, and the mountain states. Many of them tested the WRA's rigid vision of ethnic dispersal right away. Some did comply strictly with the WRA's guidelines. But others took a more realistic approach. In Chicago, the most popular destination for resettlers, lonely Nisei (second-generation Japanese) readily sought each other out for companionship, preferring the easy company of other Japanese Americans over the challenges of cultivating relationships outside the ethnic group. Racial discrimination in the city also intensified this uneasiness. Resettlers soon learned that their Japanese ancestry remained a barrier to securing desirable housing, employment, and access to public spaces such as dance halls, hospitals, and even cemeteries.[13]

Living an indeterminate present and looking toward an unknown future, countless resettlers readily dismissed the WRA's instructions to act as respectable "ambassadors" to mainstream America. Many quit their jobs unannounced, seeking better work and higher pay, to the chagrin of federal authorities who feared that such habits "reflected unfavorably" on all Japanese Americans.[14]

Eventually, the WRA conceded that assimilation would take time, given the traumatic experiences of incarceration. Federal authorities even endorsed the formation of ethnic specific organizations to support former internees through the process of readjustment. The reconstitution of Japanese American communities in the postwar period, then, can be understood as a defiance of the government's assimilationist race policy—quite the opposite of what "model minorities" were supposed to do.[15]

In tandem with resettlement, the WRA promoted military service as the route to mainstream recognition and acceptance. To federal authorities, taking up arms seemed an especially foolproof way for internees to prove their unswerving loyalty to the nation—not to mention a visible means to counter Japan's propaganda that the United States was fighting a "race war." Certain Japanese American spokespersons pushed strongly for enlistment, especially the Nisei leaders of the Japanese American Citizens League (JACL). And despite vocal protests from within the camps—including bitter denunciations of the proposed "Jap Crow" (segregated) regiments—the Army went ahead as planned.[16]

The scheme was stunningly effective. "GI Joe Nisei" became the face of an extensive and persuasive public relations campaign conducted in tandem by the state and JACL. Countless media outlets circulated stories of heroic Japanese Americans on the battlefield. *Reader's Digest*, for one, applauded the myriad ways in which Nisei soldiers fought not only to win the way but also "to prove that Japanese-Americans were basically no different in attitude or loyalty from American citizens whose forebears came from other lands."[17]

In the postwar period JACL heads continued extolling the Japanese American troops for two purposes. First, they wished to redeem their damaged reputation *within* the ethnic community for their controversial support for drafting Nisei. Second, they hoped to convince lawmakers to undo the remaining pillars of Exclusion by lobbying for Japanese American *inclusion* as the reward for the Niseis' undeniable sacrifices.[18]

The pinnacle of their PR efforts was *Go for Broke!* (1951), the Metro-Goldwyn-Mayer feature film that chronicled the valor of the famed 442nd all-Nisei battalion on the European front. (JACL officer Mike Masaoka served as "special consultant" during production.) The moral of the tale was that Japanese Americans had proved beyond a doubt their Americanism through their "baptism of blood." The movie opened with great fanfare in Washington DC, Honolulu, Los Angeles, and Tokyo. Cincinnati even declared a "Go for Broke" week honoring the city's Nisei veterans in May.[19]

Stories of Nisei in uniform fueled the momentum in favor of overturning Japanese Exclusion. Journalists and politicians followed JACL's lead, arguing that naturalization and immigration rights were due to the community as thanks for their tours of duty. Against the backdrop of the Korean conflict and the Cold War, they also convincingly added that such gestures would strengthen ties between the U.S. and Japan, America's "bulwark of democracy in the Orient." In 1952, Congress passed the McCarran–Walter Act, finally allowing ethnic Japanese to become naturalized citizens and the resumption of immigration from Japan.[20]

Nevertheless, JACL's Nisei soldier campaign had many detractors. During the war, draft resisters had refused to serve and those known as renunciants had renounced their U.S. citizenship. In the years after the conflict, some Japanese Americans continued to denounce the league for promoting what they saw as a highly problematic representation of their community, its "Uncle Tom" accommodationism, and its claims to speak for all Japanese Americans.[21]

In the 1950s, then, the JACL remained on shaky footing within the ethnic community that it purported to represent. Even its highest legislative victory—the 1952 McCarran–Walter Act—drew ire from co-ethnic critics. The law's reactionary provisions allotted more power to the federal government to exclude, deport, and denaturalize Communists. It restricted immigration numbers from colonies (especially those in the British Caribbean), a move read by many as anti-black. Additionally, it did nothing to rid the books of race-based national entry quotas. The leftist Nisei Progressives, the most visible alternative to the JACL, had lobbied President Harry S. Truman to veto the bill. After its passage, University of Chicago linguist S.I. Hayakawa criticized the League for securing Issei naturalization rights "at the cost of questionable and illiberal" policies, a compromise that was "an act of unpardonable short-sightedness of cynical opportunism."[22]

Faultfinders of JACL, however, could do little to dislodge the now-dominant image of the Nisei soldier. He had become the basis of a new popular idea of Japanese Americans as politically moderate, patriotic Americans. This, in turn, became a crucial foundation for the model minority stereotype in the following decade.

Assimilating Others: Chinese America

As with Japanese Americans, racial liberalism and U.S. foreign relations structured the experiences of Chinese Americans during and after World War II. With the United States battling against the Axis powers in the name of democracy, many liberals felt that Chinese Exclusion risked America's trans-pacific alliance with China against Japan. As one federal official brooded, severe immigration restrictions made for "bad diplomacy" at a time when China stood as "the only possibility of an allied offensive on the Asiatic continent."[23]

A coast-to-coast campaign emerged to strike down the laws. In addition to harping on the foreign policy stakes of the issue, strategists sought to reshape the imagery of Chinese in U.S. popular thinking. The Citizens Committee to Repeal Chinese Exclusion recognized that it would have to neutralize deep-seated fears of "yellow peril" coolie hordes. So it purposefully recast Chinese in its promotional materials and congressional testimonies as "law-abiding, peace-loving, courteous people living quietly among us." Fortuitously, this project resonated with the state's emphasis on racial tolerance and cultural diversity to foster national unity for the purposes of war mobilization. The outreach worked exceedingly well. National, regional, and niche newspapers and magazines opined in favor of the crusade. Mass-market periodicals featured celebratory profiles of patriotic, respectable Chinese American citizens through the war's duration.[24]

Chinese Americans' prospects thus changed decidedly after the bombing of Pearl Harbor as *inclusion* became the defining paradigm of their social standing. Congress repealed the Chinese Exclusion Acts in 1943. As a result, persons of Chinese ancestry were permitted to naturalized U.S. citizenship, while the legal immigration of Chinese resumed in small numbers—a symbolic elevation to equality with European immigrants. Opportunities also took place in more bread-and-butter forms. African Americans' "Double V" campaign for victory over fascism abroad and racism at home especially helped to open to Chinese Americans previously restricted avenues for socio-economic advancement in industry and the armed forces. The progressive activist-writer Carey McWilliams dramatically captured liberals' optimism in this moment: "The war has brought the Chinese out of Chinatown and we should lock the doors behind them." Chinese Americans themselves were thrilled: "The crisis of December 7 has emancipated the Chinese in the United States," proclaimed sociologist Rose Hum Lee.[25]

Yet even with this radical shift in U.S. attitudes, most whites never dissociated Chinese Americans from notions of foreignness. Chinese Americans remained tethered to China in the public's imagination—shaky grounds for acceptance and full citizenship given the victory of the Mao Zedong's Communist Party in China's civil war. While Chinese Americans did not break free of this linkage, the simultaneous existence of a "bad" China (the People's Republic, or PRC) and a "good" one (the Nationalists on Taiwan) after 1949 meant that they could position themselves as anti-communist disaporic Chinese committed to both Nationalist ("free") China and the United States.[26]

The PRC's entry into the Korean War in October 1950 heightened the stakes of these associations. Chinese across the United States scrambled to divorce themselves from "Red" China. Conservative Chinatown leaders masterminded this strategy to protect the community from anticipated McCarthyist repression—many feared a mass incarceration analogous to the egregious racial profiling experienced by Japanese Americans during World War II. (They also seized the occasion to crush the Chinatown left and shore up their own power within the ethnic community.) Elites launched a nationwide crusade against communism, establishing local "Anti-Communist Leagues" and planning demonstrations, parades, Korean War relief clothing drives, and other public spectacles to drive home the point that Chinese Americans were patriotic and loyal to the United States.[27]

These efforts were not entirely convincing. In 1956, federal authorities instigated a crackdown on unlawful Chinese immigration under the pretense that Communist Chinese spies were slipping into the country using false papers. The offensive—involving mass subpoenas and grand jury investigations of Chinatown organizations, prosecutions, and deportations—placed all Chinese in the United States (especially the left-leaning) under suspicion.[28]

But assumptions of foreignness had payoffs as well as constraints for Chinese America in the early Cold War years. The rise of the PRC obliged the U.S. government to pay attention to "Overseas Chinese"— members of a global Chinese diaspora with ties to each other and China— living throughout the Asia/Pacific region. The worry was that these imigrant communities were especially susceptible to political seduction by Mao's ideologies. So federal officials turned to Chinese Americans, the country's own "Overseas Chinese," to woo their assumed compatriots away from the enemy's camp.[29]

Cold War diplomacy served as a meeting ground for a convergence of state and ethnic community interests in the 1940s and 1950s. The Department of State and the U.S. Information Agency (USIA) peddled narratives of successful and assimilated Chinese Americans to these target populations in order to demonstrate the superiority of liberal democracy to communism. They disseminated the stories via newspaper and magazine articles, books, art exhibitions, and films. At the suggestion of second-generation Chinese American Betty Lee Sung, the Voice of America (the federal government's international radio operation) broadcast *Chinese Activities*, a weekly segment showcasing noteworthy Chinese in the United States. The State Department also enlisted as cultural ambassadors prominent individuals whose achievements would offer "living proof" of America's friendliness to racial minorities. Jade Snow Wong and Dong Kingman, two of the most well-known artists of the day, embarked on multi-stop tours of the region, as did San Francisco's decorated Chinese Basketball Team.[30]

For their part, the Chinese Americans who took part in these programs were not motivated by anti-communism or patriotism alone, but rather by a range of reasons to participate. While they were undoubtedly familiar with the State Department's Cold War agenda, they did not necessarily hold one-dimensional views about U.S. foreign policy. For instance, Sung, who served as head scriptwriter for Chinese Activities between 1949–1954, did not consider herself to be producing anti-communist propaganda per se. Rather, she used the opportunity to counter decades of hateful and demeaning stereotypes about Chinese in the United States. Wong, Kingman, and the San Francisco basketball players gained acknowledgment and publicity for their careers. Beyond these individual benefits, the ethnic community as a whole welcomed the official legitimization of their national belonging. Indeed, the government's tapping of Chinese Americans to serve as "goodwill ambassadors" would have been inconceivable during the Exclusion era.[31]

Closer to home, liberals convincingly turned the community's association with the "good" China into social capital in the 1950s. Amidst the country's panic over juvenile delinquency, scores of journalists, scholars, and policymakers recycled the notion of the well-behaved Chinese that first surfaced during the push for repeal in the 1940s. They lauded Chinatown households for raising exceptionally dutiful, studious children. The *New York Times Magazine* (1956) emphasized that Chinese youth displayed "unquestioned obedience" toward their elders, while

Look magazine (1958) marveled that "troublemaking" among Chinatown youths was "so low that the police don't even bother to keep figures on it." U.S. Rep. Arthur Klein praised his Manhattan constituents for their "respect for parents and teachers," "stable and loving and home life," and thirst for education. Signally, in the wake of the 1956 immigration subpoena scare, savvy Chinatown public relations coordinators pushed the family values angle to shore up the community's reputation. For example, they assisted with a flattering feature on the Chinese in the United States—including their "amazingly low delinquency rate"—for *Readers' Digest*, one of the most widely read periodicals of the era.[32]

This meme gained traction because they upheld two dominant lines of Cold War-era thinking. The first was the valorization of the nuclear family. Popular portrayals of Chinese American households that attributed their orderliness to Confucian tradition resonated with contemporary conservative mores. The second was anti-communism. Observers who extolled stateside Chinese for their "venerable" Confucianism effectively drew contrasts between U.S. Chinatowns and Mao Zedong's China to suggest the superiority of the American way of life. Paralleling the ideological work of the Nisei soldier icon in the Japanese American community, the model Chinese American household of the 1950s— characterized by deference, dutifulness, and the absence of criminality—laid the foundation for explicit comparisons between Chinese as "good" minorities and African Americans as "bad" minorities in the 1960s.

Assimilating Others: The Hawai'i Statehood Debates

Hawai'i's bid for statehood occupied a pivotal place in the origins of the model minority, paralleling and reinforcing the transformations in the continental United States. The admission campaign was one of the most visible focal points for revamping the social standing of Asian Americans after World War II. Because Americans generally considered Hawai'i to be "Eastern" in orientation at this time, the statehood question effectively functioned as a national referendum on Asian American citizenship. And as with the Nisei soldier and Chinese American "non-delinquency," it helped to pave the way for the emergence of Asian Americans as definitively not-black model minorities.

Before World War II, admitting Hawai'i to the Union had been unfathomable for many Americans largely because of the islands' majority nonwhite population. Asian laborers began arriving in Hawai'i in the late nineteenth century, recruited by the haole (white) missionary-capitalist class to labor on their industrial sugar plantations. After 1898 (when the United States formally colonized Hawai'i), the haole oligarchy benefited immensely from Hawai'i's territorial status. The arrangement allowed whites to dominate the economy and local government. By contrast, statehood would democratize Hawai'i by allowing citizens to vote for public officials and other important matters. Whites feared that Nisei—who were U.S. citizens by birth and who greatly outnumbered them—would form a powerful voting bloc as they came of age. Thus the planter class perennially thwarted attempts to push forward the statehood issue. On the mainland, anti-Asian animus in popular culture and politics, coupled with increasing tensions between the United States and Japan, guaranteed that many Americans remained hostile to the possibility of sending "Japanese Senators" and "Japanese Representatives" to Congress.[33]

The Pacific War changed nearly everything. In the wake of the Pearl Harbor bombing, Hawai'i came to be seen as an integral part of the nation. Tens of thousands of mainlanders rotated through the archipelago as military and defense industry personnel, heightening the general awareness of the territory and its significance. Nikkei battlefield sacrifices eased worries about Japanese Americans' disloyalties. The wartime emphasis on celebrating cultural pluralism amplified arguments made by area liberals since the 1920s and 1930s. University of Hawaii social scientists, in particular, had been touting the islands as a racial paradise where the Asiatic presence was harmless, if not an asset. Moreover, revised U.S. trade policies disadvantaging haole growers, coupled with the imposition of martial law on Hawai'i during the war, convinced many locals that territorial status was no longer favorable. At the close of the war, the prognosis for statehood seemed bright.[34]

Nonetheless, statehood was far from an open-and-shut case after 1945. What World War II had not upended was the ubiquitous notion that Hawai'i was "Asian." Old xenophobic allegations remained, especially that "Japs" would soon "control" the islands and infect U.S. Congress and American society with "Asiatic concepts of life" should entry be granted. Admission opponents also suggested that the islands' racial makeup made the territory susceptible to communist influence, especially the PRC. As proof, they noted that organized labor had made big inroads in Hawai'i, both in terms of unionizing and at the ballot box. Pointing to these turning tides, decriers charged that the territory had fallen under the "firm grip" of communists and should therefore be excluded from statehood.[35]

But race—like anti-communism—operated in favor of statehood as well as against it. Promoters did not disagree that Hawai'i was "Oriental." Rather, they argued these Far Eastern roots would be advantageous in the context of the Cold War and the worldwide decolonization movement. Admitting the territory would prove to the world that the United States was not racist because the act would elevate Hawai'i's ethnic Asian population to first-class citizenship. In addition, it would stand as a "concrete example of self-determination influencing all the peoples of the Pacific." Proponents depicted Hawai'i as a place of enormous ambassadorial potential, repeatedly referring to the territory as a "gateway," "springboard," "logical stepping stone," and "bridge" to Asia, among other metaphors. Statehood was a much-needed gesture to entice the newly independent Third World nations to the U.S. side of the Cold War divide. "Hawai'i's Americans of Oriental ancestry are a strong, urgent reason for Statehood, rather than the reverse," insisted territorial congressional delegate and future state governor John A. Burns.[36]

As statehood negotiations unfolded in the 1940s and 1950s, enthusiasts pitched Asian Americans as prototypical model minorities and Hawai'i as the ideal showcase for racial liberalism at work. Media outlets sang of the islands' harmonious race relations and dubbed the islands a "Pacific melting pot" and "the world's most successful experiment in mixed breeding." Sociological data confirmed that local ethnic Asian populations had Americanized (even as they maintained their Oriental essence) and were moving into the middle class. Crucially, compared to the mainland, they intermarried at astoundingly high rates with each other, Native Hawaiians, and whites. (Cognizant of the era's volatile race politics, however, statehood champions carefully reassured the public that this race-mixing was unique to Hawai'i.) All that was left to complete this picture of an idyllic multiracial liberal democracy—and thereby demonstrate to the world America's magnanimity—was the granting of formal equality (i.e. statehood).[37]

In time, such arguments proved persuasive enough to overcome lingering opposition in Congress, especially from Southern states' rights Democrats who believed that admission would weaken the grip of white supremacy in the United States. When the bill finally passed in 1959 and Asian Americans captured 42 of the 81 public offices (including U.S. Senator Hiram Fong, a Chinese American, and U.S. Representative Daniel Inouye, a Japanese American), the press saluted the event as a "melting pot election in a melting pot land." To many, the outcome denoted a watershed in American history with planetary payoffs. As the *New York Times* trumpeted, "We can now say to people of the Far East, 'Your brothers and cousins have equal rights with ourselves and are helping to make our laws.'"[38]

Although many cheered statehood as inclusive progress, the act generated its own exclusions and marginalizations. For one, it furthered assumptions about the perpetual foreignness of Asian ethnics. Even more troubling, it rendered invisible Native Hawaiians and their problems under U.S. rule. Contemporary accounts described a modern Hawai'i displacing "old Polynesia" with its "full-blooded" natives destined to fade into the mixed-race population with only vestiges of their traditional culture to remain. Asian Americans, in contrast, stood for Hawai'i's future. By ignoring the very existence of indigenous peoples, not to mention their opposition to colonization in all forms, statehood boosters evaded an uncomfortable confrontation with the consequences of U.S. occupation. In framing admission as the only possibility for Hawai'i's future, supporters legitimated the spread of U.S. global hegemony by valorizing American democracy as unique, benevolent, and superior to alternative arrangements of power.[39]

Definitively Not-Black

Within the double crucibles of global war and domestic racial reform, a cross-section of historical actors remade Asian Americans from indelible aliens to assimilating Others in the 1940s and 1950s. As racial liberalism increasingly came under attack and the black freedom movement evolved into its more radical iterations by the mid-1960s, assimilating Others underwent a subtle yet profound metamorphosis into the model minority: the Asiatic who was at once an exemplary citizen and *definitively not-black*.

Midcentury liberals believed strongly in the ability of educational campaigns and social science to transform existing ideas about race and, in turn, alter the country's racial order. Constituents of the era's race relations complex identified Nikkei citizenship as an American dilemma to be repaired in order to prove the nation's capacity for righting its wrongs, thereby protecting the United States' global position. To this end, academicians, activists, journalists, and politicians generated a series of "recovery narratives" in the 1940s and 1950s celebrating the post-internment rebound of "California's Amazing Japanese."[40]

For liberals, the recovery narratives did valuable political work. Casting internment as a "disguised blessing" and, ironically, the Nikkei's "greatest opportunity" for assimilation, they redeemed the nation's missteps. They also reinforced the tenets of racial liberalism, especially state management of the racial order. Relatedly, the discourse emphasized that racial minorities cooperate with rather than oppose the government's handling of race relations. The stories posited Japanese Americans as models of acceptable political behavior, implicitly comparing the JACL's moderation to the more confrontational tactics of African American civil rights activists.[41]

While Japanese Americans had made great strides by the late 1950s in terms of rehabilitating their collective public image, JACL stewards did not rest easy. At that time, U.S.–Japan tensions again flared up. American businesses called for boycotts of cheap Japanese goods, while many Japanese opposed the unequal treaty terms between the two nations. JACL officials dreaded that the community would suffer a backlash as a result. Moreover, they still felt insecure about the organization's standing within Japanese America as many co-ethnics continued to disagree with the league's vision and strategies. What, they wondered, could be done to further secure the footing of Japanese in America as well vindicate the JACL itself?[42]

To address these problems, JACL redoubled its public relations efforts by launching the Japanese American Research Project (JARP) in 1960. A primary aim of JARP was to produce a popular account of Japanese American history that would glorify both the community as well as the JACL itself. To potential backers and funders, the league framed the Nikkei saga as a unique "triumph of democracy in action": despite facing extreme hardship and hostility, Japanese Americans had attained "within a single generation . . . a real measure of 'Success,' greater than many Europeans with far fewer handicaps." JACL suggested that the story could boost the country's reputation in Asia and Africa by demonstrating the possibilities for racial minorities in the United States. Its reasoning worked. JARP not only found an institutional home at University of California, Los Angeles in 1962, but also received substantial support from the Carnegie Corporation.[43]

JACL directors shrewdly spun their version of Japanese American history to speak to the increasingly urgent "Negro Problem"—a discursive and political move that would have far-reaching consequences. Nowhere was this most apparent than in journalist Bill Hosokawa's book *Nisei: The Quiet Americans* (1969), the general history of Japanese America commissioned by the league as part of JARP. *Nisei* cast Japanese Americans as *definitively not-black* model minorities, citing famous examples (World Trade Center architect Minoru Yamasaki, Hawai'i Congresswoman Patsy Mink) and asking how such feats of assimilation had been achieved in the face of racial discrimination. "Looking on the extremes of apathy and militancy among Negroes and Hispanos, some Nisei from the comfort of their upper middle class homes have been led to ask: 'Why can't they pull themselves up by their own bootstraps the way we did?'" observed Hosokawa.[44]

Such sentiments infuriated many Nikkei, including some of JACL's own members. Discontents had petitioned publisher William Morrow and Company to reject the title *Nisei: The Quiet Americans*, taking issue with it as a "propaganda device to tell Black Americans and Mexican Americans to behave like 'good little Orientals' who know their place."[45] Yuji Ichioka, the young founder of Berkeley's radical Asian American Political Alliance, pointed out that the book ignored the "damages" of internment and racism. Furthermore, he noted, younger Japanese American activists were now questioning the very foundations of JACL's brand of racial liberalism: "What have we been integrating into? Into a nation conducting a politically and morally bankrupt war against Vietnamese people in the name of freedom and democracy? A nation bent upon exterminating militant Black leaders? A nation which is moving to the extreme right in the name of law and order? A nation in which the so-called 'American Dream' has turned out to be a violent nightmare?"[46] Like thousands of others who joined the nationwide, grassroots mobilization known as the Asian American Movement (late 1960s–1970s), Ichioka decisively refused to endorse what he saw as anti-black, imperialistic model minority ideology.

But Ichioka and his colleagues found themselves outnumbered. By the mid-1960s, the repositioning of Japanese Americans in the national racial order as laudably and decisively not-black had become racial "truth." Influential thinkers and doers followed in the footsteps of JACL. Notably, the league assisted sociologist William Petersen with his essay juxtaposing "successful" Nikkei with the nation's "problem minorities" for *New York Times Magazine*.[47] Assistant Secretary of Labor Daniel Patrick Moynihan appropriated the Nikkei recovery narrative to defend his controversial paper "The Negro Family: The Case for National Action." Published just days before Los Angeles' Watts Riots in August 1965, the Moynihan Report (as it came to be known) asserted that "the deterioration of the Negro family"—epitomized first and foremost by black matriarchy—was the root cause of "the deterioration of the fabric of Negro society." As a liberal, Moynihan's intent was to mobilize support for federal interventions to establish "stable" black families as a crucial means to lift them out of poverty. When the Moynihan report unleashed a torrent of controversy, its besieged author turned to Japanese Americans' "close knit family structure" to explain how Nikkei had become a "prosperous middle-class group."[48] (The percentage of white-collar Japanese Americans had increased from 24.7 percent in 1940 to 35.1 percent in 1960.)[49]

Moynihan also admired the progress made by Chinese immigrants since their arrival in the nineteenth century. "No people came to our shores poorer than the Chinese," he avowed, yet their descendants had gone on to remarkable heights of educational attainment despite continued concentration in urban centers. Harkening back to the 1950s consensus on Chinese American non-delinquency, he pointed to the "singularly stable, cohesive, and enlightened family life"—as opposed to dysfunctional African American households—as the key to Chinese Americans' success.[50] (In 1960, Chinese American men and women had attained higher mean education levels [28 percent and 24.2 percent had some college training, respectively] than their white and black counterparts.)[51]

As Moynihan made clear, the trajectories of Japanese and Chinese American racialization converged in the mid-1960s as definitively not-black model minorities.[52] As racial liberalism came under heavy fire from both the left and the right, this novel stereotype gained purchase. Liberals invested in the assimilation and integration formula for achieving racial equality, pointing to Japanese and Chinese Americans as evidence of its effectiveness. Conservatives apprehensive about the growing force of black power and the future of white supremacy also looked to these two groups as exemplars of minority "law and order." Across the political spectrum, Americans discovered that "success stories" of Japanese and Chinese in the United States—living embodiments of advancement *in spite of* the persistent color line and *because of* their racial (or "cultural") differences—could be used as potent ammunition to defend their social, economic, and political visions.

Hawai'i Senator Daniel Inouye captured this new positioning in his keynote speech at the 1968 Democratic National Convention: "As an American whose ancestors come from Japan, I have become accustomed to a question most recently asked by a very prominent businessman who was concerned about the threat of riots and of resultant loss in life and property. 'Tell me,' he said, 'why can't the Negro be more like you?'" (To his credit, Inouye dismissed the juxtaposition as unsound because Asian Americans had never endured chattel slavery or been subjected to "systematic racist deprivation" comparable to the extent of Jim Crow.)[53]

By the twilight of the civil rights era, then, the idea that Japanese and Chinese Americans were distinctly unlike African Americans had become racial commonsense.

Yet the stereotype also contained the seeds of its own critique. The model minority paradoxically served as a rallying point for the Asian American Movement and the creation of "Asian American" as an innovative, progressive racial identity. Movement participants soundly rejected the model minority myth for obscuring real problems in their communities as well as its complicity in upholding anti-black racism and U.S. imperial domination. They refused to allow themselves to be used in upholding the distinction between "good" and "bad" minorities. Instead, they embraced "Asian American" to signify self-determination and solidarity with other U.S. minorities and "Third World" peoples everywhere. The invention of *Asian America* was grounded in dreams of a different kind of nation and a different kind of world, ones grounded in freedom, dignity, and justice for all.[54]

Notes

1 "Orientals Find Bias Is Down Sharply in U.S.," *New York Times*, December 13, 1970, 1, 70.
2 William Petersen, "Success Story, Japanese-American Style," *New York Times Magazine*, January 9, 1966, 20–21, 33, 36, 38, 40–41, 43; "Success Story of One Minority Group in U.S.," *U.S. News and World Report*, December 26, 1966, 73–76. See especially the widely cited article by Keith Osajima, "Asian Americans as the Model Minority: An Analysis of the Popular Press Image in the 1960s and 1980s," in *Reflections on Shattered Windows: Promises and Prospects for Asian Americans*, Eds. Okihiro et al. (Washington State University Press, 1988), 165–174.
3 Recent historical scholarship on Asian Americans in the post-World War II decades has made important strides in this direction. We now have a much more nuanced sense of how and why Asian Americans transitioned from "yellow perils" to "model minorities" after the end of Asian Exclusion. See especially Robert G. Lee, *Orientals: Asian Americans in Popular Culture* (Philadelphia, PA, 1999); Xiaojian Zhao, *Remaking Chinese America: Immigration, Family, and Community, 1940–1965* (New

Brunswick, NJ, 2002); Lon Kurashige, *Japanese American Celebration and Conflict: A History of Ethnic Identity and Festival in Los Angeles, 1934–1990* (Berkeley, 2002); Scott Kurashige, *The Shifting Grounds of Race: Black and Japanese Americans in the Making of Multiethnic Los Angeles* (Princeton, NJ, 2008); Charlotte Brooks, *Alien Neighbors, Foreign Friends: Asian Americans, Housing, and the Transformation of Urban California* (Chicago, IL, 2009); Greg Robinson, *After Camp: Portraits in Midcentury Japanese American Life and Politics* (Berkeley, CA, 2012); Cindy I-Fen Cheng, *Citizens of Asian America: Democracy and Race During the Cold War* (New York, 2013); Ellen D. Wu, *The Color of Success: Asian Americans and the Origins of the Model Minority* (Princeton, NJ, 2014); Arissa H. Oh, *Into The Arms of America: The Korean Origins of International Adoption* (Stanford, CA, 2015); Charlotte Brooks, *Between Mao and McCarthy: Chinese American Politics in the Cold War Years* (Chicago, IL, 2015); Madeline Y. Hsu, *The Good Immigrants: How The Yellow Peril Became the Model Minority* (Princeton, NJ, 2015).

4 Recently there has been an explosion of historiography connecting mid-twentieth-century foreign policy concerns with race in the domestic arena. See for example Brenda Gayle Plummer, *Rising Wind: Black Americans and U.S. Foreign Affairs, 1935–1960* (Chapel Hill, NC, 1996); Penny M. Von Eschen, *Race against Empire: Black Americans and Anticolonialism, 1937–1957* (Ithaca, NY, 1997); Mary L. Dudziak, *Cold War Civil Rights: Race and the Image of American Democracy* (Princeton, NJ, 2000); Thomas Borstelmann, *The Cold War and the Color Line: American Race Relations in the Global Arena* (Cambridge, MA, 2001); Christina Klein, *Cold War Orientalism: Asia in the Middlebrow Imagination, 1945–1961* (Berkeley, 2003); Penny M. Von Eschen, *Satcho Blows Up the World: Jazz Ambassadors Play the Cold War* (Cambridge, MA, 2004); Nikhil Pal Singh, *Black Is A Country: Race and the Unfinished Struggle for Democracy* (Cambridge, 2004); Kevin K. Gaines, *American Africans in Ghana: Black Expatriates and the Civil Rights Era* (Chapel Hill, NC, 2006); Brooks, *Alien Neighbors, Foreign Friends*; Mary Ting-Yi Lui, "Rehabilitating Chinatown at Mid-Century: Chinese Americans, Race, and U.S. Cultural Diplomacy," in *Chinatowns in a Transnational World: Myths and Realities of an Urban Phenomenon*, ed. Ruth Mayer and Vanessa Künneman (New York, 2011), 81–100; Cheng, *Citizens of Asian America*; Wu, *The Color of Success*; Oh, *Into The Arms of America*; Hsu, *The Good Immigrants*.

5 Claire Jean Kim's seminal theory of "racial triangulation" is indispensable for understanding the racialization of Asians in the United States. Kim argues that the racialization of Asian Americans has rested in large part on "civic ostracism," whereby whites have cast them as "foreign and unassimilable." But this explanation misses a key dimension of the post-World War II period. The history of the production of the model minority stereotype reveals that whites moved to assimilate ethnic Japanese and Chinese beginning in World War II *because* of their perceived foreignness.

6 Christina Klein posits the key argument that Cold War geopolitical imperatives for the United States dictated that American elites manufacture a "global imaginary of integration" as a positive counterpoint to what many perceived as a negative ideology of containment rooted in fear. The positive image stressed affective ties between the United States and peoples of the decolonizing Third World. See Klein, *Cold War Orientalism*, 23-24.

7 On race making, see Michael Omi and Howard Winant's classic text *Racial Formation in the United States* (New York, 2014 edition).

8 This study resonates with two important critiques of Kim's triangulation model. Shu-mei Shih ("Comparative Racialization: An Introduction," *PMLA* 123, no. 5 (October 2008): 1347-1362) questions the assumed white-black-Asian triangulation (as opposed to other racial categories). Colleen Lye ("The Afro-Asian Analogy," *PMLA* 123, no. 5 (October 2008): 1732-1736) argues that the triangulation approach occludes interpretive possibilities by reducing Asian racialization "to a white supremacy that is by temporal and conceptual priority antiblack." Indeed, the invention of the model minority stereotype demonstrates that antiblack racism was but one of a range of factors grounding the changing racialization of Asian Americans in the mid-twentieth century.

9 On post-World War II racial liberalism, see Walter Jackson, *Gunnar Myrdal and America's Conscience: Social Engineering and Racial Liberalism, 1938–1997* (Chapel Hill, 1990); Gary Gerstle, "The Protean Character of American Liberalism" in *The American Historical Review* 99:4 (Oct 1994), 1043–1073; Alan Brinkley, *The End of Reform: New Deal Liberalism in Recession and War* (New York: Alfred A. Knopf, 1995); Nikhil Pal Singh, "Culture/Wars: Recoding Empire in an Age of Democracy," *American Quarterly* 50:3 (1998): 471-522; Ruth Feldstein, *Motherhood in Black and White: Race and Sex in American Liberalism, 1930–1965* (Ithaca, 2000); Gary Gerstle, *American Crucible: Race and Nation in*

the Twentieth Century (New Jersey, NJ: Princeton University Press, 2002); Alice O'Connor, Poverty Knowledge: Social Science, Social Policy, and the Poor in Twentieth Century U.S. History (Princeton, 2001); Singh, Black Is a Country; Carol A. Horton, Race and the Making of American Liberalism (New York, 2005); Thomas J. Sugrue, Sweet Land of Liberty: The Forgotten Civil Rights Struggle in the North (New York, 2008); Daniel Martinez Hosang, Racial Propositions: Ballot Initiatives and the Making of Postwar California (Berkeley, 2010); Mark Brilliant, The Color of America Has Changed: How Racial Diversity Shaped Civil Rights Reform in California, 1941-1978 (New York, 2010).

10 On the history of internment see Roger Daniels, Concentration Camps USA: Japanese Americans and World War II (New York, 1972); Michi Nishiura Weglyn, Years of Infamy: The Untold Story of America's Concentration Camps (New York, 1976); U.S. Commission on Wartime Evacuation and Relocation of Civilians, Personal Justice Denied: Report of the Commission on Wartime Relocation and Internment of Civilians: Report for the Committee on Interior and Insular Affairs (Washington, D.C., 1983; reprint, Seattle, 1997); Greg Robinson, A Tragedy of Democracy: Japanese Confinement in North America (New York, 2009).

11 Mae M. Ngai, Impossible Subjects: Illegal Aliens and the Making of Modern America (Princeton, NJ, 2004), 175-177; Colleen Lye, America's Asia: Racial Form and American Literature, 1893-1945 (Princeton, NJ, 2005), 7.

12 Wu, The Color of Success, 12-13, 19-28.

13 Wu, The Color of Success, 13, 28-33; Charlotte Brooks, "In the Twilight Zone Between Black and White: Japanese American Resettlement and Community in Chicago, 1942-1945," Journal of American History, 86 (March 2000): 1655-1687.

14 Wu, The Color of Success, 28-34; War Relocation Authority, "When You Leave The Relocation Center," n/d, densho.org.

15 Wu, The Color of Success, 33-42.

16 Wu, The Color of Success, 80.

17 Wu, The Color of Success, 78-86; Blake Clark and Oland D. Russell, "Hail Our Japanese-American GIs!" Reader's Digest, July 1945, 65-67.

18 Wu, The Color of Success, 86-88.

19 Wu, The Color of Success, 88-91.

20 Wu, The Color of Success, 92-98.

21 Wu, The Color of Success, 81-82, 90-91, 95-96.

22 Wu, The Color of Success, 98-100.

23 Bradford Smith to Alan Cranston, June 20, 1942, Folder: Chinese Exclusion Acts, Box 1075, Entry E222, NC-148, Record Group 208, United States National Archives and Records Administration, College Park MD.

24 Citizens Committee to Repeal Chinese Exclusion, "Our Chinese Wall," 1943, Box 1, Carl Glick Papers, University of Iowa Libraries Special Collections, Iowa City.

25 Carey McWilliams, Brothers Under the Skin (Boston: Little, Brown, and Company, 1943) 108, 112; Rose Hum Lee, "Chinese in The United States Today: The War Has Changed Their Lives," Survey Graphic: Magazine of Social Interpretation, October 1942, 419, 444.

26 Wu, The Color of Success, 114.

27 Wu, The Color of Success, 114-122.

28 On the 1956 mass subpoena, see Zhao, Remaking Chinese America, 152-184; Him Mark Lai, Becoming Chinese American: A History of Communities and Institutions (Walnut Creek, CA, 2004), 19-35; Ngai, Impossible Subjects, 202-224.

29 Wu, The Color of Success, 112. On the US and "Overseas Chinese," see also Meredith Leigh Oyen, The Diplomacy of Migration: Transnational Lives and the Making of U.S.-Chinese Relations in the Cold War (Ithaca, NY, 2015); Cheng, Citizens of Asian America; Brooks, Between Mao and McCarthy.

30 Wu, The Color of Success, 122-138.

31 Wu, The Color of Success, 122-138.

32 William McIntyre, "Chinatown Offers Us a Lesson," New York Times Magazine, October 6, 1957, 49, 51, 54, 56, 59; "Americans Without a Delinquency Problem," Look, April 29, 1958, 75-81; "Why Chinese Kids Don't Go Bad," 84th Cong., 1st sess., Congressional Record 101, (August 2, 1955), A5668-A5672 (originally cited in Betty Lee Sung, Mountain of Gold (New York, 1967); Albert Q. Maisel, "The Chinese Among Us," Reader's Digest, February 1959, 203-204, 206, 208-210, 212.

33 Wu, *The Color of Success*, 211-214.
34 Wu, *The Color of Success*, 214-219.
35 Ann K. Ziker, "Segregationists Confront American Empire: The Conservative White South and the Question of Hawaiian Statehood, 1947-1959," *Pacific Historical Review* 76, no. 3 (2007): 439-465; Wu, The *Color of Success*, 219-220.
36 Gretchen Heefner, "'A Symbol of the New Frontier': Hawaiian Statehood, Anti-Colonialism, and Winning the Cold War," *Pacific Historical Review* 74, no. 4 (2005): 545-574; Wu, *The Color of Success*, 220-223; John A. Burns, "Asia and the Future," letter to the editor, *Commonweal*, August 9, 1957, 474-475.
37 Wu, *The Color of Success*, 223-228.
38 Wu, *The Color of Success*, 230-231; "The State of Hawaii Votes," *New York Times*, July 31, 1959, 22.
39 Gene Sherman, "Hawaii's New Horizons: Isles Melting Pot of the Pacific," *Los Angeles Times*, May 21, 1963, 2; William J. Lederer, "The 50th State, at 5, 'Goes Mainland,'" *New York Times Magazine*, April 16, 1964, SM24; Klein, *Cold War Orientalism*, 1-17; Dean Itsuji Saranillio, "Colliding Histories: Hawai'i Statehood at the Intersection of Asians 'Ineligible to Citizenship' and Hawaiians 'Unfit for Self-Government,'" *Journal of Asian American Studies* (2010): 283-309.
40 Wu, *The Color of Success*, 156-162; Demarre Bess, "California's Amazing Japanese," *Saturday Evening Post*, April 30, 1955, 38-39, 68, 72, 76, 80, 83.
41 Wu, *The Color of Success*, 156-162.
42 Wu, *The Color of Success*, 104-109.
43 T. Scott Miyakawa, "A Proposal for A Definitive History of the Japanese In The United States, 1860-1960: The Preliminary Outline For Discussion and Review," October 1961, UCLA Young Research Library; Wu, *The Color of Success*, 150-152, 162-165.
44 Bill Hosokawa, *Nisei: The Quiet Americans; The Story of a People* (New York, 1969), 473-497; Alice Yang Murray, *Historical Memories of the Japanese American Internment and the Struggle for Redress* (Stanford, 2008), 214, 216-219.
45 "Controversy Goes to Publisher," *Pacific Citizen*, August 1, 1969, 4; Harry Honda, "'Quiet American' Controversy: Boycott threat called censorship," *Pacific Citizen*, September 19, 1969, 1-2, 6; Murray, *Historical Memories of the Japanese American Internment and the Struggle for Redress*, 214, 216-217.
46 Yuji Ichioka, "Book Review: *Nisei: The Quiet Americans*," *Gidra*, January 1970, 17.
47 JACL, Official Convention Minutes, 1966, 50, Folder 3, Box 297, Japanese American Research Project, Young Research Library Special Collections, University of California, Los Angeles.
48 Daniel Patrick Moynihan, "A Family Policy for the Nation," *America: The National Catholic Weekly Review*, September 18, 1965, reprinted in Lee Rainwater and William L. Yancey, *The Moynihan Report and the Politics of Controversy* (Cambridge, MA: 1967), 385-394; Thomas Meehan, "Moynihan of the Moynihan Report," *New York Times Magazine*, July 31, 1966, 48.
49 U.S. Bureau of the Census, *Sixteenth Census of the United States, Special Report, Nonwhite Population by Race* (Washington, D.C., 1940), 47; U.S. Bureau of the Census, *Seventeenth Census of the United States, Special Report, Nonwhite Population by Race* (Washington, D.C., 1950), 3B-37; U.S. Bureau of the Census, *Eighteenth Census of the United States, Special Report, Nonwhite Population by Race* (Washington, D.C., 1960), 108.
50 Moynihan, "A Family Policy for the Nation"; Meehan, "Moynihan of the Moynihan Report."
51 U.S. Bureau of the Census, *Eighteenth Census of the United States, Special Report, Nonwhite Population by Race* (Washington, D.C., 1960).
52 See also "Transcript of the American Academy Conference on the Negro American—May 14–15, 1965," *Daedalus* 95:1 (Winter 1966): 287–441.
53 "Transcript of the Keynote Address by Senator Inouye Decrying Violent Protests," *New York Times*, August 27, 1968, 28.
54 On the Asian American Movement, see Commemorative Issue, "Salute to the 60s and 70s; Legacy of the San Francisco State Strike," *Amerasia Journal* 15:1 (1989); Glenn Omatsu, "The 'Four Prisons' and the Movements of Liberation: Asian American Activism From the 1960s to 1990s," in *The State of Asian America: Activism and Resistance in the 1990s*, ed. Karin Aguilar San Juan (Boston, 1994), 19–69; *Asian Americans: The Movement and the Moment*, eds. Steve Louie and Glenn Omatsu (Los Angeles, 2001); Daryl J. Maeda, *Chains of Babylon: The Rise of Asian America* (Minnesota, 2009).

References

Azuma, Eiichiro. "Race, Citizenship, and the 'Science of Chick Sexing': The Politics of Racial Identity among Japanese Americans." *Pacific Historical Review* 78, no. 2 (May 2009): 242–275.

Brooks, Charlotte. "In the Twilight Zone between Black and White: Japanese American Resettlement and Community in Chicago, 1942–1945." *Journal of American History* 86, no. 4 (March 2000): 1655–1687.

Brooks, Charlotte. *Alien Neighbors, Foreign Friends: Asian Americans, Housing, and the Transformation of Urban California*. Chicago, IL: University of Chicago Press, 2009.

Brooks, Charlotte. *Between Mao and McCarthy: Chinese American Politics in the Cold War Years*. Chicago, IL: University of Chicago Press, 2015.

Cheng, Cindy I-Fen Cheng. *Citizens of Asian America: Democracy and Race during the Cold War* New York: New York University Press, 2013.

Commemorative Issue, "Salute to the 60s and 70s; Legacy of the San Francisco State Strike." *Amerasia Journal* 15, no. 1 (1989).

Heefner, Gretchen. "'A Symbol of the New Frontier': Hawaiian Statehood, Anti-Colonialism, and Winning the Cold War." *Pacific Historical Review* 74, no. 4 (2005): 545–574.

Hong, Jane H. "The Repeal of Asian Exclusion," *American History: Oxford Research Encyclopedia*, September 2015. http://americanhistory.oxfordre.com/view/10.1093/acrefore/9780199329175.001.0001/acrefore-9780199329175-e-16.

Hsu, Madeline Y. *The Good Immigrants: How the Yellow Peril Became a Model Minority*. Princeton, NJ: Princeton University Press, 2015.

Klein, Christina. *Cold War Orientalism: Asia in the Middlebrow Imagination, 1945–1961*. Berkeley, CA: University of California Press, 2003.

Kurashige, Lon. *Japanese American Celebration and Conflict: A History of Ethnic Identity and Festival in Los Angeles, 1934–1990*. Berkeley, CA: University of California Press, 2002.

Kurashige, Scott. *The Shifting Grounds of Race: Black and Japanese Americans in the Making of Multiethnic Los Angeles*. Princeton, NJ: Princeton University Press, 2008.

Kwong, Peter. *Chinatown, NY: Labor and Politics, 1930–1950*. New York: The New Press, 2001 edition.

Lai, Him Mark. *Becoming Chinese American: A History of Communities and Institutions*. Walnut Creek, CA: AltaMira Press, 2004.

Lai, Him Mark. *Chinese American Transnational Politics*. Edited by Madeline Y. Hsu. Urbana, IL: University of Illinois Press, 2010.

Lee, Robert G. *Orientals: Asian Americans in Popular Culture*. Philadelphia, PA: Temple University Press, 1999.

Louie, Steve and Glenn Omatsu, Eds. *Asian Americans: The Movement and the Moment*. Los Angeles, CA: UCLA Asian American Studies Center, 2001.

Lui, Mary Ting-Yi. "Rehabilitating Chinatown at Mid-Century: Chinese Americans, Race, and U.S. Cultural Diplomacy." In *Chinatowns in a Transnational World: Myths and Realities of an Urban Phenomenon*, edited by Vanessa Künnemann and Ruth Mayer, 81–100. New York: Routledge, 2011.

Lye, Colleen. "The Afro-Asian Analogy." *PMLA* 123, no. 5 (October 2008): 1732–1736.

Lye, Colleen. *America's Asia: Racial Form and American Literature, 1893–1945*. Princeton, NJ: Princeton University Press, 2005.

Maeda, Daryl J. *Chains of Babylon: The Rise of Asian America*. Minneapolis, MN: University of Minnesota Press, 2009.

Mah, Theresa J. "Buying into the Middle Class: Residential Segregation and Racial Formation in the United States, 1920–1964." PhD diss., University of Chicago, 1999.

Moynihan, Daniel Patrick. "A Family Policy for the Nation," *America: The National Catholic Weekly Review*, September 18, 1965, reprinted in Lee Rainwater and William L. Yancey, *The Moynihan Report and the Politics of Controversy* (Cambridge, MA: 1967), 385–394.

Murray, Alice Yang. *Historical Memories of the Japanese American Internment and the Struggle for Redress*. Stanford, CA: Stanford University Press, 2008.

Ngai, Mae M. *Impossible Subjects: Illegal Aliens and the Making of Modern America*. Princeton, NJ: Princeton University Press, 2004.

Oda, Meredith. "Rebuilding Japantown: Japanese Americans in Transpacific San Francisco during the Cold War." *Pacific Historical Review* 83, no. 1 (2014): 57–91.

Oh, Arissa H. *Into The Arms of America: The Korean Origins of International Adoption*. Stanford, CA: Stanford University Press, 2015.

Omatsu, Glenn Omatsu. "The 'Four Prisons' and the Movements of Liberation: Asian American Activism From the 1960s to 1990s." In *The State of Asian America: Activism and Resistance in the 1990s*, edited by Karin Aguilar San Juan, 19–69. Boston, MA: South End Press, 1994.

Oyen, Meredith. *The Diplomacy of Migration: Transnational Lives and the Making of U.S.-Chinese Relations in the Cold War*. Ithaca, NY: Cornell University Press, 2015.

Robinson, Greg Robinson. *After Camp: Portraits in Midcentury Japanese American Life and Politics*. Berkeley, CA: University of California Press, 2012.

Shih, Shu-mei. "Comparative Racialization: An Introduction." *PMLA* 123, no. 5 (October 2008): 1347–1362.

Wu, Ellen D. *The Color of Success: Asian Americans and the Origins of the Model Minority*. Princeton, NJ: Princeton University Press, 2014.

Yu, Henry. *Thinking Orientals: Migration, Contact, and Exoticism in Modern America*. New York: Oxford University Press, 2001.

Zhao, Xiaojian. *Remaking Chinese America: Immigration, Family, and Community, 1940–1965*. New Brunswick, NJ: Rutgers University Press, 2002.

Ziker, Ann K. "Segregationists Confront American Empire: The Conservative White South and the Question of Hawaiian Statehood, 1947–1959." *Pacific Historical Review* 76, no. 3 (August 2007): 439–465.

PART FIVE

Social Change and Political Participation

21
ASIAN AMERICAN STUDIES AND/AS DIGITAL HUMANITIES

Lori Kido Lopez and Konrad Ng

Introduction

This chapter explores the state of Asian American studies in the digital age and its intersection with the emergence of the "digital humanities" as a field of study. We are concerned with two central lines of inquiry: How does the rich scholarship and history of Asian American studies shape the concerns of Digital Humanities, and how is Asian American studies being shaped by the agendas and pedagogies of Digital Humanities? Within the realm of media and communication studies, the development of scholarly interest in digital technologies has mirrored the development of new communication technologies. In tracing the connections between communication and culture in a digital world, scholars have worked to make sense of the meaning behind shifting practices of representation, media production, information sharing, community and identity formations, and countless other practices. The use of computing tools and digital methodologies now extends beyond the field of communication to reframe the teaching and research of subjects across the humanities scholarship, forming a diverse set of overlapping research agendas and pedagogies that contend with the intersection between technology and knowledge production. Some of the field's earliest histories begin with "humanities computing,"[1] but transformed into "digital humanities" by 2006 when the National Endowment for the Humanities launched its agency-wide Digital Humanities Initiative. Much of the initial focus within Digital Humanities has centered on digitizing archival materials and working to transform images, text, and other forms of analog data into code. This process of digitization then allows for a wide variety of engagements—the data can be analyzed through algorithms or software, transformed into visualizations or maps, preserved online, made widely accessible and available to the public, or interpreted collaboratively. We can see through these modes of operation that Digital Humanities is many things, including an object of study, a methodology, a set of practices, and a political ideology. The work of digital humanists thus far has often been housed in English and Communication/Media Studies departments, but what we explore in this chapter is the way that the field can and does overlap with important inquiries within American studies, ethnic studies, and Asian American studies.

The moment is opportune to consider Asian America as a digital experience, and to theorize the way that this conceptualization bears relevance on what we see as Asian American Digital Humanities. As such, sketching this trajectory of inquiry is important to understanding Asian

American experiences. While Asian Americans studies has reached "critical mass" as a field of influence in terms of its academic institutionalization and professionalization and intellectual maturity to nurture and sustain critical self-reflexivity regarding its precepts as an "Asian American" movement,[2] the relevance of Asian American scholarship is questionable when uncontested precepts about history, culture, and complexity appear lost in the mainstream public consciousness.[3] Yet Asian Americans, it seems, are poised to shape the digital age in novel ways. Asian America is noted for being a wired and engaged online community, influencing platforms like YouTube and Twitter[4] and participating in the rise of a culture and technology innovation economy as the "Asian American creative class."[5] It is tempting to treat these observations as evidence of Asian America becoming the "model minorities" of the digital age. However, to assume this dispossessing narrative of Asian America obscures how the digital turn in Asian American experiences, and the range of complex relationships between Asian Americans and technology, offer insight into understanding the racial dynamics of the digital age. Put differently, the digital age is enabled by a racial dynamic that is often framed within a neoliberal argument for increased access. Indeed, Asian American studies during the digital age must be vigilant to avoid discourses that would position Asian Americans as digitalization's model minorities and reinscribe harmful racialized hierarchies. This way of thinking denies the discipline's founding commitments to activism and social justice, as well as later reformations and reorientations, and can fall into an uncritical embrace of Digital Humanities simply because Asian Americans appear to gain agency. To this point, we distinguish between using humanities-based inquiries to study the digital, and using digital tools to study the humanities. While the former opens up important possibilities for acknowledging the critical/cultural work that Asian Americans are conducting within the realm of the digital, the latter often seeks to erase the important nuances of context—race, class, gender, sex and history, among other intersecting and networked threads of understanding Asian American experiences, as we will explore below.

Given the diasporic sensibility of many Asian Americans, building and learning to utilize a virtually networked community is clearly a powerful endeavor. Sau-Ling Wong and Rachel Lee, in their introduction to *AsianAmerica.Net*, conjecture that Asian Americans are well suited "to take advantage of virtual reality's community-building potential given the very 'virtualness' built into the group's founding concept."[6] Yet what must be acknowledged is that these assumptions and stereotypes about Asian Americans have been harmful, and do not portray the full picture of how these individuals do or do not have access to and familiarity with communication technologies. We believe that the digital turn in Asian American studies offers a fruitful moment for reconsidering the meaning of Asian America—it provides a chance to sharpen our critiques, broaden our concerns, and rethink our loci of engagement. In exploring this transitional moment, we offer a preliminary sketch of Asian American studies at the digital turn. While Digital Humanities was not born out of Asian American studies and vice versa, our point of departure, to paraphrase Wendy Hui Kyong Chun's argument for race as technology,[7] is to consider Asian American studies and/as Digital Humanities, to map out points of intersection, and to envision what an Asian American studies during the digital age could accomplish.

Asian America and Technology

The digital age is at once about the use of technologies as well as the creation of media of communication and representation. In Asian American studies, the images and narratives that circulate across mainstream media have long been a point of departure for inquiry and activism since the emergence of an Asian American movement from the revolutionary culture of the late 1960s. Those working to establish ethnic studies as a discipline and Asian American studies as a critical field of study in universities were joined in their consciousness-raising by Asian American cultural workers—actors/actresses, artists, filmmakers, musicians, writers—and the formation of Asian American independent media arts collectives to advance social justice and empower through representation. Film, television, and other cultural forms were seen as political media—as targets of critique and opportunities to circulate narratives attuned to lived experience. In 1965, Asian American actors in Los Angeles established the East West Players theater organization to produce work that offered Asian American stories beyond popular stereotypes. Six years later, activists and filmmakers in Los Angeles also established Visual Communications with the objective of supporting Asian American filmmaking. In 1976, activists and filmmakers in New York City formed Asian CineVision to support Asian American filmmaking on the East Coast. In 1980, activists and filmmakers in San Francisco created the National Asian American Telecommunications Association (now the Center for Asian American Media) to promote independent Asian American filmmaking and Asian American productions for public broadcasting in cooperation with the Corporation for Public Broadcasting and the Public Broadcasting Service.

While concerns regarding the politics of representation across film and television have an established trajectory within Asian American studies scholarship, the study of Asian American representation in the digital age is still taking shape, and generally bridging the methods of media studies to Asian American new media. In this regard, what may be characterized as digital work in Asian American studies mirrors Tara McPherson's observation that early studies of race and the digital tend to be "a critique of representations *in* new media or the building of digital archives about race, modes that largely were deployed at the surface of our screens, or, second, debates about access to media—that is, the digital divide. Such work rarely tied race to analyses of form, phenomenology, or computation."[8] The focus of inquiry has been on the use and role of technology in Asian American cultural production and representation, prompted by observations over unprecedented forms of Asian American participation in YouTube, Twitter, blogging, among other new media platforms; for example, the activism of Phil Yu and his blog Angry Asian Man, the email campaigns launched by filmmaker Justin Lin around his film *Better Luck Tomorrow* (2001), or the rise of YouTube stars like Ryan Higa and Kevin Wu. The emergence of an alternate, oppositional arena of Asian American representational practice—what Kent Ono and Vincent Pham[9] note as Asian American independent and vernacular media—has provided wider opportunities to study the narrative and visual online representations of Asian America as well as the relationship between Asian Americans and technology.

Such examinations of the way that Asian American communities are using and responding to the changing technologies of representation and participation find precedent in earlier media studies research. Yet within these inquiries around representation, it is important to acknowledge the dominant (and problematic) discourse around Asian Americans as somehow preternaturally wired. The hypervisibility of what we might call the Asian cyborg has come to stand in stark contrast to the invisibility of Asian Americans as represented within mainstream media narratives. One article on a technology site goes so far as to ask, "Do the Asians have technology running through their veins?" This question reminds us of how Asian bodies are continually reinscribed as alien and otherized in relation to technology—a linkage that is reinforced through the sidelining of Asian actors within the routine portrayal of the "tech guy" in procedural television. Together, these linkages begin to imply that the speed of technological innovation in Asia and its adoption by Asian bodies is somehow biological or innate. Such images of the e-proficient model minority participate in recreating a kind of high-tech Orientalism where technology and Asian bodies are inextricably bound. Within techno-Orientalism, histories of economic competition between the U.S. and Japan or China become visible in depictions of Asians as alien and dehumanized—a contemporary version of Said's Orientalism, wherein the East is essentialized as primitive, exotic, and less than human. In an era when the United States fears the economic power of Asia, techno-orientalism casts a threatening pall over a population that possesses the ability to manipulate and profit from technology.[10] The fear of the Asian predilection for science and technology is particularly alive and well in the world of fictional representations—from the evil Dr. Fu Manchu and his technological warfare to an entire category of cyberpunk that relies on a decidedly Orientalized notion of the future. Science fiction movies such as *Cloud Atlas*, *Blade Runner*, *The Fifth Element*, *The Matrix*, and *Serenity* consistently include Oriental tropes and Asian iconography in their speculative visions of the future, portraying Asians as efficient technocratic robots who have somehow managed to influence every aspect of the urban landscape. As Timothy Yu states,

> The postmodern city of science fiction, while sharing some of the attributes of the globalized, transnational, borderless space of postmodernity apotheosized in the notion of "cyberspace," remains racialized and marked (if superficially) by history, exposing the degree to which Western conceptions of postmodernity are built upon continuing fantasies of—and anxieties about—the Orient.[11]

The connection between technology and the yellow peril lurks behind any discussion of the way that Asian Americans are using technology for political empowerment, community organizing, or identity development. These stereotypes are complicated by the fact that the positioning of Asia/Asian Americans as proficient in technology is not entirely unfounded. Many Asian countries are indeed at the forefront of technological innovation, exporting their high-tech goods across the globe. Moreover, research has shown that Asian Americans are the highest users of the Internet and broadband amongst all racial groups, even when compared to white users.[12] As we will demonstrate, Asian American studies in the digital age critically examines such assumptions and applications of data, arguing that the politics of race and representation is a necessary part of the digital conversation. The critical work of Asian American studies rethinks the notion of the digital divide in the Digital Humanities—that access for racial minorities is an opportunity to circumvent the barriers that prevent access to mainstream media—but that open-access itself is not detached from the politics of representation. For Asian Americans and the Digital Humanities, the discourse of the model minority and "techno-orientalism" is deeply entrenched in popular culture, and we must develop new tools for understanding and reshaping this articulation.

Asian American Digital Humanities: A Method

We can see the concern about representation in the digital age has often centered on the images and narratives of Asian Americans within digital technology. Yet it could be argued that Asian America itself is constituted by technologies—a premise that opens new approaches to understanding Asian American identity and race during the digital age, as well as the object of study for Asian American studies. The notion that race is constituted by digital technologies and not merely represented by their platforms helps us to see that Digital Humanities is an ideological—as opposed to objective—endeavor. Following Michael Omi and Howard Winant's (1994) influential work on racial formation theory,[13] the emergence of what may be described as an Asian American Digital Humanities gives us the opportunity to reflect on how the formation of Asian America assumes meaning within social relations shaped and determined by social, economic, and political forces—including the apparatuses of technology. Technology serves as an organizing principle for understanding racial identities and the deployment of technology operates within the racial categories at work. Seen in this way, "Asian America" is more complex than speaking to some unchanging racial essence, but the discourses of race and technology are intertwined. Wendy Hui Kyong Chun makes a compelling argument to consider race *as* technology, to shift "from the what of race to the how of race, from knowing race to doing race by emphasizing the similarities between race and technology."[14] The claim for a digital racial formation "displaces ontological questions of race-debates over what race really is and is not, focused on separating ideology from truth—with ethical questions: what relations does race set up?"[15] This framing allows Asian American Digital Humanities to find application beyond traditional concerns of civic empowerment and its sites of engagement.

The formation of Internet and technology culture in the latter half of the 20th century has contributed to the view of digital technology and life as an idyllic space of equality, or an opportunity to move beyond identity politics and to conflate the question of race with the answer of access. Lisa Nakamura contends that this offline view of race neglects how race and racism assume meanings online. As she points out, we must continue to ask how people of color can and do participate in new media technologies, and how the formation of racial identities is intrinsically connected to the design of online interfaces. She argues that a fuller study of digital life necessitates knowing "the specific conditions under which new media are produced as well as consumed, circulated, and exchanged. Interactivity goes both ways as well; Web sites create users who can interact with them, just as texts create their readers."[16] Digital media are unique loci of enunciation for racial experiences; they are interactive and participatory spaces where race develops a new sense of legibility within a community of online users of color. Similar to Chun, Nakamura's research in what may be categorized as Asian American Digital Humanities is less concerned about deepening coherence around the concept of Asian America, as has been a focus of debate for Asian American studies. Rather, the suggestion is to view the connection between the discourses of race and digital technologies as an opportunity to bring into being new forms of agency and new ways to critically engage the meaning of race and racism. Nakamura cites the work of Kandice Chuh,[17] who considers Asian American studies as a method addressing a set of concerns rather than instantiating an intelligible subject. The study of the relationship between Asian America and technology as being mutually constitutive positions Asian American Digital Humanities scholarship to reframe the meaning of Asian American experiences. As Nakamura writes, the study of Asian American new media, of the relationship between technology and the composition of Asian American identity, "centers on the possibility for hybrid and de-essentialized Asian identities that address contemporary narratives about power, difference, perception, and the visual."[18] It is this expression of hybridity and breaking down of borders that we see as an expanding, generative site for scholarship within Asian American Digital Humanities.

Race in the Digital Humanities

Although there has been much important work by critical race theorists on the way that minority populations are represented within digital media and the shape of their participation within digital communities, there has been a much wider chasm between critical race theory and Digital Humanities. Tara McPherson observes the dearth of discussion about the intersection between race/racial paradigms and subjects like computational systems, programming languages, or cyberstructures. This absence can be traced to the very precepts of digital culture, when the designs of technological systems during the post-World War II era embraced values of simplification and modularization in organizing knowledge. McPherson notes that, at face value, these seemingly objective computational organizing principles opposed the deeply embedded values of recognition, empowerment, and complexity espoused by the social justice movements that were forming at the same time. At the moment when digital culture and social justice movements were in formation, McPherson writes, "it seems at best naive to imagine that cultural and computational operating systems don't mutually infect one another."[19] In failing to account for the ways that racial logics undergird the very structures of digital culture, digital humanists often reify a postracial ideology where the modularity of technology and coding serve to erase the impact of social inequalities. To remedy these absences and blind spots, a number of scholars have begun to carve out a deliberate space for interrogating the assumptions behind work in the Digital Humanities and situating its development within material histories of exclusion and oppression. These kinds of discussions have taken place in many different forms—including through hashtags on Twitter; blog posts and tumblrs; sessions at conferences like THATcamp, ASA, and MLA; as well as online academic journals.[20] Two of the most active collectives of researchers who work to expand this particular line of scholarship within Digital Humanities are TransformDH and PostcolonialDH. Their interventions focus on expanding the purview of Digital Humanities to more intentionally account for vulnerable populations—including those who have been marginalized due to race, ethnicity, gender, sexuality, and class—and the way that they have been erased from more mainstream Digital Humanities discourses.

One of the ways that postcolonial scholars have worked to bring their perspective to bear within the Digital Humanities has been the development of projects designed to "decolonize the archive." Relying on the affordances of the Internet as a space that is relatively open, accessible, expansive, and durable, much work in the Digital Humanities has gone into the digitization of lost or excluded texts. For postcolonial scholars, this process of digitization and sharing takes on a political purpose. We can look at the example of Adeline Koh's project "Digitizing Chinese Englishmen," which seeks to digitize and annotate a literary magazine from colonial Singapore called *Straits Chinese Magazine*. Alongside making this literature more widely available, one of the project's broader aims is to contribute to an alternative representation of the relationship between colonizers and their subjects:

> *Digitizing 'Chinese Englishmen'* is an attempt to give voice and representation to formerly colonized subjects, and to attempt to work against the "imperial meaning-making" of the archive by implementing new types of reading and commenting technologies that disrupt the idea of dominant and subjugated knowledges.
> (Koh, *Digitizing "Chinese Englishmen"*)

This explanation reminds us that archives are often imperial projects that serve to shore up the perspective of the dominant class and subjugate those classified as inferior—whether that is through the way that histories are framed, how maps are drawn, what books are included in libraries, what images are held up as ideal, or what counts as knowledge.[21] Together, these different imperial projects contribute to an archive imbued with and reflective of the power relations that sustain it. Digital archives have often remediated these power dynamics, serving to erase subjugated histories or uphold colonial narratives and assumptions. For those working under the banner of Postcolonial DH or Transforming DH, it is important to question these commonsense practices and remedy these exclusions.

When thinking about how Asian American studies fits in to this demand for a new kind of Digital Humanities, we can first see a parallel interest in bringing subjugated histories forward for recognition and interrogation. As with postcolonial scholars, Asian Americanists posit a distinction between the object of study and the theory or approach that informs such studies. That is, they insist upon a research framework that does not merely study Asian American bodies. Rather, Asian American studies must be historically situated as a field of study with specific commitments; as Kent Ono has stated, "drawing attention to historical context and to power, to social relations, and to structured inequity remains a key feature within contemporary Asian American scholarship."[22] The category of "Asian American" is a political designation that has been given value through the recognition and validation of the collective struggles that communities of color faced in the United States. This recognition of political solidarity exists concomitantly in tension with the reality of what Lisa Lowe has famously termed the "heterogeneity, hybridity, and multiplicity"[23] of the lives and experiences of those encompassed within Asian America. Even when considering the relationship of Asian Americans to post-coloniality, Asian Americanists have called attention to the fact that Asian settlers in Hawaii are participants in the colonization of Native Hawaiians.[24] Others have criticized the field of Asian American studies for excluding, marginalizing, or tokenizing entire communities—including Pacific Islanders, South Asians, and Southeast Asians, or ethnic groups such as the Hmong. We can see that Asian American studies as a collective of individuals, communities, and institutions continues to struggle with many of these same issues of homogenization and exclusion. Thus as Asian Americanists take up work within the Digital Humanities, their interventions demand recognition of the salience of race and ethnicity in the lives of individuals and a careful eye toward the way that the fluidity of identity and the impact of history can shape data.

Digitizing Asian American: Big Data, Small Population

In order to make sense of the way that these Asian American interventions into Digital Humanities might work, let us look at an example. The Smithsonian Asian Pacific American Center has undertaken a number of different projects in the digital realm, particularly since their hire of a dedicated Curator of Digital and Emerging Media at the Smithsonian Asian Pacific American Center. In May 2014, they organized an event to contribute and edit Wikipedia entries on Asian America. With physical meetups in Washington DC, New York, Austin, and Los Angeles, the #WikiAPA event served as a catalyst for educating Asian Americans about how to become Wikipedia contributors and providing the opportunity for them to collectively participate in improving the global online resource. #WikiAPA served to call attention to the fact that there are consequences when digital resources are overwhelming authored by white men, and that we must labor collectively to remedy these problems. In particular, we can note that Wikipedia is a site that is often celebrated for its collaborative authorship, despite the fact that its hundreds of thousands of contributors are largely homogenous in gender and racial identities.[25] Yet with the recognition of this imbalance and its political consequences, we can see that Wikipedia also offers an opportunity to call upon the strengths of participatory culture—the low barriers to participation, the value placed on individual contributions, and the collective strength of the masses coming together to create a polyvocal database. Projects like #WikiAPA reflect the idea that when Asian Americanists do Digital Humanities work, there is the potential for overlap between the production of theory and the production of data—an overlap that is rare, as evidenced by the debates surrounding "more hack less yack"[26] wherein critique/theory are presumed to forestall practice/doing.

This conflict between theory and practice is of particular relevance to the Asian American studies perspective on Digital Humanities research, particularly given that one of the key projects of Digital Humanities has been to develop tools for making sense of what is known as "big data." The world has always consisted of far more data points than any researcher could ever fully comprehend or assess. Even analog objects such as newspaper articles or museum artifacts number in the millions and provide challenges for researchers, who must always draw boundaries around what they consider to be more manageable sample sizes. Yet as our world becomes increasingly digitized, data proliferate exponentially—from content that was born digital such as tweets or emails, to data automatically produced and recorded by digital sensors, to large archives of government data that are now available in digital form. With the proliferation of digital text, images, audio, and video, digital data now multiply at an unprecedented rate and are relatively accessible. Part of the work of Digital Humanities has been to corral and make sense of these data, with researchers working to develop tools for visualizing, cataloguing, and analyzing large amounts of data.

In many ways, Asian Americans have had a troubled relationship to big data. On the one hand, the project of Asian American studies has always been to create more data about this unique and understudied population. Yet the project of producing data about Asian Americans is often subject to critique, particularly when those data are used to make representative or general claims about the entire population. These issues came to the fore in 2012, when the Pew Research Center released a report called "The Rise of Asian Americans" that set out to comprehensively document the demographic characteristics of Asian Americans.[27] The study was based on a telephone survey of a nationally representative sample of 3,511 Asian Americans, and it examined topics such as values, education and career, religious beliefs and practices, economic circumstances, marriage norms, and many others. While the report provided a wealth of interesting and useful data about Asian Americans—and served to fill a large gap in Pew's data collection, which does not commonly include Asian Americans[28]—it was roundly critiqued by Asian American community organizations, scholars, and advocates.[29] In particular, they spoke out against the report's conclusions that Asian Americans are overwhelming successful in terms of income and education. A *Wall Street Journal* article summarizing the report with the headline "Asians Top Immigration Class," opened with this lede: "Asians are the fastest-growing, most educated and highest-earning population in the U.S., according to a new report that paints the majority-immigrant group as a boon to an economy that has come to rely increasingly on skilled workers."[30] As critics noted, the report's conclusions and statements of summary served to uphold the myth of model minority, or the assumption that all Asian American immigrants are successful, particularly in comparison to other minority groups like Hispanics and African Americans. This harmful stereotype neglects the extreme disparities within the diverse category of Asian American, where specific groups such as Hmong, Laotians, Cambodians, Guamanians, Native Hawaiians, and Tongans struggle with poverty and educational achievement. The report focused on the six largest ethnic groups in the U.S.—Chinese, Filipino, Indian, Vietnamese, Korean, and Japanese—and included very little study of these smaller populations. Asian Americanists argue that it is these smallest populations who demand the closest attention. It is their needs and their histories that are systemically erased in the production of big data, as their specific experiences can so easily be categorized as statistically insignificant. Indeed, within the Pew report on Asian Americans, only 176 individuals from ethnicities outside of the "Big Six" were interviewed. This means that out of the 45 ethnicities encompassed by the umbrella category of Asian America, 39 different ethnicities were represented by 176 individuals.

The responses to this form of data collection and dissemination remind us of the political dimensions of data. Although few disputed the realities that were reflected in the report's findings, the report was condemned because of its overwhelmingly positive framing, failure to meaningfully expose the limits of its disaggregation, and marginalization of so many subsections of the population. The report conflicted with an Asian American studies ethics of how and why we perform research—an ethic that can be used to shape the future of Digital Humanities.

Although big data are often celebrated for their ability to bring about innovation, insight, and increased knowledge, scholars from Asian American studies and other fields representing marginalized communities implore caution. As Crawford, Miltner, and Gray remind us in their special issue on big data in the *International Journal of Communications*:

> Big data continues to present blind spots and problems of representativeness, precisely because it cannot account for those who participate in the social world in ways that do not register as digital signals. It is big data's opacity to outsiders and subsequent claims to veracity through volume that discursively neutralizes the tendency to make errors, fail to account for certain people and communities, or discriminate.[31]

As we look forward to future research and projects that blend Asian American and Digital Humanities perspectives, methodologies, and ethics, this critique of the way that data can contribute to oppression is important to heed.

Conclusion

This chapter provided an overview of Asian American studies in the digital age and the emergence of the Digital Humanities as a field of study. We believe in the increasing relevance of Asian American studies to the Digital Humanities and the Digital Humanities to Asian American studies; an intersection that we view with cautious optimism. The pace of technological change and its integration into everyday life, the growing popularity of Digital Humanities research, and the projected growth of the Asian population in the U.S. and around the world, makes a case for the importance of Asian American studies as Digital Humanities. As our overview suggests, Asian American studies as Digital Humanities argues that the meaning of these two formations—digital technology and Asian America—can come into focus through their relationship to each other. During an era when technology continues to be embraced as an opportunity to deepen the relevance of the humanities and its institutionalization, Asian American studies provides a critical perspective on the use technology. This means treating technology not as a tool, but as a discursive formation in relation to communities of color, and as an exercise of power and ideology. In turn, research and methods in Digital Humanities suggest how Asian American studies offers a dynamic form of engagement. The conception of Asian America as technology suggests how Asian American studies may reconsider core concepts such as race and ethnicity within a different framework: identity as being constituted by technology in addition to being represented by it. This approach encourages understanding Asian American experiences in kinship with other concepts relating to the discourse of technology. As Wendy Hui Kyong Chun contends, race as technology shifts the analysis from what race is and is not, to an ethical question: "what relations does race set up?"[32] How is race interpolated with other discursive formations and concerns?

It is our hope that the notion of Asian American studies as Digital Humanities will spur novel forms of Asian American scholarly research and production. The methods and tools of Digital Humanities not only illustrate how Asian American studies can visualize its research and reinterpret the data of research about Asian Americans, but the values associated with Digital Humanities—including access, collaboration, experimentation and participation—can spark new and innovative models of scholarly engagement in Asian American studies. Instead of measuring the institutionalization of Asian American studies on campuses in terms of Asian American studies graduates and faculty, we see promise in increasing collaborations with research in digital code, design, and media studies to leverage the intellectual capital of Asian

American studies as a field with a stake in the institutionalization of other disciplines. Additionally, the adoption of Digital Humanities work[33] in Asian American studies courses can increase the relevance of Asian American studies; the digital labor and learning of Asian American knowledge add to the archive of its study as a born-digital experience. Put differently, the increase of Asian American digital output increases the relevance of Asian American studies to Digital Humanities. The promise of Asian American studies as Digital Humanities, we believe, is embedded in the process of writing this chapter, which was born out of online exchange between two researchers from different fields and neither one from Asian American studies proper. However, we share a mutual concern for rethinking "Asian America" as a digital experience, believing that this conception of Asian America not only remains faithful to the Asian American studies' founding commitments to social justice and empowerment, but that Asian American experiences offer a relevant and exciting space to understand the nature of digital life and knowledge in the 21st Century.

Notes

1 Patrick Svensson, "Humanities Computing as Digital Humanities," *Digital Humanities Quarterly* 3, no. 3 (2009), http://digitalhumanities.org/dhq/vol/3/3/000065/000065.html.
2 Kent Ono, "Asian American Studies in Its Second Phase," in *Asian American Studies After Critical Mass*, Ed. Kent Ono (Malden, MA: Blackwell Publishing, 2005), 1–16.
3 Tim Yu, "Has Asian American Studies Failed?," *tympan* (blog), December 20, 2011 (10:03 p.m.), http://tympan.blogspot.com/2011/12/has-asian-american-studies-failed.html.
4 Austin Considine, "For Asian-American Stars, Many Web Fans," *New York Times*, July 29, 2011, www.nytimes.com/2011/07/31/fashion/for-asian-stars-many-web-fans.html; Hayley Tsukayama, "In online video, minorities find an audience," *Washington Post*, April 20, 2012, www.washingtonpost.com/business/economy/in-online-video-minorities-find-an-audience/2012/04/20/gIQAdhliWT_story.html; and Hayley Tsukayama, "YouTube channel YOMYOMF launches, focus on Asian-American pop culture," *Washington Post*, June 15, 2012, www.washingtonpost.com/business/technology/youtube-channel-yomyomf-launches-focus-on-asian-american-pop-culture/2012/06/15/gJQAhEbKfV_story.html.
5 Mimi Thi Nguyen and Thuy Linh Nguyen Tu, *Alien Encounters: Popular Cultures in Asian America* (Durham, NC: Duke University Press, 2007); Richard Florida, "Race, Gender, and the Creative Class," *The Atlantic*, June 27 2012, www.theatlanticcities.com/jobs-and-economy/2012/06/race-gender-and-creative-class/2225.
6 Sau-Ling Wong and Rachel Lee, "Introduction," in *Asian America.Net: Ethnicity, Nationalism, and Cyberspace,* (New York: Routledge, 2003), xix.
7 Wendy Hui Kyong Chun, "Race and/as Technology, or How to Do Things to Race" in *Race After the Internet*, Eds. Lisa Nakamura and Peter A. Chow-White (New York: Routledge, 2012), 38–60.
8 Tara McPherson. "Why Are the Digital Humanities So White?: Or Thinking the Histories of Race and Computation." In *Debates in the Digital Humanities*, edited by Gold Matthew K., 139–160. University of Minnesota Press, 2012. www.jstor.org/stable/10.5749/j.ctttv8hq.12.
9 Kent Ono and Vincent Pham, *Asian Americans and the Media,* (Malden, MA: Polity Press, 2009), 155.
10 David Morley and Kevin Robins, "Techno-Orientalism: Futures, Foreigners, and Phobias," *New Formations,* Spring 1992, 136–156.
11 Timothy Yu, "Oriental Cities, Postmodern Futures: Naked Lunch, Blade Runner, and Neuromancer," *MELUS*, Winter 2008: 33/4, 46.
12 www.census.gov/cps/methodology/techdocs.html.
13 Michael Omi and Howard Winant (Eds.) *Racial Formation in the United States* 2nd ed. (New York: Routledge, 1994).
14 Wendy Hui Kyong Chun, "Race and/as Technology, or How to Do Things to Race" in *Race After the Internet*, Eds. Lisa Nakamura and Peter A. Chow-White (New York: Routledge, 2012), 38.
15 Ibid., 56–57.

16 Lisa Nakamura, *Digitizing Race: Visual Cultures of the Internet*, (Minneapolis, MN: University of Minnesota Press, 2008), 86.
17 Kandice Chuh, *Imagine Otherwise: On Asian Americanist Critique* (Durham, NC: Duke University Press, 2003).
18 Lisa Nakamura, *Digitizing Race: Visual Cultures of the Internet*, (Minneapolis, MN: University of Minnesota Press, 2008), 85–86.
19 Tara McPherson, "Why Are the Digital Humanities So White? or Thinking the Histories of Race and Computation" in *Debates in the Digital Humanities*, Ed. in Matthew K. Gold, (Minneapolis, MN: University of Minnesota Press, 2012). http://dhdebates.gc.cuny.edu/debates/text/29.
20 A range of online resources include: TransformDH (Twitter) https://twitter.com/TransformDH; Postcolonial Digital Humanities (blog) http://dhpoco.wordpress.com/; TransformDH (Tumblr) http://transformdh.tumblr.com/; DHPoco: Postcolonial Digital Humanites (Tumblr) http://dhpoco.tumblr.com/. Alexis Lothian, "Marked Bodies, Transformative Scholarship, and the Question of Theory in Digital Humanities," *Journal of Digital Humanities* 1, no. 1 Winter 2011, http://journalofdigitalhumanities.org/1-1/marked-bodies-transformative-scholarship-and-the-question-of-theory-in-digital-humanities-by-alexis-lothian/; Alexis Lothian, "Conference Thoughts: Queer Studies and the Digital Humanities, *Queer Geek Theory* (blog), October 18, 2011 (12:12 a.m.), www.queergeektheory.org/2011/10/conference-thoughts-queer-studies-and-the-digital-humanities/; Adeline Koh, "Postcolonial Digital Humanities Praxis: Proposal for MLA 2015," *Adeline Koh* (blog) April 1, 2014, www.adelinekoh.org/blog/2014/04/01/postcolonial-digital-humanities-praxis-proposal-for-mla-2015/; Moya Z. Bailey, "All the Digital Humanists Are White, All the Nerds Are Men, but Some of Us Are Brave," *Journal of Digital Humanities* 1, no. 1 Winter 2011, http://journalofdigitalhumanities.org/1-1/all-the-digital-humanists-are-white-all-the-nerds-are-men-but-some-of-us-are-brave-by-moya-z-bailey/.http://journalofdigitalhumanities.org/1-1/all-the-digital-humanists-are-white-all-the-nerds-are-men-but-some-of-us-are-brave-by-moya-z-bailey/.
21 Thomas Richards, *The Imperial Archive: Knowledge and the Fantasy of Empire* (London: Verso, 1993); Anne McClintock, *Imperial Leather: Race, Gender, and Sexuality in the Colonial Contest* (New York: Routledge, 1995); Ellen Cushman, "Wampum, Sequoyan, and Story: Decolonizing the Digital Archive," *College English* 76 no. 2, 2013, 115–135.
22 Kent Ono, "Asian American Studies in Its Second Phase," in *Asian American Studies After Critical Mass*, Ed. Kent Ono (Malden, MA: Blackwell Publishing, 2005), 4.
23 Lisa Lowe, *Immigrant Acts: On Asian American Cultural Politics* (Durham, NC: Duke University Press, 1999).
24 Candace Fujikane, "Foregrounding Native Nationalisms: A Critique of Antinationalist Sentiment in Asian American Studies" in *Asian American Studies After Critical Mass*, ed. Kent Ono (Malden, MA: Blackwell Publishing, 2005), 73–97.
25 Noam Cohen, "Define Gender Gap? Look Up Wikipedia's Contributor List," *New York Times*, January 30, 2011, www.nytimes.com/2011/01/31/business/media/31link.html.
26 Adeline Koh, "More Hack, Less Yack? Modularity, theory and Habitus in the Digital Humanities," *Adeline Koh* (blog), May 21, 2012, www.adelinekoh.org/blog/2012/05/21/more-hack-less-yack-modularity-theory-and-habitus-in-the-digital-humanities/.
27 Pew Research Center, *The Rise of Asian Americans*, April 4, 2013, www.pewsocialtrends.org/files/2013/04/Asian-Americans-new-full-report-04-2013.pdf.
28 Aaron Smith, "Why Pew Internet does not regularly report statistics for Asian-Americans and their technology use" Pew Research Center, March 29, 2013, www.pewinternet.org/2013/03/29/why-pew-internet-does-not-regularly-report-statistics-for-asian-americans-and-their-technology-use/.
29 Some of the organizations who criticized the report include: Japanese American Citizens League (JACL), the Organization of Chinese Americans (OCA), Asian and Pacific Islander American Scholarship Fund (APIASF), the National Commission on Asian American and Pacific Islander Research in Education (CARE), Congressional Asian Pacific American Caucus (CAPAC), Asian American Center for Advancing Justice, Asian American Pacific Islander Policy and Research Consortium (AAPIPRC).
30 Miriam Jordan, "Asians Top Immigration Class: Fastest-Growign Population Group Supplies U.S. With Skilled Workers, Study Says," *Wall Street Journal*, June 18, 2012, http://online.wsj.com/news/articles/SB10001424052702303379204577474743811707050

31 Kate Crawford, Kate Miltner, Mary Gray. (2014) "Critiquing Big Data—Special Section Introduction," *International Journal of Communication* 8 (2014), 1667.
32 Wendy Hui Kyong Chun, "Race and/as Technology, or How to Do Things to Race" in *Race After the Internet*, Eds. Lisa Nakamura and Peter A. Chow-White (New York: Routledge, 2012), 57.
33 Adeline Koh, "Introducing Digital Humanities Work to Undergraduates: An Overview" *Hybrid Pedagogy: A digital journal of learning, teaching, and technology*, August 14, 2014, www.hybridpedagogy.com/journal/introducing-digital-humanities-work-undergraduates-overview/.

References

Chuh, K. (2003) *Imagine Otherwise: On Asian Americanist Critique*, Durham, NC: Duke University Press.
Chun, W. H. K. (2012) "Race and/as Technology, or How to Do Things to Race," in *Race After the Internet*, L. Nakamura and P. A. Chow-White (Eds.) New York: Routledge. 38–60.
Cohen, N. (2011) "Define Gender Gap? Look Up Wikipedia's Contributor List," *New York Times*, January 30. Available from www.nytimes.com/2011/01/31/business/media/31link.html.
Considine, A. (2011) "For Asian-American Stars, Many Web Fans," *New York Times*, July 29. Available from www.nytimes.com/2011/07/31/fashion/for-asian-stars-many-web-fans.html.
Crawford, K., Miltner, K., and Gray, M. (2014) "Critiquing Big Data-Special Section Introduction," *International Journal of Communication* 8, 1663–1672.
Cushman, E. (2013) "Wampum, Sequoyan, and Story: Decolonizing the Digital Archive," *College English* 76(2), 115–135.
Florida, R. (2012) "Race, Gender, and the Creative Class," *The Atlantic*, June 27. Available from www.theatlanticcities.com/jobs-and-economy/2012/06/race-gender-and-creative-class/2225.
Fujikane, C. (2005) "Foregrounding Native Nationalisms: A Critique of Antinationalist Sentiment in Asian American Studies," in *Asian American Studies After Critical Mass*, K. Ono, (Ed.) Malden, MA: Blackwell Publishing. 73–97.
Jordan, M. (2012) "Asians Top Immigration Class: Fastest-Growign Population Group Supplies U.S. With Skilled Workers, Study Says," *Wall Street Journal*, June 18. Available from www.online.wsj.com/news/articles/SB10001424052702303379204577474743811707050.
Koh, A. (2012) "More Hack, Less Yack? Modularity, theory and Habitus in the Digital Humanities," *Adeline Koh*, May 21. Available from www.adelinekoh.org/blog/2012/05/21/more-hack-less-yack-modularity-theory-and-habitus-in-the-digital-humanities/.
Koh, A. (2014) "Introducing Digital Humanities Work to Undergraduates: An Overview" *Hybrid Pedagogy: A digital journal of learning, teaching, and technology*, August 14. Available from www.hybridpedagogy.com/journal/introducing-digital-humanities-work-undergraduates-overview/.
Lowe, L. (1999) *Immigrant Acts: On Asian American Cultural Politics*, Durham, NC: Duke University Press.
McClintock, A. (1995) *Imperial Leather: Race, Gender, and Sexuality in the Colonial Contest*, New York: Routledge.
McPherson, T. (2012) "Why Are the Digital Humanities So White? or Thinking the Histories of Race and Computation," in *Debates in the Digital Humanities*, M. K. Gold (Ed.) Minneapolis: University of Minnesota Press. Available from www.dhdebates.gc.cuny.edu/debates/text/29.
Morley, D. and Robins, K. (1992) "Techno-Orientalism: Futures, Foreigners, and Phobias," *New Formations 16*, Spring, 136–156.
Nakamura, L. (2008) *Digitizing Race: Visual Cultures of the Internet*, Minneapolis, MN: University of Minnesota Press.
Nguyen, M. T. and Tu, T. H. N. (2007) *Alien Encounters: Popular Cultures in Asian America*, Durham, NC: Duke University Press.
Omi, M. and Winant, H. (Eds.) (1994) *Racial Formation in the United States* 2nd ed., New York: Routledge.
Ono, K. (2005) "Asian American Studies in Its Second Phase," in *Asian American Studies After Critical Mass*, K. Ono (Ed.) Malden, MA: Blackwell Publishing. 1–16.
Ono, K. and Pham, V. N. (2009) *Asian Americans and the Media*, Malden, MA: Polity Press.
Pew Research Center (2013) *The Rise of Asian Americans*, April 4. Available from www.pewsocialtrends.org/files/2013/04/Asian-Americans-new-full-report-04-2013.pdf (accessed October 16, 2016).
Richards, T. (1993) *The Imperial Archive: Knowledge and the Fantasy of Empire*, London: Verso.

Smith, A. (2013) "Why Pew Internet does not regularly report statistics for Asian-Americans and their technology use" Pew Research Center, March 29. Available from www.pewinternet.org/2013/03/29/why-pew-internet-does-not-regularly-report-statistics-for-asian-americans-and-their-technology-use/.

Svensson, P. (2009) "Humanities Computing as Digital Humanities," *Digital Humanities Quarterly* 3(3), Available from www.digitalhumanities.org/dhq/vol/3/3/000065/000065.html.

Tsukayama, H. (2012) "In online video, minorities find an audience," *Washington Post*, April 20. Available from www.washingtonpost.com/business/economy/in-online-video-minorities-find-an-audience/2012/04/20/gIQAdhliWT_story.html.

Tsukayama, H. (2012) "YouTube channel YOMYOMF launches, focus on Asian-American pop culture," *Washington Post*, June 15. Available from www.washingtonpost.com/business/technology/youtube-channel-yomyomf-launches-focus-on-asian-american-pop-culture/2012/06/15/gJQAhEbKfV_story.html.

Wong, S. L. and Lee, R. (2003) "Introduction," in *Asian America.Net: Ethnicity, Nationalism, and Cyberspace*, New York: Routledge. xiii–xxxv.

Yu, T. (2008) "Oriental Cities, Postmodern Futures: Naked Lunch, Blade Runner, and Neuromancer," *MELUS* 33(4), 45–71.

Yu, T. (2011) "Has Asian American Studies Failed?" *tympan*. Available from www.tympan.blogspot.com/2011/12/has-asian-american-studies-failed.html.

22

ASIAN AMERICAN QUEER AND TRANS ACTIVISMS

Jian Neo Chen

Social and cultural histories of Asian American queer and trans activisms have yet to be more consistently and widely documented, cited, and transmitted. This attempt takes a relational approach to critical description and analysis—an approach developed by Asian American trans and queer embodied practices of survival and living, community-building, and political mobilization. Rather than producing a linear narrative of the emergence and continuity of Asian American queer and trans activisms, this entry will focus on moments of activity, connection, transition, and incubation that contribute to shaping still-emerging Asian American trans and queer social identities, embodied cultures and communities, and radical to progressive politics. A relational description displaces any single or complete narrative of the multiple struggles experienced and activated by queer and trans Asian Americans.

Intersectional LGBT Struggles

Queer Asian Americans became visible in the mid-to-late 1990s as an oppositional mode of social identification and cultural politics. Queer*ed* Asian American consciousness and politics builds on the intersectional political work and cultural expressions of Asian American lesbian, gay, bisexual, and transgender (LGBT) people. LGBT Asian Americans had worked within and between feminist, racial justice, Third World, anti-imperialist, economic justice, gay liberation, and HIV/AIDS movements throughout the 1960s, 1970s, and 1980s. Yet, their multidimensional struggles were not expressed or addressed by these movements. Kiyoshi Kuromiya, who was born in a Japanese internment camp in 1943, was an activist in the Civil Rights and anti-war movements and participated in numerous actions, including sit-ins in establishments that refused to serve Black people, voter registration protests, and street shut-downs. He was also a pre-Stonewall gay liberation activist, who co-founded the Philadelphia Gay Liberation Front, and, later, a leading HIV/AIDS activist. Kuromiya was often kicked out of Gay Activist Alliance meetings when he spoke out against racism (Tsang 2001: 221–222). Reflecting on his participation in the Filipino American radical left and anti-Marcos organizing in the 1970s, Gil Mangaoang states, "Initially, I felt that these two identities—Filipino and gay—were contradictory and irreconcilable" (Mangaoang 1996: 106–107). Mangaoang worried that his dual identity would put him in "double jeopardy," possibly delegitimizing his political work within the Filipino community and compounding the racism already experienced within dominant white Euro-American culture. In her poetry published in the early 1980s, Chinese American lesbian writer and activist Kitty Tsui described her experience of homophobia and alienation within her own birth family, even as she faced sexualized racism and heterosexism within dominant white American society (Tsui 2006). LGBT Asian Americans faced and fought the effects of U.S.-based systemic imperialism, racism, sexism, classism, and homophobia in their personal lives and in coalition with each other and other groups. At the same time, they negotiated the threat and reality of rejection and devaluation in the racial, ethnic, gender, and sexual communities and coalitions they helped to build.

In the 1980s and early 1990s, the intersectional specificity of Asian American LGBT social identities had become expressed in critical mass through established community groups, including National Lesbian and Gay Asian Collective (Washington, DC, 1979), Boston Asian Gay Males and Lesbians (1979), Asian Pacific Lesbians and Gays (Los Angeles, 1980), Association of Lesbian and Gay Asians (San Francisco, 1981), Asian Lesbians of the East Coast (New York, 1983), Asian Pacific Lesbians and Friends (Los Angeles, 1983), Gay Asian Rap (Los Angeles, 1984), Anamika (Brooklyn, 1985), Chicago Asian Lesbians Moving (1985), SANGAT (Chicago, 1986), Trikone (San Francisco, 1986), Pacific/Asian Lesbians (Santa Cruz, 1987), Gay Asian Pacific Alliance (San Francisco, 1988), Gay Asian Pacific Support Network (Los Angeles, 1988), Midwest Asian Dykes (Chicago and Madison, 1989), Asian Pacific Sisters (San Francisco, 1989), Pacifica Asian Lesbians (Chicago, 1989), Shamakami (San Francisco, 1990), Gay Asian Pacific Islander Men of New York (1990), SALGA (New York, 1991), MASALA (Boston, 1994), KhushDC (Washington, DC, 1994), Gay Vietnamese Alliance (Orange County, 1994), Ô-môi (Orange County, 1995), Gay Asian Pacific Islanders of Chicago (1995), Khuli Zaban (Chicago, 1995) (Shah 1993; Eng and Hom 1998: 2–3; Masequesmay 2003; Jong 2008; Dang, Vo, and Le 2015: 102). The first lesbian and gay Asian American group, the National Lesbian and Gay Asian Collective, was an informal network created by participants in the first National Conference of Third World Lesbians and Gays in 1979 in Washington, DC (Tsang 2000:117). The organizers of the Collective sought to bring together movements for sexual and racial liberation through the lens of Asian American experiences, in coalition with other Third World peoples. The majority of the groups formed in the 1980s and 1990s provided support in response to displacement from families, ethnic communities, and countries and cultures of origin, as well as racial alienation and racism in the white dominant heterosexual mainstream and LGBT movements. They sought to re-envision and build family, home, and community against these multiple displacements, while addressing the systemic societal inequalities that produce these displacements. These groups engaged in political activities, including protesting mainstream pro-gay state and city legislation that would increase the policing and targeting of immigrants and people of color (Chung, Kim, Nguyen, Ordona, and Stein 1996). They called attention to the impact of the HIV/AIDS epidemic on Asian American communities at a moment when Asian Americans were considered too numerically insignificant to target for HIV/AIDS services and prevention. Although trans identified and embodied people participated in these groups, the specificity of their experiences and struggles was rarely addressed, as reflected in the naming of these groups.

These early LGBT Asian American groups did not escape the contradictions and conflicts of pan-ethnic Asian American community organizing. Whether group membership was identified as Asian, Asian Pacific, or Asian and Pacific Islander, the racial identification used to describe shared struggles and lineages could only act as a communicated wish, hope, or activator for common ground. Each group had to actively rally together and build coalitions between people of different ethnicities, nationalities, regions, and migration and geopolitical histories under umbrella racial terms. These umbrella racial terms also had to be reclaimed against the grain of their often racist, exploitative, and regulating origins. By 1990, many LGBT Asian American organizations were using the terms "Asian Pacific" or "Asian and Pacific Islander" in naming their groups and membership. The adoption of these terms represents efforts to appropriate and re-imagine Asia-Pacific regional identity and networks, which were created and enforced through U.S. histories of imperialism, Orientalism, militarism, and resource extraction during World War II and the Cold War. In 1990, the term "Asian Pacific Islander" appeared in the U.S. Census as a fourth racial category along with white, African-American, and Native North American. Referring to use of "Asian Pacific Islander" by Asian American organizations, J. Kehaulani Kauanui and Ju Hui "Judy" Han warn that "expanding boundaries and including more does not equal being inclusive." They point out that this "misperception of 'inclusiveness' results not in Pacific Islanders being included, but being *engulfed*, swallowed whole and remaining ever invisible among (East) Asian Americans" (Kauanui and Han 1994). The term "Asian" used by Asian American LGBT groups in the 1980s and early 1990s cannot be presumed either to describe diverse and inclusive pan-ethnic coalitions. Most often, Northeast Asian Americans, especially Chinese and Japanese Americans, played dominant roles in shaping the agendas, leadership, and membership of these groups, while South and Southeast Asian Americans found their concerns and participation marginalized (Roy 1998). In describing the lumping together of Asians in the U.S. as a result of Western ethnocentrism, Indian American writer Rakesh Ratti argues "in the United States [*Asian*] is used interchangeably with the term East Asian—Chinese, Japanese, etc.—and in the United Kingdom it refers exclusively to South Asians. Even when used broadly, this term is misleading. Though they share common struggles and goals, East Asians and South Asians are distinct from one another linguistically, racially, and culturally, and yet Westerners have a tendency to refer to them monolithically" (Ratti 1993). Vietnamese American writer and chef Diep Khac Tran says, "It seems as if we [as Asian American activists] are conjuring up the idea of racial unity" (Aquilar-San Juan 2009: 41). The first South Asian LGBT groups in the U.S., Anamika and Trikone, were formed in the mid-1980s to address the specificity of the South Asian diaspora. Both used newsletters as their primary means of disseminating information and creating community dialogue across local and national boundaries (Shah 1993). Describing the creation of the Vietnamese group Ô-môi, Gina Masequesmay suggests, "The Vietnamese queer women and transgender men in Ô-môi were not content with just any queer support organization, they wanted it to be specifically Vietnamese-focused because of their unique experiences as refugees. As an ethnic group in exile, many Vietnamese feel an even greater need to hold onto their culture because they have 'no homeland left' in which to practice their customs and traditions" (Masequesmay 2003: 131). Ô-môi and the Gay Vietnamese Alliance are both located in Orange County, CA near Camp Pendleton military base, where waves of Vietnamese refugees were "processed" upon arrival in the U.S. beginning in 1975 (Masquesmay 2003). Hmong LGBTQ group Shades of Yellow (St. Paul, 2003), gender nonconforming, women, and youth focused African American and Southeast Asian group Freedom, Inc. (Madison, 2003), and Cambodian American queer-inclusive youth group Providence Youth Student Movement (Providence, 2001) together created the Queer Southeast Asian Network in 2009. Across the LGBT groups established in the 1980s and early 1990s in identification and dis-identification with "Asian America," racial, ethnic, and regional commonalities often covered over differences in class and educational privilege, abilities, gender, gender identity, sex (such as intersex), sexuality, refugee and immigration status, and language.

These groups were accompanied by a surge in cultural productions focusing on LGBT Asian Americans. Publications included stories, poetry, plays, narratives, essays, and novels by Willyce Kim, Chea Villanueva, Barbara Noda, Canyon Sam, Merle Woo, Nayan Shah, Minal Hajratwala,

Shani Mootoo, Elsa E'der, Norman Wong, Dwight Okita, Lawrence Chua, Alice Hom, and John Silva, and also anthologies such as *Between the Lines: An Anthology by Pacific/Asian Lesbians of Santa Cruz, California* (1987), edited by Cristy Chung, Alison Kim, and A. Kaweah Lemeshewsky; *A Lotus of Another Color: An Unfolding of the South Asian Gay and Lesbian Experience* (1993), edited by Rakesh Ratti; the Asian American Writers' Workshop's Asian Pacific American Journal special issue "Witness Aloud: Lesbian, Gay and Bisexual Asian/Pacific American Writings" (1993); and *The Very Inside: An Anthology of Writing by Asian and Pacific Islander Lesbian and Bisexual Women* (1994), edited by Sharon Lim-Hing. At a moment when cultural sectors including non-governmental organizations (NGOs), the mainstream art world, semi-institutionalized academic ethnic studies and gay and lesbian studies, and print and other media industries had begun to secure institutional boundaries, these writings crossed institutional sectors and resisted divisions between political activism, art, literature, cultural scholarship, and personal desire and experiences. These writings reinvented strict cultural genres, including academic essays and the novel form, to re-imagine the scope, content, and value of literature and literature's relationship to communities, knowledge, and social transformation. Published by small independent presses or self-published, these bodies of literature did not address markets or niches of readers, but instead, imagined readers who were participants in co-creating meaning, feeling, and belonging. Together, these writings and groups produced the possibility of LGBT Asian American cultures, communities, and social survival and vitality. They introduced modes and moments of cultural transmission that energized subsequent waves of cultural production, community organizing, and political activism. LGBT Asian American groups and cultural work expanded and intervened in the fractal (often failed) coalitional strategies of pan-ethnic Asian American movements by expressing and addressing the intersectional formations of sexuality and race in shaping social identity and systems of oppression in the U.S. Although less acknowledged, LGBT Asian American formations in the 1980s and early 1990s drew on the intersectional strategies of lesbian and bisexual women of color/Third World women and Asian American and women of color/Third World feminists, perhaps more so than the Asian American racial and nationalist strategies in which they often had to intervene. Many of the writers and founding participants of early LGBT Asian American literature and organizations had already contributed to building LB women of color/Third World political coalitions and cultures, including Kitchen Table: Women of Color Press, *This Bridge Called My Back: Writings by Radical Women of Color* (1984), and *Piece of my Heart: Lesbian of Colour Anthology* (1991). They had also worked to address the limitations of the white, middle-class women's movement and male privilege in the Yellow and Brown Power and other cultural nationalist movements in the U.S. by creating intergenerational, working-class inclusive, pan-ethnic Asian women's and women of color/Third World women's movements that focused on neglected issues such as the sweatshop work of Asian and Latina immigrant women in the U.S., at the U.S.–Mexico border, and transnationally (Shah 1997). These collaborations produced intersectional strategies that critiqued interlinked systems of heterosexism, patriarchy, imperialism, racism, and classism while also generating poetics based on the intimate and creative labor of negotiating life at the edges of multiple systems of oppression. Although not Asian American specific, LGBT women of color creative and cultural events like the monthly spoken word, poetry, and music events organized by "Just Us" Productions in the San Francisco/Bay Area in the early 1990s were initiated by LGBT Asian American activists such as Teiji Okamoto. Community-based organizers and healers including Milyoung Cho and Young Sohm built bridges between 1.5+ generation Asian Americans and recent immigrant women working in feminized "informal" sectors such as garment piecework, domestic service, and electronics assembly.

Jian Neo Chen

Queering LGBT Asian America

Queer Asian American identities, community activism, and cultural work emerged in the mid-1990s as an extension of intersectional LGBT Asian American struggles. "Queer" was/is a term reclaimed from its hateful, derogatory uses against people perceived as "deviant" within the confines of what is considered "normal" by presumably "common-sense" sexual and gender standards and morals. Asian Americans who adopted the term used it ironically, bitingly, and playfully to embrace outcast sexual and gender practices, bodily expressions, and relationships deemed "abnormal" under societal norms. In reworking the negativity of "queer," Asian Americans called attention to not only the heteronormative and heterosexist systems that shape everyday interactions but also the racism and Orientalism that shape common perceptions of Asian Americans. The racialization of Asian Americans has worked through attributing deviant, failed, and/or excessive gender expression and sexuality based on binary white Western standards for masculine and feminine gender, hetero- and homosexuality, and male and female sex. Queered Asian American communities embraced their *racially* queer sexualities and genders, rather than trying to re-normalize them according to binary white codes. In *Q & A: Queer in Asian America* (1998), the first anthology to mark the emergence of a distinctly queer Asian American identity and field of studies, David L. Eng and Alice Hom announce "We are queer, lesbian, gay, bisexual, and transgendered Asian Americans who are willing to engage actively in the discourses of both Asian American and queer politics but unwilling to bifurcate our identities into the racial and the sexual. This is also a historical moment, however, in which racism, sexism, and homophobia—as well as their multiple convergences—are tangibly evident from day to day" (p. 3). As in LGBT-specific Asian American movements, queer-identified Asian American communities were conscious of the intersectional labor they performed across the heterosexist nonwhite and dominant white communities and white LGBT communities in which they were marginalized. This intersectional experience informed the coalitional politics of "queer," which continued to bring together LGBT sexual orientations and gender expressions and to strive for ethnically, nationally, and regionally diverse participation in Asian American cultural and political movements. Yet "queer" also *intervened* in LGBT Asian American politics to push beyond neatly categorized identities based on "same-sex" sexual orientation and binary gender expression to include the messiness and expansiveness of sexuality, desire, and gender in living practice. For example, "queer" would include self-identified lesbians and gays who also have sex with the "opposite-sex," sexual practices and relationships that include kink, s/m, polyamory, and pansexuality, gender play and fuck including femmes and those feminine of center, butches and those masculine of center, queens, femboys, gurls, bois, sissies, tomboys, cross-dressers, drag queens and kings, and gender-fluid people.

Even as "queer" continued and reworked LGBT Asian American sexual and gender politics, "queer" also questioned and opposed the stable meaning and membership assigned to racial communities to create openings for previously marginalized and unrecognized practices, meanings, and identities. As Eng and Hom further state, "queer Asian America demands more than a deviant swerving from the narrow confines of normativity and normative heterosexuality; it requires subjecting the notion of Asian American identity itself to vigorous interrogation" (1998, p. 9). Queered Asian Americans actively rejected the presumably heterosexual and also racially homogenous and unified subject of Asian American identity. Queer Asian American identification and critical opposition emerged in the mid- to late 1990s during a period of backlash against people of color and gender and sexually non-conforming people, including divestment from affirmative action, heightened policing of immigration, English-only initiatives, antigay legislative initiates, increased anti-LGBT hate violence, and debates on abortion, gay marriage, queer parenting, homosexuals in the military, universal healthcare, and multicultural curricula (Eng and Hom 1998). This period simultaneously saw the commercialization of people of color and LGBT identities through corporate, state, and public institutions under the banners of multiculturalism and neoliberalization. This marketing of marginalized identities covered over the effects of an increasing wealth gap between rich and poor that further impoverished and disenfranchised low-income communities, especially trans and queer people of color and immigrants. "Queering" at this moment in time meant the refusal to entrench and intensify the racist, heterosexist, economically exploitative status quo. But also, in the words of Karin Aguilar-San Juan, "queer Asian America' is much more than a simple designation of a population group; . . . the phrase . . . refer[s] to the process of building a sense of collectivity, which, in its most utopian moment, strives toward community" (1998, p. 26).

Asian American queers created a new set of strategies for building coalitional communities, mobilizing politically, and producing oppositional and life-giving cultures. The mid- to late 1990s witnessed the burgeoning of queer Asian American cultural production, especially through visual media. Prior to this moment in the early 1990s, a "queer" approach to culture was being crafted by post-riot grrrl zine rebels like Mimi Nguyen, Felix Endara, Sabrina Margarita Alcantara-Tan, and Sel Hwang, even before the mass adoption of queer Asian American identity. Their do-it-yourself riffs, rants, and theories on popular culture, politics, and everyday life were etched, cut-and-pasted, and imaged in self-aware styles that pushed back against the racial and sexed politics of being-looked-at, consumed, and objectified. Their styles were also driven by the desire to speak with and create communities who could identify with them. Mimi Nguyen in her introduction to *Evolution of a Race Riot* (1997) says, "The race riot has lagged years behind the grrrl one for reasons that should be obvious by now: whiteboy mentality became a legitimate target but whitegirls' racial privilege and discourse went unmarked . . . except among those of us who were never white. Like me. Punk rocked high on the Richter scale when Kathleen Hanna screamed, 'JUST DIE!' but can a race riot get—? Zines are full of empty liberal platitudes like 'racism is a lack of love,' 'we're one race—the human race,' 'I'm colorblind' and we are supposed to be satisfied with these and maybe the occasional confession of personal racism ('I was beat once by black girls' or 'I'm afraid of people of color' or 'I called a girl a chink once')" (p. 4). Zines like Nguyen's *Evolution* queerly described the ways in which the de-linking of "race riot" from gender riot-perpetuated racism within riot grrrl culture. Their cross-media visual practices addressed readers and viewers as co-conspirators and co-creators, rather than passive audiences.

These early queer practices, before the mass adoption of the term "queer," laid some of the groundwork for the mid- to late 1990s, outpouring of queer Asian American performance, film, and video. Performance artists including Joel Tan, Denise Uyehara, Tina Takemoto, Justin Chin, Hanh Thi Pham, Erin O'Brien, and Gigi Otálvaro-Hormillosa confronted racialized sexual exotification by staging colonial racial fantasies explicitly. While the 1990s has been described as the renaissance of queer cinema including filmmakers such as Jennie Livingston, Todd Haynes, and Gus Van Sant (Yutani 1996), depictions of this moment fail to address the dominance of white Euro-American filmmakers in the analog film medium as it persists in countercultural queer filmmaking. Thus, Gregg Araki and Cheryl Dunye remain the only two filmmakers of color marginally credited with participating in the Queer New Wave. The presumed universality of white LGBT experience, over-valuation of feature length, narrative style film, and the economic and technical inaccessibility of 35 mm and 16 mm film production has pre-empted serious treatment and inclusion of film and video produced by queer Asian Americans. Prior to the awakening of queer cinema, Canadian forerunners Midi Onodera and Richard Fung used experimental non-narrative short films and video to document and re-image aspects of queer experience, racial dislocation, and migratory transience (Han and Morohoshi 1998). Fung's influential essay "Looking for My Penis: The Eroticized Asian in Gay Video Porn" discusses the racist, Orientalist ideologies that constrain popular representations of Asian male eroticism and sexuality—and also spectators' identification with these representations. Fung analyzes the sexually passive roles attributed to Asian men in gay porn and their impact on erotic pleasure, self-perception, and relationships for Asian American gay men. Throughout the 1980s, Cheang Shu Lea produced guerrilla documentaries on queer life for independent television channels Paper Tiger TV and Deep Dish TV in New York City. Building on the little acknowledged, persisting work of these artists in the 1990s, Erica "Clover" Cho, Hoang Nguyen, Yvette Choi, Ming-Yuen S. Ma, Felix Endara, Barbara Malaran, and other visual artists continue to use the new accessibility of digital video to produce a new repertoire of queer images.

Trans-ing Asian America

Although trans people participated in LGBT and queer Asian American movements, trans Asian Americans did not become more visible and mobilized self-identified communities until the 2000s.[1] By the second decade of the twenty-first century, gay and lesbian movements have made gains in de-pathologizing and de-criminalizing homosexuality. As of 1973, the American Psychiatric Association no longer considers homosexuality a diagnosable mental disorder. Currently, anti-sodomy laws targeting LGBT people have been repealed or struck down in all but twelve states after *Lawrence v. Texas* (2003). The U.S. Supreme Court legalized same-sex marriage nationwide in June 2015. Additionally, thirty-five states have laws that address hate or bias crimes based on sexual orientation. Yet, the single-issue agendas of white, wealthy, and professionalized leaders and organizations in the gay and lesbian movement have driven and financed these narrowly focused legal and medical gains. In the effort to mainstream their single-issue agendas, more race- and class-privileged segments of gay and lesbian movements have disconnected the struggle for gay rights from the struggles for self-determined gender identity and expression and economic and racial justice. For instance, the Human Rights Commission supported a version of the Employment Non-Discrimination Act that excluded protections for trans people.[2] Mainstream gay and lesbian advocacy and activism around decriminalization has also tended to emphasize the private rights of sexual minorities. This privatized approach has dis-aligned mainstream gay and lesbian rights from LGBT people of color, immigrants, people with disabilities, survival and low-income people, and youth who often experience state mechanisms as violent rather than protective. The mainstream gay and lesbian emphasis on anti-gay and lesbian hate crime laws as its primary strategy for addressing cis-heterosexist violence similarly does not take into account the targeting of people of color, especially Black Americans, immigrants, youth, and disabled and poor peoples by the police and criminal justice system. Also, while same-sex marriage rights provide symbolic and material gains for gays, lesbians, and bisexuals, access to these gains is restricted by requiring that people adopt a conventional social contract rooted in heterosexist nationalism. Gays, lesbians, and bisexuals who are not married and trans people who do not identify with the binary gender/sex system presumed by same- and opposite-sex marriage are excluded from these gains. By over-investing in mainstream rights, race- and class-privileged segments of gay and lesbian movements have de-prioritized and further marginalized the struggles of trans people, people of color, immigrants, survival and low-income people, people with disabilities, and youth.

Trans Asian American communities have become visible at the turn of the twenty-first century during a moment of disconnect from mainstreaming gay and lesbian movements. Although transgender communities and social identities surfaced earlier in the 1990s, the organizations and cultures that were most legible in representing transgender experiences were dominated by white Euro-American leaders with social class mobility (Tran et al. 1998; Stryker 2006). The broader political coalition imagined in Leslie Feinberg's redefining of transgender in the 1990s narrowed to focus on narratives of transition (male-to-female and female-to-male) that privileged the binary gender/sex system.[3] Transition narratives were encouraged and enforced by psycho-medical and legal institutions that intensified gender policing, just as gay and lesbian sexual identities were being de-pathologized.[4] White dominance of emergent transgender movements and the privileging and enforcement of binary transition as the primary mode of transgender expression and identity in the 1990s muted the struggles of trans Asian Americans and other trans people of color. This first "wave" of transgender visibility could not deal with the complexities of intersectional trans racial experiences that included negotiating not only cis-heterosexism and transphobia, but also racism, the Western binary gender/sex/sexual system, vulnerable immigration and refugee statuses, diasporic histories, poverty, and limited access to employment, stable housing, health care, and legal assistance. Trans Asian American mavericks such as Tamara Ching, Pauline Park, Christopher Lee, Richard Juang, Chino Scott-Chung, and Willy Wilkinson preceded and helped to build emergent transgender movements and lesbian, gay, bisexual movements with little recognition. Referring to the transwomen who rose up in the 1966 Compton's Cafeteria Riot in San Francisco, founding activist Ching says, "the gay movement started in the Tenderloin basically in the 60s when we decided to fight back. This was even pre-Stonewall . . ." (Silverman and Stryker 2005). Independent filmmaker and cultural activist Christopher Lee produced the first feature porn film cast by transmen and also co-created the first transgender film festival in the U.S. Activist Pauline Park co-founded Queens Pride House, Iban/Queer Koreans of New York, and New York Association for Gender Rights Advocacy and has been at the forefront of pushing the dominant transgender movement beyond its narrow focus on medical and legal recognition. Trans Asian Americans have also had to navigate transphobia and cis-heterosexism within Asian American communities, including gay, lesbian, and bisexual Asian American communities. By the 1990s, gender identity and expression, class, immigration and refugee status, and region became stronger dividing lines within Asian American communities as the U.S. state and capitalist economy continued to wear away at the already minimized civil rights gained in the 1960s and to fragment communities of color between exceptional (or model) and "failed" members.

Trans Asian Americans have become visibly mobilized during the first decades of the 2000s. Trans political and cultural activists including Ryka Aoki, Andy Marra, Wu Tsang, Yozmit, D'Lo, Kay Ulanday Barrett, Kit Yan, Kris Hayashi, Mashuq Mushtaq Deen, Ren-yo Hwang, Janani Balasubramanian, Alok Vaid-Menon, Leeroy Kun Young Kang, and Zavé Martohardjono, along with Tamara Ching, Pauline Park, Richard Juang, Chino Scott-Chung, and Willy Wilkinson, and many more continue to build social movements and living cultures that connect and energize struggles against U.S. transnational racism and white supremacy, economic exploitation, imperialism, ableism, and the cis-heterosexist binary gender/sex/sexual system. The queer and LGBT Asian American movements, cultures, and communities of which they are a part—and from which they part—continue to recreate themselves in response to twenty-first century social contexts.

Notes

1 I use the term *trans* broadly to include transgender, transsexual, genderqueer, bigender, third gender, mixed gender, gender fuck, gender fluid, genderless, MtF, FtM, Two Spirit, non-binary, androgynous, feminine/masculine of center, and other non-*cis*gender/*cis*sexual and gender variant and non-conforming identities and expressions. Nevertheless, I use the term *trans* purposefully as a prefix delinked

from gender to position *trans* as a potential intervention in the Western racially binary gender/sex/sexual system that continues to correlate gender with sex and sexuality and also to establish Western medical, political, and economic conceptions of gender, sex, and sexuality (and their relationships to one another) as the universal basis for valuing embodied experience. My use of *trans* as an intervening prefix is in conversation with Eva Hayward's and Mel Chen's work. See also the term "trans★" as a way to include more diverse gender expressions and identities as the term "transgender" becomes more codified.

2 In 2007, the Human Rights Commission refused to oppose a non-transgender inclusive version of the Employment Non-Discrimination Act.
3 As described by Susan Stryker, Feinberg's use of "transgender" called for a "political alliance between all individuals who were marginalized or oppressed due to their difference from social norms of gendered embodiment."
4 See the work of Sandy Stone on medicalized narratives of transsexuality and Eve Kosofsky Sedgwick on the shift from homosexual to gender expression and identity regulation in psycho-medical institutions in the 1980s.

References

Aguilar-San Juan, Karin. 1998. "Going Home: Enacting Justice in Queer Asian America." In *Q & A: Queer in Asian America*, edited by David L. Eng and Alice Y. Hom, 25–40. Philadelphia, PA: Temple University Press.

Aguilar-San Juan, Karin. 2009. *Little Saigons: Staying Vietnamese in America*. Minneapolis, MN: University of Minnesota Press.

Chung, Cristy, Aly Kim, Zoon Nguyen, Trinity Ordona, and Arlene Stein. 1996. "In Our Own Way: A Roundtable Discussion." In *Asian American Sexualities: Dimensions of the Gay & Lesbian Experience*, edited by Russell Leong, 91–99. New York: Routledge.

Dang, Thuy Vo, Linda Trinh Vo, and Tram Le. 2015. *Vietnamese in Orange County*. Charleston, SC: Arcadia Publishing.

Eng, David L. 2001. *Racial Castration: Managing Masculinity in Asian America*. Durham, NC: Duke University Press.

Eng, David L. and Alice Y. Hom. 1998. "Q & A: Notes on a Queer Asian America." In *Q & A: Queer in Asian America*, edited by David L. Eng and Alice Y. Hom, 1–21. Philadelphia, PA: Temple University Press.

Han, Ju Hui "Judy" and Marie K. Morohoshi. 1998. "Creating, Curating, and Consuming Queer Asian American Cinema: An Interview with Marie K. Morohoshi." In *Q & A: Queer in Asian America*, edited by David L. Eng and Alice Y. Hom, 81–94. Philadelphia, PA: Temple University Press.

Jong, Lola Lai. 2008. "API Gays and Lesbians Create Safe Spaces." In *Out and Proud in Chicago: An Overview of the City's Gay Community*, edited by Tracy Baim, 190. Chicago, IL: Agate Publishing.

Kauanui, J. Kehaulani and Ju Hui "Judy" Han. 1994. " 'Asian Pacific Islander': Issues of Representation and Responsibility." In *The Very Inside: An Anthology of Writing by Asian and Pacific Islander Lesbian and Bisexual Women*, edited by Sharon Lim-Hing, 376–379. Toronto: Sister Vision Press.

Mangaoang, Gil. 1996. "From the 1970s to the 1990s: Perspective of a Gay Filipino American Activist." In *Asian American Sexualities: Dimensions of the Gay & Lesbian Experience*, edited by Russell Leong, 101–111. New York: Routledge.

Masequesmay, Gina. 2003. "Emergence of Queer Vietnamese America." *Amerasia Journal* 29:1: 117–134.

Ratti, Rakesh. 1993. "Introduction." In *A Lotus of Another Colour: An Unfolding of the South Asian Gay and Lesbian Experience*, edited by Rakesh Ratti, 10–17. Boston, MA: Alyson Publications.

Roy, Sandip. 1998. "The Call of Rice: (South) Asian American Queer Communities." In *A Part, Yet Apart: South Asians in Asian America*, edited by Lavina Dhingra Shankar and Rajini Srikanth, 168–185. Philadelphia, PA: Temple University Press.

Screaming Queens: The Riot at Compton's Cafeteria. Directed Victor Silverman and Susan Stryker. San Francisco, CA: Frameline, 2005.

Shah, Nayan. 1993. "Sexuality, Identity, and the Uses of History." In *A Lotus of Another Color: An Unfolding of the South Asian Gay and Lesbian Experience*, edited by Rakesh Ratti, 113–132. Boston, MA: Alyson Publications.

Shah, Nayan. 2011. *Stranger Intimacy: Contesting Race, Sexuality, and the Law in the North American West.* Durham, NC: Duke University Press.

Shah, Sonia. 1997. "Slaying the Dragon Lady: Towards an Asian American Feminism." In *Dragon Ladies: Asian American Feminists Breathe Fire*, edited by Sonia Shah, xii–xix. Boston, MA: South End Press.

Shimizu, Celine Parreñas. 2007. *The Hypersexuality of Race: Performing Asian/American Women on Screen and Scene.* Durham, NC: Duke University Press.

Stryker, Susan. 2006. "(De)Subjugated Knowledges: An Introduction to Transgender Studies." In *The Transgender Studies Reader*, edited by Susan Stryker and Stephen Whittle, 1–17. New York: Routledge.

Tsang, Daniel C. 2000. "Asians in North America." In *Encyclopedia of Lesbian and Gay Histories and Cultures*, edited by George Haggerty and Bonnie Zimmerman, 117–118. New York: Routledge.

Tsang, Daniel C. 2001. "Slicing Silence: Asian Progressives Come Out." In *Asian Americans: The Movement and the Moment*, edited by Steve Louie and Glenn Omatsu, 220–239. Los Angeles, CA: UCLA Asian American Studies Center Press.

Tsui, Kitty. 2006. "The Words of a Woman Who Breathes Fire." In *Chinese American Voices: From the Gold Rush to the Present*, edited by Judy Yung, Gordon H. Chang, H. Mark Lai, 340–344. Berkeley, CA: University of California Press.

Tran, Diep Khac, Bryan, and Rhode. 1998. "Transgender/Transsexual Roundtable." In *Q & A: Queer in Asian America*, edited by David L. Eng and Alice Y. Hom, 227–243. Philadelphia, PA: Temple University Press.

Yutani, Kimberly. 1996. "Gregg Araki and the Queer New Wave." In *Asian American Sexualities: Dimensions of the Gay & Lesbian Experience*, edited by Russell Leong, 175–180. New York: Routledge.

23

"OTHER"

Reconsidering Asian Exclusion and Immigrant Rights

Sujani K. Reddy

In 2002 a group of five prisoners at San Quentin State Prison in California submitted a list of proposals to improve their education. The men were part of an accredited college program that linked university-based volunteers with inmates who could, through its courses, earn an Associate of Arts degree. Việt Mike Ngo, one of the petitioning prisoner-students, states that:

> We requested that the decision-making process concerning classes taught and who teaches them be more inclusive; that a student body committee and one veteran volunteer be created to facilitate this process. We specifically asked for more Ethnic Studies classes due to demand from volunteer professors and prisoner students. We disagreed to plans of corporate sponsorship without first seeking or receiving input from the student body and objected to the local prison policy that prohibited correspondence between prisoners and volunteers, citing that it violated prison regulations as well as the First Amendment.[1]

Much of the manner and content of these demands will sound familiar to those students and scholars of Asian/Pacific/American (A/P/A) Studies who understand our practice through the ongoing struggles for Ethnic Studies, starting with the student-led protests of the 1960s and 1970s and continuing through to the battles being waged today over the fate of affordable, accessible public institutions of higher education. A key difference, however, is that Việt Mike Ngo and his five co-petitioners were on the "wrong" side of the school-to-prison pipeline. Their demands for their right to education in general, and Ethnic Studies in particular, came at a time when prisoners and students had been effectively rendered separate populations by the Violent Crime Control and Law Enforcement Act of 1994. This legislation banned the incarcerated from eligibility for federal Pell Grants and, subsequently, eviscerated college-in-prison programs, forming part of the larger trend towards an increasingly punitive prison–industrial complex. In this context the program at San Quentin was an exception to the general rule. Nevertheless, or perhaps in part even because of this, prison administrators responded to the San Quentin prisoners' petition by placing three of the five signees in solitary confinement pending investigation. This lasted for up to one year. During that period they were subject to arbitrary transfer, some up to five times. In addition, each was denied parole based in part on the investigation, even though none of them were found to have violated prison regulations per se.

Three of the student prisoners in question are Asian/Pacific/American. I first learned of their story in a collection called *Other: an Asian and Pacific Islander Prisoners' Anthology*.[2] The volume contains writings by Asian and Pacific Islander (API)[3] prisoners and was published with help from the Asian Prisoner Support Committee. It is an attempt by all involved to bring to light a population that has been systematically rendered invisible. First, API prisoners literally don't count. As Helen Zia notes in her preface to the volume, most local and federal statistics count prisoners as "white," "Black," "Hispanic," or "Other." API prisoners get lost in this last category—thus the title of the volume. Second, the "model minority" stereotype and its uptake by immigrants themselves overshadow API communities and individuals who do not fit into its image. Prisoners are a primary example, as Eddy Zheng, the lead editor of *Other*, asserts,

> Asian prisoners have become lepers of their own communities. We're left to survive by ourselves with minimum support from our families ... I have come to the conclusion that the lack of interest from the Asian American community is its need to stay in the glass house of blissful ignorance. It's easier to neglect the problem that causes shame to its model minority status than address it. The result is the multiplying of "Asian Leprosy" in this modern day slave plantation of the Prison Industrial Complex and the continued victimization of the Asian community.[4]

In the face of this multiple silencing, the contributors to *Other* speak out as members of the API prisoner population and help us to connect their stories and situation to the mass criminalization and incarceration of communities of color, and particularly youth of color, in the contemporary United States. The U.S. is the world's leading jailor, by an alarmingly wide margin.[5] The U.S. race to incarcerate has deep roots in a nation founded on indigenous genocide and chattel slavery. As scores of activists and analysts have argued, however, incarceration took on the mass dimensions of a system of racialized control during the second half of the twentieth century, after the legal end of Jim Crow segregation. While it is not my task here to identify all of the factors that paved the path for the rise of mass incarceration, I do want to identify one major thrust forward as the criminalization of youth-led organizations such as the Black Panther Party, the Young Lords Party, and the American Indian Movement, through operations such as the FBI's counter-intelligence program (COINTELPRO) and its relationship to President Richard Nixon's "war on crime."[6] The racialized criminalization of dissent paved a path for President Ronald Reagon's "war on drugs." The policies that proliferated in the wake of this provided the teeth for the massive expansion of policing within low-wealth communities of color, the growth of increasingly punitive and mandatory sentencing, and the massive growth of what has come to be known as the prison–industrial complex. The PIC is a phrase that captures the process whereby the U.S. state and U.S.-based corporations have expanded their reach and their interrelationship through the expansion of mass criminalization.[7] The resulting system has disproportionately targeted African Americans through what some scholars have identified as the management of the economically marginalized and dispossessed, what legal scholar Michelle Alexander has popularized as the "New Jim Crow," and what activist and organizers have rallied against through the demand that #BlackLivesMatter.[8]

The contributors to *Other* draw attention to the particular place that immigrants have in the growth of the carceral state. They help us to connect API communities to other communities of color, and to complicate the divide between "good" and "bad" Asian Americans, and "good" and "bad" people of color. In this essay I ask what it would mean to place a text like this, and the API prisoners who produced it, at the center of A/P/A studies. Implicit in this question is the assertion that to do so would be to return to the roots of the field in a way that is not primarily nostalgic so much as politically, intellectually, and pedagogically urgent.

The Birth of "Asian America"

Asian/Pacific/American Studies emerged out of a demand. It was a demand by Asian Americans for recognition as members of the United States, a nation that had continued to cast Asians as one of its consummate groups of "others." To remember this is to remember the way in which "Asian" as a particularly U.S.-American racialized identity was carved out of the comprehensive exclusion of Asian immigrants and their descendants. It is to remember that Chinese laborers were the first immigrants to be excluded from the United States on the basis of race, class, and nationality; and that the forces of the anti-Chinese movement did not stop with passage or even implementation of anti-Chinese legislation. It quickly turned its vitriol towards other immigrants arriving from, primarily, Japan, Korea (then a Japanese colony), India (then a British colony that included present-day India, Pakistan, and Bangladesh), and the Philippines (then a territorial colony of the United States). Violence and agitation against all of these groups led to more restriction and exclusion. In 1907–1908 the United States and Japan negotiated the Gentleman's Agreement, restricting the emigration/immigration of Japanese and Korean laborers. And in 1917, the U.S. Congress passed an Immigration Act that was also known as the Asiatic Barred Zone Act. It prohibited the entry of immigrants from a legislatively defined geographic area that included India, Burma, Siam, the Malay States, the East Indian Islands, Polynesia, and parts of Russia, Arabia, and Afghanistan. It also reinforced the prohibition already articulated within immigration law prohibiting the entry of contract laborers, a status that had long been associated in the U.S. political imagination with Chinese and Indian indentured workers across the Americas.[9] In addition, the 1917 Act also enumerates a whole host of other "undesirables" ranging from (but not limited to) "idiots," "imbeciles," "persons of constitutional psychopathic inferiority," epileptics, alcoholics, illiterates, prostitutes, polygamists, anarchists, and anyone convicted of or admitting to a felony or a crime of moral turpitude.[10] This clear conflation of "Asian" with moral, political, and psychological deviance was of a piece with longstanding racist and Orientalist images of Asians as utterly foreign and unable to assimilate within the United States. A particular configuration of race, nation, class, sex, politics, health, and criminalization thus formed the boundaries of who or what could properly belong.

After 1917, one group still able to enter the United States from Asia were Filipinos, but this was only as long as they remained U.S. colonial subjects. The Tydings–McDuffie Act of 1934 simultaneously set a ten-year path for Filipino independence, and placed Filipino migrants under the prohibitions of the Asiatic Barred Zone. Independence, in effect, equaled illegality. The irony was indicative of larger trends within exclusion, which was about much more than legal entry. It was a wholesale effort to bar all manner of belonging. Uneven attempts by Asians to naturalize as U.S. citizens ended with two back-to-back Supreme Court rulings in 1922 and 1923. Both Takao Ozawa and Bhagat Singh Thind provided evidence of their upstanding character and practices of assimilation, but ultimately their arguments rested on skin color in the case of Ozawa and classification as Aryan under the scientific theories of the day in the case of Thind. Both were ruled as unable to naturalize, thus ending the two primary avenues through which some Asians had been able to become U.S. citizens. These rulings dealt a blow to the forms of Japanese migration that had survived the Gentleman's Agreement when, in 1924, the Immigration Act barred entry to anyone ineligible to naturalize.

If the 1924 Immigration Act halted the growth of the Japanese and Japanese American communities that had been able to grow up within the shadows of restrictions, the onset of World War II made clear the contingency of their ability to partake in the nation. Japanese and Japanese American internment was in many ways the "logical" culmination of Asian exclusion. Internees lost all land, businesses, and most of their possessions almost overnight. This reinforced the history of Alien Land Laws that had followed exclusion in many states, disabling non-citizens from legal rights to property. And in many states exclusion also included the right to marry across race, as anti-miscegenation laws barred variously defined "Asiatics" from intermarriage with white women especially (although not exclusively) in the South and West.[11] Here, Japanese migrants had the advantage of a few decades that had allowed them access to family reunification provisions, so that male Japanese workers could sponsor Japanese women as wives.[12] The second generation, or *Nisei*, were automatically U.S. citizens due to birthright citizenship, but even this failed to prevent them from being interned with their "ineligible to naturalize" elders. They were cast as the "enemy within"—linked irrevocably via biological racism to the enemy without.

War against another group of Asians, in Vietnam, Laos, and Cambodia, was also the setting for the rise of "Asian America" amidst the social movements that rocked college campuses and urban centers across the "post-civil rights" United States. Yellow power was part of the constellation of movements that were targeted and decimated by COINTELPRO and the mass media campaign against dissent. It arose most prominently amongst primarily first-generation college students who participated in the Third World Student strikes of 1968 at San Francisco State University, and later the University of California, Berkeley. Asian American, African American, Chicano/a, and Native American students stood up to demand representation of our communities and histories in the curriculum and on campus, and they linked this demand to the political, economic, and social liberation of Third World peoples in the United States and around the decolonizing world. Theirs was a global vision that encompassed opposition to the imperialist war in Southeast Asia, and that for Asian Americans also addressed the long history of exclusion that was their particular inheritance.

The Asian American movement stood at a kind of crossroads in immigration from Asia to the United States. Still connected to the communities that grew up under the shadows of exclusion, Asian American activists maintained an analysis that was connected to struggles against racialized oppression in the U.S. and Asia (particularly the war in Southeast Asia). Their perspective quickly got swamped as Asians who were disconnected from this pre-World War II history became one of the largest groups of immigrants into the United States following passage of the 1965 Immigration and Nationality Act amendments (Hart–Cellar). Hart–Cellar announced the shift in U.S. immigration law from a system anchored around race-based exclusion and nation-based restriction to one that centered on family reunification. It also included a series of occupational preference quotas that favored the entry of "highly skilled" immigrants, particularly in the expanding fields of science (due to the Cold War expansion of the defense industries) and health (due to the passage of Medicare and Medicaid as well as the expansion of healthcare for veterans).

As many subsequent scholars have pointed out, this combination created the conditions for the selection of a set of Asian immigrants who skipped ghettoized urban communities and headed straight to the suburbs. The relative economic success of Asian immigrants became proof positive that the "American Dream" had been re-racialized. Structural racism was no longer understood as an oppressive force. Now, all that anyone needed were the right values: political conformity, a heteropatriarchal family, and upward mobility through hard work and education. In this way the stereotype of an Asian American "model minority" stood against the stereotype of African American and/or Puerto Rican "culture of poverty" to provide cultural explanations for the continuity of poverty. Together they posed Jim Crow segregation as a thing of the past, even as they enabled many to look away as mass criminalization came to reincarnate institutionalized forms of exclusion from the nation and, indeed, the realm of justice and freedom.

Exclusion, Refined

This returns us to Eddy Zheng, and the ways in which his own story reveals both the limits of middle-class model minority-hood as an accurate depiction of post-1965 Asian immigration, and also the continued legacies of immigrant exclusion in relation to mass criminalization and incarceration. In 1982, at the age of twelve, Xiao Fei "Eddy" Zheng immigrated with his family to Oakland, California from Guangzhou, China. The Zhengs arrived with green cards, but little to no cultural or economic capital. With no English language skills, they began building their lives in Chinatown. Eddy's parents found jobs in the low-wage service sector, at Burger King and as a nanny. Eddy and his siblings were essentially latchkey kids, and Eddy got involved in a world of underage crime. At age sixteen, he was caught committing armed robbery, tried as an adult, convicted of multiple felony counts, and sentenced to seven years to life. During the nineteen years he ended up spending in prison, Zheng gained fluency in English, passed his high school Graduate Equivalency Diploma (GED), and went on to earn an Associate's Degree in the aforementioned San Quentin program. He also worked with at-risk youth in crime prevention workshops and fought for Ethnic Studies, for which he spent a year in solitary.

In March of 2005, at the age of thirty-five, Zheng was finally granted parole. Upon his release, the newly created Department of Homeland Security immediately transferred him to an immigrant detention facility where he was to await his deportation from the United States. This was because under U.S. immigration law any non-citizen convicted of an "aggravated felony" is subject to mandatory detention and deportation, and barred from ever reentering the United States. This law targets *legal* permanent residents, since undocumented Hart–Cellar[13] immigrants are deportable on the basis of their lack of status alone. Thus for Eddy, time served was not enough recompense. As a convicted felon and a non-citizen, his second round of incarceration had just begun.

While Zheng's re-incarceration may sound like double punishment to some, it is not, under the law, technically considered punishment at all. Instead the non-citizen stands in violation of immigration law, and their detention and deportation take place outside of the criminal justice system, in the realm of administrative law where they do not have the right to appointed counsel or trial by jury and where there is extremely limited judicial discretion. There are in fact almost no mitigating circumstances to a deportation order. It thus did not matter that Zheng had completed the sentence that was meant to serve as punishment for his crime, that he had been a "model" inmate while doing so, or that his entire family are resident citizens of the United States. For eleven years it also did not necessarily matter that community groups mobilized around his case and gathered the support of two U.S. senators, one U.S. congressperson, ten California state senators, and everyone from the district attorney who had originally prosecuted him to the 9th Circuit Court of Appeals that ruled against his deportation order in 2011, and Governor Jerry Brown of California, who finally formally pardoned Zheng in 2015. Since this was not a matter of criminal justice, the 2011 ruling simply sends Zheng's case back to the Board of Immigration Appeals for reconsideration. When it came up there (again) in 2016, immigration authorities finally withdrew his deportation order. This was not at all a necessary outcome, but an exception.[14] As a non-citizen, Zheng's case may have been accorded certain due process rights: to be heard, to examine evidence, and to receive a written decision. These rights, however, are not actually required or protected by statute and could be revoked without rebuke. This is because deportation law is not, in fact, governed by the U.S. constitution. It operates under Congress' authority to exercise sovereign, constitutionally unrestrained "plenary power." In other words, deportation is where the assertion of state sovereignty supersedes the rule of law. The degree to which deportation is governed by due process is the result of sub-constitutional rulings that are always subject to revocation by Congressional plenary power.

As Daniel Kanstroom so usefully details in *Deportation Nation: Outsiders in American History*,[15] deportation law has its origins in four interrelated legal arenas: the Alien and Sedition Laws, Indian removal, Fugitive slave laws, and Chinese exclusion. These origins provide us with a clear conceptual map for tracing the co-articulation of race, rights, national belonging, and state sovereignty. They also return us to Chinese exclusion for the way in which it raised immediate technical questions around its enforcement, and led to the development of much of what remains as the institutional and legal architecture for detention and deportation. In 1888, Congress passed the Scott Act, prohibiting Chinese laborers from re-entering the U.S. even if they had valid papers. Questions over the constitutionality of this Act reached the Supreme Court through the case of *Chae Chan Ping v. the United States*, also known as *the Chinese Exclusion Case*.[16] Ping had lived in the U.S. for twelve years when he returned to China for a visit. Aware of exclusion, although he had with him the requisite residence papers for re-entry, these were no longer sufficient. Ping contested his exclusion and in 1889 the Court ruled against him, reasoning that Congress had the right to exclude him because the power of exclusion was an incident of sovereignty. The doctrinal substratum of this ruling, the assertion of plenary power, was extended in the Court's 1893 ruling in *Fong Yue Ting v. United States*.[17]

The case arose in response to application of the 1892 Geary Act, which extended Chinese exclusion and required that all Chinese laborers in the U.S. register with the federal government and carry that proof of registration with them at all times. If caught without documentation they had to prove that failure to obtain it was "reasonable," and their legal residency had to be confirmed by at least one credible white witness. When Fong Yue Ting contested his expulsion on the basis of the Geary Act, the Supreme Court responded by ruling that Congress has absolute, unrestrained power to remove non-citizens (regardless of legal status) and that a deportation order is not a punishment for a crime. Thus, while the Geary Act was ostensibly aimed at convicted Chinese felons, this ruling effectively rendered tens of thousands of Chinese workers due for deportation. Here then lie the legal underpinnings of the extra-constitutionality of deportation law, which have yet to be overturned. Rather, its reach has steadily extended such that by the twenty-first century, noncitizens have become one of the fastest-growing segments of the particularly U.S.-American race to incarcerate.[18]

In many ways, the massive growth of immigrant detention and deportation at the end of the twentieth century took its cue from this system, even as it is, as we have seen, technically *not* considered a matter of criminal justice. Immigrant detainees are housed in both state and private jails and prisons, thus filling critical space and justifying expansion. Also, in 1996, Congress passed the Illegal Immigration Reform and Immigrant Responsibility Act (IIRIRA), which in many ways picked up on the form of mandatory sentencing associated with the "war on drugs." IIRIRA employed a "three strikes" formula to expand the list of what could count towards an "aggravated felony." "Three strikes" legislation has been a lynchpin for mandatory felonization which in turn has fueled prison growth. After IIRIRA, criminal convictions for shoplifting, possession of minor amounts of controlled substances, or driving while intoxicated can now, in effect, add up to an "aggravated felony" and be grounds for deportation, even after time has been served or a fine has been paid, even retroactively. Many analysts and activists thus date the steady and increasing growth of immigration detention and deportation to the 1996 laws, and cite these laws as laying the groundwork for the expansion that followed the attack on the World Trade Center in 2001.[19]

Even after September 11, 2001, and the rise of the increasingly criminalized U.S. racial category of "South Asian, Arab, and Muslim," the majority of U.S. deportees are Latino, not Asian. This has much to do with a long history of racializing Chicanas and Mexicans as the face of "illegality," and the ways in which this quickly came to include other Latin American and Caribbean immigrants in what Juan Gonzalez so usefully summarizes as a "harvest of empire."[20] In the face of this, I want to return to the campaign to stop the deportation of Eddy Zheng. Confronted with nearly binding administrative limits, activists emphasize the list of his aforementioned accomplishments while incarcerated, and the fact that he continues to do this work to this day. The campaign argues for Zheng on the basis of his status as a "model inmate." On the one hand, this discourse harkens us back to earlier, and at this point alternate, ideologies around incarceration where prison was meant to be a space for the "reform" of prisoners. In this model prison sentences were, at their best, spaces for rehabilitation and, subsequently, re-entry. It was, in fact, under this line of reasoning that education was brought into prisons in the first place. Zheng's sentencing as an adult while still legally a child, however, reminds us of how remote such a concept is from our current criminal justice system, structured as it is around punishment as an end in itself.[21] And yet, because Zheng is Asian American, his use of the discourse of "model inmate" also, ironically, resonates with the very image that cast him and his fellow inmates as "lepers." In a strange twist, the very image that renders them invisible may also be a source for their access to visibility and a small modicum of justice. This possibility, fraught as it is, has been a consistent and persistent theme in the politics of immigrant rights right up into the twenty-first century.

Keep on DREAMing?

On August 1, 2001, United States Senators Richard Durbin (Democrat, Illinois) and Orrin Hatch (Republican, Utah) introduced the Development, Relief, and Education for Alien Minors Act, better known by its acronym, the DREAM Act. The Act was a bipartisan effort to deliver on President George W. Bush's promise of immigration reform. It proposed conditional permanent residency to certain undocumented residents of "good moral character" who graduated from U.S. high schools after having arrived in the United States as minors and lived in the country continuously for at least five years prior to the bill's enactment *if* they either complete two years of military service, or two years at a four-year institution of higher learning. Individuals meeting these requirements could obtain *temporary* legal residency for a six-year period. During this time those who choose to attend school rather than serve in the military would *not* be eligible for federal grants such as the Pell grants that are generally considered the foundation for financial aid packages, but they could apply for student loans and work study. Lastly, the original bill repeated Section 505 of IIRIRA, which had already been interpreted by individual states to mean that undocumented immigrants were not eligible for in-state tuition.[22]

I list the details of the original DREAM Act because it has come to represent perhaps the most widely cherished possibility for inclusion at the onset of a century that has otherwise been marked, thus far, by ramped-up exercises in exclusion. The push to pass even its limited promises was quickly overshadowed by the all-encompassing push for increased security following the attacks on the World Trade Center and Pentagon a month later. Post-September 11 panic paved the pathway for what many impacted communities and their allies recognize as "the war on terror at home." Lack of due process, transparency or accountability characterized the stepped-up creation of legions of the disappeared and dispossessed. To many, the moves seemed utterly unprecedented, warranted only by the urgency of the moment, and less, anyway, than examples such as the World War II internment of Japanese and Japanese Americans. However, as we have seen, what was new was less the mechanisms themselves, and more the scale and general attention/approbation; and what was needed were not separate relocation camps, just more beds in the already existing prison industrial complex.

In a way, the DREAM Act was a kind of singular survivor of this onslaught, having been reformed and reintroduced for consideration in Congress consistently since up until 2011, when it was appended to the National Defense Authorization Act. This last version included several changes that are, again, worth listing in full. First, it does not grant resident status to anyone for two years (the original version granted that status immediately). Instead, what beneficiaries would be granted immediately is the status of "conditional nonimmigrant" and that too only if you have demonstrated "good moral character" as defined by the DHS, submitted biometric data, undergone both security and law enforcement background checks, submitted to a medical examination, registered for the Selective Services which puts you in a database for a potential military draft, and apply for consideration within one year of high school graduation, your GED or the bill's enactment. This version of the DREAM also explicitly excludes anyone who is convicted on three misdemeanors, is "liable to become a public charge," has engaged in voter fraud or unlawful voting, has engaged in marriage fraud, has abused a student visa, has engaged in persecution, or poses a public health risk.[23] If you meet all of these requirements, you would be granted legal resident status *after* two years, *if* you meet the college/military service requirements contained in the original version (with the addition that this one explicitly does not repeal the ban on in-state tuition), pay all of your back taxes, demonstrate an ability to read, write, and speak the English language and a working knowledge of the fundamentals of U.S. history and the forms of U.S. government.[24]

The 2011 version also makes explicit what you *cannot* do with your temporary and conditional legal status in the U.S. You can never use family reunification laws to sponsor extended family members, you cannot begin sponsoring your parents or siblings for at least twelve years, and if you have undocumented parents or siblings they would have to have left the United States for ten years before you could sponsor them through family reunification and then they would be added to the already decades-long backlog in those categories. It also makes clear that non-citizens are excluded from the Affordable Care Act and ineligible for Medicaid, food stamps, and other government welfare programs. Finally, the DREAM would require that you qualify for a stay of deportation while your application is pending and makes clear that the DREAM Act is *not* a safe harbor from deportation. There is in fact a chance that applying for it could put you into deportation proceedings, a chance buttressed by the fact that DHS is required to provide information from DREAM Act applicants to any federal, state, tribal, or local law enforcement agency or intelligence or national security agency in any criminal investigation or prosecution for homeland/national security purposes. Furthermore, the burden of proof is on the applicant, who needs to produce a preponderance of evidence.

This was the version that passed the House in 2010 and, much to the disappointment of many immigrants and their supporters, failed to pass the Senate.[25] Part of the DREAM's relatively broad appeal is its play on the innocence of youth who are in this country without legal status but also without willful culpability—i.e. they were brought here when they were too young to make a decision to migrate. Youthful innocence, however, is hardly a given here. Instead the DREAM Act goes to great, painstaking lengths to distinguish between qualified and unqualified candidates, deserving and undeserving youth, good and bad immigrants. It especially hardens the line between those who go to school and those who go to prison, with the addition of those who go the military, often because of lack of funds for education otherwise. What is more, for those who do qualify as "good," the DREAM Act sets up an almost impossible set of loopholes to fulfill, with an increasingly limited and partial set of benefits at the end of the road. Such a DREAM exemplifies what Subhash Kateel and Aarti Shahani have outlined as "delegalization."

Kateel and Shahani define delegalization in relation to Immigrant Apartheid: "a set of institutional and political processes leading to the creation of separate social, political, and economic spaces for citizens and noncitizens, derived from distinctions based on formal status."[26] Their definition is drawn from their praxis as the co-founders and first co-directors of Families for Freedom, a multiethnic defense network by and for immigrants facing deportation in New York City—led by and for those systemically deemed the "bad" immigrants left on the cutting table of most immigration deals, as in the DREAM Act. Delegalization expands upon the roots of exclusion I have highlighted here to include the range of ongoing practices that increasingly diminish the returns for "paths to legalization," which never grant immediate full citizenship. And yet, even if they did, we would have to consider the diminishment of the rights of citizenship in the face of mass felonization. This combination calls into question the limits of a rights-based politics, or a politics of inclusion, in the "post-civil rights" United States. This limit is one reason why so many of the undocumented youth leaders who sprung up around the DREAM Act have since left such legislation behind in their quest for justice. Some have even gone underground into immigrant detention centers to draw attention to the devastating effects of criminalization on their communities and families, and to refuse a bargain to become the "good immigrants" that so many power brokers within the movement might bargain for them to be.[27] This returns me to the central, and I would argue ultimately productive, tension that lies at the heart of A/P/A studies: the struggle between making claims for justice vis-à-vis inclusion in the very same institutions that have been the source of justice denied. It has also come time to ask: what are the alternatives?

In Lak'ech

Few places in the United State symbolize the extremes of Immigrant Apartheid like Arizona does. The state became something like the Mississippi of "Juan Crow" after passing SB 1070, otherwise known as the "show me your papers" bill, in 2010. Among the bill's more controversial provisions, it allows state law enforcement to stop anyone they suspect of being undocumented and check for their papers. Immigrant and civil rights groups immediately pounced upon it for sanctioning racial profiling and terrorizing anyone racialized as an immigrant. An article published by National Public Radio revealed that the bill had been drafted by the American Legislative Exchange Council, whose members include the Corrections Corporation of America (CCA).[28] The CCA is one of the country's largest private prison corporations, and it stands to profit enormously from SB 1070 as a "round-up" tool.

Challenges to this law, which has since been copied by several other states, have made their way to the Supreme Court. In 2012, the Court ruled against portions of the law but held up its central provisions. The verdict is not actually surprising, in spite of the fact that the argument against SB 1070 rested in large part on the constitutionality of state administration of immigration laws that are federal. Looking backwards, SB 1070 reminds us of the Geary Act; and today, SB 1070 reinforces provisions already in place at the federal level through Section 287g of the Immigration and Nationality Act. This coincidence is again evidence for the limits of seeking justice through recourse to the source of exclusion, the arbiter of apartheid.

At this point, we need to take a step outside the proverbial box. I want to contrast the limits of a court case with the possibilities presented by the May 21, 2010 occupation of the Border

Patrol headquarters in Tucson by Indigenous activists. The action was part of the larger struggle of the Tohono O'odham, who have been organizing against construction of the U.S.–Mexico border wall as it cuts across a region that for them is not defined by national boundaries but instead is marked by ceremonial sites on both sides of the militarized fence. As highlighted in Harsha Walia's *Undoing Border Imperialism*, the Tohono O'odham opposed SB 1070 as part of their struggle against border militarization as it impacted immigrants *and* indigenous peoples. Their demand was for the respect of indigenous peoples' inherent right of migration, a right that they extend to all who move across that territory.[29]

The right to migrate understood as part of struggles for indigenous sovereignty is a vision not bound to the limits of the imperial nation, but one that explicitly seeks to undo them as the grounds for the liberation of movement. It is but one moment in others that are growing through organizations like the one Walia has been involved in, No One Is Illegal (NOII). NOII is a loose affiliation of autonomous groups working across Canada, and now also in the United States, who explicitly work to link struggles for migrant justice and indigenous sovereignty. Such a framework addresses itself to the core issues brought about when we turn attention to the "P" in A/P/A studies. Here, the conflict between indigenous sovereignty and redress of Asian exclusion is made markedly clear in the work of scholars such as Dean Saranillio.[30] This analytic and movement-based work leads us towards a paradigm that undoes the binaries of good/bad, included/excluded and towards a model of both/and, a model rooted in what are, literally, outlawed ways of knowing.

Less well known than SB 1070 is another Arizona bill signed into law by then Governor Jan Brewer, HB 2281. This bill prohibits funding to any public school whose programs promote the overthrow of the U.S. government.; promote resentment towards any race or class of people; are designed primarily for pupils of a particular ethnic group; advocate ethnic solidarity instead of the treatment of pupils as individuals. Immediately after the bill became law, it forced the closure of the Mexican American Studies (MAS) program in the Tucson Unified School District (TUSD). The program had grown up to address the needs of the district's large Chicana student population, who were under-performing according to its standards. By focusing on rooting knowledge in local history, culture and practices that related to the communities where students lived, it was an exemplar of Ethnic Studies. It was also, by most standards, wildly successful. Over the fourteen years of its existence, students who enrolled in the classes graduated at higher rates than those who did not; it closed and in many cases surpassed the achievement gap between Mexican American and white youth, and matriculated to college at higher levels than their peers who did not take the classes. In spite of this, lawmakers deemed the program, open to any student in the school district, un-American.

MAS in the TUSD is rooted in a history of Ethnic Studies that exceeds the limits of a vision tied to institutions of higher education. Indeed it is wise to recognize that the Third World Student Strikers were but one part of a much longer history rooted in the struggle of Africans to preserve and transform their cultural practices across the Americas, for them to secretly learn to read and write against the will of those who enslaved them—in the struggle of Native Americans and Chicanas to preserve their languages, cultures and ways of living as the borders of white settler colonialism passed through them on the way to establishing the United States— and in the struggles of Asians to claim a place in a nation where we have been cast as the perpetually "foreign." Recognition of these legacies returns us to the demand, raised by Zheng, Ngo, and their fellow classmates at San Quentin, for more Ethnic Studies classes. Their punishment for this "crime" reminds us that it is not only certain people but also certain ways of knowing that suffer systemic delegalization. It calls our attention to the complicity between the institutionalization of certain forms of Ethnic Studies and the outcasting of certain "others."

It is against this that I invoke the Mayan code of the living heart, as recited by the teachers and students at the opening of their now illegalized classes. I quote it here as they recited it, in Spanish and English, with recognition that Mayan is the foundation for both of these as they all exist in the living histories of the borderlands between inside and out, between "us" and "other", between immigrant rights and migrant justice:

> In Lak'ech
> Tú eres mi otro yo
> You are my other me.
> Si te hago daño a ti
> If I do harm to you,
> Me hago daño a mí mismo
> I do harm to myself;
> Sí te amo y respeto
> If I love and respect you,
> Me amo y respeto yo
> I love and respect myself.[31]

Notes

1. Viêt Mike Ngo, "Lesson Learned in Prison College" in *Other: an Asian & Pacific Islander Prisoners' Anthology*, Ed. Eddy Zheng et al., Hayword, CA: Asian Prisoner Support Committee, 2007, 74. For more on and from Viêt Mike Ngo see Dylan Rodriguez, *Forced Passages: Imprisoned Radical Intellectuals and the U.S. Prison Regime*. Minneapolis, MN: University of Minnesota Press, 2006.
2. Eddy Zheng and Asian Prisoner Support Committee, Ed. *Other: an Asian & Pacific Islander Prisoners' Anthology*. Hayword, CA: Asian Prisoner Support Committee, 2007.
3. The editors of *Other* chose API as their designation to capture the range of individuals and communities who could belong to their rubric. I use API when referencing their work. Otherwise, I have chosen "Asian/Pacific/American" Studies to do the same. At times, I also employ "Asian American," for reasons that I explain when I do so. Here I simply want to note that one of the issues complicating pan-ethnic identity is precisely that of how to represent inclusion through terminology.
4. Eddy Zheng, "Intro," vii–viii.
5. This is an oft-cited statistic for which there are several corroborating sources. The most recent and complete in relation to the writing of this piece is a comprehensive report from the Prison Policy Initiative. Peter Wagner and Bernadette Rabuy, "Mass Incarceration: The Whole Pie," published on 12/8/2015, accessed January 27, 2016, www.prisonpolicy.org/reports/pie2015.html. Another widely cited source is Roy Walmsley, "World Prison Population List" (tenth edition), International Centre for Prison Studies, 2013, accessed January 27, 2016, www.prisonstudies.org/sites/default/files/resources/downloads/wppl_10.pdf.
6. An important analysis that offers another genealogical angle is Naomi Murakawa, *The First Civil Right: How Liberals Built Prison America*, New York: Oxford University Press, 2014.
7. Ruth Wilson Gilmore, *Golden Gulag: Prisons, Surplus, Crisis, and Opposition in Globalizing California*. Berkeley, CA: University of California Press, 2007.
8. Michelle Alexander, *The New Jim Crow: Mass Incarceration in the Age of Colorblindness*. New York: the New Press, 2012. Unrelatd to Alexander's work, and founded by three Black women (Patrisse Cullors, Opal Tometi and Alicia Garza) after the non-indictment of George Zimmerman for the murder of Trayvon Martin, a young unarmed Black man, the emergence of #BlackLivesMatter complicates the focus on Black men found in Alexander's work as well as many others. The founders link their work directly to the legacies of revolutionaries who the U.S. government specifically targeted in the 1960s and 1970s, such as Assata Shakur. They also bring together prison abolition and feminism as well as LGBTQ and immigrant rights. For more information see, Alicia Garza, "A Herstory of the #BlackLivesMatter Movement" *TheFeministWire* October 27, 2014, accessed on January 27, 2016,

www.thefeministwire.com/2014/10/blacklivesmatter-2/; and and a recording of the 17th Annual Eqbal Ahmed lecture, given at Hampshire College on March 30, 2015, accessed on January 27, 2016, www.youtube.com/watch?v=YpfKo10rDmA.

9   The work of Moon-Ho Jung in recovering the importance of "An Act to Prohibit the 'Coolie Trade' by American Citizens in American Vessels," signed in 1862 by President Abraham Lincoln, is critical for reminding us of how the constitutive relationship between slavery and indenture played out in the politics of the United States before Chinese exclusion. Moon-Ho Jung, "Outlawing "Coolies": Race, Nation, and Empire in the Age of Emancipation," *American Quarterly* 57:3 (2005), 677–701 and *Coolies and Cane: Race Labor, and Sugar in the Age of Emancipation*, Baltimore, MD: Johns Hopkins University Press, 2006.

10 1917 Immigration Act. H.R. 10384; Pub. L. 301; 39 Stat. 874; 64th Congress, February 5, 1917.

11 Nearly every continental state in the United States has had anti-miscegenation laws on its books at one point in its history. Anti-miscegenation laws were not ruled unconstitutional until the 1967 Supreme Court decision in *Loving v. Virginia*. For more see Peggy Pascoe, *What Comes Naturally: Miscegenation Law and the Making of Race in America,* New York: Oxford University Press, 2009; and Susan Koshy, *Sexual Naturalization: Asian Americans and Miscegenation,* Stanford, CA: Stanford University Press, 2004.

12 For some context see Eithne Luibheid, *Entry Denied: Controlling Sexuality at the Border*, Minneapolis, MN: University of Minnesota Press, 2002; and Catherine Lee, *Fictive Kinship: Family Reunification and the Meaning of Race and Nation in American Immigration,* New York: Russell Sage Foundation, 2013.

13 "Illegal," which is an administrative category within the United States, carries with it a legacy of dehumanization and degradation that extends beyond the realm of the law itself. "Undocumented" is the label chosen by immigrant rights activists, and meant to counter the dehumanization implied by "illegal." It is not, technically speaking, always accurate since many immigrants who lack and/or have lapsed legal status are, technically speaking, documented vis-à-vis employer-issued false social security cards, expired visas, etc. For this reason, some scholars choose to use "unaccounted" or "unauthorized." Unless explicitly invoking the usage of others (as I am in this instance), I will generally use "undocumented" in keeping with the social movements who have extended its meaning beyond a literal description to one that specifically counters dehumanization.

14 Zheng himself continues to fight for recognition of Asian American and Pacific Islanders who face detention and deportation. In 2015 he received an Open Society Foundations grant to work through the Asian Prisoner Support Committee (a group that mobilized around his case) to raise awareness in API communities on issues of mass incarceration and deportation.

15 Daniel Kanstroom, *Deportation Nation: Outsiders in American History*, Cambridge, MA: Harvard University Press, 2010.

16 *Chae Chan Ping v. United States,* 130 U.S. 581 (1889)

17 *Fong Yue Ting v. United States* 149 U.S. 698 (1893)

18 This has several interrelated dimensions. To begin with, it considers immigration detention part of the growing prison industrial complex, even as it is not fully part of the criminal justice system (as I describe below). Next, for the sheer growth in deportation see, for example, Walter A. Ewing *The Growth of the U.S. Deportation Machine: More Immigrants are Being "Removed" from the United States than Ever Before.* Washington DC: Immigration Policy Center, 2014. Immigrants are also more likely to be housed in for-profit prisons. Chris Kirkham, "Private Prisons Profit from Immigration Crackdown, Federal and Local Law Enforcement Practices," *The Huffington Post*, June 7, 2012, accessed January 30, 2016, www.huffingtonpost.com/2012/06/07/private-prisons-immigration-federal-law-enforcement_n_1569219.html. Recent reports have identified Latinos as the "new majority" in federal prisons. While federal prisons are not the bulk of prisons in the U.S., and Latinos are not all immigrants (consider Puerto Ricans and the fact that many Latinas are U.S. citizens), it still points to the incarceration of more and more individuals who are likely to be noncitizens. Garance Burke, "Latinos Form New Majority of Those Sentenced to Federal Prisons," *The Huffington Post*, September 9, 2011, accessed January 29, 2016, www.huffingtonpost.com/2011/09/09/hispanic-majority-prison_n_955823.html.

19 For example, see the collected essays in David C. Brotherton and Philip Kretsedemas, Eds. *Keeping Out the Other: A Critical Introduction to Immigration Enforcement Today*, New York: Columbia University Press, 2008.

20 Juan Gonzalez, *Harvest of Empire: A History of Latinos in America*. New York: Viking Penguin, 2000.

21 Angela Davis, *Are Prisons Obsolete?* New York: Seven Stories Press, 2003.

22 S. 1291 (107th): Development, Relief, and Education for Alien Minors Act
23 There is much more to say about each of these categories which have historically produced various forms of illegality cut across by race, class, gender and sexuality. Suffice it to say here that many of them are produced by the strictures of immigration law particularly as it has increasingly been characterized by temporary visas and cut across by the denial of social services (welfare) to immigrants.
24 S. 952 (112th)
25 In 2012, President Barack Obama's administration issued a policy clarification known as Deferred Action Plan for Childhood Arrivals (DACA), that emphasizes a pre-existing loophole in immigration law that allows for administrative relief from deportation for two years, on a case by case basis. Relief from deportation is for two years, after which it is renewable for an additional two more. During relief, an individual can apply for a work permit. There is, however, no guarantee that if you qualify the Department of Homeland Security (DHS) will approve your case, and DACA *is not* a path to legal permanent residency or US citizenship. DACA is outlined in a June 15, 2012 memorandum from Department of Homeland Security head Janet Napolitano.
26 Subhash Kateel and Aarti Shahani, "Families for Freedom: Against Deportation and Delegalization," in Brotherton and Kretsedemas, *Keeping Out the Other,* 258.
27 For a sense of some of the directions this movement has taken see, "DREAM Activist Speaks Out on Infiltrating Florida Detention Center to Find Wrongly Held Immigrants." *Democracy Now!* August 1, 2012, accessed January 30, 2016, www.democracynow.org/2012/8/1/dream_activist_speaks_out_on_infiltrating; and "Undocumented and Unafraid: 30 Immigrants Detained Crossing into U.S. at Border Protest." October 4, 2013, accessed January 30, 2016, www.democracynow.org/2013/10/4/undocumented_and_unafraid_30_immigrants_detained; and Von Diaz, "How 5 DREAMers Are Rethinking Their Role in the Immigrant Rights Movement." *The Huffington Post,* April 28, 2014, accessed January 26, 2016, www.huffingtonpost.com/2014/04/28/dreamers-immigrant-rights_n_5227646.html.
28 Laura Sullivan, "Prison Economics Help Drive Arizona Immigration Law" National Public Radio October 28, 2010, accessed July 19, 2014, www.npr.org/2010/10/28/130833741/prison-economics-help-drive-ariz-immigration-law.
29 Harsha Walia, *Undoing Border Imperialism,* New York: AK Press, 2013.
30 Dean Saranillio, "Colliding Histories: Hawai'i Statehood at the Intersection of Asian 'Ineligible to Citizenship' and Hawaiians 'Unfit for Self-Government," *Journal of Asian American Studies,* 13:3 (October 2010): 283–309.

Also, in a sign of growing analytical momentum, as this chapter goes to press, *Amerasia Journal,* a flagship publication in the field of Asian American Studies, has just released their Spring 2016 issue which is devoted entirely to the theme of the "carceral states," and includes analysis that highlights the intersections between immigration and indigeneity. *Amerasia Journal* 42:1 (Spring 2016).
31 "In Lak'ech," http://vue.annenberginstitute.org/perspectives/lak%E2%80%99ech-you-are-my-other, accessed July 21, 2014.

References

17th Annual Eqbal Ahmed lecture, given at Hampshire College on March 30, 2015, accessed on January 27, 2016, www.youtube.com/watch?v=YpfKo10rDmA.
Alexander, Michelle, *The New Jim Crow: Mass Incarceration in the Age of Colorblindness.* New York: The New Press, 2012.
Amerasia Journal, "Carceral States." 42:1 (Spring 2016).
Brotherton, David C. and Philip Kretsedemas, Eds. *Keeping Out the Other: A Critical Introduction to Immigration Enforcement Today,* New York: Columbia University Press, 2008.
Burke, Garance, "Latinos Form New Majority of Those Sentenced to Federal Prisons," *The Huffington Post,* September 9, 2011, accessed January 29, 2016, www.huffingtonpost.com/2011/09/09/hispanic-majority-prison_n_955823.html.
Davis, Angela, *Are Prisons Obsolete?* New York: Seven Stories Press, 2003.
Democracy Now! "DREAM Activist Speaks Out on Infiltrating Florida Detention Center to Find Wrongly Held Immigrants." *Democracy Now!* August 1, 2012, accessed January 30, 2016, www.democracynow.org/2012/8/1/dream_activist_speaks_out_on_infiltrating.

——— "Undocumented and Unafraid: 30 Immigrants Detained Crossing into U.S. at Border Protest." October 4, 2013, accessed January 30, 2016, www.democracynow.org/2013/10/4/undocumented_and_unafraid_30_immigrants_detained.

Diaz, Von, "How 5 DREAMers Are Rethinking Their Role in the Immigrant Rights Movement." *The Huffington Post*, April 28, 2014, accessed January 26, 2016, www.huffingtonpost.com/2014/04/28/dreamers-immigrant-rights_n_5227646.html.

Ewing, Walter A. *The Growth of the U.S. Deportation Machine: More Immigrants are Being "Removed" from the United States than Ever Before*. Washington DC: Immigration Policy Center, 2014.

Garza, Alicia, "A Herstory of the #BlackLivesMatter Movement" *TheFeministWire* October 27, 2014, accessed January 27, 2016, www.thefeministwire.com/2014/10/blacklivesmatter-2/.

Gilmore, Ruth Wilson, *Golden Gulag: Prisons, Surplus, Crisis, and Opposition in Globalizing California*. Berkeley, CA: University of California Press, 2007.

Gonzalez, Juan, *Harvest of Empire: A History of Latinos in America*. New York: Viking Penguin, 2000.

Jung, Moon-Ho, *Coolies and Cane: Race Labor, and Sugar in the Age of Emancipation*, Baltimore, MD: Johns Hopkins University Press, 2006.

———. "Outlawing "Coolies": Race, Nation, and Empire in the Age of Emancipation," *American Quarterly* 57:3 (2005), 677–701.

In Lak'ech www.vue.annenberginstitute.org/perspectives/lak%E2%80%99ech-you-are-my-other, accessed July 21, 2014.

Kanstroom, Daniel, *Deportation Nation: Outsiders in American History*, Cambridge, MA: Harvard University Press, 2010.

Kateel, Subhash and Aarti Shahani, "Families for Freedom: Against Deportation and Delegalization,"in Brotherton and Kretsedemas, *Keeping Out the Other*, 258–287.

Chris Kirkham, "Private Prisons Profit from Immigration Crackdown, Federal and Local Law Enforcement Practices," *The Huffington Post*, June 7, 2012, accessed January 30, 2016 www.huffingtonpost.com/2012/06/07/private-prisons-immigration-federal-law-enforcement_n_1569219.html.

Koshy, Susan, *Sexual Naturalization: Asian Americans and Miscegenation*, Stanford, CA: Stanford University Press, 2004.

Lee, Catherine, *Fictive Kinship: Family Reunification and the Meaning of Race and Nation in American Immigration*, New York: Russell Sage Foundation, 2013.

Luibheid, Eithne, *Entry Denied: Controlling Sexuality at the Border*, Minneapolis, MN: University of Minnesota Press, 2002.

Murakawa, Naomi, *The First Civil Right: How Liberals Built Prison America*, New York: Oxford University Press, 2014.

Pascoe, Peggy, *What Comes Naturally: Miscegenation Law and the Making of Race in America*, New York: Oxford University Press, 2009.

Rodriguez, Dylan, *Forced Passages: Imprisoned Radical Intellectuals and the U.S. Prison Regime*. Minneapolis, MN: University of Minnesota Press, 2006.

Saranillio, Dean, "Colliding Histories: Hawai'i Statehood at the Intersection of Asian 'Ineligible to Citizenship' and Hawaiians 'Unfit for Self-Government," *Journal of Asian American Studies*, 13:3 (October 2010): 283–309.

Sullivan, Laura, "Prison Economics Help Drive Arizona Immigration Law" *National Public Radio* October 28, 2010, accessed July 19, 2014, www.npr.org/2010/10/28/130833741/prison-economics-help-drive-ariz-immigration-law.

Wagner, Peter and Bernadette Rabuy, "Mass Incarceration: The Whole Pie," published on August 12, 2015, accessed January 27, 2016, www.prisonpolicy.org/reports/pie2015.html.

Walia, Harsha, *Undoing Border Imperialism*, New York: AK Press, 2013.

Walmsley, Roy, "World Prison Population List" (tenth edition), International Centre for Prison Studies, 2013, accessed January 27, 2016, www.prisonstudies.org/sites/default/files/resources/downloads/wppl_10.pdf.

Zheng, Eddy and Asian Prisoner Support Committee, Ed. *Other: an Asian & Pacific Islander Prisoners' Anthology*. Hayword, CA: Asian Prisoner Support Committee, 2007.

24

AFRO-ASIAN SOLIDARITY THROUGH TIME AND SPACE

Roads Taken and Not Taken

Yuichiro Onishi

When Grace Lee Boggs, an American born Chinese, was in her mid-twenties, she found herself being sucked into the vortex of the Black freedom struggle that ultimately changed her outlook on life and social change. She had just earned her doctorate in philosophy from Bryn Mawr College in Pennsylvania in June 1940. But the door of opportunity was tightly shut; the combination of racial and gender discrimination made it virtually impossible for her to secure an academic position as a professor of philosophy. Undeterred, she started to get involved in grassroots political activism.

In her autobiography, Boggs describes her experience of moving to Chicago's South Side and soon being swept up by the readiness of working-class African Americans for a new society. Catalyzed by the labor leader A. Philip Randolph's call for the march on Washington for economic justice and civil rights, Black masses decisively began moving toward the center. Commonly known as the March on Washington Movement (MOWM), Randolph's provocation to bring thousands of African Americans to Washington, DC. to demand jobs in government agencies and defense plants put President Franklin D. Roosevelt on the defensive. In the context of wartime mobilization against fascism, the government had very little option but to try to address the glaring contradiction between freedom and unfreedom in American life. In June 1941, Roosevelt issued Executive Order 8802 to begin the process of desegregation in defense industries. In the end, the march never took place. Randolph aborted it at once when the federal government responded to the demand of the Black freedom struggle. But many working-class African Americans were already in motion.[1]

Boggs, too, underwent radical transformation. Something happened to her political imagination when she witnessed ordinary African Americans, tired of waiting for racial progress to descend from the ether, begin working together and doing things on their own to confront head on the persistence of racism that narrowed their life chances and opportunities. Acutely cognizant of the hollowness of Second World War aims of the fight against fascism, those buoyed by and participating in the MOWM honed their internationalist orientations to bring together the political demands still unmet on the home front in America and the Darker World. They were not simply responding to the call for victory over fascism and victory over Jim Crow, or "Double V"; they intensified the currents of wartime mobilization by rallying around the vision of "Double D"—Democracy at home and in the wider colonial world—to bring an end to white supremacy the world over. Such a conceptual politics emanating from the globalization of the Black freedom struggle helped her achieve clarity in thought and action. She wrote in *Living for Change: An Autobiography* (1998), "I decided that what I wanted to do with the rest of my life was to become a movement activist in the black community." Until her death on October 5, 2015, she was at it, searchingly locating the gravity of myriad social movements within and beyond the inner-city neighborhood of Detroit to fulfill the vision of a truly just and democratic society.[2]

Boggs' decision to go on "living for change" best captures the hallmark of Afro-Asian solidarity. Throughout the twentieth century, Blacks and Asians in the United States and abroad have found each other in their struggles against not just racism but also imperialism and war. Engaging in the creation of a political project called Afro-Asian solidarity, they responded to the challenges of creating a new society. Then and now, Afro-Asian solidarity has never been simply about the process of coming together. As illustrated by the life story of Grace Lee Boggs, it is best defined as a deep commitment to do all that is required to transform the community of struggle they forged as a basis for a new society to go beyond wealth and inequality, hubris and violence, and rapacious exploitation and unfettered materialism. In other words, that which gives form to Afro-Asian solidarity is an uncompromising ethical stance, a set of moral principles guided by the sense of responsibility and passion for justice, albeit at times with the rigidity of theodicy.

This essay will introduce select instances of Afro-Asian solidarity across time and space in a sweeping fashion. A special emphasis will be placed on the role of U.S. wars in Asia in shaping the grounds to become productive for Afro-Asian solidarity to emerge. Starting with the U.S. war in the Philippines (1899–1902), the essay will track the ascendancy of U.S. empire in Asia and its paths toward military aggression against imperialist Japan (1941–1945), in Korea (1950–1953), and in Vietnam and other parts of Southeast Asia (1955–1975). Historically, the unspeakable scale of violence unleashed against Asians in these wars functioned like a flashpoint, bringing into sharp relief the connection between the domestic realities of racism and the destructive and violent consequences of imperial aggression. This nexus between the local and global dimensions of racism impacted the consciousness of both Blacks and Asians and brought them closer together.

Roads Taken

During the Philippine–American War, the editors of African American newspapers across the nation, both small and large, drew a parallel between rampant white terror campaigns waged across the American South and the killings of Filipinos at genocidal scale. Made explicit was the shared experience of racial violence on both sides of the Pacific. These editorials highlighted that U.S. imperial violence in the Philippines was but a lawlessness of racist southern states writ large and carried out "by the people of this country who believe in mob and lynch law." Some of the 6000 African American soldiers who fought in this war also reached the same conclusion. Writing letters home from the trenches, these dissenting African American soldiers issued a strong condemnation against the underlying white supremacy of the U.S. war in the Philippines. One soldier, for instance, wrote, "Every soldier in the Philippines who uses the term 'nigger' does so with hell-born contempt for the negro of the United States, and it is our one desire that he be cursed of his fiendish malady by a Filipino bullet."[3]

Cognizant of U.S. racial order, Filipino insurgents fighting to stem the tide of U.S. aggression often turned to the tactic of psychological warfare to convince African Americans to desert and join the cause of Filipino national liberation. Michael H. Robinson, serving in the segregated 25th Infantry, described in the published serialized accounts in March 1900 that African

American soldiers "have been warned several times by insurgent leaders in the shape of placards, some being placed on trees, others left mysteriously in houses we have occupied, saying to the colored soldiers that while he is contending on the field of battle against a people who are struggling for recognition and freedom, your people in America are being lynched and disenfranchised by the same people who are trying to compel us to believe that their government will deal justly and fairly by us." One of the soldiers who responded to the Filipino insurgents' call for desertion was Corporal David Fagan of the segregated 24th Infantry. A twenty-four-year old from Florida, he fought alongside the freedom fighters in the Filipino revolutionary army against his former combat unit. Several years later, however, he was captured and brutally beheaded.[4]

Such an act of dissent that manifested in the form of sedition was undeniably audacious, but it remained the key and persisting feature of Afro-Asian solidarity. The case in point was the growing antagonism between the United States and Japan throughout the interwar period in the 1920s and the 1930s. The symbolic significance of Japan's rise to world-power status in the international community dominated by white nations coalesced with the longstanding tradition of African American vindicationism. The image of a strong Japan helped articulate their hopes and dreams to live a life of their own unencumbered by white supremacy. As a result, some African Americans crossed over to the side of Japan to forge solidarity.[5]

This was the case particularly among the participants of the Black Nationalist movement that was influenced by Marcus Garvey and his organization called the Universal Negro Improvement Association. Guided by the vision of bringing together Africans and peoples of African descent in the diaspora for the singular cause of racial uplift to overcome the curse of Western civilization and achieve greatness comparable to the European counterpart, the Garvey movement cropped up in varying scales and momentum in African American urban and rural life, as well as in the wider Black world in Africa and its diaspora. In such a milieu, Japan appeared as an icon, embodying the history of possibility to overcome white domination among ordinary African Americans.[6]

High regard for Japan did not subside in the climate of the anti-Japanese sentiment. In some cases, it had a multiplying effect. The symbolic significance of Japan's revolt against the West through pan-Asianism continued to exert shaping power in African American life, contributing to the development of various types of pro-Japan Black Nationalist organizations in such cities as New York, Cleveland, Chicago, Detroit, St. Louis, and New Orleans. None other than historian Ernest Allen, Jr. has richly documented the largely forgotten history of pro-Japan tendencies within the African American community. Soon after the U.S. entered the war against Japan in 1942, as many as 125 African Americans associated with organizations with pro-Japan orientations—the Allah Temple of Islam, the Pacific Movement of Ethiopia, the Colored American National Organization, the Brotherhood of Liberty for the Black People of America, the Century Service Exchange, the International Reassemble of the Church of Freedom League, Inc., the House of Israel, and the Pacific Movement of the Eastern World—had come under federal custody charged with draft evasion and sedition. The most compelling account unearthed recently, building upon the work of Allen, is the work of Keisha Blain. It presents not only the involvement of a Japanese immigrant named Satokata Takahashi and a Filipino national who went by several aliases, Ashima Takis and Mimo De Guzman, in the Black Nationalist causes led by The Development of Our Own and the Onward Movement of America, but also the critical agency of the Black internationalist feminist, Pearl Sherrod, Takahashi's wife, who played the role of a pace-setter of the currents of pro-Japan tendencies within the African American community.[7]

While it is convenient to categorically declare these pro-Japan African Americans as fanatics, subversives, and traitors, as many of their contemporaries on both sides of the color line did, their vision of liberation, however much marred by the rigidity of theodicy, was suggestive of the central role that the ethos of self-determination played in forging Afro-Asian solidarity. Indeed, the suppleness with which this ethos operated in African American life is worth noting. The ethos of self-determination had a way of inciting the sentiment of righteous indignation in the face of racial injustice.

Such a sentiment appeared explicitly among individual African Americans not tied to the aforementioned Black Nationalist organizations when Japanese Americans on the West Coast experienced mass removal and incarceration. When U.S. President Franklin D. Roosevelt issued Executive Order 9066 on February 19, 1942 to carry out the policy of the forced removal and confinement of Japanese Americans, a host of African American journalists, intellectuals, and activists of diverse backgrounds, ranging from artist Paul Robeson and writer George Schuyler of the *Pittsburgh Courier*, to attorney Hugh E. Macbeth and writer Chester Himes (both Los Angeles-based), took the pro-Japanese American position to protest the action of the federal government and the treatment of Japanese Americans who were denied birthright citizenship.[8]

Historian Greg Robinson presents various ways in which the leaders of key African American institutions, such as the National Association for the Advancement of Colored People and the National Urban League, responded to the total exclusion of Japanese Americans from American life in the context of the clarion call for "Double V," victory over fascism abroad and victory over Jim Crow racial order on the home front, although largely absent was the collective movement against the policy of racial dictatorship directed singularly at the first-generation immigrants, *Issei*, and the second-generation children, *Nisei*. At the local level, some members of the Japanese American Citizens League and African Americans engaged in coalitional politics in their effort to the fight for democracy.[9]

The momentum and energy toward a more expansive democracy unleashed by the African American-led civil rights struggle during the Second World War continued to make grounds for coalition building productive for both Asians and Blacks. The global context significantly contributed to Afro-Asian solidarity. Amidst the triumphant rise of liberal internationalism in the aftermath of Allied victory over fascism in 1945 was the rising tempo of decolonization all over the world. The arrival of Mao's China and of Kim Il Sung's North Korea, as well as the expansion of the anticolonial nationalist struggle against European colonial rule in Southeast Asia and countless other darker nations' movement toward nonalignment to transcend the bipolar politics of the Cold War, also helped articulate the connection between the global color line and Cold War politics. In this context, the outbreak of the Korean War in 1950 and the subsequent U.S.-led United Nations intervention represented not simply a global Cold War hotspot. For some progressive African American journalists and thinkers tied to Left politics, it was viewed as the inauguration of a new colonialism.[10]

Speaking truth to power in the climate of anti-Communist repressive politics, African American activists opposed the Korean War on the grounds that this conflict on the peninsula was but a global manifestation of domestic racism. They risked their lives by taking the side of the cause of anti-imperialism and anti-racism rather than of Cold War status quo. Many of them, consequently, paid a huge price in the form of arrest, deportation, and ostracization. Yet such a bold expression of dissent so often animated cross-racial solidarity in an unexpected way. Historian Cindy I-Fen Cheng discusses some of the compelling and little-known cases of grassroots Afro-Asian solidarity where African American and Korean immigrant critics of U.S. Cold War imperialism in Korea found each other. When David Hyun and Diamond Kimm, Korean immigrant anticolonial nationalists committed to the creation of an independent Korea, were arrested for participation in "subversive" activities and subjected to deportation procedures, the members of the Los Angeles chapter of the Black Left organization called the Civil Rights Congress, as well as its offshoot Los Angeles Committee for Protection of Foreign Born came to their defense. Some African American activists confronted head on anti-communist repression and fought for Asian American civil rights and liberties.[11]

Equally important was the role of the Korean War in laying the groundwork for the political transformation of key activists of the Civil Rights and Black Power Movements in the 1960s and early 1970s. Both the violence of this war and persistent racism in the armed forces amidst the desegregation of the military were contexts out of which African American soldiers radicalized and fashioned themselves as anti-imperialist and anti-racist activists. Such notable Civil Rights and Black Power Movement activists as Bobby Seale of the Black Panther Party for Self-Defense, James Foreman of the Student Nonviolent Coordinating Committee (SNCC), Ivory Perry, and Amiri Baraka were all veterans of the Korean War who had come to express clear-cut disenchantment with American democracy by the end of the war. Other activists, on the other hand, either chose imprisonment or conscientious-objector status over military service, as was the case for SNCC leaders James Lawson and Bob Moses. They were all coming to take the position that the most powerful nation-state in the world was a predatory state, not the defender of freedom, that caused much harm, misery, and destruction to darker nations and people.[12]

Yet again, the escalating U.S. war in Asia, this time in Vietnam in the late 1960s and early 1970s, brought to the fore the ethos of critical resistance emanating from Afro-Asian solidarity. By then, taking giant steps to buoy the political project based on the vision of Afro-Asian solidarity were Asian American activists that had been inspired by the burgeoning Black liberation movement. Yuri Kochiyama, the Japanese American activist based in Harlem, was one of the key interlocutors of Afro-Asian solidarity during this period. Particularly important to her development as an activist was her encounter with Malcolm X in June 1964. Meeting him in a very private setting of her own home, with *hibakusha* [atomic bomb survivors] journalist-activists from Japan, was a defining moment in her life, and so was, without a doubt, becoming a witness to the tragedy of the assassination of Malcolm X at the Audubon Ballroom on February 25, 1965. Thereafter, Yuri Kochiyama made up her mind to carry forward Malcolm X's vision of the struggle for self-determination locally and transnationally to fight for justice and human liberation.[13]

Kochiyama's coming into being as a revolutionary grassroots activist in Harlem in the late 1960s coincided with large-scale opposition to the Vietnam War, a growing militancy of African American activism, and the emergent Asian American Movement. Throughout this turbulent period, Kochiyama infused Malcolm X's internationalist vision of antiracism and anti-imperialism at the grassroots to shape the Asian American Movement, and matured politically as she came into contact with old and new generations of Asian American activists. She was present, for instance, when two longtime Japanese American activists Kazu Iijima and Minn Matsuda, who had deep ties with progressive politics since the 1940s, helped organize the pan-Asian anti-war resistance group called Asian Americans for Action (AAA) in New York in 1969. The members were drawn from students at Columbia University and City College of New York who were inspired by the Black Power movement and antiwar resistance. Many of them were Chinese Americans and Japanese Americans, but other Asians, such as Vietnamese, Cambodians, Koreans, and Filipinos also entered the orbit of AAA's activism. The AAA's position was that U.S. racism at home and the justification for aggressive U.S. militarism in Southeast Asia were tightly bound up. This perspective is best encapsulated, plainly, in the following 1967 antiwar statement made by James Baldwin, one of the foremost important African American intellectuals in the twentieth century: "a racist society can't but fight a racist war."[14]

This critical perspective was reinforced, at every turn, by Third World solidarity struggles. These struggles were increasingly becoming palpable among youth on university campuses across the United States in the aftermath of the 1968–1969 Third World Liberation Front strike at San Francisco State College that sparked student activism on scales that were at once both small and large. Meanwhile, state suppressions against these radicals intensified. Out of this context of the antagonisms between grassroots insurgencies and state violence that were unfolding at local and global terrains of struggle emerged the nomenclature called "Asian America." It was a political category of struggle that was put to use in the service of building Asian American consciousness, identity, and community. As a frequent speaker at antiwar rallies and contributor to the AAA newsletter circulated within the communities of Asian American activists, Yuri Kochiyama certainly contributed to the politicization of the concept of "Asian America," along the way finding a path that led to the network of Asian American activists who were enmeshed in varying types of organizations, such as Asian American Political Alliance on both Coasts and the revolutionary Asian American group called the Red Guard Party on the West Coast and I Wor Kuen on the East Coast.[15]

Like Kochiyama, many other Asian American radicals, most notably Pat Sumi and Alex Hing, underwent what Martin Luther King, Jr. famously called "the radical revolution of values" during the Vietnam War era to emerge as anti-racist, antiwar, and anti-imperialist Asian American activists. By moving through the domain of Black and Third World Liberation, and along the way traveling to Asia to become witnesses to the causes and consequences of "the giant triplets of racism, materialism, and militarism," as King put it, many of the key Asian American radicals of the late 1960s and early 1970s fashioned themselves as a link bridging the Asian American Movement and the Black Liberation Movement. But later, making sharp analytical advances, all of them laid the groundwork, both at the level of theorization and concrete engagement, to help usher in a space of resistance where other young Asian American activists would hone a critical ethos that possessed an ecumenical authority and quality and in the process learn to articulate a distinct Asian American progressive politics capable of buoying Asian American Movement building. Stepping into the culture of liberation, they traversed, with necessary suppleness and rigor, multiple terrains of struggles—from Black liberation to antiracism to anti-war to anti-militarism to anti-imperialism to decolonial praxes. Such was the best intellectual tradition of the Asian American Movement.[16]

The dynamism of Afro-Asian solidarity that animated Asian American movement building in the late 1960s and early 1970s left an important legacy in Asian American cultural formations. According to Cheryl Higashida, Afro-Asian literary collaborations were integral parts of the development of alternative literary institutions for writers of color and women of color, such as Yardbird Publishing Company (founded by Ishmael Reed and Al Young in 1971) and Kitchen Table: Women of Color Press (initiated by Barbara Smith in 1980). These multiracial progressive communities of artists of color became an important outlet for Asian American writers to meet other writers and publish their works. Such writers as Frank Chin, Shawn Wong, Al Robles, Mitsuye Yamada, Hisaye Yamamoto, and Lawson Fusao Inada self-consciously developed themselves into Asian American writers, all the while actively shaping the Asian American literary spaces, such as Basement Workshop in New York and Kearney Street Workshop in San Francisco.[17]

During the same period, Asian American musicians, too, forged a distinct space of Asian American cultural production. A product of the Third World liberation movement of the late 1960s and early 1970s, a folk trio called A Grain of Sand comprised of Chris Iijima, Nobuko

Miyamoto, and "Charlie" Chin, for instance, made community-based musical activity and activism central to the formation of Asian American radical politics. In 1973, the trio released the album with Paredon Records that was produced by Barbara Dane.[18] Moreover, some of the Asian American free jazz artists, such as saxophonist Russel Baba, bassist Mark Izu, bass clarinetist Paul Yamazaki, violinist Jason Kao Hwang, and pianist Jon Jang, influenced by the Black Power/Arts Movement, also contributed to the development of Asian American sounds. The defining feature of these Asian American musicians' aesthetic authority was a shared commitment to go beyond the mainstream to carve out their own creative space to put the power of autonomy into practice. Modeled after cutting edge avant-garde African American artist collectives, such as the Advancement for Creative Musicians in Chicago, the Black Arts Group in St. Louis, and the Pan-Afrikan Peoples Arkestra in Los Angeles, independent Asian American artists created such groups as the Asian American Art Ensemble and the Pan-Asian Arkestra, as well as the recording label AsianImprov Records to sustain the power of self-activity and ethos of mutuality engendered by Afro-Asian solidarity.[19]

Particularly noteworthy was the role that the revolutionary artist and baritone saxophonist Fred Ho played in charting the course to create a distinct Afro-Asian political, sonic, and aesthetic authority. Combining his commitment to revolutionary socialist politics with Black and Asian American cultural radicalism, he helped bring into existence numerous creative musical projects, such as the Afro Asian Music Ensemble in 1982, the collaborative project with Kalamu ya Salaam called Afro-Asian Arts Dialogue in 1992, the multimedia Black Panther ballet titled *All Power to the People!* (1999), and the matriarchalist opera called *Warrior Sisters: The New Adventures of African and Asian Womyn Warriors* (2000). He also founded his own production company called Big Red Media, Inc., that helped define the contours of Afro-Asian solidarity and co-edited two anthologies, *Sounding Off! Music as Subversion/Resistance/Revolution* (1995) and *Legacy to Liberation: Politics and Culture of Revolutionary Asian Pacific America* (2000).[20]

Roads Not Taken

Blacks and Asians that helped forge solidarities through time and space were renegades and visionaries engaged in struggles against oppressions and injustices. These participants of Afro-Asian solidarity are still present, but the vision of liberation emanating from this collectivity and concrete engagement does demand re-visioning today. The world of Afro-Asian solidarity is not outside of the process of historical change, which is to say it is not static. It changes with new political realities. Today Afro-Asian solidarity that captured the hopes and dreams of the Third World, here and abroad, in the past is at a crossroads.[21]

One of the most visible challenges is the retreat of the vision of antiracism and anti-imperialism that was at the core of Afro-Asian solidarity throughout the twentieth century. A part of the problem has to do with the crippling effect of the discourse of model minority on Afro-Asian solidarity. The figure of a model minority, traditionally, has been associated with Asian Americans, which has been in the making since the mid-twentieth century. This racial construction greatly facilitated Asian Americans' assimilation into mainstream American society, amidst the never-ending racial stereotyping of Asian Americans as foreigners and, more seriously, anti-Asian violence. The most arresting event in contemporary Asian America was the brutal murder of Vincent Chin in Detroit in 1982 by two white men, Ronald Ebens and Michael Nitz. They beat Chin with a baseball bat by swinging four deadly blows to his skull, and got away with this heinous hate crime without any jail time.[22]

While the murder of Chin galvanized the Asian American Movement and politicized a new generation of Asian American activists in the 1980s, the face of politics was beginning to change by the 1990s and the age of Obama certainly signaled the arrival of a new politics that gave credence to the myth of post-racial America. And this idea that "race and racism are over" has given the discourse of model minority a new lease on life, transforming it into the very paradigm with which to manage U.S. race relations as a whole. For one, the representation of upwardly mobile and upstanding "citizens of Asian America," to borrow from Cindy I-Fen Cheng, has been repeatedly recycled in the media and mainstream to roll back civil rights gains in the areas of asset accumulation, political participation, and educational attainment for African Americans and Latinas. The experience of race among Asian Americans is such that they "have been racially triangulated vis-à-vis Blacks and Whites," as political scientist Claire Jean Kim argues, to maintain white domination over people of color.[23]

Such a framing of "good" and "bad" minority, to be sure, has fueled antagonisms between Blacks and Asians. The most dramatic outcome was the 1992 Los Angeles uprising in the wake of the acquittal of police officers who brutally assaulted an African American man, Rodney King. African Americans and Latinas looted countless stores in nearby Koreatown and caused much physical and psychological harm to Korean Americans. Furthermore, given that the investment in model minority discourse is tied to material progress, especially in terms of gaining access to expanded life chances and opportunities, Asian Americans have elected to participate in the perpetuation of this dominant discourse and in so doing have come to internalize anti-Black racism, all of this at the expense of the ongoing marginalization and criminalization of other, poorer Asian Americans of diverse ethnic backgrounds and other people of color, namely African Americans and Latino/as.[24]

More disconcerting is that this process of sifting out a "good" minority" from the rest of the minorities has become widespread, with chilling consequences in contemporary America. The truth is that corollary to the production of "good" minority has been the systematic denial of life for millions of people of color through the policies of indefinite detention, mass incarceration, and deportation. The following contexts tellingly highlight the mutually constitutive formation of good and bad minority and bring into sharp relief how the legitimacy of the liberal American democratic state, where "good" citizens inhabit, is enabled by state violence: (1) the rising number of apprehensions and expulsions of migrant workers crossing the southern border, categorically deemed illegal immigrants, which hit the 1.8 million mark during the first term of Barack Obama's presidency from 2009 to 2013 and neared the 2 million mark achieved by George W. Bush during his two-term presidency from 2001 to 2009; (2) the persistent hate crimes against Sikh, Hindu, Muslim, South Asian, and Arab Americans, categorically deemed citizen-suspects, since 9/11; and (3) the rising prison populations, most of whom are African Americans and Latino/as, that grew from 350,000 to 2.2 million in two decades from 1980 and 2000.[25]

What is clear then is that racism and imperialism survive precisely because contemporary statecraft of the management of difference entails the dual movement that involves, first, *inclusion* founded on the dominant multiculturalist doctrine of model minority and, second, *exclusion* founded on contempt toward people of color that is soul-murdering and devoid of ethical obligations. Some racialized people make it into American civic life, lending credence to the idea of post-racial America, while others are treated as not worthy of inalienable rights that are the hallmark of liberal modernity. Together, these two modalities of power represent the governing principle through which racialized people's life outcomes are determined. Given these political challenges, Afro-Asian solidarity cannot be the same as in the past.[26] If so, what might Afro-Asian solidarity look like in the era of the relentless war against the so-called "terrorists," "illegal immigrants," "gangsters," and "criminals"?

Such is the challenge of Afro-Asian solidarity, and to move onward, an optic must change. Can we imagine, for instance, thousands gathering, with righteous indignation, in response to the unjustified killing of an unarmed Hmong teenager, Fong Lee, in Minneapolis in 2006 by white police officer Jason Anderson—an individual with a track record of unethical conducts and abusive behaviors on and off the force who shot Lee eight times in the back as he fled? The Asian American activist and artist Bao Phi, based in Minneapolis, while deeply enmeshed in the work of building Justice for Fong Lee Campaign, wrote: "Fong Lee was a young Hmong American man. He was someone's son, someone's brother. He could have been me, or any one of us, who are unfortunately all too familiar with the devastation of violence, racism, police brutality, and systematic injustice that rips apart our families and our communities." Why can't such a pronouncement, and Asian American activism for racial justice, become a touchstone to shake up the broader discourse of civil and human rights, much in the way that a clarion call in response to the killing of Trayvon Martin and the acquittal of George Zimmerman, or the killing of Mike Brown and Eric Garner, and acquire resonance in the public sphere? Can we also imagine Afro-Asian solidarity being made anew in the context of the 2012 Oak Creek hate-crime carried out by the white supremacist gunman in suburban Milwaukee at the Sikh gurdwara that ended in the death of six worshippers? Can we invoke, for example, an Afro-Asian connection—as poet Preeti Kaur has done in her poem "Letters Home"—between the 1963 bombing of the 16th Street Baptist Church in Birmingham, Alabama that killed four girls in Sunday School, just a few weeks after the historic March on Washington where Dr. King delivered the "I Have a Dream Speech," and the shootings at the Sikh gurdwara in Oak Creek, and most recently, the white supremacist shooting at the Emmanuel AME Church in Charleston? Can we even compose a new anthem of Afro-Asian solidarity and sing it, as Kaur imagines the great African American woman singer-artist Nina Simone singing "tera bhaana meetha laage," a Sikh prayer invoking the acceptance of sacrifice, "to tune of mississippi goddamn." Can we imagine opposition to aggressive militarism and ongoing U.S. military occupation in places rarely seen as the center of Black radical politics, such as Okinawa, to become the incubator of Afro-Asian solidarity, as such writers and scholars as Mitzi Uehara Carter and Fredrick D. Kakinami Cloyd do?[27]

Black radicalism and Third World internationalism that gave form to Afro-Asian coalitional politics in the United States and globally in the past need to be redefined. But as in the past, locally, grassroots activists participating in multiracial coalitional politics are already reworking Afro-Asian politics. They are crossing over and organizing across multiple color lines to take an ethical and political stance against the conditions of injustices and oppressions against non-citizens and citizens of diverse racial, ethnic, and religious backgrounds. Herein lies the beginning of the new history of Afro-Asian solidarity, for these activists are transforming the legacy of Afro-Asian solidarity and making the culture of liberation to become the wellspring of aspirations for a new society. Such a new politics has so much potential, and we need it now more than ever.

Notes

1 Grace Lee Boggs, *Living for Change: An Autobiography* (Minneapolis, MN: University of Minnesota Press, 1998).
2 Boggs, *Living for Change*, 39; Grace Lee Boggs, with Scott Kurashige, *The Next American Revolution: Sustainable Activism for the Twenty-First Century* (Berkeley, CA: University of California Press, 2012); *American Revolutionary: The Evolution of Grace Lee Boggs*, directed and produced by Grace Lee (LeeLee Films, Inc., 2013).

3. Nerissa S. Balce, "Filipino Bodies, Lynching, and the Language of Empire," in *Positively No Filipinos Allowed: Building Communities and Discourse*, Eds., Antonio T. Tiongson, Jr., Edgardo V. Gutierrez, and Ricardo V. Gutierrez (Philadelphia, PA: Temple University Press, 2006), 55–56; Cynthia L. Marasigan, "'Between the Devil and the Deep Blue Sea': Ambivalence, Violence, and African American Soldiers in the Philippine–American War and Its Aftermath," (Ph.D., diss., University of Michigan, 2000), 2.

4. Balce, "Filipino Bodies, Lynching, and the Language of Empire," 57; Marasigan, "'Between the Devil and the Deep Blue Sea'," 1.

5. George Lipsitz, "'Frantic to Join . . . the Japanese Army': The Asia Pacific War in the Lives of African American Soldiers and Civilians," in *The Politics of Culture in the Shadow of Capital*, Eds., Lisa Lowe and David Lloyd (Durham, NC: Duke University Press, 1997), 324–353; Gerald Horne, *Race War! White Supremacy and the Japanese Attack on the British Empire* (New York: NYU Press, 2004).

6. Lipsitz, "'Frantic to Join . . . the Japanese Army'."

7. Ernest Allen, Jr., "When Japan Was the 'Champion of the Colored Races': Satokata Takahashi and the Flowering of Black Messianic Nationalism," *The Black Scholar* 24 (Winter 1994): 23–46; Keisha N. Blain, "'For the Freedom of the Race': Black Women and the Practices of Nationalism, 1929–1945," Ph.D., diss., Princeton University, NJ, 2014); Keisha N. Blain, "'[F]or the Rights of Darker People in Every Party of the World': Pearl Sherrod, Black Internationalist Feminism, and Afro-Asian Politics in the 1930s," *Souls: A Critical Journal of Black Politics, Culture, and Society* (June 2015): 90–112.

8. Greg Robinson, *After Camp: Portraits in Midcentury Japanese American Life and Politics* (Berkeley, CA: University of California Press, 2012), 157–194.

9. Robinson, *After Camp*, 157–194.

10. Daniel Widener, "Seoul City Sue and the Bugout Blues: Black American Narratives of the Forgotten War," *Afro Asia: Revolutionary Political & Cultural Connections Between African Americans and Asian Americans*, Eds., Fred Ho and Bill V. Mullen (Durham, NC: Duke University Press, 2008), 55–90.

11. Widener, "Seoul City Sue and the Bugout Blues"; Cindy I-Fen Cheng, *Citizens of Asian America: Democracy and Race during the Cold War* (New York: NYU Press, 2013), 117–148,

12. Widener, "Seoul City Sue and the Bugout Blues."

13. Diane C. Fujino, *Yuri Kochiyama: Heartbeat of Struggle* (Minneapolis, MN: University of Minnesota Press, 2005).

14. Daryl Joji Maeda, *Rethinking the Asian American Movement* (New York: Routledge, 2011); Fujino, *Yuri Kochiyama*; James Baldwin, "The International War Crimes Tribunal," in *The Cross of Redemption: Uncollected Writings*, edited and with an introduction by Randall Kenan (New York: Pantheon Books, 2010), 199–202.

15. Maeda, *Rethinking the Asian American Movement*; Daryl J. Maeda, *Chains of Babylon: The Rise of Asian America* (Minneapolis, MN: University of Minnesota Press, 2009); Fujino, *Yuri Kochiyama*.

16. Maeda, *Rethinking the Asian American Movement*; Maeda, *Chains of Babylon*; Judy Tzu-Chun Wu, *Radicals on the Road: Internationalism, Orientalism, and Feminism during the Viet Nam Era* (Ithaca: Cornell University Press, 2013); Martin Luther King, Jr., "Beyond Vietnam," delivered at New York's Riverside Church, 4 April 1967, accessed February 27, 2015, http://mlk-kpp01.stanford.edu/index.php/encyclopedia/documentsentry/doc_beyond_vietnam/.

17. Cheryl Higashida, "Not Just a 'Special Issue': Gender, Sexuality, and Post-1965 Afro Asian Coalition Building in the *Yardbird Reader* and *The Bridge Called My Back*," *Afro Asia*, 220–255; Maeda, *Rethinking the Asian American Movement*.

18. Maeda, *Chains of Babylon*.

19. Fred Ho, *Wicked Theory, Naked Practice: A Fred Ho Reader*, Ed., Diane C. Fujino (Minneapolis, MN: University of Minnesota Press, 2009); Roger N. Buckley and Tamara Roberts, Eds., *Yellow Power, Yellow Soul: The Radical Art of Fred Ho* (Urbana, IL: University of Illinois, 2013); Deborah Wong, "The Asian American Body in Performance," *Music and the Racial Imagination*, Eds., Ronald Radano and Philip V. Bohlman (Chicago, IL: The University of Chicago Press, 2000), 57–94.

20. Ho, *Wicked Theory, Naked Practice*.

21. Vijay Prashad, "Foreword: 'Bandung Is Done'—Passages in AfroAsian Epistemology," in *AfroAsian Encounters: Culture, History, Politics* (New York: NYU Press, 2006) xi–xxiii; Vijay Prashad, *The Karma of Brown Folk* (Minneapolis, MN: University of Minnesota Press, 2001); Vijay Prashad, *Everybody Was Kung Fu Fighting: Afro-Asian Connections and Myth of Cultural Purity* (Boston, MA: Beacon Press, 2002).

22 Helen Zia, *Asian American Dreams: An Emergence of an American People* (New York: Farrar, Straus, and Giroux, 2000); Scott Kurashige, *The Shifting Grounds of Race: Black and Japanese Americans in the Making of Multiethnic Los Angeles* (Princeton, NJ: Princeton University Press, 2008); Ellen D. Wu, *The Color of Success: Asian Americans and the Origins of Model Minority* (Princeton, NJ: Princeton University Press, 2013).

23 Cheng, *Citizens of Asian America*; Claire Jean Kim, "The Triangulation of Asian Americans," *Politics & Society* 27:1 (1999): 105–138.

24 Zia, *Asian American Dreams*; Claire Jean Kim, *Bitter Fruit: The Politics of Black-Korean Conflict in New York* (New Haven, CT: Yale University Press, 2000); *Sa-I-Gu: From Korean Women's Perspectives*, directed and produced by Dai Sil Kim-Gibson (Center for Asian American Media, 1993); Ishle Yi Park, *The Temperature of This Water* (New York: Kaya Press, 2004).

25 The Editorial Board, "End Mass Incarceration," *The New York Times*, 24 May 2014, accessed February 27, 2015, www.nytimes.com/2014/05/25/opinion/sunday/end-mass-incarceration-now.html; A. J. Vicens, "The Obama Administration's 2 Million Deportation, Explained," *Mother Jones*, 4 April 2014, accessed February 27, 2015, www.motherjones.com/politics/2014/04/obama-administration-record-deportations; "Obama acknowledges rising hate crimes against South Asians in American society," *The Times of India*, 1 May 2013, accessed February 27, 2015, http://timesofindia.indiatimes.com/world/us/Obama-acknowledges-rising-hate-crimes-against-South-Asians-in-American-society/articleshow/19813882.cms; The Stanford University Innovation Lab and the Sikh American Legal Defense and Education Fund, *Turban Myths: The Opportunities and Challenges for Reframing Sikh American Identity in Post-9/11 America* (December 2013), accessed February 27, 2015, http://issuu.com/saldefmedia/docs/turbanmyths_121113.

26 Eric Tang's *Unsettled* is an indispensable book of our time to embolden the strength to go on living in the present in the world where permanent unemployment, criminalization, and extrajudicial killings run deep. It offers a key blueprint to make sense of efforts to carve out the space of freedom and collective resistance for denizens in contemporary urban America who are subjected to the state of unending warfare and captivity. Eric Tang, *Unsettled: Cambodian Refugees in the New York City Hyperghetto* (Philadelphia, PA: Temple University Press, 2015).

27 Bao Phi, "Fong Lee, and Violence," *Star Tribune*, 29 September 2009, accessed February 27, 2015, www.startribune.com/local/yourvoices/62606027.html; Bao Phi, "Fong Lee: The Human Cost and the Strength of His Family," *Star Tribune*, 28 September 2009, accessed February 27, 2015, www.startribune.com/local/yourvoices/103979934.html; Bao Phi, *Sông I Sing: Poems* (Minneapolis, MN: Coffee House Press, 2011); Valarie Kaur, "Why We Must Remember Oak Creek," *Huffington Post*, 5 August 2013, accessed February 27, 2015, www.huffingtonpost.com/valarie-kaur/sikh-shooting-oak-creek_b_3706970.html; Preeti Kaur, "Letters Home," http://phulkari.blogspot.com/2012/08/letters-home.html; Bao Phi, "Letters Home: The Shootings at the Sikh Gurdwara in Oak Creek, Wisconsin," *Star Tribune*, 16 August 2012, accessed February 27, 2015, www.startribune.com/local/yourvoices/166469996.html; Shana L. Redmond, *Anthem: Social Movements and the Sound of Solidarity in the African Diaspora* (New York: NYU Press, 2014); see writings posted on Mitzi Uehara Carter's blog, http://gritsandsushi.com/ and Fredrick Cloyd's blogs, http://ainoko.wordpress.com/ and http://waterchildren.wordpress.com/.

References

Allen, Ernest Jr. "When Japan Was the 'Champion of the Colored Races': Satokata Takahashi and the Flowering of Black Messianic Nationalism." *The Black Scholar* 24 (Winter 1994): 23–46.

American Revolutionary: The Evolution of Grace Lee Boggs. Directed and produced by Grace Lee. LeeLee Films, Inc., 2013.

Balce, Nerissa S. "Filipino Bodies, Lynching, and the Language of Empire." In *Positively No Filipinos Allowed: Building Communities and Discourse*, edited by Antonio T. Tiongson, Jr., Edgardo V. Gutierrez, and Ricardo V. Gutierrez, 43–60. Philadelphia, PA: Temple University Press, 2006.

Baldwin, James. "The International War Crimes Tribunal," in *The Cross of Redemption: Uncollected Writings*, edited by and with an introduction by Randall Kenan, 199–202. New York: Pantheon Books, 2010.

Blain, Keisha N. "'For the Freedom of the Race': Black Women and the Practices of Nationalism, 1929–1945." Ph.D., diss., Princeton University, 2014.

Blain, Keisha N. "'[F]or the Rights of Darker People in Every Party of the World': Pearl Sherrod, Black Internationalist Feminism, and Afro-Asian Politics in the 1930s." *Souls: A Critical Journal of Black Politics, Culture, and Society* (June 2015): 90–112.

Boggs, Grace Lee. *Living for Change: An Autobiography*. Minneapolis, MN: University of Minnesota Press, 1998.

Boggs, Grace Lee, with Scott Kurashige. *The Next American Revolution: Sustainable Activism for the Twenty-First Century*. Berkeley, CA: University of California Press, 2012.

Buckley Roger N., and Tamara Roberts, Eds. *Yellow Power, Yellow Soul: The Radical Art of Fred Ho*. Urbana, IL: University of Illinois, 2013.

Cheng, Cindy I-Fen. *Citizens of Asian America: Democracy and Race during the Cold War*. New York: NYU Press, 2013.

"End Mass Incarceration." *The New York Times*, May 24, 2014, www.nytimes.com/2014/05/25/opinion/sunday/end-mass-incarceration-now.html.

Fujino, Diane C. *Yuri Kochiyama: Heartbeat of Struggle*. Minneapolis, MN: University of Minnesota Press, 2005.

Higashida, Cheryl. "Not Just a 'Special Issue': Gender, Sexuality, and Post-1965 Afro Asian Coalition Building in the *Yardbird Reader* and *The Bridge Called My Back*." In *Afro Asia: Revolutionary Political & Cultural Connections Between African Americans and Asian Americans*, edited by Fred Ho and Bill V. Mullen, 220–255. Durham, NC: Duke University Press, 2008.

Ho, Fred. *Wicked Theory, Naked Practice: A Fred Ho Reader*, edited by Diane C. Fujino. Minneapolis, MN: University of Minnesota Press, 2009.

Horne, Gerald. *Race War! White Supremacy and the Japanese Attack on the British Empire*. New York: NYU Press, 2004.

Kaur, Preeti. "Letters Home," www./phulkari.blogspot.com/2012/08/letters-home.html.

Kaur, Valarie. "Why We Must Remember Oak Creek," *Huffington Post*, 5 August 2013, www.huffingtonpost.com/valarie-kaur/sikh-shooting-oak-creek_b_3706970.html.

Kim, Claire Jean. "The Triangulation of Asian Americans." *Politics & Society* 27:1 (1999): 105–138.

———. *Bitter Fruit: The Politics of Black-Korean Conflict in New York*. New Haven, CT: Yale University Press, 2000.

King, Martin Luther, Jr. "Beyond Vietnam," www.mlk-kpp01.stanford.edu/index.php/encyclopedia/documentsentry/doc_beyond_vietnam/.

Kurashige, Scott. *The Shifting Grounds of Race: Black and Japanese Americans in the Making of Multiethnic Los Angeles*. Princeton, NJ: Princeton University Press, 2008.

Lipsitz, George. "'Frantic to Join . . . the Japanese Army': The Asia Pacific War in the Lives of African American Soldiers and Civilians." In *The Politics of Culture in the Shadow of Capital*, edited by Lisa Lowe and David Lloyd, 324–353. Durham, NC: Duke University Press, 1997.

Maeda, Daryl Joji. *Chains of Babylon: The Rise of Asian America*. Minneapolis, MN: University of Minnesota Press, 2009.

———. *Rethinking the Asian American Movement*. New York: Routledge, 2011.

Marasigan, Cynthia L. "'Between the Devil and the Deep Blue Sea': Ambivalence, Violence, and African American Soldiers in the Philippine-American War and Its Aftermath." Ph.D., diss., University of Michigan, 2000.

"Obama acknowledges rising hate crimes against South Asians in American society." *The Times of India*, May 1, 2013, www.timesofindia.indiatimes.com/world/us/Obama-acknowledges-rising-hate-crimes-against-South-Asians-in-American-society/articleshow/19813882.cms.

Park, Ishle Yi. *The Temperature of This Water*. New York: Kaya Press, 2004.

Phi, Bao. "Fong Lee: The Human Cost and the Strength of His Family," *Star Tribune*, September 28, 2009, www.startribune.com/local/yourvoices/103979934.html.

———. "Fong Lee, and Violence." *Star Tribune*, September 29, 2009, www.startribune.com/local/yourvoices/62606027.html.

———. *Sông I Sing: Poems*. Minneapolis: Coffee House Press, 2011.

———. "Letters Home: The Shootings at the Sikh Gurdwara in Oak Creek, Wisconsin," *Star Tribune*, August 16, 2012, www.startribune.com/local/yourvoices/166469996.html.

Prashad, Vijay. *The Karma of Brown Folk*. Minneapolis, MN: University of Minnesota Press, 2001.

Prashad, Vijay. *Everybody Was Kung Fu Fighting: Afro-Asian Connections and Myth of Cultural Purity*. Boston, MA: Beacon Press, 2002.

———. "Foreword: 'Bandung Is Done'—Passages in AfroAsian Epistemology." In *AfroAsian Encounters: Culture, History, Politics*, edited by Heike Raphael-Hernandez and Shannon Steen, xi–xxiii. New York: NYU Press, 2006.

Redmond, Shana L. *Anthem: Social Movements and the Sound of Solidarity in the African Diaspora*. New York: NYU Press, 2014.

Robinson, Greg. *After Camp: Portraits in Midcentury Japanese American Life and Politics*. Berkeley, CA: University of California Press, 2012.

Sa-I-Gu: From Korean Women's Perspectives. Directed and produced by Dai Sil Kim-Gibson Center for Asian American Media, 1993

The Stanford University Innovation Lab and the Sikh American Legal Defense and Education Fund, *Turban Myths: The Opportunities and Challenges for Reframing Sikh American Identity in Post-9/11 America* (December 2013), www.issuu.com/saldefmedia/docs/turbanmyths_121113.

Tang, Eric. *Unsettled: Cambodian Refugees in the New York City Hyperghetto*. Philadelphia, PA: Temple University Press, 2015.

Vicens, A. J. "The Obama Administration's 2 Million Deportation, Explained." *Mother Jones*, April 4, 2014, www.motherjones.com/politics/2014/04/obama-administration-record-deportations.

Widener, Daniel. "Seoul City Sue and the Bugout Blues: Black American Narratives of the Forgotten War." In *Afro Asia: Revolutionary Political & Cultural Connections Between African Americans and Asian Americans*, edited by Fred Ho and Bill V. Mullen, 55–90. Durham, NC: Duke University Press, 2008.

Wong, Deborah. "The Asian American Body in Performance." In *Music and the Racial Imagination*, edited by Ronald Radano and Philip V. Bohlman, 57–94. Chicago, IL: The University of Chicago Press, 2000.

Wu, Ellen D. *The Color of Success: Asian Americans and the Origins of Model Minority*. Princeton, NJ: Princeton University Press, 2013.

Wu, Judy Tzu-Chun. *Radicals on the Road: Internationalism, Orientalism, and Feminism during the Viet Nam Era*. Ithaca, NY: Cornell University Press, 2013.

Zia, Helen. *Asian American Dreams: An Emergence of an American People*. New York: Farrar, Straus, and Giroux, 2000.

25

THE POLITICAL PARTICIPATION OF ASIAN AMERICANS

Pei-te Lien

For most Americans, political participation is the other name for voting and elections. For Asian Americans, it refers to a multifaceted and evolving phenomenon where practice of nonvoting forms of political participation precedes voting and continues to serve as an important means of civic engagement for those who cannot or opt not to access the ballot. Research in American political behavior generally emphasizes the role of basic socioeconomic status such as education and income, other political resources such as time and civic skills, political interest and engagement, and political mobilization and contacts in determining the extent of voting and other acts of political participation (Verba, Scholzman, and Brady 1995). Although these factors have been found to influence Asian American voting behavior, for the majority members of the community who were not U.S.-born, their voting and other participation are additionally impacted by international migration-related factors such as country of birth, age of migration, length of U.S. residency, English proficiency, and maintaining contacts with the home country. These differences between Asian and non-Asian Americans are important to keep in mind as we appraise the development and current status of their political participation.

Early Forms of Nonvoting Political Participation

Compared to other major racial groups in the United States, Asian Americans have a particularly difficult time gaining access to the ballot because of restrictions set by the legislative and judicial branches of the U.S. government to block their immigration and naturalization. Before 1952, not all Asian nationals were able to petition for becoming citizens through naturalization, and it was only with the lifting of national origin quota restrictions in 1965 that Asian nationals were able to receive an equal opportunity to apply for an entry visa. During the prolonged era of immigration exclusion and political discrimination, groups of immigrant laborers and their leaders managed to flex their political muscles by forming umbrella community organizations and challenged almost every unjust law and policy through the American court system (Chan 1991; McClain 1994). They not only fought for the rights to enter and stay; they also battled for the rights to receive equal education, own business and property, and to marry outside of one's race. In the process, they also lobbied elected officials, rallied against ethnic violence, staged strikes for workers' rights, and raised funds for homeland liberation and moderation projects (Lien 2001).

In the 1960 U.S. Census, Asian Americans were less than one percent of the population and the majority of them were born in the United States and of Japanese, Chinese, or Filipino descent. These English-speaking, U.S.-born college students, social activists, and community youth formed the first stage of the Asian American Movement between 1968 and 1975 (Wei 1993; Liu, Geron, and Lai 2008; Maeda 2012). In the aftermath of the black civil rights movement and inspired by the black liberation movement, these young Asian Americans protested against the Vietnam War, participated in the San Francisco State strike that led to the nation's first ethnic studies program, and demanded fundamental social change to "serve the people." The term "Asian American" was coined out of an awakened racial consciousness and aspiration for the "yellow power" of the time to promote social justice, self-determination, and community empowerment. Another primary purpose of the creation of the panethnic group label was to help bond together a small, marginalized, and fragmented population of multiple origins and backgrounds. Although the end of the Vietnam War, economic recession, and the corporate offensive seemed to have beheaded the first and radical phase of the movement, some scholars insist that the Asian American movement has lived on and been reincarnated in numerous community-based organizations and campaigns for justice, equality, and empowerment, but under more mellow, sophisticated, and professional operations (Lien 2001; Liu, Geron, and Lai 2008). Given a changed political climate, many movement activists turned their fervor for grassroots community-based political activism to mainstream electoral politics.

Early Participation in Electoral Politics

Asian American involvement in electoral politics can be traced back to 1917 in Hawaii, where the Republican Party reached out to recruit second-generation Japanese American (Nisei) members (Hosakawa 1969). By 1922, when the first Nisei ran for office, Japanese American voters were 3.5 percent of the electorate in Hawaii. The percentage of the electorate who was Japanese rose to 31 percent in 1940 when 15.6 percent of the legislators elected to the Territorial House were Nisei (Haas 1992). Although all Nisei legislators were removed from office during WWII, they were able to recapture nearly all of the seats back in the first post-war election. Entry of heroic Nisei WWII veterans into the political arena helped significantly increase the Asian presence in Hawaiian politics, especially after the Democratic Revolution of 1954. Asian Americans have since occupied more than half of the leadership positions in the state legislature as president of the Senate, Speaker of the House, Majority and Minority Whips, and chairs of key committees of the island state. They have also been consistent in sending/returning representatives to both chambers of the U.S. Congress. Until his death in December 2012, Hon. Daniel Inoyue was the first U.S. Representative in 1959 and then the first U.S. Senator from the Aloha state for the next 50 years. Another political pioneer from Hawaii, Hon. Patsy Mink, was not only the first U.S. woman of color elected to Congress, she was noted for being a principal co-author and co-sponsor of the Title IX Amendment of the Higher Education Act of 1972 which prohibited gender discrimination in any education program or activity funded by the federal government. It was renamed the Patsy Mink Equal Opportunity in Education Act of 2002 to commemorate her premature death in that year.

On the U.S mainland, Asian Americans did not begin to run for public offices with some frequency and success until the 1970s. Their difficult start may be "directly attributed to a historically hostile racial environment and racist policies preventing immigration, public employment, equal education, citizenship, and voting" (Lien 2001, 96). Those who did run were often progressive in orientation and of Japanese or Chinese descent. When Wing F. Ong of Phoenix, AZ won a seat in the state house in 1946, he not only scored a monumental first in the electoral history of mainland Asians, he also set an example of winning high electoral office with an immigrant background and without a large number of ethnic votes (Nagasawa 1986). The majority of Asian Americans elected officials on the mainland prior to the 1970s were elected in California and of U.S.-birth, however.

Contemporary Patterns of Participation as Candidates and Elected Officials

With the advent of minority rights and the influx of well-educated and skilled immigrants from Asia made possible by the passages of landmark legislation in the mid-1960s,[1] Asian Americans on the mainland began to emerge as voters, candidates, campaign donors and volunteers, and elected officials in the 1970s and onward. Beginning in 1978, when such statistics were available, and until 2014, the number of Asian American elected officials expands from 120 to over 750. The growth rate is particularly sharp at the local level, where about two-thirds of (non-judicial) elected officials served in county and municipal governments as well as on education or school boards. Today, although those in Hawaii and California continue to dominate the electoral scene, increasingly more electoral victories are scored by Asians residing east of California, in campaigns for higher or more prominent offices, by individuals with other ethnic origins than Japanese or Chinese, and from Asian-influenced suburbs where trans-pacific capital and immigration have transformed ethnic enclaves into global cities (Lien 2001; Li 2008; Lai 2011). Consistent with the transformation observed in other groups of women of color, Asian American women have led the pace of recent growth and become regulars as political candidates and public officials. In 1985 women were 16 percent of APAs in office (Chu 1989), in 2014 it was doubled to 31 percent (Filler and Lien 2016). Although women's share of elective office-holding has increased over time, substantial gender gaps still exist.

Another enduring feature from surveying the population of APAs holding elective offices nationwide in the second decade of the 21st century is that, despite the community's long history of settlement since 1763, there are still many stories of political firsts—not unlike the legacy set by Rep. Wing F. Ong. In January 2013, when Senator Mazie Keiko Hirono (D-Hawaii) was sworn in office, she became the first Asian American woman, the first Buddhist, and the first Japan-born to serve in U.S. Senate. Hirono moved with her mother to Hawaii at age 8 and did not speak nor read English when she began elementary school. Representatives Tammy Duckworth (D-IL) and Tulsi Gabbard (D-HI) are both the first female combat veterans in Congress. Duckworth is also the first disabled woman and Thailand-born Chinese American, while Gabbard the first Hindu as well as the first Samoan American voting member, in Congress. One other new member in the Asian American congressional delegate of 2013 is former State Assemblywoman Grace Meng (D-NY), who became the first Taiwanese American female and Asian American member of Congress elected from the East Coast. Also taking office in January. 2013 is retired heart surgeon Dr. Shanti Gandhi, who arrived in 1967 to take a medical internship, becoming the first India-born and Indian American state legislator in Kansas. Meanwhile, Councilman Blong Yang, who was born in a refugee camp in Thailand and moved to America at age 3 in 1980, became the first Hmong American on the Minneapolis City Council. Across the nation, Saigon-born Tri Ta who moved with his family to the U.S. at age 19 became the first elected Vietnamese American mayor in Westminster, CA. In December 2012, former vice mayor Rob Bonta, who immigrated at age 2 from the Philippines, became the first Filipino American elected to the California State Legislature in its 163-year history. He followed the footpaths of two trail blazers in the Bay Area who made electoral history as they became two big city mayors in 2011. Former councilwoman Jean Quan became the first woman and Asian American elected to head the city hall of Oakland, CA, while former city administrator Ed Lee was first appointed then elected mayor of San Francisco. Lee, born to immigrant parents from southern China, is the first Asian American holding this post in a city that has had a prolonged history of Chinese exclusion.

The individuals named above are just a small sample of the roughly 400 (non-judicial) elected officials of API descent serving in various levels of U.S. government nationwide as of August 2014. On the one hand, their monumental success in the political arena symbolizes the viability of the American Dream, even for first-generation immigrants. The fact that close to two-fifths of the 2014 class are Asian-born—which is a lot higher than the 8 percent found among Latino elected officials in the Gender and Multicultural Leadership (GMCL) survey— also seems to support the idea of Asian Americans being a rather different and overall successful minority community (Hardy-Fanta, Lien, Pinderhughes, and Sierra 2016). On the other hand, given the community's prolonged history of engagement with the U.S. government and society, one has to wonder why Asian Americans are still considered political newcomers in so many American places. To what extent have they become politically incorporated as voters and why? What changes have occurred over time? What is their evidence of political participation other than voting and elections? In the remainder of the chapter, we begin to answer these questions by providing a brief overview of the demographic characteristics of the population. Employing the concept of voting as a three-step process, we discuss their current status of voting and registration as a whole and trends in the number and percentage share of the U.S. electorate over time. This is followed by a brief discussion of their patterns of participation beyond voting as well as their political orientations in terms of partisanship, ideology, and presidential vote. Last but not least, we discuss immigrants' participation in home country politics.

Demography is Destiny

A key reason to explain the political novice image of Asian Americans in the second decade of the 21st century is the group's distinction as the only major U.S. ethnoracial group dominated continuously by the foreign-born. Foreign-born persons constituted 32 percent among Asians in 1960, but they jumped to 59 percent in 1980 and 69 percent in 2000 (Lien 2011). In 2010, the 68 percent foreign-born rate among Asians was more than five times the national average of 13 percent and substantially above the 47 percent among Latinos. Among those migrated from Asia, over one-third (36 percent) entered in the year 2000 or later and another 27 percent entered between 1990 and 1999 (Grieco et al. 2014). Although this distribution by year-of-entry is similar to the national average, Asians' overall naturalization rate of 58 percent is only second to that among Europeans. In fact, when year-of-entry is controlled, Asian-born persons are found to have the highest naturalization rates in each entry cohort—92 percent among those arrived before 1980, 86 percent among those entered in the 1980s, and 67 percent among those entered in the 1990s. Despite their relatively fast pace of political assimilation through naturalization, close to half (46 percent) of foreign-born Asians reported speaking a language other than English at home and did not speak English "very well." The same study also finds nearly half (48 percent) of them completed a bachelor's degree or higher, a figure substantially larger than the national average of 27 percent among all foreign-born persons in 2010.

After the lifting of racist quotas in the 1965 Immigration Act, a steady stream of migration from Asia in the following decades not only helps account for the predominance of the foreign-born, it also helps explain the rapid growth of the population. Between 2000 and 2010, those identified as Asian alone or in combination with another race or races grew by 46 percent, which is faster than any other racial group and more than four times the national average of 9.7 percent (Hoeffel et al. 2012). About half of the nation's 17.3 million Asians in 2010 resided in the West, with over 5.5 million calling it home in California alone. Asians in the South, however, experienced the highest rate of growth over the decade. As in the recent past, New York City is found to be the nation's largest Asian American city and, with 68.2 percent of the population who were Asians alone or in combination in 2010, Honolulu continues to lead the nation in terms of the Asian share of the population in a U.S. city. Only two cities in Mainland U.S. were majority-Asian in 2010 and both are located in Northern California—the Asian share of the population was 58 percent in Daly City and 54.5 percent in Fremont.

In the end, although Asians experienced the nation's highest population growth rate in the first decade of the 21st century and they enjoyed leading positions in rates of naturalization and educational attainment, the community was no more than 6 percent of the U.S. population and the majority was not U.S.-born. Their ability to alter the U.S. political landscape is further complicated by geographic diversity as well as ethnic, income, and cultural diversity. In addition to being numerically small and geographically dispersed and unevenly distributed across the states, there are 23 distinct Asian ethnic groups enumerated in the 2010 U.S. Census. As suggested by the title of a major report released by a leading community organization, Asian Americans is a community of contrasts in every measurable way (Asian American Justice Center 2012). The rapid expansion of the population and the heterogeneity across ethnic groups have presented mounting challenges to the construction of a pan-Asian identity and unified political look. However, the emergence of Asian-influenced suburbs has also resulted in the formation of new political loci such as panethnic community-based organizations and ethnic media to facilitate local political incorporation (Lai 2011).

Present-day Participation in Voting and Other Political Activities

Quantitative studies of political participation in the American context typically emphasize the central importance of basic socioeconomic status. According to this theory, relatively affluent groups like Asian Americans should be accorded with relatively higher levels of voting and other acts of political participation. Socioeconomic class matters, for it influences access to political resources such as money, time, knowledge, and civic skills. In a sense, when examining only the behavior of Asian American voting-age citizens, there is empirical evidence to suggest that persons with better education and higher family income are also more likely to become registered, to report voting in elections, and to participate more frequently in activities other than voting, including writing or phoning a government official, donating money to a campaign, signing a petition for a political cause, taking part in a protest or demonstration, and other types of activities. However, when comparing the voting behavior of Asian American adults to that of other major American ethno-racial groups, past research also suggests that socioeconomic status plays a much weaker role in structuring the behavior of Asian Americans than of whites, blacks, or Latinos (Lien et al. 2001; Lien, Conway, and Wong 2004). A major explanation for this lies in the group's demography.

Because presently as many as three-fourths of voting-age Asian Americans were born outside of the United States, their ability to participate fully in the U.S. electoral process needs to be understood as a three-step process (Lien et al. 2001). In order to physically cast a ballot in an election, a foreign-born person who resides permanently in the United States must engage in the process of becoming naturalized first, followed by becoming registered to vote, and by casting a ballot either in person or via postal service before Election Day. A set of barriers or costs is involved at each step of the process. For those immigrants who have survived the naturalization process, their franchise can be wasted by their failure to become registered to vote, which is a procedure foreign to many Asian immigrants. Registering to vote and casting a vote, either in person or by mail, may be particularly onerous in a referendum-heavy state such as California, where an estimated 40 percent of the Asian American population lives. When adding to the equation such unique factors as language barriers, lack of familiarity with the American system, social discrimination, and economic hardship for working-class immigrants, it comes as little surprise that Asian Americans have one of the lowest citizenship, voting registration, and turnout rates among voting-age persons in the United States.

An analysis of the U.S. Census Current Population Survey Voting Supplement (CPS–VS) data of the November 2012 elections shows that, among voting-age persons, 68 percent of Asians as compared to 98 percent of (non-Latino) whites and 94 percent of blacks were U.S. citizens. As high as 58 percent among Asians, but only 3 percent among whites and 7 percent among blacks, acquired U.S. citizenship by naturalization. Among voting-age persons, only 39 percent of Asians as compared to 72 percent of whites were registered to vote. The registration gap between the two racial groups narrows to 17 percentage points when counting only among holders of U.S. citizenship, which is a prerequisite of voter registration. Whereas only one-third among voting-age Asians reported voting in the elections, as compared to 63 percent among voting-age whites and 62 percent among voting-age blacks, as high as 84 percent of Asians who were registered to vote turned out to vote—a rate that is only three percentage points below the national average. This exercise shows that, by taking into consideration layers of legal barriers to exercising the franchise, Asian Americans not only are not the perpetual underachiever in voting, but that their turnout rate could be nearly as high as mainstream American voters. In fact, analysis of voting rates by Asian ethnic origins shows that 87 percent of Japanese and Asian Indian Americans who were registered to vote turned out to vote in the November 2012 elections, which is the same rate for whites. Even the 82 percent turnout rate among registered Filipino and Korean Americans, which is the lowest of all major Asian ethnic groups, is only five percentage points lower than the white rate.

Studying the long-term trend of voting participation of Asian Americans as compared to other major racial groups since 1994, when the U.S. Census Bureau started to collect information for the Asian race in its CPS–VS data series, shows that voting-age Asians accounted for 2.5 percent of the U.S. voting-age population in 1994 (Lien 2011). Within 18 years, voting-age Asians grew by 179 percent to 5.7 percent of the U.S. voting-age population in 2012. In contrast, white voting-age persons only grew by seven percentage points in the period. A similar but less impressive growth rate is found regarding Asian Americans' share of the U.S. electorate. In 1994, Asian American voters were merely 1.2 percent of U.S. voters. That figure increased to 3.3 percent in 2012. The 116 percent growth rate is far higher than the 89 percent among Latinos, 46 percent among blacks, or 10 percent among whites in the same period. Nonetheless, despite their most impressive growth rates, Asian Americans' share of the U.S. electorate is still significantly below its population share in the second decade of the 21st century.

In addition to voting, Asian Americans are involved in a variety of political and civic activities that do not require U.S. citizenship but may require more time, skills, knowledge, and interest. As a result, in a pre-2012 election survey conducted by Ramakrishnan and Lee (2012), relatively few Asian Americans are found to participate in activities such as donating to a campaign (11 percent), writing or phoning a government official (11 percent), or visiting online sites (8 percent). Still fewer report taking part in a protest or demonstration (5 percent) or working on a political campaign or other electoral activities (5 percent). However, more than half (55 percent) report having engaged in political discussion with others. Similar patterns are found in surveys conducted for the 2000 and 2008 election cycles (Lien, Conway, and Wong 2004; Wong et al. 2011). In these two prior surveys, about one in five (21 percent) also report having worked with others in the community to solve a problem. Ethnic communities differ in their frequencies of participation regarding most modes of participation beyond voting. For example, in both 2000 and 2008, about one-fourth of Asian Indian and Filipino Americans report having volunteered to work on community problems. In all three election cycles, a higher percentage of Japanese Americans than other Asian Americans report making donations to political campaigns, even if the proportion is no higher than one in five. In addition, a higher percentage of Vietnamese Americans than other Asian Americans report having participated in protest rallies, even if that proportion is no higher than one in ten. Yet, recent observations made regarding the less studied refugee communities such as Cambodian and Hmong Americans also show their frequencies of participation in non-voting forms of political participation to be little different from most other Asian American groups.

Political Preferences: Political Partisanship, Political Ideology, and Presidential Vote

Being stereotyped as the inscrutable and alien race, Asian Americans' political preferences have been the subject of much (wrongful) speculation until recent years, after the emergence of large-scale, scientifically designed, national opinion surveys centering on the Asian population. From these and other survey data that include a significant number of Asians in the pool of respondents, we now have a clearer picture of the political party affiliation, political ideology, and presidential vote choice of this rising community in American mainstream politics.

Political Party Affiliation

Political party identification is traditionally the most reliable and important measure of political behavior. Extensive research done with American voters as a whole has found party identity to be a strong predictor of their candidate choice, political ideology, and issue position. Targeted research on Asian Americans affirms the utility of the party concept in studying their voting behavior—i.e., Republican/Democratic identifiers would be more supportive of Republican/Democratic candidates and the respective party platform; voters with a stronger sense of partisanship are more likely to turn out and vote than those with a weaker sense of partisanship. However, these observations are made only among those Asians who identify with mainstream American parties. The challenge in understanding the political behavior of voting-age Asian Americans is that about half of them do not identify with either of the major American parties. This is one of the major findings in the 2000–2001 Pilot National Asian American Political Survey (PNAAPS), which is the nation's first multiethnic, multilingual, and multisite survey on the political attitudes and behavior of Asian Americans. It is reaffirmed in the National Asian American Survey (NAAS) conducted in the 2008 and 2012 election cycles. This suggests that studying the reasons for the acquisition of major partisanship among this majority immigrant population is at least as important as understanding the direction of their partisan affiliation and the volatility in their nonpartisan orientation (Hajnal and Lee 2011; Harvie and Lien 2016).

In general, about one in three Asian American adults identify themselves as Democrat and one in seven as Republican. The highest share of Republican identifiers is recorded at 29 percent among Vietnamese Americans in 2008 and 27 percent among Filipino Americans in 2012. For both election cycles, the highest shares of Democratic identifiers are found among Asian Indian Americans and Korean Americans. The Democratic share in both communities was about two in five in 2008, which increased to about one in two in 2012. However, when Pacific Islanders and smaller Southeast Asian groups are included in the survey, both Samoan Americans and Hmong Americans are found to have higher shares of Democratic identifiers, at 57 percent and 52 percent respectively. Whereas only 26 percent of Cambodian Americans think of themselves as Democrats, up to 68 percent among them do not identify with any political party. In 2012, as many as 64 percent of Vietnamese and 58 percent of Chinese respondents also identify themselves as nonpartisans.

Political Ideology

Whereas prior research shows that about half of Asian American adults do not identify with the two major parties, they seem to have less of a problem describing their political orientation with American mainstream political ideological labels. In the Pew Asian American Survey of 2012, 31 percent describe their political views as liberal, 24 percent indicate they are conservative, and 37 percent indicate they are moderate; only 8 percent do not know. This distribution is quite similar to the PNAAPS findings for the 2000 election cycle, as well as in other endeavors to gauge ethnic public opinion where Asian Americans are found to lean left and be more liberal than conservative in political orientation. In a daily tracking poll conducted by Gallup for the entire year of 2009 (Jones 2010), Asian Americans are found to be the only major U.S. racial and ethnic group to have a higher proportion of liberals than conservatives (31 percent vs. 21 percent). However, a higher proportion of Asians than any other racial group also call themselves politically moderate. These statistics seem to explain the political behavior of Asian Americans being simultaneously Democratic-leaning in partisanship, lacking identification with the major parties as a whole, while willing to lend support to a more activist government in providing social services to immigrants and language minorities in principle and the general goal of affirmative action in helping eradicate social inequality.

Presidential Vote

Another key research attention to Asian Americans' political participation is their vote for the U.S. presidents. In the NAAS of 2008, 41 percent of Asian Americans indicated their likelihood to favor Barack Obama, 24 percent for John McCain, while the rest were undecided. The same study finds that the majority of Asian Americans who voted in the 2008 primary elections supported candidate Clinton over candidate Obama by a nearly 2-to-1 margin. In the 2008 general elections, national exit polls sponsored by the mainstream media found Asian American voters to have supported Barack Obama over John McCain by a roughly 2-to-1 margin. In the 2012 general elections, President Obama increased his vote share among Asian Americans by receiving 73 percent of their vote, which was 20 percentage points above the national average vote for Obama.

This pattern of a clear edge of Democratic Party candidates among Asian American voters nationwide was first systematically studied in the 2000–2001 PNAAPS. Among Asian American voters in the November 2000 elections, 55 percent report having cast a vote for Democratic candidate Al Gore and 26 percent for Republican candidate George Bush. Across Asian American groups, the percentages of voters favoring candidate Gore ranged from as high as 64 percent among the Chinese to as low as 44 percent among Korean Americans. In the NAAS of 2008, at least eight in ten Asian Indian, Cambodian, and Hmong American voters cast their vote for Democratic candidate Barack Obama, while close to half of Filipino and Vietnamese American voters cast their vote for Republican candidate John McCain. Nonetheless, the Democratic candidate received a higher proportion of the vote than the Republican opponent from each of the Asian groups in both 2000 and 2008 elections. Similar ethnic patterns are found among likely voters in the NAAS of 2012, too.

Participation in Home Country Politics

Because of overt American racism and nativism prior to the mid-1960s, which severely limited the opportunities of social and political incorporation for nonwhite immigrants, groups of Asian immigrants drew on a complicated network of transnational resources to fight racial injustice in the U.S. immigration, social, legal, and political system, to negotiate their identities between being Asian and being American, and to help improve the political and economic status of the homeland in the process (Chan 2006; Collet and Lien 2009). The overseas diaspora in the United States maintained, in turn, a prolonged and tenacious but also shifting relationship with the ethnic homeland through various transnational projects such as homeland modernization, defense, liberalization, and democratization. Particularly significant in volume and frequency are political donations, which began with giving money to political factions that had established an extensive presence in Chinese America and peaked in the eight year-long Chinese war against Japanese aggression. Similarly, early Korean and Asian Indian immigrants actively supported the homeland independence movements and attempted to influence U.S. foreign policy toward the empires of Japan and Great Britain, respectively. On the other hand, lacking power and in search of tactical resources, Japanese American immigrants in the early 20th century formed a strategic alliance with the homeland government and the social elite in Japan to combat one of California's defining acts of institutional racism: the Alien Land Law of 1913 (Azuma 2005).

In the age of global economic restructuring and waves of democratization, the frequency and variety of transnational political activities engaged in by Asian Americans only seem to have increased in the post-1965 era. Treating the pursuit of democracy in the Asian homeland as an equally important project as the protection of their civil rights in the United States, Filipino Americans organized opposition across the Pacific with Filipino nationals in the 1970s and 1980s to overthrow Philippines President Ferdinand Marcos (Espiritu 2009). Around the same time, Taiwanese Americans lobbied the U.S. Congress and worked in concert with Taiwan's *danwai* (outside of the party) elites to push for political liberalization and a democratic form of government (Lien 2007). During the Kwangju democracy movement in South Korea in 1980, Korean American students staged several rallies in Koreatown and sit-in demonstrations in front of the Korean Consulate in Los Angeles to protest against the corrupt homeland government (Chang 1988). They were part of the transnational and cross-ethnic political coalitions that helped Rep. Mike Honda (D-CA) to introduce U.S. House Resolution 121, that demands Japan's government to offer an official apology and for "comfort women" kidnapped in Korea, China, and Southeast Asia by the Imperial Army during WWII (Collet and Lien 2009). Following the collapse of the Vietnamese economy in the early 1980s, refugees from Vietnam in the United States built a transnational grassroots movement to counter but also to negotiate with the former adversary of the Communist Party in Vietnam (Furuya and Collet 2009). Prior to the signing of the India–U.S. Civil Nuclear Deal in 2006, Asian Indian American groups actively lobbied U.S. Congress to make an exception for India, a country that refused to sign the Nuclear Nonproliferation Treaty, from U.S. laws limiting trade in nuclear technology—a deal that promised to forge a closer relationship between the homeland and the hostland governments (Misha 2009).

Despite the centrality of transnational political activism to the development of Asian America, very few immigrants from Asia are found to be directly involved in home country politics after arriving in the United States. Only 6 percent among the 2000–2001 and 4 percent among the 2008 Asian American survey respondents indicate their participation in such direct activism across the Pacific. Instead, they showed substantially higher interest in following news dealing with politics and people in their home countries. In both 2000–2001 and 2012, when such statistics were available, just over half of Asian Americans indicated following closely political news of their country of origin. In both surveys, the percentages of respondents indicating having followed such news ranged from two in five among Japanese Americans to two in three among Chinese Americans. In 2012, around half of Vietnamese, Korean, and Filipino Americans, but fewer than one in three Asian Indian and Cambodian Americans, reported having followed closely news regarding their country of origin. Hmong Americans rank at the bottom, with only 12 percent reported having followed political news of the home country. Similar ethnic ranking order is found regarding the level of attention to news on U.S. foreign policy toward the home country.

Last but not least, does involvement in homeland society and politics take away interest in participating in U.S. elections? Past research has found that incidences of participation in homeland politics after an immigrant's arrival in the United States do not have a significant relationship to his or her acquisition of United States citizenship or voting (Lien 2006, 2010; Lien and Wong 2009). An immigrant's political activism prior to emigration also does not have a significant relationship to his or her rate of naturalization, voting, or participation beyond voting. Nonetheless, an immigrant's participation in homeland politics after arriving in the United States has a positive and significant relationship to his or her incidence of participation in politics beyond voting as well as to his or her participation in ethnic community organizations or related activities in the United States. This last set of relationships does not change after controlling for an assortment of possible confounding factors related to transnational political participation, such as transnational social, cultural, and political ties, degree of social and political incorporation, and personal skills and resources related to international migration. Thus, everything else being equal, an immigrant's engagement in homeland politics is associated with a greater, not lower, likelihood to participate in non-electoral activities in the United States, while it has no significant impact on voter registration and voting. These results clearly show not only that an immigrant's connections with his or her country of origin do not take place at the expense of his or her voting participation in the United States, but that there may be a complementary relationship to political activities beyond voting.

Conclusion

From exclusion to inclusion, from practices of nonvoting to electoral forms of political participation, from grassroots to mainstream platforms of politics, and from U.S. domestic to transnational political arena, Asian Americans have maintained a prolonged, multifaceted, varied, but overall growing relationships with the U.S. polity and society in its over 250 years of community history. After the lifting of restrictions to their immigration and voting rights in the mid-1960s, Asian Americans have experienced exponential growth in population size from international migration which, in turn, has contributed to the further diversification of the multiethnic community. At the beginning of the second decade of the 21st century, the community leads the nation in terms of its foreign-born share of the population, the pace of naturalization among the foreign-born, as well as the overall growth in population size and share of the U.S. electorate. Although the community has gained significant visibility and influence in U.S. society and politics in recent decades, substantial barriers remain for Asian Americans to exercise franchise and there are still substantial gender gaps among elected officials in the present day. In addition, Asian Americans continue to suffer a lack of parity in voting participation and political representation. The mixed assessment of their political incorporation points to the need for persistent and on-going efforts in citizenship education, voter education, and leadership development. It also underscores the need for strengthening the community infrastructure for political mobilization (such as panethnic organizations, community-based party or candidate organizations, and the ethnic media) so as to facilitate the translation of demographic gains into political gains.

Notes

1 This refers to the Civil Rights Act of 1964, the Immigration Act of 1965, and the Voting Rights Act of 1965.

References

Asian American Justice Center. 2012. *A Community of Contrasts: Asian Americans in the United States 2011.* Washington, DC: Asian American Center for Advancing Justice.

Azuma, Eiichiro. 2005. *Between Two Empires: Race, History, and Transnationalism in Japanese America.* New York: Oxford University Press.

Chan, Sucheng. 1991. *Asian Americans: An Interpretive History.* Boston, MA: Twayne Publishers.

———. Ed. 2006. *Chinese American Transnationalism: The Flow of People, Resources, and Ideas Between China and America During the Exclusion Era.* Philadelphia, PA: Temple University Press.

Chang, Edward. 1988. "Korean Community Politics in Los Angeles: The Impact of the Kwangju Uprising." *Amerasia Journal* 14 (1): 51–67.

Chu, Judy. 1989. "Asian Pacific American Women in Mainstream Politics." 405–421 in Asian Women United of California Eds., *Making Waves: An Anthology of Writings by and about Asian American Women.* Boston, MA: Beacon Press.

Collet, Christian, and Pei-te Lien. Eds. 2009. *The Transnational Politics of Asian Americans.* Philadelphia, PA: Temple University Press.

Espiritu, Augusto. 2009. "Journeys of Discovery and Difference: Transnational Politics and the Union of Democratic Filipinos." 64–93 in Christian Collet and Pei-te Lien Eds., *The Transnational Politics of Asian Americans.* Philadelphia, PA: Temple University Press.

Filler, Nicole, and Pei-te Lien. 2016. "Asian Pacific Americans in U.S. Politics: Gender and Pathways to Elected Office." 218–233 in Nadia Brown and Sarah Allen Gershon Eds., *Distinct Identities: Minority Women in U.S. Politics.* New York: Routledge.

Furuya, Hiroko, and Christian Collet. 2009. "Contested Nation: Vietnam and the Emergence of Saigon Nationalism in the United States." 94–118 in Christian Collet and Pei-te Lien Eds., *The Transnational Politics of Asian Americans.* Philadelphia, PA: Temple University Press.

Grieco, Elizabeth, Yesenia Acosta, Patricia de la Cruz, Christine Gambino, Tom Gryn, Luke Larsen, Edward Trevelyan, and Nathan Walters. 2014. *Foreign-Born Population of the United States: 2012.* Washington, DC: Bureau of the Census, CB14-TPS.44.

Haas, Michael. 1992. *Institutional Racism: The Case of Hawaii.* Westport, CT: Praeger.

Hajnal, Zoltan, and Taeku Lee. 2011. *Why Americans Don't Join the Party: Race, Immigration, and the Failure (of Political Parties) to Engage the Electorate.* Princeton, NJ: Princeton University Press.

Hardy-Fanta, Carol, Pei-te Lien, Dianne Pinderhughes, and Christine Sierra. 2016. *Contested Transformation: Race, Gender and Political Leadership in Twenty-First Century America.* New York: Cambridge University Press.

Harvie, Jeanette Yih, and Pei-te Lien. 2016. "Minority Voting in the United States: East Asian Americans." 283–303 in Kyle Kreider and Thomas Baldino Eds., *Minority Voting in the United States,* Vol. 2. Praeger.

Hoeffel, Elizabeth, Sonya Rastogi, Myoung Ouk Kim, and Hasan Shahid. 2012. *The Asian Population: 2010.* Washington: Bureau of the Census, 2010 Census Briefs, C2010BR-11.

Hosakawa, Bill. 1969. *Nisei: The Quiet Americans, the Story of a People.* New York: Morrow.

Jones, Jeffrey M. 2010. "Asian Americans Lean Left Politically: Asian Americans More Liberal Than Other Racial/Ethnic Groups." www.gallup.com/poll/125579/asian-americans-lean-left-politically.aspx. (accessed October 18, 2016)

Lai, James. 2011. *Asian American Political Actions: Suburban Transformations.* Boulder, CO: Lynn Rienner Publishers.

Li, Wei. 2008. *Ethnoburb: The New Ethnic Community in Urban America.* Honolulu, HI: University of Hawaii Press.

Lien, Pei-te. 2001. *The Making of Asian America Through Political Participation*. Philadelphia, PA: Temple University Press.
———. 2004. "Asian Americans and Voting Participation: Comparing Racial and Ethnic Differences in Recent U.S. Elections." *International Migration Review* 38 (2): 493–517.
———. 2006. "Transnational Homeland Concerns and Participation in U.S. Politics: A Comparison Among Immigrants from China, Taiwan, and Hong Kong." *Journal of Chinese Overseas* 2 (1): 56–78.
———. 2007. "Ethnic Homeland and Chinese Americans: Conceiving a Transnational Political Network." 107–121 in Tan Chee Beng Ed., *Chinese Transnational Networks*. New York and London: Routledge.
———. 2010. "Pre-emigration Socialization, Transnational Ties, and Political Participation Across the Pacific: A Comparison Among Immigrants from China, Taiwan, and Hong Kong." *Journal of East Asian Studies* 10 (3): 453–482.
———. 2011. "Race, Nativity, and the Political Participation of Asian and Other Americans." 24–45 in David Ericson Ed., *The Politics of Inclusion and Exclusion: Identity Politics in Twenty-first Century America*. New York: Routledge.
———, and Janelle Wong. 2009. "Like Latinos? Transnational Political Practices and their Correlates among Asian Americans." 137–152 in Christian Collet and Pei-te Lien Eds., *The Transnational Politics of Asian Americans*. Philadelphia, PA: Temple University Press.
———, Christian Collet, Janelle Wong, and Karthick Ramakrishnan. 2001. "Asian Pacific American Politics Symposium: Public Opinion and Political Participation." *PS: Political Science & Politics* 34 (3): 625–630.
———, M. Margaret Conway, and Janelle Wong. 2004. *The Politics of Asian Americans*. New York: Routledge.
Liu, Michael, Kim Geron, and Tracy Lai. 2008. *The Snake Dance of Asian American Activism: Community, Vision, and Power*. Lanham, MD: Lexington Books.
McClain, Charles. 1994. *In Search of Equality: The Chinese Struggles Against Discrimination in Nineteen Century America*. Berkeley, CA: University of California Press.
Maeda, Daryl. 2012. *Rethinking the Asian American Movement*. New York: Routledge.
Misha, Sangay. 2009. "The Limits of Transnational Mobilization: Indian American Lobby Groups and the India-US Nuclear Deal." 174–194 in Christian Collet and Pei-te Lien Eds., *The Transnational Politics of Asian Americans*. Philadelphia, PA: Temple University Press.
Nagasawa, Richard. 1986. *Summer Wind: The Story of an Immigrant Chinese Politician*. Tuscon, AZ: Westernlore Press.
Ramakrishnan, Karthick, and Taeku Lee. 2012. "Public Opinion of a Growing Electorate: Asian Americans and Pacific Islanders in 2012." www.naasurvey.com/resources/Home/NAAS12-sep25-election.pdf. Accessed October 8, 2012.
Verba, Sidney, Kay Schlozman, and Henry Brady. 1995. *Voice and Equality: Civic Volunteerism in American Politics*. Cambridge, MA: Harvard University Press.
Wei, William. 1993. *The Asian American Movement*. Philadelphia, PA: Temple University Press.
Wong, Janelle, S. Karthick Ramakrishnan, Taeku Lee, and Jane Junn. 2011. *Asian American Political Participation: Emerging Constituents and Their Political Identities*. New York: Russell Sage Foundation.

INDEX

Af-Pak: conceptual descriptor 240; military term 233, 237, 239–241; term of globality 238; *see also* Muslims; *see also* War on Terror

Aiieeeee! 1, 5, 8, 53, 56; *see also* Asian American studies: cultural nationalist approach

Anglophonicity 84–85

antipodes 88–89

Arabs: anti-Arab racism 170; Arab-Israeli War of 1967 170; conflation with Muslim 172–173; hate crimes against 172–173, 176–177; migration to the United States 167; naturalization 168; surveillance of 170–171, 174; treatment after 9/11 173–174, 176–177, 334; whiteness 166, 168, 177; *see also* War on Terror

Asian Americans for Action 346–347

Asian American Political Alliance 1

Asian American studies: assimilation paradigm 8, 10; crisis 3; cultural nationalist approach 8, 11, 53; diasporic approach 9, 66–69, 73–74; digital humanities 305–313; emergence 2, 53; institutionalization 4–5; "lost second generation of Asian American scholars" 4–5; queer theory 266; transnationalism 68–69

Asian American women: Orientalist fantasies about 262–263; *see also* Asian athletes; *see also* garment industry, New York City: 1982 strike; *see also* stereotypes: racial

Asian athletes: golfers 201–202; model minorities 200, 201; nationalism 204–205

Asian chic 203

Asian financial crisis 61

Asian Law Caucus 39

Asian settler colonialism: Asian settler colonialism (ASC) studies 144; debate about ASC 145–150; Hawaii 142–144

Association for Asian American Studies 3, 6

Bertrais, Yves, letters received 117, 120–123

Big Aiieeeee, The! 5, 8; *see also* Asian American studies: cultural nationalist approach

Blu's Hanging controversy 6

Boggs, Grace Lee 342–343

Bush, George W. 174

Cambodians: Cambodian People's Party 132; Extraordinary Chambers in the Courts of Cambodia 132, 134; Huy, Bochan 135–136; Khmer Rouge 129, 133; Killing fields 131; Phnom Penh 129–130; Pol Pot time 131–132; pop culture 194; Pran, Dith 137; Sen, Hun 132–133

Chang, Robert S. 43

Chicago School sociology 57; *see also* Hawaii: as racial laboratory 56–57

Chinatowns 223–224, 226–229, 274; *see also* ethnic enclaves

Chinese: immigration 224; model minority myth 29, 200–201, 285, 290–292; racial stereotypes 27; Tiger mom stereotype 31

Chin, Frank 11, 56: critique of *Woman Warrior, The* 11–12

Chua, Amy *Battle Hymn of the Tiger Mother* 31

Chuh, Kandice 6, 68

colonialism 54–55

colorblindness 59

conservatism 5

Counterpoint: Perspectives on Asian America 1, 2, 9–10

Crenshaw, Kimberle 41; *see also* critical race theory

critical race theory 39–42: legal realism 42; limitations 40, 46–50; origins 41–2

Index

da Silva, Denise Ferreira globality 235–237
decolonization 53; *see also* Asian American studies: emergence
diaspora 65: Asian diasporas 69–71; Chinese diaspora 212; limitations 65–68; queer critique 72–73; typological approach 65; *see also* Asian American studies: diasporic approach
digital humanities 305: Asian American 308–309, 311–312; race 309–311; *see also* Asian American studies: digital humanities
Dirlik, Arif 67–68
Do the Right Thing 43–44
DREAM Act 334–336

electoral politics 356–357: home country politics 363; political party affiliation 361–362; presidential voting 362; voting patterns 359–360
empire 60
ethnic enclaves 59–60: ethno-burbs 279; ex-burbs 279–280; *see also* Chinatowns
ethnic studies 1
exclusion laws 167–168, 249, 261, 330–331, 333

Fanon, Frantz 23
Filipinos: civic status 157–162; colonial subjects of the United States 157; musical performers 190; naturalization laws 157–162
Flower Drum Song 192
Fu Manchu 27; *see also* yellow peril

garment industry, New York City: Chinese history 222; Chinese women 222–223, 226–227; ethnic history 221–222; impact of 9/11 228; International Ladies' Garment Workers' Union 223, 226–227; 1982 Strike 226; quick time 227; *see also* Chinatowns
Gee, Emma 2
genocide 134–135: autogenocide 134
globalization: Asian America 188, 195, 198, 217–218; cultural 187, 192, 194; military bases 192–193
Gramsci, Antonio 3

Hagedorn, Jessica *Dogeaters* 32, 55
Hart-Cellar Immigration Act of 1965 169, 265, 331, 358; *see also* naturalization laws
Hawaii: Asian Americans 58; as racial laboratory 56–57; *see also* Asian settler colonialism
Hmong: literacy 119, 122–123; refugees 117–118, 122–123; RPA 118; women 122–123
Ho, Fred 348

Ichioka, Yuji 10; *see also Counterpoint: Perspectives on Asian America*
I-Hotel 1

immigration enforcement: detention and deportation 333; Illegal Immigration Reform and Immigrant Responsibility Act 333; National Security Entry-Exit Registration System 239; special registration program 174–175
imperialism 54–55, 60: model minority imperialism 54, 155

James, C. L. R. 200
Japanese: diaspora 248; internment 287–290, 345; Japanese American Citizens League 289; model minority myth 29, 285, 287–290; racism against 250; transnationalism 247–255

Kim, Elaine: critique of *Strangers from a Different Shore* 12; foreword to *Reading the Literatures of Asian America* 211
Kim Sisters 193
K-pop 194
Kochiyama, Yuri 346–347
Kuromiya, Kiyoshi 318

Lee, Christopher 6
Lin, Jeremy 211, 213–215: ancestry debate 214–215; as Asian American 215, 218; globalization 218; Linsanity 213–214, 216; participation in online culture 216–219; *see also* Asian athlete; *see also* globalization: Asian America
Los Angeles rebellion of 1992 43, 349; *see also Sa-i-Gu*
Lowe, Lisa 66

Marxist theory 40, 46
Matsuda, Mari: critical race theory 46–47; keynote speech at Asian Law Caucus banquet 39–40, 45; *see also* critical race theory
melting-pot 56–57
Mirikitani, Janice 28
Miss Saigon 192
model minority myth: Chinese as 29, 200, 285, 290–292; critiques of 7, 10, 29, 39, 331–332; Hawaii statehood debates 292–294; Japanese as 29, 285, 287–290; origins of 285–294; *see also* Moynihan Report
Mohanty, Chandra Talpade critique of Western feminist scholarship 30
Morrison, Toni *Playing in the Dark: Whiteness and the Literary Imagination* 23
Moynihan Report 29, 295–296; *see also* model minority myth
Muslims: anti-Muslim racism 233–235; as racial figure 234; *see also Af-Pak; see also* Arabs: conflation with Muslim; *see also* War on Terror

naturalization laws 158–163, 168
Ngo, Viet Mike 328
Nguyen, Viet Thanh 6

Odo, Franklin 2
Omi, Michael 3; *see also* Asian American studies
Ong, Aihwa *Flexible Citizenship* 212
Other: An Asian and Pacific Islander Prisoners' Anthology 329
panethnicity: Asian American 5; east Asian bias 5
perpetual foreigner 28; *see also* stereotypes: racial
Philippines: annexation 154; independence 164; *Insular Cases* 155; Philippine-American War 343–344; Tydings-McDuffie Act 162–163; *see also* colonialism; *see also* imperialism
postcolonial studies relevance to Asian American studies 52, 54, 69
Prashad, Vijay 241

queer Asian America 322–324: GLBTQ Asian American identities and groups 265–266, 318–321; trans Asian Americans 324–325

Reflections on Shattered Windows: Promises and Prospects for Asian American Studies 3, 6
relational analysis 235
Roots: An Asian American Reader 1, 2, 7–8

Sa-i-Gu 43–44; *see also* Los Angeles Rebellion of 1992
Said, Edward: *Orientalism* 22, 34; allegory of self and other 22–24
San Francisco State University 1: strike 3
Sartre, Jean-Paul 23
Secret War in Laos 117
Stahl, Anna Kazumi *Flores de un solo dia* 83–84, 86, 90–95
stereotypes: Asian American men 32; Asian American women 27–28, 32; Asian stock characters 26; faulty deduction 25; perpetual foreigner 28; racial 21–22; tiger mom 31; transdeductive reasoning 24
Strangers from a Different Shore 8: critiques of 11–12
success myth 7; *see also* model minority myth

Takaki, Ronald: *Strangers from a Different Shore* 8, 11–12; *see also* Asian American studies: cultural nationalist approach
Third World Liberation Front 1; *see also* San Francisco State University: strike
transnationalism: analytical limitations 68; contemporary Asian America 59–61
trans-pacific west 156–157
Trask, Haunani-Kay 56
Tratado 90
Tuan, Yi-Fu *Who Am I?: An Autobiography of Emotion, Mind, and Spirit* 33

Vietnamese: assimilation narratives 104; downward mobility 109; good refugee 107; model minorities 104; refugees 103–104; social science studies 103–104
Vietnam War 103, 130: fall of Saigon 25th anniversary 107–108; refugee resettlement crisis 103, 105, 107

War on Terror 173–174, 177, 233, 237, 241
White Boy Shuffle, The 44–45
Whiteness of Asian Americans 59–60
Williams, Patricia 48–49; *see also* critical race theory
Woman Warrior, The critiques of 11–12, 30
Wong, Anna May 35
Wong, Buck 7; *see also Roots: An Asian American Reader*
Wong, Eddie 8; *see also Roots: An Asian American Reader*
Wong, Sau-Ling C. "Denationalization Reconsidered" 9, 66–67, 212; *see also* Asian American studies: diasporic approach

Yang, Gene *American Born Chinese* 21
Yao, Ming 214; *see also* Asian athlete
yellow peril 26–27; *see also* stereotypes: Asian stock characters
Yung, Wayne *My German Boyfriend* 33

Zheng, Eddy 332, 334

Taylor & Francis eBooks

Helping you to choose the right eBooks for your Library

Add Routledge titles to your library's digital collection today. Taylor and Francis ebooks contains over 50,000 titles in the Humanities, Social Sciences, Behavioural Sciences, Built Environment and Law.

Choose from a range of subject packages or create your own!

Benefits for you
- Free MARC records
- COUNTER-compliant usage statistics
- Flexible purchase and pricing options
- All titles DRM-free.

Benefits for your user
- Off-site, anytime access via Athens or referring URL
- Print or copy pages or chapters
- Full content search
- Bookmark, highlight and annotate text
- Access to thousands of pages of quality research at the click of a button.

REQUEST YOUR FREE INSTITUTIONAL TRIAL TODAY

Free Trials Available
We offer free trials to qualifying academic, corporate and government customers.

eCollections – Choose from over 30 subject eCollections, including:

Archaeology	Language Learning
Architecture	Law
Asian Studies	Literature
Business & Management	Media & Communication
Classical Studies	Middle East Studies
Construction	Music
Creative & Media Arts	Philosophy
Criminology & Criminal Justice	Planning
Economics	Politics
Education	Psychology & Mental Health
Energy	Religion
Engineering	Security
English Language & Linguistics	Social Work
Environment & Sustainability	Sociology
Geography	Sport
Health Studies	Theatre & Performance
History	Tourism, Hospitality & Events

For more information, pricing enquiries or to order a free trial, please contact your local sales team:
www.tandfebooks.com/page/sales

Routledge – Taylor & Francis Group | The home of Routledge books | **www.tandfebooks.com**